HEALTH CARE IN THE INFORMATION SOCIETY

VOLUME 1

Health Care in the Information Society

Vol. 1: From Adventure of Ideas to Anarchy of Transition

David Ingram

https://www.openbookpublishers.com

ISBN Paperback: 978-1-80064-952-1
ISBN Hardback: 978-1-80064-953-8
ISBN Digital (PDF): 978-1-80064-954-5
ISBN Digital ebook (EPUB): 978-1-80064-955-2
ISBN XML: 978-1-80064-957-6
ISBN HTML: 978-1-80064-958-3

DOI: 10.11647/OBP.0335

Cover image: D koi, *White H2O Molecules* (27 June 2022), https://unsplash.com/photos/5nI9N2wNcBU
Cover design: Jeevanjot Kaur Nagpal

For Bożenka, whose love and encouragement made it possible, and in respectful memory of John Dickinson and Jo Milan, whose insight and friendship guided and supported me along the way

VOLUME 1

Part One—Adventure of Ideas

Bolder adventure is needed–the adventure of ideas, and the advantage of practice conforming itself to ideas. The best service that ideas can render is gradually to lift into the mental poles the ideal of another type of perfection which becomes a programme for reform.

—Alfred North Whitehead (1861–1947)[1]

VOLUME 2

Part Two—Anarchy of Transition

In every age of well-marked transition there is the pattern of habitual dumb practice and emotion which is passing, and there is the oncoming of a new complex habit. Between the two lies a zone of anarchy.

—Alfred North Whitehead[2]

Part Three—Programme for Reform

Human nature is so complex that paper plans for society are to the statesmen not worth even the price of the defaced paper. Successful progress creeps from point to point, testing each step.

—Alfred North Whitehead[3]

---

1   *Adventures of Ideas* (New York: Macmillan, 1933), p. 248.
2   Ibid., p. 14.
3   Ibid., p. 27.

Contents

Author's Biography

The author was born in 1945–a date that closely connects his life with the first digital computers and the United Kingdom's National Health Service, embodying the parallel evolving themes of health care and information technology that are woven together in this book.

His childhood was spent in a residential childcare setting, living in a large house and estate run by his parents in a tiny rural village in Hampshire in the UK. He was among the first from the village to attend a grammar school, and the first from his family to attend a university, awarded a physics scholarship at Magdalen College, University of Oxford, in 1964, and an industrial scholarship won in national competition. His work and interests have connected him widely with health and social care services, and industry, university, government, charitable and voluntary sector organizations, nationally and internationally.

His academic career from 1976–95 was in the Department of Medicine of the Medical College of St. Bartholomew's Hospital in East London and from 1995–2011 in the Centre for Health Informatics and Multiprofessional Education, at the Medical School of University College London. In retirement, he and Bożena, his wife, are citizens of St Albans, an ancient English city that is busily reshaping itself as a set of globally connected local small villages, and Krakow, in Poland, among the most beautiful of European cities. They try to keep up with four generations of family and indulge their passion for ballroom and Latin dance and Argentine Tango, hoping thereby to keep fit and well, able to continue cross-country skiing and sailing for as long as possible!

Preface

I was born in November 1945, as the Second World War came to an end. It was a time of transition out of war and into new beginnings for post-war society. In the United Kingdom (UK), it was marked by the Beveridge Report of 1942 on the causes of social disadvantage and deprivation, and the creation of the National Health Service (NHS), in 1948. Less momentous at the time, but massively significant over time, it was the beginning of transition into a new age shaped by information technology, marked by the construction of the earliest, valve-based computers. It was a both lucky and challenging time to be born!

This book is about how information and information technologies have evolved to become pivotal concerns at the heart of life and medical sciences, and health and social care services of the twenty-first century. It connects with many histories of development from earliest times–in philosophy, mathematics and logic; science, engineering, medicine, health and social care services; and society at large. These domains interact ever more immediately in the scientific, technological and social transitions of what have been called the Third and Fourth Industrial Revolutions. Electronics, telecommunications and computers heralded the Third; artificial intelligence, nanotechnology and robotics herald the Fourth. The Third created the Information Age; the Fourth is creating the Information Society. Medicine was invented in Classical times and evolved into and through the Industrial Age. Health care services have accelerated and then faltered in the Information Age and must now be reinvented for the future Information Society.

A book preface traditionally sets out how an author came to conceive of and write their book and how they became involved in its subject. In a book about the birth of a new field and era, eyewitness accounts of early participants are threads that help weave and link together different, sometimes quite loosely connected storylines, through what are typically both adventurous and anarchic times. In this book, the author is eyewitness and participant, as well as storyteller and commentator, concerning the ideas and events that unfold through its chapters. It is a tricky balance to

    https://doi.org/10.11647/OBP.0335.06

achieve, and this Preface is itself a chapter, to place the book in that personal context.

In matters of health and care, the balance of personal and professional interests and expectations, alongside population and societal perspectives, is also tricky beyond measure. It must reflect individual citizen, family and community needs and responsibilities, within diverse caring, healing and restorative environments, and respect the personal autonomy, dignity and rights of all concerned. Health and social care are essentially human matters, and we should always remember this when dreaming about and creating machine-based future 'solutions' for the complexity and difficulty they pose. These require a practised balance of head, hand and heart–a memorable phrase from the title of David Goodhart's recent book, well-suited to its 2020 publication date.[1] In writing this book, the human context of the stories told has been uppermost in my mind.

The coevolution of information technology with health care services is a story of seven decades of incremental and iterative innovation, achieving outstanding successes and persisting with perplexing failures. My career has spanned and connected widely and closely across this emerging landscape. I have been luckily positioned to listen to, read about, know and work with many who have battled and led the way–in academia, health care, professional institutions, governments, industries, non-governmental organizations (NGOs) and charities, across the world. Luck and staying power are primary qualities of successful innovators in such variable and challenging circumstances–well exemplified in many that the book describes.

The book has been written as a postscript to a career spent in exploring, supporting and connecting many and disparate interdisciplinary and multiprofessional endeavours. It emphasizes the crucial importance of creating environment and community where new approaches to the complex problems posed for health care in its transition through the Information Age can grow. It is, in turn, a preface to further transition, as the present-day communities of the Information Age create those of the future Information Society.

Histories can be told in many ways, especially when drawing extensively on first-hand experience. The book includes much personal narrative about people and teams, and their times: where and how they have worked; what they have coped with, made and done; and the connections they have forged along the way. This kind of narrative might be characterized as a Pilgrim's Progress, but that feels a bit too evangelical. Analogy with the

---

1   D. Goodhart, *Head Hand Heart: The Struggle for Dignity and Status in the 21st Century* (London: Penguin Books, 2020).

story-telling songlines of the Australian Aboriginal community culture feels more appropriate.

Songlines are assemblies of stories, songs and art describing and recording a journey through a landscape, telling of its creation and history, and of the culture and beliefs of the communities with which it connects. They are told and sung to explorers, by people they meet as they travel through the landscape over time. I have been privileged to participate in the songlines of some iconic figures of the Information Age who have made things happen—telling their stories and singing their dreams into existence, as in the Dreamtime[2]–some loudly singing or sung about and some less so. The three parts of this book form a Dreamtime-like continuum of past, present and future perspectives of health care, before and during the Information Age, and in the Information Society to come.

Of course, dreams and their dreamers are sometimes typecast as unworldly and mindless nightmares. But unrefreshed by dreams, minds create real-life nightmares, too! This book is both history and personal songline. It connects widely through an evolving landscape of imaginations, practicalities and dreams, and some nightmares, as well!

Songlines are also long marches. My career songline has been a fifty-year long march. Navigating through the Covid-19 pandemic and writing this book has been a long march–the first rough draft from March 2020 to March 2021; the second to March 2022; and the final draft, after the publisher's peer review, in the six months to March 2023. Transition of society from the Information Age into the Information Society will be another long march–searching for and establishing common ground on which to cooperate and collaborate successfully. A paradox of the Information Age is that what was promised to connect and integrate, as easily led to unravelling threads of fragmentation and isolation. The challenge for the Information Society is to weave a new tapestry that makes whole.[3]

2　'[...] the labyrinth of invisible pathways which meander all over Australia are known to Europeans as "Dreaming-tracks" or "Songlines"; to the Aboriginals as "Footprints of the Ancestors" or "Way of the Law". Aboriginal Creation myths tell of the legendary totemic beings who had wandered over the continent in the Dreamtime, singing out the name of everything that crossed their path–birds, animals, plants, rocks, water-holes–and so singing the world into existence'. B. Chatwin, *The Songlines* (New York: Random House, 2012), p. 2.

3　We need a term that represents the wholeness of health and social care. Their repetitive identification as separate entities becomes trite and tedious as well as potentially harmful. I toyed with health=care–symbolizing a bonded connection of health and care, adapting to the changing needs of society, locally and globally, today and into the future. But that becomes twee and tedious, too. From here on in the book, I use health care as an umbrella term that implies their inseparable connection. In later chapters, I introduce the idea of a care information utility,

I grew up in a small English village in rural Hampshire, and am now, as with increasing numbers of humankind, a citizen of an Internet-enabled global village. My parents were born as the first motor cars spluttered into life. They ended their days in times of traffic gridlock and environmental degradation. In 1899, the *Scientific American* journal predicted that the motor car would 'eliminate a greater part of the nervousness, distraction and strain of modern metropolitan life'.[4] Predicting the future is a dicey pursuit! How we join forces to make things happen will always matter more.

My mother went to Spain in the 1930s, to help shelter refugees from the Spanish Civil War. She and my father met in wartime when working in a residential care setting, sheltering children displaced to this country from elsewhere in war-torn Europe. Social care runs deep in my family history and personal experience. We lived for the first twelve years of my life in a large residential children's home run by my parents, caring for twenty-five English children who were separated from their broken families, and helping them develop and grow. Some have done spectacularly well, connecting with our family still, today. Good and connected human environments are a necessity for sustained growth and development, and for health. Inequalities of health have been further amplified and highlighted in the Information Age. In my childhood there was a dearth of information about health and disease and the care services. Today there is a lot of information–not all good, and not all helpful.

I was born just after Alan Turing (1912–54) and the team at Bletchley Park unravelled the secret wartime codes produced by the Enigma machine.[5] They built on insights of Polish mathematicians who had studied the machine's design, up until the time their country was invaded. The work was assisted by development of the Bletchley Park Bombe machine and Colossus computer, just a few miles from where I am writing, now. And in America, the ENIAC digital computer was created, alongside and gradually supplanting analogue computers of those times, that had been used by members of the physics team at Los Alamos in designing the first nuclear weapon–the nuclear fission-based atomic bomb. There was close connection between the ENIAC's use in calculations for military developments and

---

to embody a coherent citizen-centred ecosystem of health care information–this seemed the most appropriate simple expression of the broad purposes such a utility must serve.

4   T. Conyngton, 'Motor Carriages and Street Paving', *Scientific American Supplement*, 48 (1899), 196660.

5   Wherever I have been able to discover them, I include dates alongside referenced names, to give context of time for the people being introduced. Context is important in discussion of ideas and events, and timeline provides important, often interesting, and sometimes forgotten context.

nuclear science, and this early computer remained a secret during the early post-war development of the much more destructive nuclear fusion-based hydrogen bomb. I sit here writing, with billions of Colossus or ENIAC amounts of computational resource in use and at my disposal–smartphone, desktop computer, broadband router, central heating controller, house alarm system–and connecting with trillions more in the Internet Cloud, as tools and support for everyday work and life. A truly colossal resource!

The organization of health care services and their underpinning professions and supporting technologies have evolved continuously from the immediate post-war years of my childhood to the 2020s of my retirement. The social and political cauldrons of two World Wars, and of the Great Depression that separated them, battered and shaped the lives of my parents. They brought to the fore new leaders of the era, determined and ambitious to explore and chart a better path into the post-war world. Richard Tawney (1880–1962) and William Beveridge (1879–1963) were close friends in their college days and became talismanic figures and reforming energies, with Sidney Webb (1859–1947) and Beatrice Webb (1858–1943) of the Fabian Society. The Beveridge Report and the establishment of the UK NHS, led by Aneurin Bevan (1897–1960), and the hopes they embodied, stem from those times. They form a vivid region of the landscape that my life has passed through and been shaped by.

The book connects from the earliest stages of what has been termed an information for health revolution, set within its historical context, and ends where we are today, looking forward from the 2020s and perhaps only midway in the changes in the nature and organization of health care services that it is accompanying and precipitating. It seems appropriate to describe these changes as revolutionary because, co-evolving alongside the computer, many paradigms of knowledge and practice have changed over that timeline, significantly and excitingly, and some almost beyond recognition. This era has seen an amazing 'adventure of ideas', a term I have borrowed from the title of a book by the famous philosopher and mathematician, Alfred North Whitehead (1861–1947), written nearly a hundred years ago, to which I have often referred. Impetus has come from accelerating advance and reformulation of academic discipline and professional practice: in mathematics, science, and engineering; in law and governance; and in technology, medicine, and health care. The book interleaves personal stories with accounts of these disciplines and professions, government policies and programmes, social and economic change, and the connections they embody. History of revolution is marked by the stresses and strains of uncertain, often anarchic transition.

My pathway into a career in health informatics was an unlikely one–adventitious but also, in retrospect, uniquely advantageous. I studied theoretical physics at the University of Oxford in the mid-1960s and worked for several years in the medical engineering industry, before completing an early Master of Science (MSc) course at the innovative London Institute of Computer Science, parts of which were subsequently integrated within University College London (UCL).[6] I then completed a PhD in biomedical engineering at UCL, modelling the physiology of the human circulatory system, and worked for three years in the nearby hospital medical physics department.

Thus, by the age of thirty I had spent twelve early childhood years living in a children's home, achieved a good grounding in maths and computer science, completed a first degree in physics and a higher degree in engineering, and gained experience of work environments in large- and small-scale industries and hospital-based research and development. William MacAskill's eighty thousand hours organization[7] (this being the number of hours in a typical lifetime of work) advises that we should spend a good proportion of that amount of time considering and sampling work options, before deciding and committing to where we seek to put down roots for the longer term. My twenties were not quite that rational, but the experience gained in these widely diverse early stages of my songline stood me in good stead for a subsequent career in health informatics. There were what might have proved safer and better paid career options offered at the time–including one from a founder of the, subsequently very successful, Logica computer consultancy, and another from the scientific Civil Service–but I set off on a more adventurous path, to an academic post situated alongside clinicians at the heart of medicine and health care services. And as the poet wrote about taking paths less travelled, it did make all the difference.

In 1976, I was appointed as a lecturer in a post newly created for me in medical computing and physics, in the academic department of medicine of one of London's longest established medical schools, that of St Bartholomew's Hospital, known as Bart's, which dates from 1123. It was a bold move for them and a risky one for me and my young family!

---

6   At that time, Peter Kirstein (1933–2020), a UK pioneer of the Arpanet and co-designer of the TCP/IP electronic data transmission protocol, taught practical courses on telecommunications engineering and programming at the London Institute. In the mid-1970s, the founder of the Internet, Tim Berners-Lee, also read physics at Oxford. In more recent decades, the fields of theoretical physics and computer science have incrementally aligned at Oxford, notably in the work of David Deutsch on quantum computation, and new stars, such as Vlatko Vedral, seeking towards unification of physical law within an information paradigm, descriptive of what can and cannot happen in physical reality.

7   *80,000 Hours: How To Make a Difference with Your Career*, https://80000hours.org/

This was both the best and worst of places in which to be based for such a challenge. Best in the sense of proximity to and everyday experience of real-world community and context of health care, with freedom to explore their interplay with information technology. Worst in the sense of academic isolation and resulting, sometimes onerous, dependence on personal resource and resilience. Academic appointments usually fit within a pattern of expectations that should be met and are judged accordingly. Mine had none but was bound to be judged as if it did, nonetheless. It was precarious for some years, stepping onto a virtual ladder of career progression in computational science and medicine, for which there was no bottom rung! Moreover, being situated in a community and environment eminent in the history, pomp and circumstance of medicine, that did not understand the nature and purpose of such a ladder or have a recognized place for it.

I was sponsored and protected in those early years by John Dickinson (1927–2015), who had been my PhD co-supervisor and had by this time become the courageous and far-sighted academic chief of medicine at Bart's. I had a bench, cupboard and desk, and a telephone line, and started on my own, at ground zero, to create my ladder as I ascended it.

I had to build mission and role from below, within an existing, not unfriendly, interested but largely uncomprehending community and environment, to help generate something new. I was otherwise alone, positioned at the centre of community, environment and professions of health care, at the start of their encounter with the computer.

How this unlikely scenario played out over the following decades unfolds in the storyline of the book. It did so in ways that could not have occurred had I not been able to work and survive in an interdisciplinary and multiprofessional environment, close to everyday health care practice, education and research. Such essential environment has been rare for health informatics, as my world of endeavour became known many years later, notwithstanding the huge amounts of sometimes ephemeral and confounding artefact and literature constructed under that banner, but often at a distance from the frontline of care. That is in large part why the field has been slow to crystallize, engage and evolve. It is a picture typical of paradigm-changing innovation in many fields and the computer has changed, and continues to change, all the people, disciplines, practices and organizations engaged in delivering and supporting health care. It has changed us all, as citizens and patients, too.

Fortunately, my sometimes-perilous adventure worked out luckily and well, and in 1989, halfway through my career, I was awarded the title of Professor of Medical Informatics, the first such conferment in the UK. I was honoured, also, to be made a Fellow of the Fellowship of Postgraduate

Medicine and subsequently an Honorary Member of the Royal College of Physicians of London, for services to medicine.

Much of the book has been written while locked down for many months at home in the UK, during the Covid-19 viral pandemic. What, several decades ago, was characterized as information explosion, might today, with some justification, be thought of as information pandemic. The inflationary growth in amounts and varieties of information, and their pervasiveness across the world, continues and accelerates. It expresses and communicates an enlightening cornucopia of knowledge and experience, to nurture what Abraham Lincoln (1809–65), and more recently Steven Pinker, described as 'the better angels of our nature'.[8] It also stirs and fuels darker energies and engines, revealed from a Pandora's box of unknowable futures. And, unsurprisingly, the transition of society into the Information Age has been chaotic and stormy, as are all manner of physical, biological and social transitions. Such storms tend to focus our attention nearby and make it difficult to see ahead. Health care services are going through complicated and stormy times—especially in the recent period of viral pandemic. But as storms subside, vision and perspective improve and pathways clear—those we want and need to follow and those that are, perhaps, best avoided.[9]

It thus seems timely to take stock at this midpoint of transition, where a revolution in technical infrastructure has already substantially occurred but the transformation of personal and professional practice and changing culture of society remain unstable and unformed, between the dissolving patterns that preceded and the emerging patterns that are taking root and will follow. We find ourselves poised between ambition and optimism, and caution and concern, about how best to approach the next stages of transition into the future Information Society. This ambivalence is captured in the tempered enthusiasm of Barack Obama's writing about 'audacity of hope',[10] and the caution of Mervyn King's advocacy of 'audacious pessimism'.[11] The latter emerged from torrid times as Governor of the Bank of England,

---

8   S. Pinker, *The Better Angels of Our Nature: The Decline of Violence in History and Its Causes* (London: Penguin Books, 2011).

9   As I started to write the book, the year 2020 rang with metaphor of visual acuity. Being in possession of 20/20 vision, one can focus twenty feet ahead on detail that a normal person would be expected to see at that distance. The omen of the 2020 metaphor might not be so encouraging–20/25 vision is less acute! So, as with all metaphor and analogy, let us not take this one too far!

10   B. Obama, *The Audacity of Hope: Thoughts on Reclaiming the American Dream* (New York: Crown Publishers, 2006).

11   M. King, *The End of Alchemy: Money, Banking and the Future of the Global Economy* (New York: W. W. Norton and Company, 2016).

sceptical of science-driven mathematical models of financial markets and scarred by the near collapse of the world's monetary systems in 2008. Something like hoping for the best and preparing for the worst![12]

There is justification for both these positions. On the one hand, there is cause for optimism about the proven and now considerably more flexible, powerful and resilient connected information technologies available to us. These have significantly improved our capacity to work, iteratively and efficiently, in customizing computer applications to meet evolving and changing requirements. New software applications can be developed rapidly and spun into life on Cloud services and data stores, from anywhere on the Internet, within minutes. On the other hand, there is an accumulating legacy of considerable sunk cost in incompatible and outdated systems still in use, burdening frontline services and adding unproductive current cost. Information has become a pervasive but substantially chaotic utility, harvesting, generating, providing access to and pumping content through the globally connected infrastructure of the Internet. This proliferation has been accelerated by the pervasive standardization of methods for managing information content on the World Wide Web.

Of course, significant precursors of the 'information for health' revolution date a long way back in history–such as the perturbations caused by the work of William Farr (1807–83) and Florence Nightingale (1820–1910) in investigating and criticizing hospital statistics,[13] or Gottlob Frege's (1848–1925) formulation of the first-order predicate calculus, that led to description logic of the contemporary knowledge base era.[14] It felt fitting that, as I first wrote these paragraphs on 12 May 2020, the

---

12 My wife, Bożena, and I combine English and Polish culture and sense of humour in our marriage. It is said that the former anticipates the future and hopes the worst projections will not happen. The latter does the same and knows that they will!

13 This well-known quotation captures the flavour of Florence Nightingale's concerns in those times: 'In attempting to arrive at the truth, I have applied everywhere for information but in scarcely an instance have I been able to obtain hospital records fit for any purpose of comparison. If they could be obtained, they would enable us to decide many other questions besides the one alluded to. They would show subscribers how their money was being spent, what amount of good was really being done with it or whether the money was not doing mischief rather than good'. F. Nightingale, *Notes on Hospitals*, 3rd ed. (London: Longman, Roberts and Green, 1963), p. 159.

14 Frege made the break from formal verbal argument based on term, proposition, predicate and syllogism–originating in Classical times and associated with the names of Aristotle (384 BCE–322 BCE) and the Stoic philosopher, Chrysippus (279 BCE–206 BCE)–to argument based on formal logic, expressed as mathematical reasoning with logical predicates, as discussed in Chapter Two.

two hundredth anniversary of the birth of Florence Nightingale was being commemorated.

Subsequent months of writing saw AlphaFold–a software method based on machine learning–demonstrate prediction of the three-dimensional folding structure of a protein, based on the genetic sequence of its DNA.[15] This extraordinary success, and others that preceded it, hold out the prospect of a time to come when such machines will learn for themselves about health care interventions, based on observed and elicited facts, to devise and enact machine-based methods that reason about, interpret and even act on them in real life–controlling surgical instruments or medical devices attached to or travelling within the body, for example. Notwithstanding the promise of considerable and significant improvements along this pathway, it must be countenanced that, humans having pursued human mastery of the computing machine, there may arise increasingly capable machines that might continue to serve us, or turn the tables to our detriment–or we ourselves might unwittingly turn them–such that their needs dominate and subjugate our human values, needs and skills. Such a future scenario might constitute neither manageable nor survivable loss for humanity. For sure, it will pose new challenges and difficulties.

We have learned a great deal, often simply by trial and error, about the opportunities and pitfalls when marrying information technology with health care. We have created and improved tools and methods that enable us to succeed in areas where we have hitherto lacked insight and capacity, failed or not met expectations. And society, more widely, has substantially adapted to the use of information technology in daily life, leading to the harbouring of new hopes and expectations for customized personal health care services. There has been success in some areas, counterbalanced by burdens imposed, to little or no benefit, or to some disbenefit, in others. And regarding the increasing imbalances of health care in our ageing populations, according to the King's Fund in London, in a 2012/13 review entitled 'Time to Think Differently', resources have moved proportionally away from social care into treatments of disease which cannot yet effect a cure, connected with long term conditions and accounting for seventy percent of total health and social care expenditure.[16] This demographic shift has, in itself, reflected scientific and engineering advances of the past century, that have combated and prevented disease.

---

15 The company DeepMind, in London, announced this achievement on 1 December 2020.

16 The King's Fund, 'Time to Think Differently' (2012–13), https://www.kingsfund.org.uk/projects/time-think-differently

In an outstandingly thoughtful book, the eminent American clinician and medical scientist, Eric Topol, has emphatically and starkly attributed the accumulating, and now more widely apparent, ills of modern-day medicine to its having lost balance, through the pursuit of optimization and monetization of cure at the expense of too little time and attention paid to care ('Period', he says!).[17] I visit this book in Chapter Eight and have come to see things in much the same way, along my parallel songline. His is a physician's case history and diagnosis of what he sees as a very sick patient, and he seeks a remedy. He looks to a pathway ahead with services informed and supported by artificial intelligence, to assist in redressing the balance and enabling much greater time and attention to be devoted to care. His book focuses on doctor and patient relationships in hospital care settings of America, today. I look to a complementary, inclusive and community-wide pathway ahead, with the goal of framing, creating and sustaining a citizen-centred care information utility, anchored in the public domain, to support balance, continuity and governance of health care services.

The Covid-19 viral pandemic has starkly revealed the dynamics of unprecedentedly rapid global propagation of infection. Internet-mediated communication of malware viruses demonstrates a similar dynamic sting. Global travel routes and the Internet of electronic communication might be characterized as combinations of time compression and seven-league boots–they communicate ever more rapidly and widely. Decades of accelerating increase in the miniaturization and computational power of electronic devices, and the speed of deployment of software and systems based on them, have bypassed the additional checks and balances of time and distance that have helped society adjust to, shape and moderate diffusion and impact of innovation and change. Some kinds of stuff have always happened quickly–the Chicxulub meteorite impact or threshold phenomena in phase transitions of the natural world, for example–but information technology contributes to making man-made stuff happen on qualitatively different scales. Good stuff and bad stuff. This brings new instabilities and vulnerabilities. We shape them and they shape us.

The investments powering the helter-skelter ride into the Information Age seem now often to be out of kilter and out of control. These have been the recent Western decades of International Business Machines Corporation (IBM), Digital Equipment Corporation (DEC), Microsoft, Apple, Google, Meta (formerly Facebook), Twitter, Amazon and more, marked by trillions of dollars of expenditure and now billions of users, where inflated associated private wealth and monopoly are looming larger as international antitrust

---

17 E. Topol, *Deep Medicine: How Artificial Intelligence Can Make Healthcare Human Again* (London: Hachette, 2019).

concerns. They are mirrored today in the Eastern world of Huawei and Alphabet. Flexing muscles of government cyberwarfare and cybercrime have also amplified mutual distrust.

The World Health Organization (WHO) has estimated that the world now spends of the order of eight trillion dollars per annum on health, in its transition to more domestic, as well as more public, provision. Global spending on health information technology is rising rapidly and has been anticipated to reach around four hundred and forty-one billion dollars by 2025.[18] Some fifteen years ago, Blackford Middleton's team at Partners Healthcare in Boston (now renamed to Mass General Brigham) estimated the consequential cost of disorganization of such information at nearly eighty billion dollars per annum, for the United States (US) health economy alone.[19] A decade earlier, the UK Audit Commission estimated that clinical professional staff in hospitals were, on average, spending of the order of twenty percent of their time on tasks interacting directly with information systems.[20] In late 2022, the British Medical Association assessed that NHS doctors are losing at least four hours a week through the inefficiencies of information technology (IT) systems.[21] And on 17 January 2023, as I worked on finalizing this text, the *Times* newspaper was reporting the first meeting of its new Health Commission, established to consider reform of health care. The page one headline was 'Rising levels of ill health costing the economy £150bn a year'.[22] The detailed breakdown leading to this figure, which they described as a conservative estimate, came from a report commissioned from the Oxera economics and finance consultancy. It is sixty percent higher than the amount estimated in 2016, using the same methodology. The Information Age is clearly not well. The Information Society needs to get better.

---

18   Healthcare Facilities Today, 'Healthcare Information Technology Market to Reach $441 Billion by 2025', *Healthcare Facilities Today* (26 April 2019), https://www.healthcarefacilitiestoday.com/posts/Healthcare-information-technology-market-to-reach-441-billion-by-2025--21259

19   J. Walker, E. Pan, D. Johnston, J. Adler-Milstein, S. W. Bates and B. Middleton, 'The Value of Health Care Information Exchange and Interoperability: There Is a Business Case to Be Made for Spending Money on a Fully Standardized Nationwide System', *Health Affairs*, 24.Suppl1 (2005), W5-10-W5-18, https://doi.org/10.1377/hlthaff.W5.10

20   L. Nicholson, 'Setting the Records Straight: A Study of Hospital Medical Records Undertaken by the Audit Commission', *Records Management Journal*, 6.1 (1996), 13–32, https://doi.org/10.1108/eb027083

21   B. Ireland, 'Millions of Hours of Doctors' Time Lost Each Year to "Inadequate" IT Systems', *BMA* (5 December 2022), https://www.bma.org.uk/news-and-opinion/millions-of-hours-of-doctors-time-lost-each-year-to-inadequate-it-systems

22   Times Health Commission, 'Rising Levels of Ill Health Costing Economy £150bn a Year', *The Times* (16 January 2023), https://www.thetimes.co.uk/article/rising-levels-of-ill-health-costing-economy-150bn-a-year-x5dkcn5jg

Progressive entrainment of professional services with information systems has featured more generally in society, starting in Western economies and industries but spreading now almost universally. And yet, health care services have failed repetitively to achieve a viable and sustainable ecosystem of electronic health information systems–notably those concerned with health care records–despite very considerable, repeated and much-fêted investments. I track that reality over the past fifty years in Chapter Seven. But it is not necessary to write or read papers and reports about this to understand what is happening. Just share the experience of the logistical problems that arise, continually, through failure of continuity of record keeping and communication across different levels and regions of health care services. Or of a relative, such as me, of a recovering but critically ill patient, in months accompanying them at their bedside, day by day, through life-supporting intensive care, watching how much staff attention is forced and required to focus away from patients and onto antiquated, difficult to work with, screens.

The book tells both encouraging and alarming stories, like these, and sets them within historical and contemporary contexts. It ranges across disciplines and technologies and follows patterns of change in the professions and organizations of health care services, alongside change in the everyday life of citizens and their experiences and expectations when being cared for and caring for themselves and for others. It draws lessons from repeated failures of government policies and sets out a case for why and how we can now set our sights higher and equip ourselves to do much better in the future. Whitehead wrote of the adventure of ideas as fundamental to a continuing programme for reform. It is on the foundations laid down in this adventure that we can now, and must, ground a long-term, adaptable and incrementally sustainable programme for reform and reinvention, to meet the changing needs of health care in the Information Society of tomorrow.

The stories about health care told in the book have historical contexts spanning thousands of years, from the evolved practice of indigenous communities, the invention of medicine and first records of care in Classical times, and recent centuries of advance in mathematics, science and technology, leading into the twentieth century. They have more immediate scientific and social contexts spanning the coevolution of science, engineering and health care services of the past century, with their increasing focus on computer science and the development of information technology. And connecting these stories together, there is personal experience and perspective, looking back along the timeline of my own life and career, growing up within social care services and employed first within industry, then within health care services and academia, and now in a, thankfully, still active retirement.

Family connections with our children's and grandchildren's generations have been equally important in guiding my understanding and approach, especially considering that the computer has always featured in their lives. Indeed, they are accumulating their own professional involvement in and experience of health care and information technology. My elder son, Simon, now carries executive board responsibility for the information technology sourced and deployed in an international market research business, in countries from the USA, through Europe and Africa, to Singapore. My daughter, Katharine, is a consultant anaesthetist and has held responsibilities for the professional training programme in the NHS East Midlands region. My younger son, Tom, combined PhD research on cardiovascular disease with training as a cardiologist. He is a founding board member of an innovative new multiprofessional royal college of echocardiography, helping to shape its focus on peer-based quality assessment of services and related workforce development and leadership. And closest to my everyday life is my doctor wife, Bożena, who came to England from a very different health care system, in which she pioneered endoscopy services in paediatric gastroenterology. Her father and brother were and are much-loved physicians in their home region of central Poland and her nephew is a rising star in New York investment banking. Numerous other close relatives and friends are also clinical professionals and I had uncles who were general practitioners (GPs) and surgeons long ago. My father had an extensive network of social work colleagues. In his later career he was head of training and then of childcare services for the London and South-East region of the Barnardo's charity in the UK.

These wide-ranging personal connections with family and friends, and with people, organizations, ideas and initiatives widely further afield, have stayed in my mind and helped crystallize my learning in this book. Much of the wider learning needed for success in shaping the transition of health care services into the future Information Society will centre on the experience of citizens and health care professionals in using and shaping the information technology that underpins them. For most of them, if the IT system is seen to meet their needs, it will become largely invisible. Few know about tuning and maintaining the engines of their cars these days and would be ill-advised to try! It will be the same with the information engines we come to depend on in health care. But the human values, goals and methods that underpin them will matter–they must be transparent, and their governance must be trusted.

This breadth of personal experience has also encouraged and led me to a forward-looking, largely optimistic view on how best, now, to address the wrongs that have accumulated and supersede the increasingly unsustainable legacy of technologically and clinically dysfunctional, burdensome IT systems that currently dominate much of everyday health care services. This view further aims to achieve a practical rationale for constructive engagement with new ideas and their advocates, such as those encouraging us on from the stormy current dystopia of the Information Age, to a promised, but not proven, resolution, supported by connected, micro-electronically instrumented, information-driven, machine intelligence. This is a domain populated by many with the mindsets that led King to his advocacy of an approach based on audacious pessimism rather than hope. The world often proceeds through unintended consequences and many such may arise over the horizon of what has been termed an approaching Novacene era of intelligent systems.

There are good reasons not to despair of progress through times of such great change and uncertainty, as Pinker maintains in his book *The Better Angels of Our Nature*.[23] First, there is much that is amazingly good and remarkable in what has already been learned and achieved in the very wide range of endeavours encompassed in the book. Second, there remain complex intellectual and practical challenges that call for invigorated interdisciplinary, multiprofessional and community-wide commitment and cooperation. Third, scientific advance, combined with the technology and infrastructure resources now available, seventy-five years on, brings qualitatively new opportunities for tackling these unresolved challenges and connecting them successfully with core goals of affordable and high-quality health care services, supporting individual citizen health and wellbeing.

I do not seek, and am not well-equipped, to describe the details of all the domains of academic discipline, professional practice and health care services that the subject matter of the book traverses. There is almost no topic covered that could not be written more precisely or expertly than I am able to or have space for here. I have tried to communicate enough of their flavour, content and context, at levels that show how they connect with and have contributed to health care in the Information Age, and how and why they matter. Many of the stories and topics covered connect closely, and uniquely, with and along the timeline of my own career in the field, which has coincided with the emergence of health informatics as both discipline and practice. Health informatics has been termed a 'grand challenge' and such challenges have been a recurring theme of academic discourse of recent decades.[24]

---

23   Pinker, *The Better Angels of Our Nature*.

24   Neil Gershenfeld at Massachusetts Institute of Technology (MIT) described the increasing grouping and cross-fertilization of disciplines, and the defensive boundaries between them that encourage and incentivize non-communicating silos of knowledge. He proposed the regrouping of academic disciplines around grand challenges facing society, in which all disciplines have a part to play–such as ageing society, artificial intelligence and clean energy. He wrote that 'The greatest

Success in meeting them transcends governments, organizations, industries, disciplines and professions. It requires cooperation and collaboration that engages these groups and the communities they serve, united in pursuit of common purposes and goals, honed by incrementally and iteratively tested implementations in real-world practice. This in turn depends on a trusted common ground of knowledge that is openly shared and sustained among participants and within the global public domain.

As will already be clear, the attempted scope of my book is very ambitious, and perhaps foolishly so! It travels widely into many and disparate histories, disciplines and professions, seeking connections on a common ground of health care services and the information systems that support and integrate them. This breadth of coverage risks becoming too complicated, and indeed of limited interest, even if admittedly of major potential impact, for those involved in the separate domains the book concerns. Its principal audience is therefore likely to be centred on those recognizing the importance of and engaging in endeavours which are intrinsically collaborative, interdisciplinary and multiprofessional. A key requirement for such endeavours is that there is an understood shared goal of the collaboration and that each contributing partner group is able and prepared to work towards mutual understanding of where its partner groups are coming from, and to learn, adapt and co-evolve with them, accordingly. In today's discourse and society, such polymath capacities are a receding reality. Culture, practice and leadership of teamwork across widely disparate disciplines, professions, services and communities are central to successful ventures–emphasizing all-important human factors, once again.

Recognizing the limitations that it entailed, the physicist and father of quantum mechanics, Erwin Schrödinger (1887–1961), opened with a caveat when introducing his book *What Is Life?*, in which he set out to characterize living organisms within then contemporary concepts and language of physics.

> We feel clearly that we are only now beginning to acquire reliable material for welding together the sum total of all that is known into a whole; but on the other hand, it has become next to impossible for a single mind fully to command more than a small, specialized portion of it [....] I can see no other escape from this dilemma (lest our true aim be lost for ever)

---

consequence of improving information technology may be to organize intellectual inquiry around grand challenges rather than traditional disciplines', saying that 'if this turns out to be so, then a title like "the physics of information technology" may eventually become triply redundant. The truth is that none of those words can properly stand without all of them' (N. Gershenfeld, 'Bits and Chips', *New Scientist*, 169 (2001), 55).

than that some of us should venture to embark on a synthesis of facts and theories, albeit with second-hand and incomplete knowledge of some of them–and at the risk of making fools of ourselves.[25]

Schrödinger framed a very broad-ranging purpose and goal for his book–an elusive answer to the question he posed. He probed disciplinary insights directed to that end, illuminating the question as much as providing an answer. It was quite a short book, but a mind-stretching read for the audiences it sought to connect with–for the physicist familiar with that world but new to the life sciences, and vice-versa for the life scientist. It penetrated detail of these different disciplines and their bodies of knowledge when looking for useful connections that might throw light on his quest.

A similar caveat from me, about 'risking making a fool of myself' with this book, is infinitely more due! However, there seems little harm that can arise from it and not a lot to lose. It seems necessary to risk foolishness in venturing so widely, to seek greater understanding. And thereby to help facilitate traction in coping with and navigating the landscape of often anarchic encounters of information technology with life science, medicine and health care services, and in envisaging and shaping what might lie ahead. I am hugely indebted to Alessandra Tosi and Rupert Gatti, the founders of Open Book Publishers, and those who have contributed to the costs of publication, for trusting, encouraging and supporting me in bringing it to life as an open access work.

There is a very wide range of past and present participants closely involved and implicated in these matters, and the needs and available means to help join their disjoint goals, motivations and actions also vary greatly. Were we to place members drawn from all the constituencies involved in developing, delivering, receiving and regulating health care services in one room, they would likely mostly succeed only in swapping their stories, or discussing football or the weather! As the philosopher Arthur Schopenhauer (1788–1860) remarked, 'The doctor sees all the weakness of mankind; the lawyer all the wickedness, the theologian all the stupidity'.[26] Much confusion and confabulation of perspectives still pervades the airwaves! And yet, the human biology that accompanied the ideas attributed to Hippocrates (*c.* 460 BCE–375 BCE) and Galen (*c.* 130 CE–210 CE), from around 2000 years ago, leading to the invention of medicine, is very much the human biology of today. Schopenhauer also said that all human history

---

25   E. Schrödinger, *What Is Life?* (Cambridge, UK: Cambridge University Press, 1948), p. 1.

26   A. Schopenhauer, *Parerga and Paralipomena: A Collection of Philosophical Essays* (New York: Cosimo, 2007), p. 66.

was encompassed in Herodotus's *Histories*, which was assembled some decades before *The Epidemics*, indicating that humankind does not change much, either!

In fairness, the landscape of new ideas, methods and practices involving information technology that has unfolded onto the health care scene along my songline, and much of it disappeared out of sight, has often been bafflingly multi-faceted and complex for everyone, me included. Each participating constituency has sought its own answers and asserted its own clarity. Few meaningful and useful answers can arise that way these days, save perhaps through extreme good luck or the diktats of *force majeure*. They require environments and common endeavours that join across disciplines, professions, services, industries, jurisdictions and society at large.

This is the inclusive perspective that the book is organized around and one of its principal goals is to describe and lay foundations that can help to support future inclusive endeavours. The audience for such a goal is not well-defined or formed in the fragmented world of health care in transition that we have come to inhabit. Such audience must be created and persuaded, it being characteristic of the reception of new and yet unexplored ideas, that they can be quickly dismissed as irrelevant and of no interest, or perceived as too difficult to engage with, or be allowed to pass by under the radar before being afforded opportunity and space to develop. I devote a section at the end of the Introduction to a more detailed consideration of the potential audience for the book and, to the extent that it has not existed hitherto, how, and why it can and needs to be created. This process will include a wider coming to terms with the realization that informatics, the science of information, is, like mathematics, now increasingly central to the framing of ideas central to many disciplines, and not just as a computational tool used by those disciplines. Bioinformatics is now central to life science and health informatics increasingly so to health care.

I was, in my academic grounding, a proficient mathematician and a capable theoretical physicist. Vainly, I can boast that I have the double first-class honours degree to show for that, though have not used it as once I might have hoped to–perhaps also wisely recognizing that I would probably not have succeeded! Theory and abstraction based on clear and critical thinking are important in physics. But they only progress beyond abstraction when grounded in experiment. And in such widely ranging domains as health care and information technology, they only make sense when grounded in wider social context and culture, and advances in engineering. Like medicine and politics, engineering is an art of the possible. Engineering advances, often underappreciated and overlooked, have been the driving force behind much of the scientific progress that has been made.

Like any skill, medicine included, people learn it and become good at it, by doing it and reflecting on their performance. This is a thought I return to often in the book, in recognizing and celebrating the importance of pioneers–makers and doers working at the interfaces of science, health care and society. Key figures I introduce have combined intellectual prowess with determination to see ideas into practice, experimentally at first, and progressively by turning their hands to making and doing things that work, putting them to use, and learning, thereby, how to make and do them better. A crucial liberation of the potential of information technology came from its democratization in this way, from the domain of its specialists into the multiple domains of its users, enabling them to use it themselves, creatively, in their own very different worlds, to create their own stories. We should focus more, now, on how to place health care back more closely into the hands of individual citizens and their communities.

By chance, my career has always been a marginal one. But from it has grown an international community and organization, the not-for-profit openEHR Foundation, created from my Department at UCL in the second half of my career in health informatics, and the openEHR International Community Interest Company (CIC), working within the framework of the Creative Commons, to which operational activity and governance is now devolved. Such entities are organic in nature and expressions of the many people and organizations in many countries that make them a reality. openEHR is a tree that I conceived of, planted and nurtured through its early decades and helped to grow into an increasingly successful and influential forest, with thousands of members and participants, now in a hundred countries, and an increasing number of successful businesses, health care organizations and municipalities in partnership. Most importantly, it now thrives and governs itself, without me occupying any role other than the self-indulgent celebratory one of its Founding President. It seeks to share the values and goals we set twenty years ago, and the culture and spirit of cooperation and ways of doing things that were adopted from the outset. It is doing influential work and involving and motivating a new generation of pioneers, much more able than I am, or ever was, to carry it forward. It has had its perilous and dispiritingly vulnerable moments, too, of course! This is a story, that of openEHR and its mission, that I tell in Chapter Eight and a Half. I explain, there, the inspiration for the half chapter in its connection with the novelist Julian Barnes. It probably should have a book of its own. Maybe and zobaczymy [we will see], which is the Polish response when confronted with all imponderables in life! More fatalistically, in English, we say that 'time will tell'.

The second initiative I have participated in for fifteen years is the OpenEyes open-source software for ophthalmology electronic medical records, which had its origins nearby UCL, at the world-renowned Moorfields Eye Hospital. It is now being taken forward by the Apperta Foundation and a growing international and multiprofessional partnership of participants. This story is also told, but in less detail, in Chapter Eight and Chapter Eight and a Half. Like openEHR, it has been accelerating on a long runway spanning two decades, to the point where it is now creating records for approaching fifty percent of eye care consultations in the UK health services and flying over the Internet Cloud to be used by clinicians elsewhere in the world. In January 2023, OpenEyes was accredited by the Digital Square organization (Digitalsquare.org) as a global public good. In health care, these are described as '[...] tools that are impactful, scalable, and adaptable to different countries and contexts. These free and open-source digital health tools look to reduce fragmentation and duplication to accelerate scale and health impact'.[27]

Building and sustaining good teams and creating and supporting inspiring and creative environments that enable them to flourish, is central to success. The approach to the challenges of health informatics that I have pursued carries risks but is relatively inexpensive and already has vibrant communities of practice and substantial worldwide installed bases. In Nassim Taleb's terms, it is surely antifragile.[28] The potential upside benefits are very large, and the downside risks very limited. The time has come to open eyes, to projects and communities like those of openEHR and OpenEyes. There are many such initiatives emerging across the world in the Information Age and they need and deserve greater attention and support. They are tackling problems that have proved beyond governments, professions, communities and industries, alone, to solve, but which require solution if information is to extend beyond its technology into an essential utility, supportive throughout health care.

The balance, continuity and governance of care services form a trifecta of challenges faced in reinventing and reforming health care. In openEHR and OpenEyes we have come halfway, as dreamers, along a pathway of learning how to create and sustain what we might call an openCare utility, supportive of such reinvention and reform. In his epic history, *Seven Pillars of Wisdom*, T. E. Lawrence wrote thus of two kinds of dreamers: 'All men dream, but not equally. Those who dream by night in the dusty recesses of their minds,

---

27   S. Bochaberi, V. Rathod and C. Fourie, 'Digital Square Announces New Software Global Goods Approved through Notice G', *Digital Square* (16 February 2023), https://digitalsquare.org/blog/2023/2/16/digital-square-announces-new-software-global-goods-approved-through-notice-g

28   N. N. Taleb, *Antifragile: How to Live in a World We Don't Understand* (London: Allen Lane, 2012).

wake in the day to find that it was vanity: but the dreamers of the day are dangerous men, for they may act on their dreams with open eyes, to make them possible'.[29] The openEHR and OpenEyes communities are hopefully neither vane nor dangerous, and certainly not all men! But they are, for sure, acting (i.e. implementing!) their dreams to make them possible!

After starting my life living in a small and isolated rural village, I am now living in the ancient English city of St Albans, which is busily reshaping itself as a set of globally connected local small villages, where daily life and relationships are both global and local, in both scope and application. I look back along my songline with a mixture of amazement and bemusement. Amazed by the advances in science and engineering and my personal good fortune to have lived and worked so closely with people who have been at the heart of those achievements. Bemused by the countervailing tensions that have arisen in the wider context and global reach of information technology and communications, and their demonstrated capacity to reshape everyday life in ways that both improve and draw people together and impoverish and split them apart. I look forward with equal amazement as AlphaFold, ticking away just a few hundred metres from UCL–its chess- and Go-playing co-founding genius having commenced his professional life at the UCL Queen Square Institute of Neurology–demonstrates the progression of machine learning into the life science and clinical domains. Perhaps Jeremy Bentham (1748–1832) would have been pleased to observe how my story connects with engineering and medicine at UCL, the University that celebrates its close connection with him to this day. I am delighted by its many connections, also, with physics and engineering at my alma mater, Magdalen College at the University of Oxford, and medicine at Bart's.

The book has been growing and metamorphosing in my mind for several years, alongside the very diverting new obsession with my wife, Bożena, in keeping fit and getting rather good and having fun in all manner of ballroom, Latin and Argentine Tango dance–we have drawers full of medals to justify that boast! It was a happy moment when youngsters in the teaching crew at a sailing club in Greece, saw us dancing at the social evening, asked to dance with us, and enquired whether we had been professional dancers! We wish! With these diversions, it has never felt a good time to sit down and spend the many months I have, to write the book. Marcus Tullius Cicero (106 BCE–43 BCE) may or may not have written that 'Times are bad. Children no longer obey their parents, and everyone is writing a book', as legend avers. But bad times, recently, facing enforced house lockdown for many months because

---

29   T. E. Lawrence, *Seven Pillars of Wisdom* (Chatham: Wordsworth Editions Limited, 1997), p. 7.

of the pandemic, presented an opportunity and accelerated my writing of this one, now.

I started to write at the beginning of what, it seemed, might progress into a twelve- or twenty-four-month period of locked-down life, at the start of the first wave of the Covid-19 pandemic. The science on which hopes are pinned for better treatment and prevention of the infection, making the world safe again, would have been unimaginable to those who lived through the Spanish flu, immediately after the First World War. The communication of and about the virus itself–the speed of its transmission and of cooperative responses seeking to understand, treat and guard against it, in countries across the globe–would likewise have seemed dreams about another planet. They would have been Utopian dreams in the 1950s at the start of my songline, when many of the people I encountered and the ideas they brought to fruition in science and technology (transforming medicine and underpinning the networks of communication, data processing and computation on which everyday life now depends) were in their early adult lives and formative career stages.

The imperative to write the book also resonated with me strongly when in receipt of the piercing interrogations of the young. 'What have you been up to, grandpa?' is a great question–for me as much as for our family's nine gorgeous, growing, enquiring and challenging grandchildren. It is wonderful to have them alongside, at the start of their own songlines and with more acute eyes and ears, peering forward and listening. The Information Age is just normal life for them. Like any grandad, I am anxious for the Information Society to evolve well for them.

This has been a long preamble aimed at illuminating the origins and content of the book. There are very many people acknowledged throughout for their contributions. With regards the content of the book itself, of course, the buck stops with me. I hope it is interesting, fair, balanced and useful. And, hopefully, also thought-provoking and controversial. Nothing useful could be written about this very wide-ranging field, that was not! It has been a privilege to have been trusted with freedom in my work, to focus on creating and enabling innovation that is significant and will endure alongside the uncertain and changing contingencies of our anarchic times, mirroring how MacAskill has encouraged us to focus, when deciding what to do in our lives.[30] My greatest hope is that my family, friends and colleagues will feel pleased and proud to have been part of it all, alongside me, while also, no doubt, quite relieved, as I am, that the writing is now done!

David Ingram, St Albans, March 2023

---

30   W. MacAskill, *What We Owe the Future* (New York: Basic Books, 2022).

Prologue

What's past is prologue, what to come, in yours and my discharge.

–William Shakespeare (1564–1616)[1]

How the past perishes is how the future becomes.

–Alfred North Whitehead (1861–1947)[2]

We may become the makers of our fate when we have ceased to pose as its prophets.

–Karl Popper (1902–94)[3]

The ultimate hidden truth of the world is that it is something we make and could just as easily make differently.

–David Graeber (1961–2020)[4]

A prologue is traditionally a curtain-raiser in the telling of a story–it arouses and prepares us for what is to come. It is like a birth or dawning. We talk of human birth and development and dawning of civilization. The computer was also born, and its powers are developing. Its scope and capability are starting to dawn on us, now.

Each human life is conceived and endowed with a biological inheritance– shared from its parents and connected with its mother. This inheritance channels the nurtured growth from a single cell to a maturing embryo, born as a child into the world. The child discovers, learns, lives and copes. They experience the world and connect with it. They grow and evolve in context of family, community and society at large. On these many levels and stages of life, the computer is now never far from their side. We are learning to live with the computer. It shares in what we sense and know, and how we act. It

---

1   *The Tempest*, Act 2, Scene 1.
2   *Adventures of Ideas* (New York: Macmillan, 1933), p. 228.
3   K. Popper, *The Open Society and Its Enemies: The Spell of Plato* (London: Routledge and Kegan Paul, 1957), p. xxxvii.
4   D. Graeber, *The Utopia of Rules: On Technology, Stupidity, and the Secret Joys of Bureaucracy* (New York: Melville House, 2015), p. 97.

    https://doi.org/10.11647/OBP.0335.07

has the potential to empower and enrich our lives, but with a catch for the unwary. Where we know our mind and keep our head, it is an invaluable resource. Where we do not, it exposes and amplifies inconsistencies in our approach and expectations. It does so without heart and can come to haunt us. Our hands can become entangled and tied, and we will have tied them.

By design and by stealth, an increasingly pervasive computerized reality is emerging and unfolding, channelling and modulating human experience and creating virtual worlds with which we engage. In health care, there is a growing profusion of computer software and applications: sensing the world, collecting and analyzing data, and reasoning about, guiding and determining action. This is an embryonic information utility–universal and flowing, like water in a river. A river carrying diverse kinds and qualities of information, much of it meandering through tributaries, without direction and purpose, hydrating and flooding some parts of the human, social and environmental landscape and missing others that remain dry.

David Deutsch, a doyen of quantum computation, has characterized knowledge as information with causative power. What is this information, where does it come from, what does it cause to happen and why? And how should we envision and create coherent and purposeful information as a utility for everyday life? These are central questions for our present and future health care. What we make of them, and how we act as a result, affects us now and will form our legacy to those who follow us. It will be their inheritance.

This book looks back, around and forward, to celebrate people and ideas, regret wasteful and burdensome failings, and propose an optimistic programme for reform. It addresses the most significant, and thus far least successfully answered, of these questions. How? It is not a prescription–it is a story about how the past and present were made, and about shaping the future. It is a story of the admixture of human-mediated material reality with computer-mediated virtual reality.

We can imagine being born into life and awareness of the world–that world appearing, and experienced, as a jumble. Being born as a nourished and functioning organism, with senses bombarding the mind, starting to breathe and giving voice. Being born with an embryonic inner world, already connecting, communicating, maturing and learning. An embryonic mental world of signals colliding and resolving into touch, vision, sound, taste and smell–into feeling and expression–into patterns and languages–making sense. A formative world of experience of community and culture. An integrative world of living and coping. A being pre-formed in the womb, in transition to a person existing and performing in the world, and becoming one of an evolving humankind.

The computer is a machine that has mirrored much of this developmental panorama. We have made it that way. It was conceived of, given embryonic form and function, attended to lovingly and let loose to grow within, pervade and learn about the world. Its sensors, language and memory–and its power to process, analyse, decide, communicate and act–have massively matured. In its own ways, it sees, hears, touches, tastes and smells. Its communications and connections with the human world have embedded ever more widely. This is where we have got to. The story is still unfolding.

A nourished and functioning body is each healthy individual's inheritance at birth–the inherited mechanism of life itself. Wider inheritance from the outside world accelerates from birth and accumulates through life. We inherit, add to and subtract from inheritance in our lives, share its learning and pass it on. Each unique human life adapts and passes on its biological inheritance, learning and experience. Each human era embodies experiences of present and past reality, and of transition into the future. Each era bequeaths a legacy–environment, culture, knowledge and belief.

Human civilization has itself emerged and evolved, also mirroring much of this same developmental pattern and panorama–from embryonic beginnings to present-day community and society. Now with an accumulated inheritance of language and discourse–words, philosophy, number and reason. With tools and technologies for making and doing. With literature and libraries. With law and governance. With a science of theory, experiment, analysis and record. With education, medicine and health care. From a world with none of these ideas and connections, now emerging into an embryonic new world–that of the Information Society. This transition is perturbing nearly every aspect of society that existed before the birth of the computer. It is a very bumpy ride. There is much that it is helping to improve and re-form, and much that it is destabilizing and deforming.

The legacy of the computer is, thus far, a modern-day curate's egg. A half-mature technology interacting with a half-helped, half-impeded, but universally impacted, world and society. It is both a success story and a cautionary tale, but universally costly, burdensome and disruptive. We look forward with both hope and pessimism, audaciously emboldened and thoughtfully cautious.

The computer is a machine. Its design has evolved from simple embryonic structure and function, to hugely more complex but still evolving form and capability. It connects with sensors that measure and record appearances of the world. It has memory. It embodies methods that model and represent these appearances and analyse and reason with them. It interacts with and influences what humans make and do. It enacts a play, holding a mirror up to life and experience of the world. It connects with what we know and believe. It can deceive and lead astray. Human awareness is connecting with and adapting to the computer and its virtual reality, bringing new sensations and appearances of the world, and enabling and creating a new sense of the possible.

What is happening to health care as life and medical sciences metamorphose in all these giddying contexts? What means and methods should we be adopting, now, in our work to create a good information utility for health care? What is the purpose of such a utility and what should be its goals and governance? Who should participate and where should they come from and work?

Today hosts the last human generation with direct experience of the world before the advent of computers, and of the transformative impact their invention has had. It is a unique time of transition–it will not reverse direction and it will not come again. The Information Society, brave new world or otherwise, is being created. This world is characterized by global and universal machine-based experiences, connections, communications and computations. It introduces a new realm where human senses, feelings and consciousness interact at an accelerating pace within an infinite ensemble of future minds and possibilities.

To understand and engage with health care of the future, we must listen to the experiences and needs of those for whom good health care can feel an unachievable or very unequal reality. To understand how to create a good future information utility to support the values and goals of health care services in the emergent Information Society, we must know and think about history. History that played out before the computer, across many and disparate domains, encompassing philosophy, logic and mathematics; science, engineering and medicine; materials, methods and machines; environment and community. This historical progression extends from eras without medicine to our current context of health care in the Information Age: from the earliest recognition and description of disability and disease, through the utilization of tools such as thermometers and stethoscopes for observation and measurement, to the modern development of pharmaceuticals, body scanners, portable and networked sensors, and machine intelligence. It encompasses the progression of health care settings from asylums and workhouses to specialist hospitals and hospitals at home; and the evolution of practitioners, from wandering healer and Good Samaritan, to primary, secondary and tertiary care teams, and self-care.

An inherent complexity in the handling of health care as a topic of debate and decision, is that almost every discipline, profession and social constituency contributes–seeing itself mirrored in, and being actively interested in, the matters arising. Almost by definition, there is a lack of unifying perspective. Closeted rooms populated with learned philosophy, mathematics, science, professions, services, ethics and law, tend to issue clouds of white and black (yes and no) smoke. These blow in different directions in the world at large and their constructs can easily tend towards chimeric aggregations rather than wholes. And yet, no credible and cohesive policy and plan for health care can be constructed and implemented without them. Health and social care services are 'wicked problems' of social policy. They exist as costly and unduly fragmented domains–governed under political fiat and managed through persuasion, money and resource, and such evidentiary justification as their component communities can assemble and agree on. And they keep changing. Wicked problems and how we approach them feature strongly in the landscape this book traverses.

Such differing and changing perspectives can become more ingrained as we map them into our efforts to computerize. How far are we distorting or constraining the nature of the biological and clinical reality that the computer is being required to compute about, as we grapple with representing this natural world within the available forms of computer-generated virtual reality? Humankind copes with and resolves incoherence and inconsistency, and keeps going, as best it can. The machine world is less forgiving and gives up easily, but at a cost. As the saying goes, 'to err is human, to really mess things up, buy a computer'!

A sound handle on coherence and consistency, or lack thereof, is a prerequisite for safe and logical computation. One way or another, a functioning computer program asserts an order. At the machine code level, computer processors do not tolerate ambiguity, albeit that the quantum era of computation promises to bring greatly increased power to methods for tackling complex problem formulations, by exploiting the quantum superposition of qubit states in the search for solutions.[5]

There is also a recurring clash of perspectives when we start to compute about a disputed reality. First between the perfection of our knowledge and the facilitation of our practice–debated in philosophies of ontology and epistemology. On another level–played out in moral philosophy–there is the clash between the general and the particular regarding principles (which serve as standards, truth-tellers and guides). Generalists look for and emphasize general principles, and 'particularists' argue against them, citing exceptions.

Writing from Harvard University in 1932, Whitehead commented on this dilemma:

---

5   Algorithms that would grind for many millennia on the most powerful of today's supercomputers, might now, in time, be circumvented in minutes by quantum circuits running in laboratory lash-ups of a few dozen qubits, connected to the Cloud. These prototypes are objects of contemporary awe–making real the musings of visionary theoretical physicists sixty years ago

The first step in science and philosophy has been made when it is grasped that every routine exemplifies a principle which is capable of statement in abstraction from its particular exemplifications. The curiosity, which is the gadfly driving civilization from its ancient safeties, is this desire to state the principles in their abstraction. In this curiosity, there is a ruthless element which in the end disturbs [...] The generality stands with a cold impartiality, where our affections cling to one or other of the particulars. [...] All the world over and at all times there have been practical men, absorbed in 'irreducible and stubborn facts'; all the world over and at all times there have been men of philosophic temperament, who have been absorbed in the weaving of general principles. It is this union of passionate interest in the detailed facts with equal devotion to abstract generalization which forms the novelty of our present society.[6]

And how can moral philosophy find its way into the encoded virtual reality? Probably it cannot (and a coming Novacene era of artificial intelligence might not see the point, anyway!), but what then?

It is interesting to think back to how a sense of reality unfolded in classical times. For some strange reason, my brain still remembers this from schooldays:

τυφλός τα τ' ὤτα, τον τε νουν, τα τ' ὄμματ' εί

Phonetically, this sounds like: typhlos ta t' ota, ton te noun, ta t' ommat' ei. It was a tongue-twister to amuse Greek classes. Education was all about Greece and Rome to my wonderfully eccentric headteacher, and all Greek to most of his language pupils, including me in my one year of accelerated attempt, at his insistence, to learn the language! I can still pronounce the words but cannot now translate them. Google translates them like this: blind in ears, mind and eyes, blind in hearing, intellect and sight. This appears to pertain to the relationship between our senses and our comprehension and interpretation of reality: the mind makes sense of the reality sampled by the bodily senses. There is trial and error, and patterns take root. Most of the brain is devoted to interpreting and controlling bodily sensation and function. As Leonard Cohen (1934–2016) said–or, rather, gravelly intoned for us, as we listened, spellbound, at one of his last concerts, in London–'everybody knows', and I think we might interpret that as 'every body' knows! The mind has a conscious will and wends its way–another complicated and much-debated story!

Okay, all a bit sophistic, maybe, but translated to the computer it gives pause for thought. Human senses are different from and often inferior

---

6   *Adventures of Ideas*, p. 138.

to many in the animal kingdom. Bees sense ultraviolet light and earthly magnetism, where humans do not. Some shrimps have twelve kinds of light detecting cells where humans have three. They 'see' differently. And the computer is rapidly enhancing device technology and outscoring biology in the ability to sense the natural world, not just in kind but also in scale and duration. It, too, 'sees' differently. With the computer, we can now map and track every tree on earth and much else in the universe. So what of our human relative 'blindness' in the senses and corresponding relative blindness in 'intellect'?

As well as tongue-twisters, the Greeks were good at mind-twisters! The nature of reality (ontology) became a vortex of debate among philosophical minds. Professional philosophers who debate ontology are forever accusing one another of egregious error! Whitehead describes a study of inconsistency among logicians, where twenty distinct meanings of the term 'proposition' were revealed; the distinctions reflecting different purposes and points of view. He writes, 'it is safe to affirm that this situation can be repeated over every technical term in philosophy'.[7] Such might equally now be said of much of the historic terminologies of computer science and medicine!

Health care informatics proved a brain twisting domain, too, as it sought to formalize language and description of health and disease in the company of professional 'ontologists' (Microsoft Word suggests that I might be thinking of professional otologists or oncologists, here, so perhaps there are no such people, after all!). Experience of this history should perhaps caution us not to concern ourselves, too quickly or too closely, with the complexities of ontology as a regulator of our ideas and debates. Stories of making and doing, over time and in close touch with people and events, and stories of coping with complexity and challenge, are instructive when seeking common ground on which to build what comes next. 'What is true and what to do' joust one another in contesting that space. This book is about the quest for common ground on which to base, create and sustain a care information utility that is supportive of citizen-centred, coherent, integrated and equitable health care systems and services of tomorrow.

---

7   Ibid., p. 221.

PART ONE–
ADVENTURE OF IDEAS

Bolder adventure is needed–the adventure of ideas, and the advantage of practice conforming itself to ideas. The best service that ideas can render is gradually to lift into the mental poles the ideal of another type of perfection which becomes a programme for reform.

–Alfred North Whitehead (1861–1947)[1]

Part One of the book concerns the adventure of ideas that has powered the rise of computer science and technology, and its impact on the advance of life sciences, medicine and health care, as they have moved into and through the Information Age.

The adventure began in ancient and classical times and has connected over many centuries in the evolving ideas and histories of philosophy, mathematics, logic, science and engineering. Many worlds have been turned upside down by the invention and evolution of the computer.

The five chapters span a long history and scan a wide panorama: knowledge, language and reason; observation and measurement; models and simulations; and information technologies. These have evolved side by side in the Information Age. And society, too, has evolved and innovated, bridging from the adventure of ideas into practices that have shaped, and now underpin, health care services today.

---

1 *Adventures of Ideas* (New York: Macmillan, 1933), p. 248.

1. Introduction–Connecting for Health

Only connect! That was the whole of her sermon. Only connect the prose and the passion, and both will be exalted, and human love will be seen at its height. Live in fragments no longer. Only connect, and the beast and the monk, robbed of the isolation that is life to either, will die.

–E. M. Forster (1879–1970)[1]

A good environment is not a luxury; it is a necessity.

–Richard Wollheim (1923–2003)[2]

Sometimes reality is too complex. Stories give it form.

–Jean-Luc Godard (1930–2022)[3]

This book connects two domains that are integral to every human life and increasingly to almost every other domain of human knowledge, appraisal, decision and action. The first of these, the unity of health and social care, has become progressively fragmented into separate entities, and needs wholeness restored. This reunification has been a long-expressed ambition of national policy in the United Kingdom (UK). Other countries, such as Finland, in my observation, are taking this more seriously and doing better. The second domain, information technology, can play an important role in fulfilment of this ambition, but as a component of an organic information utility, not as a machine. Organic, that is, in the sense of 'relating to, or derived from living organisms' and, in the context of health care, in the sense of being adaptable, evolving and human-centred.

---

1   *Howards End* (London: Edward Arnold, 1910), p. 174.
2   Quoted in J. Z. Young, *Programs of the Brain: Based on the Gifford Lectures, 1975–7* (Oxford: Oxford University Press, 1978), p. 1.
3   NB: this quote is widely attributed to Godard, but no explicit source has been identified.

       https://doi.org/10.11647/OBP.0335.01

Connection, environment and storytelling are central themes of this book, hence the introductory quotations above. It seems fitting to start here by revisiting the often-quoted perspective of Forster, writing a hundred years ago, when cars and telephones were new and electronic computers unknown. He was prescient of the potential for harm wrought by technology on social interaction. In his novel, *Howards End*, 'only connect' was about the connection of opposing elements of human personality–beast and monk, prose and passion–and the importance of the quality, not the number, of personal relationships. In the short story *The Machine Stops*, Forster painted a picture of a future society that had become dependent on connection with and through a worldwide machine–for shelter, food, communication and health care–and where personal life characterized by ubiquitous connections had retreated into a state of isolation and immobility, communicating only via 'the Machine'.

Connection is about joining and binding together; about nexus–a common theme and method and means of binding. Communication is about sharing and making common–common ground joins community and environment. I shared common ground with Richard Wollheim, who I also quoted above in relation to the importance of environment. Wollheim was as an undergraduate at the University of Oxford (where he studied Philosophy, Politics and Economics (PPE)) and a professor of philosophy at University College London (UCL). A 'good environment', as Wollheim suggests, in which to connect and communicate is essential for creativity, growth and development. Many strive to make connections and help build and sustain good environments and communities–some are lucky and successful in this, and some are not. People work and feel better, and trust more, in environments where they feel connection and a sense of personal identity and worth.

It would be naive not to recognize the power of disconnection, too. Polarization of opposites is a feature of the physical world, and, as Primo Levi (1919–87) expressed in *Other People's Trades*, the tendency to gravitate to repelling poles of extreme perspective is a natural human trait, seeking and prizing a feeling of certainty over the pain of confronting uncertainty.[4]

The storyline of this book opens onto a field of view encompassing the connection of information and information technology with the multiple disciplines and professions, and social and organizational contexts, of health care services. There are abundant connections that can and might be made across these domains, viewed from historical, contemporary and future perspectives. Nonetheless, the connections that persist throughout

---

4   P. Levi, *Other People's Trades* (London: Sphere Books, 1990).

are with the lives of individual citizens and the environments in which they live, work and receive or give care.

The book is a story of these many and disparate connections and interactions. It offers a perspective on how they can assist and support health care services as they evolve in the decades to come. Information, as a scientific construct, has emerged as a unifying concept of science and communication. Information as a utility akin to water and electricity supply, has emerged as an essential resource for everyday living. Information utility will be central to the future balance, continuity and governance of health care services. It is more complex than water, though: it is organic and can thus exhibit pathology. And it will reshape relationships of trust between individual citizens and the multiprofessional teams that serve them. Information utility for health care, as a co-creation of citizens and health care professionals, will be an essential shared and growing repository of knowledge and a resource for everyone, for learning and living.

As also quoted above, Jean-Luc Godard spoke of the importance of stories in giving form to complex ideas. As a film maker, he would likewise have spoken up for film and image, which also give form to ideas. Such an image as that in Figure 1.1 might be taken to symbolize the exploratory and incremental connections of multiple disciplines and professions in simultaneously creating and ascending a staircase of new knowledge and services in support of health care. It was produced by an online artificial intelligence program[5] that creates images from text.[6]

---

5   Several of the images that I had originally hoped to include in the book were not available under an open-access license. This led me to experiment with Stable Diffusion Online (https://stablediffusionweb.com) to create images using artificial intelligence software, based on descriptive text in the book. The images that the software created from extracts from poems by William Blake and T. S. Eliot (quoted at the start of Chapter Two (Vol. 1) on knowledge) were fascinating, thought-provoking and funny!

6   Thinking of the start of my career in health informatics, as described in the Preface (Vol. 1), the image might also be taken to represent me, 'stepping onto a virtual ladder of career progression in computational science and medicine, for which there was no bottom rung! [... starting] on my own, at ground zero, to create my ladder as I ascended it. I had to build mission and role from below [...] to help generate something new'.

Fig. 1.1 Ascending a staircase of new knowledge, professions and services. Image created by David Ingram using Stable Diffusion Online (2023), CC0 1.0.

The connections of information with medicine, health care and society today, have historical context of more than two thousand years. The book draws on a personal and subjective set of these connections–people and community, discipline and profession, science and practice, team and environment. It is a collection of stories, drawn from many sources and expressing many points of view. History as told by Herodotus (*c.* 484 BCE–420 BCE), often characterized as the father of history, was, I have read, constructed that way. He was writing some decades before the time of Hippocrates (*c.* 460 BCE–375 BCE) and his *Epidemics*, when oracles and omens were favoured predictors of the future, so one must bear this in mind when drawing on his insights.

For Herodotus, sources were categorized on three levels. The most reliable and useful were stories recorded in eyewitness accounts. Then came hearsay, based on stories derived from eyewitnesses. Finally came sources descriptive of official lines–expressions of politics and orthodoxy of the day, which he deemed the least reliable of sources! His reputation as a historian has waxed and waned–from charming but naive purveyor of other people's accounts to artful and intelligent overseer and shaper of sources, with the aim of creating a wider model and view of history. He was, it seems, attuned to a modern day anthropological and ethnographic approach to history, recorded through stories of culture and diversity, custom and practice, as much as through accounts of military and political events. From this diversity of sources and stories, listened to and accumulated along his wide-ranging songline, he shaped his narrative, concerned with questions of who was telling what stories, where and in what context, and from what perspective. He did not focus on veracity of individual sources so much as on a kaleidoscope of truths and untruths being told and shaped to different ends, thus assembling an overview culled from multiple sources and communities of storytellers.

This historical analogy echoes in contemporary experiences of social media and its polyphony of stories and accounts: it speaks to how we, individually and as a society, shape and make sense of such stories; how, within the Internet-connected environment, we modulate and moderate these stories to serve personal ends; and how, in the parallel contemporary surge of artificial intelligence and software like ChatGPT, the computer is being used to assimilate, generate and propagate stories, challenging human ability and capacity to distinguish information from misinformation, and reason from unreason. As Herodotus believed, we are under no obligation to believe stories but do, nonetheless, need to shape our understandings from the patterns and contingencies they present and reflect.

This perspective has strong echoes, too, within health care professional practice. Listening to, capturing, recording and responding to a patient's story along the timeline of their care–documenting the observations, measurements, interpretations, decisions made, actions initiated and resultant outcomes–traverses social culture, academic discipline and professional practice. The clinician is akin to both historian and eyewitness participant in this encounter, working like Herodotus to piece together understanding from disparate sources and assembled collections of evidence and accounts that may at times be conflicting and dissonant. The narrative of these histories is drawn together and connected within records of care. And artificial intelligence will bring new capacity for entwinement there, in unpredictable ways, accomplishing many beneficial and desired outcomes. However, it also carries the risk of admixing its own, potentially detrimental, virtual caricatures of the scene into the storyline of care, shaping both machine and human action.

The science and art of professional practice intermingle. Clinical skills depend importantly on what Gillian Tett has termed 'anthro-vision'. This is the title of her 2021 book, which is further discussed in Chapter Eight (Vol. 2).[7] The term characterizes the focus of the anthropologist on making sense of and engaging with histories in the human context of individuals and

---

7   G. Tett, *Anthro-Vision: A New Way to See in Business and Life* (New York: Simon and Schuster, 2021).

their families and communities. Here, health and care become increasingly indivisible, and issues of personal trust and autonomy reign supreme.

There is a further relevant perspective about such records, running parallel to these historical and anthropological ones, concerning holism in science and shifting emphasis onto the whole as greater than the sum of its parts. In his 1953 BBC Reith Lectures, *Science and the Common Understanding*, the physicist Robert Oppenheimer (1904–67), who led the wartime Manhattan Project, discussed what he termed the 'malignant ends' arising from a systematic belief in the idea of total knowledge, where all truth is one truth, all potential can exist as actual, all community as one community, all experience compatible with all other.[8] He drew on the idea of complementarity of the particle and wave descriptions in quantum theory, showing there how richer understanding comes from holding these two seemingly incompatible ideas in mind at the same time, in order to 'get things right'. He extended this idea into the quest for understanding of the complexity of wider human knowledge and society.

In the concluding chapter, he writes:

> If we err today–and I think we do–it is in expecting too much of knowledge from the individual and too much of synthesis from the community. We tend to think of these communities, no less than of the larger brotherhood of man, as made up of individuals, as composed of them as an atom is of its ingredients. We think similarly of general laws and broad ideas as made up of the instances which illustrate them, and from an observation of which we may have learned them. Yet this is not the whole. The individual event, the act, goes far beyond the general law. It is a sort of intersection of many generalities, harmonizing them in one instance as they cannot be harmonized in general.[9]

This echoes with the nature of clinical practice in its marrying of knowledge about patients in general with care of the individual, and the challenge faced in capturing this reality faithfully and usefully in computer software. In the light of the intrinsic limitations of what we, as humans, know and can know, Oppenheimer goes on to make a case for open access to knowledge, describing it as providing 'unlocked doors and signs of welcome, [...] a mark of a freedom as fundamental as any'.[10] He quotes Bishop Thomas Sprat (1635–1713), writing in the 1680s about the scientific purposes of the newly established Royal Society, and talking there about the central importance

---

8   J. R. Oppenheimer, *Science and the Common Understanding* (Oxford: Oxford University Press, 1954).

9   Ibid., p. 103.

10   Ibid., p. 105.

of diversity and the joining of different points of view. He describes 'the open society, the unrestricted access to knowledge, the unplanned and uninhibited association of men for its furtherance' as 'what may make a vast, complex, ever growing, ever-changing, ever more specialized and expert technological world nevertheless a world of human community'.[11] In discussing how we should seek to accommodate and learn from incompatibilities and diversities he says that achieving balance of these is both a required goal and a process that defines who we are. The quest for balance is necessary to make progress and, at the same time, it is a process that defines what we should aim for–a connection between the balance we seek and how we seek it–a feedback between goals and methods, and between means and ends.

Once again, this echoes our struggles to deploy the computer for the benefit of health care in the Information Age, and the task we face in finding balance, continuity and governance of health care services for the future Information Society.

This seems an appropriate moment to emphasize complementarity more widely. Oppenheimer used complementarity of particle-wave theory as his example. James Clerk Maxwell (1831–79) wove together experiment and theory of electric charge and current, and magnetic pole and field, in his theory of electromagnetism. Much of what had been separate–motor and dynamo action–became one. Complementarities, sometimes elusive ones, pervade this book–knowledge and experience, observation and measurement, information and life, and health and social care. Health and social care as 'healthocarism'–a shame that that sounds so awful! The binary logic of truth and falsehood, and yes and no decisions, has been fundamental to how information systems function and how they broker the complementarities of our understandings of, and feelings about, the world.

I introduce here another trail-blazing series of Reith Lectures, also near the beginning of my songline. These were the very first Reith Lectures, delivered by the mathematician, philosopher and social activist, Bertrand Russell (1872–1970) in 1948–49. The two series, Oppenheimer's and Russell's, resonate strongly today, seventy-five years later, with where we find ourselves in the transition from Information Age to Information Society, and with the choices that we face in how we marry information technology with both individual and population health care.

Russell's title was *Authority and the Individual*, and he covered the topic under headings of social cohesion, human nature, government, individuality, conflict, control, initiative and ethics–all seen through contrasting individual

---

11   Ibid., p. 106.

and societal perspectives and motivations.[12] Russell was, as ever, incisive (if not always practical!) in his judgements:

> Broadly speaking, we have distinguished two main purposes of social activities: on the one hand, security and justice require centralized governmental control, which must extend to the creation of a world government if it is to be effective. Progress, on the contrary, requires the utmost scope for personal initiative that is compatible with social order.
>
> The method of securing as much as possible of both these aims is *devolution*. The world government must leave national governments free in everything not involved in the prevention of war; national governments, in their turn, must leave as much scope as possible to local authorities.
>
> [...] People do not always remember that politics, economics, and social organization generally, belong in the realm of means, not ends. Our political and social thinking is prone to what may be called the 'administrator's fallacy', by which I mean the habit of looking upon the society as a systematic whole, of a sort that is thought good if it is pleasant to contemplate as a model of order, a planned organism with parts neatly dove-tailed into each other. Society does not, or at least should not, exist to satisfy an external survey, but to bring a good life to the individuals who compose it. It is in the individuals, not in the whole, that ultimate value is to be sought. A good society is a means to a good life for those who compose it, not something having a separate kind of excellence on its own account.[13]

Information systems bring these same issues of individual autonomy and social cohesion, of global order and local devolution, of personal ethics and national and international law, under a new spotlight. They reveal and challenge us with complex technical, organizational and clinical issues, for which we must seek new balance, continuity and governance of care.

How do these diverse perspectives of Tett, as anthropologist, Oppenheimer, as scientist, and Russell, as philosopher and social reformer, connect with the world unfolding in the Information Age? What light do they throw on the human, scientific and ethically-challenging kaleidoscopic pattern of connections of the computer with the health care of individuals, communities, and societies, locally, nationally, and globally? Where do issues of balance, continuity and governance of health care services lie within these wider contexts of the individual and society?

---

12   B. Russell, *Authority and the Individual: The Reith Lectures for 1948–9* (London: Allen and Unwin, 1949).

13   Ibid., pp. 107–08 and 116.

One key message that recurs is that we must work practically at ground level, and that this process will both define and reflect who we are. First, we must look at the connections of information with health care.

Information and Health Care–A History of Connections

Narratives of life and death have found expression in beliefs, cultures and practices of society, and their clashes, from ancient and classical times, East and West. They are pieced together from documentary and archaeological record and interpreted by historians. They are preserved, supplemented with new discoveries and perspectives, studied, reshaped and passed down through recorded history. Such record is captivatingly present in Edward Gibbon's (1737–94) *magnum opus* history of the Roman Empire.[14]

In classical times, failing health, accident and disability were perceived as afflictions from the gods. They were mitigated by mystical and religious beliefs and practices, and sacrificial offerings. A systematic approach to health slowly gained sway, as recorded in the writings attributed to Hippocrates and Galen (*c.* 130 CE–210 CE). Accounts emerged of the carefully observed progression of ill health and interventions enacted, with experiences of bodily functions and correction of dysfunctions crystallizing as ideas of disease. Such concepts of the nature of health and illness evolved, finding expression in mythology, philosophy, arts and science. Over time, they were refined and gained wider explanatory context from later experience, new ways of thinking and growing bodies of knowledge. Medicine is a human invention. It started to emerge, in record, practice and discipline, in ancient and classical times, as recently pieced together with scholarly authority by the historian, Robin Lane Fox, in his book, *The Invention of Medicine*, which centres on the story of Hippocrates and his *Epidemics*.[15]

Philosophy, mathematics, logic and science evolved in sequence and in parallel. Measurements of space, weight and time, and reasoning with these, advanced for purposes of agriculture, commerce, construction and navigation. Medicine, ever a matter of life and death, stayed close to craft and religion, guarded by the priesthoods of successive eras. Folklore prevailed alongside belief and law of church and land. The idea of the body as a homeostatic and conscious organism dawned slowly, engaging philosophy,

---

14   E. Gibbon, *The History of the Decline and Fall of the Roman Empire* (London: Strahan and Cadell, 1788).

15   R. Lane Fox, *The Invention of Medicine: From Homer to Hippocrates* (London: Penguin Books, 2020).

mathematics and science in lengthy, earnest discourse and contention. Until the twentieth century, the interaction of measurement and science with the practice of medicine was mainly treated as irrelevant, an unwelcome intrusion. In the early stages of my songline, information technology was treated with much the same brand of ridicule, amusement and professional disdain in life science and medicine, as that afforded to the thermometer and stethoscope in their respective infancies.

And alongside all this, has evolved the story of information, as encompassed within the scope of this book. The story starts from earliest times, with human knowledge and the quest to classify books and documents and organize libraries. Over many centuries, religion, philosophy, logic and mathematics traded arguments about knowledge and its description in language. The terminology of this discourse evolved, as we sought to communicate within and among different disciplines and articulate and clarify differing positions and perspectives. This has often led to a restrictive appropriation of the use of words, to mean different things within diverse disciplines and contexts.

Models in mathematical form were used as expressions of the phenomena being measured or reasoned with. This enabled the rules of mathematics to be applied in abstract analysis, enabling the discovery of new knowledge. Formal logic evolved. Mathematics gave birth to theoretical foundations of computation and computer science. With the advent of the computer, mathematical models extended to more complex and comprehensive representations and reasoning. These mapped the observed and measured reality, expressed in words and numbers, to one expressed in the language of computation.

Information technology translated the world of knowledge, measurement and mathematical models to the world of the computer. Measurement technologies advanced and became ever more central engines of scientific advance. What was observed and measured, captured and reasoned with, as narrative and number, and analyzed with mathematics, extended into a world of codes and symbols. The computer focused first on calculation with numbers and then on processing of all manner of these data, captured and communicated from sensors and keyboards, stored in and accessed from databases, modelled and analyzed with program algorithms. Multiple descriptions of reality and its appearances lifted off and started their climb into and beyond the data stratosphere, into a universe of data and 'dataism'.

For example, consider the evolution of weather forecasting (a story of great success, from a very different world than health care).[16] From the feel

---

16   I have used many wide-ranging stories and examples throughout the book, to give context and perspective to what happened within health care in the Information

of seaweed hung on a door peg, a moistened finger in the air and observation of clouds; to weather stations on land and at sea, collecting and charting temperature, humidity, pressure and airflow; to the grouping and drawing together of these separate sets of data, by eye and mathematical fitting of curves, into contour maps used to display and reason about weather patterns; to mathematical models of the physics of the atmosphere, ever more granular and widely distributed sensors and systems of measurement, computer models and computations. Prediction of the trend and variability of weather was progressively tamed within newly discovered bounds of chaos and complexity theory. All rather a long way from useful models of biological systems, and their intrinsic and contextual variability. What works for the weather system cannot necessarily be expected to perform equivalently, and provide useful insight, for the systems of biology, medicine and health care.

Measurement devices and models are tools of science, designed and built by scientists and engineers of their times–some as trained professionals and others as gifted artisans. With arrival of the computer, engineering entered a new era of information engineering, underpinned by at first pragmatic, and then more principled, theoretical models of computation and data. Software tools evolved to support design and development of information systems, to manage ever-expanding amounts and complexity of data and ever-more powerful programs to process and analyze them. The rise of telecommunications engineering gave impetus to this advance, focused initially on electrical signals and their accurate transmission from a source device, through wires and junctions, to a destination. These systems evolved into networks of digitized information flow across the world, standardized progressively into a World Wide Web.

The idea of information as a science of order gained ground in the eighteenth century, from the thermodynamics of gases and steam engines

---

Age and what is to come. Readers reviewing and advising me about earlier drafts of the book sometimes found them to be tangential and distracting from its core themes, and in part they are. They cover topics that have connected with and assisted me in making sense of experience accumulated along my personal songline. I have removed or abbreviated several of them. In real life, songlines do, though, tend to meander off track! Herodotus's multi-volume *Histories* is renowned for heading off track into 'rabbit holes' of story and anecdote, so I feel in good company! The writing of history and the creation of the future are both acts of imagination. I hope my storytelling is suitably and usefully imaginative! I have sought to retain the predominant flavour of an eyewitness account in the book and avoid *post hoc* rationalizations that might appear as a pretence that there was always a clear pathway ahead. When including such 'tangential' examples, I do, though, seek to show their relevance for illustration of the wide-ranging health care and information technology themes of the book.

and the physical concept of entropy. The idea of information as a science of signal gained ground from mid-twentieth-century theoretical analysis of the digitization and accurate transmission of electrical signals in telecommunications networks. The connection of these ideas with biology permeated scientific study of the nervous system and the propagation of the nerve action potential, and growing interest in the special nature of living systems that enabled them to sustain order and procreate, in apparent contradiction with known physical law. 'What is life?' and 'Why is life as it is?' became interesting questions connecting the physical and biological sciences. Over the ensuing decades, these ideas enmeshed with the elucidation of the mechanisms of cellular biology, their basis in genomics and bioenergetics, and the struggle to capture, organize and analyze the scale and complexity of data unfolding in these sciences. Information became a topic of central scientific interest, bridging computer science with life science and medicine. And with mathematics, physics and chemistry, as well, but more on that later!

The impact of evolving information technology on life science was closely paralleled in the science and engineering of clinical measurement and the diagnosis, treatment, monitoring, description, codification and classification of diseases and treatments. It spread more widely into the monitoring and analysis of the health and wellbeing of populations. The computer rapidly became a tool for the management of health care services. This paralleled its emerging role in commerce and industry, as a tool for the control of machinery and technical infrastructure, and the transaction and management of businesses. These innovations brought medicine towards a summit of connections of science with what was termed 'Industrial Age medicine' and its specialisms. Eric Topol characterized this as 'Shallow Medicine'![17]

And where we now stand, the computer has opened new frontiers of knowledge and posed new challenges for how we create, reason with and use that knowledge. It has transformed opportunities for how we connect with and depend on others in society and what we make and do for ourselves. However, all along, advances in capability to identify, prevent and combat disease have played out on a checkered and inequitable landscape of need for and provision of health care services. Balance, continuity and governance of services have proven increasingly difficult to afford and sustain. There is thus an increasingly pressing case for a coherent programme for reform, addressing fundamental issues of equity, quality and sustainability of health care systems and services, and caring relationships among citizens,

---

17   E. Topol, *Deep Medicine: How Artificial Intelligence Can Make Healthcare Human Again* (London: Hachette, 2019).

patients and professionals. Achieving this will require far greater coherence of supporting information systems than is presently in play.

We are learning experimentally, both excitingly and painfully, how the computer can assist us in the ways we create and share knowledge–how we can deploy it to help us apply and sustain the new insights and strengths it brings, while coping with and putting right the weaknesses and limitations it exposes and amplifies. Furthermore, as citizens and professionals, we must also consider the necessity of adapting our own roles, expectations and behaviours in this emerging world of the Information Society.

For from an economic perspective, we are increasingly challenged to interpret global expenditure estimated at eight trillion dollars each year on health services, and rising now towards four hundred and fifty billion dollars on information technology, with key policy priorities established half a century ago still remaining unmet. How should we respond to further estimations suggesting that our failure to get a sound grip on health care data has led to hundreds of billions of dollars of unnecessary additional annual cost, in repetitive, uncoordinated and ever-more expensive practices? And from a policy perspective, why have governments clutched repeatedly at empty promises, when investing in information technology for health care?

Information policy, more essential than ever to enable services to cope, has meandered wastefully through a landscape where remediable poor health of citizens persists, and continuity of health care services has become fragmented. The industrial age of medicine appears disconnected from the social determinants of health and wellbeing. The five giant evils of society described by William Beveridge (1879–1963) in 1942–want, disease, ignorance, squalor and idleness–were revisited in Michael Marmot's landmark reports of 2010 and 2020,[18] which documented the social determinants of health arising from inequalities and inequities of health and social care provision.[19]

The multiple dimensions of new technology and social change, that rose to a crescendo in the second half of the twentieth century, transformed society, shaking the foundations of education and professionalism, management and governance, and experience of health care services by both patients and professionals. They transformed norms and expectations.

---

18   M. Marmot, *Fair Society, Healthy Lives: The Marmot Review: Strategic Review of Health Inequalities in England Post-2010* (London: Marmot Review, 2010); M. Marmot, 'Health Equity in England: The Marmot Review 10 Years On', BMJ, 368 (2020), m693, https://doi.org/10.1136/bmj.m693

19   My childhood experience in a children's home, and later work in the voluntary sector and social housing movement, connected me closely with this reality. Marmot was an illustrious colleague as Head of the Department of Epidemiology at University College London (UCL), in my time as a Head of Department there.

The struggle to find balance of individual patient care and management of services for populations of patients, and the need for appropriate experimentation with the rapidly evolving, but serially immature, new technologies of information, were overridden by inappropriate, premature and widescale adoption. This was trumpeted and expected to perform, and depended upon to sprint before it could crawl, let alone walk. Giga-systems of information technology are not good at supporting incremental change, when they innovate inappropriately and disrupt without benefit, at giga-scale. They then create unaffordable waste and confusion, ultimately leading to destabilization and demotivation.

There have been many success stories, as well! Information technology in support of health care services has advanced spectacularly in its exploitation within the science and engineering of clinical measurement, treatment and pharmacy. But in the management of services, it has advanced in unfortunate ways. Central policy for health care information systems in the United Kingdom's National Health Service (NHS) proceeded in roughly quinquennial, electoral limit cycles of local delegation and central imposition, with little consistent and sustained focus on the need and capacity to experiment, learn and adapt. In these anarchic episodes, large monetary transactions between buyers and sellers equilibrated unhealthily with opportunism among those who sought to sell, consult and profit. Those who bought, ill-advisedly, and had to live with the consequences, lost out. Those who talked, wrote and consulted at a distance, came and went. Many who stuck with the task, on the ground, and sought to create a better future, by coping and improving, also paid a price. It is important to remember and learn from this period. As an eyewitness account of the times—and the people who lived through and experienced them—this book tells good and bad stories.

In that chaotic period, the adoption of information technology often proved a succession of Faustian bargains. Immature and rapidly-obsolete installed technology and methodologies interacted with distractions, confabulations and doom-mongering narratives surrounding the arrival of new technological waves. Serially unsuccessful attempts at imposing 'big idea', top-down innovations and reorganizations of services compounded the inevitable uncertainties associated with transitioning into the Information Age. They produced a destabilizing effect through the assertion of pretended knowledge and ability to predict and manage, while neglecting the greater imperative to cope and learn.

Information technology widened scientific vision to the extremes of the ultra-large and ultra-small. Humans tend to think big, but solutions to intractably complex big problems may sometimes only come, more simply, when the method is focused, more pragmatically, on the small—on the little and incremental things that count. Expected largescale cost-benefits were not often achieved, and the costs and disruptions caused to services were excessive and severe. The resulting legacy of incompatible and progressively obsolete systems, and the data they martialled, made the necessary, but lacking, standardization ever more difficult to achieve.

Full circle, the revolution of the Internet and the refinement of tools and methods of information engineering have brought more rigorous and resilient technologies. These advancements are leading us into an era when information will become a utility, rising as a phoenix from a wide-ranging and battle-scarred landscape of accumulated obsolescence. Information viewed as a service, not a technology, that can be depended upon; that becomes a burden in daily life principally due to its *absence*, rather than to its *presence*. This vision emphasizes the importance of a dependable and incrementally sustainable flow of information, resembling a clean and sufficient water supply.

To achieve this emerging vision requires that we take a step back, to reimagine and reform health care information as a continuously evolving, citizen-centred utility and make new connections by looking beyond what currently is, under the bonnet, a piecemeal and fragmented landscape of information systems. Of course, as with the story of advice given to the motorist seeking directions on how to get to Dublin, it is not helpful to be told that one would have been better off not to start from here! We must, of course, start from here, and the key question is how to create a tractable and beneficial way forward, in the face of the combinations of undue trust and distrust that prevail in situations and times of transition and uncertainty. The way forward must cope with this challenge in all its dimensions, and not trample over or exacerbate it. It must start from small beginnings with things that can be achieved, envisioned within a practical framework that can be extended, adapted and generalized, as requirements naturally evolve. It must engender trust by delivering value at an affordable cost and with acceptable burden on current health care services, that will, necessarily, be adapting and evolving along the way. And it must build new environments and communities to create, sustain, operate, govern and own what is needed.

The challenge is huge—we may note how influential contemporary writers have viewed this scene. In his *Homo Deus: A Brief History of Tomorrow* (itself a good deal longer than Stephen Hawking's (1942–2018) *Brief History of Time!*),[20] Yuval Noah Harari divided human history into three

---

20   S. Hawking, *A Brief History of Time: From Big Bang to Black Holes* (London: Random House, 2009). Remarkably, time can now be measured with a strontium atomic

phases–conquering, giving meaning to and losing control of the world. The foreboding of the final chapter is captured in its title, 'Data Religion':

> The world is changing faster than ever before, and we are flooded by impossible amounts of data, of ideas, of promises and of threats. Humans relinquish authority to the free market, to crowd wisdom and to external algorithms partly because they cannot deal with the deluge of data. In the past, censorship worked by blocking the flow of information. In the 21st century, censorship works by flooding people with irrelevant information.[21]

His sense of loss of control is mirrored in the Guardian newspaper this week, as I write, in an interview with the novelist Kazuo Ishiguro.[22] This piece accompanied the publication of his latest short novel, *Klara and the Sun*, dreaming about a world of artificial intelligence and artificial friends, which I immediately read.[23] I love it that he says his novels, even this quite short work, typically take five years of deep contemplation and working out. The academic world has stretched itself rather too far, in seeking to entrain its outputs to Internet time!

Reflecting similar concern about loss of control, in February 2023 the fiction writer, Ray Nayler (author of the speculative novel *The Mountain in the Sea*), urged new legislative focus that is directed away from predicting the near-future for technology, to one imagining the worlds that emerge as a result. He imagines:

> 'Parliaments of the Future'–groups of technologists, social scientists, economists, legislators and perhaps even writers–who should game out the effect of emerging technological developments and [...] prepare framework legislation ready to ensure better protection of human and consumer rights, as well as civic freedoms. [...] It isn't that governments aren't trying to predict the future–they are. It is that these predictions aren't linked back to creating better legislation, lack transparency, and are over-reliant on the false promises of quantitative data and artificial

---

clock to a precision equivalent to less than one second in the age of the universe, but yet the nature of time remains a mystery!

21   Y. N. Harari, *Homo Deus: A Brief History of Tomorrow* (London: Random House, 2016), p. 396.

22   L. Allardice, 'Kazuo Ishiguro: AI, Gene-editing, Big Data... I Worry We Are Not in Control of These Things Anymore', *The Guardian* (20 February 2021) https://www.theguardian.com/books/2021/feb/20/kazuo-ishiguro-klara-and-the-sun-interview?CMP=Share_iOSApp_Other

23   K. Ishiguro, *Klara and the Sun* (New York: Knopf, 2021).

intelligence. The future can't be 'solved for'. It isn't a mathematics problem. Predicting the impacts of change demands human creativity.[24]

In this spirit, Part Three (Vol. 2) of the book is couched in imaginative terms, thinking ahead to values, principles, scope, methods, and governance for creating and sustaining care information as a public domain utility.

An 80:20 Landscape View–The Structure of the Book

The storyline of the book traverses an extensive landscape along a lengthy personal songline, experienced during a uniquely formative era of both information technology and health care. Organizing and communicating such multi-dimensional subject matter is challenging. And as Erwin Schrödinger (1887–1961) surmised about his book, *What Is Life?*, perhaps foolishly so. The landscape surveyed is multidisciplinary, multiprofessional, multisectoral and multinational. The various stories and storytellers come from many times, places and walks of life. The conceptual and practical domains encompassed are, in themselves, huge, and impossible to cover in detail.

Thus, the book is what might potentially have been structured as several different books, directed at different audiences. Given the publishers' policy of making each chapter separately downloadable, and as readable as possible as a free-standing piece of writing, it might also be thought of as ten-and-a-half short books. This also acknowledges that few may wish, or find it possible or useful, to connect in both breadth and depth, throughout. A specialist may not find adequate detail of what interests them. A generalist may not find adequate coverage of all that concerns them. The material and stories the book brings together do, though, cover and connect through one personal career songline, and that has seemed a good reason to try to bring it all together in a single work.

I have sought to draw material from the many different landscapes that I have traversed, into an authentic, interesting and useful whole. My purpose has been directed towards showing the timeline and nature of the connections and disconnections that have been in play, and the impact they have had, and less towards encapsulating and grouping the detail according to what have become many, and increasingly fragmented, areas of health care endeavour. It is an 80:20 landscape view, which aims to cover key features of the wider scene, while acknowledging that as such it cannot

---

24   R. Nayler, 'Parliaments of the Future', *New Scientist*, 257.3427 (2023), 27.

offer a comprehensive or precisely definitive account. I therefore provide pointers to where greater detail can be found.

The connections and interrelationships of people, teams and ideas are a central feature of this history and my knowledge of them is heavily biased to the UK and its universities and health care services, and their related organizations in the public, private and voluntary sectors. Much of the UK landscape is recognizable elsewhere in the world, in similar form, and much of its domestic scene has played out alongside stories from other countries, internationally.

As ever, enduring features are remembered, celebrated and mythologized. But many failed or defeated endeavours, and successes that became obsolete (or otherwise disappeared out of sight), were also worthy of their place in the book. Many important stories will inevitably be absent, reflecting my personal lack of knowledge and awareness of them. The rapid evolution of new and incompatible technologies of the Information Age has swept over and buried lifetimes of effort, as did the transformation of society in the Industrial Revolution.

The book is structured to connect with the communities of many and disparate domains of academic discipline and professional practice, in context of their significance and enduring contribution to health care, and the inevitable imperative that they adapt and change over times ahead. It achieves this by encompassing perspectives of history before the computer, the experience of transition through the present-day Information Age and the joining together of contributions towards balance, continuity and governance of health care for the Information Society of tomorrow. As such, it addresses a multi-faceted and still evolving audience.

The book is also drawn together, in parallel, along the personal songline of its author, who has been closely involved in many of these communities since the advent of the computer. It uses extensive quotations from the stories of people encountered along the way, both in person and through their roles and writings. It lets them speak for themselves–it does not speak for them. As such, it is an eyewitness history of those times, and the book seeks to steer a straight course in describing many differently directed paths that have been encountered, experienced and navigated over time. In *The Art of War*–a text now much-used text in prestigious Master of Business Administration (MBA) courses on leadership–Sun Tzu (*c.* 544 BCE–496 BCE) wrote that 'Victory belongs to the man/ Who can master/ The stratagem of/ The crooked/ And the straight'.[25] Whether or not this songline has proved a victorious campaign (not really!), the book describes

---

25   J. Minford, trans., *Sun Tzu: The Art of War* (London: Penguin Classics, 2008), p. 43.

a personal journey through a landscape and, like walks in the countryside, interesting and fruitful experiences often lie tangentially, off the beaten track. Countryside walks meander and so does the storyline of the book, seeking authenticity and avoidance of *post hoc* rationalization. At the end of each chapter, I have reflected, in parenthesis, on general issues raised and challenges faced in introducing information technology to the domain on which the chapter has focused.

In terms of its intention, the book seeks to contribute towards a shared goal for the reformulation of health care, and a common ground of discipline and practice around which to achieve it. Coherent and trusted information will be central to this common ground. Throughout its pages, the book:

- asserts the importance of health care service governance and resource management that is maximally devolved towards the citizen;

- asserts the importance of knowledge that is openly shared, to create and sustain the common ground;

- asserts the importance of standardization of information systems as coordinated and regulated components of this common ground, centred on the shared requirements of the devolved communities of health care practice and connecting nationally and internationally with the disciplines and professions of health care that are needed to frame and address them;

- doubts that this quest can be expressed in the language of right and wrong answers, but rather through experiment and pursuit of practical goals, where complementary approaches can sometimes coexist to support and benefit shared endeavours.

Informatics must and will evolve as a central discipline of the communities, disciplines and professions of health care. It must grow in the context of the changing needs of both users and providers of services, through education, research and development, peer review and governance of services delivered, and through relationships with supporting businesses that provide information systems and services.

With all these considerations in mind, the structure of the book is a compromise that will, inevitably, not please or interest all. It is principally a songline and has been through three advancing drafts, with extensive peer review, both personal to the author, by numerous colleagues, and independently for the publisher, in reaching this published version. It is structured in three parts. Part One (Vol. 1) concerns what Alfred North Whitehead (1861–1947) called an adventure of ideas, this one being that which has powered the rise of computer science and technology and the advance of life science and medicine as they moved into and through the Information Age. Part Two (Vol. 2) is about the ensuing transition of health care-related disciplines, professions and services, with its share of what Whitehead referred to as the anarchic pattern of such major transitions. Part Three (Vol. 2) imagines and sets out a programme for reform, drawing on Whitehead's characterization of how adventures of ideas guide transitions through anarchic times, towards a new order. This programme focuses on the creation of a coherent, citizen-centred care information utility, to support integrated health care systems and services, alongside citizen engagement in meeting their personal health care needs and those of people they care for.

A key interest of Part Three is in the changing nature of knowledge sharing and collaboration within and between public and private sectors domains, as increasingly evidenced in the growing influence of initiatives such as the Creative Commons and community-interest endeavours. In keeping with this philosophy, the book has been designed for open access electronic publication as well as print-on-demand hard copy. Each chapter seeks, as far as possible, to be a freestanding and self-contained component, that can be downloaded and read in that way, linked together in the book as a set of stories and reflections on connected themes. This requires that some material about people and their ideas and endeavours be repeated, to maintain continuity between chapters. Introductory sign-posting boxes seek to link and align the component chapters into a coherent whole. In keeping with the aim for self-contained chapters, page footnotes rather than book endnotes have been preferred, albeit that this inevitably sometimes disrupts the chapter flow. Some of the footnotes are used to anchor the themes being discussed in the chapter, to people and events featuring along my songline.

In aiming for an original and hopefully appealing and illuminating way to write about this wide-ranging material, which is both orderly and authentic, it seemed a good idea to start by recognizing the numerous connotations of the term information. This was the approach I took in an invited talk I gave at the Royal Society of Medicine (RSM) in London in 1991. I was asked to reflect there on a then much-discussed new phenomenon, that of 'information explosion', under the title: 'Coming to Terms with the Information Explosion in Clinical Medicine—Can Information Technology Help?' The audience was populated with illustrious professors of medicine of the era, some trading on reputation as the traditional rottweiler, but usually, in my experience, with noisy bark much worse than bite, and warm and generous people—assuming, of course, that one had prepared well!

It was risky—I was a marginal figure. A mathematician and physicist with an engineering PhD and experience of working in industry, subsequently immersed in computer science, physiology and medical physics research and development, and later (due to the good fortune of having had a brave and forward-looking academic supervisor and subsequent sponsor), on the academic staff of the Department of Medicine of a medical school dating back now nine hundred years. I was an outsider in all these different but connected worlds and had ended up a professor in a central position at their intersection. Quite an unusual case, and imaginative medics are curious about those!

Although somewhat daunting in prospect, it turned out to be a satisfying and productive encounter for me, leading to invitations to attend and speak at events around the world. I had prepared by digging for two months into the literatures of physics, life science, medicine, engineering and computer science, for their narratives about information explosion. The unpolished and now rather dated notes I compiled for this talk are lodged as Appendix I in the archive of additional resources associated with the book, accessible from the Open Book Publishers' website listing for this book.[26]

In my research, I read through learned society perspectives cataloguing the growth of publications over time, and through critical reviews of the literatures of different subject domains, mined for their new content or lack thereof, and showing accelerating rise on both counts. It was amusing to discover that accelerating frequency with which the term 'information explosion' cropped up in papers catalogued in the Index Medicus over the preceding decade. I am sure there was not enough data to indicate that it was an exponential rise, and do not wish to offend any mathematician readers by describing it as such! It did, though, give me a good joke in showing a slide, albeit based on small numbers, suggesting that the information explosion was itself exploding!

Many proposals for reform were being suggested in this literature, including restricting an individual's published output to fifty publications during a career! Seeing some people's names over the years, attached to hundreds of strikingly similar publications (many of which have been long forgotten and seldom read in detail beyond a limited audience), such a restriction might arguably have helped! Albert Einstein (1879–1955) and Richard Feynman (1918–88) set an opposite example, nowadays far too risky, of publishing as infrequently as possible! (Theirs were brains and personalities that could get away with anything, of course.)

In the talk, I went on to discuss how information technology was supplementing and enriching the tools and methods of science, through mathematical modelling, signal processing and expert systems–now the domain of artificial intelligence. I described how, within the context of

---

26   Available at https://www.openbookpublishers.com/books/10.11647/
      obp.0335#resources

weather forecasting, a pattern of increasing accuracy and range of forecasts had been demonstrated, as measurement and computational models advanced synergistically and in parallel. I mentioned some areas where similar efforts to model systems and use them predictively were being made in life science and medicine. I identified some reasons why this was an especially uphill struggle in the diffuse, variable and highly context-dependent world of medicine and health care practice, and its related data.

Having commented on common usage of the term information and realizing that I might need to defend my interloper credentials a bit, I proceeded to talk about information and order as concepts fundamental to physics, emerging as the discipline came gradually to terms with the profound nature of the second law of thermodynamics and the elusive concept of entropy. How and why do physical systems move from states of order into states of disorder? How can description of these states, and transitions between them, be captured within an overarching theory. How do living systems survive for a while, and procreate, sustaining order and defying decline into disorder?

This is an interesting topic, yet arguably still rather esoteric in relation to matters of health care. I explore its relevance to the unfolding story of the book in Part Two. The 1991 RSM talk was not an occasion for discussing further what has sometimes been described as the most important equation in the world of science ($S=k\log\Omega$) or indeed the scientist Ludwig Boltzmann (1844–1906) whose grave is inscribed with it–a life sadly and, given this illustrious accolade, poignantly ended by suicide. But from these beginnings have grown new and progressively refined concepts of information, which have arrived, centre-stage, in scientific discourse.

In my presentation, I went on to talk about Claude Shannon (1916–2001) and his seminal work in what became known as information theory, coming to terms with digitization and communication of electrical signals.[27] In providing theoretical foundations of design for reliably error-free electronic communication, he led the way towards the new devices and technological infrastructure of the Information Age, on which the methods of physical and life sciences and medicine now depend. Advances in physics and chemistry of the earlier half century (which had culminated in the discovery of the double helix structure of DNA) combined with the growth of computer science and technology to bring new focus on and development of the bioinformatics-driven discipline of molecular biology.

I moved on next to the challenge faced by librarians in managing their rapidly accumulating collections of books and documents, where they

---

27   C. E. Shannon and W. Weaver, *The Mathematical Theory of Communication* (Urbana, IL: University of Illinois Press, 1949).

had coined the term 'information science' to describe efforts to tame their classification. I showed examples of the explosion of numbers of publications catalogued in the Index Medicus, in different sub-disciplines, and quoted from review articles of the time concerned about their quality. Cheekily, I reflected that the disorder evidenced might, to a physicist, suggest an era of ignorance explosion, rather than knowledge explosion! I had unearthed reviews suggesting that, in some areas, less than two percent of new papers contained new data or findings, but were, rather, repeating and reworking previous publications.[28]

In contrast, I then discussed information from the practical engineering standpoint of the design and programming of computer systems: the principles of data acquisition, communication, storage, retrieval, processing and display, and the associated hardware and software. In this context the term informatics had come to be used for 'the rational scientific treatment, notably by computer, needed to support knowledge and communications in technical, economic and social domains'. I recalled one of the first lectures on medical informatics that I had attended many years before, at St Thomas's Hospital in London. This was hosted by Walter Holland (1929–2018), the Professor of Epidemiology at that time, who was taking a close interest in information technology, and was delivered by Thomas Lincoln (1929–2016) from the RAND Corporation in California. He showed a slide that stuck in my mind, charting the numbers of clinical investigations, measurements and subclassifications of disease identified in treating patients with pneumonia, before and through the advent of the first antibiotics (sadly, slides he showed there have been lost from my archive). This showed that the number of investigations rose at an increasing rate before, and declined rapidly after, there was an effective treatment for these patients. The overarching message was that the less we know what to do, the more we tend to amass measurements and other information describing and reflecting that incapacity.

I showed a related slide from one of the first international encyclopaedias of medical informatics, edited by my eminent Dutch colleague of that time, Jan van Bemmel, charting the rapid increase in hospital investigations over a ten-year period, set against an unchanging baseline of numbers of hospital admissions. From another, but related perspective, I showed a slide created by my luminary sponsor John Dickinson (1927–2015), Professor of Medicine

---

28 Translated to 2014, 'a new paper is published every 41 secs. The 2% that is relevant to them would require practitioners to devote 21h per day every day to read it'. Quoted in R. E. Susskind and D. Susskind, *The Future of the Professions: How Technology Will Transform the Work of Human Experts* (Oxford: Oxford University Press, 2015), p. 48.

and Head of Department at St Bartholomew's Hospital (Bart's). This charted the increase in numbers of separately identified causal mechanisms in the regulation of human blood pressure, since discovery of the Cushing reflex a hundred years before (see Figure 1.2). These followed the timeline unravelling the story of essential hypertension, in which John remained a world authority until his death.

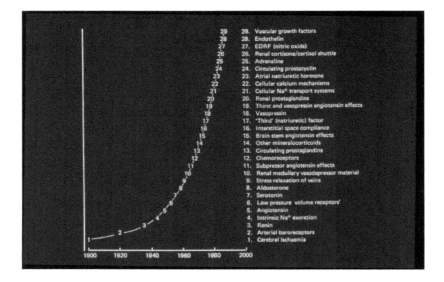

Fig. 1.2 John Dickinson's graph showing the growth of principal factors identified over a century as causative influences in the regulation of blood pressure in the human circulatory system, used in my 1991 Royal Society of Medicine talk. Image created by John Dickinson (*c.* 1990), CC BY-NC.

Turning to the professional issues encountered when dealing with such rapidly extending and ubiquitous sources of information, I showed slides illustrating the difficulties for clinical decision making that arise, the implications for overloaded content in curricula of medical education and the ways of continuing to learn about and access knowledge relevant to everyday practice. I touched on their implications for new relationships of patient and practitioner, governance of services, standardization and effectiveness of information systems and their ease of use. Finally, I suggested the importance of open information architecture, governed in the public domain. There was a new imperative for harmonizing information across connected health care services, avoiding the cost and dysfunction of data silos. This quest, which interested and absorbed me from then on in my career, was crystallized in the establishment of the Creative Commons organization in 2001.

I have rehearsed the above-described talk in some detail as it has provided an initial template, nearly thirty years later, for thinking about how to organize the chapters of this book. Each chapter covers broad areas of discipline and practice. Each has historical context, contemporary relevance and significant implications for the future. Each has a relationship with the rise of information technology and its applications in health care services. I think of these chapters as stepping-stones along pathways of social and technical transition into and through the Information Age. I have stepped on many of these, along my songline, and the book is a story of how I have connected them. Each chapter theme has featured in my work and experience and shaped my understanding. Whitehead described such pathways as transitions of ideas, of ways of thinking and acting. He cautioned that they can be dangerous and risk undermining the foundations of society.

After this introductory chapter, Part One proceeds with Chapter Two on the theme of knowledge, beginning in ancient and classical times with knowledge thought of as an encyclopaedia–a circle of learning. It is a long chapter–arguably itself the content of a short book–exploring the development of ideas that underpin and provide context to health care of the Information Age. It connects perspectives from philosophy, logic and language with those of mathematics, natural science and computer science of the modern era. It traces the librarian's dilemma over the ages–where to place books and documents within their collections, and how to search them in pursuit of learning. The chapter then moves on to language as an expression of knowledge, and the many forms of such expression–spoken, written, artistic, mathematical and computational–and how they connect and contrast in different ways of reasoning with knowledge, and in their precision of expression. It touches on mathematical and computational disciplines that grew from the development of formal logic and the reformulation of the foundations of mathematics, in their transition from the nineteenth into the twentieth century, and now into the twenty-first-century world of machines and artificial intelligence. Moving on to the bemusing and complex world of medical language and terminology, the chapter illustrates the difficulties that have been faced in moving *corpora* of descriptive terminologies from pragmatic organizations into computable forms. Some notable pioneering initiatives and participants in these endeavours are profiled along the way.

Chapter Three (Vol. 1) is about observation and measurement and their connections with number, symbol, code, logic and ethics, traversing, over time, from cubits to bits and qubits. It starts from a historical perspective and links to the present-day scene in clinical measurement, exploring connections with science of the past century and information technology of the past half century. This leads to a discussion of data and records. The chapter considers both large- and small-scale devices. It links from the start of my songline in the 1950s, offering stories of people, devices and systems that underpin measurements in medicine and life science today. It traverses between worlds, where the computational capacity of yesterday's largest computer is now exceeded by devices built into a wristwatch or handheld devices. These devices monitor, communicate and advise about bodily systems and signs, and they exceed the computational power that shepherded the first voyage of humankind onto and back from the moon in 1969. This week, as I write, a high-definition video camera and computer system are memorializing and transmitting to us the automated arrival of a Mars lander on the Red Planet.

Chapter Four (Vol. 1) is about models as representations of reality. Models of different kinds–physical, mathematical and computational–and their use in different domains and for different purposes. Modelling and simulation as a third branch of science, alongside theory and experiment, enabling and supporting discovery, insight, understanding, reasoning, prediction and action. In the examples described, I focus on pioneers I have been taught by or collaborated with: my physics lecturer John Houghton (1931–2020), on weather and climate modelling (to give a perspective from a non-medical domain); my supporters and sponsors Arthur Guyton (1919–2003) and John Dickinson, on modelling of clinical physiology.[29] Further examples are drawn from later work that I have been privileged to see first-hand, as a reviewer of largescale research projects across the European Union: the Virtual Physiological Human project and the modelling and simulation of tumour dynamics (CHIC), led by Norbert Graf, in Germany, and Georgios Stamatakos, in Greece. Exploratory clinical and health care related applications of mathematical models are then introduced, as applied, for example, to analyzing and supporting clinical decisions, tracking and predicting the course of epidemics and guiding patient management.

---

29   There have been two reminders of John Houghton as I wrote this book. He died from Covid-19 infection in March 2020, and today, on 9 August 2021, as I write this note after listening to the United Nations (UN) global news conference launching the new report of the International Panel on Climate Change (IPCC), it was poignant to hear the report dedicated to his memory. I describe his contribution to climate modelling and leadership of the first UN IPCC report in Chapter Four.

Chapter Five (Vol. 1) focuses on information engineering and the design of information systems. It is often the engineer–positioned at the interface of science and society, between the commissioner and the user of the information system–who shapes and navigates the pathways leading to success or failure. I draw on Samuel Smiles's (1812–1904) 1884 book, *Men of Invention and Industry*, a wonderful account of engineering innovation through the English Industrial Revolution, to draw parallels with innovation in the information revolution of our age.[30] Stories drawn from shipbuilding and steam power illustrate the enduring character of such innovators and the manyfold challenges they face. The connection of steam engines with information engines resonates pleasingly with both science and society! Smiles campaigned with the Chartist movement for government reform, believing that progress would depend more on changing attitudes rather than laws, and on greater empowerment of citizens. This resonates with present day thoughts about the necessary reform and reinvention of health care.

The chapter connects the discussion of models and simulations in Chapter Four, with data models, information models and knowledge models of today, focusing on database and knowledge base systems. It connects varieties and groupings of data that are captured, processed, stored and retrieved, with the devices and systems employed. It considers how these have evolved from the village of my childhood, through school and university days, to my desktop today in the global village and the Cloud of computational resources with which it immediately connects. It highlights how characteristics and limitations of devices and evolving programming paradigms have channelled both theoretical and practical developments and determined their usefulness. It explores standardization of these methods and the transforming infrastructure of the Internet and World Wide Web.

The chapters in the first part of the book follow a common pattern, building from historical context and example and charting their changing scientific, technological and social contexts over time. To introduce Part Two, Chapter Six (Vol. 2) takes a step into another dimension, to consider where information itself, as an idea, now connects within life science and medicine. Information as somewhere between material and measurable entity and immaterial abstraction. The use of the term is now so widespread that it sometimes seems akin to a holy grail–a sought after but unattainable mystical essence of the natural world. The question 'What is Life?' and its connection with the nature of information as a scientific concept, has captivated luminary scientists who have written landmark books on this

---

30   S. Smiles, *Men of Invention and Industry* (London: Read Books, 2013).

theme. I examine an eclectic selection of such works, written from physics, life science, mathematics, computer science and cognitive neuroscience perspectives.

The anarchy of transition of health care services into and through the Information Age has correlated with the experimental coupling of new science and technology of living systems and health care, with new science and technology of information. The pace of advance in technology has impelled corresponding progress in medical science and health care. New technology leads to new data and new data leads to new technology: for instance, smart watches amassing non-coherent datasets monitoring chronic disease; chronic disease datasets tuning non-coherent and opaque artificial intelligence models for collecting, monitoring and interpreting smart watch data. Apart from signal noise and bias, there might prove to be something akin to self-referential feedback, here–computer models of information feeding as input to measurement, and measurement feeding as input to computer models of information. Feedback systems can be unstable. The health care data ecosystem is, perhaps, inevitably always going to be somewhat messily unstable.

In matters biological and clinical, if one looks for 'dysfunction' one will surely find something. Whether it matters is another matter. Deciding it matters when it truly does not, and vice versa, can matter a lot to all concerned, including those who pay, of course. We must be informed, wise and careful about such matters ('care full', maybe!). That is why we need professional and local people in the same loop, who are able, have time and are willing to empathize and care–how, where and when it matters for patients.

The Whitehead quotation heading Chapter Four warns of the risks incurred by intermixing putative abstract models with the real-world phenomena they depict. One wonders, perhaps provocatively, how far non-coherent information models underpinning policy and management for the Information Age of health care services have exacerbated the costly and burdensome anarchy of transition these services have been subjected to. In this, I am not in any way querying the importance of a coherent data ecosystem to underpin well-evidenced methods for diagnosis, treatment and management of disease. Quite the reverse: I am, rather, emphasizing concern about the harm and costly confusion that can arise from the non-coherence of such data.

Plunging then into the evolving world of health care, Chapter Seven (Vol. 2) goes on a long journey, covering in detail the seventy-five years that have connected it with information technology. Another whole book, perhaps! It highlights the associated transition in methods and organization of services, professions, education and research. It moves from health care in the local context of village life that I experienced in childhood, to that experienced in global village life today. It introduces Horst Rittel (1930–90) and Melvin Webber's (1920–2006) ideas about the 'wicked problem' of social policymaking, in the context of the difficulties of design, implementation, operation and governance that have been faced in developing and sustaining information systems of the Information Age.

This transition has been described as turning the world of health care upside down, from the Industrial Age to an Information Age.[31] The then editor of the *British Medical Journal*, Richard Smith, addressed this future perspective in a landmark editorial in 1997. He showed a figure comprised of two triangles, one inverted above the other, depicting health care services turned upside down in the Information Age, from the industrial to the personal. In this figure, which I have redrawn for inclusion in the chapter (Figure 7.10), Industrial Age medicine is depicted as centred on the health care service providers, with citizens, as patients, largely dependent on decisions and actions of the professionals looking after them. By contrast, future Information Age medicine is depicted as centred on the patient and their needs and experience, with citizens achieving greater personal autonomy–making informed personal choices, participating in decisions about treatments and implicitly sharing more responsibility for how these turn out.

I have already introduced in this chapter Oppenheimer's Reith Lectures and his lucid reflections on the theme of complementarity. It is a theme that I build on in many places throughout the book. We may more fruitfully see these two perspectives of Smith's editorial as complementary, albeit that they are often positioned as conflicting. They are not half and half, as it were, zero sum games, with clear winners and losers, as the world turned upside down metaphor of the origins and outcome of the English civil war tends to imply.[32] As Oppenheimer emphasized, the whole can be greater than the sum of the complementary halves.

'Upside down' also carries the metaphor of up-down and down-up, a familiar lens through which we examine these matters: we talk of top-down and bottom-up approaches to problems. Any attempt to build a supportive framework or utility of health care information must recognize and accommodate complementary perspectives. This requires articulation

---

31   The phrase 'world turned upside down' was used by historians to describe changes in English society in the seventeenth century, in the chaotic transition from despotic rule to parliamentary government, through civil war between the armies of Roundheads and Cavaliers.

32   In fact, the geographical distribution of the Roundhead and Cavalier allegiances of that civil war resurfaced in the voting allegiances on Brexit!

of shared vision and the drawing together of complementary threads that contribute to the task of its implementation. I discuss ideas about the leadership for such an endeavour in Chapter Nine (Vol. 2). Health care itself is struggling for a new vision, as is health informatics, yet both continue to approach this struggle predominantly from a top-down perspective. Part Three of this book envisions a care information utility that supports the needs of the future Information Society. It addresses how we can and must learn how to identify and address these needs, by collaborating to imagine and implement this vision collectively, by working from the ground up, while also finding creative and imaginative solutions to the complementary top-down challenges of global standardization and cost-effective and affordable services.

With the arrival of new measurement and computational methods, from genome to population level informatics and machine intelligence, the Information Age has brought health care to another pivotal transition– between the Third and Fourth Industrial Age. This is the prospect of widescale machine learning and artificial intelligence. People who have pioneered key innovations along this pathway are introduced.

Moving on from the fragmented and worryingly unsustainable reality of health care systems today, Part Three of the book envisions a different path ahead; it describes how this path is already, in embryo, being developed in many parts of the world, across languages and jurisdictions, not from the top down but from below. It focuses on the idea of a coherent, person-centred care information utility, co-created by citizens and their supporting professionals, drawn together within collaborating local health care services and centred on care records that deploy computational methods and tooling that are standardized globally and locally customized. The utility would best be governed and shared, and the essentials made freely available, in the public domain. It is envisioned as an evolving common ground of collaborating health care organizations and companies, and the citizen, professional and academic communities that create and sustain it.

Chapter Eight looks at the form this utility might take, as a public domain ecosystem, and the values and principles required for creating and sustaining it. These rest on foundations of openness, sharing, governance and trust–an emphasis reminiscent of the advice given by the Chinese philosopher Confucius (*c.* 551 BCE–479 BCE) to his disciple, Tsze-Kung, on the three essentials for government: food, weapons, and trust. The first to sacrifice *in extremis* is the weapons and the one to hold on to until the end is trust, 'because without trust we cannot stand'.[33] The chapter emphasizes the

---

33   Analects, 12.7.

organic nature of such a utility, in analogy with the ecosystem of the natural world. It makes a parallel analogy with the monetary ecosystem, discussing the relevance for health care information policy of the lessons drawn by Mervyn King, when writing about the 2007–08 financial crisis.[34] These he attributed to an underlying 'crisis of ideas' reflected in the prevalence of 'hubris' and 'pretence of knowledge'. He called this the 'alchemy' of money. I compare his perspective with a similar alchemy of information.

The chapter charts the framing and implementation of information policy for health care over the past five decades, drawing again on people and stories encountered along my songline. I reflect on the unique character of some great innovators I have known and worked with, who have pioneered and laid foundations for transformational information infrastructure and services for health care, from small-scale and local, to large-scale utilities. They have all, in their different ways, been engineers. It is a tribute to such great clinical, technical and organizational engineers–operating at the interface of science and society–that they have demonstrated how wicked problems can, patiently, and sometimes necessarily impatiently, be tamed and overcome. The chapter then looks at contemporary trends in global village life, health care services, professionalism, education and research. From these, it seeks to envision the culture and principles needed to underpin a future public domain-anchored care information utility, identifying the issues affecting its implementation, sustainability and standardization.

The second half of Chapter Eight, numbered Eight and a Half (Vol. 2), for reasons I explain, is an account of the openEHR movement and, in lesser detail, that of OpenEyes, and how such initiatives originated and are forming as kernel components of future care information utility. These innovations are described to show that an embryonic utility already exists and is growing rapidly in archives of co-produced and shared clinical data models, software products and collaborating health care services and systems, worldwide. These initiatives have grown from the ground up, nucleated in the efforts of small teams of collaborating innovators, working with minimal funding and resources in comparison with the multi-billion, unsustainable sums that have been spent by governments, companies and health care organizations. Heavily funded endeavours that have been substantially funded in mutually non-coherent ways, arguably, conspired (in the word's sense of 'breathing together') to constrain and disrupt much creativity and progress in the domain.

The freely shared openEHR care record platform technology and its methodology are now central to products and services of a rapidly

---

34   M. King, *The End of Alchemy: Money, Banking and the Future of the Global Economy* (New York: W. W. Norton and Company, 2016).

expanding group of partnering companies and organizations in many different countries. The openEHR International community interest company now hosts a worldwide community of some one thousand clinical data modelers, working with common tools to define interoperable care record data structures–now the largest coherently curated, openly and freely shared knowledge base of such models in the world. openEHR has a growing constituency of health care organization adopters and is embodied in international standards for the field. It has been refined experimentally, iteratively and incrementally, and scaled across health economies, in multiple languages, over three decades. It has a growing footprint in the Nordic countries, Germany, Slovenia, Netherlands, Spain, South America, India, Australia, Russia, China, Japan, Italy... and now within the UK NHS, following several decades of fits and starts. It is argued that such a utility, and crucially, the way it is created and sustained, will be central to enabling the trusted and equitable citizen and professional relationships needed to underpin provision and support of citizen- and home-centred (or 'home first', as my colleague Sam Heard has characterized them) health care services in the future. openEHR started quite tentatively for me, as it came at a time of great flux in my life. It spun into a thread that has woven and connected my working life together to this day, now no longer its leader but often still its advisor and mentor.

OpenEyes, the brainchild and creation of my colleague at the Moorfields Eye Hospital in London, Bill Aylward, is an open-source software for eye care records. It has attracted a formidable team of active clinician designers and implementers, led in turn by the formidable polymath clinician, James Morgan, after Bill retired to a life sailing with his wife! Like openEHR, OpenEyes is lifting off, internationally, and today handles the care records for approaching fifty percent of eye care consultations in the UK, including for the whole of Scotland and Wales and some ten NHS Trusts in England. Both openEHR and OpenEyes are now managed by self-governing, self-funding community interest companies, providing access to their now considerable globally accessed and used Internet Protocol (IP), which is protected within not-for-profit organizations and made available under liberal Creative Commons, Apache and General Public Licenses (GPL).

Chapter Nine has been the most difficult to conceptualize. It concerns issues that are perhaps the most consequential to grasp and address–those of coherent and sustained implementation of information systems, at scale, in support of health care. That these remain urgent matters is evidenced by serial failure in tackling them, over decades. The principal motive in writing this book has been to document history and experience and give a future-facing perspective of how now to do better. The chapter is a work in progress, drawing together past, present and future perspectives, akin to a Dreaming of the Dreamtime. It reflects on core challenges of implementation that are central to successful and scalable reform–from the start, I characterized the three top priorities of openEHR as implementation, implementation, implementation!

The chapter grapples with three essential threads of implementation. The first is about approach and method–that is *how* the care information utility can be created and sustained, connecting communities served with professional and academic work, and public and private enterprise and institutions. It highlights the importance of Creative Commons and operational governance that preserves the non-exclusive relationship of public with private enterprise. The story and cultural significance in the UK of common land, and its appropriation to new private interests through the eighteenth century and the Enclosure Acts, is visited as a parable for intellectual commons in the Information Age. It discusses the harm that restriction of intellectual property does in blocking innovation that tackles wicked problems, which requires connection and cooperation within diverse communities of practice.

In this respect, there are lessons to be drawn for health care from how antitrust concerns in the United States of America (USA) and the European Union (EU) are starting to inform the framing of protections needed to prevent socially harmful and exploitative tech industry monopoly. Big Tech, Big Data and 'Big' everything else are ringing alarm bells of concern. In these ways, the story of information and information systems is starting to connect more closely with the changing culture of national and corporate governance, internationally, and its increasing emphasis on environmental and social governance factors, as captured in the acronym, ESG.

The second thread of implementation is about endeavour, focusing on *who* will do the work of creating and sustaining the utility, and *where*. It considers the implementation endeavours needed and the teams of people who will be required to create and sustain a care information utility. It considers the qualities of environments where they can connect effectively with health care services, in a shared culture of learning by doing. This is about the teamwork needed to imagine, develop, lead and sustain the information systems of tomorrow, iteratively and incrementally. The chapter looks at the different qualities of leadership that pioneering endeavours along my songline have exemplified, and, for fun, ticks them off against the classic, much used text on leadership of Sun Tzu in *The Art of War*.[35] Commitment, insight and alliance are *sine qua non* attributes of communities that confront wicked problems, in combination with the most important

---

35   Minford, trans., *Sun Tzu*.

of all–staying power. Stubborn people often have extra staying power and thank goodness for all such people that I have been privileged to know, learn from and work with. Such communities are not well led by people who strut too far above them–they are sometimes best led from below, and sometimes most effectively when least visibly. The third thread of implementation is governance, and the chapter considers new requirements that the care information utility will pose.

Chapter Ten (Vol. 2) is a review of where we have reached in the transition to the Information Society of the future. It combines with a Postscript, offered as a preface to new personal songlines that are just starting to unfold, or those in mid-journey. Echoing Bon Jovi, the chapter builds on the theme of being halfway there! Human society defines itself by its values and how it adapts and changes. This is true for individual lives, challenged greatly in chaotic times, and for societies in transition. Wherever we travel as individuals and global villagers in the coming years, the story of health care services, health care systems and the information technology and utility they embody and utilize, will only be half of what determines their usefulness and fruitfulness. I recount, with her permission and approval, aspects of my wife's extraordinary personal struggle through critical illness, over a two-year period. Her survival and recovery, half about health care services she experienced–both good and bad–and half about her personal nature, struggle and resilience. The chapter reflects briefly on James Lovelock's (1919–2022) book, *Novacene*, which he published at age one hundred, as a guide and pattern for human civilization with the advent of hyperintelligent machines, and health care in future society with the advent of artificial intelligence.[36] A stimulating counterpoint is Ian McEwan's imaginative recent novel, *Machines Like Me*, about life lived alongside an extremely futuristic cyborg![37]

In the Postscript, my songline comes full circle and, in the spirit of T. S. Eliot's (1888–1965) *Little Gidding*, looks again at the 'unknown, remembered gate' that I first passed through into this field, some fifty years ago.[38] But with new eyes, having connected a full cycle around Shiyali Ramamrita Ranganathan's (1892–1972) circle of knowledge and completed an encyclopaedic personal circle of learning.

---

36   J. Lovelock, *Novacene: The Coming Age of Hyperintelligence* (Cambridge, MA: MIT Press, 2019).

37   I. McEwan, *Machines like Me* (Toronto: Knopf Canada, 2019).

38   T. S. Eliot, *Little Gidding* (London: Faber and Faber, 1943).

The following, supplementary materials can be found in the additional resources tab for the website listing of this book:[39]

Appendix I: Royal Society of Medicine Talk Notes, 1991

Appendix II: NHS Acts of Parliament, Policies and Organizations Relating to Information and Information Technology since 1946

Appendix III: Forty Years of Policy and Implementation in the UK NHS

Appendix IV: A Reflection on Health Informatics

Appendix V: A Wider Acknowledgement of Contributions

Appendix VI: Annexes to Chapter Eight and a Half–openEHR Documents of Record:

Annex I: The Original openEHR Manifesto, 1999

Annex II: Origins of openEHR

Annex III: Transcript of Lecture about openEHR for Medinfo 2007, Brisbane

Annex IV: openEHR History from 2002–18

Annex V: openEHR Vision and Mission–Co-written with Thomas Beale, 2018

A 2020 Portrait View–People and Ideas

Throughout this book, I draw on material from many other books and reports and combine it with stories of many people and their ideas and contributions. I call this a 2020 portrait view, not just because of the date it was first being compiled and its focus on people, but also to convey a sense of balance. The stories of people relate to meetings and shared endeavours at many times throughout my fifty-year career songline. Some of the books are personal and reflective summations of their diverse authors' expert insights, accumulated and tested over long periods of time.

I have drawn substantially on a personal collection of such books that have influenced me and proved useful in connecting across disciplines,

---

39   Available at https://www.openbookpublishers.com/books/10.11647/obp.0335#resources

professions, and domains of health care, science and information. They have stood as navigational beacons, akin to the inuksuk signposts used as markers and guides by the Inuit communities of northern Canada. Inuksuks are rock cairns fixed at key and enduring points in the landscape and used as guideposts. For example, some are placed to be visible from afar in the seasonally changing landscape–alternating ice, snow and flood–to navigate on journeys through and along valleys and rivers below. I have a small model of an inuksuk on the shelf above my writing desk. Nowadays, few of us are, or can be, highly original thinkers. Our originality is increasingly expressed in how we use and combine ideas, resources and circumstances, to achieve interesting and useful things. In this quest, we all need our inuksuks. I call these special books, my 'inukbooks'!

An early inukbook was *The Songlines*, by the travel writer, Bruce Chatwin (1940–89); the inspiration for the characterization of my storyline, as recorded in this book.[40] He wrote there of the tradition of storytelling in the Aboriginal culture of central and northern Australia–legend woven around people, landscapes and journeys. The explorer and the storyteller alternate roles–an explorer moves along the songline, experiencing the changing landscape and meeting and listening to storytellers who attach their stories to the features of the place where they meet. Explorers sometimes stop in their journey, to become storytellers along the songlines of other explorers, who travel along the same or different intersecting lines to meet them, and then pass by. The stories told are records–data and narrative, commemoration and explanation–of the past and present, and provide a focus for the future. Having travelled quite extensively in former days, I am now much more of a stationary landmark!

In contrast with such enduring, inuksuk-like books, the exploding volume of published outputs in the Information Age has catalogued often ephemeral formative experiences of still largely anarchic domains of knowledge and endeavour, prone to large amounts of obfuscating noise. Reliable signposts are sorely needed through this confusing maze. At the time of writing (22 May 2021), *New Scientist* has two articles germane to this theme.

The title of the first is 'Machine Churning', a play on machine learning![41] It describes a review from the Cambridge Image Analysis Group (in the Department of Applied Mathematics and Theoretical Physics, University of Cambridge) of more than three hundred papers published between January and October of 2020, reporting applications of machine learning methods to

---

40   B. Chatwin, *The Songlines* (New York: Random House, 2012).
41   M. Roberts, 'Machine Churning', *New Scientist*, 250.3335 (2021), 23, https://doi. org/10.1016/S0262-4079(21)00873-3

diagnose Covid-19 from chest scan images and predict how patients will fare.[42] None of these was deemed of use in clinical settings. The authors describe this as a kind of publication bias that promotes inadequate experimental rigour and unreliable claims of success over careful experimentation–'churning' out of papers over the consolidation of learning. ROC (Receiver Operating Characteristic) sensitivity versus specificity charts provide a standard way to map and compare the performance of methods promoted in such a spectrum of publications. The collection of high-quality datasets with the necessary large numbers of data subjects that are typically required for the development of such methods, and then their prospective testing, is in itself a considerable challenge. Christian Leibig and colleagues followed this approach in their 2022 paper comparing the strengths of radiologists and an artificial intelligence (AI) method for breast cancer screening, as further discussed in Chapter Ten.[43] This scale of research, which is assuming greater importance as AI advances in capability, will be more readily achievable as the objectives of Part Three of this book start to bear fruit, establishing a coherent care information utility.

The second article is a book review of *Power to the Public: The Promise of Public Interest Technology*, which argues for greater government focus on meeting everyday needs of citizens, and catalogues how they have fallen down on this imperative in the transition to the Information Age.[44] The second and third parts of this book catalogue a similar pattern that has come about in health care and imagine new common ground on which we can achieve a better balance for the digital citizen and Information Society of the future.

To provide potentially many thousands of connected references for this book, would almost certainly prove an erroneous, easily misleading and quickly outdated exercise. Many of the inukbook references I have provided are, themselves, more narrowly focused and referenced than this book. Some date from over one hundred years ago but remain clear and relevant today. I have adopted this approach, also, because more specific and up-to-date connections are today quickly and potentially more sensitively made through keyword searches in easily accessible and extensive electronic reference works, such as the multi-disciplinary compilations in

---

42 M. Roberts et al., 'Common Pitfalls and Recommendations for Using Machine Learning to Detect and Prognosticate for COVID-19 Using Chest Radiographs and CT Scans', *Nature Machine Intelligence*, 3.3 (2021), 199–217.

43 C. Leibig, M. Brehmer, S. Bunk, D. Byng, K. Pinker and L. Umutlu,, 'Combining the Strengths of Radiologists and AI for Breast Cancer Screening: A Retrospective Analysis', *The Lancet Digital Health*, 4.7 (2022), e507–19.

44 T. D. McGuinness and H. Schank, *Power to the Public: The Promise of Public Interest Technology* (Princeton, NJ: Princeton University Press, 2021).

archives like Oxford Reference, to which I have access through university subscription, and the evolving and open access commons of Wikipedia, to which I personally subscribe. Readers can further view other resources and developments in the field using the additional resources tab on the website listing of this book.[45]

The organization of literature that encompasses and connects domains of knowledge became an increasingly complex edifice in the anarchic transition into the Information Age. I review its history in some detail, in Chapter Two. Wikipedia attracts some disdain, but it is a much utilized and improving experiment in the Creative Commons. Used carefully, it and other such online encyclopaedias of the Information Age provide increasingly valuable resources. This book has been constructed with Creative Commons licensed open-access publication in mind, and that principle, along with the widening public ownership of knowledge and related intellectual property, is a pathway along which information about, and supporting, health care will emerge as a sustainable care information utility for the future. Combining reports of data with the methods employed to analyze them, such that the analysis can be critically replicated by others, is increasingly important for the publication and communication of knowledge.[46]

Almost all the books that I have referenced come from my library at home, and there is one custom-built oak bookcase where I keep the many inukbooks that have interested and guided me most, at different times. It covers a wide range of themes: in philosophy, mathematics, physical sciences, life sciences, medicine and health care, economics, engineering, the arts, history, religion. I have sometimes allowed myself to be interested in too many things! These books are close at hand and often looked at or picked off the shelf, to read and refresh my memory. Some in the collection have more personal and sentimental value, such as books that helped my father in the 1930s, as he found his way on from an impoverished childhood, having lost both his parents from desertion and disease, and having left school at age fourteen. Writings of William Blake (1757–1827), Aldous Huxley (1894–1963), George Orwell (1903–50), and many more, are there, including an early edition of Huxley's *Brave New World*, published in 1932, and a first edition of Orwell's *1984* (published in 1948, when I was three years old–he died shortly after at University College Hospital, my alma

---

45   Available at https://www.openbookpublishers.com/books/10.11647/
      obp.0335#resources

46   Some years ago, I worked for a while on behalf of the British Library and the
      Wellcome Trust, to participate in and chair groups they established to consider
      and oversee developments contributing towards this end, including, initially, for
      the PubMed library resource in the UK.

mater of later years).[47] There was my early school-leaver Dad, eighty years ago, reading two authors prescient about the concerns of the Internet age of the 2020s! Huxley, concerned that human life would become trivialized and egotistical, surrounding itself and drowning in a sea of inconsequential information, and Orwell, concerned that the potential for malign official censorship would restrict access to information, to control and enchain society. These books remind me of all that I owe to my parents. I introduce several others of them, here, to give their flavour.

My mother's brother, my Uncle Geoffrey, a Casualty Surgeon at the Royal Northern Hospital and then the Whittington Hospital in North London, had a lifelong interest in history and astronomy. He was a member of the British Interplanetary Society and I have some of his early books about the solar system. He had collected some early printed volumes of the histories of Herodotus, but these have sadly decayed beyond repair. Also from him, I have an 1830 edition of the combined seventy-one chapters of Gibbon's *The History of the Decline and Fall of the Roman Empire* and an 1881, seventeenth edition of Joseph Haydn's (1786–1856) *Dictionary of Dates and Universal Information–Relating to All Ages and Nations*.[48]

Gibbon's *magnum opus* in my 1830 Galignani edition totals one thousand and three pages, with around one thousand two hundred words per page. This amounts to a creditably compact ten-megabyte account of history, spanning some one thousand five hundred years! In Haydn's nine hundred and nineteen pages of tiny typescript–packing in about four thousand words per page, and thus comprising about twenty-five megabytes of data or the equivalent of just a few jpeg images on our smartphones today. As recorded in his brief Preface to the 1841 first edition, Haydn set out 'to attempt the compression of the greatest body of general information that has ever appeared in a single volume, and to produce a Book of Reference whose extensive usefulness may render its possession material to every individual'.[49] There you have it: information selected and communicated for its general usefulness–not exactly the spirit of our age! Two ancient, thick and decaying, yet remarkable intact and readable, volumes on my shelf!

In 1945, Encyclopaedia Britannica published its 'new survey of universal knowledge' in the form of twenty-three volumes, alphabetized from A to Z and with a twenty-fourth volume comprising maps, indexes and lists of contributors. My parents bought this edition when they started their family and just after I was born. They are bulky–parallel columns of around

---

47   A. Huxley, *Brave New World* (n.p.: DigiCat, 2022); G. Orwell, *Nineteen Eighty-Four* (London: Hachette, 2021).

48   B. Vincent, *Haydn's Dictionary of Dates* (Frankfurt: Salzwasser-Verlag, 2020).

49   N.p.

seventy-five lines and twenty words per line. The index to the maps extends to three hundred and eighty-nine pages, that of the twenty-three volumes of content to four hundred and ninety-seven pages, and the list of contributors to thirty-three pages. The instructions for how to use the indexes run to five pages. These hefty volumes are safely stored in our summerhouse. The pious incantation on the title page is 'Let knowledge grow from more to more and thus be human life enriched'.[50] A rough estimate says twenty-four thousand pages and (24000x75x20x5) around one hundred and fifty megabytes of data.

Grown, this body of knowledge certainly has! Wikipedia extends now to petabytes and Internet data sources extend by zettabytes each year! Maybe a DNA level of data storage minimization will reduce the sub-ocean, electricity-guzzling and heat-emitting Cloud data stores to the size of Gibbon's and Haydn's books, before long, as Internet-linked digital storage volumes continue their seemingly inexorable expansion! Maybe they will be archived on another planet that does not destabilize our environment on Earth! By way of sobering perspective, Chapter Six delves into a comparison of the capability and capacity of computer technology with that of the human brain and living cells, in its discussion of the landmark inukbooks of John von Neumann (1903–57) and Paul Davies.[51]

I have collected dictionaries on many subjects and the eight kilogram, two-volume 1971 Oxford English Dictionary has sometimes been helpful in pinning down the imprecise use of words and their misuse or hijacking within specialist jargons. This is hard to achieve in any domain, let alone when embarking on a work that intertwines experience along a songline through landscapes of health care and information technology.

Other historical works of Henry Hallam (1777–1859), Thomas Macaulay (1800–59), Karl Marx (1818–83), H. G. Wells (1866–1946) and Norman Davies are there on the shelves–the latter with his connection, for me, to Oxford and my wife Bożena's homeland of Poland and his special expertise in Central European history. I cannot claim to have read all of them but have browsed through and continue to benefit from knowing they are there. They sit alongside the writings of science laureates of the past century, especially in physics, and of modern-day writers. There is also an eclectic collection of novels that I have especially enjoyed, including those of Julian Barnes,

---

50 W. Yust, ed., *Encyclopaedia Britannica: A New Survey of Universal Knowledge* (Chicago, IL: University of Chicago Press, 1945).

51 J. von Neumann, *The Computer and the Brain*, Mrs. Hepsa Ely Silliman Memorial Lectures (London: Yale University Press, 1958); P. Davies, *The Demon in the Machine: How Hidden Webs of Information Are Solving the Mystery of Life* (Chicago, IL: University of Chicago Press, 2021).

whose life briefly brushed alongside mine at Magdalen College (University of Oxford) in the late 1960s and whose *A History of the World in 10½ Chapters*,[52] inspired my half chapter and the ten and a half chapters, here.

Another inukbook that I treasure, for personal reasons, is *Atoms in the Family* by Laura Fermi (1907–77), wife of the renowned physicist Enrico Fermi (1901–54), who was one of a generation thought to have damaged their health and died young as a result of exposure to harmful radiation during their experiments.[53] The book is the songline of her family life from the 1920s to the 1950s, featuring people and events at the centre of the unfolding of atomic and nuclear physics. It extends through to the Manhattan Project and the dropping of the atomic bomb on Hiroshima, which, she says, neither she nor other wives she was close to, had understood to be the work on which their physicist husbands were engaged.[54] It was from this closely connected community and era that the ENIAC computer emerged. Fermi was one of the great physicists of the time that saw the ascendancy of quantum mechanics. He shared the Nobel Prize in 1938 for his work on slow neutron nuclear reactions. Many lived through and were conditioned by the social and political strife that forced them to leave Europe and emigrate to America. This book was given to me by Elisabeth Ullmann, a physiology lecturer colleague at the Medical College of Bart's. She told me about key players of the age that she had known, such as Niels Bohr (1885–1962). I collaborated with her to introduce my work on simulation models of clinical physiology with John Dickinson, the then Professor of Medicine at Bart's, into her classes for medical undergraduates–a story I tell in Chapter Four.

Laura Fermi's songline was from the pre-war era and it intersected with that of Richard Feynman, the physicist who made the imaginative breakthrough leading to the theory of quantum electrodynamics, for which he was awarded the Nobel Prize, with Julian Schwinger (1918–94) and Shinichiro Tomonaga (1906–79), in 1965.[55] I have as complete a collection of

52   J. Barnes, *A History of the World in 10½ Chapters* (New York: Knopf, 1989).

53   L. Fermi, *Atoms in the Family: My Life with Enrico Fermi* (Chicago, IL: University of Chicago Press, 2014).

54   Among the Fermi family's closest friends were the Peierls family. Rudolf Peierls (1907–95) ended his career in the late 1960s as Head of Department and Professor of Theoretical Physics at the University of Oxford, where I attended his lectures. It is amusing to recall the fluency of such great figures of the time, who taught us, with such aplomb, things we now know not to have been true, and to recall us students, who sought to emulate them and were graded for our own dextrous aplomb in explaining the untruths that were truths of the day! I admire and am excited by physics to this day, but not sorry that I took a different path.

55   Enrico Fermi had joined the Los Alamos Manhattan Project in 1944 and, with other physicists of the era, played a key role in designing the atomic bomb. Feynman joined while still a graduate student at Princeton University. He

books in Feynman's name as I have been able to lay my hands on–his clear and illuminating style was a notable inspiration for me when discovering physics for the first time, at the University of Oxford. Feynman had an aversion to writing–many of these books comprised his ideas and notes compiled into book form by others. One of them, by Anthony Hey, is based on Feynman's highly original lecture notes for a California Institute of Technology (Caltech) course on computation. I worked alongside Tony Hey when he created and led the innovative UK e-Science Programme in the early 2000s.

Such has been the rapidity and impact of changing information technology at all levels of society, and extending throughout the world, that chaos along my songline was inevitable. Expensively misguided and sometimes disreputable stuff did happen. Another of my inukbooks, to which I have already referred several times, is Whitehead's *Adventures of Ideas*. As also quoted on the front page of Part Two of this book, he captures the chaos of such times very well:

> In every age of well-marked transition there is the pattern of habitual dumb practice and emotion which is passing, and there is the oncoming of a new complex habit. Between the two lies a zone of anarchy [...][56]

One wonders how he would have characterized the anarchic transition through the Information Age, with which his life scarcely overlapped. He was, though, a key figure, along with Russell, in the transition of mathematics and philosophy onto new foundations, around the turn of the twentieth century. This contribution was drawn together in their treatise, *Principia Mathematica*,[57] and progressed into ensuing decades of debate about the logical foundations of mathematics, blown open again by Kurt Gödel (1906–78). From this era, came ideas that laid the foundations of computer science, set down in the landmark contributions of the mathematicians John

---

delighted in teasing the team by cracking the safes in which the results and designs were secreted each day, leaving mischievous notes to unnerve his colleagues when they opened them the next time. Joseph Rotblat (1908–2005), who pioneered radiation biophysics and was subsequently head of physics and a senior colleague at Bart's Medical College in London, had joined the project from the UK. Rotblat devoted much of his life, thereafter, to promoting understanding and cooperation among scientists, between East and West, through the Pugwash Conferences. Jointly with the Pugwash Conference, he was awarded the Nobel Peace Prize for this work in 1995.

56   Whitehead, *Adventures of Ideas*, p. 14.
57   A. N. Whitehead and B. Russell, *Principia Mathematica* (Cambridge, UK: Cambridge University Press, 1925–27).

von Neumann, Alan Turing (1912–54) and Alonzo Church (1903–95) in the 1930s, centred on the universal computer and theory of computation.

Russell and Whitehead wrote more widely about philosophy and social change. Following Whitehead's phrase, we might interpret a well-marked transition as one where there are well-delineated differences, before and after, and well-characterized causative factors at work, which illuminate our understanding of how and why change comes about. This understanding may not help a lot in characterizing and coping with change, when living through the anarchic zone he describes as lying in between. One could probably, if feeling so inclined, fill many books with examples of the kind of 'dumb practice and emotion' that Whitehead wrote about, many of them my own!

Too much musing and writing about imponderables can easily dominate too little thought and action about making and doing things iteratively and incrementally better. That was the slippery slope in antiquity that Gibbon cautioned against. It is best to write only when there is something useful to say, and not do so, or be incentivized to do so, otherwise. There has been hard-won progress and good practice, achieved by brave innovators, to stand against the opposing battalions of hubris and despondency that broadcast loudly in such times. Given the vagaries of national and institutional policy and allocation of resources in anarchic times of transition, success in making a useful difference as a pioneer can prove especially hard-won, and staying-power and good luck are key ingredients of the remembered storytellers. The inukbooks introduced throughout this book have been chosen to illustrate a diversity of stories that illuminate the anarchic transition of the past seventy-five years. It is a personal and eclectic selection.

Transition and Anarchy

We see and describe transition in terms of what happens and seek to understand and explain why. Change and transition are about past, present and future; about events occurring. We look for and make connections. All change over time is transition of one kind or another, sudden or gradual.

Today, the passage of time is tracked over unimaginable billions of years and fractions of seconds. Its subdivisions are variously described as eons, eras, periods, epochs and ages, to the present day. Cosmologists straddle imagination of time from 10 exp (-50) seconds to 10 exp (100) years, describing the past and expected future of the universe in terms of key transitions. They track time and energy in the universe from its unimaginably rapid and high energy creation and inflation, after the imagined Big Bang. This progression is marked in terms of radiation, particulate matter, stars, planets, galaxies and black holes, projecting into equally unimaginable multitudinous eons of slow decay into low energy radiation and nothingness.

Geology spans from the formation of the earth to the present day, in billions of years. It tracks the sedimentary record of rocks, marked by many tens of stages of evolution of the earth, as it took shape and adapted in its orbit within the evolving solar system, flexed and buffeted from afar. Life scientists track the emergence of life on earth and its evolution, marked by transitions between simple and complex life forms, fuelled by the energy of the sun, constrained by underlying and emergent mathematical and physical patterns and properties. In these Covid years, we are focused on very short-term biological transitions, arising from movements and mutations of a virus and their consequences. Archaeologists map the emergence of human societies in different regions of the world, marked by tools, lifestyles and cultures. Historians describe and characterize the evolution and transition of human societies, marked by infinite contexts of stuff and stuff happening–good stuff and bad stuff–war, revolution, discovery, reformation, renaissance, enlightenment and industrialization. Sixty thousand years of Indigenous culture in Australia supplanted, under European influence, over just four hundred years.

Transition and anarchy are described in different ways in different contexts. In the physical world, maths and physics describe threshold phenomena, such as phase transitions, in terms of models of networks, forces and energies–from ice to water to steam, sometimes skipping phases. Heat energy is absorbed, exciting and destabilizing the water molecules in ice, breaking them from one kind of order and its prevailing forces and interactions (solid state) into another (liquid and then gas). The transitions in the reverse direction release energy as the energetic gaseous water molecules condense into liquid water and freeze into solid ice. Different forces operate and predominate at different ranges, to establish a new stable state or phase. Though precisely marked at scale, such phase transition is nonetheless chaotic at the molecular level.

The take-off of an airplane is a transition, as it lifts from the ground. Air flows at differential speed, above and below its aerofoil wings, and the Venturi effect characterizes the observed net upward lifting force. Thermodynamics describes this effect. It does not enlighten us, should we attempt, in vain, to understand what is going on by studying what happens to individual air molecules as the plane rushes through and perturbs them. In the natural world, cell division is a transition from a state of one to a state of two. Mitosis and meiosis proceed through waves of chaos in transition between well-marked states.

The forces in play, that drive transitions, may be extreme or subtle. The Chicxulub meteorite was a sudden extreme event, arriving out of the blue, and the transition that followed extended across the physical and natural world in both immediate and long-term, irreversible changes. Transitions may occur suddenly, even when caused by slowly incremental change that has accumulated to a chaotic breaking point between an old and new order, as in an earthquake. For the animal kingdom, Stephen Jay Gould (1941–2002) described such rapid jumps and characterized them as a punctuated equilibrium.[58] The natural world defends itself, adapting to changes of season, climate and predator. It often seems okay until not okay, and then is very much not okay. The human body and mind, and their health and defences, are like that, too.

The terms anarchy and chaos describe lack of form and order. When we say the outcome of successive spins of a coin is a random process–50:50, heads or tails–we mean we do not know which way it will fall, but the two possibilities are equally likely. When we select a card at random from a pack of fifty-two, we do not know which of them will turn up–unless, of course, there is cardsharp practice in play! Random means essentially that we do not know–with 50:50 prior probability, if we want to predict, we might as well spin an (unbiased!) coin. In human affairs, a great deal is written and computed about situations like this (excessive words/watts about fifty-fifty life events–a good acronym would be e-waffle!). There is upside and downside risk and utility in all of life's balances, and how we act to protect and influence them. Nassim Taleb's *The Black Swan*[59] and *Antifragile*[60] and Daniel Kahneman's *Thinking, Fast and Slow*[61] are books rich in insight about balance and transition, and human behaviour when faced with uncertainty.

Human society is in the throes of a long transition marked by the rise of information technology. We talk of transition twelve thousand years ago, from prehistoric times of hunting and gathering to settled agriculture; of ages characterized by stone, bronze and iron materials and tools; of eras deemed ancient, classical, medieval and modern. The modern world looks back over many centuries, to successive and interacting ages of renaissance in arts and culture, reformation of church and state, and enlightenment in philosophy and reason, that led into new ages of commerce, industry and science. The past hundred years of science and engineering transformed medical practice and seventy-five years of information technology has changed everything again. Much now unfolds in dramatically new ways,

---

58   S. J. Gould and N. Eldredge, 'Punctuated Equilibrium Comes of Age', *Nature*, 366.6452 (1993), 223–27, https://doi.org/10.1038/366223a0

59   N. N. Taleb, *The Black Swan: The Impact of the Highly Improbable* (London: Random House, 2007).

60   N. N. Taleb, *Antifragile: How to Live in a World We Don't Understand* (London: Allen Lane, 2012).

61   D. Kahneman, *Thinking, Fast and Slow* (New York: Macmillan, 2011).

year on year. The sequencing of the human genome took years of multicentre collaboration to assemble. The SARS virus was sequenced in a few weeks and the corona (Covid-19) virus sequencing, alongside routine human whole genome DNA sequencing, can now be completed within hours if not minutes. It is both an exhilarating and frenetic time.

My fifty-year career songline has moved through an oftentimes anarchic landscape. The stories I encountered and participated in reflect an amazing mixture of creativity, staying-power, luck, muddle and confusion. Given the uniqueness of the times, there was fortunate opportunity to meet and learn from heroic storytellers. And, unfortunately, sometimes to experience the beguiling but ultimately busted forays of hubristic mortals whose optimistic and confident predictions and promises were too readily believed by powerful ears, ill-equipped, ill-tuned or sometimes not interested, to discern pretence of knowledge. Diverse funding streams floated many computerized boats, and land-based admirals sent them to sea, where they were subsequently found unseaworthy or quickly obsolete. The wreckage left below the waves imperilled navigation of other boats, thereafter. The sinking of the massive ship, Vasa–now amazingly restored and preserved in the Vasa Museum in Stockholm–as it left harbour into a stiff breeze on its maiden voyage from Stockholm, is a memorable nautical parable of this sort of debacle.[62]

---

62   John Dickinson and I visited the Vasa on a trip to give talks at the nearby Karolinska University Hospital in Stockholm, nearly forty years ago. According to Wikipedia, 'The ship was built on the orders of the King of Sweden Gustavus Adolphus as part of the military expansion he initiated in a war with Poland-Lithuania (1621–1629). She was constructed at the navy yard in Stockholm under a contract with private entrepreneurs in 1626–1627 and armed primarily with bronze cannons cast in Stockholm specifically for the ship. Richly decorated as a symbol of the king's ambitions for Sweden and himself, upon completion she was one of the most powerfully armed vessels in the world. However, *Vasa* was dangerously unstable, with too much weight in the upper structure of the hull. Despite this lack of stability, she was ordered to sea and foundered only a few minutes after encountering a wind stronger than a breeze'. Wikipedia contributors, 'Vasa (ship)', *Wikipedia, The Free Encyclopedia* (9 June 2023), https://en.wikipedia.org/wiki/Vasa_(ship). Wikipedia has further interesting and illuminating details of this story, which resonate with unstable computer systems finding their way into everyday life. Take the NHS Covid App, for example–a doctor well known to me, who had been busy helping to cope with the flood of Covid admissions to their hospital, told me that staff had had to switch it off on their phones as its unreliable and unhelpful alerts risked the workforce becoming overwhelmed, because so many of them would have had to be sent home, unnecessarily. False positive alarms were a cacophony in the care home where my dad spent the last months of his life. What might we face from a non-coherent ensemble of unreliable alerts from AI-enabled smart phones monitoring illness?

At times it has felt as though the landscape unfolding was moving under foot–accelerated continental drift and frequent earthquakes, combined. Some explorers achieved iconic storyteller status and those stories have passed on into later decades. Others disappeared or gave up. It was all too easy to struggle up what turned out to be blind alleys, meeting storytellers who were stuck there, blocked from or unable to move forward onto a different, more prosperous path. Some had started with great energy, ambition and fluency, but had become exhausted and dispirited. Some were tied to technology and methods that had become quickly obsolete and unsustainable. Exploration of a problem may reveal previously unforeseen requirements that indicate or necessitate a completely different approach to it. New methods of working may require different skills, and reskilling requires willingness, aptitude, time and opportunity that may not be available. The information technology scene changed considerably, year on year, in the anarchic transition into and through the Information Age.

When thinking and writing of this more human and organizational chaos, I picked up another book, *In the Margins of Chaos*, describing relief work between the First and Second World Wars, led by an indomitable woman, Francesca Wilson (1888–1981).[63] She described the plight of refugees throughout Europe and the concerted efforts on many levels to help and support them. Her title is significant. It is hard to make a constructive and peaceful impact at the centre of a battle, but in the margins of the battle there is always opportunity, given courage and persistence. The book, given to me by friends of a friend of Francesca Wilson, and great friends of mine today, is one of my inukbook treasures. My mother worked with Francesca Wilson in running a centre situated behind Tibidabo in Barcelona, supporting refugees fleeing General Franco's advancing army, towards the end of the Spanish Civil War.

How, then, are we to characterize and understand the anarchy of transition into the Information Age? There can be no turning back, and it is a challenging and sobering time, the like of which King wrote of in his valedictory book about world financial crisis.[64] In his term 'pretence of knowledge', he was mirroring Friedrich Hayek (1899–1992) in his criticism of what he called 'scientism'. King reflected on what he called the crisis of ideas underlying recurring crises of the international monetary system. Whitehead, too, was given to sobering judgement about anarchic social change:

---

63   F. M. Wilson, *In the Margins of Chaos: Recollections of Relief Work in and between Three Wars* (New York: Macmillan, 1945).

64   King, *The End of Alchemy*.

It is the first step in sociological wisdom, to recognize that the major advances in civilization are processes which all but wreck the societies in which they occur [...] Those societies which cannot combine reverence to their symbols with freedom of revision, must ultimately decay either from anarchy, or from the slow atrophy of a life stifled by useless shadows.[65]

The term *symbol* has special relevance when describing transition through the Information Age. Whitehead would have been fully cognizant of symbolic logic, although not of the coming era of computer science. Chapter Two tracks the evolution of mathematics and logic and the emergence of computer science, in representing, manipulating and reasoning with symbols–letters, words, numbers, codes, logical propositions and predicates. Logical truth became the touchstone of formal semantics, expressed and played out in terms of machine-based symbols. How powerful are these symbols? Can we, in Whitehead's terms, revere symbols that arise in and shape machine discourse, and are revised there, in ways we progressively no longer control or understand? Can we distinguish symbolism that arises in human culture and symbolism imprinted from machine culture, if one calls it that, just to emphasize the question? Are these boundaries whereby we can have our cake on one side of the transition and continue still to eat it on the other side? A divide is being crossed and we should listen to and reflect on these forebodings.

Charles Dickens (1812–70) wrote *A Tale of Two Cities* in describing the transition of the French Revolution and the Reign of Terror. It has these memorable and much quoted opening few lines: 'It was the best of times, it was the worst of times, it was the age of wisdom, it was the age of foolishness, it was the epoch of belief, it was the epoch of incredulity'.[66] He might, might he not, have been writing about the Information Age! For me, the transition of the Information Age has been a tale of two villages– the rural hamlet where I grew up, from 1945, just as the UK NHS and the computer were being invented, and the global village in which I now live, in retirement. In the 2020s, I connect with both these villages. Between those times, a lot of both good and bad things have come and gone, and many good things remain. The transition is also a tale of science, before and after the rise of computer science and technology, in which all of science has developed ever more rapidly. And it is a transition with a social phenotype

---

65   A. N. Whitehead, *Symbolism, its Meaning and Effect* (New York: Macmillan, 1927), p. 88.

66   C. Dickens, *A Tale of Two Cities* (London: Chapman and Hall, 1868), p. 1.

of the pandemic—infectious unrest and political divisiveness played out in individually-targeted disinformation and nationally-targeted cyber-warfare.

I have lived, throughout my life and career, close to health and social care services in anarchic transition, linked with the rise of information technology. The technology transition is well-marked, but the human health care transition is not. The information revolution has starkly exposed disjoint perspectives on physical and mental health and social care, and how these services should be organized and managed.

From Physics to Biology

The science and technology of measurement that underpins our understanding and treatment of disease, and the promotion and safeguarding of health today, have accelerated along a runway of scientific advance over several hundred years. In the late nineteenth century, information emerged as a unifying concept for shaping and linking the physics of thermodynamics, entropy, statistical mechanics and order, increasing the scientific understanding of equilibrium and non-equilibrium physical systems.

In its rise during the second half of the twentieth century, information technology became inexorably rooted within scientific method, underpinning the capture and management of data from an ever-widening range and scale of observations and measurements. Information concepts also took root in the arts, in new paradigms for study of language and media. In science, measurement reached down and out over many tens of orders of magnitude towards 'zeptoscopic' granularity and 'zottascopic' giantism—prefixes of scale such as micro-, mega- and, even, giga- quickly became outdated! Science now peers at and grapples with Planck units, with blank incomprehension! And numbers characterizing the scale of the observable universe are similarly unimaginable.

New physics, building on the shoulders of earlier giants of electromagnetism, atomic physics, relativity and quantum theory, heralded new devices and experimental methods for chemistry, biology and medicine. Mathematicians, physicists and engineers pioneered computer science and the first electronic computers, which heralded the rise of pervasive information technology. In these ways, pioneering mathematics, science and engineering of the first half of the twentieth century powered biology, life science and medical science of the second half of the twentieth century.

This pattern of advance challenged understanding of living systems—did they somehow defy those same physical laws? The concept of information started to permeate more widely into electrical engineering and life science of the mid-twentieth century. Concepts of epistemology and ontology fuelled philosophical debate about theory of knowledge and theory of mind. 'What is reality, life, truth ...?' is always a puzzled line of questioning, but philosophy is devoted to such puzzles, and it is good to seek clarity, even when not always useful! 'What is information?' has also raised its hand. Philosophy and mathematics, as with pure anything, seek Platonic distance from, while depending on, the nitty gritty of material reality, life and living. This is not a criticism—we need them.

As mentioned in the Preface, at the beginning of the Information Age, in 1944, Schrödinger published *What Is Life?* Reasoning from the physics of that time, he imagined, with remarkable prescience, some key aspects of the form and function of DNA. With modest and straightforward style, he laid an influential foundation for what developed over the coming decades into a story of immense detail, scale and complexity. In 2015, the biochemist, Nick Lane, a UCL colleague, wrote what read to me as another landmark book, to pose *The Vital Question—Why Is Life the Way It Is?*[67] It would have enthralled Schrödinger to read there the life stories of electrons and protons, operating in vast numbers across biological membranes within minute volumes, and at miniscule energy levels in comparison with those powering the semiconducting interfaces of the transistors at the heart of the electronic circuits of the computer, to constrain, channel and power living systems. Life harnesses and channels the energy of solar radiation to power and sustain itself. Cascades of electrons move along pathways of biochemical reactions, giving up energy and releasing protons that establish chemiosmotic potential gradients across cell membranes. These, in turn, provide energy required to fuel cellular processes. Critical of what he saw as overemphasis on the story of information, Lane added the story of bioenergetics, in proposing an answer to his question Why? I tell these stories in Chapter Six, alongside others bringing summative reflections about the nature and understanding of information and life.

From Mathematics to Informatics

In the first half of the twentieth century, new mathematical ideas, drawn together by Russell and Whitehead and further evolved from there, provided the foundations for computer science as they progressed into and through the 1930s. Mathematics advanced and connected more widely in

---

67   N. Lane, *The Vital Question: Energy, Evolution, and the Origins of Complex Life* (New York: W. W. Norton and Company, 2015). NB: the British edition is subtitled 'Why Is Life the Way It Is?' while the American edition is subtitled 'Energy, Evolution, and the Origins of Complex Life'.

science, through the continuous probing of topics like theory of number, set, network, symmetry and topology, and what they offer in clarifying physical, chemical and biological form and function. It has further connected with topics like the analysis of thresholds of transition in complex physical systems, the structure of complex hierarchies of data (such as genomics and proteomics data) and the largescale modelling of public health systems (such as those which guide the management of protection from epidemics). As human mathematicians battle the limits of what they can imagine and do in expanding the scope of their discipline, the computer is emerging as an essential tool in their pursuit of progress. In the not-too-distant future, software systems may bear the names of such renowned mathematicians as Erdős[68] and Ramsey,[69] with the creators of these systems acting as collaborators in their published endeavours! Will software start to win Fields Medals and Nobel Prizes, one wonders?

The range and virtuosity of mathematical methods has expanded and diffused rapidly across disciplines in the Information Age. In Chapter Six, where I explore ideas about the nature and relationship of information and life, I introduce my Ian Stewart inukbook that positions mathematics at the heart of understanding of the living world.[70] Mathematics, spoken of as both science and art, has defied definition. Some resorted to describing it circularly, and no doubt with tongue in cheek, as 'what mathematicians do'! Informatics took root in similarly wide-ranging contexts, also defying distinctive definition.[71] This all feels a bit like Nathan Bailey's supposed copout, in his *Dictionarium Britannicum* (1730), in describing a dog as 'an animal well-known'.[72] With increasing cross-fertilization, hybrid disciplines emerged, and their boundaries blurred–biomathematics, computational physics, medical informatics and so on.

Informatics evolved as a wider currency of scientific discourse, notably so in the reshaping of biology in the second half century. Molecular biology built on the physics and chemistry of crystallography, pioneered by father and son, William Henry Bragg (1862–1942) and William Lawrence Bragg (1890–1971) from the turn of the twentieth century. It led in the early 1950s to the discovery of the double helix structure of DNA. This had, it seems,

---

68   Paul Erdős (1913–66).
69   Frank Ramsey (1903–30).
70   I. Stewart, *Life's Other Secret: The New Mathematics of the Living World* (New York: John Wiley and Sons, 1998).
71   The celebrated physicist, John Wheeler (1911–2008), agreed about the indefinite nature of mathematics and mused further that, at the most basic level, everything is information–informatics being what informaticians do, perhaps! More on this theme in Chapter Three.
72   N. Bailey, *Dictionarium Britannicum* (London: T. Cox, 1730), n.p.

already been characterized by Schrödinger as a 'code-sequence'. The double helix was announced at the University of Cambridge in 1953, when the younger Bragg was head of physics there, as Director of the Cavendish Laboratory. His father had worked at UCL in the post-First World War years. Schrödinger connected with physics at Oxford, spending some time at Magdalen College, my alma mater. These ties to Oxford and UCL add connective warmth for me, in my story.

As with mathematics, informatics spread its wings. It was principally concerned with computation: methods for recording, processing and analyzing data in the engineering of information systems; methods for building representations or models of branches of knowledge, to assist reasoning about them, and for use in predicting their behaviour. Computational power and volumes of stored data grew extremely rapidly over decades. By the turn of the twenty-first century, bioinformatics had emerged, as characterized by my UCL colleague of that time, later the founding director of the European Bioinformatics Institute at Cambridge, Janet Thornton, as a core discipline of biology.

And *medical informatics* was consolidating itself as a discipline at the heart of medicine, as exemplified in the title of a conference held at the British Medical Association (Clinical Information–The Heart of Medicine, December 1994) addressed by the then Chief Medical Officer, Kenneth Calman. It extended further into health care where it was explored in the context of the delivery of services and interfaces with patients. This wider compass, characterized as *health informatics*, gained currency, as did *biomedical informatics* (both of which are often treated synonymously). *Bio-health informatics* also raised its standard, although I am not sure how many troops have rallied there. I will stick with health informatics, on which my first UCL lecturer appointee, Paul Taylor (now a UCL professor), and my Australian colleague, Evelyn Hovenga (like me, the first professor of health informatics in her country), write and communicate so well.

Over the decades traversed in the Information Age, the linkage of information and health care has evolved in fundamentally new directions. Methods of data capture, analysis, reasoning and communication have advanced, hand in hand. The skills and resources required for clinical practice, efficient and effective health care delivery, and self-care, have likewise evolved in parallel, and expanded. The advent of ever more powerful information technology, marked by the exponentially increasing rate of advance described by Moore's Law, has been fundamental. As Walther Ch. Zimmerli wrote for a Ciba Foundation Symposium in 1989, information technology is 'the one and only existing "horizontal technology", a technology that pervades each and every part of social life and all the other technologies as well'.[73]

Emerging from and through all these anarchic forms and connections, health informatics is now more widely understood as playing a crucial role at the heart of health care. Fifty years ago, such thoughts were tolerated or puzzled over with a mixture of incomprehension, amusement and anger, and widely dismissed as pretentious, eccentric and irrelevant. Such is the perception and reception of adventurous new ideas and focus for reform. It is not unknown for clinical scientists close to Nobel Prize recognition, to be under pressure for a perceived lack of quality and progress of their work and publications. I have listened to one such person speaking in the series of annual clinical prize lectures at UCL.[74]

The transition of health care into the Information Age has challenged expectations, behaviours, and capacities: in education and professional roles, organization and financing of services, and their governance. It has seen many engineering and science-based industries come and go and others adapt, evolve, and extend to global reach. It has brought new focus on opportunities and requirements for every citizen to engage constructively and realistically with their personal health. New context of ethical dilemma, such as about personal privacy, preservation of life, and scarce and costly resource allocation, has arisen, while inequalities in health remain as a scourge on society, globally and more locally.

Health informatics, as the broad field that embodies the transition of health care into the Information Age, matters a great deal, has many aspirant owners and has achieved significant things, of which some have taken root. And it has often gone badly wrong. Most academic initiatives launched into the field have lasted just a few years, until their priming funds

---

73 Universität Bern. Akademische Kommission and Law Symposium on Human Genetic Information Science, *Human Genetic Information Science, Law and Ethics*, Ciba Foundation Symposium 149 (Chichester, NY: John Wiley and Sons, 1990), p. 94.

74 This was Stanley Prusiner, who unravelled the story of misshapen prion proteins– one wonders how quickly AlphaFold might now accelerate such discovery. Working at Penn State University, Prusiner was the first researcher to suspect that a misshaped protein, which does not contain genetic material that allows viruses and bacteria to reproduce themselves, could cause disease. The idea was controversial and dismissed by many in the scientific community, including colleagues who judged him unsuited for tenure in his post. Fortunately, he had influential colleagues like Britton Chance (1913–2010), who counselled in his support. Prusiner was awarded the 1997 Nobel Prize in Medicine or Physiology for his work in proposing an explanation for the cause of bovine spongiform encephalopathy (Mad Cow Disease) and its human equivalent, Creutzfeldt-Jakob disease. I well remember that lecture at UCL, describing his career.

ran out. Most pioneering health information systems in use have peaked and declined. Many national implementation initiatives have failed. All of this has cost a huge amount of money and involved much waste of effort and opportunity. And a great deal of learning has been lost along the way. It has made companies and careers and destroyed them. The story of health informatics parallels that of the transformation of society through the Industrial Revolution, starting several centuries before. Its scope is, though, more immediately and globally pervasive, and the anarchy it has brought is, in that sense, pandemic.

A Halfway View

In the extensive, anarchic and costly domain joining health care and information technology, admixtures of commercial, academic and professional issues and rivalries have become, and remain, controversial and strongly contended. Health informatics of the second half of the twentieth century set the scene for, and is now powering, health care systems of the first half of the twenty-first century. It is a transitional bridge between health care before and after the Information Age and this book is a view from halfway across that bridge, midstream in Whitehead's anarchic zone.

The term *pontiff* comes from the Latin for bridge. It conveys leadership in making and communicating connections. There are those that build bridges and those that travel and communicate across them. There are those that wish them into existence but themselves lack the expertise to design or build them—pontificators about impractical bridges. Practical grounding is essential when deciding what and where to build, and how to build, not just technically but also in terms of teams, organizations and communities of builders and users. This is necessary foundation for trust and cooperation, whereby combined efforts accumulate and augment one another, and are sustained.

Information technology has shown great promise in establishing and facilitating important new connections in science and society. It has in very many respects delivered on that promise and will surely continue to do so. It has also disturbed and disappointed, by letting loose a Pandora's box of unknowable connections and disconnections. These have been vectors of instability in economic and social life, loosening and weakening some human connections that have served society stably and well. The transition through the Information Age has become a communicator of fragmentation in society, as Whitehead's words about the anarchy of transition might, in retrospect, have foretold. This transition has not yet settled to a new order, save, perhaps, for the sometimes rather trite observation that change is the nature of things.

Parenthesis–Audience

This introductory chapter began with E. M. Forster and 'only connect'. It closes here with a reflection on the book's connections with and relevance for the intended audience. Why would I attempt such work–both as a career and now as a book of record? This poses another question–the first one that my college friend, Duncan Gallie, asked when I told him of my plan to write the book. What is the audience it will address? Who would wish or need to read it? My off-the-cuff response was that I, myself, was one in the audience as I wanted to see if I could succeed in writing it and having it published, peer-reviewed, by a reputable publisher, believing that I had a unique and worthwhile story to tell. In a sense, writing the book has been an exercise in framing and creating its potential wider audience. How would what I wanted to record and express connect with the interests of others who might read it? Duncan is an eminent social scientist and historian and was at one time Foreign Secretary of the British Academy, and I was duly encouraged when he replied that this was a good reason to write it–albeit clearly not enough of a reason, of course!

The transition of health care from a time when the computer played no part in the science, professional practice and organization on which it draws, through the greater part of the subsequent decades when it was treated with airy disdain, to a time when it has emerged as central to health care, has been an astonishing and highly significant era. It has relevance and personal impact for multiple audiences, present and future, far larger than those who have time to engage with a book like this. The transition needs to be understood and communicated from a forward-looking perspective, and, adopting such a stance, this book addresses many of the audiences that are practically engaged in health care services, be it as inventors, developers, providers, users, researchers, educators, policy makers, administrators, managers or regulators.

In so doing, the book looks ahead to the coming decades of an imagined radical reinvention and reform of health care, focused on achieving and sustaining the best possible coherent, integrated and adaptable citizen- and home-centred supporting information systems and services. It tries to avoid superficial rationalizations and hubristic predictions of the future, that often prevail in times of uncertain change, leading to unwarranted confidence in the potency of preferred magic bullet 'solutions'. I believe that is called 'optimism bias', but there is, of course, 'pessimism bias', as well, which should also be avoided.

The book seeks, rather, to connect constructively with the disciplines, professions and industries currently engaged in health care and health informatics, by presenting an eyewitness story of the ideas and communities of endeavour that have played out over time, in relevant contexts of their wider philosophical, scientific, engineering and societal contingencies. One way or another, information systems and services join them all together, and, when poorly construed and implemented, they can come to impede, fragment and disconnect component health care services from their shared purpose and goals.

As discussed in the Preface, the book focuses in large part on interdisciplinary and multiprofessional endeavours and communities, which are essential to a domain like health informatics. Members of such communities need to acquire and maintain mutual understanding of where fellow members are coming from, and this is a justification I offer for the breadth and depth of the book's coverage, chapter by chapter. Along the way, the building blocks of health informatics are visited, some in more detail than others, placed in context of the histories of both health care and information technology and how they have connected. Sources invoked from beyond the health care domain are used to illustrate their wider contingencies. Viable future reform may arise through connections made from way outside the current comfort zones of orthodoxy. It is necessary to explore widely beyond our current scope and reality of services to discover these.

The book also seeks to connect with citizens of the upcoming Information Society, regarding what health care services may look like and the changing roles and expectations incumbent on them, as well as on those implicit for the providers of services. Finally, the book seeks to connect with those who serve society more generally, in the politics of provision, management and administration of health care, on behalf of citizens.

In the final chapter of his recent book, *What We Owe the Future*, entitled 'What to do [in making the future]', the philosopher William MacAskill advises that we should focus on 'making plans [...] as if we were walking backwards [looking at the past and present] into unknown terrain'.[75] In this book, Part Three is centred on an imagined future reality of Information Society that we are backing into, anticipating a new audience that is being created along the way. My personal songline has involved participation in many of the interdisciplinary and multiprofessional endeavours that the

---

75   W. MacAskill, *What We Owe the Future* (New York: Basic Books, 2022), p. 224.

book describes. Making viable connections within such domains requires direct engagement and experiment within the different disciplines and practices involved, and judgement at their intersection and overlap. This truly is a matter of exploring and learning from 'what works' in practice. **Work**, as in **w**orkforce, **or**ganization and **k**nowledge! And to have things work**ing** together more widely brings the need to harmonize with **in**dustry and **g**overnance. If there were a letter **p** to qualify **work**, I would assign it to **p**ersonal, **p**ractical and **p**rofessional, much more than **p**olitical!

The book adopts a personal and conversational style, with the intention of being easily readable by a broad audience. However, it does often delve into detailed explanations of specialist knowledge, which may be less accessible, and thus of more limited interest and relevance, to some groups of the intended readership. Such readers may prefer to skip some sections and jump from chapter to chapter. To maintain the book's comprehensive overview and wide range of sources, keeping the length within hard-print publication limits, some relevant and supplementary content has been moved into the online additional resources.[76]

As mentioned, when discussing the book's structure, some might understandably prefer it to have been written as several books, not just one, each with a more narrowly defined scope and selectively focused discussion, in part to assert a more rational and abbreviated order for this anarchic domain. That is not my way; I prefer a book that challenges me to think more widely, and this is what I have aimed for, warts and all. By making the book open access, I wish it to be available to an audience of anyone, anywhere, who is curious about the subject. It is an open-ended invitation, which I encourage readers to draw from, incorporate their own insights, and build upon in their own reflections and endeavours. I hope it may help to create a new audience which continues to develop in its own way, making its own contributions to health care in the Information Society of tomorrow.

---

76 Available at https://www.openbookpublishers.com/books/10.11647/obp.0335#resources

2. Knowledge, Language and Reason–From Ancient Times to the Information Age

The story starts long ago, with the gradual conceptualization of knowledge as an encyclopaedia–a circle of learning. This chapter traces a path from the invention of medicine in classical times, through philosophy, language and logic, and through mathematics, natural science and computer science into the modern era of information technology and health care. It follows the librarian's dilemma over the ages–discovering how best to position books and documents within collections and search them in pursuit of learning.

The chapter proceeds to consider languages as expressions of knowledge, and the different forms they take–spoken, written, artistic, mathematical, logical and computational. This sets the scene for introducing computational discipline that grew from endeavours to formulate rigorous logical foundations of mathematics, in earlier times, and the development of formal logic in support of rigorous reasoning. From there, the computer has become integral to how we express and reason with knowledge, and to problem solving and the discovery of new knowledge. These are twenty-first-century frontiers of machine learning and artificial intelligence.

Moving to the complex world of medical language and terminology, used in representing knowledge about medicine and health care, the chapter discusses difficulties faced in evolving their *corpora* of terms and classifications, from pragmatic organizations into reliably computable forms. Notable pioneering initiatives and their leaders are profiled, highlighting some ideas that have acquired staying power and others that have not, looking for patterns of success and failure.

Finally, the chapter moves to a discussion of some pioneering computer-based systems for capturing, storing and reasoning with medical knowledge, such as for guiding the prescription of antimicrobial drugs. It closes with a light-hearted take on how we use the terms knowledge, information and data, and a reflection on the traction that is needed in the unfolding of new knowledge and its application in practical contexts.

   https://doi.org/10.11647/OBP.0335.02

It seems like we all seem to know what 'to know' means. It is one of only 100 or so words that have a comparable translation in every language on earth.

–Marcus du Sautoy[1]

The story begins with knowledge, but how to begin with knowledge? It is an elusive idea. Maybe a picture is best (see Figure 2.1).

Fig. 2.1 Knowledge as earth, air, fire and water–and the passage of time. Photo by Andranik Sargsyan (2020), Pexels, https://www.pexels.com/photo/silhouette-of-unrecognizable-woman-jumping-above-sea-beach-at-sunset-4149949/

In ancient times, humans experienced and came to know earth, air, fire and water, and had a sense of passing time. The concept of a 'beginning' was expressed through words, and through a belief in many and powerful gods. In the classical Greek and Roman sense, encyclopaedia denoted a circle of learning. Learning begins with awareness and experience of reality. In our sense of beginning, there is the hypothesis of science known as the Big Bang, which gives the universe a history and challenges belief. Humans find inspiration and illumination in science and art, and in culture and belief.

Maybe we could begin with one grain of sand–from the opening lines of a poem by William Blake (1757–1827), loved by my dad:

---

1   M. du Sautoy, *What We Cannot Know: Explorations at the Edge of Knowledge* (London: Fourth Estate, 2016), p. 413.

To see a World in a Grain of Sand
And a Heaven in a Wild Flower
Hold Infinity in the palm of your hand
And Eternity in an hour[2]

There are less lyrical perspectives of knowledge, also based on sand–reality as an arid desert landscape and shifting sands of time and experience. We talk of structures built on sand.

In the works of T. S. Eliot (1888–1965), we find poetic lament of pointless knowledge:

The endless cycle of idea and action,
Endless invention, endless experiment,
Brings knowledge of motion, but not of stillness;
Knowledge of speech, but not of silence;
[…] Where is the wisdom we have lost in knowledge?
Where is the knowledge we have lost in information?[3]

Human knowledge is much discussed. It connects and communicates throughout the worlds of experience, learning, imagination and action. The book's Introduction started with a quotation about connection. We connect, communicate about and reason with knowledge through language and logic. And in the Information Age, machines connect and communicate through language and logic, too–machine and program languages and formal logics.

Human knowledge and learning, and machine knowledge and learning, which we now also speak of, evolve in time. They may cooperate and they may diverge, in different dimensions, on different scales, and according to different values. David Deutsch has described knowledge as information that has causal power. Charles West Churchman (1913–2004) and his doctoral student Russell Ackoff (1919–2009) expressed the relationship the other way around, describing information as knowledge for the purpose of taking effective action. Information, too, is a central but elusive idea. Knowledge and information pervade the eternal world of ideas about the nature of reality and the everyday world of appraisal, decision and action.

Information technology also relates to sand–silicon crystals and embedded impurities at the semiconducting interface, transistors that shape and direct electron flow, and the electrical circuitry of computers. Proton gradients energize and shape electron flow across membrane interfaces and along the pathways of chemical reactions and molecular transport enacted

---

2   'Auguries of Innocence' (c. 1803), ll. 1–4.
3   'The Rock' (1934), ll. 6–9, 15–16.

in living systems. And information technology connects and communicates information flow at the interface of machine and human worlds.

Other luminaries provide further avenues into knowing and knowledge:

I neither know nor think that I know.[4]

Nosce te ipsum [know yourself].[5]

Knowledge is always accompanied with accessories of emotion and purpose.[6]

Pure logical thinking cannot yield us any knowledge of the empirical world; all knowledge of reality starts from experience and ends in it.[7]

It is as du Sautoy says: everyone knows about knowledge! One sometimes resonates with several lines recorded in *The Rubáiyát of Omar Khayyam*—I have my grandfather's 1928 illustrated edition of this gem close-by on my office bookshelf. Omar Khayyam (1048–1131) was born in eleventh-century Persia, and, so the story goes, the Vizier to the Sultan Alp-Arslan granted him 'sufficient provision to enable him to devote himself to the pursuit of knowledge'.[8] Despite his achievements in the science of astronomy and as a poet, and his high-level patronage, his worldly concerns in those pursuits ran into opposition from the mystics of the day. He records his frustration with their philosophy, thus: 'Myself when young did eagerly frequent, doctor and saint and heard great argument, about it and about: but ever more, came out by the same door wherein I went'.[9]

I used to use this quotation as a joke in talks about information technology and health care–substituting 'it' with 'IT'! My colleague, Thomas Beale, pointed out the coincidence that Khayyam was alive around the time of the founding of St Bartholomew's Hospital (1123), when we first worked together (in 1992).

Here is my own, not very serious, starter about knowledge:[10]

A is for: Alphabet, Appearance, Attribute, Alpha, Acquisition, Antiquity, Authority, Alchemy, Astronomy, Astrology, Aristocracy, Abstraction, Argumentation, Abduction, Acceleration and Age. Knowledge is an Alphabet of learning, distilled from a kaleidoscope of Appearances. It has

---

4   Socrates (470 BCE–399 BCE), recorded in Plato, *Apology*, section 21d.
5   Carl Linnaeus (1707–1778), describing humans in *Systema Naturae* (1735).
6   A. N. Whitehead, *Adventures of Ideas* (New York: Macmillan, 1933), p. 12.
7   A. Einstein, *Ideas and Opinions* (New York: Crown Publishers, 1954), p. 271.
8   O. Khayyam, *The Rubaiyat of Omar Khayyam*, trans. E. Fitzgerald (London: George G. Harrap & Co. Ltd, 1928), p. 8.
9   Ibid., p. 41.
10   I had the idea of starting each succeeding chapter with a paragraph like this, based on succeeding letters of the alphabet. But it didn't work out—this is a one off!

an infinity of Attributes. It starts from Alpha and stops short of omegA. Stories of the pursuit and Acquisition of knowledge date from Antiquity. They demonstrate knowledge as both manifestation and instrument of Authority. Science in its earliest days was embroiled with mythology and mysticism–early chemistry with Alchemy, and Astronomy with Astrology. The pursuit of knowledge engaged the rulers and Aristocracy of church and state. Theory of knowledge, embodying processes of Abstraction, Argumentation, induction, deduction, Abduction and more, has evolved over centuries, as it challenged the shaping confines of mysticism and religious belief. This unending process has seen huge Acceleration in the Information Age.

Concepts of knowledge and truth seem destined always to be strongly coupled together in the human mind. Discussion of knowledge is encircled by perspectives of discipline, and discussion of truth by schools of philosophical thought. There is much diversity in these discussions and debates, which engage the finest of minds. Karl Popper had little time for their deliberations. At his ninetieth birthday party, he is quoted, loose-lipped, as follows(!):

> I think so badly of philosophy that I don't like to talk about it. [...] I do not want to say anything bad about my dear colleagues, but the profession of teacher of philosophy is a ridiculous one. We don't need a thousand of trained, and badly trained, philosophers–it is very silly. Actually, most of them have nothing to say.[11]

Ridiculous or not, and very much not, I think, philosophy endures. The issues debated are defined and refined in the languages, logics and contexts of their times. Language has extended from the grammar, meaning and symbolism of the spoken and written word to the language of mathematics and computer science. It has entered the complex world of information systems that represent and reason about health care. Differences of perspective can then become embedded and buried within software. The use of this software connects back into human experience of the material world. We must keep our wits about us, lest we fall, unsafely and unaware, under the whim of computer and virtual reality.

I have neither the credentials, nor strong interest, to engage in the detail of philosophical debates, but have observed and followed some of their progression, and read many reams of printed pages through which they have played out. This chapter is built from and expresses that personal experience–no more than that.

---

11 E. Y.-C. Ho, 'At 90, and Still Dynamic: Revisiting Sir Karl Popper and Attending His Birthday Party', *The Karl Popper Web* (29 January 1997), http://www.tkpw.net/hk-ies/n23a/

When we talk of knowing, we debate theory in the realm of epistemology ('The theory of knowledge and understanding, especially with regard to its methods, validity, and scope, and the distinction between justified belief and opinion').[12] When we talk of truth, we jostle over belief within the realm of ontology ('The nature of reality and being'). With this linguistic etymology, science (*scire* [to know]) is bounded within the domain of epistemology. Epistemology seeks definition and is evolutionary. Ontology seeks truth and is a historical and intellectual battleground of competing perspectives and beliefs.

The nature of truth has been much debated by philosophers of logic and science. Colleagues tell me that: 'Is this an ontological question?' has become ever harder to answer in the Information Age, as we grapple with the space between the material reality of human experience and the virtual reality of the computer. The word ontology has become more narrowly appropriated to mean a set of concepts and categories in a subject area or domain that shows their properties and the relations between them. Concerning ontology, the Oxford Dictionary of Philosophy, 2nd Edition 2008, has this to say:

> Philosophers characteristically charge each other with reifying things improperly, and in the history of philosophy every kind of thing will at one time or another have been thought to be the fictitious result of an ontological mistake.[13]

Brief and to the point! It brings to mind the send up of modern-day political gobbledygook in Michael Dobbs's novel, *House of Cards*: 'You might very well think that. I couldn't possibly comment' (the catchphrase of the character Francis Urquhart).[14]

Francis Bacon (1561–1626), an English philosopher who wrote influentially about scientific method, developed the idea that knowledge should be comprehensively classified and universally shared, for the greater good of humanity. He has a close connection with my home city of St Albans, the location of the Roman city of Verulamium. He is remembered in the phrase: 'Knowledge itself is power', from *Meditationes Sacrae* (1597).

Bacon was devoutly religious, believing that knowledge is the rich 'storehouse for the glory of the Creator and the relief of man's estate'.[15]

---

12 'Epistemology', *Oxford English Dictionary*, https://www.oed.com/
13 S. Blackburn, *The Oxford Dictionary of Philosophy*, 2nd ed. (Oxford: Oxford University Press), p. 261.
14 M. Dobbs, *House of Cards* (London: Harper Collins, 1990).
15 F. Bacon, *Advancement of Learning*, ed. J. Devey (New York: P. F. Collier, 1901), p. 66.

He sought scientific method rooted in his Christian faith. This shaped his idea that philosophy and nature must be studied and reasoned about by process of induction, founded on unquestioned divine revelation, but illuminated through observation and experiment and leading incrementally to the steady accumulation of knowledge. That was his theory, and it suited orthodox thinking of his time.

Theory of Knowledge

I would be foolish and will certainly not attempt a comprehensive survey or summary of the theory of knowledge over the ages. My purpose, here, is a limited one. I seek to highlight its historical development from earliest times, alongside language, logic, mathematics and computer science, and its interface with the organization of books and documents, and now computerized databases and knowledge bases. I extend from this to its contemporary interface with life and medical science, health care and the computational problems these have encountered in their transition into the Information Age. The problems reflect, and reflect in, language and terminology descriptive of these domains and methods for representing and reasoning with medical knowledge, more generally. By analogy with databases that store and manage data and records, computer systems that represent and reason with knowledge have been termed knowledge bases.[16]

Theory and practice intertwine. Theory involves abstraction and simplification, consistent with the domain and purpose it serves. Leonardo da Vinci (1452–1519) wrote that:

> Those who are enamoured of practice without theory are like a pilot who goes into a ship without rudder or compass and never has any certainty where he is going. Practice should always be based upon a sound knowledge of theory.[17]

I am not sure if he was a sailor–possibly he was, given his wide range of talents and interests–but he would surely also have known that there is a lot more to sailing safely than knowledge about winds, headings, charts and weather forecasts. These must be experienced–the knowledgeable pilot on board is more oracle than mariner in good sailing and survival at sea.

---

16 A. Rector et al., 'On Beyond Gruber: "Ontologies" in Today's Biomedical Information Systems and the Limits of OWL', *Journal of Biomedical Informatics: X, 2* (2019), 100002, https://doi.org/10.1016/j.yjbinx.2019.100002.

17 Leonardo da Vinci, *Notebooks*, comp. I. Richter (Oxford: Oxford University Press, 2008), p. 212.

That said, Whitehead makes these points about theory of knowledge and method in matters of science and philosophy:

> A great deal of confused philosophical thought has its origin in obliviousness to the fact that the relevance of evidence is dictated by theory. For you cannot prove a theory by evidence which that theory dismisses as irrelevant. This is also the reason that in any science which has failed to produce any theory with a sufficient scope of application, progress is necessarily very slow. It is impossible to know what to look for and how to connect the sporadic observations. [...]
>
> No systematic thought has made progress apart from some adequately general working hypothesis, adapted to its special topic. Such an hypothesis directs observation, and decides upon the mutual relevance of various types of evidence. In short, it prescribes method. [...]
>
> A method is a way of dealing with data, with evidence. [...]
>
> Every method is a happy simplification. But only truths of a congenial type can be investigated by any one method or stated in the terms dictated by the method. For every simplification is an oversimplification. Thus, the criticism of theory does not start with the question, True or False? It consists in noting its scope of useful application and its failure beyond that scope. It is an unguarded statement of a partial truth. Some of its terms embody a general notion with a mistaken specialization, and others of its terms are too general and require discrimination of their possibilities of specialization. [...]
>
> In the preliminary stages of knowledge, a haphazard criterion is all that is possible. Progress is then very slow, and most of the effort is wasted. Even an inadequate working hypothesis with some confirmation to fact is better than nothing. It coordinates procedure.[18]

So much has changed in the one hundred years since Whitehead wrote these words about science and philosophy. Perspectives on the relationship of theory, practice and meaning have unfolded within new domains of knowledge, such as psychology, anthropology and behavioural science, forming fresh connections between science and society, politics and economy, and lifestyle and ecology. In human affairs, theory and practice coexist within the context of the art of the possible, and programmes for reform inherit from adventures of ideas. The story of the computer in medicine and health care is characterized by counterflows of knowledge and meaning, in both theory and practice. There is an adventure of ideas in theory extending towards a programme for reform of practice, and there

---

18   *Adventures of Ideas*, pp. 213–14.

is experience of meaning in practice, feeding back to illuminate and help improve both theory and practice.

The struggle to match theory, evidence and practice in medicine has been a recurrent and haphazard thread running through the Information Age, as it has explored and struggled with its roles and credentials that lie midway between life science and health care practice. This anarchic zone has been further highlighted and amplified by the haphazard nature of forays to computerize, as the capacity to make measurements has accelerated beyond imaginable bounds.

The first part of this book is mainly concerned with the adventure of ideas. The middle section highlights the anarchy that the computer has unleashed in the haphazard collision of new ideas with current practices. Programme for reform takes centre stage in the final part of the book, aiming and pointing towards a fruitful and meaningful experience and practice of personal health care for the individual citizen, drawn together around a more principled theory and practice of information that connects health care services with individual citizens, in their home settings and within populations.

Returning now to theory of knowledge, it is impossible for me to think, let alone start to write about knowledge, without feeling a sense of inadequacy, and awe of Bertrand Russell (1872–1970), who, with Alfred North Whitehead, did much to establish logical foundations of pure mathematics, as set out in 1910–13, in their *Principia Mathematica*.[19] My wider admiration of Whitehead will already be clear. Russell, too, was an extraordinary person, combining aristocratic demeanour, ruthless logical argumentation and loudly expressed pacifist belief.[20]

In 1946, Russell published *History of Western Philosophy*,[21] of which the historian G. M. Trevelyan (1876–1962) wrote in his review (as quoted in the cover notes for the seventh imprint): 'It may be one of the most valuable books of our age'. I have a copy from 1963 on my desk as I write, presented to me as the Bishop Burroughs' Prize for Science, and inscribed by my eccentric, classics enthusiast headteacher of the Bristol Cathedral School. It is one of my early inukbooks, spell binding in its incisive clarity, traversing two thousand years of Western philosophical thought.

---

19   A. N. Whitehead and B. Russell, *Principia Mathematica* (Cambridge, UK: Cambridge University Press, 1925–27).

20   K. Willis, 'Russell and His Obituaries', *Russell: The Journal of Bertrand Russell Studies*, 26 (2006) 5–54, https://doi.org/10.15173/russell.v26i1.2091

21   B. Russell, *History of Western Philosophy: Collectors Edition* (New York: Routledge, 2013).

Of course, there has been much else of philosophy argued through the seventy-five years since it was written, but this book is a marker, published at the very start of my life, and it seems appropriate to start from there, leaving perspectives arising from more recent relevant traditions of thought, such as philosophy of mind, to be introduced later in the book.

Russell writes: 'To teach how to live without certainty, and yet without being paralysed by hesitation, is perhaps the chief thing that philosophy, in our age, can still do for those who study it'.[22] For Russell, that aim is principally served through clarity and logical precision of thought and reasoning. He was not beyond the occasional incisive moral judgement, though! In the Preface to his *magnum opus*, apologizing for writing a book covering such a wide field, Russell says, 'If there is any unity in the movement of history, if there is any intimate relation between what goes before and what comes later, it is necessary, for setting this forth, that earlier and later periods should be synthesized in a single mind'.[23] That belief is to be pondered in our era of information explosion, where Deutsch speaks of knowledge as information with causative power. Is humankind any longer capable of such synthesis of knowledge, and thus awareness of its causative potential?[24]

Setting out his stall further, Russell writes:

> Philosophy, as I shall understand the word, is something intermediate between theology and science. Like theology, it consists of speculations on matters as to which definite knowledge has, so far, not been ascertainable; but like science, it appeals to human reason rather than to authority, whether that of tradition or that of revelation. All definite knowledge—so I should contend—belongs to science; all dogma as to what surpasses *definite* knowledge belongs to theology. But beyond theology and science there is a 'No Man's Land' exposed to attack from both sides; this No Man's Land is philosophy.[25]

---

22   Russell, *History of Western Philosophy*, p. 14.
23   Ibid., p. 7.
24   Advances in machine learning have caused the champions of the games of chess and Go to be deposed by machines, guided by the brilliant, Turing-like minds of those such as the inventor Demis Hassabis. As I revise this chapter, the company DeepMind has just triumphed again with AlphaFold, working from the known nucleic acid sequence of many millions of proteins to derive their three-dimensional topology. Of course, there are more dimensions of protein function still to unfold. Having accepted defeat to the machine in many areas, wise synthesis of different threads of knowledge is the next humanly-perceived boundary that is claimed to distinguish humans from machines—a noble thought somewhat thrown into question by the pervasive political turmoil of the summer of 2020!
25   Russell, *History of Western Philosophy*, p. 13.

According to Russell, philosophers through the ages have divided into disciplinarians–characterized as advocating some form of old or new dogma, that could not be proved empirically, and thus tending to be hostile to science–and libertarians–characterized as 'scientific, utilitarian, rationalistic and hostile to violent passion and profound forms of religion'. Russell's personal conclusion, in reviewing the ebb and flow of this philosophical debate was sombre, observing 'endless oscillation' between these 'partly right and partly wrong' parties.[26]

From its origins alongside those of science, in the philosophy of Thales of Miletus (*c.* 624 BCE–548BCE), Western philosophical thought has been dominated by a succession of 'ologies', 'doxies' and 'isms' (and 'isn'tisms'!), characterizing perennial dispute! Religious doctrine became dominant up to and through the Middle Ages, and then, through Renaissance, Reformation and Enlightenment times, science and logical thought became more dominant. Nowadays, philosophical debate is also framed within the scientific and technological contexts of the Information Age. As Russell remarks, philosophical arguments seldom achieve resolution. Some may, in time, come to be conceived as wrong-headed or logically unsound–he is cholerically vituperative about what he sees as non-sense, or ideas contrary to common-sense–but may, even so, re-emerge, re-framed and re-expressed, and argued anew, in contemporary contexts.

In thirty-one chapters comprising over eight hundred and forty-two pages, Russell situates each philosopher as the product of the *milieu* of their times, in whom 'crystallized and concentrated thoughts and feelings which, in a vague and diffused form, were common to the community of which he was a part'.[27] In turn, he observes 'a reciprocal causation: the circumstances of men's lives do much to determine their philosophy, but, conversely, their philosophy does much to determine their circumstances'.[28]

Much philosophical argument centres on the use of words and language. In Grecian times, philosophy was propagated in open debate, and by people moving from city to city. In increasingly stark contrast, much knowledge and theory of knowledge in the age of the computer (such as knowledge entailed in artificial intelligence algorithms) is moving out of reach of communities of scholarship, to be embedded in software and owned or appropriated as property of commercial organizations with global reach. This is a new structure of scientific revolution, with considerable practical and philosophical implication for the balance of public and private enterprise in society. At many points as the storyline of the book develops,

---

26 Ibid., p. 22.
27 Ibid., p. 7
28 Ibid., p. 14.

it highlights contemporary movements to fulfil Bacon's vision of open knowledge within Popper's vision of Open Society, expressed variously as open access to knowledge, open data and open-source software. The key to this future, if that is the way society evolves, is in the three taken together. The expression of knowledge, the data on which it rests and the software used to reason about and utilize the two, must demonstrate their mutual connections, to justify their correctness and useful application.

Consideration of the nature of knowledge devolves into that of truth and belief. Chapter thirty of Russell's book is devoted to John Dewey (1859–1952), a New Englander most known for his book *The School and Society*, and much admired by Russell, personally and professionally.[29] Dewey was the leading proponent of instrumentalism and a critic of traditional notions of truth as 'static and final; perfect and eternal'. Russell writes:

> Since Pythagoras, and still more since Plato, mathematics has been linked with theology, and has profoundly influenced the theory of knowledge of most professional philosophers. Dewey's interests were organic rather than mathematical, and he conceives thought as an evolutionary process, and human knowledge 'as an organic whole, gradually growing in every part, and not perfect in any part till the whole is perfect'.[30]

Dewey maintained that inquiry is the fundamental concept of logic and theory of knowledge. Russell writes that Dewey defined this as follows: 'inquiry is the controlled or directed transformation of an indeterminate situation into one that is so determinant in its constituent distinctions and relations as to convert the elements of the original situation into a unified whole'; and later, 'unified wholes are to be the outcome of inquiries'.[31] Russell took issue with Dewey over the primacy of inquiry, substituting his own concept of truth as the yardstick of logic and theory of knowledge. This got him into further mathematical and logical complexity, in tackling so-called Russell Paradox that his ideas led him to puzzle over. The instrumentalist view was also criticized by George Santayana (1863–1952), who Russell quotes as saying: 'In Dewey, as in current science and ethics, there is a pervasive [...] tendency to dissolve the individual into his social functions, as well as everything substantial and actual into something relative and transitional'.[32]

29   J. Dewey, *The School and Society and the Child and the Curriculum* (Chicago, IL: University of Chicago Press, 2013).
30   Russell, *History of Western Philosophy*, p. 775.
31   Ibid., p. 778.
32   Ibid., p. 781.

As we delve further into the nature of truth and falsity of knowledge, we encounter debates about language, and words and terms, such as: belief, meaning, significance, thing, fact, common sense and reality. Profusion of differently understood terms also characterizes the discussion of knowledge in the context of computation and I return to this problem in the discussion of computer knowledge bases, later in the chapter.

In 1912, Russell advanced the correspondence theory of truth, writing that: 'truth is understood in terms of the way reality is described by our beliefs. A belief is false when it does not reflect states-of-affairs, events, or things accurately. In order for our beliefs to be true, our beliefs must agree with what is real'.[33] In *History of Western Philosophy*, Chapter XXX, he produced examples whereby Dewey's reasoning leads to positions he believed absurd, based on what he saw as common sense, writing that:

> Dewey's divergence from what has hitherto been regarded as common sense is due to his refusal to admit 'facts' into his metaphysic, in a sense in which 'facts' are stubborn and cannot be manipulated. In this, it may be that common sense is changing, and that his view will not seem contrary to what common sense is becoming.[34]

These words chime with the buzzwords of recent months–'alternative facts' and 'fake news'.

Chapter thirty-one is devoted to the philosophy of logical analysis, in which school of thought Russell was a leading figure. It has come to the fore in formal logic of the Information Age, which has been influential in the evolution of knowledge bases. Russell describes its origins in the work of mathematicians such as Karl Weierstrass (1815–97), in placing the infinitesimals of the calculus of Gottfried Wilhelm Leibniz (1646–1716) onto a logically secure foundation, and Georg Cantor (1845–1918), whose theory of continuity and infinite number, he says, put to bed a good deal of 'muddled and mystical philosophical musings' over the ages! He did not mince *his* words!

The historic connections of knowledge with philosophy, language, mathematics, logic and reason are mirrored in the transition into the world of the computer, and its languages and logics. This transition is developed further in sections below, but first I make another historical detour, this time into the world of librarianship and the age-old struggle to organize the increasing scope and proliferation of books and documents. There are illuminating parallels between this story and the quest to curate, classify

---

33   B. Russell, *The Problems of Philosophy* (Oxford: Oxford University Press, 1912), Chapter XXXI (n.p.).

34   Russell, *History of Western Philosophy*, p. 780.

and reason with knowledge, using computers in the Information Age, very much a story playing out in medicine and health care of the Information Age.

Libraries and their Classification of Knowledge

A book is a fragile creature, it suffers the wear of time, it fears rodents, the elements and clumsy hands. So, the librarian protects the books not only against mankind but also against nature and devotes his life to this war with the forces of oblivion.[35]

Librarians provide access to knowledge and maintain order in and between bodies of knowledge and the communities of their producers and users, for research, education and practice. Libraries are also often custodians of historically important collections of books and other artefacts. Wear of time, rodents, elements and clumsy hands all have their correlates in the computer age! The forces of oblivion do not change much; ultimately, they are just physics! The protection of knowledge remains hard and complex, spanning lifetimes of work.

I have chosen to continue this chapter's exploration of knowledge in the world of libraries, and not just because I like books and spend a lot of time with them. My purpose is to draw out parallels between difficulties faced by librarians over the ages, in organizing the storage and retrieval of the written word, and those faced in the evolving Information Age, in envisioning and creating computerized databases as well as knowledge bases.

The advent of electronic publishing has transformed libraries into organizations that connect continuously, both locally and globally, with many communities and languages of disciplines and users. This has brought new challenges to the standardization of methods, bridging from local to global content and organization. Library information systems are, perhaps, not quite as complex in their semantics as are health care record systems, but they are challenging, nonetheless.

Mine is a small personal collection of books, and libraries have always curated collections specific to the interests and needs of their client users. In medicine, the specialist libraries of the Royal Society of Medicine, the British Medical Association, The Wellcome Trust and the Royal College of Physicians are well-established, located close by to my university (University College London). As with many capital cities, there are myriad such libraries, both specialist and general, in central London. As with any

---

35   U. Eco, *The Name of the Rose* (London: Pan Books, 1984), p. 38.

university, in ours there are multiple libraries distributed across the separate academic campuses and within the academic departments established there over many decades. They are places to work in as much as to access books. Coherent and standardized information technology (IT) infrastructure and services are now crucial for both purposes. Mergers of previously independent institutions and library teams, changing academic needs over time and the alignment of library systems with IT infrastructure more generally have posed major transitional challenges on many simultaneous fronts, over many years.[36]

The world of books and documents and the world of data have increasingly converged during the Information Age. This convergence requires curation that connects knowledge with the data and methods on which it is based, so that findings can be replicated, and the knowledge created more openly shared and accessible, within and between communities of discipline, practice and use. Science places a high priority on the ability of different teams to replicate one another's experimental findings. A recent study showed that fewer than half the results published in twenty-three highly cited papers in preclinical cancer biology research could be successfully reproduced.[37] Such findings are of increasing concern and reinforce the need for curation of both knowledge and the data on which it is based, when publishing research findings.

The history of libraries deserves to be appreciated and learned from in the interconnected domains of knowledge and practice for health care in the Information Age. Books in libraries are not databases but there are some analogies. Waving hands somewhat: persistence of data is the placing of books on shelves; indexing of data is the tagging or coding of books and documents within the library classification system; inheritance of properties of data is the reuse of patterns of subdivision in library classifications.

---

36 During the course of my career in London, latterly at UCL from the mid-1990s, I worked in many libraries and with their communities of librarians and users. I observed and helped in the transition of university and national libraries, and those specific to medicine, through the Information Age. In those years, I passed and saw daily the emergence of the magnificent new British Library, close by to UCL and St Pancras station. The head of information systems, there, approached me to join and then chair a group overseeing the development of a new system for the PubMed electronic library in the UK, and also serve on the UK advisory board for a Research Information Network across disciplines. The interface of library IT systems with the wider IT infrastructure of our university was a world I experienced closely as a member of its Information Strategy Committee, where I chaired the Information Infrastructure sub-committee for some years.

37 T. M. Errington et al., 'Reproducibility in Cancer Biology: Challenges for Assessing Replicability in Preclinical Cancer Biology', *Elife*, 10 (2021), e67995, https://doi.org/10.7554/eLife.67995

Library history demonstrates the importance of interpreting knowledge within historical contexts: assumptions made and understandings reached; skill and motivation of writer, curator and reader; resource deployed; power exercised. The efforts made to bring sustainable and useful order to library classifications, notably over the past one hundred and fifty years, parallel attempts over recent decades to systematize the language, methods and procedures used in organizing medical knowledge and information systems supporting medicine and health care. There is a continual interplay of theory, pragmatism and edict in these stories.

It is understandable that such breadth of ambition and quest for generic method, proves too risky and intractable for many to encompass. An often-made pragmatic compromise is to narrow the focus and effort into a domain-by-domain approach. That was the decision of the US Library of Congress a century or so ago, in the world of library classifications. It is often the only practical way forward–grand schemes addressing grand challenges are risky and prone to failure! However, the price of pragmatic simplification in the shorter term can be escalating confusion in the longer term. The underlying problem does not go away–it is ignored or deferred down the road until another day. And of course, that day will bring new contexts–including new kinds of problems.

The experience gained and limitations encountered when attempting to formulate and refine a useful and applicable general method, by conducting experiments that implement and use the proposed method in practice, play out in context of the motivation and capability of the participants in the experiment and the availability of resource. The outcomes inform choices that are made about the standardization of method. The twentieth century history of the computer system and its designers and users, in creating and operating health care-related knowledge bases and maintaining records of practice, has interesting historical parallels in library science. It reflects issues of scope, rigour, flexibility to change, cost, utility and governance. In the Information Age, librarianship has extended to open curation, access to and governance of electronic sources of knowledge and data, for example in the arenas of Creative Commons and open-access publications and data. Citizens, in both their personal and professional roles, can now more readily, and usefully, take part as creators, reviewers, curators and governors of these resources. Citizen science is emergent in many fields.

In the next section, I trace the story of the organization of knowledge within libraries, as book and document stores stretching back over more than two thousand years. I do this with Edward Gibbon (1737–94) as my early guide, and later draw inspiration from conversations I had some decades ago with a friend who played a leading role in the UNESCO project entitled the Broad System of Ordering (BSO). This initiative had, and retains, a close link with my alma mater, University College London (UCL), to which its copyright is now assigned.

Historical Origins

Gibbon's one thousand-page history, written from 1783–88, has been my introductory inukbook and source for the following survey.[38] His writing is often richly polemical and controversial, but some of the ancient sentiments expressed amuse, more than offend, and some ring true in the frustrations of our age!

In Gibbon's discussion of progress in the sciences, he adds, dismissively, that:

> The libraries of the Arabians, as with those of Europe, were possessed only of local value, or imaginary merit [...] The shelves were crowded with orators and poets, whose style was adapted to the taste and manners of their countrymen; with general and partial histories, which each revolving generation supplied with a new harvest of persons and events; with codes and commentaries of jurisprudence, which derived their authority from the law of the prophet; with the interpreters of the Koran, and orthodox tradition; and with the whole theological tribe, polemics, mystics, scholastics and moralists, the first or the last of writers, according to the different estimate of sceptics or believers.
>
> The physics, both of the Academy and the Lycaeum, as they are built, not on observation but on argument, have retarded the progress of real knowledge. [...] the human faculties are fortified by the art and practice of dialectics; the 10 predicaments of Aristotle collect and methodise our ideas, and his syllogism is the keenest weapon of dispute. It was dexterously wielded in the schools of the Saracens, but as it is more effectual for the detection of error than for the investigation of truth, it is not surprising that new generations of masters and disciples should still revolve in the same circle of logical argument. The mathematics are distinguished by a peculiar privilege, that, in the course of ages, they may always advance and can never recede.[39]

There have been efforts to classify writing, in the form of clay tablets, papyrus manuscripts, documents and books, from earliest times. As such archives grew, this became a significant challenge, and the library and librarian profession were born. No small undertaking—essentially any

---

38 E. Gibbon, *The History of the Decline and Fall of the Roman Empire* (London: Strahan and Cadell, 1788).

39 Ibid., p. 982.

writing, from any domain of scholarship, be it in a narrow discipline or multi-disciplinary, needed to be placed somewhere, and known about so it could be discovered, retrieved and used.

Where there is a relatively small set of items to store, one can stack them in piles–just as the numerous source books are stacked as I write and refer to them, here, and rely on the human eye to find and retrieve them. Maybe one can group them in some way, again in piles, as I have done for each chapter, or along shelves in order of size or date of publication, or alphabetically by the name of the author. What about finding the book according to the name of the second or subsequent authors, though, and how should they be managed when they cross different zones of classification? Creating lists and indexes to keep track of library contents became a necessity.

Bibliographies and indexes have grown in scale and detail as human knowledge has grown. Modern day data processing has brought new opportunity and likewise also become a necessity in keeping track and enabling access. Searching recent medical literature just fifty years ago was a laborious and time-consuming process, involving scanning of the microscopic print of hefty annual indexes with a magnifying glass, on frequent treks to libraries.

Clay tablets in the royal archives of the Assyrian king, Ashurbanipal (685 BCE–631 BCE), were organized in a catalogue divided into classes of grammar, history, law, natural history, geography, mathematics, astronomy, magic and religious legends, each divided into subclasses. The poet and scholar, Callimachus (*c.* 310 BCE–240 BCE), is reported as having organized the Great Library of Alexandria, using a classification of poets, law makers, philosophers, historians, rhetoricians and miscellaneous writers, subdivided by form, subject and time. According to Gibbon, the library was described by the Roman historian and philosopher, Livy (*c.* 59 BCE–17 CE] as *elegentiae regum curaeque egregium opus* (Google translates this as 'The elegance and care of kings, an excellent work'), an encomium with which the Stoic philosopher Seneca (*c.* 1 BCE–65 CE) disagreed. That is the way with philosophers! Gibbon has a waspish turn of phrase, here, criticizing that their 'wisdom, on this occasion, deviates into nonsense'![40]

Liu Xiang (77 BCE–6 BCE, a Chinese astronomer, poet, politician, historian, librarian and writer) and his son Liu Xin (*c.* 50 BCE–23 CE, a Chinese astronomer, mathematician, historian, librarian and politician) devised the first library classification for the Seven Outlines ('Qi Lue') in the Han Dynasty of China. Libraries of China in the West Han period, around the first century CE, used a classification of philosophy, poems and songs, military art, sooth saying and medicine.

---

40   Ibid., p. 956.

Gibbon gives a lively story of the historical context of those times, particularly the Saracen invasion of Egypt in 638 CE, led by Amrou (Amr ibn al-As al-Sahmi, *c.* 573 CE–664 CE), the defeat and retreat of the Greek rulers, and the demise of the Great Library of Alexandria. This history has been substantially pawed over and re-written in modern times, but Gibbon records that Amrou discussed the status of the library with John Philoponus (490 CE–570 CE), a Byzantine Alexandrian philologist, Aristotelian commentator, and Christian theologian, famed for his 'laborious studies of grammar and philosophy':

> Was the library an inestimable gift, in the eyes of the Greek, or contemptible, in keeping with the contempt for idols of their conquering successors? The Caliph Omar was consulted and gave the opinion that 'if these writings of the Greeks agree with the book of God, they are useless and need not be preserved: if they disagree, they are pernicious and need to be destroyed'.[41]

Magisterial having and eating of cakes! As the story goes–which Gibbon doubted, but it is a good story–the paper and parchment was distributed to four thousand baths in the city and fueled their heating for six months! One wonders how many baths the hot air associated with today's Cloud-based knowledge stores could heat!

Culture, belief and learning went hand in hand and stirrings of science occupied a lowly position in the order of things. The early astronomers maintained their credibility by combining their observations with astrology and the mysticism of the Zodiac. They were careful not to challenge the abstract geometry of the heavens described by Claudius Ptolemy (*c.* 100 CE–170 CE). Discovery of the solar system rested in wait until the Copernican revolution broke the mould of established doctrine many centuries later. The books and documents were collected and organized in line with the predilections and pragmatic choices of their times; the common goal was to give each item a place in a collection.

Around the turn of the sixteenth century, in the England of Elizabeth I (1533–1603), the classification of knowledge proposed by Bacon sought to organize all types of knowledge into groupings of history, poetry and philosophy. He understood information to be processed through human memory, imagination and reason, but his methods for the categorization of knowledge were based on inductive principles of experiment and reasoning, proceeding from divine revelation, which he insisted on as the basis of his scientific method.

---

41   Ibid., p. 952.

William Torrey Harris (1835–1909) built on Bacon's ideas about knowledge structure and scientific method. He created a library catalogue for the St. Louis Public Library School and his ideas were widely influential. He proposed a practical system of rules for the classification, ranging from the generic to the specific. There were main divisions, ultimate divisions, appendices and hybrids. Bacon's approach sought to define all knowledge within a predetermined structure of classification. Harris used generic main divisions to provide a 'guiding principle' of the form of knowledge and dealt with the detail of knowledge content more flexibly in minor divisions and sections.

Enumerative and Faceted Classification

In this section, I explore the origins of more formal library classification systems–how they describe the subject matter of books and documents such that they can be placed efficiently within a library collection and readily discovered there by its enquiring users. In passing, we might note that the computer has a similar problem to solve with data, as we come to consider in Chapter Five. In that context, the computer, as data librarian, must be able to decide how and where to store data as efficiently as possible, in different data storage media, such that they can be efficiently managed and retrieved, as required, for use in the computations specified by its programs, as the data library users.

Enumerative classification focuses on the place for the book. Faceted classification focuses on the content of the book.[42] The section draws on historical detail from *The Encyclopaedia of Library and Information Sciences*;[43] a more recent appraisal of theory and practice of library classification schemes is provided by S. Batley.[44]

First, a simple and rather fanciful example to set the scene. Imagine you are a librarian, and you receive a shipment of new books for the library from a publisher, packed in a large box. You open the box, take out a book and

---

42   In library classification, 'facet' refers to a particular aspect of a subject or train of characteristics—e.g., in literature, there may be four facets: language, form, author and work. An enumerative classification contains a full set of entries covering all defined concepts. A faceted classification uses a set of semantically cohesive categories that are combined as needed to create an expression of a concept. In this way, the faceted classification is not limited to already defined concepts. Wikipedia contributors, 'Faceted Classification', *Wikipedia, The Free Encyclopedia* (24 May 2023), https://en.wikipedia.org/wiki/Faceted_classification

43   R. Wedgeworth, ed., *World Encyclopedia of Library and Information Services* (Chicago, IL: American Library Association, 1993).

44   S. Batley, *Classification in Theory and Practice* (Oxford: Chandos Publishing, 2014).

glance at the title and brief description of the work on its cover, and perhaps the table of contents. It is a book about Euclidean geometry, say–geometry as a subdomain of mathematics. It might devote some of its content to the history of mathematics in classical times, in Greece. Leaving aside all the administrative steps in registering the book in a library catalogue, your imagined task is to take the book up staircases, along corridors and into aisles of shelving, to place it within the library. It must go somewhere. There is a limited number of spaces available.

One can imagine several possible procedures–the first, a purely pragmatic one. You and your librarian colleagues have previously put your heads together and decided on the layout of the library, dividing it into a fixed number of zones for the principal subject domains: mathematics, literature, science, history, technology etc. These zones may be associated with separate buildings, floors or rooms of the library. In each zone, you have subdivided the space available: mathematics might encompass sub-sections of algebra, probability, numerical methods, combinatorics and geometry etc., again each with a limited and fixed capacity to house books. Likewise in the history zone, its space has subsections organized by time, region of the world, and kinds of history: social, military, economic etc.

Further choices have been made to define the structure of this very inflexible imaginary library, allocating a numeric code to each book position in the subsection of the library in which the new book is to reside. Your thinking heads have thought through this conundrum and decided upon a divisional structure to deal with all possibilities, and how many book slots to allocate to each subdivision. It is an 'enumerative coding system' (i.e., based on numbers, but essentially an orderly set of symbols) that covers all the possibilities and expresses the structure of the cascading subdivisions of the library book locations ('pigeonholes').

You opt to classify the new book under history and allocate the code that then guides you through the labyrinth to the fixed slot on the shelf, within the room, on the floor, and within the building that is to be this book's home. And so on with the rest of the box of new accessions to the library. I did say it was fanciful!

Assuming there is a space available, this works for placing the book, but there are further difficulties: what about the library users, who come to the library with a topic in mind in search of relevant books? A history student enters looking for information about Euclid's place in the history of Greece, they browse the history shelves dedicated to history of mathematics in classical times. Had you opted for this book to be housed in the mathematics building, they might not have found it so easily. Likewise for a mathematics student who seeks out a book comparing the pros and cons of Euclidean geometries alongside non-Euclidean geometries–they might not have been so lucky, after trekking expectantly to the mathematics building. It is unlikely that many users will be sufficiently determined and resilient to visit every building and browse the shelves there, according to the possible combinations of topics whereby the sort of book they seek might be located.

Both librarian and student have choices to make; they get harder as the scale and granularity of content in the library collection grows in terms of numbers of books, diversity of subjects covered, and their interconnections–history connecting with mathematics, science connecting with technology, politics and economics connecting with pretty much anything. New subjects arise that undermine the integrity of the structure that has been imposed. If one part of the enumerated code has space for four numeric digits, the ten thousandth book that would legitimately be represented by that code segment will have nowhere to go. A valid book classification has overflowed the fixed number of slots available for books thus classified. The material needing to be positioned cannot be accommodated within the structure of permissible classifications of content. The library may yet have spare slots elsewhere–perhaps books about performance of Beethoven symphonies in nineteenth-century Tbilisi have not yet filled their allocated slots!

In theory, you and your librarian colleagues could juggle the enumerated structure of the classification to use the available number of slots more efficiently, moving the books around accordingly. But a 'general post' of books, relocating them to different shelves of a dynamically evolving library, to provide valid positions for new books, is not an attractive option. The frequent users of a particular reference book would be unhappy for it to be moved from place to place. You fiddle with the scheme, and over time it becomes untidy and does a poorer and poorer job.

An alternative strategy might be to disconnect the problem of classifying the book content from that of allocation of slots on bookshelves. Each book is to be uniquely classified according to different facets of that content. In principle, such flexibility should allow for the addition of new divisions and subdivisions of content of the book. But, as ever, the devil is in the detail; the choice of available facets and how they are combined become rather fundamental issues.

A cut diamond is structured with many facets (faces) to reflect and channel incident light that passes through and issues from the whole diamond, in different ways and directions. The quality and appeal of the diamond is expressed and perceived via the cutting of its facets. The content of the book is expressed in a common language of facets. The user can interrogate the facet-based classification and the language can extend in time to introduce new domains of content, and connections between them, that the enumerative procedure is not equipped to handle. We still have the problem of optimal physical placement of books within library collections, but this can now become a separable concern, no longer a tail wagging the dog of a satisfactory system of content classification. An automated book storage and retrieval system sounds a good idea—well, the database engineer and Amazon warehouse manager think that, too, and it is a more realizable one in their worlds of data storage persistence and warehousing, where there are no browsing users who persist in liking to experience the look and feel of books!

This has been a rather artificial and hand-waving introduction to a complex field with a complicated and anarchic history. The librarians' problem over the ages has emerged from and intertwined with the unfolding world of knowledge and technology which they struggle to curate and manage. In passing, we might note analogy with the computer's problem, as knowledge and data librarian, emerging from and intertwined with that same world. There is a difference, of course. The book librarian is not responsible for the problem they confront, but, in the Information Age, the computer is closely implicated in the problem—itself integral to the creation of the exponentially growing body of knowledge and data that it struggles to curate and manage. We are sometimes a bit like the latter-day Christopher Marlowe's (1564–93) Dr Faustus: frustrated with the vicissitudes of medicine, law, logic and theology, seeking to acquire magical mastery over the world, accepting, albeit with similar repeating misgivings, the services of a Mephistophelian computer!

Let us not dwell here on Faustian bargain and fate—it does not have to be that way, but we should be aware and beware! The bargain with the computer can penetrate deeply into health care services. The complexity of challenges to their balance, continuity and governance in the Information Age reflects the intertwinement of problems in management of the data explosion created by and with the computer, and the battle for understanding the proliferating detail and nuance of practice that it creates and exposes. Best not to pass that problem back to Deep Mephistopheles for resolution. We need human hands on how we judge and contain the fractal complexity of data and knowledge—otherwise we risk escalating and intractable battle between signal, bias and noise in human judgement, of the kinds that Daniel Kahneman and colleagues are signalling.[45]

The library story illustrates a general tension between an aesthetically appealing, open and theory-based approach, enabling any book or document to be classified as exactly as is desired, and a more tied-down and pragmatic approach that limits classification in a predetermined manner. It affords no wholly satisfactory solution and requires compromise. It remains

---

45   D. Kahneman, O. Sibony and C. R. Sunstein, *Noise: A Flaw in Human Judgment* (New York: Little, Brown Spark, 2021).

a continually evolving story and how it has played out is best followed along its historical timeline, as, for example, set out in *The Encyclopaedia of Library and Information Sciences*, which I have used, here. There has been a mixture of enumerative and facet methods of classification. Shiyali Ramamrita Ranganathan's (1892–1972) method of colon classification, the subject of its own section below, stayed true to a wholly facet-based approach but proved too challenging to implement at scale in practice.

There are instructive parallels between this story and that of medical language and the terminologies and classifications descriptive of medical knowledge and clinical practice, as told in the succeeding sections. Computer-based knowledge and library management systems have evolved to tackle the limitations of enumerative and facet-based methods, enabling new tools that work better, now, in both library curator and user contexts. In the medical domain, formal logics have emerged to play a new part in taming the complexities of medical language and knowledge bases. This is a topic that joins my storyline as it moves on into the world of mathematical and formal logic. For now, we continue with the history of library classifications.

Melvil Dewey (1851–1931) was a pioneer of educational reform and librarianship. An early trailblazer in library classification systems was the 1873 Dewey Decimal Classification (DDC), originally enumerated in a thousand subdivisions over twelve pages and criticized at the time as overly detailed! Here is how the Encyclopaedia describes it:

> Dewey's innovation was to use numbers (decimal fractions) as subject (class) markers, infinitely expandable in size, over time, within existing classes and with limited ability to expand within a hierarchy of classes, integrating new subjects within a single unified scheme. Further detail could be added in ancillary tables. And some representation of relationships between subjects was provided for by allowing the subdivision of one class with numbers built (inherited) from another.[46]

As with the much earlier examples, the chosen organization reflected the assumptions and outlook of the times. However, the principle adopted– of maintaining integrity of the numbers–prevented restructuring of outdated classification schedules to incorporate new subjects. Cognate areas of knowledge, such as technological applications of basic sciences, were separated in the number schemes. And new ways of providing generic patterns of structure, such as faceted classification and the later contribution of Ranganathan, with his colon coding scheme, were not well

---

46 Wedgeworth, ed., *World Encyclopedia*, pp. 209–12.

accommodated. The DDC received powerful backing from the US Library of Congress, which established an organization to take the work forward.

In the 1880s, seeking to break away from the pragmatic (enumerative and pre-coordinated) 'pigeon-hole' filling approach of DDC, Charles Ammi Cutter (1837–1903) proposed an Expansive Classification (EC), aiming to reflect 'evolutionary order in nature'. This initiative did not survive his death, but his idea of encompassing a more philosophically enriched, ideal ordering of subjects influenced subsequent policy and developments at the Library of Congress and the work of Henry Evelyn Bliss (1870–1955) in the United Kingdom (UK).

In the 1890s, seeking an international approach, a Universal Decimal Classification (UDC) was proposed under the auspices of the International Federation for Documentation (FID), now the International Federation for Information and Documentation. Substantially but not fully DDC-compatible, this introduced colon notation to link two or more codes. It was championed by the Union of Soviet Socialist Republics (USSR), which made it mandatory in 1963, and had a wide-ranging user base in Eastern Europe, Japan, Brazil and Latin America.

With the pragmatic foundations of the Dewey system proving difficult to maintain and sustain in the changing and rapidly growing libraries of the time, and with Dewey himself unwilling to agree to substantial revision of his scheme, the US Library of Congress Classification (LCC) proceeded to introduce a Federation of twenty-one loosely coordinated classifications. The notation adopted was a mix of letters and numbers for main classes and it left space for expansion. Each classification adopted its own approach to subdivision of classes. Management of the classifications became rather haphazard, with arbitrary use of vacant spaces, deletions and reuse of blocks of allocations and movement of subjects to different schedules.

Bliss devoted his lifetime of work to devising a scheme of bibliographic classification (published from 1935–53) to represent the 'order of things and ideas'. This had twenty-six main classes (A/Z) and anterior classes (1/9). It was flexible in allowing alternative locations or treatments for many subjects. Though considered a significant advance in the underlying principles adopted, the investments of US libraries in DDC or LCC made it infeasible for them to branch their efforts to a new and unproven system. A hundred UK libraries made slow progress with its improvement.

Thus far in the library story, some common themes and stages have started to emerge.

- Pragmatism–every book or document must have a place in the library and the classification system serves the main purpose of defining and providing that place: a set of 'pigeon-holes' such that everything can find its home somewhere;

- Idealism–whereby the method of classification seeks to be configurable and evolvable, providing a coherent description of the content of any book or document, based on an underlying theory;

- Context and choice–decision about what constitutes a logically consistent, practically achievable and useful home, and how that should be coded for within an index, to cater to prevailing needs, ideas and cultures;

- Pattern–in exploring and experimenting with different systems, the possibilities, and their relative strengths and limitations, emerge over time and general patterns crystallize;

- Growing pains–strength of personality and the commitment and staying power of innovators, combined with organizational and national rivalries, assert themselves;

- Power–sponsorship is dominant.

A not dissimilar story to this has played out along my songline, in its encounter with endeavours to formalize the description of medical knowledge and link this with records of health care practice. Progress in such domains is made slowly and then in jumps, as in the Niles Eldredge and Stephen Jay Gould (1941–2002) characterization of 'punctuated equilibrium' in biological evolution.[47] As for the state of the art today, one might remark, as the Chinese leader Zhou Enlai (1898–1976) was said to have done, when asked his opinion of the success of the French Revolution: 'it is too early to tell'![48]

The Colon Classification of Shiyali Ramamrita Ranganathan

Trained as a mathematician, Ranganathan worked as a librarian in Bombay and is recognized as a founding father of modern-day librarianship, which he called library science. He is credited as the last person to single-handedly envision and enact a library classification that was used in practice. He is also credited as the person who broke decisively with the pragmatic tradition of

---

47   S. J. Gould and N. Eldredge, 'Punctuated Equilibrium Comes of Age', *Nature*, 366.6452 (1993), 223–27, https://doi.org/10.1038/366223a0

48   It was a misunderstanding, apparently, but a good story, nonetheless (see, further, 'Not Letting the Facts Ruin a Good Story', *South China Morning Post*, https://www.scmp.com/article/970657/not-letting-facts-ruin-good-story).

classification in libraries and sought an underlying theory. Encyclopaedia Britannica records his influence thus: 'Perhaps the most important advance in classification theory has been made by the Indian librarian, SR Ranganathan, whose extraordinary output of books and articles has left its mark on the entire range of studies from archival science to information science'.[49]

I discovered an extensive archived collection of his works online at the University of Arizona (search keyword Ranganathan at repository.arizona. edu), but little evidence survives elsewhere today. He introduced his facet-based colon classification of library contents in six editions between 1933 and 1960.[50] In this system, facets describe 'personality' (the most specific subject), matter, energy, space and time (PMEST). These facets are generally associated with every item in a library, and so form a reasonably universal sorting system.[51]

Ranganathan grounded his ideas in what he set out as Five Laws of Library Science: books are for use; books are for all; they should be openly accessible as if in the reader's private library; and organized to protect the reader's time from laborious search. Finally, the library should be seen as a growing organism and thus needs to be organized around strong enough and flexible enough foundations, so that its communications could be complete, concise, considerate, concrete, courteous, clear and correct. He certainly knew the alliterative power of C lists! His sentiments were sound and the organic characterization resonates strongly with similar requirement for life-long digital care records.[52]

In anticipation of the later UNESCO Broad System of Ordering (BSO), he set out to devise a theory-based method for expression of the content of books, and thus of the full range of knowledge contained there. He conceived of a circle of knowledge, which was described to me as a twenty-four-hour clock face, starting with philosophy at midnight and proceeding counterclockwise through successive domains of knowledge. The hour hand moved on through mathematics and sciences devoted to theory and experiment, from the physical world into the living world, and

49   D. J. Foskett, 'The Dewey Decimal System', *Britannica*, https://www.britannica. com/topic/library/The-Dewey-Decimal-system

50   S. R. Ranganathan, *Colon Classification*, 6th ed. (Bangalore: Sarada Ranganathan Endowment, 1989).

51   Wikipedia contributors, 'Colon Classification', *Wikipedia, The Free Encyclopedia* (7 May 2023), https://en.wikipedia.org/wiki/Colon_classification

52   S. R. Ranganathan, *The Five Laws of Library Science* (Bangalore: Sarada Ranganathan Endowment, 1989) https://repository.arizona.edu/handle/10150/105454; S. R. Ranganathan, *Philosophy of Library Classification* (Bangalore: Sarada Ranganathan Endowment, 1989), https://repository.arizona.edu/handle/10150/105278

then to education and social sciences. At about twelve noon it moved into demography, politics and law.

It then proceeded through economics and finance and on to technologies and industries, language and literature, arts and religion, and finally to the occult and mystical, where, at the reverse striking of midnight, it emerged again into the world of philosophy. Here is a slide I constructed to illustrate this ordering; a previous version was used in my lectures of thirty years ago (see Figure 2.2).

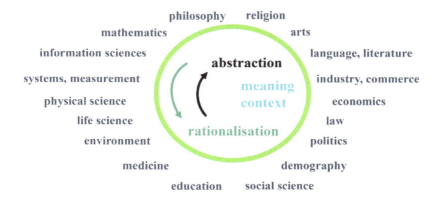

The Circle of Knowledge –after Ranganathan, ·
The Broad System of Ordering, UNESCO, 1950

Fig. 2.2 The Ranganathan Circle of Knowledge. Image created by David Ingram (2022), CC BY-NC.

Ranganathan set out to create a set of general principles for an evolving and enduring classification of books and documents. He abandoned the pragmatic approach of enumerating a set of fixed pigeonholes, each for a preconceived and precoordinated class of things and ideas, with ever more detailed subdivisions. By contrast he proposed what he termed an 'analytico-synthetic method of classification', the Colon Classification. Analytico-synthetic scheme, according to Ranganathan, is used 'to denote any scheme in which a compound subject is first analysed into its facets in the idea plane, and later synthesized in the verbal plane and in the notational plane respectively'.[53]

---

53   S. R. Ranganathan, 'Colon Classification Edition 7 (1971): A Preview', *Library Science with a Slant to Documentation*, 6 (1969), 205.

The term resonates with philosophy, descriptive of human reasoning (particularly that of Immanuel Kant (1724–1804))–involving analysis as a rational process working from *a priori* assumptions, and synthesis as an empirical process working from *a posteriori* evidences. Perhaps Ranganathan saw his ideas as bridging these two. The following quotations are from the American Library Association *Encyclopaedia of Library and Information Services* and Wikipedia description of colon classification, to give the flavour of his approach–its detail is best followed up in the references given.

> Colon Classification lists relatively few and simple objects and ideas as main classes. These are combined, at will, with what were called facets as opposed to precoordinated subdivisions–facets are class markers or tags. These are combined, using a formal punctuation notation, to express exact document subject, from a formal vocabulary and notation capable of unlimited variety of expression and extension. His other main innovation was an alphabetical chain indexing mechanism.
>
> The classification enables 'all possible subjects' to be constructed from a set of standard units covering what Ranganathan calls main classes (mathematics, physics, [...] zoology, [...] medicine, [...] arts, law, economics), common isolate, time isolate, space isolate, language isolate, phase and intra-facet relationship. The colon syntax acts to join these parts together and build a so called analytico-synthetic classification.

This avoided the rigidity of previous systems and gave new flexibility to incorporate new subjects and their various relations over time. Describing his ideas, Ranganathan likened the Colon Classification to Meccano–a favourite construction toy of my childhood and a predecessor of Lego. In this analogy, the classification of a particular book or document is depicted as a Meccano model, nut and bolted together by the colon syntax, from Meccano plates, girders, axles, cogs, wheels and so on, representing the component facets that are the building blocks of the system.

I discovered this Meccano model analogy quite recently, when researching his work, and was immediately struck by its parallel with the Lego model analogy we have used in describing the openEHR methodology for constructing clinical data models. openEHR (discussed in Chapter Eight and a Half) used the analogy to illustrate its compositional method of construction of these models, which provide generic patterns of data entered into electronic care records. The building blocks (Lego blocks) are selected from a set of predefined types and groupings of data, comprising the openEHR Reference Model. These are joined together to create clinical data models (Lego models) known as openEHR archetypes. The record itself is thus akin to a Lego village, such as the Bekonscot Model Village not far from my home, in Beaconsfield, and the one at the home of Lego–Billund, in Denmark.

The UNESCO Broad System of Ordering (BSO) for Documents and Books

In 1951, in pursuit of wider dissemination and adoption of his theory, Ranganathan took on the role of coordinator of the International Federation for Information and Documentation. From this base, his work had a strong influence on future developments in the field. However, his colon classification, and derivatives from it, as adopted in the BSO, ultimately lost momentum some fifty years later, notwithstanding the efforts to support them by UNESCO.[54] I doubt that many now know of its existence, and so I have taken space here to record some of its history and introduce and honour one of its principal adherents and advocates, Eric Coates (1916–2017).[55]

There were important general lessons from the decades-long efforts and final burned-out failure of the BSO. They have parallels in the difficulties and impediments encountered in bringing innovation in information technology to fruition at a comprehensive scale, in support of health care services today. It is a common and costly characteristic of the Information Age that rather than recognizing and learning from past failure, failure is often rationalized, swept under the carpet and forgotten about, as credulous attention switches to new predictions and aspirations.

I knew nothing of Ranganathan until his name came up in a chance discussion with Eric Coates in 1990, where I learned that he had been a key figure in establishing British technical standards in the post-war years and the Director of the British Technology Index publication. I had known Eric as an attender at Quaker meetings for many years before that chance event–a quiet, wiry, civil and slightly austere man, who came each week, never spoke in the meetings and left rather quickly at the end. Eric knew my father well and we talked about him and another young person who my dad knew from a Quaker family of the wartime era, Fred Sanger (1918–2013), who went on to become a double Nobel Laureate, a founding father of molecular biology.[56]

---

54   For detail of the BSO, see the archive maintained at University College London, *BSO* (2000), https://www.ucl.ac.uk/fatks/bso/

55   For an appreciation of Eric Coates's contributions, see K. Kawamura, 'In Memoriam: Eric Coates, 1916–2017', *Knowledge Organization*, 45.2 (2018), 97–102, https://doi.org/10.5771/0943-7444-2018-2-97

56   Fred Sanger and my father were members of a Quaker community at Spiceland, on the Blackdown Hills in Devon, which sought to establish effective community action in wartime. I remember my dad pointing to its towering chimneys on a distant hilltop, when, years later in my childhood, we drove to Devon from the

At our meetings, I told Eric about a major switch in my career, around 1990, when I set off in a new direction, having just been appointed to the first UK Chair in Medical Informatics, at London University. Among my new directions was the leadership of the European Union AIM research and development initiative to formalize the architecture of electronic health records. This was the GEHR (Good European Health Record) Project, which evolved over the coming decade, through a succession of further projects and collaborations, into openEHR, as described in Chapter Eight and a Half.

Connecting with this topic, Eric told me about Ranganathan and provided me with some early documents–sadly lost in a flood at our home in later years. Eric himself featured prominently in the story of the BSO right through until his retirement, when its copyright was assigned to UCL. The story is recorded by Keiichi Kawamura,[57] who covers two hundred and sixty-two summaries of reports, articles and meetings between 1973 and 2011.[58] I have selected excerpts that illustrate the human dimension of the struggle that Eric led, which I connect with struggles for methods of standardization in the medicine and health care domain.

In Reference 261, the following appears:

> Eric Coates was working as a cataloguer and classifier at the then recently established British National Bibliography. Earnest, sometimes a little severe, transparently sincere, and humane, Eric later became the first editor of the British Technology Index and wrote a book, *Subject Catalogues: Headings and Structure*, much influenced by facet ideas. He has also played a major part in constructing and testing the Broad System of Ordering, a high-level classification system.

---

children's home he and my mother ran in Hampshire, and we stopped for a break and to admire the rhododendrons on the hills. The history of this self-reliant community—men and women, some four hundred strong—is recorded by Stanley Smith, with the amusingly telling subtitle *Cups without Saucers*, nodding towards a rather spartan life (*Spiceland Quaker Training Centre, 1940–46: Cups without Saucers* (York: W. Sessions, 1990)). I have it on the shelf above my desk and see, on p. 35, that Sanger worked at the time as a ward orderly in the local Winford Hospital— quite a modest setting and role, and perhaps a signal of why and how he achieved so much thereafter.

57 K. Kawamura, *BSO–Broad System of Ordering: An International Bibliography* (Koshigaya: K. Kawamura, 2011), https://repository.arizona.edu/ handle/10150/129413

58 I was interested to see that a key meeting, among many where BSO struggled to be heard, had been held at Helsingør in Denmark, in 1964. This location (in dramatic full view of Hamlet's castle!) hosted a similar meeting many years later, bringing together leaders of national health IT programmes and the HL7, IHTSDO and openEHR organizations, at which I represented the openEHR Foundation.

In Reference 262, his contribution and staying power, pitted against institutional inertia, obstruction and vested interest, is recognized:

> [...] the works of Eric Coates who put into practice and advanced Ranganathan's thought mainly through the British National Bibliography (BNB), the British Technology Index (BTI) and the Broad System of Ordering (BSO) [...] these three systems demonstrated: (1) how his works are connected with each other, (2) why his achievements should be estimated by a global standard, and (3) which of his contributions will throw light on unsolved problems in knowledge organization. The conclusion is that the underlying conceptual coherence in the work of Coates should be highly regarded as the persistent survival of interest and concern about classification, despite its marginalization.

Eric described himself as 'in favour of a revolution, not of classifications but of the management of classifications' (Reference 1). He was, in essence, seeking a grounded and sustainable method. In his work for the BNB and BTI, he perceived (Reference 62) 'key issues for furthering their work were in distinguishing methods and techniques from sciences and products of human activities, including technologies and religions'. Promoted through the UNESCO UNISIST Programme (United Nations International Scientific Information System), the BSO was conceived as a 'switching system' to enable interconnection and cooperation between information systems, standardizing communication of content among the key classifications of books and documents. The underpinning theory, providing coherence and a *lingua franca* for this communication, was the conceptual framework of Ranganathan's circle of knowledge and the colon classification. Initial efforts were geared towards defining and grouping thousands of subject fields. By 1984, four editions had been published (Reference 78). By 1990, the BSO had expanded to three times the size of the first published form in 1978 (Reference 86).

A review in 1980 (Reference 133) highlighted the problems it faced:

> The progress in library classification has been slow in its long history. But there was a drastic change in the 1960s due to the rapid development of science and technology, an increase in number of publications, and the advanced information processing technology. Looking back on the theoretical studies and practical activities in library classification for the last 10 or 20 years, the following are recognized: (1) the trend towards faceted classification, (2) unified view of classification and indexing, (3) mechanization and automation, and (4) standardization.

This review illustrated these trends with examples of national and international perspectives on the situation. The BSO's aim to provide a generalized 'switching language' for the UNISIST standardization programme implied generalization and was recognized to be at a price in terms of its lack of particular specificity. This was subsequently regarded as a serious defect and the suggestion was made to combine use of BSO with UDC, to attempt to overcome it. The trade-off between general and particular considerations and means to broker coherently between the two has become a widely enduring feature of design and standardization endeavours for health care information systems.[59]

Reference 134 provides a historic flavour of the issues and underlying tensions in play, because of the diversity of disciplines:

> The paper traces the main lines of development of scientific and technical terminology (STT) and the sub-languages of individual scientific and technical subjects. It is emphasized that for a long time virtually every branch of science and technology developed in isolation and has evolved its own closed terms system. In the 20th century, when sciences are interpenetrating on a wider scale and new and promising research trends emerge at discipline interfaces, the interactions of isolated terms systems have wrought havoc in the STT sphere. This tells on the evolution of indexing languages, both classificatory and descriptor ones. The situation is aggravated by the fact that most indexing languages have been developed to serve the needs of one organization or a group of organizations and seldom crossed national boundaries.
>
> Main merits and demerits of the UDC are discussed and an assertion is made that the underlying principles and main scheme of this classification are not consonant with the present-day condition of scientific knowledge. It is pointed out that the Broad System of Ordering (BSO) has a big role to play in perfecting STI exchange processes and in information organization in major information centers, above all international ones. However, BSO is not without fault either, its chief drawbacks being a strong influence of Anglo-American STT, an overly pragmatic nature, the difficulty of classifying multisubject documents, and a potentially strong dependence on political and ideological factors. A crisis of traditional hierarchical classification is postulated. The rapid proliferation of thesauri adversely affects STI exchange and the use of large information networks. It also happens that practically all thesauri,

---

59   There are interesting parallels in this story with the issues faced and highlighted by Alan Rector and colleagues ('On Beyond Gruber'), seeking viable combinations of 'open world' methods from description logic, 'closed world' frame-based methods, and *ad hoc* annotations, to achieve alignment and harmonization of the important SNOMED and ICD medical terminologies and classifications. These issues of medical language and terminology are discussed in further sections below.

including international ones, are semantically and logically incompatible even where they refer to one knowledge area. It is suggested that the basic concepts of hierarchical classifications and upper-level descriptors be integrated, and thesaurus systems be established on a common conceptual and logical basis. Latin American nations provide a good testing ground for such a global-scale experiment.

There is a lot to digest and reflect on in that long summary. With Eric already retired, and the failure to replace his breadth of knowledge and engagement as the driving and anchoring force at the heart of its leadership, the BSO lost steam in the standards arena. And FID bowed to the inevitable, passing its copyright to the BSO panel members in 1990 and backing UDC. In 1993, the panel members established a not-for-profit company for distribution of the BSO. In 2000 the copyright was vested in the School of Library and Information Sciences (SLAIS) at UCL.

It is of note that by 2004, the year after the openEHR Foundation was launched, Reference 169 in Kawamura's bibliography records:

The need for structured machine-readable data and not just 'simple text' and thereby to have a common standardized data model was highlighted. This would enable automatic classification and management and control of concept hierarchies and vocabulary facets and sub-facets. Proprietary data formats in applications are seen as costly and limited. The requirement for independence and integrity of data elements is emphasized.

This motivation has much in common with that addressed in the mission of openEHR, as covered in Chapter Eight and a Half.

The language of these extensive quotations reflects that they derive from an era where manual, facet-based method, which influenced medical terminologies and classifications of the times, was state of the art. Computer science pioneers of the description logics of more recent decades developed theory and method for tackling these goals on a higher level of abstraction. But in seeking to raise endeavours to this level, historic investment in what had become intractable legacy inhibited and contended progress. In turn, the semantic complexities of medical knowledge uncovered in these endeavours challenged the available and tractable methods of description logic. Change of approach required radical new thinking and reform, which further challenged the communities involved with each standard, internationally. This set of related problems was the focus of pioneering research in small, not widely visible, or recognized projects, such as Alan Rector's GALEN project, that grew alongside the GEHR project and its successors in the EU AIM Programme, as discussed later in this chapter, in the section on medical language and computation.

Confusions of the times and struggles for greater clarity are evident throughout the long history I have traced here. There is a sense of an elusive perfection of theory that bedevils practical efforts. Although always imperfect, theoretical models can nonetheless prove valuable, and we seek always to improve those we have and make them more useful–this is a theme developed in Chapter Four. We need a clear sense of why we are building new systems, what our goals are in this, when, where and with whom we are going to tackle them, and, most importantly and most overlooked, the method that embodies how we will achieve these goals. Fulfilling a useful purpose must reign over achievement of perfect execution.

With the benefit of hindsight, one can see in histories like that of the BSO, all these dimensions of challenge playing out in a theatre of life. As William Shakespeare (1564–1616) wrote in *Hamlet*, the play holds a mirror up to nature, and we must learn from the images it provides for us.[50]

As highlighted at the beginning of this chapter, we express, communicate and reason with knowledge through language and logic, and now, in the Information Age, machines do, too, through machine languages and logics. As with many other generic themes encountered along the storyline of the book, language and logic are, in themselves, extremely deep and wide-ranging subjects. My purpose, here, is to emphasize how they have connected with where we have reached in the evolution of computer-based health care records and related knowledge-based information systems.

Languages and their Expression and Communication of Knowledge

For last year's words belong to last year's language
And next year's words await another voice.[61]

In the evolving quest to make and express their sense of the reality of the world, the Greeks became absorbed with metaphysics–τὰ μετὰ τὰ φυσικά [*ta meta ta physika*]. *The Metaphysics of Aristotle* (384 BCE–322 BCE)

---

60   'Suit the action to the word, the word to the action, with this special observance, that you o'erstep not the modesty of nature: for anything so o'erdone is from the purpose of playing, whose end, both at the first and now, was and is, to hold as 'twere the mirror up to nature: to show virtue her feature, scorn her own image, and the very age and body of the time his form and pressure'. *Hamlet*, Act 3, Scene 2.

61   T. S. Eliot, 'Little Gidding', *Four Quartets*, ll. 118–19.

concerned matters 'after the things of nature'. This was a domain envisaged to lie beyond objective study of material reality–idea, doctrine, the nature of reality. Not a domain that the embryonic biological mind had much time or use for. But one of enduring interest and perplexity to the enquiring, embryonic, civilizing mind, concerned with making sense of and interacting with the material and human worlds.

More Greek words came into play–ὄντως, δόξα, δοκεῖν, ἦθος, λόγος, πάθος, ἐπιστήμη, ἐπίσταμαι, τέχνη [ontos, doxa, dokein, ethos, logos, pathos, episteme, epístamai, techne]. Here is a rough run down, based on my ten-kilogram Compact Edition of the Oxford English Dictionary (published complete with essential magnifying glass!)–better-informed readers than me may justly roll or avert their eyes.

ontos–being, nature of reality

doxa–opinion or glory

dokein–to seem or to seem good–led to **dogma** and **paradox.** More distantly to **decent** (in connection with seeming 'good')

ethos–custom or habit–connecting with ἠθικός [ethikos]–showing moral character–more generally, characterizing the spirit of a culture, era or community as expressed through its beliefs and aspirations

logos–word, reason, discourse, study–from λέγειν [legein]–to speak

pathos–suffering, experience

episteme–science or knowledge

epístamai–to know, to understand, to be acquainted with–about knowledge of principles

techne–craft, art–making or doing–concrete, variable and context-dependent–also a kind of knowledge

Adding the suffix λόγια [*logia*] (plural of logos), describes an associated oral or written expression. Combining with stems leads to 'ologies'.

Οντολογία [*ontologia*]–ontology is about how we answer the question, What is reality? It affects how we approach our subject. It quickly gets complicated and convoluted when we dig deeper into detail. But a key feature of an approach is that it be accepted, appear to be a good one, and be right. In matters beyond the senses this is argued and judged in the realm of belief. It becomes a matter of ownership, assertion, power and persuasion–of rhetoric, logic and reason. **Ontos, ethos** and **logos** became central to argument. Knowledge became prescribed and proscribed.

> **Doxology** became connected with praise and glorification, as expressed orally, first appearing in English around 1645. It became liturgy.

> Λειτουργία, **liturgy**–divine or public service; function, operation, service, working.

> Ορθοδοξία, **orthodoxy** (ορθό [*ortho*], 'right') became authorized or generally accepted theory, doctrine or practice. It extended to 'right' thinking elsewhere–e.g., monetarist orthodoxy.

> Ετεροδοξία, **heterodoxy** is another doxology (ηετερο [*ietero*], 'another'). Someone quipped that orthodoxy is my doxy–yours is heterodoxy (or even heresy)!

> *Επιστημολογία*, **epistemology**–The theory of knowledge; especially pertains to its methods, validity and scope, and the distinction between justified belief and opinion.

Plato (*c.* 428 BCE–348 BCE) contrasted **episteme** with **doxa**–common belief or opinion. The term **episteme** was also distinguished from **techne**–a craft or applied practice.

For Aristotle, **pathos** was a means of awakening people's emotions in order to sway their opinion towards that of the speaker. **Rhetoric** embodied **pathos**, **logos** and **ethos**. Disease was suffering and suffering became disease. *Pathology* became the study of disease.

The ether (or aether) of classical times was the fifth element (quintessence), after earth, air, fire and water. It was a medium filling the universe above the terrestrial sphere. Science later conceived of light propagating in the universe through an ether. We now talk of other universal media–communication systems and the information they transmit. These bear some (pharmacological) resemblance to chemical ether! As Marshall McLuhan (1911–80) wrote in a different context, the medium is the message.

When we reason, express and communicate, we do so through language, of which there are many kinds. Good use of spoken and written language enables and stabilizes communication, as a medium for the expression of thought. It evolves. It reflects and describes domains of knowledge and understanding, and their different jargons. It is conditioned by purpose and context–of culture and practice, geography and time. Interestingly, I've read that some believe that language evolved first as a means of misleading rather than informing, to confuse and discourage potential jungle predators in threatening situations. Information pandemic, a term used to describe confirmatory bias in communications about the Covid pandemic, has born some resemblance to cacophony in a jungle!

Poor use of human language harms communication and risks misunderstanding, distortion and confusion of meaning. Overly elaborate language becomes a linguistic Tower of Babel, overly simplistic expression a Dalek drone, to the human ear. Finding the right words is a struggle for personal understanding as well as for its expression–words may fail us due to overthinking them, as much as not thinking about them enough. It is easy to overthink or be careless with words. Words connect on different levels of meaning and intention: simple and complex, vague and precise, gentle and harsh. Ideas thought through and framed in language, no matter their significance, connect on different levels of expression, too.

Psychologists tell us that the greater part of human communication is non-verbal. Human language has infinitely variable and subjective contexts that impacts its meaning and its integration with wider non-verbal communication. Words toe a line between a defining framework of the language in which they are expressed–we speak of syntax–and communication of their meaning–we speak of semantics. Poetry taps into meanings, feelings and emotions beyond the words and forms expressed. We say that music and art speak to us, and silence speaks volumes.

Human language was born into the cradle of civilization. Philosophy, logic and mathematics evolved from and around natural language. The philosophy and 'term logic' of Aristotle and the philosophy and 'Stoic logic' of Chrysippus (*c.* 279 BCE–206 BCE) were launched, clothed in natural language. They disappeared and resurfaced over the centuries, formalized in new languages of mathematics, science and computation. Now, language of logic permeates and underpins foundations of mathematics and language of mathematics permeates foundations of logic. The *linguae francae* of the world now extend through the languages of mathematics, logic and computation.

The Language of Mathematics, by Frank Land (1911–1990), is the title of my first book prize at school, sitting above me at the far end of the shelf. Over recent centuries, the languages of mathematics, and then computation, have become intertwined with scientific methods. They are now intrinsic to the modelling and analysis of complex systems, and no systems we work with in this way are more complex than living systems. In the Information Age, theory of computation progressed alongside experimentation with novel forms of computer language whereby computing machines could be made to enact human instructions, manipulating first numbers and then data, symbols and reasoning, more widely. Experimental programming languages were in their infancy at the start of my songline. Languages of computation now underpin the rigour, expressiveness, reliability and trust in computer systems and communication.

Fluency in many and diverse languages of communication is increasingly significant for understanding what medicine is and what it does–the science on which it is based and how health care services acquire and use knowledge to investigate, reason, act and communicate. This spectrum of languages is akin to a spectrum of electromagnetic radiation–from the long, medium and short waves of radio transmissions in my childhood, now transmitted and detected at ultrashort wavelength and measured, manipulated and transmitted in digital form, with tools and methods that vary across the spectrum.

When we seek to enhance our lives by intermixing language and communication of machines with human language and communication, we must be careful as this may risk impeding and harming both. As the use of language fails to satisfy and cohere, it is patched by narrow and diverse approximations and appropriations of words and meanings. As Russell wrote, logical formalization of reasoning must be carefully pinned down within its applicable context, as logic grapples with the nature of appearance, reality and truth.

In health care, that is a very hard bar to rise above, and not always or necessarily a useful one. Simpler approximations may suffice and be more effectively enacted and communicated than more complicated and precise ones. As technology advances towards artificial intelligence and the *Novacene* era that James Lovelock describes in his 2019 book, the language of the machine encroaches, superimposes on, and supplants the predominant languages of former eras.[62] Some of that potentially for the good, and some for the not so good. Zobaczymy [we will see]![63]

Facing these numbingly wide-ranging issues, I was undecided about where and how to write about language in the context of health care information systems. Specialists at all points of the circle of knowledge have something to say, splitting the spectrum of languages into all the colours of the rainbow. Spoken, written and machine languages differ and differ differently, in different languages. Language integrates and language differentiates. Language unifies and language divides.

So where to begin? I will cop out and start somewhere else, with some personal, linguistically untutored reflections about my experience of learning two new languages, in later years–the very tricky Polish language, having married into that wonderful country and culture, and the language

---

62 J. Lovelock, *Novacene: The Coming Age of Hyperintelligence* (Cambridge, MA: MIT Press, 2019).

63 On this Polish expression, see Preface.

of dance, which has preoccupied our home life for two decades, now. Encyclopaedia, in its classical context, was a circle of learning before it became a circle of knowledge. Language, too, starts with learning.

Learning a Language

I learned Polish when marrying again, and the motivation was huge. My newly extended family had few English speakers. Hugs and kisses and the punctuating *dzień dobry*, *dziękuję* and *dowidzenia* pleasantries can only get one so far, as with the broken German on both sides, which is where we started! A brilliant young teacher, Ela Wolk, at the London School of Slavonic and Eastern European Studies, now part of UCL, taught a small group of dedicated learners for three years. We were all seeking out Polish connections and/or heritage in our lives.

On opening one's eyes and ears in a new country, there is a richness of culture to be shared, that would be substantially inaccessible without the language of that country. Ela drilled into us grammar and marked our homework; she took us with our partners to experience Polish theatre and music. One thing we learned quickly about Polish is that you must listen hard to catch the words. Ela used to tell us to pause from analyzing the puzzling, consonant-riddled written forms and consider instead, how does it sound? She would ask 'what do you think it means?', encouraging us to identify what similarities it had with other words we already knew. But, hm...! Here, on the one hand, we were facing the extraordinary complexity of written Polish language, with its somewhat pedantically Latinate formal grammar, while, on the other hand, everywhere in sight the rules were being broken to make pronunciation easier. In principle, the phonetic structure and the spelling go hand in glove in Polish, more than any language I have studied. It requires a special configuration of jaw and tongue to get it right. English does, however, get its revenge–Polish people have difficulty with 'th', just as I do with ę and ą–try them with fifth or thistle!

Languages have spelling and grammar–the structure of sentences parsed into subject and predicate, noun phrase and verb phrase, main and subsidiary clause, noun and adjective, verb and adverb, associated inflexion, mood, gerund and gerundive, pronoun, preposition and the rest–or maybe all new descriptors, now. I had learned Latin and Greek at school. Latin was quite pleasant to my mathematically inclined mind as it kept pretty much to the rules. Greek was a blur as I had a year to study the language and did not quite get there. My scholarly, eccentric head teacher–who persuaded my parents I should study both Latin and Greek, when I would rather have skipped Greek–had lifted me from my surreptitiously-preferred geography class to study Greek with him in a tiny group of four. I am now very glad that he did as it gave me a rusty key to many doors, discovered and walked through years later.

Expression in spoken language is a mix of formal, blurred and broken rules of grammar, and an enveloping contextual and cultural mishmash of associations and meanings. My doctor wife trained as a medical linguist in the UK. She acts as interpreter across health, education, social care and law. The communication she brokers is from different languages, cultures and experiences, of both client and service provider. Sometimes in English, sometimes in Polish, sometimes with native English-speaking professionals, sometimes with professionals from other cultures and tongues, speaking English as a second language. This is the world; and this is health care language and communication.

Esperanto is one approach to overcoming the dividing lines of language– everyone sharing a common auxiliary language–might that be a solution? Incidentally, Esperanto is a nice vignette of Poland and medicine–it was created by the Polish ophthalmologist Ludwik Zamenhof (1859–1917) in 1887. The word translates into English as 'one who hopes'. Clearly its time has not yet come, though hope springs eternal and it is a living movement, still pleasing and enriching to those who keep it alive. Context of language always matters. Languages merge and standardize and then pidgin languages take flight. Now the dangled offering is Google Translate. What cultural implications and perturbations may lie lurking when leaving to the machine, the brokering of human communication?

It is important to remember that human communication is substantially non-verbal. I think of that in the context of dance. We talk about dancing around the point when not quite communicating with one another and being (badly) led a dance. One of the things my wife and I discovered was that we both loved dancing. She expressed it in her nature and drew it out of mine. We did not share a mother tongue and communication through dance proved foundationally important for us in lots of ways and has shaped our lives together amazingly.

One learns that communication on a dance floor is both subtle and dramatic, rife with potential for miscommunication and mistake. Dance is a language of connection and flow. It comprises human form, emotion, fitness and balance, all of which must be nurtured and practised. Dance needs good teachers who love dancing and know how to dance. We have Tom and Ali, who teach teachers of Tango, and Sarah, who performed in the Royal Ballet and toured with the prima ballerina, Darcy Bussell. Dance has a musical context of melody, structure, rhythm and interpretation, and that must be listened to and communicated, sometimes best with eyes shut– more so for the led partner, of course! My wife will often say 'I do not feel that in the music', as I chide her that she is taking the lead when I feel she should not be! Dance may appear unbalanced along gender lines in leading and following, but that is not true for the dancers themselves: gender no longer determines dance partnership, and dance is better for it. Some of the best and most artistically-led partners are the emotionally and physically strongest. And the best leaders know the best dance can only be led, in all moods and stages of the music, when the partner is listened to, given space and with leadership negotiated and flowing, to and fro. If you like jazz, you will probably resonate with tango.

There are several lessons about language that I draw from these two very different learning experiences. Learning language is about listening, experiencing, practising, performing and enjoying. Different languages are not isolated domains, they cross-fertilize in both method and context. The bedrock of fluency in language lies in *how* we learn it, and, specifically, in whether we learn it within its rich cultural contexts. Learning and knowledge go hand in hand. Literacy, in the sense of the effective use of language, is the foundation of knowledge and wisdom. Literature is an account and record of knowledge, the organized expression of thoughts, feelings and ideas–a medium that further connects and flows. In the era of ubiquitous information, we, too easily, talk and write as if we know before we have experienced and learned. We learn from experience and that requires expression and testing of yet unformed ideas.

Some questions then arise. We use words (literately, literacy) and information (informedly, 'informacy'?) well and we use them carelessly and blindly (ignorantly, ignorance). In moving beyond words to information more generally, what are fluency and literacy in the combined use of the many different kinds of language that underpin the Information Age? This ability was once the preserve of the polymath, an expert in many disciplines. But those days have receded beyond the horizons of human capability and capacity. What characterizes a polymath of the Information Age and what distinguishes them from a Jack of all trades? Is the computer fluent and literate? If so, how is it learning languages and what does it know? Will we come to think of it as wise? And how does the information that it communicates connect and flow, in human terms, between machine and human worlds? In 2023, the likes of ChatGPT are dramatically raising the stakes in relation to how we approach these matters.

Language and Machine

In the Information Age, we speak of language that specifies instructions to a computer to execute programs. When the computer reads program instructions from its memory store and follows them to enact the computational steps they specify, there are three different but closely interconnected considerations in play. Taken together, these determine how the enactment plays out, each reflecting and depending on a different language. The first concerns the machine itself and the kinds of operations that it is capable of enacting, commonly referred to as its machine code or machine language–precise and readable within the computer CPU, although opaque and unreadable binary code to most human eyes. The second concerns the programming language chosen to specify the computational process and task to be performed, in a manner intelligible to and reflecting the purposes of the programmer. Precise and readable, here, by the compiler or interpreter program that runs on the machine, first to translate from the programming language into the machine's language, enabling the machine to perform the instructions generated there. The third concerns language descriptive of the data that the program enactment causes to be captured or generated, processed, stored and communicated.

Precision of language matters in all these contexts but is not in itself a guarantee that the machine can or will function as the programmer intends. Machine, program and data descriptive languages each embody and exhibit precise expressive capabilities and rules for how they are used. They also embody precise limitations. The enacted program utilizes these capabilities and must combine them correctly and circumvent their limitations. It needs to be done efficiently. The data provided to the program must exist in a form consistent with the requirements and capabilities of both program and machine.

And for all this to be meaningful, program and data must be jointly expressive and representative of the task the program addresses. This involves considering the relevant context in which the data is generated and processed, as well as ensuring that the results computed are to be properly understood and interpreted. The machine and program must likewise perform together efficiently and acceptably, in terms of the time and resource they require.

Where the program goal served is purely concerned with manipulating data within a particular machine environment, as a closed system (reading a block of data from a disc store, adding up a column of numbers) no wider practical issues of meaning arise. Where the program goal is integral with concerns outside that environment–making a weather forecast, predicting numbers of cases in a global pandemic or results in an election (like today, as I first write this section, with election and viral pandemic both raging on 6 November 2020 in the United States of America)–the question 'What does it mean?' is embedded within a wider context and the answer potentially a matter of human controversy!

The programming of the machine is, in a sense, an art of the possible, seeking to pitch at a sweet spot between the capabilities of the machine and the framing of the nature and requirements of the task being addressed. Sweetness consists in operating within those capabilities and limitations, and with outcomes perceived as useful and meaningful for the task at hand. It can, though, become a sour spot, where delegation to the needs of the machine is a derogation of the human needs that the task addresses. As new boundaries of the possible are approached and explored, the potential for doing harm needs to be understood. This can then be better balanced against the curiosity and excitement about the potential of the new, and the value anticipated from its realization. This is the nature of innovation. The bridge between science and society created by the innovation of information systems and technology is a focus of Chapter Five on information engineering.

What can different computers, or any computer, compute? What can systems of logic or any logic express, prove and decide? What can different languages of computation express and represent? What can be measured and described? These kinds of questions, and the limits they probe, arise within the languages of mathematics, logic, computer science, natural science and engineering. They ramify all around the circle of knowledge, as the Information Age spreads more pervasively into and across human affairs.

Precision of Language

Writing can either be readable or precise, but not at the same time.[64]

There speaks the logician, in his wide-ranging work spanning from precise language of mathematics to logical precision in communication of thought and meaning, connecting with discussion of the nature of truth. On my bookshelf is Russell's, *An Inquiry into Meaning and Truth*.[65] We talk of a computer reading and writing when it transfers information to and from data storage devices. We say that programmers write programs and computers read and execute them. In this transfer of information, precision and readability go hand in hand.

In Russell's world of philosophical logic, consistent, clearly-framed and articulated use of language are the bedrock of thought and reasoning. Expressive range and use of language are also the bedrock of human culture, arts and communication. And in the Information Age, the language

---

64   Quote attributed to Bertrand Russell, unknown source.
65   B. Russell, *An Inquiry into Meaning and Truth* (New York: Routledge, 2013).

of computation is fundamental to the integrity of data and algorithm, and to the efficiency, effectiveness and robustness of computer systems. All these dimensions matter in the context of health care information systems. How they fit and work together is complicated!

Russell was very much aware of and actively engaged with the social context of the times in which he lived. In his philosophical works, he maintained that logical abstraction and definition must be precisely stated within relevant context. Herein lies a considerable challenge for the domain of health care in the Information Age. How, where and to what extent is logical precision a valid and achievable goal in reasoning with knowledge in this domain? How, where and to what extent does the limitation of logical precision of language matter? Every model of appearances, as with language and logic, is a simplification of the reality it purports to represent. The world of model-based representation is the subject of Chapter Four.

Physics is thinking and discovering its way through a multidimensional maze of experiment, theory and mathematical language, in its quest to describe and understand physical reality in greater detail. Scientifically, this is an exciting pursuit; it focuses research on unsolved but potentially experimentally tractable areas of current unknowing. This is not solely about instruments of ever more precise and specific measurement. Whitehead quotes Jules Henri Poincaré (1854–1912) in pointing out that instruments of precision, used unseasonably, may hinder the advance of science–giving the example that knowledge of the tiny relativistic imperfections of Johannes Kepler's (1571–1630) law of planetary motion might have delayed the imagination by Isaac Newton (1643–1727) of the law of gravitation.[66] Truth must, he says, be seasonable (Microsoft Word does not recognize 'seasonable' and suggests I probably mean 'reasonable'!). That is perhaps another way of saying that meaning and truth must be considered in relevant context.

Formalism of Language

My maternal grandfather, who I never met but whose picture is on the wall to the left of my desk as I write, was an English teacher at Westminster School in London. He was a stickler for grammar and wrote numerous textbooks used for teaching the 'rules'. His writing style in these books and in his articles for the school magazine that he edited reads now as primly pedantic flourish–not very readable although immaculately well-formed. And he, as a teacher then, was always formally dressed, of course! In my student days, too, there was a lot more formal stuff–the balance is better, now. The

---

66   Whitehead, *Adventures of Ideas*, p. 232.

formalism of a language is meant, here, to cover its definitions and rules of use. Rules of grammar are a formal model of the structure of language. Communication is improved to a point by attention to formal grammar, but when pushed to extremes, this becomes restrictive of expression–words and their usage constantly evolve over time.

English lessons devoted to grammar were an oft-practised routine in my secondary school days–it was a Grammar School! We were given complicated sentences and set to compete, to see who could succeed first in breaking the structure into its different parts of speech and their groupings, linking and labelling them, and arriving at a final standard, hierarchical diagrammatic form. The method for constructing and deconstructing (parsing) natural language sentences might now, I understand, be termed a 'phrase structured grammar following the constituency relation'. It is quite complicated to remember and apply such formalism unless one deals with it on a regular basis! Here, a constituent is 'a word or a group of words that function as a single unit within a hierarchical structure'. The constituency relation comes from the subject-predicate division of sentences, with their clause structure understood in terms of binary division between subject (noun phrase) and predicate (verb phrase). The parts of speech (terms) constituting a complete sentence, and the stepwise reduction of the sentence structure, through binary division of its different kinds of clauses and phrases, maps to a tree structure. The sentence terms and their groupings at successive stages of this reduction appear as nodes in the tree. Such formalism connects with the term logic of Aristotle, as discussed further in the sections below.

Natural language, logic, mathematics and computer science evolved over many centuries, along connected pathways of formal method–mysticism, religion and philosophy initially intertwined. Logic from the time of Aristotle and Chrysippus was expressed in sentences of natural language, and more abstractly characterized and expressed as premise, proposition, predicate and syllogism–a 'sentential logic'. Concept of number, and calculation with numbers, intertwined with philosophy and logic of reasoning and argument, and the glimmerings of science. Mathematics and logic of inference intertwined with philosophy and method of science. Mathematics of infinitesimals and infinities gave birth to calculus. Logic and mathematics intertwined in 'logical calculus', reimagining mathematics in the language of logic.

By the time of Gottlob Frege (1848–1925), mathematics and logic had reached a competing understanding of the logic of sentences. He broke away from Aristotelian logic, built around binary divisions of the structure of the sentence, aiming to replace it with a mathematically rigorous formalism. And two runways of lift-off ensued. The first was directed towards the reinvention of the foundations of logical inference, providing new mathematical reasoning about propositions and predicates. This was no longer formalized in the grammar of sentences comprising words as atomic elements, but in manipulation of mathematically precise constructs that could be seen as either true or false, using logical operations applied to symbols and formulas as the new constituents of a mathematical language of logic. Logic itself became a calculus. The second and parallel runway inherited these ideas and was directed towards unifying mathematics within a framework of logical deduction from a small set of basic axioms.

The language of mathematics and logic of the nineteenth and early twentieth centuries led to and cross-fertilized with language of computation and algorithm, today–a revolution led by mathematicians. Computer technology was a physics and engineering revolution and the Information Age an Industrial Revolution. Medicine of the twentieth century was a scientific, professional and computational revolution, and health care, today, is embroiled in a twenty-first-century cultural and social revolution. I will pick up on the two runways and the post-Frege story of the past one hundred and fifty years in the next section on the language of mathematics and logic, and its embedding within the history of reasoning with knowledge, in the succeeding section. First, I will look briefly at where it led in the formal study of grammar.

The languages used to write computer programs require rules of grammar whereby program sentences (statements) can be rigorously and reliably generated and parsed. Noam Chomsky developed an overarching theoretical foundation for a hierarchy of grammars which underpinned this quest, from the 1950s.[67] In linguistics, Chomsky is known for his theory of universal grammar as an inherited 'hard-wired' human capacity to learn grammar. Wired or not, most people find natural language grammar gets harder as the complexity of meanings expressed increases. Unsurprisingly, the same holds true for the computer and its program languages!

Natural language and programming language share a common feature. Richness of expression correlates with complexity of its analysis. With increased richness and diversity of natural language, comes greater difficulty in mapping or parsing to reveal underlying grammar. And likewise with formal grammar of machine programming languages, grammar with greater power of expression brings harder problems in its parsing. In natural language, the boundaries of correct and incorrect use of grammar

---

67 Chomsky categorized four types of grammar, with each higher numbered category subsumed within the lower numbered category: regular (Type 3), context-free (Type 2), context-sensitive (Type 1), unrestricted (Type 0). Each had a set of associated rules for generating syntactically correct statements in the language.

are a fuzzy space, and usually not a huge problem, except to the more insistently rigorous of minds. This fuzziness is not possible in the realm of program language and computation, save within a framework that precisely defines what it is to be fuzzy! The programmer may specify valid program code that obeys the grammatical rules of the language used for creation of a program, but the machine used to implement it may, nevertheless, find the task too complex or impossible to execute. The problem of tractability of computation is studied in the machine language of the Turing machine, which features in Chapter Five on information engineering.

Two final questions arise about expressiveness of language in the Information Age. Are we, as some fear, on an *Académie Française*- or Esperanto-like path, risking loss of meaning by overly normalizing and constraining language to a common denominator that serves principally the purposes of machine communication? In refining information systems and infrastructure, accommodating the standardization they require, and adding artificial intelligence overlays, are we also implicitly deskilling and disqualifying humankind, such that it will no longer be able to understand and express itself, and thereby control its own fate? There are no persuasive answers to be had in response to such questions about how emanations from Pandora's box will play out. At best, as yet, both yes and no, potentially, and not necessarily! How we approach them will largely determine events.

We should not look back for answers. As Whitehead wrote a hundred years ago, and it remains true:

> Today the world is passing into a new stage of its existence. New knowledge, and new technologies have altered the proportions of things. The particular example of an ancient society sets too static an ideal and neglects the whole range of opportunity.[68]

We should rather look forward, with somewhere between Barack Obama's audacity of hope and Mervyn King's audacious pessimism. Zobaczymy! First, I will explore how the languages of mathematics, logic and computation came together to advance how we think about thinking and know about knowledge.

The Language of Mathematics and Logic

Leibniz argued that human thinking can be grounded in laws described in the language of mathematics. He was born at a time of turmoil and civil war in England, in the era of Oliver Cromwell (1599–1658), which overturned

---

68   Ibid., p. 261.

the 'Divine Right of Kings' to govern and established government by Parliament. Those times were described in the eponymous English ballad of that era as the 'world turned upside down'. The term was borrowed by the historian Christopher Hill as the title of his book describing the history of the era.[69] Leibniz was a father of mathematics who overturned the divine nature of inference, turning the world of logic upside down! This was the taxiing zone before the first runway.

Logicism asserts that mathematics is reducible to logic and that pure mathematics can be deduced from a few simple axioms (sometimes called primitive notions) through a process of formal logical argument. Russell wrote that it is the logicist's goal 'to show that all pure mathematics follows from purely logical premises and uses only concepts definable in logical terms'.[70] This was what I described as a second and parallel runway of advance, in the previous section.

There is as much learned dispute among logicians about theory of logic as there is among philosophers about ontology. The topic would quickly move to a level of detail that disrupts the flow of the book, by delving too deeply into what may be unnecessary, distracting or bemusing explanations and examples. It seems better to provide some brief outlines, footnotes and pointers to detail elsewhere. Wikipedia or a good logic primer are reasonable starting points for exploring further.

The domain of mathematical logic, which was also called formal logic, intersected early on with the mathematics of algebra and set theory.[71] In 1847, a self-taught, religiously devout English mathematician, George Boole (1815–64) published an essay entitled *Mathematical Analysis of Logic* that laid the foundations of what became known as Boolean algebra. In this algebra, statements in logic are expressed as algebraic equations. The symbols in the equations represent groups of objects (mathematical sets) and statements in logic. Their algebraic manipulation provides a rigorous method of logical deduction, thus representing logic as algebra. This algebra provides a

---

69   C. Hill, *The World Turned Upside Down: Radical Ideas During the English Revolution* (New York: Viking Press, 1972). The turmoil of seventeenth-century England has also been described as a reflection of a society challenged in its norms and beliefs as it came to terms with new ways of communicating the printed word and managing the explosion of information that this heralded. This polarized society into civil war between Cavalier and Roundhead armies, although historians differ as to how these loyalties segregated along political, economic, religious and demographic lines. The parallels with our Information Age turmoil, in this case coming to terms with the computer, are tempting to opine!

70   B. Russell, *My Philosophical Development* (London: George Allen and Unwin, 1959), p. 74.

71   Wikipedia contributors, 'Mathematical Logic', *Wikipedia, The Free Encyclopedia* (222 May 2023), https://en.wikipedia.org/wiki/Mathematical_logic

basis for analyzing the validity of logical statements, capturing the binary character of statements that may be either true or false. Boolean logic has been described as akin to a mathematics restricted to the two quantities, 0 and 1.

Boole worked at Cork, in Ireland, a few miles from the location of the Blarney stone. I was taken there once, when visiting to talk at his old University, but was not brave enough to stretch down over the cliff edge, to kiss it! In 1858, Augustus De Morgan (1806–71) was the first to propose the term mathematical logic. He was a close contemporary of Boole, based for many years at London University, the predecessor of my alma mater in London, UCL, which was established in those times as a non-conformist institution, countering the conformist religious regimes of the era, at Oxford and Cambridge.

De Morgan expressed logic in the language of set theory and logical propositions were cast into theorems of mathematical, logical inference. Rules used in translation and reduction of these logical expressions into a standard, not further reducible or simplifiable form, bear the name De Morgan's Laws. The precision this afforded enabled new insight and clarification of principles and methods of logical inference.

The wider application of the ideas of Boole and De Morgan into the realm of reasoning with knowledge, started with John Venn (1834–1923). He proposed the term symbolic logic and is remembered in the Venn diagram, used to represent the overlap of sets of objects arising in logical reasoning. Different kinds of logical formalism evolved over time, specialized for different requirements arising in the representation of verbal logical argument. It is a blurry panorama of separately identified and named branches of logic. I provide here just brief notes and introductory pointers to easily accessible further explanations.

The increasing semantic richness of formalized logic gave rise to different levels of what became known as logic calculus. Boole's work focused on the formal logic and algebraic manipulation of logical statements. There arose what was variously termed propositional logic, propositional calculus, statement logic, sentential calculus, sentential logic.[72] It deals with propositions and relationships between propositions, including the construction of arguments based on them. Frege, with Charles Peirce (1839–1914), made what is seen as the crucial break from the Aristotelian tradition

---

72 K. Klement, 'Propositional Logic', *Internet Encyclopedia of Philosophy*, https://iep.utm.edu/propositional-logic-sentential-logic/

of logical argument, replacing his term logic with what was called a first-order logic, which became known as the first order predicate calculus.[73]

Seeking greater order and precision of logic languages over subsequent decades, different levels of logical expressiveness became known as zeroth,[74] second-[75] and higher-order logic, such as multi-valued logic (a calculus of propositions permitting of more than two truth values, worked on by Jan Łukasiewicz (1878–1956) and Alfred Tarski (1901–83)).[76] Logical operators, or connectives, have evolved to encompass various sub-specializations, including modal logic (expressing statements about necessity or possibility), temporal logic (expressing quantification over time), deontic logic (expressing obligation and permission) and relevance logic (expressing relevant connection of antecedent with consequent of inference). Each of these languages of logic sought rigorous expressiveness of the subtlety of different strains of natural language and verbal reasoning, pricking up the ears of philosophers defending their own boundaries of discipline. Some eminent philosophers would have none of it—notably Willard Van Orman Quine (1908–2000).

As the foregoing brief account well exemplifies, the names and descriptions of the different kinds of language of logic calculus that have been explored are, in themselves, confusing. Proposition, predicate, statement and sentence mixed with propositional and sentential logic, and with propositional, sentential and predicate calculus. The terminology of this rather chaotic domain became a bit like that of medicine of recent decades! My chief aim here is to illustrate the complexity that mathematization (and then computerization) of commonly expressed human logical argument can foist upon us.[77]

The story continues in the next section on logic and reasoning with knowledge. This section is focused on the language of mathematics and

---

73 See Wikipedia contributors, 'Term Logic', *Wikipedia, The Free Encyclopedia* (19 June 2023), https://en.wikipedia.org/wiki/Term_logic; Wikipedia contributors, 'First-order Logic', *Wikipedia, The Free Encyclopedia* (21 June 2023), https://en.wikipedia.org/wiki/First-order_logic

74 Wikipedia contributors, 'Zeroth-order Logic', *Wikipedia, The Free Encyclopedia* (20 May 2023), https://en.wikipedia.org/wiki/Zeroth-order_logic

75 Wikipedia contributors, 'Second-order Logic', *Wikipedia, The Free Encyclopedia* (28 May 2023), https://en.wikipedia.org/wiki/Second-order_logic

76 Wikipedia contributors, 'Higher-order Logic', *Wikipedia, The Free Encyclopedia* (20 June 2023), https://en.wikipedia.org/wiki/Higher-order_logic

77 I am, at least, in good company in my perplexity: Encyclopedia Britannia likewise throws up its hands over the persistent disagreements among expert logicians over the connections of theory of logic with discourse on language (The Editors of Encyclopedia Britannica, 'Logical Relation', *Encyclopedia Britannica* (20 July 1998), https://www.britannica.com/topic/logical-relation)!

logic, the next on the problems it is used to address. Clearly, these two considerations intertwine, and things then get even more complicated!

I return, now, to the second runway, that I described as following from the seminal contributions of Frege. This is Russell's logicism–the quest for a reformulation of mathematics that proceeds from simple axioms using formal logic. Many well-remembered nineteenth-century mathematicians laid foundations to underpin the development and tools of formal logic of the coming century. Mathematical logic was consolidated by Giuseppe Peano (1858–1932) and later taken up by Russell and Whitehead, in their work towards establishing secure logical foundations for mathematics. By the late nineteenth century, there was broad consensus that a great deal of mathematics could be formally derived in logical progression from a small number of simple axioms. Frege's work set out such a framework, but it was seen not to perform in resolving paradox, including Russell's own eponymous paradox. This inspired Whitehead and Russell to work together to extend their own current thinking, as expressed in their earlier books on these topics: Whitehead's 1898 *A Treatise on Universal Algebra* and Russell's 1903 *The Principles of Mathematics*. Russell worked particularly on the theory of descriptions, and the no-class theory, in which he argued that to be meaningful, set or class terms must be placed in well-defined contexts.

In 1910, 1912 and 1913, Whitehead and Russell published the three volumes of *Principia Mathematica*. The drafts circulated between them and Russell wrote that: 'There is hardly a line in all the three volumes which is not a joint product'.[78] The title echoed Newton's *Philosophiæ Naturalis Principia Mathematica*–also three volumes but in Latin, and first published in 1687. Whitehead and Russell's work posed a different linguistic challenge, introducing new mathematical notation that frustrated colleagues! Nevertheless, these mathematical giants enlivened and recast the foundations of mathematics.

The quest entered new territory over the following decades with the landmark findings of Kurt Gödel (1906–78), who showed that within any consistent formal system of mathematics based on axioms, there are statements that are undecidable–neither provable nor disprovable. The formal system is said to be incomplete. 'Formally consistent' means that within the system there can be no statement such that both the statement and its negation can be proved. This put the cats among the pigeons and the debates trod widely on the toes of philosophy and logic–peering at and disputing language and terminology, as ever, about: assumption, axiom, type, class, category, context, predicate, proposition, fact, meaning,

---

78   Russell, *My Philosophical Development*, p. 74.

description, appearance, reality, truth, beauty… This era and these debates were the mathematical crucible of computer science, where the now legendary names of John von Neumann (1903–57), Alonzo Church (1903–95) and Alan Turing (1912–54) appeared to heat and stir the molten mix and pour it into new moulds of theory of computation.

Philosophical and mathematical debate extended into the discourse of computer science and its program languages. It seems that the connections of logic, mathematics and computer science are strong but not watertight in the sense of being fully and consistently argued and proven from common axioms. Frege's 1874 *Habilitationsschrift*, a tough read, set the scene for a hundred years of transition in logic, mathematics and computer science. Tractable elements of the first-order predicate calculus have been assimilated within description logics today, such as within the Web Ontology Language (OWL), introduced in the section on computational reasoning, below. The goal of aligning mathematics and formal logic is still worked on. Some of Frege's original constructs, such as his second-order calculus of predicates, proved not to be watertight, and the full richness of his first-order calculus is, in some cases, intrinsically not computable, and, in others, not yet feasibly implementable in computer systems of today.

In many areas of interface of theory and practice, a decision is required about where to pitch pragmatic compromise in the choice of method for tackling a problem. Both are important but create bias in different directions. How far should we simplify and blur precision of theory, as a compromise in favour of tractable practical application? How far should we pursue precision of theory and, by so doing, compromise practical relevance and ability to implement? It is a balance decided in context, and such balance shifts in time, accommodating new considerations of theory and new methods and technologies of implementation. Advancing precision and range of measurement makes possible new balance and interaction of theoretical and experimental physics. New things that can be measured help in refining theories about the phenomena observed, and new theories of these phenomena helps ground further experiments; together advancing the field. Each aspect is provisional and imperfect but in combination they work towards greater insight and capability–searching for a sweet-spot of theory and practice. Such compromise can alight on sour spots where neither theory nor practice advance and may regress. They may become a sweetshop of readily accessible goodies that taste nice but turn out to do harm. Short term sweetness can evolve or turn to sourness as times move on.

The first-order predicate calculus of Frege was a transforming insight–a sweet spot of formal logic and practical reasoning with knowledge. It broke from the classical language of logic to a mathematical language. It advanced the alignment of mathematics with logic and evolved over the next century to set computer science on a pathway to knowledge engineering and then machine learning. In practice, its theoretical potential had to be reined in considerably, to render computable the answers to the questions it asked, and the calculations required.

The debates are far from over, as they never seem to be when they tread deeply into matters of language, logic, ontology and epistemology. Advocacy against formal logic emphasizes its limitations. It asserts that the restrictions implicit in mathematically-precise logic and reasoning do not match well with the variability of detail, context and nuance of human knowledge and affairs, and the ways in which we express and reason about them in words. Quine and others have argued that the limitations lead to ambiguity in both the formal syntax and semantics of knowledge thus represented. Advocates in favour counter by arguing for a narrowed and more precise scope of philosophical discourse, limiting the context of application of formal logic to one based on realism and practicality rather than abstraction. Others argue that all perceptions of reality are subjective appearances, reflecting belief as much as reality. Logicists counter that 'facts', expressed in a precise context, are not matters of appearance–they can be relied on, axiomatically, to underpin unambiguous logical argument. And so on...

Khayyam's eleventh-century verse could readily be updated to Information Age discourse about knowledge! As could Jean-Baptiste Alphonse Karr's (1808–90) much-quoted saying from the January 1849 issue of his journal *Les Guêpes* [The Wasps]: *Plus ça change, plus c'est la même chose!* [The more it changes, the more it's the same thing!] Philosophers might both agree and disagree, I suspect, and perhaps even take this as a profound statement and compliment–it all depends on how you take the meaning of the words.

Whitehead's writing on these matters from a hundred years ago, in *Adventures of Ideas*, rings true to me. He explored the philosophical issues arising in discussion of logical proposition and predicate,[79] in his examination of the appearance, and truth, of reality. Here are some quotations that characterize his approach:

> Truth is a qualification which applies to appearance alone. Reality is just itself, and it is nonsense to ask whether it be true or false. Truth is the conformation of appearance to reality.[80]

> A proposition is a notion about actualities, a suggestion, a theory, of things.[81]

---

79   Whitehead, *Adventures of Ideas*, p. 234.
80   Ibid., p. 231.
81   Ibid., p. 233.

No verbal sentence merely enunciates a proposition. It always includes some incitement for the production of an assigned psychological attitude of the proposition indicated. In other words, it endeavours to fix the subjective form which clothes the feeling of the proposition as a datum. There may be an incitement to believe, or to doubt, or to enjoy, or to obey. This incitement is conveyed partly by the grammatical mood and tense of the verb, partly by the whole suggestion of the sentence, partly by the whole content of the book, partly by the material circumstances of the book, including its cover, partly by the names of the author and of the publisher. In the discussion of the nature of a proposition, a great deal of confusion has been introduced by confusing this psychological incitement with the proposition itself.[82]

The most conspicuous example of truth and falsehood arises in the comparison of existences in the mode of possibility with existences in the mode of actuality.[83]

He is, though, forward looking and I like that, too. He cautions against what he said might be called an 'out with the new, in with the old approach!'

Logic and Reasoning with Knowledge

Nothing illustrates better the danger of specialist Sciences than the confusion due to handing over propositions for theoretical consideration by logicians, exclusively.[84]

My purpose in this section of the chapter is to introduce how the connected histories of mathematics, logic and computer science, and the methods of formal logic that have evolved from them, have led to new ways of framing and reasoning with knowledge. It introduces how the computer now reasons about real world problem domains. This leads on to sections discussing the application of these methods in medicine and health care.

Improvement in how we think about, express and reason with our knowledge of the world around us is an important and infinite quest. It reflects what we believe, can observe and measure, wish to see and think about, and thus seek to organize, express and systematize. I think Whitehead was saying that logic is important in this broad endeavour, but perhaps not *that* important! Clearly *that* depends on what we are talking about. Errors of machine logic in the processing of electrical signals in a computer chip or

---

82   Ibid.
83   Ibid., p. 234.
84   Whitehead (ibid.) discussing truth and appearance, predicate and proposition.

circuit board, are clearly crucial to put right. Whole worlds would collapse if 2+2 did not make 4!

When we think about and reason with problems and ideas, we say we turn them over in our mind and sometimes that we sleep on them, relegating them to the unconscious mind. When awake we think and reason instinctively and seek to do so, also, logically and with balance and perspective. In Kahneman's terms, this is *Thinking, Fast and Slow*.[85] It is a mix that is matched to our capabilities and the purposes our bodies and minds are addressing. We navigate between the capabilities and limitations of our brains and the languages they employ to represent and reason; likewise, we grapple with the motivations that drive us to understand and act. These languages have extended our canon beyond biological signals and words into mathematics and logic, and into computation.

If mathematics, logic and computation are to be in harmony, rigorous computational methods of mathematical logic that we can depend on (whilst being cognizant of and allowing for their limitations) are very important. As we become increasingly dependent on computer systems that use these methods to reason with clinical knowledge, similar attention to their applicability is needed. Each language or tool has its characteristic applicability and limitations in what it seeks and is able to do in support of thought and reasoning and the solution of problems. The models of the problem domain that they express are representations of reality and must be understood in the context of the purposes they serve and how well they are achieved. And it is thus with computation, as we construct languages and methods and write programs utilizing them to represent and reason with ideas, analyse observations and measurements, and determine, control and regulate actions.

Apart from a passing reference to Aristotle and his Organon in classical history classes at school, I cannot recall the study of logic cropping up anywhere in my education until the names of Boole and De Morgan appeared in the Theory of Computation module of the Masters course in computer science of the University of London, that I attended in 1970. In my school-day mathematics, the good marks came when one had mastered calculus, vector methods and conic geometry. These foundational methods had been envisioned, refined and evolved in the practical context of problem-solving, over centuries. Exposure to the mathematics of symmetry, set and group theory and topology was extremely limited–school curricula were only slowly catching up with these directions of travel and their contributions in physics.

---

85   D. Kahneman, *Thinking, Fast and Slow* (New York: Macmillan, 2011).

In my university physics days, the mathematical problems got harder and partial differential equations, and matrix and tensor algebra loomed large. Statistics played only limited roles, given the measurements and data we encountered, as then characteristic of the physics domain–five sigma it was not! Mathematics and theoretical physics were closely intertwined. Principles of mathematical symmetry, illuminated and characterized through set and group theory, were emerging into the world of particle physics and field theory. Early progress got even the greatest of minds a bit carried away. My scientific hero, Richard Feynman (1918–88), was quoted as having commented–after the discovery of the omega-minus particle in 1964, which theory had predicted would exist to complete a modelled symmetry of elementary particles–that particle physics would be done and dusted within fifty years!

Theory of computation was nowhere in my education in physics and not very persuasive in the very practically focused Masters course in computer science that I followed at the end of the 1960s. A decade later, in the early and mid-1980s, Feynman envisioned and created one of the best introductions I know to the subject, first for his physics students at the California Institute of Technology (Caltech) and then more widely. He approached it from the physics of computing devices and spread the net wide to theory of computation, information and coding theory, quantum mechanical computers and parallel computing. I review the edited collection of these horizon-scanning lectures in Chapter Six.

Before getting too starry-eyed about the prospects for reasoning based on formal and computational logic, first a story about stars in the sky and how knowledge about them grew two hundred years ago. Perhaps no other endeavour has captivated the human imagination as greatly as the observation, appreciation and quest for knowledge of the night sky.

The Babylonians knew about the revolving planets but not until the late eighteenth century was Uranus added to the list. It had of course been seen but was thought to be a star, until William Herschel (1738–1822) learned to plot its distant orbit. It was through advent of the Newtonian reflecting telescope and its refinement to much greater sensitivity by Herschel (thus conferring ability for observers to reflect more clearly and systematically on what they saw), that the paradigm of astronomy changed. Newton had given up on the challenge of improving the blurring imperfections of the refracting glass lenses of telescopes and substituted mirrors. Herschel conceived of and painstakingly polished single metal reflecting mirrors to a new scale and precision. No one could help him–there was no commercial basis for such production. The measurement of star position for purposes of navigation did not require such precision.

Observation and measurement of the night sky thus moved up an octave and so did reasoning about the observed stars and their constellations. The long observed cloudy nebulae resolved into galaxies of stars. In time, the term nebula came to characterize gas clouds as the factory of stars. Herschel discerned Polaris as a double star–observation over time of their optical parallax revealed their relative distance. In time, binary stars, lacking such observed parallax, were revealed as gravitationally coupled neighbours. He was so far ahead of contemporary observatories that his results were difficult for professional astronomers to confirm. Some thought his ideas 'fit for bedlam'. But he had the credibility of having discovered Uranus as a planet, to protect him against such assault. In using coloured glass filters to process the images, he experienced heat originating from the red end of the spectrum and, by checking with a thermometer, discovered the infrared. He introduced the time dimension of the observed night sky–how long the light took to reach the earth, speculating that it might be millions of years.

Herschel was a gifted amateur astronomer, long earning his living as a musician. Only once famous was he given patronage and honour to be accepted into the brotherhood of astronomy. It was his sister, Caroline Herschel (1750–1848), who made it a sisterhood, too. She had a similarly sharp and focused mind but had struggled to be allowed to branch beyond domestic life, being constrained by the expectations of their parents. She was helped to escape by her brothers, who surreptitiously enabled her to work alongside William in England. She recorded his observations, called down from the pitch blackness enveloping the position in which he worked, at the end of his twenty-foot telescope tube. She took the opportunity to use the telescope independently and discovered comets. She attended to the rigorous documentation of the new more precise observations and found errors in the then classic Flamsteed catalogue. She added five hundred stars to the previously recorded three thousand. It was called a New General Catalogue and I understand that its coding system survives to this day in their naming. She introduced what we might call a new ontology for this record–moving beyond classification within constellations to one based more systematically and painstakingly on geometry of angles.

Much of the reasoning in the foregoing story was based on a combination of measurement and mathematical analysis. No formal logic was needed, which is the way advances in science have long played out. Indeed, the mathematically based methods of formal logic, introduced in the previous section along the timeline of developments in the logical foundations of mathematics, have mainly connected with reasoning about knowledge within the disciplines of mathematics, logic and computer science, themselves. Their application to provide the theoretical underpinnings of life science and medical knowledge bases is growing but has still quite limited and partial practical application in health care delivery. There have been brave attempts along my songline but not many have persisted.

This pattern has started to change in the data intensive world of the computer, where we increasingly depend on formal logic to help us cope and reason with the huge volumes of data, and complexity of their detail, that land on our doorstep. Systematizing and reasoning with domains of knowledge is becoming mainstream computational science. I survey this scene in the concluding sections of this chapter.

I continue, here, with my brief historical overview of logic and reasoning with knowledge. And to clear my head for this, I spent a day collecting and comparing dictionary entries in Oxford Reference, for common terms describing them that have entered different fields of discourse. I interrogated the learned dictionaries of philosophy, mathematics, logic, computer science, psychology and mind, and some from wider domains–religion, biology and medicine. In practice, I could have gone right around Ranganathan's circle of knowledge, but I called a halt at thirty-five pages of comparative study. The hardest to follow tended to be elaborated at the greatest length. Philosophy excelled in length, followed by mathematics and computer science. These disciplines swapped in order, computer science then coming first when I compared the extent to which they used specialized appropriations of the meanings of commonly used terms.

To communicate successfully with the computer about logic and reasoning with knowledge, we clearly have to define the meaning of words used in that discourse more narrowly than when we share them with one another in everyday life. In normal life, it is often rather easier to construct arguments and reach agreement when we can talk across one another a bit, using words loosely to mean different things in different contexts. That is the necessary ambiguity of politics, after all–the art of the possible and making things possible in the human world! Look no further than the tipping point in the dramatic final session at the COP26 United Nations Climate Change Conference, last week as I write, which hinged on one word, 'down' replacing 'out', in relation to the future trajectory of the use of fossil fuel, on which depends reversal of the habitable earth's trajectory towards 'down' *and* 'out'!

I conducted another exercise in relation to the usage of words. I checked with my weighty and now ancient Compact Oxford English Dictionary (OED), to see how it defines some of the words now descriptive of computer-based information systems. These have become blurred, appropriated and fertile ground for misunderstandings in the fragmented discourse of the Information Age. I was interested to see how the classical wordsmiths of OED define some of them–at least I could confidently give them an alphabetical order! I list these words, here, just to illustrate the complexity that arises when mixing natural and specialist languages to express, communicate, and reason with knowledge, and share this, formally, with the computer.

Class: In logic: a class differs from a catalogue by virtue of a common resemblance in the midst of diversity. Way of grade or quality. Grouping by common attributes.

Classify/classification: modern verb/noun–to arrange or distribute in classes, according to a method or system. Especially in relation to general laws or principles. Department of science that consists in or relates to classification. First use in medicine–1799 by Took: the diseases and casualties are not scientifically classified.

Encyclopaedia: Greek: circle of arts and sciences considered to be essential for a liberal education. The circle of learning–a general course of instruction. Word derives from general education. From seventeenth century: a literary work containing extensive information on all branches of knowledge, usually arranged in alphabetical order.

Language: the whole body of words and methods of combination of words used by a nation, people or race, a 'tongue'.

Nomenclature (*nomenclatura*, Pliny): the act of assigning names to things. A list of collection of names or particulars; a catalogue or register.

Taxonomy: early nineteenth century. *Taxis*: origin Greek: arrangement, order. From *tassein*, to arrange.

Term: A limit in space, duration–that which limits the extent of anything. Or a limit or space in time. Limiting conditions. Uses leading up to the sense of an expression:

- in maths, quantities used;
- in logic, each of the two elements, the subject and predicate, which are connected by the copula;
- in relation to a syllogism, the subject or predicate of any of the propositions composing it and forming one of its three elements: major term, minor term, middle term, each of which occurs twice.

Definite use of word or phrase in a particular subject. Expressing a notion or conception or denoting an object of thought. Manner of expressing oneself. Way of speaking.

Terminology: system of terms belonging to any science or subject; cf. nomenclature.

Type: (There are seven usages recorded for the noun, four for the verb!) That by which something is symbolized or figured. Distinguishing mark or sign. Characteristic form of a fever. The general form structure or character distinguishing a particular kind group or class of beings or objects. Hence a pattern or model after which something is made.

As will already be clear, and leaving aside the vagaries of terminology, which feature in the section below on medical language and computation, the applications of formal methods of logic are often hard to grasp and understand–in their details, capabilities and limitations. I studied theoretical physics and had testing experience of ideas that were mathematically 'hard' to understand when I came across them, and that was just within the discipline of physics! It is burdensome for a newcomer to read across disciplines, disentangling what is written about logic in the engagements between learned minds, parsing this into one brain, and sharing it with others.

I am labouring this point, here, only to now point out that the computer is also burdened by the effort required to compute with terminology and logic expressed in such convoluted terms; its elaborations blow fuses of computability. There is an evolving ping-pong match of what the human mind envisages and what the machine can recognize and work with. There is experiment and learning in this game, occupying nimble and learned minds, and, when let loose too soon, it risks creating confusion and burden that becomes entrenched in the wider world.

Verbal and Mathematical Reasoning

As we have seen, the search for precision and consistency of thought and verbal reasoning about the material world and human affairs, has long been the domain of philosophy. Historians trace this quest to early civilizations. Hundreds of volumes were written about it in classical times, and some survived to be pored over and debated in succeeding contemporary contexts. How this inheritance has transmogrified into mathematical and computational reasoning with knowledge, today, is, again, as we have already seen, a long and interconnected set of stories. Natural language of speech and writing has gradually assimilated into specialized language of logic, used to reason about appearances in the natural world. It has assimilated into a meta language of abstraction, to generalize ways of describing and reasoning: words about words, data about data, language about languages.

From classical times, observation and measurement of the natural world and the study of paradox evolved and revolved, encompassing new ideas about the nature and meaning of words, numbers and symbols. The study of reasoning evolved and revolved, encompassing new ideas about grammar, statement and argument expressed in natural language. Philosophy evolved and revolved within schools of thought about the nature of reality and its consonance with ways of reasoning about the world. This Pandora's box of challenge and insight–of discipline struggling to be born–had the lid pressed firmly down for many centuries by the force of prior belief, expressed in the language of mysticism and religion. The power of authority and orthodoxy, and fear of the new, are ever with us.

In the history of Greece, the name Parmenides (born *c.* 515 BCE) carries a flag for metaphysics and ontology–about existence, being, becoming and reality. Aristotle and Chrysippus were flag carriers of two emerging schools of logical thought. Aristotelian logic was based on terms and their conjunction in expressing ideas, and syllogism in reasoning with them. Stoic logic was based on proposition. Stoicism has been remembered mainly in context of philosophy of life. Diodorus (*c.* 90 BCE–30 BCE) was also later associated with propositional logic.

In the time of Aristotle, logical reasoning was pursued through verbal argument and seen as the organon (described as 'an instrument of thought, especially a means of reasoning or a system of logic') through which we come to know anything about the world. Aristotle described logical syllogism as 'a discourse in which certain (specific) things having been supposed, something different from the things supposed results of necessity, because these things are so'.[86] The study of logical reasoning requires the parsing of sentences like that! Formal rules of (deductive) reasoning were the basic principles of this logic, which was accepted in Western philosophy until the nineteenth century, when it was notably disrupted by the mathematical advances of Frege.

Stoic propositional logic fell away, to be rediscovered and built on many centuries later, including by the Polish mathematical logician, Łukasiewicz, influential as a historian of logic and in making bridges from mathematics and logic to computer science. He was the originator of Polish Notation of operators and operands, from as early as 1924–in Polish, and so not widely translated or read!

Bacon produced his *Novum Organon* (1620), to replace the Aristotelian deductive reasoning with inductive reasoning. He advocated the eponymous Baconian method for reasoning inductively from observation to abstract concept, through scientific method and experiment. Immanuel Kant promulgated his *Critique of Pure Reason* (1781). Other notable philosophers of the changing times, as ever, had their say.

---

86   Aristotle, *Prior Analytics*, ed. and trans. by R. Smith (Indianapolis, IN: Hackett Publishing Co., 1989), p. 2.

Patterns of syllogism and the reduction of logical propositions to a set of normal forms were explored extensively in classical times and evolved in stages. They jumped many centuries into mathematical and computational logic, embodied and debated in many systems of logical inference that covered increasingly diverse and semantically rich kinds of logic, reflecting more complex styles of reasoning, such as the modal, temporal, deontic and relevance logic sub-specializations mentioned in the preceding section about the languages of mathematics and logic. Subsets of these were explored, conditioned by practical considerations of feasibility, correctness of enactment and proof of consistency.

Terms like sentence, subject and predicate, proposition, premise, class, category, inference, truth, causality, existence, universality, necessity, possibility, obligation, permission... came to populate philosophy, grammar, linguistics, mathematics, logic, computer science, psychology and religion... through the ages and to this day. They have provided plenty of scope for people to talk past one another, plenty of reasons to be clear and careful, and difficulties aplenty in connecting logical thought and reasoning with the programming of computers.

When feeling bemused by the rapid inflation of the universe of knowledge in the Information Age, it is salutary and steadying to read Whitehead's critique about such adventure. In his extensive review of the classical philosophical and scientific foundations of knowledge and reasoning with ideas, he writes that 'Where Aristotle said "observe" and "classify", the moral of Plato's teaching is the importance of the study of mathematics'.[87] In his *Seventh Epistle*, Plato had opposed the notion that a final system of reasoning could be verbally expressed. His thinking revolved around seven main notions: ideas, physical elements, psyche, eros, harmony, mathematical relations and what he termed the receptacle. Whitehead expressed caution about logic disconnected from mathematics, saying that 'Aristotelian logic, apart from the guardianship of mathematics, is the fertile matrix of fallacies. It deals with propositional forms only adapted for the expression of high abstractions; the sort of abstraction usual in current conversation where the proposed background is ignored'.[88]

He further argues:

We can never get away from the questions: How much–In what proportions–and, In what pattern of arrangement with other things? The exact laws of chemical proportions make all the difference; CO will kill you, when CO_2 will only give you a headache. Also, CO_2 is a necessary

---

87 Whitehead, *Adventures of Ideas*, pp. 137–55 (p. 148).
88 Ibid., p. 150.

element for the dilution of oxygen in the atmosphere; but too much or too little is equally harmful. Arsenic deals out either health or death, according to its proportions amid a pattern of circumstances. Also, when the health-giving proportion of CO_2 to free oxygen has been obtained, a rearrangement of these proportional quantities of carbon and oxygen into carbon monoxide and free oxygen will provide a poisonous mixture.[89]

It is interesting that, as a philosopher and mathematician, Whitehead used an example from physiology to make this point. Similar arguments about the importance of context, when reasoning with knowledge, can be made with even stronger force, using examples from the medicine and health care domain. He also argues that 'the essential connectedness of things can never be safely omitted' and that all languages witness to the 'error' of 'investing each factor in the Universe with an independent individuality'. Here, as well, 'even the appeal to mathematics is too narrow, at least if mathematics is taken to mean those branches hitherto developed' and 'in the absence of some understanding of the final nature of things, and thus of the sorts of backgrounds pre-supposed in such abstract statements, all science suffers from the vice that it may be combining various proportions which tacitly presuppose inconsistent backgrounds'.[90]

This line of reasoning was crystallized in Whitehead's 'process philosophy', described as a philosophy of organism which envisions reality as composed of processes rather than material objects, defined by their mutual relationships. This organic characterization lends support to how I have come to characterize care information as an organic utility, as developed in Part Three of this book. Also, interesting (at least for me!), is the physicist Carlo Rovelli's current pursuit of a similar idea, in proposing theory of relationship as a fundamental unifying ground of theoretical physics. Other physicists are grounding their 'What is reality?' quests in ideas based on theory of information. Theories of information, relationship and process seem to be circling one another in the physical, biological and virtual worlds!

Later in his book, Whitehead writes that 'All knowledge is conscious discrimination of objects experienced'.[91] Here, he sounds to be at one with the Einstein quotation at the beginning of the chapter: 'Pure logical thinking cannot yield us any knowledge of the empirical world; all knowledge of reality starts from experience and ends in it'. Machine intelligence is, though, beginning to experience and learn for itself, about the world and

---

89   Ibid., p. 149.
90   Ibid., p. 150.
91   Ibid., p. 173.

the problems we, as humans, face in it. Thus far post-Aristotle and post-Frege; henceforward post-artificial intelligence (AI)?

It is apparent when thinking about this substantially and continuingly anarchic scene, that we have much still to learn about logic and reasoning with knowledge. It has made all manner of human reasoning more complicated, as well as offering opportunity, and necessity, to make it better. In the panorama of medicine and health care, the full spectrum of this adventure and the programme for reform it makes necessary, is playing out all around us. How is the computer coming to grips with this scene? The story now moves into the decades during and after which Whitehead was writing, to the rise of computer science, the computing machine and machine intelligence.

Computational Reasoning

The quest to connect logic and reasoning with knowledge, with computationally tractable axioms and proofs, is a complex challenge. It is playing out in the invention of new computational methods that are being explored across multiple problem domains. Given current uncertainties, it seems a reasonable concern about this direction of travel that, even if new mathematics, science and computation do succeed in representing knowledge, measuring phenotype and analyzing data about human physiology and behaviour, to provide tractable new methods of logic and reasoning about human health care, in useful ways, the methods thus employed may ultimately prove beyond the capacity of human minds to understand and regulate. The machine may then be left to establish yet another sense, adding to the many that du Sautoy remarks already exist, of what it is to know, and what it is to reason, and to decide what should be made of and done with that knowledge.

With that caution in mind, I start here by drawing together a historical timeline of the challenge of computational reasoning. In much of scientific endeavour, whole communities share both task and credit. The communities of actors are large and widespread, and progression a complex mix of shared and contested insight and activity, context and staying power. That is not to deny the inuksuk-quality significance of the insights and historical contributions of key individuals, and I have opted to highlight a few.

Charles Babbage (1791–1871) was both an engineer and mathematician and his interest in building his first mechanical computer was as a tool for mechanizing the labour of calculating astronomical tables. A hundred years later, the system of Boolean logic, and theorems based on it, such as De Morgan's laws, became a central motif of circuit design for electronic computers, applying logical functions to binary data and performing binary arithmetic.

Theory of mathematical logic became foundational to and increasingly intertwined with computer science of the twentieth century. As we have seen, this evolution accelerated in the decades either side of the turn of the century, with the landmark contributions from such as Cantor, Frege and David Hilbert (1862–1943) in Germany, Whitehead and Russell in England, Łukasiewicz, Polish-born in the then Austro-Hungarian province of Galicia, and Gödel, from then Czechoslovakia. Such people were giants and recognized the giants on whose shoulders they stood. Modern-day theory of proof treats the reasoning employed in proving mathematical theorems and verifying their correctness within a framework of mathematical logic. It grew from the work of Cantor and Hilbert and connected with theory of computer science as it got to grips with the expression and correctness of algorithm and program.

Church and Turing focused on theory of computation and its mathematical limits. Turing developed the idea of an abstract universal computing machine, on which any computational process could be performed. This gave traction to the study of computability–what computers could and could not, in principle, compute, from a mathematical standpoint. Church invented the lambda calculus as an abstract theory of computation, also drawing on Łukasiewicz's Polish Notation and the mirror Reverse Polish Notation used in describing functions. This part of the story links with Chapter Five on information engineering.

Theory of computation enabled and helped formal logic to grow, and limitations of computer power and computability guided and constrained its applicability as a method for solving problems. Some computational tasks arising within theory of formal logic defied feasible program implementation and available computing resource. Exploratory implementation efforts were restricted to handling subsets of the expressions that the formal logic could, in principle, handle.

The story became more complex and specialized as it extended more widely across cognate disciplines, framed by their different language and discourse. Philosophy of mind debated with neuroscience and computer science, giving new context to the study of logic and reason. Reasoning about knowledge extended in the context of the computer science of program languages and development of early knowledge base systems. The idea of self-referential systems entered discussions of consciousness and mind, as the cognitive psychologist, Douglas Hofstadter explored in his book, *I Am a Strange Loop*, which I introduce in Chapter Six.

This history has, thus far, trended towards philosophical bemusement and computational intractability! The perplexity it presents is reminiscent of René Descartes' (1596–1650) philosophy of mind and body dualism, once memorably batted off with: 'What is mind? No matter: What is matter? Never mind'.[92] And in response to the still baffling physics question, What is reality?, a similar response has been: don't think about it, just solve the Schrödinger equation! Reducing theoretical physics to its simplest axioms has long been a recurrent work in progress and the quest has involved much new mathematics.

Notwithstanding the fractal complexities and contingencies of human affairs, we decide and enforce rules whereby society operates, and individual components are required to function and behave, presided over by judicial systems. These change over time and exceptions are made—the rules are said to be 'defeasible'. Rules that do not admit of such change are 'indefeasible'. Where we seek generality, we focus on the indefeasible. Where we recognize and allow for variability and contingency, we are in the defeasible realm of the particular. The more we seek to allow for and define the contingent and defeasible, the more complex and ungovernable the computational edifice we create. Today's national tax codes that look after every nook and cranny of compliance and default, extend from hundreds to thousands of pages—those of some countries are much more complex than others. Judicial functions are challenged, too, and human judges teeter on the limits of their oracular finesse and prestige. Human judgement admits of increasing noise and bias and, as Kahneman, Sibony and Sunstein suggest, assumes the character of imprecise measurement.[93] Health care knowledge and clinical records populate a highly defeasible domain.

What problems does the ingestion of this noisy and uncertain world of discourse present to the machine? One might say that it tends to exhibit the machine equivalent of indigestion, burping and adding to the noise and general disarray! It needs a digestive system for the data it eats and the information it processes and promulgates. It causes problems with the use of terminologies and their change over time. It creates problems of burdensome legacy as knowledge evolves while knowledge base systems are unable, or fail, to keep track. It causes problems in the navigation of a middle ground that attempts to represent and reason with what we deem indefeasible axioms of knowledge and what is contingent.

Problems of how to embody the generalism of knowledge about the human circulatory system—what it is and how it works—and the particular knowledge about individual patients who, given an underlying disorder, may present with a generalized pattern of symptoms, but not always so. Myocardial infarction generally, but not always, exhibits a pattern of

---

92   Ibid., p. 173.
93   Kahneman, Sibony and Sunstein, *Noise: A Flaw in Human Judgment.*

radiating right arm pain. Most might imagine that putting a lower bound on blood pressure compatible with life might be framed as an axiom, but someone, somewhere, for sure, will put up their hand, in all seriousness, to ask about cryogenic preservation of frozen bodies–whether they have a blood pressure and in what sense they are still alive!

Computational logic and reasoning lie within evolving, both theoretical and empirical domains of endeavour. Logic is concerned with provable truths. Formal logic has struggled to represent uncertainty and contingency. Computational logic endeavours have come to lean more to the theoretical than the practical side of the purposes they serve. Statistics helps us with uncertainty and Bayesian statistical methods help us with incremental learning to improve reasoning, in the context of evidence elicited and the framework of concepts we use to measure, model and analyse the system being studied or worked with. Computer software sets us free to create and reason with representations of knowledge that are detached from enforced mathematical correctness. That may be a good or a bad idea depending on the situation. This approach is sometimes called heuristic–applying 'rules of thumb'. At least we should be aware when we are usefully employing heuristics and when we are just getting our sums wrong!

All methods of computational logic require wide-ranging appraisal of their rigour and applicability in particular situations: how faithfully can they mirror a desired way of describing a system; are they formally rigorous and consistent in their statements and proofs; and how useful can they be in refining the knowledge they embody, and improving the services that teach, use, sustain, promulgate and update that knowledge?

Machine learning methods, as further discussed in the next section, widen the software scope further, to provide the ability to learn an optimum method for reasoning in a defined context of questions asked or decisions to be made. What is the three-dimensional structure that this DNA sequenced protein molecule will fold to? What is my best next move in a game of chess or Go? The method trains itself in this skill through an experimental process of trial and error, to create its own heuristics, based on historic databases of known and classified cases and other relevant knowledge about rules of the game or domain–rules of chess, a bank of known protein folding structures, scientific knowledge about the domain concerned.

These many and varied exploratory methods butt horns with human discourse. Formal logic has butted horns with philosophy in discourse of ontology. Mathematical and computational formulations of reasoning have butted horns with other communities and their methods of measurement, analysis and reasoned judgement, such as health professionals making judgements about the patients they care for.

In the realm of medical terminology, we are trying to arrive at both expressive and consistent vocabulary that can reliably be used to codify knowledge and pass it for further use and analysis. We must expect changing concepts of health and disease, that develop in line with changing means of measurement and analysis, and new representations of this knowledge in computer systems. A formally rigorous logical representation is required to ensure that consistent and correct inferences can be made when joining together elements from diverse computer representations of knowledge. Combined in this endeavour are validated methods for representation of the modelled reality with mathematically provable methods for inferences then drawn. Medical terminology has proved a fruitful area for exploration of the potential of the branch of formal logic known as 'description logic'. Medical language and terminology and the representations of knowledge about them are further discussed in the section below.

In the wider context of the use of knowledge bases in support of clinical reasoning and decision making, we encounter a mixed world of indefeasible and defeasible (contingent) statements, and consideration of how well and usefully different computationally anchored representations handle them. The methods explored have evolved considerably over at least six decades and I trace some landmark systems in the section on medical knowledge bases. One approach is to operate as a law maker and use the program to express rules to be followed, with embodied reasoning anchored to these rules. Early 'rules-based expert systems' adopted this approach.

Often, a hierarchy of knowledge representation is postulated, seeking to give a sense of the structure of central and subsidiary detail required. Sometimes this is expressed as a span from a background knowledge base about generalities and a foreground database about particulars. In clinical contexts, this database may include care records of patients and other defeasible and contingent knowledge that is relevant to the purposes served. Another consideration when deciding on a formal method for modelling a domain of knowledge, is how we are to interpret and act on results arising from computations involving the knowledge base thus created. This leads us to consideration of 'closed-world' versus 'open-world' assumptions.

The closed-world assumption is more prescriptive–if a statement is not provably satisfiable within the context of the knowledge base under consideration, it and statements that logically follow from it are deemed false. It is sometimes expressed as taking the view that all knowledge relevant to the purposes served by the knowledge base is represented within it. And thus that, if a proposition or statement can be shown not to be satisfied in this knowledge base context (sometimes called a 'world'), it can reasonably be treated as false, and all consequential propositions or statements that follow from it, likewise.

The open-world assumption is more restrictive and sets a higher bar of proof for a statement, requiring that its negation is provably untrue in the context of any possible 'world' consistent with the defined knowledge base framework. Otherwise, the matter remains undecidable. It recognizes that no system can have complete knowledge and that future changes in the knowledge base may render statements that were formerly undecidable, decidable.

Knowledge bases using a mixture of open- and closed-world assumptions have been explored. These assumptions become of great significance when searching for information by interrogating the knowledge base with logically constructed queries. The semantics of such query constructions become all important in guarding against incorrect, misleading, or unintended results.

Two principal approaches have predominated in this exploratory era of computerized knowledge bases–substantially pragmatic approaches called frame logics, which adopt the closed-world assumption, and later, substantially theory-based, approaches drawing on description logics, which follow the open-world assumption. Over time, the two have been admixed, rather as we saw in the world of library classifications. All this quickly becomes a highly context-dependent discussion and the arguments adduced, one way or another, need to be based on a clear statement of goal and definition of method, informed by experiment with implementation. Such uncertain endeavours seem easily to become entrenched in debate over mutual understanding of methodology, between subject domain and logic domain specialists, more than experimental findings in practical implementations.

Wider historic and up-to-date reviews of the field of clinical decision support, have been provided by luminary figures such as Mark Musen, Blackford Middleton, Robert Greenes, Dean Sittig and Adam Wright.[94] The previously cited paper of Rector et al.[95] is essential reading for understanding how this field has played out in attempts to harmonize the knowledge bases of two state-of-the-art terminologies, SNOMED (Systematized Nomenclature of Medicine) and ICD (International Classification of Diseases), as introduced in the section below. This incisive and battle-hardened overview of the state of the art is magnificent and Rector's personal advice has been generously given in helping me make my own, considerably more limited,

---

94   M. A. Musen, B. Middleton and R. A. Greenes, 'Clinical Decision-Support Systems', in *Biomedical Informatics*, ed. by E. H. Shortliffe and J. J. Cimino (Cham: Springer Nature, 2021), pp. 795–840; B. Middleton, D. F. Sittig and A. Wright, 'Clinical Decision Support: A 25 Year Retrospective and a 25 Year Vision', *Yearbook of Medical Informatics*, 25.S 01 (2016), S103–16.
95   'On Beyond Gruber'.

sense of this domain. I hope I have not departed too far off beam in this. The paper is a tough read but a worthwhile one–as with the Frege papers on predicate calculus it is best approached with a cold towel around the head!

Frame Logic

Frame-based methods emerged as a mechanism for capturing knowledge concepts and relationships among concepts, expressed as descriptive data structures and tools for reasoning with these. They seek to represent what is known and deemed relevant in a particular domain of application. The set of frames thus defined, and connections between them, form the basis of reasoning about the domain of knowledge represented. Frame logic is a pragmatic, cut-and-dried methodology and computer programs can more readily navigate the interface of defeasible and indefeasible domains of knowledge that it may encompass.

Notable tools to support frame-based knowledge systems have been pioneered by Musen at Stanford University. His team's renowned Protégé system became a widely used open-source ontology editor and knowledge management system in the field of biomedicine. In its later evolution, Protégé frames methodology moved on to adopt the OWL (Web Ontology Language) description logic methods alongside the frame structure, enabling the language of OWL also to be used to reason with the knowledge about the domain of application.

Protégé was a generation further on from an earlier pioneering initiative, the MYCIN rule-based expert system, created to represent and reason about antimicrobial therapy in clinical practice.[96] Even earlier initiatives originating from the same team, notably at Stanford and Massachusetts Institute of Technology (MIT), had led to the first expert systems, such as the Heuristic Dendral system of Edward Feigenbaum, known as the father of expert systems, and his team. This system identified chemical structures from their mass spectrometry profiles; one of the pioneering examples of knowledge bases that I introduce in a separate section below.

The evolving Stanford team, environment and field of work has made connections all along the timeline and songline of this book. It illustrates many of the lessons that recur throughout. It has been a sustained source of effort to construct knowledge bases useful for the support and improvement of clinical decision making in the Information Age. These experimental endeavours have connected new and evolving methods of observation and

---

96   E. Shortliffe, *Computer-Based Medical Consultations: MYCIN* (New York: Elsevier, 2012).

measurement, modelling and engineering (Chapters Three, Four and Five in Part One) with the transition of medicine into the Information Age (Part Two). From the early days, the experiments went hand in hand with the research of computer scientists, such as Ivan Sutherland, exploring new programming languages like John McCarthy's (1927–2011) LISP, tuned to reason with formal expressions of knowledge, just as they now connect with the unfolding field of machine learning.

Description Logic and the Web Ontology Language (OWL)

Description logics are languages designed to express and reason with knowledge about real world entities, utilizing methods of mathematical logic. Statements in these languages are used to represent what is known about a domain of knowledge, in a computable format. They are used to describe the logical structure of the domain and populate, manipulate and interrogate an associated knowledge base with content that fits within this structure. There are many such languages, and they utilize different levels and constraints of mathematical logic.

They are used to check the mutual internal consistency of both the knowledge structure and the entries placed within it. The logic statements expressed in the description logic language are treated as mathematical axioms and used to prove theorems based on them, to assist in reaching conclusions and informing decisions. An underlying inference engine, embodying formal rules for logical reasoning about the knowledge represented, such as *modus ponens*, is used to prove the consistency of the logical statements made and infer further true statements relevant to the purposes the knowledge base system serves. These might be to place the entities being described into a logical structure or taxonomy, showing where they fit within a hierarchy, and how they otherwise interrelate. This reasoning enables the construction of a logical network of relationships.

In knowledge bases programmed using the methods of open-world description logic, the representation of knowledge is in the form of indefeasible statements (axioms) about the things described–these brook no exceptions and are called invariant in formal logic. The computer may understand these axioms, but they may, nevertheless, prove impossible to compute with (be intractable) when attempting to reason about this knowledge representation, for example due to mathematical limitations or the scale of 'combinatorial explosion' (escalation in amount of computation) involved.

A growing range of description logic languages has evolved to represent and reason with knowledge. They occupy a sweet spot between theory and practice, comprising a set of formal logic methods that are capable of computing with the knowledge in the form they represent it, which can be implemented efficiently. In the main, those in use today are said to be more expressive than propositional logic and less expressive than first-order predicate calculus.

Description logic provides for two areas of reasoning and these exhibit different scales of computational complexity. There is T-box reasoning about what are sometimes called 'necessary truths' about classes of descriptive knowledge (for example, axioms about the classes of lungs, pneumonias and bacteria) and A-Box reasoning, which covers assertions made about individuals (for example, London, Manchester and Bristol as examples of English cities). The system might be designed to reason about cities, with some axioms being statements about the characteristics of any city, in T-box style, and some being assertions about London or Manchester, in A-box style.

In the health care domain, description logics have proved useful in furthering the quest to ensure consistent use of terminology for representing, analyzing and communicating its wide-ranging and complex hierarchies of knowledge (sometimes called terminological knowledge). To quote Rector et al. directly:

> In general, reasoning about classes ('T-Box reasoning') can be optimized computationally (although in expressive dialects it is worst-case intractable). However, reasoning about individuals ('A-box reasoning') is much more difficult. Conveniently, it is primarily axioms about classes that are relevant for terminologies.[97]

The Web Ontology Language (OWL) is a family of description logic languages that brought formal logic to the Internet, as a foundation of the Semantic Web.[98] This built on the World Wide Web Consortium (W3C) standards for data description on the web, notably Extensible Markup Language (XML) and the Resource Description Framework (RDF). OWL is for the interchange of knowledge representations, what XML and RDF have been for the interchange of data. OWL has been used as a tool for the formal representation of many different domains of biomedical knowledge.

Computer systems that represent and reason with knowledge about different domains of study, using methods of formal logic, have increasingly found their way into exploratory real-world applications. In medicine, methods of description logic have principally found application in

---

97 Rector et al., 'On Beyond Gruber', p. 4.
98 Wikipedia contributors, 'Web Ontology Language', *Wikipedia, The Free Encyclopedia* (17 April 2023), https://en.wikipedia.org/wiki/Web_Ontology_Language

endeavours aiming to provide logically consistent and useful representation and management of medical terminologies, such as SNOMED, and in creating models of biomedical structures, such as the Foundational Model of Anatomy (FMA). I follow both in sections below. And in recent times, the advance of machine learning and artificial intelligence, to analyse, reason with and make decisions, based on data collected from widely across the domain under consideration, has created a new buzz. I often tend to elide the two terms as 'machine intelligence'.

How and where different kinds of formal logic and machine intelligence can be applied, and prove reliable and useful, in well-characterized domains, and in relevant practical contexts, is an open question. Time will tell and a lot will change along the way. The hope is that they will enhance human health and wellbeing and improve the ways in which society operates and develops. The concern is for caution, lest this trend prove an overly Faustian bargain, heralding an era of machine intelligence that acquires and maintains momentum in directions that quickly deskill, demotivate and degrade human endeavours, adding to social inequalities and divisions. We must create and navigate this future songline, guided by King's audacious pessimism and Obama's audacity of hope.

Machine Learning and Artificial Intelligence

Machine learning adopts a naive approach to solving problems. In theory, it starts from almost nowhere in terms of knowledge assumed, save for some nascent capabilities for structuring information, using, for example, 'neural network', 'genetic algorithm' and database, with statistical and algorithmic dexterity–a bit like the Chomsky idea of an inbuilt human capacity for grammar. But if the problem posed is to learn to play a game, it seems only fair to let it know and make it follow the rules! And in setting it to tackle any problem, the machine might also, advantageously, be pump-primed in some way with human experts' accumulated knowledge and expertise in solving that problem–track record and strategies acquired in becoming good at winning in a game like chess or GO, for example, or a 'test set' of cases for identifying abnormalities in clinical images, where the answers deemed correct are given, and the problem posed is for the machine to become good at arriving at these answers on its own.

The machine kicks off with a best guess idea of a computational method or solution it seeks for solving the problem posed to it–playing its chess moves, for example–a bit like starting from a prior probability in a Bayesian method of inference. Equipped with its internal computational method for managing and learning from experiment, it tries this idea out, observes the outcome it achieves, revises its guess and tries again, seeking improvement. And it does so again and again, iteratively homing towards better and better method or solution for the problem posed.

Such a quest for improvement can be rapidly played out over many millions of iterations in virtual reality. And such systems consume electricity in gargantuan amounts! It is a method akin to the proof of a pudding being in the eating, as the computer eats the numbers and digests them to become a more useful tool! This tuned and continuously updated resource can then be applied prospectively to newcomers–for example, to play chess for real against an opponent, having tired of playing itself, or to propose a three-dimensional folding structure of a protein, for which the proteome sequence is known but the corresponding structure has not yet been found. The machine learner becomes a skilled pattern recognizer by working out its own patterns. All this is somewhat akin to humans who say that they will sleep on a problem. On waking with an answer, they may struggle to articulate in humanly accessible ways, how they arrived at this solution. Just as skilled clinicians may struggle to explain their immediate ability to recognize and interpret a pattern in what they see, when caring for a patient. The machine, and it is just a machine, may likewise become good, and even better than humans, at discerning patterns in, and interpreting, observations and measurements recorded, as, for example, in medical images and biochemical profiles. And as with any such tool, its results tend to prove better, prospectively, for well-defined and -circumscribed problems, and such constraint may not be easy to pin down in the highly contingent world of clinical practice. At some level of description, each patient is unique, and, in that sense, their associated contextualized data exist in a sample space of one.

The machine learner surveys all manner of recorded appearances in its circumscribed problem domain, or 'world', and searches out more, learning to make its own connections and adapting its learning, guided by the experience gained in trying and failing, as it iterates to improve. In its simplest form, this is an empirical process of learning from experience, naive because childlike–the way the newborn starts to experience, learn and acquire knowledge. This process might now be termed heuristic and I further connect the storyline with pioneers of 'heuristic programming' later in this chapter and in Chapter Five. It is much as the Greek philosophers confronted the foundations of mathematics and logic, learning to reason, faced with paradox and inconsistency revealed in the application of their arguments. It is much as the world learned to become systematic about medicine, in the evolving practice of wandering healers, bridging from concepts of divinely conferred affliction to descriptions and management of treated disorders. The machine-learning algorithm is a naive learner, its neural networks a childlike (but inhuman) learning brain.

At first glance, human factors may not appear to feature in the machine. This level of machine intelligence will not seek to psych an opponent in a game and nor will it get emotionally tired, drained or frustrated, and tip up the board, or become erratic and go home with a headache! One can imagine that machine intelligence may, though, subtly, and perhaps harmfully, distort the human world it samples and learns from, as it evolves. It may break down or get too difficult or expensive to sustain. As it interacts with and influences the wider world, that world will change, and the problems addressed there with machine intelligence will, too. New challenges to human governance will arise.

Digging deeper in one particular 'world' of specialism does not necessarily lead to a 'better' solution, when set against the immense breadth and variability of human phenotype, knowledge and behaviour intrinsic to the wider 'world' of health care. It may create new problem domains where machine intelligence, itself, becomes part of the 'problem'. What might a world look like where a Go or essay-writing competition is battled between AlphaGo- and ChatGPT-like machines? Of course, they will have come up with much more taxing pastimes! Machine fusion, powered by nuclear fusion, resulting in human confusion is probably best avoided! Such are some of the real and imagined issues that look to face us in coming to terms with what the world now recognizes as AI, and these have to be weighed experimentally, in human ways, in the real world.

In September 2019, a thoughtful and fluently interesting article appeared in the *Times* newspaper, characteristic of its well-respected journalist author, David Aaronovitch. It headlined the potential future benefits of AI in medicine, drawing extensively on a visit to see the work of a DeepMind AI company team collaborating with clinicians at my nearby Royal Free Hospital.[99] A patient, doctors and nurses at the hospital were quoted as expressing strong endorsement of the revolutionary benefits flowing from a DeepMind software App called Streams, that they had been piloting on their wards. They described the clinical insight it provided, by monitoring and alerting the team to significant deterioration of a patient's kidney function, in a timely manner that enabled effective intervention to support and stabilize them.

The article made a sharp comparison of the reported frequent failings of the breakdown-prone hospital-wide information system in use, with

---

99   D. Aaronovitch, 'DeepMind, Artificial Intelligence and the Future of the NHS', *The Times* (14 September 2019), https://www.thetimes.co.uk/article/deepmind-artificial-intelligence-and-the-future-of-the-nhs-r8c28v3j6

the clinical utility of this free-standing App. The App itself accessed a limited subset of the patient record, as stored on the hospital system, and communicated directly with mobile devices carried by clinicians treating the patient concerned, alerting them to imminent and acutely threatening kidney injury (AKI). The article made further connections with pioneering work on AI in the USA, including in the Veterans Administration health system, exploring the efficacy of AI systems to help analyze patient data–for example providing accurate interpretations of clinical images and timely alerts about detected adverse trends–and optimize and streamline workflow for clinical teams.

There are a number of issues here, which illustrate the checkered pathway along which AI is rapidly evolving, today. I consider these further in the context of factors shaping future health care, in Chapter Eight. There, I describe an authoritative 2019 book (surely an inukbook) by the eminent clinician and medical scientist, Eric Topol, in which he reviewed and provided a wide perspective on the field.[100] He quotes what he calls a published 'sharp critique' of the domain and key points made there, including about the lack of transparency in its methods and 'growing (often self-interested) misinformation and mystification of the field'.[101] He was interviewed, and his book cited, for the *Times* article.

When I read the article, I was both impressed and surprised. The message about AI was a good one but the lead-in and main story about a patient and clinical team, which served effectively to humanize and dramatize its impact, was misleading. First, the Streams App reported was apparently a version based on a straightforward calculation using measurements of creatinine level in blood samples, not on any much more complex computation associated with and conjured in the reader's mind by the term artificial intelligence. Thus, the approval reported was not a reflection of AI, but rather of an important much-improved clinical workflow that the App enabled. Apparently, the measurements of creatinine level that the App used were already being collected and filed in the hospital IT system, but their significance was not being detected there, and was thus not alerted to the clinicians overseeing care. The long article did say, later on, that the Streams App was not based on AI. But then, if so, why use it in this way to promote a message about the potential benefits of AI?

In this regard, I recalled a paper from forty years ago, with authors including the current President of the Royal Society, the eminent statistician of Bayesian methods, Adrian Smith. This reported that a Kalman-filtered time

---

100 E. Topol, Deep Medicine: *How Artificial Intelligence Can Make Healthcare Human Again* (London: Hachette, 2019).

101 Ibid., p. 94.

series of essentially the same creatinine measurements, enabled a similar, up to several days, advance warning of imminent failure of kidney function, relative to that which was otherwise evident to attending clinicians–for renal transplant patients in that case.[102] I remembered collecting the paper and communicating with its authors at the time. A later section of the *Times* article described progress in development of AI methods, achieving similar detection and advance warning of significant clinical problems. It reported a visit to a Veterans Health Administration (VA) hospital in the US, where AI researchers extolled the potential of AI in enabling these benefits.

If this level of clinical impact is now seen as revolutionary, and on the face of it, it certainly appears so, why has it not been pursued with the statistical methods explored and reported forty years ago, and become a recognized standard practice over those intervening decades? Does labelling it as an example of AI somehow give it a magical status and justify its realization now, through AI becoming a priority?

All that said, it is entirely feasible that present-day state-of-the-art machine learning algorithms will progress to make immense contributions in preventive medicine and the further enhancing and streamlining of health care services–whether providing AKI alerts, detecting adverse pathology in radiographic images or retinal investigations, identifying and monitoring population subgroups at specific risk of disease, guiding patient self-care, or the like, and whether used in the patient's home, or a care home or hospital setting. Based on that reported experience at the Royal Free Hospital, it was, though, incautious exaggeration to align AI with the benefits reported– clinically, economically, and in both staff and patient appreciation–since no machine learning method was then involved. Unfortunately, hyped and uncritical projections about the health care benefits of AI are rather common at present. Such Apps as the one described in the article are a front end of the improved information flow on which AI can and will feed. A key observation, also made by Topol in his landmark 2019 review of health care workforce for the NHS, and in his book, is that to work well and beneficially, such new method will require coherent, accessible and timely digital care records, which is a central concern for the patient-centred care information utility advocated in this book.

There is a further relevant and evolving perspective about AI arising from the analysis and prediction of weather systems. Today, as the modelling of these systems combines with machine intelligence, both are proving differently advantageous in forecasting of weather and what is

---

102   I. M. Trimble, M. West, M. S. Knapp, R. Pownall and A. F. Smith, Detection of Renal Allograft Rejection by Computer', *BMJ*, 286.6379 (1983), 1695–99, https:// doi.org/10.1136/bmj.286.6379.1695

being called its 'nowcasting'. For an immediate (now) prediction of local weather trends, machine intelligence can nowcast based on measurements of the current weather, including wind, temperature, cloud cover and time of day, to outperform complex physics-based model predictions. Longer-term and wide-area forecasts are still the preserve of complex models of atmospheric physics.

At this point in the book, and after peering briefly to a future reality of AI-supported health care, it seems appropriate to come back down to earth, in the here and now. The applications of computational logic and reasoning are experimental; however, as their ambition broadens in scope, the feasibility of conducting controlled experiments to study and make informed decisions about them diminishes. Somehow, our age has become of the mind that such applications are not of an experimental kind– often treating them, in embryo, as mature in form. Treating principles of computation as purely technical abstractions has had a harmful influence on the interplay of information technology and medicine. The interaction of science and technology with health care engages with personal and social problems as much as with mathematical and scientific ones, and the field of health informatics has often lacked, and not sufficiently prioritized, practical engineering interface between these related scientific and social domains. The framing of policy for services that bridge them has been characterized as a 'wicked problem'. Such problems feature throughout the book, though I discuss them in the context of health care policy specifically in Chapter Seven.

The interactions of theory with experiment and practice, accumulate as the storyline and chapters of the book moves around the Ranganathan circle, through the worlds of philosophy, mathematics, science and engineering, into the worlds of life science, medicine and health care information systems. The importance of efforts to study and experiment with their interconnections, in the context of the grand challenges they illuminate and address, is common sense. But a relevant community and environment in which to achieve a credible balance of theory with tractable and sustained implementation, where such experiment can proceed and prosper, has proved exceptionally hard to create and manage. There have been notable exceptions and I describe a number in Chapter Eight, and the pioneers who created and led them, and enabled good things to happen there.

The story now moves into the world of medical language and computation. In this, I focus on two examples of knowledge representation taken from the medical and clinical domain–the clinical terminology SNOMED, and the Foundational Model of Anatomy (FMA). They exemplify the state of the art in software whereby knowledge can be represented and used to create programs that organize, search and reason in these domains. They illustrate two general forms for representing hierarchy of knowledge, termed 'compositional containment hierarchy' (as exemplified by the FMA) and 'subsumptive containment hierarchy'(as exemplified now by SNOMED).[103] Here the container aims to provide a full and consistent description, at a chosen level of detail and within a chosen context of use. These initiatives illustrate the evolutionary interplay of knowledge, logic and machine capability in the practical problems tackled. They have been important foundational experiments–SNOMED, over many decades in exploring and developing theory and method in the context of practical health care requirements.

These two examples then bridge to the topics of Chapter Three, connecting from knowledge, language and reason to observation and measurement, and Chapter Four, broadening the discussion to the modelling of different kinds of systems, to represent and reason about their structure and function and the way they work.

Medical Language and Computation

In the storyline thus far, we have visited the historical evolution of library classifications, in their aim to achieve ordering of knowledge, and parallel quests to express, communicate and reason with knowledge, through verbal language, mathematics, logic and then computation. These histories have touched on examples from health care while setting the scene more generally for discussion, now, of the quest of recent decades to tame and computerize medical knowledge.

It has proved a perilous and contested terrain! One on which unsuspected dragons have revealed themselves, to become fired up and magnified in the Information Age! The quest to computerize always brings us face to face with what we know and do not know about a subject, how we express and communicate it, and how we reason with and from it. It challenges us as to why we are doing what we are doing, to what end and how well.

Medicine and health care appeared to offer enticingly rich pickings for computerization, in all these dimensions of expression, communication and reasoning with knowledge. Early endeavours focused on creating dictionaries and databases of medical and health care language and terminology. These evolved into quests for logical rigour and consistency in taming the huge and multi-faceted corpora of terminologies and classifications of knowledge

---

103 For basic definitions of these subtypes of hierarchy, see Wikipedia contributors, 'Hierarchy', *Wikipedia, The Free Encyclopedia* (21 June 2023), https://en.wikipedia.org/wiki/Hierarchy

that emerged, reflecting different but overlapping purposes, goals, methods and governance. It has been a torturous escapade of discovery, with some, but not much, low-hanging fruit found on these growing computerized trees of knowledge. They were more like a coconut palm–a very tall trunk to climb before reaching the fruit, with the coconuts often falling on the brave climbers' heads before they reached them!

Terminologies used in expressing ideas are noisy and imprecise and so may be the judgements based upon them. A connecting thought caught my attention when re-reading Whitehead's *Adventures of Ideas*, as I was considering how to construct this section of the Chapter. In Chapter XV on Philosophic Method, where he is discussing how we use language to express and generalize experience, he says that what may appear a redundancy of terms used, is in fact required and that 'the words correct each other' in conveying meaning. In this sense, tying expression to a limited vocabulary risks limiting and harming communication of meaning.

On another occasion, preparing for writing Chapter Six, I was re-reading an equally wonderful book, *Feynman Lectures on Computation*, where binary coding and transmission of electrical signals are discussed in relation to the methods used to correct errors generated by the electrical noise experienced during their transmission.[104] Here again, redundancy in the transmitted binary data is key to its accurate communication. Error-correction methods, without which no digital network infrastructure can function, work on the principle of transmitting redundant additional data, which is generated from the signal being encoded and tagged onto it during transmission. The system of coding is designed such that the undamaged transmitted data can be reconstructed, to an extremely high degree of accuracy, from the noise-beset erroneous data received. This is at the expense of transmitting the redundant bits of the digital signal and the encoding and decoding process needed to set up the transmission of messages and detect and correct for any errors encountered.

Communication of meaning about individual health care is prone to all manner of noise, discontinuity and imprecision. During my career, I sat for many years within hearing distance of the lunch-time discussions among clinicians about their patients. It is a very efficient channel but not widely scalable to the high-intensity, multi-faceted, distributed settings of health care today. Where we computerize these records and communications, it is essential that their human meanings are communicated well. Clinical meaning is poorly communicated between today's non-coherent digital care

---

104 R. P. Feynman, *Feynman Lectures on Computation* (New York: CRC Press, 2018).

record systems. The motivation of openEHR, as discussed in Chapter Eight and a Half, has been foursquare focussed on improving this reality.

Records of health care are both narrative and structured datasets. They connect with the personal story of the individual patient and the professional record of their care. The records of individuals also need to be shared and integrated within the wider health care system. Achieving expressiveness in the natural language of the record and formal structure that facilitates meaningful access, analysis and communication, more widely, places natural language in apposition to language of the computer system. These goals pose complex requirements and the solutions thus far evolved have been a complicated mix.

Natural Language and Medicine

Joseph Weizenbaum (1923–2008) expressed concern about language in relation to medicine and computation. His seminal book, *Computer Power and Human Reason*, features strongly in my Chapter Seven, where I move on to discussion of health care services.[105] He spoke of language used for the organization of facts and assertion of axioms and theorems, in the context of processes.

> Human language in actual use is infinitely more problematical than those aspects of it that are amenable to treatment by information theory [...] language involves the histories of those using it, hence the history of society, indeed, of all humanity generally. And language in human use is not merely functional in the way that computer languages are functional. It does not identify things and words only with immediate goals to be achieved or with objects to be transformed. Human use of language manifests human memory. And that is a quite different thing than the store of the computer, which has been anthropomorphized into 'memory'. The former gives rise to hopes and fears, for example. It is hard to see what it could mean to say the computer hopes.[106]

Notably, he comments:

> Even the kinds of knowledge that appear superficially to be communicable from one human being to another in language alone are in fact not altogether so communicable. Claude Shannon showed that, even in abstract information theory, the 'information content' of a message is not

---

105 J. Weizenbaum, *Computer Power and Human Reason: From Judgment to Calculation* (Harmondsworth: Penguin Books, 1993).
106 Ibid., p. 209.

a function of the message alone but depends crucially on the state of knowledge, on the expectations, of the receiver.[107]

The quest to constrain expressiveness by enforced normalization of language has a history. In his book *Medical Nemesis*, Ivan Illich (1926–2002) records that, in 1635, Cardinal Richelieu (1585–1642) set up an Academia of distinguished scholars of French literature, for the purpose of protecting and perfecting the French Language.[108] They imposed and mandated an elite language of the bourgeoisie and made it normative for all social classes. The term 'normal' has history as well. Illich also wrote that in England of the 1830s, normal was a geometrical term for perpendicular, or standing at a right angle. In the 1840s it was generalized to mean conforming to a common type. And around 1840, Auguste Comte (1798–1857), in France, talked of the laws relative to the normal state of an organism as a basis for study of comparative pathology. In that era, pathology was largely used to classify anatomical anomalies, and, towards the end of the century, Claude Bernard (1813–78) started to label and catalogue functions and homeostasis of the body. Clinical normality gradually became associated with wellbeing.

Specializations of medicine have led to ever more extensive vocabulary and complexity of language used to name, group, describe and record thoughts, ideas and reasoning. In the Information Age, these have extended beyond dictionaries to databases. Terms and their interrelationships have been grouped and expressed as hierarchies, enabling computer programs to meaningfully and rigorously handle a vast corpus of terms that would otherwise be unmanageable for humans. Here have arisen clinical terms as codes used to label and integrate medical knowledge with the procedures and reasoning of clinical practice. It is hard for humans to master consistent use of the hundreds of thousands of terms of the language that have arisen in this way. Their selection and use are increasingly enacted using machine software.

Nomenclature and Terminology

There is a story told of a blinded set of observers presented with a huge elephant and each asked to feel its body and describe it in words. One encounters the tail, another the tusks, another the trunk and another the legs. The contrasting descriptions they give are all true, but incomplete and inadequate to describe the elephant. How they connect would be missing

---

107 Ibid.

108 I. Illich, *Limits to Medicine: Medical Nemesis: The Expropriation of Health* (London: Boyars, 1995), pp. 115–16.

from these descriptions, even if they are simply concatenated together. Neither medicine, nor health care, more generally, nor the individual citizen cared for, are elephants, but they are huge in the sense of the domains of knowledge and data that they encompass. The descriptive range covered in these domains is likewise huge, and prone to intractable problems when seeking to draw together disparate descriptions, connections and communications, to in some way faithfully represent the wholeness of health care, as it affects and is experienced by individual citizens. This has been an elephant in the room, where blinded observers have often flailed and failed to connect reality with the computer, from the outset of the Information Age. That story is told in Part Two of the book.

The decades-long struggle for the standardization of electronic care records serves as a persistent testament to wider endeavours that have involved and implicated the computer in the ways we understand and express our knowledge of what medicine and health care services are, and what they do. Care services require and depend on good records that are faithful to this understanding and kept up to date with relevant new knowledge. Record plays a central role in the connection, communication and application of the wholeness of this knowledge–logically, consistently and ethically. Central to faithful records are the terms and systems of terms (nomenclatures) used, the structure of relevant knowledge they reference and contain, and the logic of the reasoning and decisions they reflect.

It has proven extremely hard, if not as impossible as once it might have seemed, to compartmentalize the personal, professional and organizational content and context of records kept about each citizen and patient. As in the domain of library classifications discussed earlier in the chapter, this has developed into a battleground of rivalries and special interests–national, commercial, institutional and professional–with the patient, who is the focus of the record, spoken of and for, but too often left in the margins of the circle of those speaking. In the Information Society of the future, citizens will reclaim both their personal data and the common ground on which care record systems are centred and shared. That is the vision and perspective informing Part Three of the book, which looks forward to how it can now be created. In the story of how electronic care record standardization has evolved, there are illuminating parallels with the experience of library science in its efforts to move beyond enumerative hierarchies of terms and codes towards a compositional approach, using generic building blocks applicable at different levels of hierarchy and detail of content.

Lancelot Hogben (1895–1975) studied medicine at Trinity College, Cambridge and worked then as an experimental zoologist.[109] His wider interests extended to medical statistics, etymology of language and experimental biology. He recognized the struggle students had in learning the terminology of biology, especially those unfamiliar with etymology and classical language, and worked on an *interglossa*–a language for international communications–believing that eight hundred words constructed with very simple grammar, rooted in Latin and Greek, would suffice as a basic vocabulary across languages! He believed that an international committee could easily take it on and make it happen! It is hard not to smile wryly at this expression of belief, looking back over the years, but he was a great and lauded thinker, and such were the times.

Recent decades have seen rapid escalation in the scale and complexity of nomenclature and classification used in records descriptive of health care practice. The history of medical terminology, the clinical tasks it addresses and the challenge of adopting formal method, were covered in a 1980 review by Roger Côté and Stanley Robboy[110] and later reviews by James Cimino[111] and Cimino and Xinxin Zhu.[112]

There is continuing struggle to tame what might be called the linguistic noise and accumulating entropic disorder present in records, through their incorporation of imprecise and changing terminology and categories and structures of content, over time. If records are to be computable and sustainable throughout patients' lifetimes, consistent use of terms is important. GIGO (Garbage In, Garbage Out) may overstate the impact but NINO (Noise In, Noise Out!) is physical reality. Pretending otherwise is a no-no! One can artfully filter signal from noise, but noise remains noise, at whatever level of resolution–'random' signifies 'don't know'. Leaving aside

---

109 Lancelot Hogben's book, *Mathematics for the Million* (1936), was described by the historian and imaginer of future worlds, H. G. Wells (1866–1946), as of first-class importance and was praised by Einstein, Russell and Julian Huxley (1377–1975). He was socialist and atheist—in the First World War, he served in the Red Cross and Friends Ambulance Unit and in the second as curator of the army's medical statistics. His work in experimental zoology was recognized by the Royal Society in his fellowship there in 1936.

110 R. A. Côté and S. Robboy, 'Progress in Medical Information Management. Systematized Nomenclature of Medicine (SNOMED),' *JAMA: The Journal of the American Medical Association*, 243.8 (1980), 756–62, https://doi.org/10.1001/jama.243.8.756

111 J. J. Cimino, 'Desiderata for Controlled Medical Vocabularies in the Twenty-First Century,' *Methods of Information in Medicine*, 37.4–5 (1998), 394–403, https://doi.org/10.1055/s-0038-1634558

112 J. J. Cimino and X. Zhu, 'The Practical Impact of Ontologies on Biomedical Informatics', *Yearbook of Medical Informatics*, 15.01 (2006), 124–35, https://doi.org/10.1055/s-0038-1638470

the many frustrations and differences of opinion that have prevailed in this area, they do reflect real, and very difficult, problems experienced at the coalface of health care services.

Multiple perspectives and interests are in play when seeking greater clarity, coherence and usefulness of medical language. The benefits sought, and the burdens imposed in attempting to realize them, are experienced differently, in the contexts where professional practice is performed, and in those where it is managed and regulated. At the coalface of practice, the benefits are often fewer and the burdens often greater than they are perceived and experienced to be when sitting away from that front line, in places where policy is set and designs and plans are made and mandated for implementation.

Safe use of language for coding and classification of care records requires consistent methods and the availability of resources–people, time and money. It can assist rapid browsing and access to the relevant content of the record, during a consultation. It can enable subsequent extraction of data for secondary analysis elsewhere, in support of audit and resource management of clinical services, research and budgetary control. In UK hospitals, dedicated local teams navigate the immense collections of terms that are selected from when making, coding and classifying clinical records. They make decisions about how to use these terms to tag individual records and provide aggregate statistics descriptive of the care processes and outcomes of the services that the institution provides. This can bring further work for the clinicians whose records are being analyzed, drawing them into the checking of judgements made, where ambiguities have arisen. All this embeds closely with cost and remuneration of services, and the pursuit, and sometimes gaming, thereof.

A good way to meet these important but different requirements, in a less burdensome manner, has long been, and remains, urgently needed. Achieving this requires that the data can be drawn together across different component services, simply and accurately, within a coherent information framework. There has been considerable and costly redundancy of efforts in this regard. For example, as mentioned to me by a former UK Chief Medical Officer some years ago, there were then some thirty or more different systems in everyday use across the NHS, for generating the nationally mandated critical incident reports–collecting, structuring and mapping local disparate datasets to a centrally defined report template, as further discussed in Chapter Seven. And I have read that during the Covid pandemic, data from a hundred differently structured spreadsheets were regularly cut and pasted into an aggregated report for senior NHS management purposes.

If we decide to keep trying to improve record keeping–and as Chapter Seven will unfold in detail, over the past fifty years this has been recognized as a *sine qua non* of progress in health informatics–coherent, robust and connected specification and implementation of the related computational methods programmed and deployed, and clarity about their bounded domains of application, are imperative requirements. E. M. Forster's 'only connect', says it all, here, too. Otherwise, disconnection will propagate and the entropy of information and information system legacy will grow, because of the lack of such discipline.

Historically, considerable momentum was injected into coding and classification of medical language, long before rigorous methods of description logic had or could have crystallized. Today's health care information systems remain strongly influenced by the early methods that were used to organize them, substantially through 'pre-coordination' of pragmatically-structured lists of terms. This has inevitably led to a considerable legacy of codes and methods of coding that must now be accommodated within new methods experimented with. The complexity is compounded by the continuous emergence of requirements for new terms and the need to extend or redesign the structures of the systems into which they fit. 'Post-coordination' of terms (creating new terms from combinations of existing ones), though tractable, has been found a difficult and onerous method to implement and sustain rigorously in practice. The result has been shaky edifices that have struggled, after initial enthusiasm and support, to reinforce or underpin their foundations with new more formal methods, and thereby reinvent themselves within changing contexts. However, the legacy of systems in current use was hard to achieve and expensively won, and it is hard to justify and seldom if ever seems timely to change them.

The limitation and Achilles' heel of pragmatic decisions about medical and health care language (focused on the here and now of the domains represented, and adjusted piecemeal to changing requirements over time) is the incremental complexity and blurring of the imposed order of the system of terminology adopted. Entropy accumulates within the system and impedes further evolution and change, requiring continuous work for maintenance of the current system, to keep it in order and functioning. That is physics and that is life!

The promise of a stable and expressive description logic is that its adoption would provide rigorous discipline and tooling in support of this curation task. It would provide a framework whereby the coherence and consistency of the nomenclature could be validated and analyzed, using generic software tools based on the adopted description logic formalism. Once established and well-grounded in custom and practice, this would facilitate smoother evolution alongside changing requirements. Of course, a model of the term set expressed in formal logic is itself a complex design. It requires anchoring expertise and engagement, spanning mathematics, computer science and engineering as well as medicine and health care, and suitable environments in which to draw them together.

In recent years, the SNOMED, ICD and UMLS (Uniform Medical Language System) systems–leading international initiatives that I introduce below–have experimented with description logic for restructuring their extensive and 'multiaxial hierarchies' of terms. The tools available to support this effort have continued to evolve, and, as ever, pragmatic choices have been needed to balance evolving theory of the underpinning computational methods and established practice in their application. The essence of these endeavours has been to represent the system of terms as an ensemble of logical descriptions of their form and content, expressed as a 'subsumption hierarchy'–one that subsumes and generalizes terms within hierarchies of detail, reflecting the knowledge they represent and how it fits together.

The brave and difficult SNOMED International initiative has received multi-government backing, initially orchestrated by my colleague, Martin Severs, as I describe below. Over recent years, merged with the UK NHS Read Codes project, they have taken the plunge and adopted description logic methods. Yet more recently, the ICD, the most venerable, and arguably most successful, of medical terminology initiatives, has also put its toes in the water to weigh up whether to jump in and swim towards the adoption of description logic methods. Another great colleague, Alan Rector, worked with a SNOMED- and ICD-knowledgeable team to confront the methodological issues that would need solutions to update ICD methods in this way, and facilitate alignment with the UMLS.[113] They reviewed the functionalities required and tools available to realize them, and described a combination of state-of-the-art description logic, frame-based logic and ad hoc code, that appeared suitable for the experiment.

In earlier years, Rector had pioneered a green field description logic approach to medical language, encyclopaedia and nomenclature, the 'len' of the 1991 EU GALEN Project, which I also introduce in a separate section below. As with the BSO for classification of books and documents, it failed, but Rector and his team's work has, nonetheless, been widely influential in the field. Failure to recognize and support this pioneering experimental initiative and help it achieve traction, was a highly consequential failure of policy of recent decades. Not that it was necessarily going to prove a successful approach in the short term, but the creation of a well-anchored and competent academic and professional environment and community of

---

113   UMLS is an initiative of the US National Library of Medicine, seeking to draw together the current medical language standards used in publication and record keeping, within a common framework. It is introduced briefly, below, alongside several other initiatives of note.

endeavour in description logic and medicine would have been a good goal to support, enable and sustain.

It is a struggle to keep one's feet on the ground in these emerging adventures of ideas, but that is what is needed to improve quality and achieve traction in the development of methodology and implementation of electronic care records. Staying power is also needed and this requires sponsorship. Lacking this cohesion, developments typically proceed piecemeal, and pragmatic choices made at each stage easily lead to sub-optimal combinations of the old and the new. These choices are fiercely debated by rival interests and critics of all the parties in play, whose teeth tend not to be biting the bullet of hard work involved in tackling the task at hand, on the ground.

Achieving expressiveness and rigour of computation and applying it efficiently and effectively in diverse health care contexts (while accommodating legacy systems and coming to terms with the opportunities and constraints of newly evolving, but often rapidly obsolescent, computational methods) is a multiplicative set of challenges. These play out alongside the rapid change, intrinsic uncertainty and difference of perspectives, implicit in individual patient care. It has been said that health care is the most fertile domain for proposing problems likely to benefit from the application of information technology, while, at the same time, the most difficult in which to realize the hoped-for benefits.

Experience of three attempts to underpin the concrete foundations of our house here in St Albans, have shown that such efforts can often be only temporary fixes! Problems continue to recur. Building a new house, possibly in a different place, might often prove a better long-term bet, but it costs money, and location matters! In a universal domain like an academic or professional discipline, we often wait for the structure to collapse before being forced to build anew. Thomas Kuhn (1922–96) and Gould have had something to say along these lines, about how paradigms of knowledge change through resistance to change and punctuation of equilibria.[114] Pressure towards a new home sometimes pushes the old one towards tipping over before it is ready to fall. Leaning structures, such as the famous Tower of Pisa, somehow manage to persist against seemingly poor odds, with the burghers of Pisa no doubt very keen and active, behind the scenes and viewing their tourism statistics and cash registers, that it should not fall!

On the following pages, I briefly highlight global initiatives working to standardize the language and nomenclature of medicine and health care,

---

114 T. S. Kuhn, *The Structure of Scientific Revolutions: 50th Anniversary Edition* (Chicago, IL: University of Chicago Press, 2012); Gould and Eldredge, 'Punctuated Equilibrium Comes of Age'.

drawing heavily on the up-to-date websites describing their work. I focus first on the two that are connected with my close colleagues of the era, Severs and Rector. They have played stellar roles in clinical and scientific leadership along the timelines of the SNOMED and GALEN initiatives.

SNOMED™–Systematized Nomenclature of Medicine[115]

SNOMED started as a library-like enumeration of terms used in records of care, organized and grouped under axes (facets) of topography (anatomic site), morphology (form), aetiology (origin) and function. It has grown into a present-day incarnation of hundreds of thousands of terms, each with unique code and linked in twenty hierarchies, organized as subsumptive containment structures.

SNOMED CT (Clinical Terms) describes itself as a multi-lingual, multinational logic-based health care terminology. It traces its origins to the Systematized Nomenclature of Pathology (SNOP), published in 1965 by the College of American Pathologists (CAP).

Here is the paraphrased story of its subsequent evolution, as told on the International Health Terminology Standards Development Organization (IHTSDO) website, now the SNOMED website. The IHTSDO now owns, develops and maintains it, trading under the name SNOMED International.

SNOMED I and II were released in 1974 and 1979.

SNOMED-RT (Reference Terminology) was released in 2001.

1999: Agreement was reached between the NHS and the College of American Pathologists to bring together the NHS Clinical Terms Version 3 (formerly known as the Read codes) and SNOMED-RT, under the umbrella of a new terminology, SNOMED CT. The final product was released in January 2002.

2003: The National Library of Medicine (NLM), on behalf of the United States Department of Health and Human Services, entered into an agreement with the College of American Pathologists to make SNOMED CT available to U.S. users at no cost, through the National Library of Medicine's Unified Medical Language System (UMLS) Metathesaurus.

2007: The International Health Terminology Standards Development Organization (IHTSDO) was established as an international SDO. SNOMED CT intellectual property rights were transferred from the

---

115 SNOMED, https://www.snomed.org

CAP to the IHTSDO, in order to promote international adoption and use of SNOMED CT. IHTSDO subsequently adopted the trading name, SNOMED International.

Rather than paraphrase, the following is quoted directly from the 2020 website, to give the flavour of the rapidly evolving initiative which now has received powerful and wide-ranging international backing.

> SNOMED RT, with over 120,000 concepts, had wide coverage of medical specialties and was designed to serve as a common reference terminology for the aggregation and retrieval of pathology health care data recorded by multiple organizations and individuals. The strength of CTV3 was its terminologies for general practice. With 200,000 interrelated concepts, it was used for storing structured information about primary care encounters in individual, patient-based records. The January 2020 release of the SNOMED CT International Edition now includes more than 350,000 concepts.

> SNOMED CT's primary purpose is to support all health care professionals in their recording and sharing of detailed patient information within Electronic Health Records (EHRs) and across health care communities globally. Its ontological foundations allow SNOMED CT data to support detailed data analytics to meet a variety of use cases from local requirements to population-based analytics. With the help of SNOMED CT, programs can translate different medical terms into an internationally standardized numerical code. In this way, clinical data from different countries can be compared and used for research. This creates the prerequisites for treating diseases more effectively in the future, recognizing them faster and supporting prevention. The networking of routine care data and top medical research has great potential–for better medical treatment and for strengthening business and science.

> With a complement of 39 Members, SNOMED CT now represents approximately one third of the global population. Adding to that complement with our affiliate licensees, SNOMED CT is now used in more than ninety countries globally.

> SNOMED CT is currently available in American English, British English, Spanish, Danish and Swedish, with other translations underway or nearly completed in French and Dutch.

> SNOMED CT cross maps to other terminologies, such as: ICD-9-CM, ICD-10, ICD-O-3, ICD-10-AM, Laboratory LOINC and OPCS-4. It supports ANSI, DICOM, HL7, and ISO standards.

The ontology foundations of SNOMED have evolved considerably over recent years. SNOP, SNOMED-RT, Read and CTV3, as well as LOINC, ICD-11 and UMLS do not employ formal logic at their core, with the inbuilt proof and checking of consistency that this provides. Multiaxial hierarchy and class overlap were introduced within the constraints of the EL++ subset of description logic–which lies between propositional and first-order logic, allowing overlapping of classes, in contrast to ICD-11. It provides for post-coordination of terms, drawing together pre-coordinated terms. Laterality and negation are not currently allowed for.

GALEN–Generalized Architecture for Languages, Encyclopaedias and Nomenclatures in Medicine

The GALEN project arose from the computer science community at the University of University, through the work of Rector's luminary team. Although transformational in potential, it suffered from a lack of parallel, everyday health care service support and grounding.

If there was ever a name to fit the acronym, this must be it! GALEN is remembered for his role in the invention of medicine and contributions to the evolution of Aristotle's logic. The parallel is fitting–Rector, father of this initiative, was a notable pioneer. In the language of Ranganathan, GALEN is an 'analytico-synthetic' method for composing codes. In this respect, its approach, as specifically characterized, below, in bullet point five, bears resemblance to the 'switching language' concept of the BSO.

Again, quoting extensively from the now no-longer hosted GALEN website (as with others mentioned in the following section, like ICPC, this is no longer maintained):

> GALEN is the name given to a technology that is designed to represent clinical information in a new way and is intended to 'put the clinical into the clinical workstation'. GALEN produces a computer-based multilingual coding system for medicine, using a qualitatively different approach from those used in the past. GALEN is attempting to meet five challenges:
>
> - To reconcile diversity of needs for terminology with the requirement to share information
>
> - To avoid exponentially rising costs for harmonization of variants
>
> - To facilitate clinical applications
>
> - To bridge the gap between the detail required for patient care and the abstractions required for statistical, management, and research purposes

- To provide multilingual systems which preserve the underlying meaning and representation

To do so, GALEN advocates five fundamental paradigm shifts to resolve the fundamental dilemmas that face traditional terminology, coding and classification systems:

1. *In the user interface*, to shift from selecting codes to describing conditions. Interfaces using GALEN technology allow a central concept to be described through simple forms. If required, a precise code for reporting can be generated later automatically.

2. *In the structure*, to shift from enumerated codes to composite descriptions. Correspondingly, GALEN handles terminology internally analogously to a dictionary and a grammar so that indefinitely many descriptions can be composed from a manageable number of base concepts. Traditional coding systems are more like a phrase book; each sentence must be listed separately. No one would think of trying to list all the possible sentences in any natural language in a phrase book; listing all possible disease or procedure terms in a coding system is equally fruitless.

3. *In establishing standards*, to shift from a standard coding system to a standard reference model. Existing coding and classifications differ because they are used for different purposes. Finding a single fixed set of codes for all diseases, procedures, etc. which will serve all purposes is a chimera. The GALEN Common Reference Model provides a common means of representing coding and classification systems so that they can be inter-related–a common dictionary and grammar. The project's slogan is 'coherence without uniformity'.

4. *In delivery*, to shift from static coding systems as data to dynamic terminology services as software. Terminology is now at the clinical software. GALEN originated the idea of a terminology server and is participating actively in the CorbaMed effort at standardizing the software interface.

5. *In presentation*, to shift from translations of monolingual terminologies to multilingual terminologies. GALEN separates the underlying concepts from the surface natural language that presents them.

The founders established OpenGALEN as a not-for-profit organization to enable the widest possible exploitation of some of the results of the GALEN Programme. GALEN is built around what is called the GALEN Core:

> The GALEN CORE Model for representation of the Common Reference Model for Procedures contains the building blocks for defining procedures–the anatomy, surgical deeds, diseases, and their modifiers used in the definitions of surgical procedures. This document describes the structure of the CORE model and gives a detailed account of its high-level schemata followed by a detailed example of the use of the ontology for a portion of the model of the cardiovascular system and diseases.
>
> The ontology for the GALEN CORE model is designed to be re-usable and application independent. It is intended to serve not only for the classification of surgical procedures but also for a wide variety of other applications–electronic health care records (EHCRs), clinical user interfaces, decision support systems, knowledge access systems, and natural language processing. The ontology is constructed according to carefully selected principles so that the reasons for classification are always explicit within the model and therefore available for processing and analysis by each application. This leads to an ontology in which most information lies in the descriptions and definitions. The hierarchies are built bottom-up automatically based on these definitions.
>
> Note that the word ontology has acquired a range of meanings in various communities. Following the usage of Guarino [Guarino and Giaretta 1995], it is used here with a lowercase *o* or in the plural to indicate the set of primitive, high-level categories in a knowledge representation scheme together with any taxonomy which structures those categories.
>
> Quality assurance of the model is an ongoing process. The most important quality assurance of the building blocks comes from the checks on the correct classification things built with them–the model of procedures and the other models for subspecialties being built in collaboration with other projects. Preliminary results from such checks are extremely promising.
>
> The structure of the model is now believed to be complete, but there remain many details of anatomy and diseases to complete for each subspecialty area. Future development of the model is governed by the requirements of the applications and the needs of the centres who are using it to develop classifications of procedures. The next areas to be addressed will be based on the needs of vascular, ENT, orthopaedic, and gynaecological surgery to meet the requirements and priorities of those centres.

Some authors succeed in summarizing a field so well, at a point in time, that it would feel almost an insult to paraphrase them. The seminal paper describing the challenges of aligning ICD-11 within a framework of formal logic, where Rector played a leading role, has been previously cited. The conclusions provide a classic account of the state of the art in 2019. Again, it would be a disservice to paraphrase, albeit that the quotations here abbreviate the authors' deep understanding of the domain, and further insight requires engagement with the paper itself and its references.

> In general, reasoning about classes ('T-Box reasoning') can be optimized computationally (although in expressive dialects it is worst-case intractable). However, reasoning about individuals ('A-box reasoning') is much more difficult. Conveniently, it is primarily axioms about classes that are relevant for terminologies, *e.g.,* axioms about the classes of lungs, pneumonias, bacteria, penicillin preparations, etc.

> [...] The reasoning path, or 'justification' leading to inferences in OWL/DLs can be surprisingly difficult to work out by manual inspection. Unlike the closed world reasoning in logic programming methods such as Prolog or MYCIN, there is no way to accumulate a simple explanatory trail in the course of the proof. This has led to a body of research on methods for generating 'justifications' computationally.

> [...] Almost all statements about signs and symptoms in medicine– and many characteristics in genetics, genomics, and biomedicine more widely–are subject to exceptions, *i.e.,* they are 'defeasible' or, in our vocabulary, they are 'generalizations'.

> [...] To summarize: in closed-world representations, 'not' means 'not found or derived based on the individuals explicitly in the knowledge base'; 'all' means 'all found or derived'.

> [...] The Information Retrieval and Librarianship communities have a long history of systematic methods for organizing and classifying terminologies, thesauri and other knowledge artefacts, much of it shared with the linguistic community. Standards based on this work include the work of ISO TC-37, especially the ISO standards 704 and 1087. The most important example in biomedicine is the UMLS Semantic Network.

> [...] Description logics were a major advance for expressing invariant/indefeasible statements but are fundamentally unable to express generalizations/defeasible statements. The conflict between expressiveness, logical completeness and computational tractability has been a recurring theme in the knowledge representation research, see for example Doyle and Patil. Regrettably, frames, description logics, and ICD-like structures were often seen as rivals rather than complementary. The ICD-11 project required articulating their complementarities, an instructive example of practical development helping to elucidate theory.

> [...] Conclusion

In summary, OWL has been a major step forward for representing terminologies and the invariant part of background knowledge bases. However, the W3C's standardization on OWL has led to pressure to use OWL, often beyond its limitations, and contributed to confusion over vocabulary and to neglect and misunderstanding of other representations.

The experience in the ICD-11 project is that, although it is not possible to express frames in OWL or OWL in frames, it is possible to combine them in hybrid systems that take advantage of the semantics of each without violating the semantics of either. Likewise, while it is not possible to represent systems such as ICD based on JEPD (Jointly Exhaustive Pairwise Disjoint) mono-hierarchies in either Frames or OWL, it is possible to link them through queries. Associations for navigation and language are needed by most applications but should be distinguished from statements with other semantics. SKOS (note: Simple Knowledge Organization System, is a W3C standard, based on other Semantic Web standards (RDF and OWL)), often provides a useful set of relations for this purpose.

If symbolic knowledge representation is to continue to play a role in biomedical information systems, our experience is that such architectures need to be further developed and standardized, preferably within an integrated environment.[116]

In this last paragraph, the paper connects back to a general theme exemplified in the storyline of this book. One might say, *plus ça change, plus c'est la même chose*! GALEN was a seminal initiative towards modernization of health terminology systems in the Information Age, comparable to the BSO of former decades. And like BSO, it drifted onto the rocks when it failed to connect and develop at scale, within the practical and everyday context of coding and classification of medical records, which it was designed to support.

Further Notable Medical Language and Terminology Initiatives

The history of medical terminologies is a long one, and impossible to encompass in detail within the broad range of this book. As with the forgoing truncation of discussion of formal logic, the following section aims only to give the flavour of key initiatives. It relies on, and quotes from, their current websites, where detailed and up-to-date descriptions can be found.

---

116 Rector et al., 'On Beyond Gruber', pp. 4–13.

UMLS–Uniform Medical Language System[117]

This initiative of the National Library of Medicine has built on its substantial role in collating, first the paper-based Index Medicus of publications and then the online version known as Medline/Medlars. It 'integrates and distributes key terminology, classification and coding standards, and associated resources to promote creation of more effective and interoperable biomedical information systems and services, including electronic health records.

The component parts of UMLS are:

1. The Specialist Lexicon

The SPECIALIST Lexicon is an English lexicon (dictionary) that includes biomedical terms as well as commonly occurring English words. The lexical entry for each word or term records the following information:

- Syntactic (syntax information)
- Morphological (inflection, derivation, and composition information)
- Orthographic (spelling information)

Currently the SPECIALIST Lexicon contains over 200,000 terms and is used by the lexical tools to aid in Natural Language Processing. Words are selected for entry into the Specialist lexicon from a variety of sources:

- The UMLS Test Collection of MEDLINE abstracts
- *Dorland's Illustrated Medical Dictionary*
- *The American Heritage Word Frequency Book*
- *Longman's Dictionary of Contemporary English*
- Current MEDLINE citation records[118]

2. The Metathesaurus

Over 100 vocabularies, code sets, and thesauri, or 'source vocabularies' are brought together to create the Metathesaurus. Terms from each source vocabulary are organized by meaning and assigned a concept unique identifier (CUI).

---

117 'Unified Medical Language System', *National Library of Medicine*, https://www.nlm.nih.gov/research/umls/index.html

118 'The SPECIALIST Lexicon', *National Library of Medicine*, https://www.nlm.nih.gov/research/umls/new_users/online_learning/LEX_001.html

Sixty-two percent of the Metathesaurus source vocabularies are in English. However, the Metathesaurus also contains terms from seventeen other languages such as Spanish, French, Dutch, Italian, Japanese, and Portuguese.[119]

3. The Semantic Network

The Semantic Network consists of semantic types and semantic relationships. Semantic types are broad subject categories, like Disease or Syndrome or Clinical Drug. Semantic relationships are useful relationships that exist between semantic types. For example: Clinical Drug treats Disease or Syndrome. The Semantic Network is used in applications to help interpret meaning.[120]

[...] The Semantic Network consists of:

- Semantic types (high level categories)

- Semantic relationships (relationships between semantic types)

The Semantic Network can be used to categorize any medical vocabulary.

There are 133 semantic types in the Semantic Network. Every Metathesaurus concept is assigned at least one semantic type; very few terms are assigned as many as five semantic types. Semantic types are listed in the Metathesaurus file MRSTY.RRF.

Semantic types and semantic relationships create a network that represents the biomedical domain.[121]

---

119   'The Metathesaurus', *National Library of Medicine*, https://www.nlm.nih.gov/research/umls/new_users/online_learning/Meta_001.html

120   'The Semantic Network', *National Library of Medicine*, https://www.nlm.nih.gov/research/umls/new_users/online_learning/OVR_003.html

121   'The Semantic Network', *National Library of Medicine*, https://www.nlm.nih.gov/research/umls/new_users/online_learning/SEM_001.html

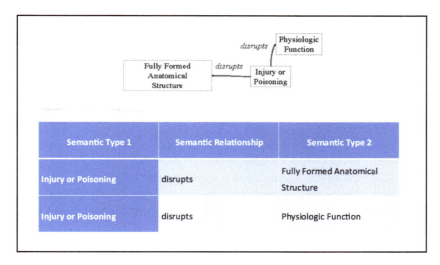

Fig. 2.3 An illustration of semantic relations. Image created by David Ingram (2022), based on details from the USA National Library of Medicine website, https://www.nlm.nih.gov/research/umls/new_users/online_learning/SEM_001.html

Semantic types and relationships help with interpreting the meaning that has been assigned to the Metathesaurus concept. This graphic adapted from the website (Figure 2.3) illustrates two semantic relationships. There are currently some fifty-four semantic relations defined. Tools are provided to assist parsing of natural language about any biomedical topic, seeking to recognize words, in whatever form they are expressed or spelt, by reference to the two hundred thousand-strong semantic lexicon. These are then mapped to what is sometimes called a 'controlled vocabulary', in this case that of the vocabulary or concepts of the Metathesaurus. In this usage, the controlled vocabulary being built on is the set of source vocabularies, each of them a thesaurus, embodied in the Metathesaurus. The Metathesaurus is a thesaurus of thesauri! Following on in the website description, 'The UMLS Metathesaurus organizes all of the original data from the source vocabulary including unique identifiers, definitions, or term spelling variants into a common format'.[122]

---

122 'The Metathesaurus', *National Library of Medicine*, https://www.nlm.nih.gov/research/umls/new_users/online_learning/Meta_001.html

The next step is to take the resulting words–that re-express the originals in the terms of the controlled vocabulary–and map their meaning, in the sense of semantic 'type' and 'relationship', as specified in the semantic network, and the much smaller, but still very wide-ranging model of types and semantic relationships that it provides.

So far and so good. When creating or invoking any model, an important first step is to know why we are doing it and what we plan to use it for. We then come better equipped with a sense of how it will be employed and how it will enable things to be done better. In these respects, the librarian's perspective is, quite rightly, predominant, given the organization (the US National Library of Medicine) that is leading these efforts. The purpose of UMLS parallels the librarians' challenge described earlier in the chapter. It is one of organization of materials, but here the challenge is not where to place the document or book as much as: what is being discussed here and how can I group and generalize all potentially relevant resources within a simplified, useful and computable structure? The driver is one of automation to support management of the exploding contexts of both knowledge semantics and scale of curation required. There is still human control applied in defining the methods adopted. We should be aware that an initiative like this appears to be progressing towards a time when such a purpose will be wholly within scope of machine control, when it will no longer be just human knowledge that is being organized.

The UMLS is reaching its capable arms around the very substantial and still growing challenge of managing medical literature. The integrative methods that it embodies, embracing the many vocabularies, semantic types and relations of medicine and health care, has scaled satisfactorily thus far. It has not dropped the ball, but at some future point, the balance of human and machine effort required may well fail again, and a heavier ball will drop. The benefits to student, researcher and librarian, alike, in managing the new world of literature, are phenomenal, as compared with the time and effort required for the hit-and-miss work involved in reading through and taking notes from Index Medicus of yesteryear, and sending off letters requesting to borrow copies, or receive reprints, of published books and papers. But these very limitations shaped as much as constrained academic discourse of the times. Set free from such limitations, with machine software making decisions required to carry the load, the new methods reflect into a qualitatively different human discourse. Scale and metrication of publication has exploded, bringing new burden and constraint. When we step from the world of education and research into the world of providing and recording services for direct health care, expectations of well-curated documents and records impose new burdens on practitioners, where they require new expertise to interface with an ever-increasing and evolving standardized use of language and codification of knowledge. If the machine takes over that burden in ways that do not chime with human meanings, the real and virtual worlds will further divide.

MeSH–Medical Subject Headings[123]

The MeSH initiative started from the other end of the scale, with the purpose of creating standardized descriptors of a document, to assist in the positioning and retrieval of relevant information from a collection of documents, by giving them a consistent and coherent system of headings. Again, the following rests heavily on up-to-date reference to its website.

> The Medical Subject Headings (MeSH®) thesaurus is a controlled vocabulary produced by the National Library of Medicine and used for indexing, cataloguing, and searching for biomedical and health-related information and documents.
>
> MeSH includes the subject descriptors appearing in MEDLINE®/ PubMed® and other NLM databases. MeSH provides a consistent way to find content with different terminology but the same concepts. MeSH organizes its descriptors in a hierarchical structure so that broad searches will find articles indexed more narrowly. This structure also provides an effective way for searchers to browse MeSH in order to find appropriate descriptors.
>
> The MeSH vocabulary is continually updated by subject specialists in various areas. Each year hundreds of new concepts are added, and thousands of modifications are made.
>
> Many synonyms, near-synonyms, and closely related concepts are included as entry terms to help users find the most relevant MeSH descriptor for the concept they are seeking. In NLM's online databases, many terms entered by searchers are automatically mapped to MeSH descriptors to facilitate retrieval of relevant information.[124]

The MeSH website records the history of its evolution since 1954. Many of the issues encountered in the development of the BSO initiative resurfaced there, such as alterative choices of headings and subheadings to group under, depending on topic, and overlap among chosen groupings. It was

---

123 'The Metathesaurus', *National Library of Medicine*, https://www.nlm.nih.gov/ research/umls/new_users/online_learning/Meta_001.html

124 'Medical Subject Headings: Preface', *National Library of Medicine*, https://www. nlm.nih.gov/mesh/intro_preface.html

a cultural change within NLM to bring together what had previously been separately designed and managed methods for compiling book catalogues and periodical article indexes.

The main heading-topical subheading combination is a pre-coordination of terms, reducing the problem of term permutation, which looms large in most manual retrieval systems in book form.

From its beginning, MeSH was intended to be a dynamic list, with procedures for recommending and examining the need for new headings. The content of the vocabulary related to the usage of terms in the literature itself and evolved to meet new concepts in the field. The use of the computer made revisions more practical and systematic, despite the difficulty in updating printed indexes and card catalogues.

Categorized lists of terms were printed for the first time in the 1963 *Medical Subject Headings* and contained thirteen main categories and a total of fifty-eight separate groups in subcategories and main categories. These categorized lists made it possible for the user to find many more related terms than were in the former cross-reference structure. In 1963, the second edition of *Medical Subject Headings* contained 5,700 descriptors, compared with 4,400 in the 1960 edition. Of the headings used in the 1960 list, 113 were withdrawn in favor of newer terms. In contrast, the 2015 edition of MeSH contains 27,455 descriptors and in 2021 there are 29,917 Descriptors and 270,373 Supplementary Concept Records.

In 1960, medical librarianship was on the cusp of a revolution. The first issue of the new *Index Medicus* series was published. On the horizon was a computerization project undertaken by the National Library of Medicine (NLM) to store and retrieve information. The Medical Literature Analysis and Retrieval System (MEDLARS®) would speed the publication process for bibliographies such as *Index Medicus*, facilitate the expansion of coverage of the literature, and permit searches for individuals upon demand. The new list of subject headings introduced in 1960 was the underpinning of the analysis and retrieval operation. MeSH was a new and thoroughly revised version of lists of subject headings compiled by NLM for its bibliographies and cataloging.[125]

---

125 Ibid.

ICD–International Classification of Diseases[126]

ICD describes itself thus on its website:[127]

> [as] the foundation for the identification of health trends and statistics globally, and the international standard for reporting diseases and health conditions. It is the diagnostic classification standard for all clinical and research purposes. ICD defines the universe of diseases, disorders, injuries, and other related health conditions, listed in a comprehensive, hierarchical fashion that allows for:
>
> - easy storage, retrieval and analysis of health information for evidenced-based decision-making;
>
> - sharing and comparing health information between hospitals, regions, settings and countries; and
>
> - data comparisons in the same location across different time periods.
>
> - Uses include monitoring of the incidence and prevalence of diseases, observing reimbursements and resource allocation trends, and keeping track of safety and quality guidelines. They also include the counting of deaths as well as diseases, injuries, symptoms, reasons for encounter, factors that influence health status, and external causes of disease.

And:

> The first international classification edition, known as the International List of Causes of Death, was adopted by the International Statistical Institute in 1893.
>
> WHO was entrusted with the ICD at its creation in 1948 and published the 6th version, ICD-6, that incorporated morbidity for the first time. The WHO Nomenclature Regulations, adopted in 1967, stipulated that Member States use the most current ICD revision for mortality and morbidity statistics. The ICD has been revised and published in a series of editions to reflect advances in health and medical science over time.
>
> ICD-10 was endorsed in May 1990 by the Forty-third World Health Assembly. It is cited in more than 20,000 scientific articles and used by more than 100 countries around the world.

---

126 'International Classification of Diseases (ICD)', *World Health Organization*. https://www.who.int/classifications/icd/en/

127 The text here is from the 2021 version of the ICD website which has now been superseded.

A version of ICD-11 was released on 18 June 2018 to allow Member States to prepare for implementation, including translating ICD into their national languages [...] Member States will start reporting using ICD-11 on 1 January 2022.

Bringing ICD-11 and SNOMED CT within a unifying framework of description logic has proved challenging. Rector et al. give a forensic review of the internal structure of ICD and the still intractable (because too expensive to rectify) methodological limitations it imposes on its future development.[128] Similar 'too big to fail' limitations came to wider attention when methods of formal logic were deployed to analyze their mutual consistency and coherence.

LOINC–Logical Observation, Identifiers, Names and Codes[129]

The longstanding and influential LOINC resource, first developed in 1994, started as a database and standard for identifying medical laboratory observations. It was created and is maintained by the Regenstrief Institute, a US non-profit medical research organization.

The initiative describes itself as follows:

[LOINC is] a common language (set of identifiers, names, and codes) for identifying health measurements, observations, and documents. If you think of an observation as a 'question' and the observation result value as an 'answer.' LOINC codes represent the 'question' for a test or measurement.

Where needed, codes from other standards (e.g., SNOMED CT) represent the 'answer.' Of course, you don't always need a code for the result value. For quantitative results, the 'answer' is just the numeric value–with its associated units of measure.

Most laboratory and clinical systems today are sending data out using the HL7 version 2 messaging standard).

The system allows for local coding standards to be applied, as synonyms, within the universal standard it provides.

---

128 'On Beyond Gruber'.
129 LOINC, https://loinc.org/

ICPC–International Classification of Primary Care[130]

ICPC was developed in stages, from 1987, originally under the name HICPIC. Its last published update was ICPC-2, in 2003, from Oxford University Press. It was recognized by the WHO Family of International Classifications (FIC) as a means for classifying reason for encounter in primary care and general practice, wherever applicable. It takes account of the frequency distribution of problems seen in these domains and allows classification of the patient's reason for encounter (RFE), the problems/diagnosis managed, interventions, and the ordering of these data in an episode of care structure.

The website of the WHO describes the ICPC structure as follows:

> It has a biaxial structure and consists of 17 chapters, each divided into 7 components dealing with symptoms and complaints (component 1), diagnostic, screening and preventive procedures (component 2), medication, treatment and procedures (component 3), test results (component 4), administrative (component 5), referrals and other reasons for encounter (component 6) and diseases (component 7).[131]

There is clearly huge overlap with the services of secondary care and the standards of terminology and classification used there. Although high profile in its time, the lack of update for the past almost twenty years, indicates that it has largely disappeared from use.

Two Illustrious Pioneers

It has been one of my great good fortunes to know and work alongside pioneers of our field, and two such are Martin Severs and Alan Rector. They have been strong and indomitable thinkers about fundamentals, and orchestrators of change at the coalface of practice. Alan has pushed for incorporation of the methods of description logic in organizing medical terminology and knowledge representation. Martin has pushed health care delivery to the centre of national policy for health informatics, breaking down barriers and building international collaboration, notably in establishing the IHTSDO (International Health Terminology and Standards Development Organization) and becoming its founding chair. Their contributions are akin to those of Ranganathan and Coates, whose stories I told in the first half of this chapter.

---

130 'International Classification of Primary Care, 2nd edition (ICPC-2)', *World Health Organization*, https://www.who.int/standards/classifications/other-classifications/international-classification-of-primary-care

131 Ibid.

It is one of the rewards of academic life to supervise doctoral students and it was an illuminating honour for me to be invited to examine some of Alan's great cadre of PhD students, some of whom continued very successfully in the world of health informatics. The role of reviewer of research, especially of large-scale projects bridging across disciplines, organizations and countries, is another such experience. It brings disjoint worlds of endeavour and enterprise together in dialogue among assessors, in hearing and responding to the evolving story and drama of research teams and their work. I will describe more such experiences in the next chapter, exploring biomathematical models of cancer treatment in cancer research. Here, I draw on my personal experience of working with Martin and Alan.

Martin Severs

Fig. 2.4 Martin Severs–clinician and founding father of SNOMED International and medical director of NHS Digital, curating the NHS data forest. Now wielding a chainsaw to curate his own forest near Portsmouth and enjoying the great outdoors. Photograph by Martin Severs, CC BY-NC.

Martin provided leadership, organizational and political skills, clinical expertise and insight, professionally and nationally. He showed extraordinary commitment and staying power in raising SNOMED International into the worldwide position it occupies today. It is a great regret that our combined efforts over two years, some fifteen years ago, to merge the openEHR mission within this organization that he created, were unsuccessful. Some twenty carefully constructed working papers and plans were voted down by its more influential international government representatives, perhaps because the project was seen as too disruptive of contemporary interests and legacy. I have preserved all these working documents in my personal document archive of the field and consulted them when writing here.

I first knew Martin through his several leadership roles: of the Royal College of Physicians of London Computer Committee and afterwards the Medical Informatics Group, then of SNOMED, internationally, and finally as Medical Director of NHS Digital. He immediately stood out in his concern for those at the coalface of health care services, helping them to adapt to and survive the increasing burdens faced in managing information resources and responding to increasing, managerially driven, audit and governance process demands.

He was always a doughty, honest and loyal warrior and friend. He understood that the practical exigencies and burdens of clinical practice imposed exacting limitations of time and capacity on what was achievable there in standardizing the coding of records. Whole departments were being devoted to manual determination of codes descriptive of clinical records. In the electronic capture of records, necessary and sufficient explanatory codes should arise and be recorded integrally with the workflow of care, although this workflow itself, and the skills required by clinical professionals, would necessarily need to evolve, too. He realized that the transition from individual practice to organizations and wider groupings of services would encounter differences of perspective when defining requirements and implementing standards at each level and scale, from local to national and international levels. It was thus a highly political, human and professional endeavour, requiring new organization and clout to cope with and counter operational intractability, inertia and dispute. The same sort of context that Coates had encountered and fought against, for many years, as I described above in the history of the BSO.

Martin's foremost achievement was his leadership of the SNOMED organization for a decade. As a practicing clinician, he had become interested in the coding of clinical practice through observing the inside story of Read Codes, named after James Read, a general practitioner who had composed a loosely structured compendium of the terms used in general practice. From this background, he achieved reputation, trust and sponsorship at a national level, supporting its extension into the wider NHS Clinical Terms project, as a foundational level of recording in electronic patient records.

Established terminology such as the long-established International Classification of Diseases, was focused on what might now be termed static knowledge–although that characterization is, as ever, philosophically contentious. Static tends to mean what is included in and taught from contemporary textbooks of medicine. It consisted of a hierarchy of names of disorders, pragmatically structured and grouped according to discipline, and using the language of the day.

Read and SNOMED terms and codes branched further into new nomenclature for coding medical records, to enable the creation of more coherent and consistent textual accounts–thus more readily and reliably used, cross-referenced, searched and communicated. The terms covered the presenting problems of patients, investigations, clinical reasoning, actions and outcomes–the who did what, when, how and why of health care. They were generalizations and these mushroomed in range and detail, attempting to keep track of the almost infinite variety of patient journeys, treated in context of time, place and person. They started with pragmatic choices in representing this complexity, mirroring the history of library classifications of the content of documents and books, emerging from pragmatic and enumerative approaches towards a theory-based compositional structure of codes. SNOMED metamorphosed into SNOMED-RT to absorb the Read Codes. Read was substantially rewarded for assigning his copyright in these to the NHS.

Under Martin's determined leadership, SNOMED became an internationally backed and fast-growing organization, with United Nations (UN) formula-based national subscription to support its operations and strong defense of its copyright.

Alan Rector

Fig. 2.5 Alan Rector–pioneer of formal logic and its application to the curation of medical records and terminology. Now creating order in his vegetable garden and playing the piano, he tells me. CC BY-NC.

Alan was the intellectual powerhouse behind the GALEN initiative, on which he set to work around 1990. This was, in many ways, an analogous quest to the colon classification initiative of Ranganathan and conducted in very much the same pioneering spirit. Like Octo Barnett (1930–2020), a founding father of medical informatics, Alan brought personal grounding in both medicine and computer science.

I knew about Alan's alma mater, the University of Manchester, through its pioneering contributions in Computer Science and Engineering in the UK, in the days when it was world-leading in semiconductor physics and electronic engineering. Alan led a wide range of projects in electronic health records, most notably in application of description logic to formalizing medical terminology. Also at Manchester were Christopher Taylor, who worked in medical biophysics and imaging science, another pioneer I knew from earliest days when we were both members, with Jo Milan (1942–2018), of the Hospital Physicists' Association Computer Topic Group, subsequently the IPSM (Institute of Physical Sciences in Medicine).

I got to know Alan when we arrived together at a meeting room in Brussels, in 1991, under the auspices of Niels Rossing, the outstanding leader of the EU AIM (Advance Informatics in Medicine) initiative. We had both led successful proposals–he for the GALEN project, described above, and I for the GEHR Project (Good European Health Record), the forerunner of openEHR.

Alan was concerned with the computational integrity and expressiveness of medical knowledge bases. He worked to explore the development and use of description logic as the basis of open-world representations of knowledge–open in the sense of dealing with any possible logically conformant world of content. He proposed new thinking to replace pragmatic rules of enumeration of content with logical models defining content, supporting composition and analysis. This was a close parallel with the transition from enumeration to analytico-synthetic composition exemplified by Ranganathan and Coates's endeavour in the UNESCO Broad System of Ordering, as described earlier in the chapter.

Alan faced an uphill struggle in maintaining and enhancing his position and departmental support in Computer Science, while securing ongoing engagement at the coalface of clinical practice–he did not practice as a doctor when I knew him. At the time, I was in a mirror world, working to establish a position in the clinical environment of a Medical School Department of Medicine, with struggle in the reverse direction, maintaining and enhancing broader connections with computer science and other cognate academic disciplines. He was recognized internationally for his research contribution and looked after a small group of devoted colleagues and students, with whom he maintained contact into his retirement years. His manner had a North American phenotype, from where he came and that I had come to recognize–a sometimes rasping and angular mental toughness, and sometimes rather intimidating! It was a 'no nonsense' and honest style, as was that of Martin, which I admired and appreciated.

Alan brought the greatest of minds to his domain of research, surveying across description logics and their intersection with medicine. He kept abreast of all these tools, alongside others of the era used in natural language processing techniques for analyzing bodies (corpora) of texts descriptive of different domains of medical knowledge. His students' theses moved the field forward. I especially recall examining Nicholas Hardiker's thesis on the use of description logic as a metalanguage for comparing and analyzing several existing and pragmatically constructed terminologies descriptive of nursing care. In this, he concluded that it was impossible to translate meaning from one to the other.

Medical Knowledge Bases

> Knowledge is in part kinaesthetic; its acquisition involves having a hand, to say the very least. There are, in other words, some things humans know by virtue of having a human body.[132]

> Knowledge is only a rumour until it lives in muscle.[133]

As this chapter has unfolded, we have seen how the advent of the computer has brought new perspective and focus to the understanding and communication of human knowledge and reasoning. The Ranganathan circle of knowledge has encircled human reasoning–clockwise in abstraction of theory and counterclockwise in rationalization of practice. Stories of this evolution permeate the book. Joseph Weizenbaum (1923–2008) conjectured about knowledge that is accessible only to humans. We now conjecture about knowledge accessible only to the computer. The Asaro tribe saying connects knowledge and muscle. What is the computer's muscle? What will govern arm wrestling competitions between computer and human muscle?

Earlier sections of the chapter included discussion of the historical development of library classifications and medical terminologies and progressed to describe initiatives reaching from their pragmatic origins towards more rigorous and sustainable theoretical foundations. They tracked the scope and methodology of these evolving endeavours, into the Information Age, and alongside the evolution of formal logic and reasoning embodied in computerized knowledge bases.

---

132 Weizenbaum, *Computer Power and Human Reason*, pp. 207–08.
133 A saying of the Asaro tribe of Indonesia and New Guinea.

The nature of the book as a whole requires a mixture of organizing principles in its presentation of material, chapter by chapter. These reflect the timeline of events, my personal songline of experience and the thematic development of the ideas covered. The combination of these is a pragmatic one and the coverage of health care knowledge bases is introduced in increments along the way, as methods and applications arise in other contexts. This section is by way of an introduction to this ever-widening domain of experimentation, recently surveyed by Musen and colleagues.[134] It is a field full of promise for the careful and rigorous, and of pitfall for the careless and imprecise. As has so often happened, terminology descriptive of the field has evolved in confusing ways. In their paper, Rector and colleagues made suggestions for how such terminology might be usefully standardized.[135]

As further unfolded in the following chapters, developments in mathematics, formal logic and linguistics, and theory of computation and abstract automata, co-evolved with scientific and technological advance to place computational method on increasingly rigorous foundations of discipline. As discussed in Chapter Five, mathematics and computer science combined to shed new light on computation, through the unconventional genius of Turing and exploration of his eponymous Turing Machine–a conceptual but practically implementable device. Study of the potential solutions of classic problems, such as calculation of the optimum route among clients to be followed by a travelling salesman, revealed new complexity, and led to new analysis, of computational problems and the intrinsic difficulty in solving them–what could or could not, in principle, be solved, and with what resource of time and machinery. Proof of the consistency and correctness of the decision logic representations of knowledge bases mirrored proof of mathematical theorems.

Philosophy has debated 'knowledge that' and 'knowledge how', and the ways they connect–knowing that something is true and knowing how to make or do something. Knowledge bases deal in both these aspects–as a discipline for maintaining good order in the representation of a domain of knowledge and as a tool supporting its effective use in practical contexts.

As with all matters philosophical, there are contrary perspectives, of course. Gilbert Ryle (1900–76), the erudite philosopher of mind who passed me by every day, near my rooms at Magdalen College, considered this a false dichotomy. But humans are fond of arguing in terms of dichotomy, distinguishing supposedly disjoint ideas, and arguing about their connections. Dividing lines between them are often matters of much

---

134 Musen, Middleton and Greenes, 'Clinical Decision-Support Systems'.
135 Rector et al., 'On Beyond Gruber', p. 3.

musing, and rather less moment. Ontology and epistemology get typecast somewhat in this way, as do health and care, and dare I breathe it, messages and information models in context of meaningful communication of data between health care computer systems! Emoticons are not allowed in the book's text but take it that a smiling one is due from me, here! Some of my colleagues might likely choose to emote in more dramatic moods and modes!

As Robert Oppenheimer (1904–67) argued in his Reith Lectures that I discussed in Chapter One, in relation to scientific understanding, 'both and' can be a more fruitful approach than 'either or', in the pursuit of sound reason, good decision and effective action. 'Either or' often tends towards a playground of zero-sum gamers and their winners and losers.

Many computerized knowledge bases have straddled the 'that/how' dichotomy of knowledge. They have combined formal representation of *that* which is known in a particular domain of knowledge, with methods for reasoning with this knowledge and reaching decisions about *how* to act in its light, to achieve a desired end or solve a problem. The knowledge represented may be of problem, discipline and individual subject–heart attack, cardiology, John Smith presenting with chest pain, for example.

There has been a myriad of such examples, differently specialized as to how they approached and combined their 'that' and 'how' dimensions of knowledge. Among the earliest I worked with were radiotherapy treatment planning programs, which combined the 'that' knowledge of dose-absorption characteristics of ionizing radiation incident on human tissue, with the 'how' knowledge reflecting the state of the art in deciding the alignment and time course of application of the beams of radiation delivered in cobalt and linear accelerator radiotherapy treatment of cancer.

One pioneering medical knowledge base, which has already been mentioned in other contexts, combined knowledge descriptive of antimicrobial therapeutic agents with rules for their use in identifying and treating threatening pathogens encountered in caring for an individual patient. This was the MYCIN system, further described below, that evolved over many years from a team that included luminary figures like Feigenbaum, Bruce Buchanan and Edward Shortliffe, founding fathers of biomedical informatics in the USA. They made foundational contributions to the field of expert systems, a front runner of artificial intelligence.

A common fate of pioneering innovations in the field, such as this one, is that they were gradually disrupted and nudged aside by more generic tools, such as OWL, the OMG-pioneered knowledge representation language. As we have seen, open-world description logics have found fruitful application in the context of organizing medical terminologies, but both these methods and closed-world frame logics, and their combinations alongside other pragmatic software fixes, have struggled to provide and sustain adequate methods for useful and sustainable formalized medical knowledge bases more widely. And more generic tools of artificial intelligence, which are now rapidly coming of age, are poised to disrupt this domain, once again.

As was also introduced above, this machine intelligence has provided a different, and more simplistic and naive, approach to some such problems, which are seemingly now poised to prove more usefully competent there. It largely dispenses with 'knowing that' and restricts itself to 'learning how'. Knowing *that* can be of more limited use than knowing how, in making decisions about something that is required to be made or done. People and machines both learn to play games, and how to play them to win. Broadly speaking, the 'that' knowledge of chess is simply the rules of play with the pieces on the board. And the 'how' knowledge (its 'know-how') is an infinitely more subtle and massive ensemble of pattern, strategy, experience and expertise, which includes weighing up the opponent during the course of play and studying their previous form. Nowadays, the machine can discern what the human does not see in the game, or perhaps cannot articulate. The 'that' and 'how' of the game of Go are yet more simple and yet more subtle, we are told. I do not know, so could not say. Again, the naive but capable machine has scored.

The ideas underpinning medical knowledge bases continue to feature in later sections of the book. To conclude this section, I will briefly introduce some further pioneering examples, whose pioneers I have known and followed in their initiatives to explore clinically relevant knowledge bases in the Information Age.

Pioneering Examples

Heuristic Dendral–Analyzing Mass Spectra[136]

I remember collecting the impressive early work at Stanford of Edward Feigenbaum, from the 1950s, a pioneer in the field of expert systems who coined the term heuristic programming to describe this algorithmic approach

---

136 B. G. Buchanan, G. Sutherland and E. A. Feigenbaum, *Heuristic DENDRAL: A Program for Generating Explanatory Hypotheses in Organic Chemistry* (Stanford, CA: Stanford University Department of Computer Science, 1968); G. Sutherland, *Heuristic DENDRAL: A Family of LISP Programs* (Stanford, CA: Stanford University Department of Computer Science, 1969); R. K. Lindsay, B. G. Buchanan, E. A. Feigenbaum and J. Lederberg, 'DENDRAL: A Case Study of the First Expert System for Scientific Hypothesis Formation', *Artificial Intelligence*, 61.2 (1993), 209–61.

to reasoning. Written in LISP, a pioneering programming language of the era, Dendral was designed to study hypothesis and discovery in science. The Heuristic Dendral and Meta-Dendral programs reasoned with mass-spectrometer profiles of known molecules, to deduce the composition and structure of unknown molecules, based on their measured mass spectra. Knowing the atomic mass of a compound, a search of known elements was used to create a candidate list of potential composing groupings of atoms. For water, with atomic mass eighteen, this is not a large list, but for larger compounds the list of potential combinations explodes in size and has somehow to be reined into a manageable group for further study. This narrowing down was achieved by applying a set of general rules, based on knowledge of the science governing the formation of compounds. The initiative thus focused on a specific problem domain, and the rules pertaining within that domain, while exploring more widely the general issue of representation and reasoning with data and knowledge.

MYCIN–Prescribing Antimicrobial Therapy[137]

I also read and collected early books on exploratory applications in medicine, including, notably, the rule-based expert system, MYCIN, developed by an early colleague of Feigenbaum, Buchanan, and then spearheaded within the domain of medical informatics over the coming decades by another luminary figure, Shortliffe. MYCIN, one of many so-called rule-based expert systems in medicine, embodied knowledge about microbial diseases and rules governing and justifying an automated reasoning process, to elicit information about the patient, identify the disease and propose the drug treatment that was indicated. MYCIN embodied a database of antimicrobial drugs and their properties and uses. It thus combined knowledge of the clinical and scientific domain with expertise in diagnostic reasoning about individual patients.

Through Musen, Stanford also led the way in evolution from rule- to frame-based knowledge base systems. This generic approach to closed-world knowledge representation and reasoning was disseminated in the Stanford Protégé system, which now combines with the description logic of the OWL language, as introduced above. It populates and edges outwards the current practical limits of computability, implementing tractable elements of predicate calculus.

---

137 Shortliffe, *Computer-Based Medical Consultations*.

PROforma–Modelling Clinical Decision-making Processes

Closer to home, my colleague and friend, John Fox (1948–2021), who, sadly, died as this book was being written, was a career-long tiger in the jungle of clinical decision support systems, in his career spanning the invention of tools and their testing in clinical applications. He created and ran the Advanced Computation Laboratory of the Imperial Cancer Research Fund at Lincoln's Inn Fields in London, from where he created and led the OpenClinical initiative.[138] He and his team invented PROforma, an agent technology for modelling clinical decision making, and Tallis, a visual design studio for creating such models, and much more.[139] Standout future leaders in health informatics, such as Enrico Coiera and my subsequent colleague at UCL, Paul Taylor, launched their careers in his team. This was a fertile environment bringing together pioneers of the age. Nearby at the Royal College of Surgeons, was the home of a luminary contributor to clinical measurement, Denis Hill, working there with John Bushman and James Payne. He in turn connected with William Mapleson (1926–2018), at Cardiff, a pioneer of the mathematical modelling and control of anaesthesia, who I got to know during the first half of my career, devoted to educational computing and the modelling of human physiology, as described in Chapter Four.

The Foundational Model of Anatomy (FMA)[140]

The Foundational Model of Anatomy is a frame-structured hierarchy and closed-world representation. Human anatomy is complex and so is this model, which provides a computational representation of how an anatomist views the human body.

The architecture of the model is a very large compositional containment hierarchy. As of 2020, it described itself as comprising seventy thousand concepts, one hundred and ten thousand terms, six and a half million instantiations and one hundred and seventy kinds of relation. The hierarchical class relationships descriptive of anatomical structure proceed from anatomical entity and subsume structure, organ and cell classes.

---

138 *OpenClinical*, http://www.openclinical.net

139 D. R. Sutton and J. Fox, 'The Syntax and Semantics of the PRO Forma Guideline Modeling Language', *Journal of the American Medical Informatics Association*, 10.5 (2003), 433–43.

140 C. Rosse and J. L. V. Mejino Jr., 'A Reference Ontology for Biomedical Informatics: The Foundational Model of Anatomy', *Journal of Biomedical Informatics*, 36.6 (2003), 478–500, https://doi.org/10.1016/j.jbi.2003.11.007

Concepts, classes and instances are represented as frames. Continuity and physical adjacency of entities in the hierarchy are handled as relationships. Connections between frames are handled through slots. One has to see the detail to understand the precise meanings intended by these descriptive terms–a controlled vocabulary of such descriptions, perhaps with the admirable Rector as stern rector, would help a lot!

Overlying the structural hierarchy there are physiological/functional, radiological, surgical and biomechanical system hierarchies. A difficulty faced is how to handle problems of change in the applicable model during ontogeny, as the body develops and grows. Describing the change in lung anatomy and function at birth would be one such transformation.

Knowledge, Information and Data

In the oncoming chapters, the storyline of the book moves from the world of knowledge into one of data and information. It traces this path through successive chapters on observation and measurement, models and simulations, and information engineering. In passing, I interpose a reflection about the oft-enunciated trichotomy of knowledge, information and data.

As the quotations at the head of this chapter signified, it does not pay to apply our mind too seriously to defining what we mean by knowledge, these days. Such attempts often seem self-referential; knowledge is what we know! Hofstadter has gone so far as to suggest that the mind itself is a self-referential system–as discussed in his book, *I Am a Closed Loop*, introduced in Chapter Six. Whitehead wrote that reality just is, and we can connect only with appearances of reality.

The differentiation of knowledge, information and data is another topic that has involved much mental exercise. Again, self-reference abounds–information is how we inform ourselves, to guide our actions, and data are, as Latin indicates (*do, dare, dedi, datum*), 'givens' that we capture, collect and collate. Such abstractions often elude singular definition and are described in multiple ways, each adding to the wholeness of the ideas expressed.

It seems that it does not pay to spend too much time defining mathematics, either. As mentioned earlier in the Introduction, some say that mathematics is what mathematicians do. They explore rigorous tools for reasoning about the manifolds of number, shape and form, that they care, and find it useful, to reason about in that way. They enact connections throughout science, providing a unifying framework and thread. Mathematics of physics connects with physics of chemistry, chemistry of biology, biology of life, and the lives of people, ecosystems and societies.

As with mathematics, it does not pay to spend too much time defining informatics, nowadays, either. We might cop out in a like manner and say that informatics is what informaticians do. They explore rigorous tools that connect *how* we capture, process, codify, analyze, communicate and reason with knowledge and data, at all levels of science and society, in support of *how* we understand their meanings and *what* we make and do. Informatics is to knowledge more broadly, as mathematics is to science, including now computer science. It is elusive to capture and define information as an abstraction, as it is the manifolds that mathematicians imagine and deal with when describing number, shape and form. Some, as does Paul Davies, conjecture that information may be found to be a fundamental component of physical reality and measurable as such–as I discuss in Chapter Six, in the outline of his book, *The Demon in the Machine: How Hidden Webs of Information Are Solving the Mysteries of Life*.

Mathematics and informatics are central to *how* we connect the science and practice of health care with the computer, helping to frame answers to questions about the way things work. Ranganathan placed them side by side, after philosophy, in his circle of knowledge. *How* connects with causal power–information connects knowledge with action.

In the computer era, fragmenting the world into disjoint domains of knowledge, information and data–K, I and D–has sometimes degenerated into kids' play, digging bottomless pits of abstract and unconnected conjecture and distraction! Wholeness reflects the three in concert. If one follows Einstein's thinking, as also highlighted at the beginning of this chapter–'all knowledge of reality starts from experience and ends in it'–and John Archibald Wheeler's (1911–2008) observation, that appears again in Chapter Six–that during his career, 'everything is particles', gave way to 'everything is fields', and then to 'everything is information'–one might assert the primacy of information in characterizing all knowledge.[141] The KID stuff is then all information and informatics is science that seeks rigorous and trusted tools for engaging and reasoning with, and making sense of experience.

A highly abstract and philosophically Olympian perspective, for sure, and speculative, no doubt. But, who knows, in time, in a future Information Society, it may make sense to connect human quests to 'know', in that way. Mathematics connecting domains of number, shape and form, and informatics connecting domains of knowledge, experience and action. The

---

141 J. A. Wheeler, 'Information, Physics, Quantum: The Search for Links', in *Feynman and Computation*, ed. by A. Hey (Boca Raton, FL: CRC Press, 2018), pp. 309–36, https://doi.org/10.1201/9780429500459-19

'What is life?' and 'What is information?' questions, and what connects their answers, are considered in Chapter Six.

Concern for clarity and consistency of discourse in the languages of philosophy, mathematics and logic have fed into the evolving language and discourse of computer science and medicine. Study of the logically-deduced framework of mathematics proposed in *Principia Mathematica* led to its axioms and reasoning coming under a new spotlight. In similar manner, the evolution of medical language, terminology and classification, and programming languages that manage them in computable form, have brought new focus on the consistent and coherent use of language descriptive of medicine and health care. This has been a slow process of discovery, refinement and standardization, based on how ideas have worked out in practice, in managing information that embodies and connects knowledge and data with logic and algorithm. Along with this must come consistent and coherent information, framed within coherent discipline of informatics.

Progress towards health and care made whole, which will underpin their reinvention in the Information Society, will rest substantially on information and informatics relating to them made whole, which will rest on knowledge and experience of them, made whole. These are, of course, most unlikely ever to be 'made whole' in any absolute sense and must therefore always be treated as provisional and evolving understandings, with recognition of their limits. The computer is both a central ally in this quest and a powerful adversary. Concern for clarity, consistency and transparency in this evolving discourse will become ever more important as reasoning about them increasingly disappears into the inner worlds of ever more capable machines.

Health and care are intrinsically grey and messy areas, where noise is rife and context all important. Will computing machines have the capacity or the 'will' to handle the symbols they work with, cautiously and within a humanly recognizable rationale of provisionality and conditionality? Or will this evolution of the machine lead to assertion and imposition of a more machine-based rationale , and how will that play out? The recent advances in machine learning and the potential of quantum computation to widen capability in formal logic systems portend a long road ahead in which these technologies will play out, from playing with checkers to playing with Go, to engaging with life and health care. Chapter Six charts the connections being made between the science of information and the science of life. These seem destined to play forward into Lovelock's *Novacene* era of machine intelligence. It was interesting to observe the amazement in the world of life science, reacting to the announcement of AlphaFold, as if of magic, as I first wrote this section some weeks ago.

Parenthesis–Traction

Vehicle traction is force applied that achieves grip and creates movement. Travel and steering depend on it. Physical traction depends on connection and synergy. We generalize the idea in mathematics and computation–the intractable problem is one where we lack a viable method for its solution. In health care, traction is more organic in nature, contributed to and experienced by both carer and cared for. This traction is one of human connection and flow, on which tractable balance and continuity of services depend. Information policy for health care services, in general, has become an intractable problem. Here, I reflect on why that is and what might be done to improve matters.

A driver who skids and spins their vehicle on ice has connection but not traction between wheels and road, lacking friction between tyre and ground. Applied torque force, car momentum and direction of steering are out of balance. The car is difficult, if not impossible, to drive and can become dangerously out of control. Anti-skid technology can assist in maintaining traction between car and ice, making its control more tractable. Where traction is elusive or not possible, we speak of an intractable situation. New technology can make the intractable more tractable. What was unimagined or practically impossible can become feasible, albeit sometimes still very hard–perhaps requiring adaptation of purpose, goal and method in what we are attempting to make and do.

In everyday life, we seek traction between our efforts and their desired outcomes. The pursuit of knowledge seeks traction between ideas expressed and the context in which they arise and are applied. In science, this is traction between theory and experiment, and in everyday life between theory and practice. New ideas can enable progress on previously intractable problems and dilemmas. Advance in knowledge increases our sense of the known, unknown and unknowable. And advance in technology increases our sense of the tractable, intractable and impossible.

It is, though, a phenomenon of our times that fundamental underpinning utilities, on which everyday life depends, tend to become noticed only when they fail. We used to know about what was going on under the bonnet of our car, because we had to. But now we do not, and mostly cannot; it is opaque to us, and we have come to rely on services that keep our cars on the road. How far are we content to allow a similar derogation and delegation of power over and governance of personal data about our health care, to what might be, or become, opaque information engines and utilities? Software and data systems and services can also become opaque and inaccessible, or unusable, when they become technologically obsolete. In this sense, advance of technology may render a previously accessible and tractable utility no longer so. This is another kind of slippery surface on which we need to navigate with better traction!

Traction matters when tackling difficult immediate needs and concerns, faced with cost of effort, risk of harm and uncertainty of outcome. Good government requires that policy, goal and implemented plan of action have traction. Information technology has brought revolutionary advances in measurement devices and analysis of data. But the policy level encounter of information technology with health care has struggled to achieve tractable balance, continuity and governance of high quality and affordable services. Considerable applied torque has spun often threadbare wheels, failing to achieve commensurate movement on the ground! The UK NHS is pointed to from across the world, as having been the home of the biggest public sector procurement failure ever, with its early twenty-first century eleven-billion-pound National Programme for IT. Not all bad but not yet good enough.

This chapter has highlighted issues of traction between theory and practice in relation to knowledge and computation. Theory and practice are both implicated, and both lacking, when new ideas unfold in new practices. A sweet spot is needed, on which to concentrate in gaining traction. This is only discoverable with adventurous people and their environments, ideas, luck, hard work and staying power. Successions of hubristically championed and expensive sour spots have impoverished the pathway of much of health care service computerization and made it slippery. The evidence of growing dysfunction in the vehicles navigating this slippery ground is under their bonnets, out of sight, or observed with poor eyesight, in the many string-and-sealing-wax legacy information machines that pertain there. The issue of *New Scientist* this week, as I write, has a telling article on the hidden crisis of legacy software that is facing the world at large. There must be a more tractable way forward. I will describe one that I favour and have experimental and experiential knowledge of its formative stages, in the third part of the book.

Learning about *what* we assert to be true of something and connecting it with *why* and *how* we reason and decide about what to *make* and *do* in the context of this knowledge, has surfaced new issues of computational traction, as knowledge bases have advanced in the Information Age. Learning both *why* and *how* to make and do something involves *experience* (*expiri* [to try]), which comes from a combination of *discovery*, *experimentation* and *practice*.

Making and *doing* things is about *methods* employed. *What* we do and *why* we do it is tightly bound up with *how* we are able and chose to *implement* it. A tractable method must be *grounded* and *understood*, with awareness of both its scope and limitations. Grounding of method requires *consistent theory* matched with *achievable practice*. This depends on resource, community and environment, as well as capability. In that spirit, too narrow a consistency may not be compatible with a useful practice. As Ralph Waldo Emerson (1803–82) famously wrote in *Self-Reliance* (1841), 'a foolish consistency is the hobgoblin of little minds, beloved by philosophers, politicians and divines'! User community support for implementing, testing, refining and sustaining new ways of working, are essential for them to gain and sustain traction. Where this is lacking, innovations (however promising and much needed) may likely prove burdensome and unacceptable to those expected or required to use them.

Experiment and practice have *errors and uncertainties* which must be understood and accommodated. These can, to advantage, be tamed and narrowed, and thus made tractable, but not eliminated. In facing errors and uncertainties, and finding tractable method for coping with them, human beliefs and values are both motivators and demotivators of action–to stay as we are, asserting *status quo*, or to cope with fear of the unknown, innovate and seek to change. An overly idealistic or visionary approach risks obfuscating, as much as helping efforts to improve. An overly cautious and limited approach risks stasis and decay. Neither will likely gain and retain traction.

Theory and practice can quickly detach from one another within unclear and confusing experimental contexts. The story of the decades of implementation experience in the encounter of information technology with the delivery of health care services is one of failure of traction between policy, goal, method, team and environment. Policy must focus practical health care *engagement*, computational *rigour* and public *trust*, as a tripod of supportive legs on which to create good standing of method, team and environment.

The close connection of innovation in computational methods with everyday presence in, and experience of, practical problem-solving environments is exemplified in many of the stories in this book. Turing's foundational contribution in computer science, which I further describe in Chapter Five, related to his success in aligning theory of computation with machinery of computation–an abstract machine but a palpably implementable one. The wartime code-breaking exploits at Bletchley Park exhibited interplay of theory and implementation, to solve the most immediate and practical of problems–breaking the code of the ENIGMA machine. The story of Barnett and the MUMPS language, featured in Chapters Five and Eight, played out in practical context of the limited capabilities of the DEC minicomputer machine environment available to him and the characteristically sparsely filled and continuously changing data ecosystem of everyday clinical practice. More recently, advances in tractable description logic have played out in the context of problems encountered in creating orderly foundations of medical terminology.

This close connection with implementation was why and how my colleague, Jo Milan, was so successful in building coherent and effective information systems for the Royal Marsden Hospital in London, as I describe in Chapter Eight. Lack of awareness of the nature and depth of his contribution, and its significance, revealed harmful and costly disconnectedness of health information policy and policy makers, from such everyday realities on the ground. In failing to detect and understand this quality, although seeing it performing there, in plain sight, they failed to support this contribution and enable it to gain wider traction. Governments need to rethink their constructive roles in such creative endeavours or they will continue to drain away resources and make worse the problems that they believe themselves to be addressing, in what prove serially disjointed policy initiatives.

These many aspects of traction were all contributory reasons that led me to frame the three top priorities of the openEHR mission as implementation, implementation and implementation. This initiative spearheaded a new approach to achievement of a coherent and soundly based architecture for digital care records, as described in Chapter Eight and a Half. I also described the mission, in a letter to my colleague and friend, the chair of SNOMED International in those early times, Martin Severs, as prioritizing 'Little Data' first, ahead of 'Big Data'. This novel methodology–established, iteratively and incrementally, in and from its foundational team and environment–laid the foundations for the subsequent incremental traction of the openEHR mission.

Surveying the field of medical terminology today, SNOMED has established traction, and now occupies a key position in the context of names and structures for coding and mapping care record entries to a description logic style of knowledge base of clinical terms, and related expression language. ICD also has traction. More narrowly focused on classification of diseases, it remains poised between a history of largely pragmatic methodology, and a future moving towards a mixture of OWL-based subsumption and frame hierarchy and annotations, that together capture the richness of what it seeks to describe. The LOINC codes, which focus on clinical laboratory findings, is performing well in its domain of application. For these terminologies and classifications to increase their traction with health care service delivery, they need to be better aligned with coherent reference models that overarch record, analysis and communication of data expressing the wholeness of individual patient care. The ways in which this might best be approached and achieved remain matters of interest, experiment and debate, currently being played out, principally and in principle, among four communities: HL7, IHE, openEHRInternational and SNOMED International.

A good heuristic for achieving and maintaining traction is to keep close to priorities for things that need to be done, and for which we can establish a clear and practical plan for how they should and can be done better. In this we must prioritize learning from successes and failures of traction along the way, and how they came about. The detailed history set out in Chapter Seven shows that coherent, integrated and interoperable digital records of care, providing a comprehensive, balanced, meaningful and ethically acceptable account, and supporting continuity of care, have long been and stubbornly persist at the head of these priorities. Traction in this endeavour requires synergy across communities of health care practice, research, education and industry. It requires teams and environments in which mutual collaboration can be nurtured and sustained.

Ethical traction of science within society is an increasingly complex matter, when seeking to achieve and ensure wise balance, maintain effective continuity and assure trusted governance of services. These three legs of a tripod—balance, continuity and governance—emerge strongly along the storyline of the book, as it evolves towards a perspective of care information as a public utility that connects and flows organically. This utility is envisioned to be centred on individual care records, owned by autonomous and enabled citizens, as a symbol of their ownership of their individual health care needs. It is envisaged to be co-created by them and the professional teams that treat and support them, as a symbol of the essentially connected roles and responsibilities of both parties, and the mutual dependencies and duties that connect them in their pursuit of traction in both personal health care, centred where they live, and public health care services.

The Quaker short book entitled 'Advices and Queries', which I used to read at one time in my life, advises that a useful test of our knowledge is that we should 'know it experimentally'. In the world of artificial intelligence and Big Data, what is the relationship between what the computer gets to know experimentally and what we do? Society today is observing artificial intelligence at a moment of awe in its evolving power, comparable to that when chess playing machines first challenged and defeated human mastery. Health care is not a game, and the human stakes are far higher. Are we going to tip over our King in resignation, as we had to with the chess game? If not, how will we secure traction in the future balance, continuity and governance of health care, such that Big Data and AI are our servant and do not conspire, by default, to impose what I have heard described, in another context, as a 'confederacy of virtual caricatures' that shape human life and experience in unwished for ways? The story of Dr Faustus and Mephistopheles is not without parallel; I certainly do not impute any devilment, but the hype of AI is a bit magical and different incarnations of Mephistopheles may be lurking, or emerge, there! At least doctors today should think about the other doctor, Doctor Faustus, and the warning to him–*homo fuge*! No one would wish for his fate! I reflect further on this issue, a bit more seriously, in Chapter Eight.

The historical axis of this first long chapter of the book has tracked through philosophy, spoken language, mathematics and logic. It introduced Ranganathan's circle of knowledge, and it is further round this circle, into the natural and clinical sciences, that the storyline of the book now progresses. The next chapter enters the world of observation and measurement, where the Information Age has seen transformational change in science and technology. Medicine and health care have been enticing and sometimes controversial domains in which this evolution has played out. What and how we can now measure has extended almost beyond bounds. Why and to what ends we measure, and how we share and regulate measurement, and records of measurement, have become of increasing ethical concern as we employ ever more powerful and autonomous computational methods.

3. Observation and Measurement– From Cubits to Qubits

The story now moves on to consider observation and measurement, and their relationship to number, symbol, code, logic and ethics. Once again, this chapter starts from a broad historical context, setting the scene for discussion of the connection of life science and clinical practice with science and engineering of the past one hundred and fifty years, and information technology of the past seventy-five years.

The chapter visits large- and small-scale measurement and tells stories of people, devices and systems that have revolutionized science and health care in the computer era. It spans between worlds in which yesterday's largest computers are now exceeded in computational capacity by devices built into a wristwatch or handheld device, monitoring, communicating and advising about vital signs. It describes the growing dependence of scientific enquiry on computer technology and software methods, and the new measurement modalities that have grown from these connections, in support of everyday health care. It reflects on the challenge to computation posed by the orders of magnitude increases in variety, scale and volume of measured data and the curation of care records based on these.

As an example, the chapter tracks a century of research, starting with the story of X-ray diffraction methods for the study of crystals, in piecing together the structures of proteins. It describes how databases of such structures began to be organized and shared in the founding era of bioinformatics. It discusses the juxtaposition of measurements with theoretical models, and computational methods that search databases of known structures, to assist interpretation of data about newly studied protein molecules. The chapter concludes with a reflection on the challenges to balance, continuity and governance of health care services. These challenges arise from the explosion of new methods of observation and measurement in the Information Age, and the numerous, huge and disparate silos of data accumulating–containing data about individual citizens that is often non-coherent, proprietary and increasingly impossible to anonymize.

    https://doi.org/10.11647/OBP.0335.03

Everything is numbers.

> –attributed to Pythagoras (*c.* 570 BCE–490 BCE)

Men, I still think, ought to be weighed, not counted. Their worth ought to be the final estimate of their value.

> –Samuel Taylor Coleridge (1732–1834)[1]

All things physical are information-theoretic in origin and this is a participatory universe [...] Observer participancy gives rise to information; and information gives rise to physics.

> –John Archibald Wheeler (1911–2008)[2]

My Uncle Geoffrey, a casualty surgeon, told me the following joke when I was about ten years old–strange that my brain still remembers and pictures him as he spoke. Question: What is the difference between a physician, a surgeon and a pathologist? Answer: Physicians know everything and do nothing; surgeons know nothing and do everything; and pathologists know everything and do everything... a day too late!

Reminiscent of in-crowd banter among doctors, such jokes about professionals are staple comedy fare; this one is maybe now a bit dated! It does, though, give me a link from Chapter Two and the world of knowledge to the world of observation and measurement, with the pathologists observing down microscopes and measuring in test tubes. Incidentally, a more cerebral and knowledgeable surgeon than my uncle, you could not imagine. He used to visit me when I was a student at the University of Oxford and took me out for dinner at the swish Mitre restaurant. He had long since retired from his work in charge of the Emergency Department of the Whittington Hospital in London and died several years before I arrived to work there. One of the doctors I met and chatted to, remembered him with great affection.

Observation and measurement connect hand in hand with science and technology. They underpin scientific method and are, in turn, underpinned by technologies that determine what and how we can observe and measure in the world. Computer technology and computational science have augmented our senses and provided new eyes, and nowhere more so than in health care. This chapter is a story of this coevolution–about its origins and pioneers and their practical impact.

---

1   S. T. Coleridge, *Lay Sermons* (London: Edward Moxon, 1852), p. 243.
2   J. A. Wheeler, 'Information, Physics, Quantum: The Search for Links', in *Feynman and Computation*, ed. by A. Hey (Boca Raton, FL: CRC Press, 2018), pp. 309–36, https://doi.org/10.1201/9780429500459-19

The Greeks observed the world, confronted paradox in ways of describing and measuring it, and thought about term and number. John Wheeler, colleague of Niels Bohr (1885–1962) and tutor of Richard Feynman (1918–88), is a doyen of theoretical physics. He confronted measurement in the quantum age and thought about information. Information is to science, today, what number was to science, and to Pythagoras, two and a half thousand years ago–that is, an unfolding enigma! Wheeler might have said that everything is information! Carlo Rovelli might now drop the observer and say that everything is relationship, mirroring, it might appear, Alfred North Whitehead's (1861–1947) process philosophy that we encountered in Chapter Two. In this, he moves from description based on the concept of entity, characterizing 'thing with independent existence', to description based on the concept of relationship, characterizing how 'things are connected, or the state of being connected'. That also sounds to connect with Wheeler's 'participancy' of the observer, as captured in his paradigm changing ideas which he characterized as 'it from bit'!

Electronic care records are to health care today what descriptive narrative was to the emergence of medicine in the times of Hippocrates (*c.* 460 BCE– 375 BCE) and Galen (*c.* 130 CE–210 CE)–that is, contentious! Forgetting for a moment that weight is a measure, Coleridge's enjoinder was caution about dependence on metrication as a record of human life–what might now be called 'data-ism'. Pythagoreans believed in the connectedness of body and soul–an early expression of *mens sana in corpore sano* [a healthy mind in a healthy body]. Yuval Noah Harari depicts data-ism as magnifying body and diminishing soul.[3]

Whitehead described the world we observe and measure as one of appearances of reality. These unfold more complexly as the range of scientific enquiry extends over both orderly and disorderly phenomena. Science seeks to crystallize the principles underlying these appearances as simply as possible. The computer is both assisting this endeavour and, at the same time, expanding the range and complexity of what we seek to describe and understand. In his long-ago lecture that I described in the Introduction, Thomas Lincoln (1929–2016) gave an example of how in one branch of medicine before antibiotics, much more was measured when much less could be done for the patient. A kind of hopeful fishing expedition. The computer has cast a net over ever-increasing amounts of inedible fish. I remember a time when the miracle of early data-devouring statistical analysis packages led researchers astray to hunt for supposedly significant statistical correlations in their data, to record as markers of success.

---

3   Y. N. Harari, *Homo Deus: A Brief History of Tomorrow* (London: Random House, 2016).

The reems of paper circulating in the hospital-based department I worked in during the early years of my career in health informatics bore witness to the huge volume of medical notes and the often-tiny amounts of detail in the surgical notes–for example, 'inguinal hernia, TCI', recording an outpatient consultation and covering a diagnosis and instruction to the clinic secretary to arrange admission of the patient (TCI = to come in) for an operation. What matters is not big or small but appropriate to the task at hand. We easily fall into valuing and rewarding volume of data and in this we mirror the computers' capacity to support us in producing it.

Measurement has a dimension of timeliness. Returning to my uncle's joke, the pathology lab team might once have taken a day or two to collect and test a blood sample or prepare a specimen for detailed microscopic investigation and then report back, during which time an urgent clinical situation might have moved on. As I write, there is a contemporary example of the importance of time in the tracing and tracking of infection from Covid-19. Methods of measurement that detect the presence of the virus in saliva samples, completed within minutes–potentially replacing laboratory analysis of samples collected in nose swabs, analyzed by slower PCR tests, reported back several days later (notwithstanding stories of chaotic logistics in the transport, handling and processing of these samples)–are news items being discussed today (19 August 2021). Rapid testing and tracing of contacts of people who test positive for the virus are seen as key to successful containment of its spread in the population.

Notwithstanding the poetic caution of Coleridge, and the counsel of well-seasoned clinicians–that medicine is art as much as it is science–observation and measurement have become fundamental to health care today. Charles P. Snow (1905–80) described the counterpoint of sciences and arts as the clash of two cultures.[4] The clash has persisted from classical times into the emergence of science from countervailing cultures and beliefs. The modern-day father of the analysis of computational algorithms, Donald Knuth, who I write about in Chapter Five, is widely quoted to have once observed, somewhat narrowly and contentiously, that 'Science is what we understand well enough to explain to a computer. Art is everything else we do'. The programming of computers is a challenge to the articulation of knowledge and reasoning within a framework of engineering discipline. Engineering, as with medicine, operates at the interface that unites science and society. It helps us bridge between Snow's two cultures–think of the artist David Hockney and his iPad art! Eric Topol, more recently, has painted a picture of

---

4   C. P. Snow, *The Two Cultures and the Scientific Revolution* (Cambridge, UK: Cambridge University Press, 1959).

the engineering of artificial intelligence, as providing a bridge between what he describes as 'shallow' and 'deep' medicine.

As mentioned in Chapter Two, Gilbert Ryle (1900–76) argued against the separation of theory and practice and stated two theses: 1) Knowledge-how cannot be defined in terms of knowledge-that; 2) Knowledge-how is a concept logically prior to knowledge-that. This sounds akin to Albert Einstein's (1879–1955) statement that I quoted in Chapter Two, that the only source of knowledge is experience.

In seeking mental traction with this philosophy, cold towel wrapped around the head, it is good to keep in mind a sense of what is unknown and may never be known, or indeed be knowable through any conceivable experience of the appearances of reality. This is the theme of two of my inukbooks. At the turn of the twenty-first century, John Maddox (1925–2009) retired as editor of the journal *Nature* and published *What Remains to Be Discovered*, visiting the frontiers of science and the unanswered questions being pursued there.[5] In 2016, Marcus du Sautoy published *What We Cannot Know*.[6] They are great, and mentally satisfying reads!

As the Coleridge quotation reminds us, health care is a balance, and services must weigh multiple perspectives when reaching general decisions with and about particular individuals and groups. Lifespan and lifestyle are balances of bodily functions and human and social behaviours. From images of the earliest weighing scales, metaphor of balance has featured in matters of truth and justice. We speak of weighing evidence in deciding what is true. The gold-coloured statue of justice, Britannia, a woman standing tall and holding the scales of justice in one hand and a sword in the other, sits atop the Old Bailey Central Court in London and was visible just one hundred metres from my office window, during my fifteen years working in the Department of Medicine at St Bartholomew's Hospital. Such statues, dating from the ancient mythology of Themis/Justicia, adorn courts of justice across the world.

Datum as 'Omnuscle'

Observation, measurement, mathematics and logic connect with sensors and senses, and ever more closely with machine computation and ethics. When thinking about this chapter, I invented the term 'omnuscle' to capture

---

5   J. Maddox, *What Remains to Be Discovered: Mapping the Secrets of the Universe, the Origins of Life, and the Future of the Human Race* (New York: Macmillan, 1998).

6   M. du Sautoy, *What We Cannot Know: Explorations at the Edge of Knowledge* (London: Fourth Estate, 2016).

this connected world.[7] It sounded right–omnuscle as datum that embodies observation, measurement, number, symbol, code, logic and ethics as well. A quick search shows that 'phonosemantics' is indeed attested in linguistics! The world of computing is an 'omnuscular' world. *Musculus* in Latin means 'little mouse', perhaps because that is what some muscles look like. I like the idea of 'omnuscle' as small or little data! 'Small data' is a term I long-ago coined in personal correspondence with Martin Severs, as big data started to preen its feathers–it is what big data is composed from, although the 'big' sometimes neglects its 'small' provenance. Ernst Schumacher (1911–77) reminded us that 'small is beautiful'.[8]

As usual, I start by digging back in history. Here were spun, woven together, reasoned with and recorded, 'omnuscular' threads that connect health care with the binary worlds of big science and big data today.[9] They connect from the Epidemics of Hippocrates and the origins of medicine to the Covid-19 pandemic and health care services today. In the Information Age, the 'omnuscular' has stretched the world of appearances in every dimension, on every level and at every scale, changing our lives profoundly. We should remember and keep attached, the 'e' of ethics at the end of 'omnuscle'.

Observation and Measurement

In Chapter Two, ontology and epistemology appeared as co-evolving ways of framing human thought and debate about the nature of reality and the articulation of knowledge–two halves of a whole. Colloquially, we speak of measurements as typically expressed and recorded in numbers, and observations as spoken about and recorded in words and images. Philosophically, such distinctions of meaning are blurred. There is recurrent debate about their nature. They have long been batted to and fro in physics–considered (by physicists, of course!) the hardest of sciences–seeking interpretation and resolution of puzzles arising at the interface of theoretical and experimental quantum physics. It has kept physicists and philosophers enwreathed in scientific puzzles and linguistic knots for almost a century!

Lancelot Hogben (1895–1975) published his much-remembered book, *Man Must Measure* in the mid-1930s, tracing methods of measurement from

---

7   I should maybe call it an 'omnuscule', by adding 'u', for understanding!
8   E. F. Schumacher, *Small Is Beautiful: A Study of Economics as if People Mattered* (London: Abacus, 1973).
9   I notice that high-scoring words that drop from my invented word, 'omnuscular', in the TV game of Countdown, that I am no longer any good at, are 'unmoral' and 'raucous' as well as a lower scoring, 'normal'!

earliest times. It was where I first encountered the pyramids at Giza.[10] Aimed at children but read by all ages, it was a book my parents bought for me, but is now, sadly, lost. I recall reading there about measurement in classical times. Years earlier, Hogben wrote *Mathematics for the Million*, described by the historian and imaginer of future worlds, H. G. Wells (1866–1946), as a book of first-class importance.[11] He also wrote *Science for the Citizen* (1936)[12] and edited *The Loom of Language* (1943)[13]–language as a tapestry. He was classically well-versed and connected language, and problems of language, with mathematics, science and medicine.

Anyone who has visited Cairo will have marvelled at the skill and force whereby the huge boulders of the Great Pyramids of Giza (*c.* 2580 BCE–2560 BCE) were hewn into shape, manhandled and manoeuvred into position, and made, layer by layer, to rise from a square base to a point summit. The makers had rudimentary measures of length, compasses, observation of the sun and the shadows it cast, rollers, levers, ropes and human labour, at their disposal. Such exploits, combining observation and measurement with making things, led to concepts of shape and volume (γεωμετρία [*geometria*], 'earth measurement'), and calibration of angles by degrees.

Although it was no doubt practised in some shape or form much earlier, medicine was first documented from the fifth century BCE, when descriptive accounts of disease first appeared in the *Epidemics of Hippocrates*.[14] Systems of weights and measures are recorded from the third century BCE, in Egypt and Babylon/Mesopotamia (μέσω ποταμος [*meso potamos*], 'middle river'; the land between the Tigris and Euphrates rivers in modern day Iraq). These were driven locally by the needs of agriculture, trade and construction. The cubit unit of length, about half a metre, used the convenient instrument of the human forearm, from elbow to third finger or wrist. There was local variation in such measure, of course, and over time some convergence towards a common standard across the region. It was not until the eighteenth century, in part prompted by Benjamin Franklin's (1706–90) 'Experiments and Observations on Electricity', that the need for wider standardization took root, and from this the modern-day science of metrology.

Edward Gibbon (1737–94) describes how, in later classical times, the length measure of Rhiyyal, or Hashemite cubit, was calibrated with

---

10 L. T. Hogben, *Man Must Measure: The Wonderful World of Mathematics* (London: Rathbone Books, 1955).

11 L. T. Hogben, *Mathematics for the Million: A Popular Self Educator*, 2nd ed. (London: Allen and Unwin, 1937).

12 L. T. Hogben, *Science for the Citizen* (London: Allen and Unwin, 1938).

13 L. T. Hogben, *The Loom of Language* (New York: W. W. Norton and Company, 1944).

14 R. Lane Fox, *The Invention of Medicine: From Homer to Hippocrates* (London: Penguin Books, 2020).

astronomical observation (Microsoft Word hears and records cubit as qubit! The Riyal is now the unit of the Saudi Arabian currency).[15] Astronomical tables were compiled from recorded observations:

> They cultivated [...] the sublime science of astronomy which elevates the mind of man to disdain his diminutive planet and momentary existence. The costly instrument of observation was supplied by the Caliph Almamom (786 CE–833 CE), and the land of the Chaldaeans still afforded the same spacious level, the same unclouded horizon. In the Plains of Sinaar, and the second time in those of Cufa, his mathematicians accurately measured the degree of the great circle of the earth and determined at 24,000 miles the entire circumference of our globe.[16]

Relating this to angles and the division of the circumference into 360 degrees, he writes:

> This degree most accurately contains 200,000 Rhiyyals, which Arabia had derived from the sacred and legal practice both of Palestine and Egypt, this ancient cubit is repeated 400 times in each basis of the great pyramid and seems to indicate the primitive and universal measures of the East.[17]

Gibbon further describes how astronomers had to tread cautiously in the 'clash of Greek and Eastern culture and despotism' of the times. The 'Eastern Saracen [...] disdained knowledge of antiquity [...] the heroes of Plutarch and Livy were buried in oblivion [...] Truths of science could be recommended only by ignorance and folly' and 'the astronomer would have been disregarded had he not debased his wisdom or honesty by the vane predictions of astrology'.[18]

Robin Lane Fox describes how medicine in the era of Hippocrates was in part humane and philanthropic service, to be carefully balanced against personal gain for its exponents. Its early medicaments were based on plants. He describes how medicines were prescribed in amounts weighed in balance with several coins. In his forensic appraisal of the documents of the times, he sets out to identify the writers of the Epidemics and the times they were written, making connections with the archaeological record of different systems of coinage and the places where they were used.

In the later centuries described by Gibbon, medicine was already a profession. He records that that there were '860 physicians licensed to pursue their lucrative profession in Baghdad'. This later era paralleled

---

15   E. Gibbon, *The History of the Decline and Fall of the Roman Empire* (London: Strahan and Cadell, 1788).
16   Ibid., pp. 982–83.
17   Ibid., footnote on p. 983.
18   Ibid., p. 983.

the emergence of chemistry, converting 'alkalis and acids, and poisonous mineral to soft and salutary medicines', alongside the quest to transmute metals and find the 'elixir of health'. He describes a world in which 'reason and fortune of thousands were evaporated in the crucibles of alchemy, promoted by mystery, fable and superstition'.[19]

From ancient times and over many millennia, the recording of time employed sun and sundial, flow of water and sand, and burning of candles. Escapement mechanisms arrived in third century BCE Greece, to assist calibration of elapsed time, although the human body as a system, yet alone heart rate as a thing, was not yet imagined. Escapements started with water and evolved over centuries into wheels and gears, and portable clocks and watches regulated by springs. Pendulum clocks arrived in 1656, to calibrate Gottfried Wilhelm Leibniz's (1646–1716) day. These set the standard of time until the electronic era took over, bringing quartz oscillators in the 1930s and atomic clocks at the start of my songline in 1945. My uncle Geoffrey collected clocks and we have the two-hundred-and-fifty-year-old family longcase pendulum clock calibrating our day now. This clock started ticking as the world moved from the Enlightenment into the Industrial Age, leaving behind its agrarian landscape. It ticks today as the world clicks on in its transition into the Information Society.

Number and Logic

Logical reasoning with and about numbers sprung to life in Greece of the fifth century BCE, the era of Parmenides (born *c.* 515 BCE) and his student and colleague Zeno (*c.* 495 BCE–430 BCE), living in what is now Southwest Italy. There were likely similar awakenings in those times in China, as discussed by the historian Joseph Needham (1900–95), although the record of these has been largely lost. The study of paradox (παράδοξο [paradox], 'beyond or outside of thinking; contrary to expectations'), immortalized in such as Zeno's paradoxes of dichotomy–Achilles racing a tortoise, and arrow in flight –were central to debate about concepts of number, space and time, in context of observation and measurement.

Paradoxes are thought experiments–ways of exploring thinking, and how we think about thinking. The debaters contest one another's assumptions and reasonings about the paradox, whereby wrong or seemingly implausible conclusions are reached (travel over any finite distance can neither be started nor completed; the fast runner can never overtake the slower runner; the arrow is stationary) to defend and refute different understandings about

---

19   Ibid.

the nature of space and time. These thought experiments were a testbed of ideas of their times, just as the real experiments of psychologists like Kahneman are advancing thinking about thinking today.[20]

Discussion of paradox shaped widening philosophical and scientific debate in the eras of Pythagoras (*c.* 570 BCE–490 BCE), Socrates (470 BCE–399 BCE), Plato (*c.* 428 BCE–348 BCE), Aristotle (384 BCE–322 BCE) and Archimedes (*c.* 287 BCE–212 BCE). 'Common sense' ideas about number, based on experience acquired in observation and measurement of the world, were found wanting in the quest for abstract underlying concepts. This opened the way to new thinking about numbers and counting. In these debates, ways of expressing and defending reasoning–resting on stated assumptions and defined rules and methods of logical argument, thereby open to scrutiny–came to the fore. Disagreements about ways of reasoning revealed in discussion of paradox, and attempts to understand and unravel them, led to new concepts of number: of zero and infinity, of point in space and time, of strange properties of numbers–such as irrational numbers that appeared neither odd nor even. Many centuries later, the calculus of Isaac Newton (1643–1727) and Leibniz in the seventeenth century arose from experimental and observational science of that time–such as in describing the orbits of the planets. It introduced new mathematical methods for describing and integrating infinitesimal change. Two centuries later, paradox of self-reference in logical statements triggered and shaped advance in theory of number and its relationship to theory of computation in the twentieth century.

Paradox also played a part in discussion of natural language, relating to fuzzy definitions of words used. One such example concerned the term baldness. As the number of hairs on the head increases from zero, at what precise event of addition of a single hair does a subject being described change from being bald to not being bald? Can one hair make the difference? We recognize the term, and it somehow relates to number, but the relationship is unclear. Similarly, as one throws logs together, one at a time, at what addition of a single log does the assembly of logs become a pile?

Such debate shaped the interplay of number and logic with experimental observation and measurement, and with philosophy and belief.

Symbol and Code

---

20 D. Kahneman, *Thinking, Fast and Slow* (New York: Macmillan, 2011); D. Kahneman, O. Sibony and C. R. Sunstein, *Noise: A Flaw in Human Judgment* (New York: Little, Brown Spark, 2021).

Chapter Two introduced the representation of knowledge expressed in terms of symbol and code. The S and C of 'omnuscle' reflect these attributes of data-processing in the Information Age. George Boole (1815–64), Augustus De Morgan (1806–71) and John Venn (1834–1923) took logic into the realm of symbolic logic and computation, where these symbols lie at the heart of how computers work, and how observation and measurement become integral with models of reality programmed in software.

In *I Am a Strange Loop*,[21] Douglas Hofstadter described human reasoning as enacted in the brain on the level of symbols. In Chapter Six, I introduce this as one of my inukbooks on the themes of What is Life? and What is Information? It might have been seen as a mixture of speculative, incomprehensible or whacky, by many cognitive neuroscientists, but his earlier classic book, *Gödel, Escher, Bach*,[22] which showed his immense knowledge of patterns and symbols in mathematics, art and music, gave him the right to be read respectfully. His book describes the brain as 'a chaotic seething soup of particles, on a higher level it is a jungle of neurons, and on a yet higher level it is a network of abstractions that we call symbols'.[23] Eminent molecular biologists, such as Paul Nurse, now speak in the language of information circuits as integrative mechanisms of biology. Hofstadter talks of 'a high-level picture of information-manipulating processes alone'.[24]

That said, and as I describe further in Chapter Six, Feynman cautioned against thinking that the computer needs to be, in any way, brain-like in how it tackles the same tasks that humans do. The emerging field of neuromorphic computing, pursuing implementation of now much more fully understood neuron- and brain-like features, with which to cast and solve computational problems, might now somewhat temper that advice.

Ethics

Incrementally through the Information Age, as the granularity and ease of dissemination and dispersion of data became ever more magnified by the computer, the ownership and governance of data came under ever greater scrutiny. What is personal to be kept private and secure and what is public to be freely shared? What should and must be shared with governments and in the context of professional relationships within health care services? Ethical concepts and considerations framed discussion of ownership and sharing

---

21 D. R. Hofstadter, *I Am a Strange Loop* (New York: Basic Books, 2007).

22 D. R. Hofstadter, *Gödel, Escher, Bach: An Eternal Golden Braid* (New York: Basic Books, 1979).

23 Hofstadter, *I Am a Strange Loop*, cover text.

24 Ibid., p. 174.

of personal data and became embodied in law. Demonstrated conformance to the legal rights of the data subject, whose permissions regarding use of their data were required to be obtained and recorded through a process of informed consent, became a key attribute of personal data. This extended to the safeguards that must operate when using the data, including potentially difficult and onerous obligations on those handling it, to anonymize the identity of the data subject and correct any propagation of errors seen to have occurred when computing with their data. These requirements became central to how computer systems represent, work with and manage personal health records. The need for this to be done in a demonstrably rigorous, coherent and regulated manner became a significant driver of standardization of such systems.

The 'e' at the end of 'omnuscle' became a long tail (and tale!), sometimes wagging the dog a bit too hard, perhaps. Humans have proven cavalier in how they behave in, and care about, the sharing of their data, with and by computers–such as through their Google, Facebook and Twitter accounts– while trenchantly protective about how official and professional bodies they consult and engage with are allowed to share it. Big Brother is now having an identity crisis, and lawyers, administrators and politicians, a field day. After first framing intractable law married to intractable computational assumptions, they have switched to prosecuting and defending inevitable defaulters through the courts. Zobaczymy [we will see]![25]

Philosophy and Natural Science

And what of philosophy in relation to observation and measurement? René Descartes (1596–1650) differentiated body and mind–he of Cartesian dualism and the Cartesian coordinate axes of graphs. Modern science seeks to integrate and make whole. The nervous system and brain integrate functions of the body. Bodily homeostasis is regulated lower down in the brainstem and is largely subconscious. Conscious thought and sensation and control of bodily movement reside higher up in the cerebral cortex and cerebellum. Observation, originating through the sensory nervous system–hands, eyes, ears, nose, tongue and touch, all included–travels upwards. Thoughts and actions travel down–the two lines connect. Does what we see, hear and feel echo what our mind is set on seeing, hearing and feeling? There are subtle and subtly manipulable echo chambers in our interactions with and through computers, too. And, as discussed in Chapter Two, philosophy of mind has sought, and some think failed, to distinguish

---

25   On this Polish expression, see Preface.

intelligence–'knowledge that'–from the application of intelligence through action–'knowledge how'. Philosophy of mind interacts with psychology and neuroscience in clarifying debate about consciousness, thought, intelligence, and now also artificial intelligence (AI).

Observation and measurement intricately interconnect with theory and experimental method of science. Theory provides concept and framework around which to structure knowledge and understanding. Observation and measurement, and tools for analyzing and reasoning with them, anchor detail, rigour, utility and sustainability of that knowledge. And the experimenter is an observer, with potential to interfere and introduce bias throughout.

In twenty-first-century physics, these connections remain unclear. The quantum theory describes reality in terms of wave functions and probabilities. Newtonian classical mechanics embodies a deterministic model of space and time relationships. Somewhere and somehow, they connect. Both have rested on experimental data that verified their predictions, within their respective domains of observation and measurement. There are different schools of thought and substantial continuing experiment at the interface of quantum and classical descriptions. One has it that the act of observation changes (collapses) the uncertain quantum state of the system being observed, as described by its wave function, thereby aligning it with the certain state of the classical description. But what exactly is the nature of observation associated with collapse of quantum wave function probabilities? And how can we characterize transition between a system, like a balding head acquiring hairs, that changes from a quantum system to a classical system, such as a carbon buckyball of incrementally increasing size. And what about entanglement, action at a distance, and John Stewart Bell's (1928–90) inequality–the mood music sometimes seems to change by the week?

Quantum theory has brought to the surface modern-day paradoxes of observation and measurement. It is deep stuff at the level of the meaning of existence and relationship. Erwin Schrödinger's (1887–1961) both dead and alive cat is perhaps among the best known. The Quantum Zeno paradox also now reflects on the meaning ascribed to observation and measurement. My 2019 inukbook, *What Is Real*? seeks to summarize this confusion.[26] It is already out of date. Non-local action–seemingly instantaneous communication of signal between entangled quantum entities–required by quantum theory and with plausible experimental evidence in support, yet seemingly defying tenets of relativity theory which constrain such transmission to the speed of

---

26   A. Becker, *What Is Real?: The Unfinished Quest for the Meaning of Quantum Physics* (London: John Murray, 2018).

light, defies satisfactory resolution. There are libraries of books descriptive of this state of unknowing. No one knows–maybe there is a Gödel-like theorem of mathematics lurking, making it an ill-formed question or an unknowable truth! Or, as Rovelli maintains, is physics barking up the wrong tree and should better envisage reality in terms of relationship rather than entity? Some, such as Wheeler, have sought an explanation based on information; in his case the idea of 'it from bit'.

Unfortunately, 'I don't know how to solve the equations' is not a highly prized answer in a theoretical physics exam paper, notwithstanding that no one knows what they mean. Students are still expected to show they can do the maths. Neither would I have gained good marks in my final exams, fifty plus years ago, for explaining the elusive neutrino other than as a zero-mass particle, and I would have had next to nothing to say about the mathematical basis today of quantum field theory and quantum gravity.

If physics is in this sort of quandary about observation and measurement, what hope is there for the highly variable domains of biology and medicine, and health care? They have different problems to deal with. I emphasize their different characteristics in the following sections, but not intending complete separation of domains. Words describing observations and measurements and how we reason with them, that have shared and generally accepted, if somewhat fuzzy, colloquial usages (such as object, class, type, quantity and attribute), have acquired narrower meaning within specific contexts of discipline–such as with these same terms in computer science. Even within disciplines, debate focuses on different ways of narrowing these definitions still further. Between disciplines, debates focus on whether there can exist a sound basis for mutually meaningful exchange of information and ideas. Linguistic, scientific and clinical ambiguities surface frequently along the evolutionary timeline of the systems of terminology described in Chapter Two, seeking to standardize the language of health care records.

Biological Variability

There is an important difference of methods tuned to the study of the biological and physical worlds. The search for useful generalization targets simplification of the complexity of observed reality, to an essence that enables reasoning with and about it. In the biological world, there is naturally occurring and 'normal' variability. Healthy people exhibit wide-ranging blood pressure. It varies with age, circumstance, time of day and in many other such contexts. It needs to be adaptable like this, for the organism to survive. And experiment seeking to understand blood pressure in health and disease must accommodate that reality. It can be mitigated by standardizing posture and method when making measurements, but there remains a distribution of results that pertain, when seeking to test hypotheses about cause and effect–does this drug usefully control blood pressure in this clinical situation? The general classification of clinical conditions encountered is similarly impacted by the immense variety of people and environments being surveyed and grouped together.

Characteristically high biological variabilities, known about in general, and widespread particularities (special cases), encountered in practice, limit the scope for useful simplification. This is not to say that simple principles cannot provide useful insights into the nature of complex systems–why they are as they are, in general–and useful ways to reason about and cope with their complexity. When faced with a particular individual phenotype, in practice, it can be difficult to relate such simplification to the presenting case and circumstance, unambiguously, and base useful action upon it.

Methods that can be made to work in a pilot and experimentally constrained context, are liable to falter or fail when pitted against unconstrained, real-life situations, at scale. And in systems devised to categorize and classify the highly variable and contextualized appearances of the biological world, to organize and manage its variety and guide related actions, the handling of special cases that arise is liable to lead to increased complexity of those systems. This might be attempted either with increased complexity of the rules used in making a classification or with expansion of the number of different categories recognized as a basis for classification, and thereby a smaller sample space for each. Such are the arts of analysis and statistics!

In the physical world, scientific method is targeting a different situation. Experience supports the hypothesis that general laws apply, and that we can learn about them experimentally and apply them usefully. Such experiment can more feasibly be conducted within defined and controlled settings. There is thus created a common ground that makes possible reliably testable and sharable answers to the questions the experiment is designed to probe, in the search for principles and laws that underpin the measured reality. Implementation of the experiment will often still pose considerable engineering challenge: to control the environment in which experiment is conducted, measure relevant properties reliably and distinguish the signal looked for from associated contextual noise generated in the experimental process and apparatus.

In the physical sciences, scientists hone their model of a system and analyze and compute the precision with which it describes the modelled data. They focus on minimizing experimental variability, making it possible to ascribe difference between measurement and model prediction to either experimental error or inadequacy of the model. They set a high bar for recognizing new discovery. Five sigma is a level of significance test that requires a one in thirty-three million chance that the signal observed is simply due to background noise (leaving aside, here, the finer points of clarification about the applicability of one- or two-tailed statistical tests). There can then be a virtuous circle, with continuing improvement of both theory and experiment. Biology and medicine feel lucky just to be able to track the difference between the experimental and control group, reliably, let alone discriminate among alternative theories as to how that difference might have arisen.

Notwithstanding the intrinsically fragmented landscape of methods of observation and measurement, analysis, inference and action in the biological and clinical domains, working with what we have is a powerful imperative. One way or another, a rampant tumour must be combatted, now, or a life may be lost. The nature, quality, meaning and impact of data, weighed in individual and population human context, now threads throughout health care.

Clinical Measurement

The foundation of reality upon which appearance rests can never be neglected in the evaluation of appearance.[27]

Appearances are finally controlled by the functionings of the animal body. These functionings and the happenings within the contemporary regions are both derived from a common past, highly relevant to both.[28]

Taken together, these two quotations serve to emphasize the dual importance of theory and context in weighing evidence. In clinical medicine, observation and measurement arise and play out within complex personal and practical contexts. The balance of theory and practice is difficult to achieve and navigate in clinical practice. It is like holding and adjusting a course when sailing a dinghy–you know and apply the theory but capsize and dowsing is an ever-present risk in gusting winds!

The traditional picture has been of the clinician as the observer and measurer and the patient as the one being observed and measured. Patients experience and observe their maladies, and how these are treated and cared for, in and through their own bodies and minds. Clinicians experience and observe their patients in and through *their* own bodies and minds, too. The two observe and experience one another, and how they interact and

---

27   A. N. Whitehead, *Adventures of Ideas* (New York: Macmillan, 1933), p. 293.
28   Ibid., p. 241.

collaborate matters. The connectedness does not end there. It extends within the clinical team and community, to the patient's family and community, and across countries. Clinical practice, and the outcomes it achieves, plays out across all these levels, and therein lie the art and science of health and healing–they do not work well as divided or clashing cultures. The dynamic between clinician and patient has evolved from the invention of medicine in classical times and continues to evolve in the Information Age.

According to surviving documentary records and art from the times of Hippocrates and Galen, medicine as a practice started to emerge in a noticeable way in Greece, in the five centuries BCE and the early centuries CE. Its invention as science and early evolution as a profession is traced meticulously in Lane Fox's recent account. In the sixteenth century, specific gravity of urine was measured accurately and imbued with many diagnostic and curative meanings. Galen had taught that urine came directly from the *vena cava* and thus directly reflected the state of the patient's blood. Until about 1800, reliance on measurement in treating disease was still widely thought of as quackery. Doctors were dismissive of the taking of a temperature or a pulse and it took thirty years for the stethoscope to be accepted into clinical practice, around 1845.[29] With the increasing metrication of patient state, arose the ideas of normal status and wellbeing. As we saw in Chapter Two, the term 'norm' was first used to designate things conformant to a common type, then usual state or condition, of people as well as things. By 1900, norms and standards had become central to diagnosis and treatment of disease. Ease was wellbeing and dis-ease was pathology, and in Ivan Illich's (1926–2002) apocalyptic view, as discussed in Chapter Seven, this was evidence that 'society has become a clinic, and all citizens have become patients'. He saw the way ahead diverging into two alternative paths: increasing 'sickening medicalization of health care' or 'demedicalization of the concept of disease'.[30]

The science and technology of measurements available for the practice of medicine, to characterize and illuminate problems and to enable and guide treatments, have advanced beyond recognition over the past century. The capture of images displaying body state and function now involves a substantial assembly of measurement devices and computations. Theory of measurement (metrology) became established, and in 1944 a professional Institute of Measurement and Control was formed, now based close to University College London (UCL). It brings together engineers and scientists interested in measurement, automation and control systems. The

---

29   For a review of this period, see I. Illich, *Limits to Medicine: Medical Nemesis: The Expropriation of Health* (London: Boyars, 1995).

30   Ibid., p. 116.

initial focus was on national utilities, industrial infrastructure and logistics. This has broadened in the digital age, to cover sensors linked with machine intelligence, the Internet of Things and personal health monitoring devices. Measurement theory now covers many dimensions. The frequency and breadth of usage of the term 'dimension' increased manifold to an asymptote over the century.

Measurements sample the state of the measured system. Measurement is performed by some measuring agent or device–such as a thermometer measuring temperature within the human body or a human counting the number of blood cells in a specimen slide observed under a microscope. The measuring device exhibits a state that couples to the state of the system it is being used to measure–with increasing temperature, the mercury of early thermometers expands along a tube and the degree of expansion reflects the temperature of the measured system. In this simple and dated example (toxic mercury no more!), a human then sees and records the temperature exhibited along a scale set out to calibrate the expanding mercury column in the device.

Brought together in this simplest of examples is the scientific knowledge embodied in the device (knowledge about the expansion of mercury with temperature), the design engineering expertise that ensures it can sample the state of the measured system (a bulb with suitable thermal conductivity such that heat can flow and temperature can equilibrate quickly between body and device, without unduly disturbing the body), and a suitable volume of mercury that can be heated quickly enough and at the same time exhibit an accurately readable expansion, given the range of temperatures it will be exposed to in normal use.

What is measured, the state of the system that this measurement relates to, the properties of the materials used in the device to probe this state of the system, the signal generated as the device responds to the state of the measured system (in the body thermometer example, this is the movement of the expanding column of mercury, but most devices now generate and record electrical signals and their digitizations, in some shape or form), the means whereby this signal is captured, shaped, communicated and recorded, the quality of signal propagated and accumulated along the way, the faithfulness and interpretation of the final recording made–all these contribute to theory of measurement. Scientific advance in physics, chemistry and biology, engineering advance in materials and methods, electronics and electrical circuit design, mathematical and computational methods for processing signals, ranging from single numbers or sets of numbers to arrays of numbers in multidimensional arrays or images–all of these are specialisms of science and engineering, and of mathematics and computation.

The handling of bias and error requires that any method of measurement be systematically validated and calibrated. The tuning of device characteristics is a compromise to achieve a signal that faithfully (and without bias) reflects the state or function of the system that it is designed to sample, while minimizing extraneous signal arising due to perturbing factors within the system or in the measuring device and measurement process. What we want to see is spoken of as measurement signal. What we want to peer through, and that may obfuscate what we want to see, is spoken of as measurement noise. The design of the system is a compromise between signal and noise. Efforts to tune out noise may also reduce the useful signal. Efforts to amplify the useful signal may increase the associated noise. Design mitigations seek to eliminate bias and improve signal to noise ratio.

The interpretation of measurement connects with the knowledge, skills and experience of the measurer, be they human or embodied in machine and algorithm. This draws on knowledge of the form and function of the measured system and the context within which the measurement is being made. In the simple example of body temperature, has the subject just drunk a hot cup of tea, for example? That is important to know, of course, but, more seriously, where in the body was temperature measured and what aspects of the state of the body system are exhibited at this location. In the context of a blood pressure measurement taken by a human with a sphygmomanometer, was the patient calm, and what was their posture, and how skilled the operator? What does the measurement tell us about the state of the patient's cardiovascular system? How relevant and significant is this kind of measurement, in this particular context, when reasoning about the patient's state and deciding on any actions needed?

To a trained and knowledgeable ear, a stethoscope reveals much more than is heard by a lay person listening in, to whom Korotkov sounds– Nikolai Sergeyevich Korotkov (1874–1920)–might go largely unremarked, if remarked on at all. Even drawing fully on the skills of a highly trained human operator, the desired goals of the measurement may only be achieved by extensive computational analysis of the recorded data. Buried within the signal measured may lie unseen or unsuspectedly useful further information about the state of the system probed, perhaps treated as noise–for example, the tell-tale chance observation of the oscillating radio signature of the first observed quasar (pulsar), discovered by Jocelyn Bell Burnell during a night-time stint at the astronomical observatory where she was conducting her PhD research, lurking in an astronomical chart record being collected for another purpose.

The usefulness of a device or method is often characterized by the specificity and sensitivity of the measurements made with it, in relation to the question that has motivated them. Is this person Covid positive, for example? Sensitivity (true positive rate) characterizes how well the actually positive (true positive, TP) cases are detected, avoiding false negative (FN) results. Specificity (true negative rate) characterizes how well the actually negative cases (true negative, TN) are detected, avoiding false positive (FP) results.[31] It is always possible to detect all the positive cases simply by declaring every case to be positive–this requires no measurement! Though absurd, that method is sensitive, in that it succeeds in identifying all the positive cases that exist. The approach lacks specificity, however, in that all the negative cases would be misidentified as positive–the measurement thus not providing useful information for specifying the separation into the groups of true positive and true negative cases. How the sensitivity and specificity of measurements are weighed, depends on context–of the characteristics of the population sampled (its actual distribution of positive and negative cases) and the clinical importance of correct decision–is it so important that actual positives be detected that the impact of the associated number of false positives results can be tolerated?

Medicine today is practised as a combination of skilled observation, measurement, reasoning and action, its observations potentially combining all sensory awareness–of sight, touch, hearing, taste and smell. The relative importance of these and the need for skilful practice in their enactment (reliable, consistent and reproducible, as well as being handled well with the person being cared for), varies according to time and context. The nature of these different clinical roles embodied in observing and measuring requires a high degree of awareness on the part of the practitioner. Interpretations made, actions taken and outcomes monitored are, likewise, contextual.

Clinical observation–feeling a pulse, listening to a chest or voice–is a human skill. Different clinicians within a single specialty will evolve these skills differently, according to their experience and capabilities. My late and beloved Polish father-in-law, with a lifetime of clinical experience in his combination of hospital and home-based practice, decided the time had come to hang up his stethoscope when he felt he no longer had the sense of touch and hearing on which he had built his diagnostic skills, practised with only rudimentary machine-based imaging and laboratory chemistry available.[32] The diagnostic skills in different specialties are tuned

---

31   On true positive rates and true negative rates, see further Wikipedia contributors, 'Sensitivity and Specificity', *Wikipedia, The Free Encyclopedia* (16 June 2023), https://en.wikipedia.org/wiki/Sensitivity_and_specificity

32   This was when he was in his mid-eighties and he still had devoted and dependent patients of many years standing, who he charged very little, and who he continued to visit at their homes. My wife tells me that the local chamber of doctors, where he still attended regular professional events, had suggested that he would have to be disbarred if he didn't put up his fees!

to interpret different kinds of observations, measurements and contexts. There are yet wider and more important subtleties! A sense of timeliness is also important. Situations evolve and clarify–timely action or inaction, timely pauses for observation and reflection, times requiring immediate response, whether prompted by urgent instinctive reasoning or in adhering to mandated protocol.

Dialogue and storytelling feature strongly in clinical communication. Dialogue with patients and their family and friends, and within clinical teams, serves to unravel presenting problems and their contexts. Dialogue with others further afield, including from different specialty domains, helps to guide decision and action. Capturing human observations in words and drawings, calibrating, scaling and quantifying them, and relating them to measurements, is a complex and sensitive matter.[33]

Diagnosis of clinical problems and decisions about treatments, based on observation and measurement, can be viewed as an intrinsically experimental method–ideas (hypotheses) crystallize, and actions are taken to test them. The Greek etymology of the word 'diagnosis' attests to reasoning or understanding arrived at through or based on knowledge. Sometimes that knowledge was of mythology or scripture. Diagnostic process attests to a situation where the boundaries of the system being investigated are well defined and the available means for stimulating it and observing a response are well encapsulated in terms of both theory and practice. In clinical medicine, such boundaries are highly permeable, leaking noisy information into the melting pot. An experimental testbed approach to measurement, combined with practical experience of it, that enables patterns of malfunction to be spotted and recognized, based on intuition

---

33 To take a rather extreme example, the observation and recording of colour is a well-trodden field. Universalists would take the view that the human biology of the eye is the same and the frequency spectrum of a light source is the same, independent of the context in which it is being seen by the human eye. Thus, they argue, a colour terminology must have universal constraints. Relativists are interested in cultural and geographical factors impinging on perception of colour, which lead to many diverse manners of expression—some recognize only very few basic colours, others many more, with different regions of the spectrum attracting different amounts of attention. The complexity and range of words used in the Arctic to describe colour, as described in M. Fortescue, 'The Colours of the Arctic', *AMERINDIA*, 38 (2016), 25–46, illustrates how elusive any attempt would be to calibrate such observation within a clinical context, other than in the broadest of terms, or to generalize among different regions of the world where the emphasis and range of colour terms varies from minutely detailed, to very much more broad brush. I recount this example to give context to the reality that the computer has brought qualitatively different contexts to the scale and range of all manner of sensing devices that are now feasible, well beyond what the human brain will ever be able to handle and reason with.

and observation, are two sides of a coin. They play together in sorting out a malfunctioning car engine or electronic circuit board, escalating in some sequence towards a decision that may be to repair or discard and replace. The situation is of a different nature with living systems, where boundaries and interdependencies between component parts are more amorphous, and experiment is typically conducted within a context of uncontrolled influences and behaviours. Causes and effects inter-react through feedback, and replacing or discarding parts of body systems is not often lightly or easily undertaken!

If a train of thought leads to elicitation of confirmatory evidence, a plan of action is decided on and implemented. The clinician may suspect diabetes and decide on conducting a glucose tolerance test. This test challenges the body with fasting or injection of a bolus of glucose and measures the effect this has on glucose metabolism over the ensuing hours. The details of the measurements may vary but all are directed at inferring something about the state of health of the presenting patient and deciding among options for future management of the disorder they may exemplify. The record kept is, in a sense, a laboratory notebook. With growth of experience comes the skill to recognize and anticipate patterns of illness and their optimum management. In some situations, such as emergency medicine, immediate action is imperative to mitigate harm. Thinking and action designed to tackle underlying damage must wait. In such situations, where time is of the essence and pause for thought a sharply limited possibility, a protocol such as ATLS (Advanced Trauma Life Support, developed by the American College of Surgeons) is best followed–going by the book, where evidence shows this is, in general, the most effective strategy in the interests of the patient. Connecting the best of investigative practice with effective treatment protocol is a key challenge and opportunity of the Information Age, drawing on accurate, reliable and reproducible measurement in support.

In everyday medicine, there is a natural tendency and wish to respond to need by doing something. This is tempered by caution, encapsulated by the exhortation attributed to Hippocrates–probably erroneously, according to Lane Fox–to do no harm and to palliate intractable disease. 'Wait and see' is a common heuristic employed to deal with such uncertainty. Clinicians can work only with the understanding and tools of their times, and risk reputation in straying unwisely into untried or untested territory. What can in principle and in practice be done, what should be done and what is done, reflect different facets of the art and science of medicine and its human context more broadly. As ever, there is also an economic balance of choices to be made. How these are weighed, and how well, depends heavily on the quality of information and the tools and resources available. The art of medicine is, like politics, the art of the possible.

Weighing the costs and benefits of the multiply expanding and expensive dimensions of clinical measurement and observation, coupled with the similar explosion in feasible prevention and treatment of disease, has proven an ever more ambiguous and contentious quest. It sometimes feels that as we come to expect greater vitality in living longer, we somehow come to fear our inevitable mortality more! One wonders what AI will make of these challenges. Perhaps, it will throw up its metaphorical hands–post an emoji and decide not to bother, treading instead a different, perhaps more limited, purely presenting-data-driven pathway of diagnosis and treatment of disease. For sure, from the human perspective, there will need to be a caring and careful balance.

Measurement and Professional Practice

Bodily disorder can be very hard to pin down and manage within the lexicon of known and treatable conditions and situations, as can reasoning about the probable outcome of clinical action or inaction in addressing the disorder. In professional practice, recognition of patterns of disorder, based on clinician experience, is relied on heavily to sort out signal and noise in the welter of data from multiple observations and measurements, that may present.

Machines may in time prove more reliable and effective in finding patterns in this data, which is useful in determining and effecting successful action. In a sense, the machine is learning over time, discovering what works, experimentally, by progressively aggregating and structuring the data from records of clinical practice, to discover an optimal subset that is effective when deciding the best route forward, prospectively, for newly presenting cases. This algorithmic contribution to the diagnosis and management of disorder needs to fit, in an understandable way, with the human needs and goals set in caring for the individual patient. The marriage of machines and humans in this endeavour is a key challenge for AI in health care.

In the previous chapter, the potentially harmful impact on human communication, arising from the delegation of translation between natural languages to machine translators or natural language generators, raised its head as a concern. Here, the potential impact arising from delegation of clinical decision making to machines, is similarly uncertain. In some areas, clinical practice has already long done this and adapted beneficially and with ease. For example, computerized radiotherapy treatment planning has relegated to a distant memory the bench-based graphical methods that were used, during my early career in medical physics, for deciding the radiation beam timings and alignments. But what about choices among heavily impactful diagnostic procedures imposed on the weakest and most distressed of patients? I vividly recall being alongside my wife as she was turned back–lying on a stretcher and inside the radiology department, having been wheeled through long subterranean corridors for a much-needed MRI scan. She was a critical care patient and proved too prone to sickness and too weak to safely undergo the lengthy constraint within the narrow scanning chamber of the machine. These are heart-wrenching moments of clinical decision and not likely well-addressed by 'computer says yes, or no'.

Medical and life science have evolved pervasive new interfaces with mathematics, physics, chemistry and computation. Clinical practice has evolved a correspondingly immense menu of measurements and actions, and a burgeoning lexicon of associated terms used, classifications ascribed and observations, measurements and reasoning recorded. As biological and clinical science advance, so the ensemble of such datasets multiplies, with the potential to illuminate, confuse and contradict, to varying degrees. Just look at the immense and complex detail that must be mastered in the clinical polypharmacy encompassed by state-of-the-art treatment protocols for combatting all manner of different cancers today.

Feynman cautioned against undue digging in matters of scientific enquiry. 'If we look at a glass of wine closely enough, we see the entire universe [...] if our small minds for some convenience divide this glass of wine, this universe, into parts–physics, biology, geology, astronomy, psychology, and so on–remember that nature does not know it!'[34] Investigating clinical professionals also know more than nature knows and may be both well and badly informed. The way they become informed, how well and to what end they are informed, become key issues as the book extends to information utility, from Chapter Eight. At the centre of enquiry in clinical practice, there are diverse individual patients, their diverse families and friends, communities, cultures and populations, and constraining contexts of present need, available resource and potential action. Noise and bias multiply in scale and lead to misinformation alongside information explosion. I have sat and discussed with highly trained and experienced intensive care unit (ICU) staff, who proved right after having said and acted on saying 'I am going to ignore this, this, this and this because of this, which matters more'. Such combined human and scientific insight in interpreting

---

34   R. P. Feynman, R. B. Leighton and M. Sands, *The Feynman Lectures on Physics* (Beijing: Beijing World Publishing Corporation, 2004), I, 3–10. Also illustrated audio recording at Be Smart, 'Universe in a Glass of Wine (Richard Feynman Remixed)', online video recording, *YouTube* (31 December 2013), https://www.youtube.com/watch?v=b3_n7TDL7lc

clinical observation and measurement is a very high bar to rise to at the level of machine learning. Adaptive machine learning along a timeline of clinical measurement is different from interpretation of a static situation at a particular moment in time.

How does Illich's diagnosis stand up fifty years on in the Information Age? Is medicine heading further towards the factory production line nemesis that he luridly foresaw? Or will health care, rather, become 'demedicalized', as he believed essential, making room for greater personal stewardship of health care needs and choices? In his critique of two different schools of philosophy, Bertrand Russell (1872–1970) believed that truth resided somewhere in between. In this case, might we find a middle course, characterized in a balance of two halves, which I designate in Chapter Seven, in a simplistic way, as a balance of lifestyle and lifespan? This balance, and how it will play out in the Information Society, is the integrative theme I explore further in Chapter Eight. In this chapter, I will continue to explore how observation and measurement are evolving in Information Age medicine, continuously reshaping the art of the possible, alongside changing patterns of health and disease in society.

Measurement and Personal Health Care

In many countries, lifespan is increasing; people are living longer in good health and living longer with chronic illness. Whereas an ideal life for all might be wished to be long, able, active, fulfilled and healthy, these attributes may alternatively be short, disabled, inactive, unfulfilled and unhealthy. All binary compositions of these are possible, and vary over time in the opening, active and closing phases of a life. Different needs and priorities pertain, different organization of health care services are needed to meet and support them, and, thereby, there are also different information needs. It is a continuing characteristic of our age that variation across the spectrum of healthy lifespan and fulfilled lifestyle show marked inequalities, within and between countries. These reflect the natural and social environments lived in, as well as availability and access to health care systems and services.

Chronic illness–illness that does not immediately threaten life, that can in the main be controlled and managed away from hospitals but does not dissipate–has become more common as medicine has succeeded in offering a healthy lifespan and postponing the inevitability of its closure. Nowadays, ageing itself is approached as akin to an illness that can be treated. Staying fit and able into old age has become a more achievable goal, seen to be dependent on choices and control of a healthy and fulfilled lifestyle, as much as through medicine that prolongs lifespan.

Life has evolved to defend itself for survival against odds. The human body is resilient in self-defence and self-repair. And humankind has evolved to cope with, adapt to and help care for the adversities of ill health, both personally and for other people, where personal resource and capability is lacking, or lapses. And where a human body and human society is unable to fulfil those roles, medical science and health care services have acquired a huge repertoire of supportive and corrective interventions. Science has atomized disease to reveal function and dysfunction of the human body and enable intervention at ever greater depth and detail. All this is now better understood and communicated, including in scientific terms.

The past century has witnessed considerable change on all these fronts, and this has accelerated in the Information Age. But some earlier defences have weakened. Families have scattered more widely, not close enough to provide mutual support in coping with challenging events and stages of life. Generally more affluent lifestyles have highlighted the inequalities experienced by the less fortunate. The burden of managing an unhealthy lifespan has increased in duration and volume. It is perhaps not without significance that the first half of the twentieth century, culminating in the early decades of the NHS, saw the 'upswing' decades of politics, care and community in America, and the second half, coinciding with advent of the Information Age, were 'downswing' decades, pivoted to in the 1960s. This inverted U-shaped curve was characterized as 'we-to I, I-to-we', by Robert Putnam in his 2020 book, *The Upswing*, with its forensic data analysis of societal change over the twentieth century in the USA.[35] He did not correlate any of his charts with the rise of information technology, but there looks to have been a crossing of straight lines, forming the letter X–a descending line from community cohesion into a more selfish individualism and a rising line, in counterpoint, of the growth of IT and virtual reality. Putnam is convinced that the coming decades will bounce back towards greater respect for community values and cohesion, to tackle societal failings in stewardship of environment and economy and address concern for equality in matters of race and gender. In this scenario, information as utility could grow in line with this upswing, to help put right the societal failings that unbridled information technology has amplified and brought to a head in the Information Age.

New requirements and methods have emerged. There are many more ways open for the individual to monitor, manage and control their health care needs and for health services to prevent and pre-empt their disease progression. Just as hospitals emerged and grew some centuries ago,

---

35 R. D. Putnam, *The Upswing: How America Came Together a Century Ago and How We Can Do It Again* (London: Simon and Schuster, 2020).

and primary care services multiplied over the past century, 'personalized medicine' has brought new options and possibilities for cost-effective and safe individual self-care, and hospital at home. There is again a confusion of terminology, here. For the patient, personalized medicine has come to mean an increasing array of options for managing on their own, at home or with their family and immediate carers. For the disease specialist, personalized medicine has come to mean the more precise calibration of professional interventions, drawing on knowledge of the situation and characteristics of each individual patient.

Simple-to-use and quite small devices can enable a patient, or someone attending them at home, to monitor their blood chemistry and vital signs, alerting them to initiate prescribed interventions to control and manage their disorder. Diabetic patients can follow their blood glucose levels at home, on demand, from a pricked sample of blood. Sales of pulse oximeters have mushroomed during the Covid epidemic, based on infrared light shone onto the skin by a finger-clipped sensor. Much more will be possible as sensor biophysics and cellular biology and biochemistry advance, and their technologies are miniaturized and become nanotechnologies. Some will piggyback on the mainframe of yesteryear scale of computational capacity now embodied in a smartphone. For acute, but perhaps only intermittently expressed, conditions that require specialist oversight (such as cardiac arrhythmias), continuous and wearable monitoring devices, active throughout daily life, may offer safer, more effective and more achievable options for management of those conditions. These devices are monitored from wireless domestic networks, linked to specialist centres, thereby avoiding or minimizing the necessity to be hospitalized.

In these ways, advances in device technology are bringing a new balance of personal and professional care, combining new means of measurement and treatment with more detailed computation and analysis of data collected. While this can form the basis of useful information and guidance for both citizen and professional, about actions they can and should take, it risks increasing the fragmentation and incoherence of associated records, impacting adversely on continuity of care. If the diabetic patient can manage the monitoring of their glycaemic state at home, and adjust diet and behaviour, accordingly, how will professional surveillance in the wider context of health and disease be maintained, when there is less personal contact with clinicians trained to look for and detect the unexpected. There are new issues of governance, too, as sharing of data spreads ever more widely, centred more on the wishes and discretion of the individual citizen, and less on that of the professionals who serve them.

And in areas of acute illness and specialism, a treatment for breast cancer, for example, traditionally managed through treatment protocols extending to all patients, can now be customized to individual patients, based on knowledge of individual genotype and sensitivity and specificity of available treatments, relative to known genotypes. A drug that has hitherto shown limited efficacy for the whole group of breast cancer patients may prove highly effective for a defined, genome-characterized subgroup, and relatively ineffective for others. Huge and growing archives of time-series connected clinical and genomics data–uniquely identifiable with individuals, and on into their families–are extending from research into utility in support of everyday practice. This is an active area of research in multinational teams, such as those I have worked with over the past two decades.[36]

Science and Computation

Much of the measurement involved at the leading edge of scientific discovery and professional practice today is intimately integrated with computation. Quantum theory and device physics have transformed chemistry and opened the door to computational chemistry. This, in turn, has transformed computational biology and computational medicine. New concepts of information and information technology have permeated physics, chemistry, biology and medicine, horizontally across disciplines and increasingly over time. As Walther Ch. Zimmerli wrote, information technology is a 'horizontal technology'.[37] Horizontal technology has evolved into horizontal and citizen science. This trend has led to the reshaping of academic endeavour away from siloed domains of discipline and towards a more collaborative focus, grouped in hybrid disciplines to tackle 'Grand Challenge'. At UCL, new academic institutes have drawn together researchers from different disciplines, such as in the CoMPLEX Institute, which stands for Computation, Mathematics and Physics in the Life Sciences and Experimental Biology.

Some years ago, I represented the UK Medical Research Council on the national body overviewing research on what was termed eScience, and as a member of an advisory board of the Council for the Central Laboratory of the UK Research Councils (CCLRC), drawn from across disciplines. CCLRC is based at Harwell, near Oxford, the home base and coordinating centre for large-scale research facilities such as a high energy laser source,

---

36   The Advancing Clinico-Genomic Trials on Cancer (ACGT) and P(ersonalized)-Medicine initiatives of the European Union (EU) Framework Programme.

37   W. C. Zimmerli, 'Who Has the Right to Know the Genetic Constitution of a Particular Person?', *Ciba Foundation Symposium*, 149.93 (1990), 93–110, https://doi.org/10.1002/9780470513903.ch8

synchrotron light source, neutron pile and telescope observatory. These committee memberships included people responsible for major physics facilities at the Culham Centre for Fusion Energy (CCFE) and the Conseil Européen pour la Recherche Nucléaire (CERN).

Such facilities are stretching the limits of capability of both device and computation, in the scale of measurements of space and time, from the smallest to the largest, and volumes of data collected and analyzed. This evolution has gone hand in hand with the extension of computer processor power, memory size, dynamic and archived storage capacity ard network connectivity. Some of the devices themselves are engineering masterpieces—the particle accelerators, telescopes, satellites, lasers and fusion devices are extraordinarily impressive human constructions of our era. It was a privilege to see them and have them explained by their international teams of expert scientists, engineers and operators, at close hand.

It was at Harwell, in 1932, that John Cockcroft (1897–1967)[38] and Ernest Walton (1903–95) first demonstrated nuclear fission, by firing protons at high speed into a metal target. This landmark achievement followed three decades of extraordinary advance in experimental physics: experiments at the University of Cambridge conducted by Joseph John Thomson (1856–1940), moving the image created in cathode ray tubes in applied electric and magnetic fields, and by Ernest Rutherford (1871–1937), firing alpha particles at a thin metal foil and observing back scattering, also at Cambridge, leading to the discovery of the electron and nucleus of the atom. Observing the huge power consumption required by the machine used by Cockcroft and Walton, and the small amount of fission energy released in the experiment, the accomplished and illustrious Lord Rutherford said, in an address to the British Association in 1933:

> These transformations of the atom are of extraordinary interest to scientists, but we cannot control atomic energy to an extent which would be of any value commercially, and I believe we are not likely ever to be able to do so [...] Our interest in the matter is purely scientific, and the experiments which are being carried out will help us to a better understanding of the structure of matter.[39]

---

38   I had a connection with the Cockcroft family in the 1950s, through their daughter, Elizabeth, who came for a while to work on the staff of the children's home in Hampshire run by my parents.

39   Quoted from A. S. Eve, *Rutherford–Being the Life and Letters of the Rt. Hon. Lord Rutherford* (Cambridge, UK: Macmillan, 1939), p. 374.

A very different future was created than the one he, one of its most luminary progenitors, had predicted![40]

Knowing this historical background, the experience of touring the Harwell and Culham devices of today is breathtaking. We were given conducted tours during the construction of the Diamond Light Source, an electron synchrotron to probe structure and function of materials at the molecular level. The multiple beam lines for mounting experiments on small samples of material, probing them with pulses of X-rays radiating from the electrons accelerated near to the speed of light, are finely tuned in frequency and sensitive to the tiniest amounts and structural properties of the material being studied. The five hundred and sixty-two-metre storage ring is engineered to millimetre precision and held stable on foundations drilled into the chalk substrate of the land on which it is built. The data centre nearby, with row upon row of high-performance computers, is networked with researchers studying subjects arising widely around the circle of knowledge, and around the world.

The nearby Culham Laboratory has been the European research centre for fusion research. A robotic arm sealed away inside the spherical tokamak achieves pinpoint precision in lifting, moving and fitting the panels that line and insulate its wall. The highly skilled and athletic operator activates its movement with hand-operated equipment in the control centre. It looks like a fitness machine in a gymnasium. Five or more technical staff work nearby at screens, to supervise. Vastly more computational resources are deployed to land a small panel in its desired position in the tokamak wall than was used to land the lunar lander from Apollo 11. Jokingly, our guide said they look on the fusion reactor as a peripheral device of the robotic arm, so great is the functioning reactor dependent on it, and so great have been the engineering and computational challenges faced in making it work. Similar challenges posed by the robotic devices employed in the current Mars lander mission,

---

40   The advancing wave of science eludes the predictions of the most eminent of its progenitors. Richard Feynman, the physics icon of my earlier years, buoyed by the then recent discovery of the predicted omega-minus particle in 1964, completing a group of symmetry in the standard model, predicted that particle physics would be a done deal fifty years hence! Incidentally, this was the year that I arrived at the University of Oxford after reading Volume I of his Freshman Lectures in Physics to students at the California Institute of Technology (Caltech). Fifty years must have seemed a safely long interval—no one would remember! Waiting for a unified field theory of forces and elementary particles to be strung together is a bit like Ionescu's *Waiting for Godot*, if not for the God particle (the Peter Higgs boson), which has now declared its existence! The predicted date of arrival of practical nuclear fusion reactors has been thirty years hence, for many years! During the writing of this book, net release of energy has been demonstrated in experimental prototypes of future fusion reactors.

to drill for and analyze samples of materials to be brought back to earth, are described to be as great as those of getting safely to and from the planet.

On my visits over more recent years, back to old haunts in the Physics Department at the University of Oxford, I have listened to researchers who are working on new devices and technologies of quantum computation, a level of computational resource that may break the secrecy of technologies on which systems of cryptography currently depend. These are outstanding advances to be admired–sadly, well beyond my brain power now! They involve huge new investments, while at the same time contributing to attrition of previous investments, as the devices and infrastructure of the facilities, and the skills in ways of working with them, are often quickly superseded, and made obsolete.

This overview of science and computation may seem rather far-removed from the everyday realities of health care, and no doubt in large part it is. But in the Information Age, science and instrumentation created at the leading edge of scientific endeavour have often evolved and connected extraordinarily quickly into the everyday devices used in laboratories and services, in universities, hospitals, industry and at home. As solid-state physics, molecular science and nanotechnology have advanced, much measurement previously restricted to high-end and expensive laboratories, can now be customized within small and easily handled devices. These can be operated by smart phones, wrapped around with software to analyze and chart information collected during our everyday lives–about the environment around us, what we are doing and how our body is functioning.

Nearly sixty years ago, the physics of nuclear magnetic resonance (NMR) was taught to me as a mix of experimental and theoretical physics, where problems involving the Felix Bloch (1905–83) equations were used to tease our mathematical skills. NMR is now the basis of magnetic resonance imaging (MRI) scanning, a central tool of clinical imaging, and NMR spectroscopy is used routinely in the life sciences to probe the chemistry of life. From electrons revealing themselves to Thomson as what he described as 'corpuscles', to electrons accelerated in synchrotrons and emitted X-rays tuned to probe materials at femto-levels of sensitivity–all within one hundred years! From demonstrating fission of the nucleus to nuclear powered electricity generators, first in Russia and then in the UK, in just over twenty years, and, more soberingly, to the destructive potential of nuclear weapons in less than ten years. From the establishment of paper and thin film chromatography as a method of separating, identifying and measuring amounts of different molecules in a prepared biological sample, starting with Mikhail Tsvet (1872–1919) in Russia around 1900, to the gas and liquid chromatography of today and the flow techniques for rapid detection of Covid-19 virus.

The life science of genetics and molecular biology moved from discovery of the double helix structure and molecular coding of DNA, seventy years ago, building on X-ray crystallography of earlier decades, to the unravelling of its human sequence in a collaborative international research partnership of the 1990s, to new measurement devices that mirrored such results within days, hours and increasingly minutes, and to scientific databanks and population-wide clinical biobanks that aggregate and curate sequences and structures, measured and computed in populations, over lifetimes, throughout the world.

Such measurements and capabilities and the related science and informatics of genome and proteome have reframed genetics research and clinical genetics services. They have enhanced and accelerated discovery and refinement of pharmaceuticals, through new capability to visualize drug action–matching chemical attachment of candidate molecule to target cellular receptor. This imagery has been displayed to illustrate daily news about the Covid virus infection. And in December 2020, AlphaFold has shown that machine learning can succeed in accurate prediction of the three-dimensional folding structure of proteins, working only from the measured sequence data and the already known structures and properties of other proteins.

All these ideas, from the largest to the smallest scales of endeavour, have been made real in a new era of computational physics, chemistry and biology. It is a triumph of computational science and device engineering. It is an inspiring world of science and the appliance and appliances of science. But we must not lose sight of the many problems it poses for creating and sustaining balance, continuity and governance of citizen-centred health care services appropriate to an emerging Information Society. These have loomed on several fronts. First, in overreliance on and overinterpretation of poor-quality data, relating to how we view and value health care services, and based on sometimes highly conjectural abstract models of the real-world. Second, in the additional burden that non-coherent experimentation and implementation place on already overburdened health care services, which struggle to keep abreast of more basic needs. And third, in the business models underpinning health care information systems at large, which are based, in the main, on closed source and proprietary software, lacking adequate and rigorously defined and shared common ground with other software, in their semantic foundations. Lack of this common ground renders coherent overview, from dual professional and citizen perspective, and fruitful collaboration and mutual participation in health care related endeavours, increasingly difficult and burdensome to achieve, if not impossibly so.

Delving into software designed to support discovery at the limits of science and compare it with software in practical, widescale use in daily support of health care services, is sometimes a sobering and rather shaming experience, as illustrated in the following chapters of this story. There is a reason for this–the science and engineering communities that I have described have shared key knowledge and knowhow that has enabled them to collaborate and integrate across disciplines and nations. Governments have enabled that to happen. The health care world has chosen not to invest in this way, preferring to support industry business models that sustain competitive position through proprietary information models, and the records based on them. Future citizen-centred information utility for health care needs to be drawn together on common ground, to share knowledge and methods whereby the data needed can integrate effectively and facilitate coherent records and continuity of care. Proprietary and legacy information systems cannot keep pace with this changing scene, unless functioning, effectively, as monopolies. This is a key issue for the fundamental reinvention and reform of health care services that is now needed–long evident and now increasingly recognized.

Data

The content of records is covered under the blanket plural term, data. The Latin root of the word is about giving and so a reasonable question might be: What does data give us? Apart from the ruefully obvious answer, a headache, we might be forgiven for thinking that it serves no intrinsic purpose! It just is, and it is up to us to accept it more as a gift, leaving with us what we see in it and get from it. I suppose, as in the Latin saying (but with no offence intended to my wonderful Greek friends, whose culture's gifts to civilization are beyond doubt!), we should be cautious of gifts–*timeo Danaos et dona ferentes* [I fear the Greeks even when they bring gifts]! Diverse in form, fuzzy and uncertain in definition and precision, data that we compute with (computable data) must have a clear and consistent provenance, as with the shelf location of books in the library of Chapter Two, if we are to be able to rely on them when building our own knowledge and basing our decisions and actions safely around them. Each type of data has its qualities and limitations, as do combinations of data collected and shared from disjoint data sources–as another saying goes, data is not the plural of anecdote!

In the immense variety of systems supporting measurement in health care, all manners of data are in play. Numeric variables range through nominal, ordinal, interval and ratio levels of measurement. Numeric, textual and image data and standardized terms and codes are used to record, group and classify data, reflecting the disciplines and contexts in which they arise, and the statistical analysis and algorithms (and now machine learning) used to interpret and reason with them.

Chemistry quantifies interactions of atoms and molecules. It defines units of amount in terms of atoms and molecules. Today, measurements of time and space range over the infinitesimally small and the astronomically large.[41] Scientists experiment with atto-second ($\sim 10^{-18}$) laser pulses, detect femto-mole ($\sim 10^{-15}$) concentrations of material with spectrometers, and peer to distances at the gigaparsec limits of the observable universe. One gigaparsec = 3.26 billion light years = 3.086×10^{13} kilometres. The age of the universe based on observations from the Max Planck satellite observatory, named after the founding father of quantum theory, is 13.82 billion years.[42]

In my 1991 talk at the Royal Society of Medicine (Appendix I),[43] I said that in thinking of these spectacular human accomplishments, I knew of no more powerful balancing reminder, to place such successes in the context of what the biological world achieves, than two facts from the science of human sensory systems: 'The kinetic energy of a pea after free falling for a distance of 5 cm would be sufficient to stimulate the retina of every person

---

41   The cardinality of sets of things studied involves unimaginably large numbers—this is not new. Avogadro's number, the number of units in one mole of any substance is equal to $6.02214076 \times 10^{23}$ and has been known for one hundred years. We now know that the human body contains billions and trillions of cells, bacteria, nerve synapses or corona virus particles in an infected lung. DNA sequences within the cell extend to some three billion base pairs, within the twenty-three pairs of chromosomes. Astronomers estimate that there are two trillion galaxies in the observable universe and twenty sextillion (10^{21}) planets, a number which far exceeds the number of seconds since the Big Bang, leaving aside quandaries about the nature and relationship of time and gravity at that point! More down to earth, the number of ways that a pack of 52 cards can be arranged (factorial 52, written 52! and meaning 52x51x50x....3x2x1) is a very much bigger number, still.

42   At the other end of time, in the realm of quantum mechanics, the Planck time (tP) proposed by Max Planck (1858–1947), is the unit of time in the system of natural units known as Planck units. A Planck time unit is the time required for light to travel a distance of 1 Planck length in a vacuum, which is a time interval of approximately 1.911×10^{-43} s (Lorentz-Heaviside version) or 5.39×10^{-44} s (Gaussian version). All scientific experiments and human experiences occur over time scales that are many orders of magnitude longer than the Planck time, making any events happening at the Planck scale undetectable with current scientific knowledge. As of November 2016, the smallest time interval uncertainty in direct measurements was on the order of 850 zeptoseconds (8.50×10^{-19} seconds). See Wikipedia contributors, 'Planck Units', *Wikipedia, The Free Encyclopedia* (23 April 2023), https://en.wikipedia.org/wiki/Planck_units for more information.

43   Available at https://www.openbookpublishers.com/books/10.11647/obp.0335#resources

who has ever lived', and 'The average energy carried in the sound of the human voice three hours per day for a lifetime, would be sufficient just to boil one cup of water'—both from Primo Levi (1919–87), in *Other People's Trades*.[44] It does say average and I have not checked the calculations but have a feeling that Levi probably did!

As these numbers are chosen to emphasize, data is pervasive and 'given' in overwhelming amounts. Twenty years along my songline, the amount of data collected and stored in the earliest computer databases and processed within computer programs running on millisecond cycle time computer CPUs, was reckoned in kilobytes and (then 'huge'!) megabytes. The achievements of engineers in that era were, nonetheless, frugally remarkable, in what they achieved with what now seems so little. I celebrate some of these pioneers in Chapter Five and Chapter Eight. The machines I used for my PhD studies in the 1970s were already displayed in museums that I visited, just a few years later! The size of file for a typical digital radiograph today (fifteen megabytes) would occupy ten of the spinning discs of the early 1970s and the file sizes for MRI or CAT scanner studies may extend to five hundred megabytes.

Today, data collected in scientific experiments probing at the limits of these Information Age scales of measurement is at the level of exabytes (2×10^{60} bytes) and beyond. Meteorologists use these information technology-based resources to measure pressure, temperature, humidity, wind, rain, solar radiation, at land and sea, and monitor weather patterns with satellite-based sensors, providing fine detail from throughout the globe. Sonar-powered underwater sensors are being developed to provide an underwater Global Positioning System (GPS), setting the stage for mapping the earth's undersea geography. The UK Biobank project is following a cohort of 500,000 people over time and collecting genotype and phenotype data—now, for example, including functional MRI on 100,000 of the cohort. Life scientists use these resources to create three-dimensional computational models of proteins and drugs and markers of diseased cell surfaces that can be targeted by drugs designed to lock there They use synchrotrons to generate pulses of X-rays that scatter on impacting material samples of interest, measuring and analyzing the scattered radiation to infer its structure. In this way, foot and mouth disease vaccine was studied and a structural modification designed and tested, to improve its rigidity and increase its natural decay lifetime, enabling it to be used further away from its production facility.[45] PET scanner radioisotopes must be sourced from

---

44 P. Levi, *Other People's Trades* (London: Sphere Books, 1990), p. 114.

45 R. David, 'New Vaccine Promise', *Nature Reviews Microbiology*, 11.5 (2013), 298, https://doi.org/10.1038/nrmicro3019

close-by cyclotrons. Foot and mouth vaccine cannot be manufactured close to cattle herds throughout the world.

Scientific experiments now employ arrays of computing machinery connected through global networks. Data processing is conducted on linked grids of nanosecond-speed processors and petabyte-scale storage devices. Capacity to tackle currently intractable processing tasks is emerging in quantum computers, based on optically linked arrays of quantum entangled devices. storing qubits of data interacting within multiple quantum states.

A 2008 International Data Corporation (IDC) white paper described the world we live in as awash in digital data: 'An estimated 281 exabytes (2.25 × 10^{21} bits) in 2007. This is equivalent to 281 trillion digitized novels but less than 1% of Avogadro's number, or the number of atoms in 12 grams of carbon (6.022 × 10^{23})'.[46] By these estimates, the scale of digital data in our cyberworld will surpass Avogadro's number by 2023. We marvel at these achievements and worry about their energy dissipation, rising rapidly to replace mineral oil consumption with that of snake oil!

Health care brings another scale of measurement to the forefront; that of the size of populations covered, with eight billion, heading towards ten billion, people living in the world today. The investigations incorporated in health records cover data collected throughout a person's lifetime. They contain measurements from many kinds of laboratory tests, many varieties of physical images, many kinds of signals from physiological sensors, all feeding into capturing the data about who did what, when, where, how and why, and with what outcome, of health care services. These are recorded by different practitioners, by patients themselves, and directly from devices making the measurements, at different times, drawing on different knowledge bases and in different individual, discipline, profession and service contexts.

Health and care also bring into focus the importance of following the time course of measurements made. There is natural variation in living systems. from minute to minute, through the day, with eating, physical exercise and rest, and in changing conditions throughout the year. Living systems are dynamic. They are energetic and they move and adjust, maintaining balance and adjusting to context. The measurement of bodily function in the varying contexts of being healthy, becoming ill, and being treated, layers dysfunction over normal function. Onset and recovery from illnesses reveal themselves as a function of time. Single measurements

---

46   L. Mearian, 'Study: Digital Universe and Its Impact Bigger than We Thought', *Computerworld* (11 March 2008), https://www.computerworld.com/article/2537648/study--digital-universe-and-its-impact-bigger-than-we-thought.html

adjudged to be within a normal healthy range, may, in context of a series of such measurements, or in conjunction with other measurements, be judged as indicators of illness. And the reverse may apply. Dysfunction may also arise sporadically–an abnormal heart rhythm–and require a continuing sequence of 'normal' measurements to detect an abnormality among them.

Record

These many aspects of measurement and relevant context of data impinge on the importance for health care of maintaining appropriate, coherent, consistent, accountable and accessible records over time, for individuals and for populations. This need extends across all levels of care, from tertiary, secondary and primary care into the growing domain of home-based care and self-care, all of which interrelate and must communicate in terms of their meanings and contexts.

The wide-ranging types of clinical data and their personal and confidential character place exacting requirements on acceptable methods for their handling in care records, the potential risks arising from their misuse being especially acutely felt when they are held in electronic form. Record systems must show themselves to be technically rigorous and sustainable, clinically and economically feasible and trusted. Complete and timely records must be securely and confidentially accessible across organizations of health care and connected with patients at home and in their local community. Methods and heuristics employed to reason with and act automatically on these records, usefully and acceptably, must have trusted governance, independent of system supplier and technology employed in their construction. Standardized protocol and procedure must be balanced against limitations of clinical freedom to interpret and prescribe on behalf of the individual patient, and the right of the patient to be involved at all levels. The records are a co-creation and owned by the data subjects–the patients. All professionally and personally involved must have the wherewithal to be involved, as appropriate to their status, and to participate and collaborate.

Experience of inadequate performance of software in systems sitting in oversight of the tripod of clinical measurement, decision and action, may frequently be interpreted as signalling a need for more data, rather than as an indication of a dysfunctional machine or system. This may lead to additional burdening and bending of human activity, to treat and feed the sick machine's disorder, thereby degrading the human quality of care that can be offered to the patient and their disorder.

I have seen and experienced the focus on more, and repetitively poor quality, redundant, or inaccessible data, in years working close to wards, and in months of watching ward level activities, sometimes continuously, in day- and night-times and through dangerously deskilled and understaffed weekends, alongside my very sick wife. I have heard similar stories from informatics colleagues, themselves going through serious illness, lamenting almost unusably archaic computer systems on view to them in hospital wards. Poor data and record discipline adds to uncertainty in clinical decision and action.

This is a deliberately pessimistic perspective, to highlight the audacious challenge to create the future otherwise. The transition from Information Age to Information Society is principally an integrative challenge:

- to support and sustain balance, continuity and governance of health care services, over time, connecting more locally in the homes and communities where people live and are cared for, and more globally in diverse organizations of specialist care;

- to enable personalized medicine, in terms of customization of methods for the care of individual patients and support for their personal autonomy;

- to provide and connect with coherent and trusted curation of care records and open access to and sharing of knowledge, to mutually inform and enable professional teams and citizens, alike;

- to enhance education, research and professional development, again enabling the participation of citizens and professionals, alike.

Care records cannot ever hope and should not pretend to be in any sense complete; the clinical and personal context is highly variable and the pathway ever-changing. There is different perspective and bias naturally arising within communities of people involved and methods employed. Some components of observation and measurement are well-bounded in context and can be rigorously standardized. Some combine reasoned argument, reference to precedent and personal narrative, alongside observation and measurement.

Hundreds of billions of dollars per annum, extending now over the past fifty years to plausibly many trillions, have been spent in seeking to keep pace with, and rationalize, failure in the lucrative but serially underperforming endeavour to computerize health care records. I chart the story of those decades in Chapter Seven. But we should not need to rely on such documentary trail and decades of hand-wringing journalistic accounts of disappointments. Ask friends who have experienced the discontinuity of services across different sectors and regions of care, today. It was a deliberately provocative maxim that I coined for openEHR: that we can now do ten times better, ten times more economically and ten times as fast, if freed from past legacy and sunk cost. The second part of the book focuses on understanding how and why this situation came about, technically, clinically and organizationally, and still continues today. It is a story not without hope for doing much better in the future, as the third part of the book seeks to show. The programme for reform set out there seeks to be audaciously pragmatic, complementing Mervyn King's audacious pessimism and Barack Obama's audacity of hope.

The first twenty years of my professional songline charted my move from physics into medical physics and engineering, life science, and medical informatics. This focused on building computational models of human physiology, based on data and knowledge about bodily systems and their application in education and practice. This is the topic I move on to in the next chapter. At the start of that era along my songline, patient records typically took the form of thirty-centimetre-high stacks of paper in folders; summarized after each clinic attendance, Dictaphone in hand, by hurrying senior registrars. Today, they still sometimes take this form, but more often are partly or wholly captured within digital record systems. Methods for representing and structuring the record and rendering the expanding content such that it can be reliably computable, sustainable and easily accessed, in different contexts of practice, audit and research, have figured greatly over recent decades. This topic, central to my mission of the past thirty years, is centre stage in Part Three, from Chapter Eight of the book.

I move on, here, to describe how new measurement and computation that constitute the clinical data and content of records, have co-evolved over the past century, using examples of key technologies of measurement that have emerged at the interface of science, engineering and computational method in support of health care.

Measurement Sciences, Technologies and Devices

The mathematical advances from the nineteenth century tracked in Chapter Two and the computer science and technology that followed in the twentieth century, were mirrored in the advances in physical science and engineering fifty years later, and in what these have led to in the life, clinical and population sciences today.

These broad domains of science, engineering and practice have mixed and matched with new devices and methods supporting observation and measurement. The computer now captures, records, analyzes and displays the data, and controls the devices, just as it does, and will, with coming generations of space probes and autonomous motor vehicles. In the connections they have made from the science of measurement devices to their practical applications, computer technology and computational method have changed everything. I will give examples of some that I have connected with most closely along my songline.

Over the past one hundred and thirty years, a succession of advances in the physical and life sciences and medicine–many recognized in Nobel Prizes–have underpinned the engineering of new measurement devices fundamental to life science and medicine. Much of today's repertoire of clinical measurement has its scientific origins in physics of the late nineteenth and the first half of the twentieth century, taken further in chemistry and applied within life sciences and medicine in the second half of the twentieth century. and continuing in the molecular biology and bioinformatics of today. Taken together, these have been transformative; their practical potential realized alongside advances in computer science and technology from the middle decades of the century.

Here are some key examples. They link with radiation physics, electromagnetism, optics and photonics, nuclear physics and ultrasound.

X-ray imaging

1890s: Wilhelm Roentgen (1845–1923)–X-rays, 1901 Nobel Prize in Physics–X-ray imaging.

1970s: Godfrey Hounsfield (1919–2004) and Allan Cormack (1924–98)–Computerized Axial Tomography (CAT) scanner, 1979 Nobel Prize in Physiology or Medicine.

Electrocardiography

1901: Willem Einthoven (1860–1927)–electrocardiogram, 1924 Nobel Prize in Physiology or Medicine.

Microscopy

1930s: Ernst Ruska (1906–88) and Max Knoll (1897–1969)–electron microscope, 1986 Ruska awarded half of Nobel Prize in Physics for his work on electron optics.

1930s: Frits Zernike (1888–1966)–phase contrast microscope, 1953 Nobel Prize in Physics.

Magnetic Resonance Imaging

1940s: Edward Purcell (1912–97) and Felix Bloch (1905–83)–Nuclear magnetic resonance, 1952 Nobel Prize in Physics.

1970s: Paul Lauterbur (1929–2007) and Peter Mansfield (1933–2017)–Magnetic resonance imaging (MRI), 2003 Nobel Prize in Physiology or Medicine.

Nuclear Medicine

1950s: Positron Emission Tomography (PET).

1970s: Michael E. Phelps–PET camera and scanner for animals and humans.

Diagnostic Ultrasound

1950s: Ian Donald (1910–87)–ultrasound as tool in obstetrics and gynaecology–1963, the diasonograph.

Medical devices probe body systems ever more widely, deeply and precisely, interacting with and sensing the state of health. The sciences and technologies on which they are based, combine and overlap. To understand a PET/CT scanner, one might travel through nuclear physics, electromagnetism, radiochemistry, mathematics and computational science, before even starting to think about and marvel at the design engineering and clinical skills on display, that enable everything to be made to work together, to achieve useful and reliable goals in the diagnosis and monitoring of disease.

Sound pressure waves permeate from the anxious voice, through the air, to a human ear, and from the pulsing heart, through the body, to stethoscope diaphragm and human ear. They feature in pulsed measurement of intraocular pressure and ultrasound scans for non-invasive dynamic imaging and measurement of body state and function. Electromagnetic waves–gamma rays, X-rays, light waves and radio waves–propagate everywhere. Science and technology track and tune them throughout the spectral frequencies and wavelengths of radio, infrared, visible and ultraviolet light, and on down in wavelength to X-rays and gamma rays of highest energy, harmfully absorbed within body tissue. Atomic and nuclear physics, electromagnetism, photonics, optics, chemistry, biology and electronics combine to underpin the science of clinical measurement devices. The computer now takes all such modalities of measurement in its stride.

Measurement devices are transmitters, receivers, transducers and processors of signals. Light waves illuminate the microscope and the sample it views. They transmit through and interact with tissue at infrared wavelengths, in pulse oximeters and neonatal brain scanners. Electron microscopes and other probes and sensors extend signal and image resolution beyond what can be achieved with light waves. Radiation and radioisotope physics have made historic contributions in crystallography, clinical imaging, clinical chemistry, nuclear medicine and molecular and cellular biology. Nuclear magnetic resonance has become central to life science and medical imaging. Bioinformatics and health informatics are burgeoning new domains of life science and clinical practice.

The scientists and engineers have a reverence for their hard-won and satisfying creations. Clinicians, in general, have quite limited bandwidth for understanding these levels of scientific and engineering detail–they use the resulting machine rather like a car, sometimes not very sensibly or carefully! I have several in my family and some–well, mostly my wife (she laughs when I write this!)–are not so good at taking care of machines like toasters, radios and cars! Today, it is easy to develop a false sense of security or insecurity, when driving computational machines that are akin to early motor cars, which needed constant checks and adjustments by their drivers, when being driven cautiously on highly variable road surfaces and past startled humans. It is beguilingly easy to use these still early computational machines and applications as if we were Lewis Hamilton in a modern-day Mercedes racing car, but with none of his skills! In virtual worlds, this is especially easy; the gaming industry catapults gamers into the excitement of Forza Horizon 4. In real life, we may find ourselves, marginally rope-and piton-protected on a risky mountain face of computerization, with little computer mountaineering skill or sense of the rock face we are navigating, or the plunge below.

In the following sections, a principal aim has been to paint a picture of the interconnectedness of scientists and engineers and the teams and environments in which they have worked in advancing medicine in health care services. There are also underlying stories of how science before the computer's arrival, connected with science after its arrival, and key personalities and teams that bridged the two eras. It does not claim comprehensiveness or balance. The discovery of the structure of DNA was built, Newton-like, on the work of many shoulders. The happy coincidence of one with eyes to see, and opportunity to observe a chance event, has marked greatness in the scientific lexicon. Bell Burnell is one very famous example, as previously mentioned. Such heady moments of insight and discovery help lift people to a new level. An environment centred on common ground, enabling cross-fertilization of ideas among colleagues in closely connected teams, from different disciplines and areas of research, is an important determinant of their creativity.

X-Rays–Radiation Physics

Imaging

The penetrating and destructive power of X-rays was experimented with and experienced by physicists, long before being understood at the level of particle physics and the quantum theory. The lethal potential of the radiation only slowly imposed itself on those experimenters, told in the stories of Marie Curie (1867–1934) in the late nineteenth century, through to the atomic physicists of the 1930s; some–perhaps many–probably died young as a result.

X-rays found application in metallurgy, to study dislocations of metal structure and check quality of welds that affected its material strength. Holes were cut out from structural members in the fuselage of aircraft, to reduce weight and thus improve fuel efficiency in flight. Metal fatigue led to terrible accidents, such as in the Comet airliner crashes of my childhood. Hidden dangers of this kind are often not easily mitigated. I remember working one summer in a disused aircraft hangar, rearranged for testing new designs of linear accelerator for cancer treatment. It was at South Marston, near Swindon in the UK–subsequently the site of the, now closed, UK Honda car factory. The machine under test was partly shielded by huge concrete blocks, but with probably at most fifty percent of the sphere of emitted radiation covered and no allowance for scattering. Nearby testing of metal welds for defects, based on exposure of X-rays onto photographic gels, was conducted in open areas.

X-ray imaging measured the absorption and scattering of the radiation, as it was transmitted through the body and exposed onto a silver-halide film. It was immediately useful in imaging damaged bones. Barium meals were given to patients, in the form of liquid contrast media that sharpened the X-ray images obtained when the meal entered and passed through the gastro-intestinal tract, improving the ability to localize and observe abnormalities such as stomach ulcers. This sort of investigation has been largely superseded by endoscopic imaging, which passes a camera, sometimes somewhat unpleasantly for the patient, from either end of the body into the tract. It can also enable less invasive surgical interventions, to deal with problems that previously had to be enacted through invasive laparoscopic surgery, opening the abdomen.[47]

---

47   Notable pioneers of endoscopic investigation, like Christopher Williams, working at St Mark's Hospital in London, and now the lauded author of his landmark early textbook of endoscopy, were my colleagues at Bart's in the 1980s. As were Parveen

X-ray technology is also used to track leakage from gastrointestinal (GI) tract into the peritoneum, occurring in regions that cannot be reached with the endoscopic camera. In other instruments, cardiac catheterization and injection of boluses of contrast-enhancing radiopharmaceuticals create real-time X-ray images of blood flow through coronary blood vessels, revealing potentially life-threatening blockages. Similar methods guide intravascular interventions to excise thrombi and mitigate occlusion of blood vessels by positioning stents.

In the early 1970s, I was working in the medical physics department of University College Hospital in London when the story of the first EMI Company Computerized Axial Tomography (CAT) X-ray scanner started to unfold. There were rather dismissive opinions voiced about the computational method employed, termed Algebraic Reconstruction Technique or ART. The rather snooty and snide title of one article questioning the significance of its pioneering iterative reconstruction method was 'Is ART science?'!

CAT technology constructed a cross-sectional image from a set of scans of the radiation transmitted from X-ray source to detector, through the body, reflecting absorption and scattering of incident X-ray beam by the body tissue through which it passed. This was the computer algorithm central to the measurement made. The set of scans was collected, step by step, at each angle sampled, in a 360-degree circular sweep of the device around the body cross-section of interest. The EMI engineers had created what proved a world-changing innovation for clinical practice, and scientists and clinicians of the day were a mixture of nervously excited and arrogantly dismissive in their opinions of it–a not uncommon story about engineering innovation, as further exemplified in Chapter Five!

The images obtained greatly improved the precision of anatomical localization possible–first demonstrated in brain scans. The computational method remains fundamentally the same today, although optimized and considerably enhanced. The computation now extends to three-dimensional image reconstruction and visualization of the body over time. The range of clinical applications has extended from anatomical into functional imaging studies, able to probe dynamic behaviour of body systems, such as the heart and lungs. The computational methods it pioneered have been taken into other modalities of medical imaging, such as radioisotope, nuclear magnetic resonance and ultrasound scanning. Methods for imaging three-dimensional and four-dimensional (three-dimensional plus time) manifolds of data have cross-fertilized with scientific disciplines beyond medicine. For example, the CAT scanner has been used by archaeologists

---

Kumar and Mike Clark, whose landmark textbook of medicine has now found its way to into a passing mention in the latest series of Netflix's *The Crown*, I noticed!

for study of mummified bodies in museum collections dating from ancient times–a field now referred to as paleoradiology.

The engineering of the devices and their computational methods has continued to evolve. Those forming medical images today, the level of anatomical and functional detail they reveal, the safety of the investigative procedure they enable, and the ways in which the machines capture, record, and communicate the resulting images, are of a completely different order from the early CAT scanner prototypes of the 1970s. They bring new eyesight to clinical investigation and new metrics of quantification and classification of disorder.

Radiotherapy

As with electromagnetic radiation, particle radiation from a radioisotope or linear accelerator source causes destructive harm to tissue it passes through. In medical treatments, radiotherapy harnesses this to target and destroy cancer cells, while avoiding harm to healthy tissue nearby. In my time in medical physics of the 1970s, the targeting was an embryonic art of manual optimization, enacted by radiotherapist and physicist, working with paper charts, and supported by dose-depth calibration curves depicting the absorption of the radiation from the machine in tissue.

The science of radiation physics and biology was unfolded by notable medical physicist researchers of earlier decades. Jack Boag (1911–2007), at the Royal Marsden Hospital, Jack Fowler (1925–2016) at Mount Vernon and Joseph Rotblat (1908–2005) at Bart's, who described himself as a 'Pole with a British passport', were leaders of that era alongside radiation biologists, such as Rotblat's colleague at Bart's and co-organizer with him of the Pugwash Conferences, Patricia Lindop (1930–2018).

Experiments with animals and later with phantoms made from tissue equivalent materials, quantified dose distribution and harm to life, to understand and quantify the interaction of radiation with tissue in clinical imaging devices and radiotherapy, and devise risk management protocols protecting both the patients and the teams operating the machines. Computer-based treatment planning developed rapidly, as further discussed in Chapter Eight, where I describe a team that pioneered innovation within hospital physics at the Royal Marsden Hospital, from the 1960s. Today, such science and engineering are carried forward in product development programmes of the multinational industries of medical technology, exploring and developing new treatment modalities, such as proton beam therapy.

Crystallography

In the early decades of the twentieth century, X-rays were used to reveal the ordered structure of crystalline matter, through the patterns revealed by scattering from successive layers of its structure, captured in images recorded onto film. The wavelength of the incident X-ray radiation matched the regular spacing of atoms aligned within the material, leading to measurable patterns of interference in the image. This image was an average over the scattering from all the molecules aligned in the crystal lattice, thus achieving a usable signal to noise ratio. The physics underlying this process and leading to the interpretation of the patterns it produces, by crystallographers and life scientists, was formalized by William Henry Bragg (1862–1942) and William Lawrence Bragg (1890–1971), the father and son who shared the 1915 Nobel Prize for Physics 'for their services in the analysis of crystal structure by means of X-rays'. They certainly established 'bragging rights' as the founders of this field, which grew and diversified, very rapidly, over the coming decades! Henry Bragg was a UCL physicist, chemist and mathematician. In the following years at UCL, the crystallographer Kathleen Lonsdale (1903–71), his student, further developed the technique in its application to chemistry. A Quaker luminary of the era, she is remembered through the naming of the building where she worked, and which now houses the Physics Department and once housed the Chemistry Department, as well.

X-ray diffraction technology laid the foundations of a step change in study of the biology of the cell. The physicist William Astbury (1898–1961) worked as a student of Lawrence Bragg at UCL and later at Cambridge. He was a pioneer of its application to the study of cell function. This developed into the field of molecular biology, in the 1930s, and from there into the rise of bioinformatics, in later decades, the theme of the next section of this chapter. The chemist Linus Pauling (1901–94) built on Astbury's work and connected it with the atomic physics of the era, in pioneering quantum chemistry. He used ball and rod models to capture the structure of the chemical substances he was studying.[48] With advancing detail of evidence

---

48   Linus Pauling was one of four scientists to have been awarded two Nobel Prizes, one of his being the Peace Prize. There were two physicists and two chemists: the Polish physicist Marie Curie, recognized for her work on X-rays, and the American, John Bardeen (1908–91), whose prize in 1956 recognized his contribution to the invention of the transistor; the other chemist was Fred Sanger (1918–2013), who laid foundations for key measurement technologies that enabled molecular biology to scale to the level of the first whole genome sequence of an organism, Haemophilus influenzae, in 1995. Peter Pauling (1931–2003), the son of Linus Pauling, was working at UCL, studying protein structure, when I arrived

from crystallographers, notably the biophysicist Maurice Wilkins (1916–2004) and chemist Rosalind Franklin (1920–58), the histories were drawn together in the discovery of the double helix structure of DNA in 1956, by Francis Crick (1916–2004) and James Watson, at Cambridge. Cambridge has continued as a powerhouse of this scientific era.

Another luminary figure of the times was John Bernal (1901–71), who focused the field on mathematical methods for unravelling molecular structures, starting first with study of graphite and bronze, and moving on to viruses. His son, Michael Bernal, taught computer science in the London Institute course I attended in 1969. Like Astbury, John Bernal was also a student of Lawrence Bragg, and Max Perutz (1914–2002) and Dorothy Hodgkin (1910–94) were his students. Crick, in turn, was a student of Perutz–it was a truly remarkable and formidable lineage, that forged formative connections of physical and life science, computer science and engineering, and medicine and health care of the coming decades.

The 1962 Nobel Prize for Chemistry was shared by Perutz and John Kendrew (1917–97), for their work on the structure of haemoglobin and myoglobin molecules. They combined expertise in biochemistry, molecular biology and crystallography but their major advance was described by Perutz as 'pure physics'. He worked for most of his career studying the three-dimensional structure of haemoglobin, the full model of which he published in 1959, and from which he deduced the conformational changes that occur when the molecule loads and unloads oxygen in the human respiratory system.[49] Dorothy Hodgkin was awarded the 1964 Nobel Prize in Chemistry for her work using X-ray crystallography in deducing biochemical structures, including that of the protein hormone, insulin.

there in 1969. This was laborious work and the preparation of the experimental material, and its crystallization took many months. I remember meeting and talking to him in the Department, where he would often be found sitting on a stool and looking at pages of X-ray images, laid out in front of him on the floor. He would move the stool around and peer at them from different angles, trying to piece together what he could deduce from them about the atomic composition and structure of the crystal, revealed by the images. He was creating his own mental axial tomography!

49   I once had the pleasure of attending a lecture by Perutz. His was an extraordinary life and his book of essays is beside me as I write (M. F. Perutz, *I Wish I'd Made You Angry Earlier: Essays on Science, Scientists, and Humanity* (Oxford: Oxford University Press, 2002)). He recalls the twenty-two years he devoted to finding the structure of haemoglobin; the three-dimensional model which he published in 1959 is pictured opposite the title page. This he described as being based on 'pure physics', with no assumption of the chemical nature of the protein and no idea of what it would look like.

John Bernal connected teams and environments in London, Oxford and Cambridge. Later in his career, he led research at Birkbeck College (now Birkbeck, University of London), situated a very short distance from the UCL environment pioneered by the Braggs. One of his close colleagues, there, was Andrew Booth (1918–2009), who forged links with the mathematician and pioneer of computer science, John von Neumann (1903–57), at Princeton University, to pioneer early electromechanical computing devices for assisting in crystallographic data analysis.[50] Kathleen Booth (1922–2022), his centenarian wife, was a pioneering computer scientist, mathematician, and researcher at Birkbeck, who wrote one of the earliest books on programming.[51] Her recent obituary records that they left England to embark on a more peaceful, recognized and productive life in Canada–hence, perhaps, her one hundred years!

Franklin also worked in John Bernal's department at Birkbeck College. She obtained some of the first X-ray diffraction images of DNA and was engaged in the quest to understand their meaning for its structure. Crick and Watson used the familiar chemical models of known molecules of the era, in the form of spheres of different sizes representing constituent atoms, connected by rods of different lengths, at different angles, to represent chemical bonds. Working in this way, and armed with crystallographic X-ray images, including Franklin's then unpublished results, they inferred the double helix structure of DNA–a flash of genius for which they were awarded the 1962 Nobel Prize in Physiology or Medicine, jointly with Franklin's former colleague, Wilkins, 'for their discoveries concerning the molecular structure of nucleic acids and its significance for information transfer in living material'. Franklin died very young and her team member, Aaron Klug (1926–2018), continued their joint work and was awarded the Nobel Prize for Chemistry in 1982.

Gamma Rays–Nuclear Physics

A radioactive nucleus (radionuclide) is an unstable atomic nucleus that exhibits spontaneous nuclear decay, emitting elementary particles and/ or electromagnetic radiation. In *in vivo* medical investigations, tracer

---

50   For further information on the role played by Booth in the early computer developments in London and the UK from the late 1940s, see R. Johnson, *School of Computer Science and Information Systems: A Short History* (London: Birkbeck, University of London, 2008), https://www.dcs.bbk.ac.uk/site/assets/files/1029/50yearsofcomputing.pdf

51   W. J. Hutchins, ed., *Early Years in Machine Translation: Memoirs and Biographies of Pioneers* (Amsterdam: John Benjamins Publishing, 2000).

substances are used to track and identify bodily function and disease. A radioisotope is an atom with a radioactive nucleus. Radioisotopes that emit gamma radiation are employed as labels attached to these tracer molecules, to enable them to be tracked through the body, by gamma ray detectors. The labelled tracer is injected into the blood stream, to circulate, permeate and attach within the body, to assist discovery of the nature and location of disorder.

Because their radiation causes harm over time, radioisotopes need to be short-lived, present only for the time needed to arrive at their target location in the body and be observed there using detectors positioned to measure the radiation that they emit. Radioisotopes of long duration arise and decay naturally in the world. Short-lived radioisotopes also arise in the interactions involving radiation and particulate matter–medical cyclotrons are used to create these radioactive nuclei. These are then customized with bench chemistry methods to incorporate them within tracer molecules. Such labelling methods were perfected in chemistry laboratories to create highly sensitive radioimmunoassay methods used for measuring the tiny concentrations of molecules that pertain in the chemical reactions of living systems.

The diagnostic imaging field of nuclear medicine employs cameras and scanners that detect gamma radiation from decaying radionuclides– the gamma camera is an example. The team I worked in at University College Hospital (UCH) in the early 1970s, experimented with connecting data captured by these devices with early Digital Equipment Corporation computers. The signals generated were used to create and optimize images showing where the administered tracer molecule had become localized within the body, and from this infer details of the body functions it linked with.

Radioactively labelled tracer molecules are used to investigate a wide range of pathologies–for example: brain, respiratory, cardiac and metabolic function, and malignancy. Rather than relying on the transmission of X-rays to highlight regional damage and disorder, this technology uses knowledge of body chemistry and pharmacology to deploy tracers that can home in on specific mechanisms of interest, providing additional information on which to base clinical interpretation–radiolabels of glucose, for example, to target malignancies. There is a trade-off between level of precision achieved in determining anatomical location and detail of bodily function, and safety of what are significantly invasive procedures.

Positron emitting radionuclides were first used in transverse tomography in the 1950s. In Positron Emission Tomography (PET), the detection of the two gamma rays emitted at the same time and in opposite directions, from mutual annihilation of a positron with a nearby electron, requires detectors wired together to detect these two simultaneous events. Labelled positron-emitting radionuclides enable imaging of bodily function–notably enhanced metabolic activity in tumour cells. The method thus gave new insight in checking for secondary cancers anywhere within the scanned region of the body. The anatomical localization achievable was poor by comparison with other imaging modalities but gave additional specific information about presence of malignancy.

In like manner to CT X-ray scanners, advanced PET scanners used a circular ring, or succession of rings, of detectors. Electronic coincidence of detection of emitted gamma rays was used to position the disintegrating nucleus within the cross-section area covered by each ring, thus creating a three-dimensional volume image of where the injected radioisotope had lodged. To implement this detector in electronic circuitry was a complex challenge, quickly handed over to computer-based methods, enabling control by program algorithm rather than electrical circuit logic.

The resolution of the images obtained with PET scanning, seeking to localize abnormality, was still inferior to the CAT machine. But in acute situations, a combination of imaging modalities could be employed, supplementing one another to improve positional and functional resolution, including in time. The hazard imposed and benefits and risks for the patient–immediate and longer term–must be balanced as best possible. In further advanced iterations of these methods, machines delivering both PET scan and CAT scan, in a combined procedure, were developed. These machines, and their extensive supporting infrastructures and teams, form the (extremely expensive) state of the art, today.

There are many such examples, and the ones described here have been chosen principally from those of which I was an eyewitness, to illustrate the thread whereby science, measurement technology, and computation have proceeded hand in hand and towards medical applications. PET/CT scanning draws on physics, chemistry, biology, mathematics and computer science in the images it produces. It is a triumph of its science, engineering and clinical practice pioneers, and can now be safely operated by radiographers–a profession now enhanced to cover far more than X-ray-based modalities alone–supported by teams of clinicians and engineers.

Electrophysiology

Other connections along my songline, with people I encountered working at or linked with UCL from the late 1960s, opened windows for me into new areas of computation in the life sciences. Two such were Andrew Huxley (1917–2012) and John Zachary Young (1907–97).

Huxley, who had previously been awarded the 1963 Nobel Prize for Physiology or Medicine with Alan Hodgkin (1914–1998) and John Eccles (1993–97), was then Head of the UCL Physiology Department. It is difficult to imagine more prestigious intellectual aristocracy of that era than a combination of the Huxley and Hodgkin names. They are remembered for the Hodgkin-Huxley mathematical model of the propagation of the nerve action-potential. Huxley spent a whole summer, before the computer era, working through the solution of these partial differential equations, using a hand-operated mechanical calculator, and becoming expert in optimizing that method. From this field developed that of electrocardiography, as a measurement science, computational analysis and topographical mapping of electrical signals collected from around the chest wall. This topic and its computational aspects are further discussed in Chapter Four on models and simulations.

Young, known for his work characterizing the action-potential in the squid axon, was Professor of Anatomy at around the same time. Young's interest in the integrative properties of the nervous system had followed from that of Charles Sherrington (1857–1992) in the 1920s. Sherrington held the Oxford Waynflete Chair of Physiology at Magdalen College from 1913 and he and Edgar Adrian (1889–1977) were awarded the 1932 Nobel Prize in Physiology or Medicine for their work on the functions of neurons. Young is author of one of my inukbooks, *Programs of the Brain*,[52] which I discuss in Chapter Six. I remember this tousled, grey-headed figure pounding along Gower Street from the Darwin Building of UCL, nearby to my first perch in the Medical School, in about 1971.

Emerging within the life science domain have been new ideas about bioenergetics and bioelectricity, which look poised to help clarify fundamental principles of the development and function of living systems.

Ultrasound

Diagnostic ultrasound measurement was first applied to blood flow measurement, detecting the Doppler effect in sound scattered from the moving blood corpuscles. I remember my late colleague in the UCH Medical Physics Department, Roland Blackwell, studying this and showing me his results; he also worked on its use in imaging methods in obstetrics and gynaecology. Gail ter Haar, the daughter of my Oxford physics tutor, Dirk ter Haar, made her name in ultrasound research at the London Institute of

---

52   J. Z. Young, *Programs of the Brain: Based on the Gifford Lectures, 1975–7* (Oxford: Oxford University Press, 1978).

Cancer Research, close by to the Royal Marsden Hospital and its tertiary cancer services.

Ultrasound waves are now routinely transmitted, reflected and scattered from different volumes of tissue, and detected in two-dimensional cross sectional images generated by sweeping a directional sensor or array of sensors across the body. They are used to measure distance and build images progressively, showing variation over time. Greater safety in the balance of nature and quality of image achievable with ultrasound, set against implicit risk to embryo, made this of particular interest in scanning the health and growth of a baby, *in utero*.

In the 1970s, my late colleague Jo Milan (1942–2018), at the Royal Marsden Hospital in London, switched his attention from the computerization of radiotherapy treatment planning to diagnostic ultrasound imaging. He obtained his doctorate for work that connected ultrasound probe with computer, producing early two-dimensional digitized diagnostic images. I tell the story of his illustrious contribution to hospital information systems and electronic health care records in Chapter Eight. Diagnostic ultrasound measurements combined with computation now provide a range of mappings of body state and function in gastroenterology and cardiology—probing for abnormal structure and fluid collections in the abdomen and disorders of cardiac anatomy and function, for example.[53] They feature in measurements of corneal thickness in the eye and increasingly in hand-held devices usable beyond hospital settings.

Photonics

Advances in microscopy have spearheaded new methods of life science and clinical measurement and investigation, over several centuries. The optical microscope revolutionized biological science and the electron and scanning electron microscope extended the magnification and resolution of images deep into the living cell. Atomic force microscopy further extended the range of measurements possible and the environments in which these could be made.

The term photonics now brings together an extraordinary range of technologies, devices and applications, drawing signals from widely across

---

53   My younger son, Tom, is leading a UK national initiative to support continuing professional development and support of echocardiography teams and services, at the coalface of care. This endeavour can now be organized more easily and effectively using the network and image sharing opportunities of the Information Age. It portends a new and more sustainable culture of teamwork, peer review and support for the governance and improvement of services.

the spectrum of electromagnetic waves.[54] These have progressively been combined with electronic devices and computation to advance scientific understanding and clinical capability. For example, advances in fibre optics and cameras have led to new opportunities to investigate the GI tract with endoscopes. The combination of a miniaturized camera, x-ray angiography and machine intelligence software has led to more precise methods of imaging. Optical coherence tomography has been combined with angiography to guide the sizing and positioning of stents used to strengthen damaged blood vessels. Advances in thermal infrared imaging technology have enabled non-invasive monitoring of neonates. And the ever-greater precision and range of time and distance measurement, as, for example, made possible by optical frequency comb technology, is opening yet-wider vistas of the ultra-small and ultra-large. John Lewis Hall and Theodor Wolfgang Hänsch shared half of the 2005 Nobel Prize in Physics 'for their contributions to the development of laser-based precision spectroscopy, including the optical frequency comb technique'.

Nuclear Magnetic Resonance Spectroscopy and Imaging

Nuclear magnetic resonance (NMR) is a physical phenomenon used to probe the perturbed energy levels of atomic nuclei when placed in a strong static magnetic field and subjected to a weak oscillating field probe. The probe is tuned to detect resonance with the perturbed energy levels of the nucleus, which occurs at a frequency dependent on the magnetic properties of the nucleus and the medium in which it is situated. This phenomenon was unfolded in the 1940s and has found worldwide application in magnetic resonance imaging (MRI), now a leading clinical imaging technology. NMR spectroscopy, used in studying the physics of molecules and properties of crystalline and non-crystalline materials, has notably advanced the study of the structure of organic materials, such as proteins. Used to probe body tissue, the technique is relatively non-invasive. It is used to probe the energy levels of protons in the water and carbon nuclei of the tissue being studied.

Studies of protein structure have employed intricate, multilevel combinations of experimental and computational method, to analyze nuclear magnetic resonance (NMR) spectra that probe atom by atom, nucleus by nucleus, through the spine and side chains of protein molecules, over nanometre distances, and detect motions occurring in picosecond time

---

54   Amiri, I. S., S. R. B. Azzuhri, M. A. Jalil, H. M. Hairi, J. Ali, M. Bunruangses and P. Yupapin, 'Introduction to Photonics: Principles and the Most Recent Applications of Microstructures', *Micromachines*, 9.9 (2018), 452, https://doi.org/10.3390/mi9090452

intervals. Applying NMR spectroscopy in this sort of probe is complex and time consuming. It proceeds systematically, marking different parts of the molecule studied, such that they can be recognized and analyzed, and using the measurements made to infer three-dimensional structure. These intricate laboratory procedures have progressively become automated, just as hospital chemical pathology laboratory tests were automated fifty years ago. X-ray crystallography is still a preferred method, in terms of the positional resolution it can achieve. But purifying samples and growing crystals is a slow process–it does not progress in Internet time! NMR spectroscopy has the advantage of allowing the liquid state to be probed.

X-ray crystallography and NMR spectroscopy have strong and longstanding scientific pedigrees. Devices that enable sequencing of molecular structures of interest have advanced in scale and speed, setting the pace for, and keeping pace with, scientific enquiry. Three-dimensional visualizations are intrinsic to the study of the function of these molecules but obtaining them experimentally, for the hundreds of thousands of molecules for which chemical composition and sequence data are known, is prohibitively costly and time-consuming.

It was at this stage that bioinformatics began to come into its own and take off as basic science. Computational methods have progressively filled the gap in providing new approaches to infer structure, less precise but much faster to implement, based on sequence data alone. Sequencing methods, too, have advanced spectacularly in their speed and cost-effectiveness, now utilizing automated laboratory devices based on nanopore technologies. Libraries of known sequences and their structures are used to piece together candidate structures of other proteins. Many-body problems, such as these, might be thought tractable by applying the methods of quantum mechanics to determine atomic and molecular state. They are hard enough in the abstract realms of theoretical physics and controlled physical experiment, however, let alone in biological context. This was the challenge addressed by Tom Blundell, described in the following section, whose career has spanned Oxford, Cambridge (where he was a student of Dorothy Hodgkin) and London.

Molecular Biology and Bioinformatics

Molecular biology was thought of as completing a circle with biochemistry and genetics, in seeking understanding of the functions of proteins and genes in the living cell.

In its earliest days, Astbury described molecular biology as follows:

> [...] not so much a technique as an approach, an approach from the viewpoint of the so-called basic sciences with the leading idea of searching below the large-scale manifestations of classical biology for the corresponding molecular plan. It is concerned particularly with the *forms* of biological molecules and [...] is predominantly three-dimensional and structural—which does not mean, however, that it is merely a refinement of morphology. It must at the same time inquire into genesis and function.[55]

Leaving aside Astbury's implied disdain for the niceties of what counts as basic or pure science (which somewhat mirrors the ring fence between pure and applied mathematics), this biological quest has drawn in other disciplines, pure and applied, creating a widening mix of bioscience. After biochemistry, have come biophysics and bioengineering, with bioenergetics, as a subdomain of biophysics, and biomechanics as a subdomain of bioengineering. At further levels of abstraction around the Ranganathan circle of knowledge, have come biomathematics and bioinformatics. And bioethics—which must patrol somewhere in the same region as biophilosophy, biolaw and bioreligion—has long been a field and afield! They each grasp, define, measure and describe a different perspective of the one elephant, the living organism, both enriching and complexifying discourse.

Bioinformatics emerged as a science, described as being concerned with measuring and modelling the genome, proteome, transcriptome and metabolome. It provides the central measurement and computational STEM of biology. STEM, here, is a play on words, emphasizing computation as a spine holding together the coherence of the science, technology, engineering and mathematics discipines that the biology draws on. This stem has been described as the central discipline of biology. I once opined to a group of clinical researchers at a departmental seminar at Bart's, that the topic of my talk, which was medical informatics and the GEHR (Good European Health Record Project), in its work towards designing a coherent information architecture for the digital health care record, was, similarly, a computational stem of all the topics they would likely ever have on their agenda! They looked shocked, surprised and unbelieving more than affronted–I surprised myself!

The scientific foundations of the interplay of molecular biology with bioinformatics have rested first on measurement of the biochemistry of the cell, then on its development and evolution through cell and organ lifetimes, and over evolutionary time, seeking to piece together a picture

---

55   W. Astbury, 'Molecular Biology or Ultrastructural Biology?', *Nature*, 190 (1960), 1124, https://doi.org/10.1038/1901124a0

and model of cell structure and function. This is a subtle and connected series of bioscience stories, way beyond sensible narration by me, but resting on a further set of pivotal and illustrious career contributions, recognized by more Nobel Prizes. There have been many such pioneering prize winners, some of whom I have already touched on. I add further mention, here, of Fred Sanger (1918–2013), Sydney Brenner (1927–2019), John Sulston (1942–2018) and Paul Nurse, who have spanned and led in this era of scientific transition into bioinformatics.

Sanger was born one year after my dad and died one year after him. Their paths crossed and they lived in the same community for several years, in wartime, when, as mentioned in Chapter Two, both were undertaking Quaker relief work. Sanger struggled with maths and physics, taking three years to get past the Part One Cambridge Natural Sciences Tripos. He focused, thereafter, on biochemistry and achieved first class honours. He laid foundations of experimental method for the genomics era, being awarded the 1958 Nobel Prize in Chemistry 'for his work on the structure of proteins, especially that of insulin'. He also shared in the 1980 Nobel Prize in Chemistry, awarded to Paul Berg (1926–2023) 'for his fundamental studies of the biochemistry of nucleic acids, with particular regard to recombinant-DNA', and the other half jointly to him and Walter Gilbert 'for their contributions concerning the determination of base sequences in nucleic acids'. Gilbert was Quaker school and Cambridge physics educated, supervised there by Abdus Salam (1926–96), Nobel Laureate in Physics in 1979 with Sheldon Glashow and Steven Weinberg (1933–2021), for their contributions to the unification of the weak force and electromagnetic interaction between elementary particles. It is interesting to note how the contribution of one who struggled with physics and maths, aligned so fully with one whose insight was tutored from the heart of theoretical physics!

Sulston and Brenner shared the 2002 Nobel Prize in Physiology or Medicine with Robert Horvitz, awarded for their contributions to 'understanding of organ development and programmed cell death'. Brenner was a key figure in piecing together how cells function, working first at Oxford, then at Cambridge and in the USA, puzzling over experiment and theory of the role of DNA and ideas about information flow within biological systems. He created a computer-based matrix that pulled together the relationships, to guide his thinking.

Sulston studied how genes regulate tissue and organ development via a mechanism called programmed cell death. In his Nobel lecture, he remarked that having chosen the right biological organism (the nematode worm) to work on turned out to be as important as having identified the right problems to address. He led the Cambridge arm of the Human Genome Project, from 1990–2003, seeking, successfully and at considerable cost and effort, to be first to map the full sequence and thus be able to ensure that detail of the genetic code would reside on common ground, within the public domain. In this they set out to defeat the competing US efforts led by Craig Venter, who tackled the sequencing with an alternative approach termed 'shot-gun sequencing'. This used computer algorithms that mixed and matched sequences obtained from small fragments of DNA. It had promised faster progress but was thought likely to prove unreliable, given the complexity of the genome that was envisaged to be involved. His controversial approach aimed towards the patenting of genetic sequences, thereby making them proprietary intellectual property. Sulston was a leading campaigner against the patenting of human genetic information.

Paul Nurse pioneered research on the control mechanisms active in the cell. He was awarded the 2001 Nobel Prize in Physiology or Medicine along with Leland Hartwell and Tim Hunt, for their discoveries of protein molecules that control the division of cells in the cell cycle. He has been a doughty advocate and campaigner for science in public life, enacted in leading roles, such as his appointment as the founding head of the Crick Institute, newly built, near to UCL, and recognized in a stellar range of personal awards.

The bioinformatics discipline accelerated from the early 2000s, capitalizing on rapid advances in measurement technology and combining new rapid sequencing methods with computational algorithms for mining and analyzing largescale databanks of known molecular sequences. These were used to explore the structure and function of the macromolecules they code for and how they fit together in the enactment of the machinery of the cell. This still rapidly evolving story is proving considerably more complex than might have been envisaged in the early days of protein chemistry and DNA sequencing.

The network of connections discovered has been compared to the electrical circuits of electronic systems, with their component resistors, capacitors, inductors and transistors, organized into rectifiers, logic gates and switches, filters, amplifiers, and so on. In the cell, the multitudes of macromolecules are organized in a similar pattern of component groupings, responsible for the diverse and linked processes that power and enact the chemistry of life. These synthesize and transport molecules around the cell, across membranes between different compartments, engaging in different roles and reactions, there, and moving material into and out of the cell. At an atomic level, these processes can also be described in terms of the physics of electron and proton gradients, electrochemical forces and energy balances. This evolution in scientific thinking is a synthesis of experimental, mathematical and computational physics, chemistry, biology and medicine. And overarching all of this are predicted to lie certain information networks and mathematical symmetries, yet to be understood, that determine the structures and functions that can exist, and thus constrain what does exist. Chapter Six takes a side journey along this route of discovery in the science of life. Here, I continue to follow the connection from measurement and computation into clinical practice.

The progress made in scaling and speeding up measurement is evidenced by the new reality that the three billion or so base pairs in two metres or so length of DNA in the cell, grouped within the twenty-three chromosomes, can now be quickly sequenced and analyzed for individual subjects. The Sanger Institute and the adjacent European Bioinformatics Institute (EBI) at Cambridge and now the Francis Crick Institute in London, provide a focus for assembling the data and creating the analytical methods of bioinformatics, now central to life science research and its connection with clinical genetics and clinical practice. Much focus, in the near term, is directed towards understanding and potentially treating inherited conditions.

The NHS in England has pioneered the 100,000 genomes project scaling these efforts to population level. Other such biobank initiatives around the world are following a similar pathway. Inherited diseases are highly varied and many extremely rare. Pulling together genotype and phenotype data from affected patients across a country, and across the world, is crucial for both scientific enquiry and effective clinical management, requiring capture of coherent data from investigation and treatment in different centres. This is a significant factor in the push for an open platform of digital care records, as pioneered by openEHR. The openEHR community, led in this aspect by researchers in Sardinia, has played a part in efforts to align phenotype data collected in care records with the evolving new methods and practice of genomics medicine.

As I arrived back at UCL in 1995, the Provost, Derek Roberts (1932–2021), asked me to meet Janet Thornton, and I visited her office in the then Human Biology department, now grouped under the umbrella of UCL Life Sciences. Herself trained as a physicist; she was engaged in research characterizing protein folding. It was she that characterized the then emerging discipline of bioinformatics as the central discipline of biology–an assessment encapsulated in the title of a Royal Society Symposium she organized at that time. Brave words for a physicist, but persuasively evidenced by its subsequent evolution. Janet has gone on to create and lead the European Bioinformatics Institute (EBI) at Cambridge.

In the early days of bioinformatics, life science had to come to grips with the expanding databases of gene sequences assembled from the plant and animal kingdoms, and in clinical research. Algorithms that mined, characterized, searched and analyzed these sequences, mushroomed.

Looking for the codes and patterns governing the structure of genes and gene expression in all stages of the growth and reproduction of an organism is a huge enterprise. There was uncertainty as to how many such genes there were in the human genome and about the role of much of the genetic material that seemed not to be directly connected with them–termed junk DNA or non-coding DNA, but with the suspicion, as with stuff hidden in long-forgotten loft-stores in our houses, that it might hide unknown but important gems!

The mapping of gene sequences to the historic language of genetics, based on breeding experiments, and the study of inherited rare diseases and the susceptibility to them of family members, added further detail and complexity. Computer scientists became active in devising computational methods to go further, mining DNA sequences to look for underlying patterns of gene structure, transcription and expression in the biochemistry of the cell and organism, and in family histories. They extended sequencing methods to the study of the gut flora, assembling a further huge data domain, in what was, by analogy with the genome, termed the gut biome. Study of the hundreds of thousands of proteins expressed by genes within the cell gave rise to a sub-discipline of proteomics. Viral and bacterial DNA and RNA were studied, recasting these fields within the framework of bioinformatics. Bioinformatics extended to characterization of plant biology and ecosystems.

The idea of inferring protein structure from sequence data was attractive in prospect. The jigsaw puzzle-like challenge was first to identify the pieces of the puzzle (the atoms and chemical bonds), as revealed in multiple measurements made, and then fit them together to solve the puzzle and thereby infer a possible three-dimensional structure of the complete protein molecule. This systematic process was gradually supported by computational methods that inferred details of position and connection of component atoms, molecular spine and side chains. Numerical optimization methods were then used to infer ways in which the structure might fold in on itself, to achieve a stable energetic state, thus completing the structure prediction.

The emerging field of structural biology took this world further away from the laboratory bench and into the computational world of bioinformatics. Today, computer databanks house hundreds of thousands of protein sequences. Tom Blundell had explored computational methods for piecing together three-dimensional structures by looking for homology (common pattern, such as in position and structure of components) between sections of the sequence data of a molecule under investigation, and sequences for which structures were already known and recorded in international protein databanks. These databanks were data mined to discover likenesses.

Structural biologists devised software to apply constraints in how the discovered homologues might be combined, stereo-chemically, in terms of bond lengths and angles, and then employed numerical optimization methods to derive a feasible and minimum energy state combination of these, embodying all the protein's known constituents.

And on 2 December 2020, the DeepMind company, based at King's Cross in London, owned now by Google, capped their triumphs in mastery of chess and of the game of Go, with AlphaGo. They announced that their new program, AlphaFold, had succeeded in deriving protein folding structure from the sequence data of a protein to a very high degree of accuracy in placement of its atoms within the structure. It will be fascinating to understand, if we are told and can understand, the process it embodies–step by step, breaking the sequence into sequences of known folding structures, then gradually integrating them together towards a structure of the complete sequence. This story has continued to unfold at a dizzying pace. Equally interesting will be to see what resemblance it may bear to Blundell's strategy for tackling the problem. It is difficult to imagine that it has been able to approach the problem at the level of atomic orbitals, quantum wave functions and energy minimization. In whatever way it has been achieved, it will be at least on the level of achievement of Alan Turing (1912–54) in decoding the ENIGMA messages, which was a triumph of insight in combinatorics combined with knowledge of the physical mechanism of the machine itself. Maybe, one day soon there will be an AlphaEnigma able to replicate Turing's feat.

Academic computer science, a bit dizzy with its unfolding roles and contributions, across science, engineering and society, claimed bioinformatics as a subdomain of its own discipline. It had done this also, for a while, with computational physics and biology, until such subclassifications became rather pointless–rather like making biochemistry, biophysics, biomathematics and biomedicine subdivisions of the discipline of biology. Many such meta disciplines arose, grouping sciences across disciplinary boundaries into more holistic frameworks, and so arose systems biology and systems medicine.

The Science of Systems

The term system crops up everywhere these days. Everything seems either to be a system, or to exist and function within a system. Systems of thought and reasoning (for example, formal logic); systems of measurement (for example, SI units, *Système Internationale*); systems of structure and organization of the natural world (solar system, periodic system of the elements) and of human edifice and activity (Dewey decimal system, health care system). The term is widely appropriated across science, engineering and society. There is systems science, systems engineering and there are social systems. The system has become an all pervading and sometimes disturbing presence and paradigm–we blame the system!

The evolution of the systems approach in science, has reflected situations where measurements of complex natural phenomena exist within, and interrelate with, one another in a defining overarching context. It only makes sense to measure, record and reason with measurement made on the system where this context is considered, too. Measurements of blood pressure, cardiac output and heart rate make sense as a grouping within the context of the human circulatory system. And, depending on the purpose of our measurement, so also will depend how we capture, record and reason with these measured data. There has evolved a branch of science called systems theory, that addresses the issue of how we deal with ensembles of data and record pertaining to measurement and analysis of systems. There is instructive history of how systems theory and systems science have evolved.

Quite early in my reading into the world of mathematical modelling, as discussed in the next chapter, I came across the work of the chemist, Ilya Prigogine (1917–2003), at the Centre for Complex Quantum Systems of the University of Texas, Austin. He studied emergent properties of systems and their connection with the behaviour of living systems. His work on irreversible thermodynamics and the concept of dissipative structures and their role in thermodynamic systems away from an equilibrium state, led to his award of the Nobel Prize for Chemistry in 1977.

From this reading, I became aware of Ludwig von Bertalanffy (1901–72), who is credited with early attempts to draw multiple threads together within a general concept of systems theory. He was a biologist and is said to have coined the term systems biology. He wanted to restrict use of the term to refer to principles common to systems in general, saying:

> There exist models, principles, and laws that apply to generalized systems or their subclasses, irrespective of their particular kind, the nature of their component elements, and the relationships or 'forces' between them. It seems legitimate to ask for a theory, not of systems of a more or less special kind, but of universal principles applying to systems in general.[56]

He believed that systems theory 'should be an important regulative device in science', to guard against superficial analogies that 'are useless in science

---

56 L. von Bertalanffy, *General System Theory: Foundations, Development* (New York: George Braziller, 1968), p. 32.

and harmful in their practical consequences'.[57] The theory was couched in and drew together some familiar, and some newly coined terms–boundary, homeostasis, adaptation, reciprocal transaction, feedback loop, throughput, microsystem, mesosystem, exosystem, macrosystem, chronosystem.

According to Wikipedia, systems theory is 'a transdisciplinary, interdisciplinary, and multi-perspectival endeavour' that 'emerged in multiple contexts of academia' and 'brings together principles and concepts from ontology, the philosophy of science, physics, computer science, biology and engineering as well as geography, sociology, political science, psychotherapy (especially family systems therapy), and economics'. It 'promotes dialogue between autonomous areas of study as well as within systems science itself'.[58]

This scope is an extremely broad canvas on which to discern a theory of systems and paint a picture–extending over space, time, context, purpose, structure, function and behaviour. I will leave it there, for now, although the term information system, does require more discussion. I delay this until Chapter Five, where the context is of information engineering, and where systems analysis and systems engineering also feature. In scientific method, the term system segues into the domain of models of systems. In the next chapter, I will describe and discuss how mathematical and computational models have evolved over time, and especially during the Information Age, propelled forward by information technology.

A major international initiative pitched at the level of systems physiology and medicine is the Virtual Physiological Human (VPH) Institute, championed by Peter Hunter, Denis Noble and Peter Kohl. The VPH is:

> [...] a methodological and technological framework that, once established, will enable collaborative investigation of the human body as a single complex system. The collective framework will make it possible to share resources and observations formed by institutions and organizations, creating disparate but integrated computer models of the mechanical, physical and biochemical functions of a living human body.[59]

I discuss VPH further as one of my examples of mathematical models in biology and medicine, in Chapter Four.

---

57   Ibid., p. 81.
58   Wikipedia contributors, 'Systems Theory', *Wikipedia, The Free Encyclopedia* (25 June 2023), https://en.wikipedia.org/wiki/Systems_theory
59   Wikipedia contributors, 'Virtual Physiological Human', *Wikipedia, The Free Encyclopedia* (27 January 2021), https://en.wikipedia.org/wiki/Virtual_Physiological_Human

Parenthesis–Manifold and Balance

In the mathematics of topology, shapes are thought about and grouped within manifolds and their properties explored. Mathematicians continue to search for new manifolds and the rules that define them. In measurement we talk of three- and four-dimensional manifolds of data–capturing and recording events within dimensions of space and space-time. Classifications of disease are akin to manifolds, albeit sometimes rather arbitrary and unruly ones! Oxford Reference describes that 'In the philosophy of Kant, the manifold is the unorganized flux presented to the senses, but not experienced, since experience results from the mind structuring the manifold by means of concepts. The nature of the unstructured manifold is unknowable (transcendental)'.[60]

In both these usages of the term, manifold relates to grouping and classification as a means towards understanding. The Information Age has tested our intelligence and capacity in this regard, to the limits. Observation and measurement have focused over ever greater and ever smaller scales and extents. Academic discourse has ramified fractally, towards smaller distinctions and greater diversifications of theory and practice. Finding reliable and trusted methods for sharing, guiding and containing this boundless inflation of data and meanings, challenges human purposes, values and cultures. It is very confusing.

In times of confusion and anarchy, human societies oscillate unstably, locally and globally, in cycles between opposing limits of victory and defeat, triumph and disaster, boom and bust. Such limit cycles reflect imbalances and inequalities we have created and allowed to emerge. They lead to wars of culture, politics, ideology and criminality, now pursued through manyfold manifolds of information warfare, which have also exploded in range and scale. To be able to come to terms with the destabilizing potential of these new manifolds of the Information Age, and the imbalances, inequalities and inequities they can magnify and disseminate, we need to better understand, and share understanding of what is in play.

The human body has evolved the property of homeostasis, to enable it to balance and navigate the internal and external environments that it contains and encounters, and their perturbations. The Information Age has extended these environments and perturbations, worldwide. The thus connected world society finds itself and its environments increasingly unstable and must evolve quickly to achieve new balance–a more secure, both social and environmental homeostasis that enables humankind to navigate the pace

---

60 'Manifold', *Oxford Reference* (2023), https://www.oxfordreference.com/display/10.1093/oi/authority.20110803100130846

and impact of machine evolution and social change. What kinds of manifold and balance might that entail for navigating health care? We do not yet have understanding that helps us know, but the history of navigation at sea might provide useful analogy.

The shaping power and impact of new measurements, of global reach, is well illustrated by this history, which was transformed by accurate and feasible measurement of latitude and longitude. From earliest times, estimation of the position of a boat had rested on determination of its direction and speed of travel, relying on astronomical observation, compass, knotted rope and calculation based on the recording of speed and direction of travel. The science and precision of navigation evolved through the creativity and determination of artisan instrument makers of compass, sextant and clock escapement, and mathematical calculation to create complex lunar charts, providing methods that could be feasibly implemented onboard a ship at sea. The sextant stabilized measurement of latitude and the Harrison escapement clock enabled timekeeping, to keep track of elapsed time and thereby the longitude displacement of the boat relative to a common reference meridian–the Greenwich meridian. Pendulum clocks, the former instruments used for measuring time, were of no use on a pitching and yawing boat at sea!

The forces of mercantilism, empire and looting quickly cottoned on to the exploitative potential of these new accurate means for navigation. They sought, for their own interests, to maintain secrecy of the increasingly essential maps and charts that could then be created, to make navigation accurate, detailed and safe. James Poskett's book, *Horizons: A Global History of Science*, has a fascinating historical account of how maps were evolved in this way.[61] Private enclosure of global charts and maps would have served those narrow interests but done nothing for the cooperation and benefit of other travellers. As the challenge of accurate measurement of position on the earth's surface was gradually met, so too came recognition of the importance of new international public institutions that were created to maintain the navigational commons and defend against destabilizing and unbalancing forces. A new manifold and a new balance.

There is a parallel struggle facing software technology today, to defend the common ground underpinning information utility for the Information Society. The Information Age has taken science and society into new and virtual worlds of measurement and modelling of data, along new axes, and manifolds of life science, clinical and population data. The Internet and Cloud technologies on which these operate rest on accomplishments of worldwide

---

61   J. Poskett, *Horizons: A Global History of Science* (London: Penguin Books, 2022).

science, technology and collaboration. They are products and resources of the modern-day intellectual Commons. The gene sequencing technology of today has grown from similar scientific worldwide collaborations in the Commons as has much of artificial intelligence.

Appropriation of such accomplishment and resource into proprietary software parallels the way in which the Enclosure Acts of 1773 destroyed the culture and enrichment of common land in England. Information enclosure is a symbol and threat of our age, because of its wide-ranging causative power –it extends from life science and clinical science to social media and artificial intelligence. Appropriation of the Commons of intellectual property is cloaked as a free-enterprise good and daggered as an impoverishment and disempowerment of society more widely. Opportunity for shared understanding of the theory and practice of the virtual worlds in which we now model and analyze data, risks becoming stymied by knowledge and know-how sequestered in proprietary domains. Knowledge of the engineering of information systems in which these worlds are enacted, and the vital information about life and wellbeing, on which they rest in supporting the health care services that serve and protect the living, must not be lost to society in this way.

Models and simulations of reality, operating in the virtual domain, are the subject of the next chapter. Engineering, which exists at the interface of science and society, is the subject of Chapter Five–a place where theory and practice contend. It is there that we must look for progress and there that the future will unfold. In all aspects of data capture, management and processing there are escalating engineering challenges of precision, scale and sustainability. There are ethical, social, economic and political implications to be faced, and choices to be made. Lying at the interface of science and society, these choices challenge vested interests and establishments, often remaining poorly understood, resisted or unrecognized, until too late in the day for efficient and effective preventive, mitigatory, or interventional action.

Creating, sustaining and collaborating on common ground is the essence of these challenges that lie ahead. It is central to the quest for good balance, continuity and governance of health care, and the creation of a care information utility to support it, centred on the needs of the individual citizen in the future Information Society, focused on support and delivery of care as locally as possible to their home, and standardized as globally as possible to ensure mutual coherence and cost-effectiveness of services.

4. Models and Simulations– The Third Arm of Science

Modelling and simulation have arisen as a third branch of science alongside theory and experiment, enabling and supporting discovery, insight, prediction and action. The Information Age gave rise to an upsurge in the use of models to represent, rationalize and reason about measured and predicted appearances of the real world. This chapter describes different kinds of model–physical, mathematical, computational–and their use in different domains and for different purposes. Solutions of mathematical model equations that defied analytical method and required huge amounts of mental and manual effort for the calculations made, before the computer, became considerably more straightforward to deal with using computational methods and tools developed and refined in the Information Age.

In the examples described, the focus is on pioneers I have been taught by, got to know or collaborated with: John Houghton (1931–2020) on weather and climate modelling, to give a perspective from a non-medical domain; Arthur Guyton (1919–2003) and John Dickinson (1927–2015) on modelling of body systems and clinical physiology; Louis Sheppard on model-based control systems for intensive care, and mathematical models applied to track and predict the course of epidemics and analyze clinical decisions. Other examples are from teams I have been privileged to see firsthand, as a reviewer and advisory board chair of largescale research projects across the European Union.

With colleagues in the UK and Canada, I previously published the Mac Series models of clinical physiology with Oxford University Press. I have established a Cloud-based emulation environment to provide access to these working models–created in the first half of my career and thus now archaic in terms of software interface–to accompany their description in one of the chapter's examples.

     https://doi.org/10.11647/OBP.0335.04

The most conspicuous example of truth and falsehood arises in the comparison of existences in the mode of possibility with existences in the mode of actuality.

–Alfred North Whitehead (1861–1947)[1]

Science may be described as the art of systematic over-simplification–the art of discerning what we may with advantage omit.

–Karl Popper (1902–94)[2]

The story now moves from knowledge, observation and measurement to modelling and simulation, which are sometimes described as the third arm of scientific method, alongside theory and experiment. These in turn connect with information and engineering, which is where the story moves to in the following chapter. We build models to see how our ideas hang together and might pan out, when observed or implemented for real in everyday practice and context. Simulation is the enactment of a model, and science seeks new understanding by hypothesizing and exploring the enactment of candidate theoretical models, matched against experimental data.

There are many kinds of model in everyday use–in physical or abstract logical, mathematical or computational forms. Some are continuously grounded in experiment and measurement, and closely track observed physical reality. Some synthesize and reason with accumulated knowledge spanning different disciplines and domains. The knowledge bases introduced in Chapter Two embody models of domains of knowledge.

Alfred North Whitehead's words can be taken as a caution not to confuse the real world and the model, in this process. Models can be powerful tools, but it is beguiling easy to become a bit too fixated on them. Karl Popper's remark may be taken as another kind of caution; about how we delineate the purpose that a model is to serve and reduce to its essence the detail that we include, so that the model can be both tractable and useful. Too many particular adaptations, and the generality of the model loses its power and appeal. Too much blanket generalization and the real world loses touch. These issues have come to the fore in how models are designed, validated, communicated and used. In 2020, mathematical epidemiologists built and refined many mathematical models to guide government policies, seeking to manage and combat the future progression of the Covid-19 pandemic. In the first half of my academic career, from 1970–89, I was closely involved in

---

1   A. N. Whitehead, *Adventures of Ideas* (New York: Macmillan, 1933), p. 234.
2   K. Popper, *The Open Universe: An Argument for Indeterminism from the Postscript to the Logic of Scientific Discovery*, ed. by W. W. Bartley III (Abingdon: Routledge, 2012), p. 44.

the development and application of computer models of clinical physiology and pharmacology; it is a world I have known well.

The Egyptians built pyramids using a toolbox of methods, combining astronomical observation, standardized measurement, machinery and human labour. They might have built a small-scale model of the Grand Pyramid to test their ideas, or maybe they just went for broke and got lucky in attaining its summit. They had built smaller pyramids first, and if you have seen them, their summits do look a bit flatter—rather like the summit of Mont Blanc. They are not at all as sharply geometrical as the Grand Pyramid. Maybe a point summit was not aimed for or just not attained for these. Maybe they reflect erosion through time of less hardy construction materials. Or maybe they reflect gradual improvement of initially not so successful pyramid construction methods, through successive attempts to build them, and learning from the experience.

This speculation serves to introduce an important general point: that there is iterative learning involved in making and deploying useful models, and risk in extrapolating their use, precipitately or too widely, in real life. That said, innovators always push on and pursue adventures of ideas, beyond the bounds of what may, in retrospect, look to have been safer and more logical ways of proceeding into the unknown. There are always first prototypes, and these may not work—they are models used in developing and improving designs. John Archibald Wheeler (1911–2008) has a memorable quotation in his seminal 'it from bit' paper that I introduced in Chapter Three, where he writes that the 'The policy of the engine inventor, John Kris, reassures us, [about the importance of testing our ideas in practice] "Start her up and see why she won't go"'![3] Of course, medical practice must be more cautious! But, medical science and clinical practice are always proceeding into the unknown, both at the level of first encounter with a presenting patient, or in exploring in further detail, with new methods, a presenting situation that goes beyond or does not quite fit with current knowledge and practice.

The terms modelling and simulation arise widely in everyday life: mathematicians, scientists, engineers, clinicians, economists, businesspeople and politicians all create, use and talk about their models. Philosophers of mind talk of it as encompassing a model of the world it inhabits. At Magdalen College (University of Oxford), I lived for a year two floors above the study of Gilbert Ryle (1900–76), who devoted his life's work to philosophy of mind. He has been succeeded by luminary figures like Daniel Dennett. Philosophy of mind, and ideas about the nature of consciousness and intelligence,

---

3   J. A. Wheeler, 'Information, Physics, Quantum: The Search for Links', in *Feynman and Computation*, ed. by A. Hey (Boca Raton, FL: CRC Press, 2018), pp 309–36 (p. 310), https://doi.org/10.1201/9780429500459-19

weave in and out of contemporary neuroscience, psychology, economics, computational science and engineering, and artificial intelligence (AI).

A seven-foot-tall machine called MONIAC (Monetary National Income Analogue Computer–the name amusingly close to the root of another word that seems suitably adjectivally-descriptive of the world it models!) was one of the first economic models, built in 1949 at the London School of Economics. I have seen it on display at the London Science Museum, consisting of a collection of tanks and tubes designed to simulate the flow of money around the economy. The human circulatory system has variously been modelled as a hydraulic mechanism, a set of biomechanical equations, and as analogue and digital computer programs. Embodied in simulations, models are used to explore structure and function of the modelled system in ways that may not be open to direct experimentation–such as to think about what will happen when a currency is devalued, or a patient's cardiac pump performance suddenly decreases by a half. Or in an imaginary enactment of what has been described as happening in 'The First Three Minutes' of the universe, remembering the graphic storytelling in the book by Steven Weinberg (1933–2021).[4] Not much scope for experiment there, but he was a co-recipient of the 1979 Nobel Prize in Physics for his outstanding range of theoretical contributions to more testable ideas, as noted in Chapter Three.

Early simulations posed new requirements for analytical solutions of complex mathematical equations. At the start of my career, simulations of analytically intractable equations, such as those describing the propagation of the nerve action potential, were cranked out, iteratively and laboriously, on hand-operated mechanical calculators, over many months, as discussed in the previous chapter. Now, intrinsically more complex, large scale and multilevel model equations require numerical methods for their solution, which are provided in computer software.

Models of many different kinds are used in research, education and training, and in the design, implementation and operation of devices and systems. They are used in guiding policy and managing organizations, large and small, spanning from the logistics of product manufacture and distribution to the performance of national economies, and the spread of international pandemics. This wide range of usage is informative of the different purposes served, and the methods used to build, test and apply the models to simulate the domains they encompass. The examples in this chapter are mainly focused on medical science and health care.

In managing the Covid crisis, models have played a strong supportive role. It has been reported that some seven different mathematical models

---

4   S. Weinberg, *The First Three Minutes* (New York: Bantam Books, 1979).

have been used in the United Kingdom (UK), to predict and reason about likely patterns of infection and morbidity, and their mitigation. Probably many more than that, I would imagine; nowadays, they tend to be quite easy to conjure into existence but often remain very difficult to tune to practical ends and advantage. Different models, based on different assumptions, differently structured and differently interpreted, have predicted strikingly different courses of events. Their design and application are theoretical, experimental and applied sciences. Politics may feel a need to cover its tracks, to be seen as guided by (clear and accepted) science. It is less attractive to admit dependency and reliance on the appliance of (unclear and uncertain) research in progress. Although there may indeed be some wisdom in deferring to a crowd of models in this situation, if any model is relied upon too greatly, or used incautiously, the conclusions drawn may mislead and distort reason, and perhaps distract unduly from simpler approaches that might play out as well, or better.

Second-guessing the behavioural impact of different phases of population lockdown to contain spread of infection has been a difficult area in which to weigh model prediction against the gut instincts of political judgement. The impact of the viral mutation that set the infection in the UK on a markedly different trajectory around Christmas 2020 was a Black Swan event that could not have been predicted, although the possibility of such an event was clearly always there. Viruses mutate and this mutation turned out to be highly impactful. The wild card this morning, as I write, has been a sudden and unexpected announcement of a significant reduction in vaccine supply from a manufacturer. Again, always a possibility, but a Black Swan occurrence defying prediction, other than in general assessment of potential risks, their impact, and mitigation strategies. It is costly to allow for the many such potential contingencies, where none or several might arise and would, in combination, interact. Chance events can be a both lucky and brutal amplifier and leveller. Some we are born to, and some are cast upon us.

All this is an extremely complex domain to seek to model! Some of the mathematical modelling flown into the stormy Covid pandemic has not flown too well. Policy choices in managing the crisis, predicated on modelling studies, were impactful in the spread and impact of the infection and in the economic consequences—many lives and livelihoods were at stake. It would be interesting to discover how policy has played out in places where there was no modelling community to draw on for advice. The many imponderables about the modelling work, and how the issues it sought to predict played out in coping with and managing the pandemic, will be the subject of important and critical review, as the current crisis recedes into the past. It has been a real-life (substantially uncontrolled) experiment that none, other than the most centrally controlled of societies, could have conducted, or wished to do so!

There is a wider problem, here. Gaining a handle on managing complex systems often looks a very good candidate for a model-based approach. In the social domain–and managing a pandemic is as much a behavioural challenge as a scientific, clinical and logistical one–models are nigh on impossible to validate experimentally, in their real-life context. In science and engineering, it is of the essence to propose and dispute alternative models as a means for gaining insight and testing ideas. It seems unlikely that the designers of simulators for training aircraft pilots would allow multiple alternative models into everyday use. They would be more specific about the purposes served and provenance of the models proposed, and test them rigorously, before deciding on use. There was no such option in reacting to the crisis of pandemic. The modelling of world economies was subjected to a not dissimilar 'experiment', with the financial near-collapse of the world monetary system in 2007–08.

We now have models of complex global weather systems, used to forecast the local weather that we can expect, with considerable precision. They have taken many decades to improve and scale, in balance with the feasible measurement of the weather systems they represent, the logistics of continuous collection of the data needed, and the computational capacity required to simulate and communicate the weather patterns predicted by the solution of the model equations. And these forecasts need to balance with and be tuned to the needs of different audiences–citizens, event organizers, local farmers and airline pilots.

If we only consult the weather App on our smartphone, we may yet step out into a vigorous local downpour. Somewhere along the line, individual judgement receives and processes multiple sources of information, balances risks and decides what to do–whether to stay home, what clothes to wear if going out and whether always to carry an umbrella, just in case. And it is a good idea to have a look outside the front door, first. In well-defined and monitored domains, machine intelligence may, in time, prove decisive in such judgements. If so, we must accept the loss of autonomy and self-reliant capacity to observe and think, that this dependency may engender or entail. There is an element of bargaining involved–we bargain on it not raining and leave our umbrella at home. With the Mephistophelean computer involved, it might prove a Faustian bargain.

Purpose and Method

The term model is now very widely appropriated. As a noun, it carries a connotation of ideal form, to be adhered to or followed as a way of presenting or acting. As a verb, it is a creative action, abstracting and representing something–an aeroplane, chemical structure, or body system. We talk of human role models–people we observe and follow, and thereby feel helped to shape and improve our own roles and contributions in life. Good role models are not perfect people, but they are authentic, demonstrating quality and balance in what they achieve, and how they do it. They are, in a sense, representations of who we might aim to be and become. We need to see and feel some connection between them and their lives, and us and ours, and to have belief and trust in them. The pursuit of better things needs always to be balanced by a sense of what we have, being perhaps good enough already. As the paediatrician Donald Winnicott (1896–1971), a close colleague of my parents in the 1950s, used to write, parents should not aim at perfect parenting–good enough parenting is a good enough goal to aim for. There is a wider issue, here–how do we decide what is good enough in the models we create and adopt?

Models are pervasive: in research, education and training; in practical support of design, manufacture and operation of devices; in systems and services of everyday life. They are integral to control engineering. They assist in reasoning about complexity, exploring consistency of theory and experiment, and discerning and focusing on relevant and essential detail. Purpose of use and method of design and operation connect closely. We seek good enough models.

For Science

Mathematical models and simulations have featured in theoretical physics since long before my songline. They employ differential equations to describe physical phenomena that evolve over time, solve the equations analytically, and present the results as columns of numbers and graphs. The integration of the equations is a simulation of the model they represent. Many such representations are of a scale and complexity that defies such analytical solution, and simplifications are adopted for the purpose of making analytical solutions more tractable. Non-linear relationships are linearized, for example, and large scale and distributed systems are divided into a set of smaller equivalent compartments.

Such models now range from the atomic to cosmic dimensions of physics, and living organisms and systems are modelled from molecular to earthly (Gaia) dimensions. Discussion of the nature of consciousness and intelligence has been known to scale theoretical models, conceptually, towards the current Planck boundaries of measurement! And the quest to create new mathematical methods that better serve the modelling of complex physical and biological systems goes on. Mathematics has long sought to go beyond the integer realm of calculus, where we have the first, second and higher order derivatives of traditional calculus, and their integrals, to explore what a fractional calculus might look like, lying between those integer orders. New tools have emerged to populate models with these functions and thereby achieve a more faithful and tractable representation of complex system dynamics, for example where they cross over between different domains of behaviour and require memory of past behaviour when predicting how the future will unfold. These methods are finding increasing application in science, including the disciplines of biology and medicine, for both modelling and controlling system behaviour.

In physics, models range over field theory and particle physics of the exceedingly small, to cosmology of the exceedingly large. They simulate and match experimental data from particle colliders that accelerate matter towards the speed of light, and laboratory-, land-, ocean- and satellite-based environmental sensors, and telescopes probing to the limits of the observable physical universe. In more recent decades, models ranging from the atomic level, to the molecular, cellular, organ, body and population levels, have spread through life science, medicine and health care.

I had early encounter with the theoretical foundations of atmospheric physics that underpin today's weather forecasts, and use this as my first example, below. Coming from a field far removed from biomedicine, the story of their evolution over time provides useful counterpoint to later discussion of models in life science and health care. Rather as the story of the evolution of approaches to library classifications of knowledge, in Chapter Two, showed parallels with that of computerized medical terminologies, classifications, and knowledge bases. In like manner, stories about engineering innovation in the Industrial Revolution are invoked, in Chapter Five, when surveying the engineering of information systems in the Information Revolution of our age. I still follow with interest, but sadly no longer as much understanding, the model-related discussions, and conjectures about unification of quantum theory and general relativity. Today, as I write (18 January 2022), tidying the second draft of the book before submitting it for the publisher's peer review, I have been reading about new experimental results leading to renewed conjecture about the idea of a potential fifth fundamental force. Such glimmers stimulate hopes that they might help to clarify, and fill some of the outstanding gaps between theory and experimental observation, in what the current Standard Model of physics can account for.

In computer science, the Turing machine arrived in the 1930s as an abstract model of computation used to represent algorithm and computer program. Models of logic, expressed by mathematical logicians and argued over by philosophers, took on computational form. Computer languages (for example, Simula (1962) and Prolog (1972)) evolved for expressing different ways of representing, simulating and reasoning with different kinds of computer-based models. Algorithms and computer programs evolved, expressed in these languages, to use these models in real life contexts. With the advance of the computer came ever more extensive computational methods and models of complex systems. These could be designed to represent the modelled system in finer detail and predict its behaviour more extensively. They used newly devised numerical methods, implemented in computer programs, to converge on accurate and stable solutions of the model equations, by iterating successive approximations in many steps.

X-ray imaging and the rod and sphere models of chemical structure of molecules, provided the methods and resources that guided Francis Crick (1916–2004) and James Watson to their imagination of the double helix of DNA, in perhaps the best-known scientific example of such physical models.[5] What are called 'animal models' of disease have been extensively bred for researchers to test potential treatments, as a preliminary stage in creation of safe human therapeutics. These *in vivo* model experiments can, to an increasing extent, be replaced by *in vitro* and computer-based testing, drawing on extensive databases of the properties of already known and described macromolecules, pharmaceutical materials and products. An early example of such databases was the Swiss-Prot protein sequence databank, developed in the Geneva University Hospital, in the department of my late,

---

5   As I was first drafting this section, the *Times* newspaper (20 May 2020) reported the Princeton/Bergamo study of the design of Renaissance domed churches and cathedrals—at the interface of abstract geometry, architecture, engineering, and construction. The domes of Antonio da Sangallo (1484–1546), built around the 1530s, were known for their engineering feats, including foundations for building on unstable land. One such dome, built in two self-supporting layers, comprised a 'cross-herringbone spiral pattern'—a double helix—constructed from vertical bricks and filled in with horizontal bricks. This construction avoided the need for expensive wood support framing. It felt a beautiful analogy with the chemical bonds stabilizing the flexible DNA double helix molecular structure—a double helix design of vertical 'bricks' (A, C, G, T), with bonding horizontal 'brick courses' (chemical bonds), creating a stable 'Renaissance dome' (DNA molecule) on 'unstable ground' (the living cell)! Maybe a foolish aside, but fascinating and fun!

much-respected colleague there, Jean-Raoul Scherrer (1932–2002). As early as 1969, he worked on pulling together the DIOGENE patient-centred care record for the hospital information system.

The mapping of genomic sequences to computational models of stereochemical molecular structure has evolved very rapidly in recent decades, and from this came new understanding of normal and abnormal folding of protein structures, as discussed in Chapter Three, and much else. The amazing new scientific edifice of pharmaceutics that has resulted has, in large part, been a creation based on the work of very many scientists collaborating within the public domain. One wonders what might have happened had commercial intellectual property patenting norms prevailed over these innovations at that time. Drug and vaccine design have advanced rapidly from these beginnings, with the advent of three-dimensional computer-generated models to assist in matching their molecular design to target cellular receptors and processes.

In Education and Training

The flight simulator is a well-known example of the use of a model to assist training and assessment of a skill. The Harvey simulator, used in training doctors, nurses and paramedics in common clinical skills, is an example of the use of simulators in the clinical domain. Harvey focuses on practical handling and interpretation of clinical signs and interventions, such as intubation of breathing apparatus, intravenous injection of drugs and cardioversion. My work of two decades from the 1970s, at St Bartholomew's Hospital (Bart's), was largely devoted to the development of a range of highly experimental computer-based models, and their testing and use as simulators within educational and clinical environments. These models, known as the Mac Series, were created by a team of which I was a member, led by my then head of medicine at Bart's, John Dickinson (1927–2015), in the context of his close connection with the pioneers of the Medical School at McMaster University in Ontario, Canada. This history recurs in the examples below, of computational modelling pioneers I have known, and their related initiatives that I connected with and worked on, along my songline.

The Mac Series models were distributed widely across the world, first by me, on nine-track magnetic tapes, for incorporation within preclinical, clinical and professional educational curricula. They even cropped up and surprised my medical student daughter in her respiratory physiology course at the Nottingham Medical School, where I had previously got to know her lecturer! As I further describe in the next section, the graphical versions that I created at the start of the transition between the minicomputer and microcomputer technology eras, were published by the IRL Press (no longer in existence), based near Oxford, as part of a trial of where computer software might fit within their future publishing business. I was a member of their Software Advisory Board, and then that of Oxford University Press, at that time. These published versions of the models received favourable review in a special issue of the *Times Higher Education Supplement*. I have resurrected them—nowadays just historic artefacts of early and now obsolete educational technology—from the only extant copies I know of. The programs are on ancient floppy discs together with their published manuals, and I have preserved them at home for now over thirty years, along with some related books written at the time.[6] Through these years, I also collaborated closely with Leonard Saunders at the University College London (UCL) School of Pharmacy, to extend the drug pharmacokinetic modelling work into pharmacy education and research.[7]

Three Sliding Doors

This seems an appropriate point in the storyline of the book, to interleave the context of some major transitions in my career in health informatics during the years around 1990. These were marked by a switch from a career focused on the computer modelling of body systems and medical education, to one concentrated on imagining and evolving a standardized architecture for electronic health care records. They broadened the interdisciplinary and multiprofessional flavour and scope of my work, bringing unique new opportunities in the decades that followed to link health informatics within

---

6   These graphics versions of the Mac Series models have been reconfigured to be made available, open-access and online, with permission of the surviving authors, as part of an electronic archive of additional resources to accompany this book (available at https://www.openbookpublishers.com/books/10.11647/obp.0335#resources). In Chapter Five, I tell the story of how a community of programming enthusiasts, working in the public domain and dedicated to sustaining the long obsolete MS-DOS microcomputer operating system and applications that ran on it, recently enabled me to resurrect the programs in this way, and hopefully now keep them preserved in working form—something I had long-considered unachievable.

7   L. Saunders, D. Ingram, C. J. Dickinson and M. Sherriff, 'A Comprehensive Computer Simulation of Drug Metabolism and Pharmacokinetics', *Computers & Education*, 6.2 (1982), 243–52; L. Saunders, D. Ingram, and S. J. Warrington, 'The Pharmacokinetics and Dynamics of Oxprenolol: A Simulation Study with Six Subjects', *Journal of Pharmacy and Pharmacology*, 37.11 (1985), 802–06; L. Saunders, D. Ingram and S. H. D. Jackson, *Human Drug Kinetics: A Course of Simulated Experiments* (Oxford: Oxford University Press, 1989).

the mainstream of health care education, research and practice. There were three sliding doors that I stepped through, along with close colleagues at that time, into new environments that we created together.[8]

Door One

On becoming a professor in 1989, one of the first innovations that I was asked to take forward for the Bart's Medical College was a proposed new joint medicine and nursing clinical skills centre supporting undergraduate and postgraduate education. The project brought together a small team drawn from the local medical and nursing academic communities, which I was asked to lead. The way in which this first sliding door arose, and the innovative health care environment that, by stepping through it, we were enabled to create over the coming years, placed me at the centre of a widening multiprofessional scope and context of the evolving field of health informatics.

This Clinical Skills Centre, as it was later characterized, was the first such initiative in the UK and arose from growing concern about rigour in the assessment of clinical skills, in formal examinations framed around the traditional apprenticeship model of bedside, in-practice teaching. The concern extended from undergraduate education into the assessment and regulation of professional practice, and the clinical team that came together around me at Bart's, then, and later at UCL–especially Jane Dacre and then Lesley Southgate, in this context–went on to lead much wider initiatives of medical royal colleges and the General Medical Council. These sought to improve accreditation and regulatory roles in the assessment of the performance of doctors, through formal examinations and continuing improvement and review of clinical professional practice. These were, and remain, complex, multifaceted and contentious concerns; highly dependent on how they are approached, the information on which they are based, and their professional leadership and acceptance. They are in some parts highly political in nature, and in others not political at all–true of wicked problems, more generally, as I discuss elsewhere in the book! Lesley and Jane both enjoyed stellar subsequent careers, elected as Presidents, respectively, of the Royal College of General Practitioners and Royal College of Physicians, and were honoured with Damehoods by the Queen.

---

8   Further detail of these environments is covered in Chapters Eight and Nine.

Fig. 4.1 Jane Dacre–pictured here as President of the Royal College of Physicians of London. A leading figure in undergraduate and professional medical education and a close colleague at Bart's and UCL. CC BY-NC.

Interprofessional collaborations are never easy–between medicine and nursing, professional and personal history, and some rivalry, are seldom far from the table! For our new centre to be successful, it was crucially important to work together across this divide, with a shared goal and intention to build a good environment and team culture, to deliver it. My then dean, Lesley Rees (1942–2022), had recently become the first woman dean of the venerable Bart's Medical College and had a good relationship with the head of the adjacent Nursing School, Susan Studdy. It was heart-warmingly adventurous of them, and personally motivating for me, not being clinically trained and thus inevitably an outsider in the medical school hierarchy, that I was called on and trusted in this way to lead the initiative.[9] I reflect further

---

9 The project needed someone willing and able to lead from below in the hierarchy and I seemed to fit that bill—a senior professor of medicine or nursing would, likely, not have done! My sponsor professor of medicine, John Dickinson, took on the building project, liaising with the architects, and we recruited Jane Dacre as the lead medic and Maggie Nicol as the lead nurse—both then in their early careers, but clearly destined for great things—to forge a professional doctor/nurse alliance and work on the clinical skills teaching curriculum. They got on very well. I drew everyone together in running the project team, which included Diana Holroyd and Sonia Crow, senior nursing school staff who represented Sue Studdy. Together we set out to, and succeeded, in creating an effective and trusting team environment, respectful to both traditions and the sensitivities that could easily have become inflamed. That was, I think, in large part because we all approached

on this endeavour, as an example of the creation of a new environment, in Chapter Nine.

This was one of several wider leadership roles that I found myself moving into during those years of career transition: being hands-on in creating a computer infrastructure and support service, *de novo*, for the clinical departments of the Bart's Medical College; creating a novel videodisc-based educational resources to support multiprofessional training in support of cancer care in the community, for the Marie Curie Foundation; writing machine code software for a twenty-three videodisc series aiming to support the teaching of human anatomy, for an A-V industry-based project; helping to stabilize a project team that had got into team relationship difficulties when producing a computer-based resource supporting tropical medicine, for the Wellcome Trust; and then, most impactfully of all, leading the GEHR (Good European Health Record) academic, industrial and health services consortium and project of the European Union (EU), from 1990 to 1994, creating new foundations for electronic health record architecture. This latter opportunity–brought to me, persuasively, by Sam Heard and Alain Maskens, who overcame my initial nervous scepticism–led over the next twelve years to the establishment of the multiprofessional and interdisciplinary Centre for Health Informatics and Multiprofessional Education (CHIME) at UCL, in 1995, and creation of the openEHR Foundation at UCL, in 2003.

The successes and failures experienced along these separate but connected and evolving pathways of my career in health informatics have permeated widely in the narrative and framing of this book. They flowed from my presence over many years, working at the centre of health care communities and being given permission and freedom to explore. These beginnings led to conferment of more than ten full professorships in informatics and medical and health care-related fields, over the coming fifteen years. The huge amount I owe to many colleagues, in making this possible and making it work, cannot be overestimated. Their contributions feature and are acknowledged in multiple places throughout the book. Several of them have been reading and advising as its writing has progressed.

Door Two

During the time of the Skills Centre project, I was also busy thinking about creating a new environment for my academic work in health informatics. This would have had quite limited prospects within the Department of Medicine, after my sponsoring professor's approaching retirement. It was

---

the project in that way. Jane Dacre et al., 'The Development of a Clinical Skills Centre', *Journal of the Royal College of Physicians of London*, 30.4 (1996), 318.

an uncertain time and led to a second sliding door. Lesley Rees agreed that I could move my small team out of the Department of Medicine on the hospital site in Smithfield, and to rooms adjacent to the Medical College General Practice Department, situated at Charterhouse Square. This was at the generous invitation of its Head of Department, Lesley Southgate, and her colleagues, who included my subsequent close colleagues and team members, Marcia Jacks, Sam Heard and Dipak Kalra. In 1991, Jane Dacre and I established a small new department there, brashly called Clinical Skills and Informatics, and moved to Charterhouse Square, along with colleagues in my small team of that time. It was a staging post that positioned us for new opportunities to come, as the different stages and directions of our careers played out. It was a brave leap of faith into the unknown for us all!

The name of the department was a statement of ambition–the sort of outlandish idea that a new professor in a new field is sometimes indulged and encouraged to come up with! Such indulgence tends to wear thin if not fruitful, and unsuccessful indulged heads tend to be lopped within a couple of years or so–luckily mine survived intact in academic life for twenty more years, until my retirement!

Little could either Jane or I have imagined how far and how rapidly the interrelationship of the nature and skills of health care and professional practice, and their connections with the computer and its burgeoning aspirations and progress towards AI, were destined to advance during the following years, as unfolded in the storyline of this book! The advancing story of health informatics, and especially, now, of a hoped for benign and humanly supportive AI, has profound and increasing implications and impacts throughout the spectrum of health care education, professional practice, service delivery, research, governance, regulation and legal accountability. It has equally profound implications for every citizen in context of their access to, engagement with and expectations of health care services. It is a vector of continuous disruption of the markets and industries that support health care, in their products and services. And, thus, it is politics and business writ large and an unrelenting headache for the politicians and civil servants struggling to advance policy and strategy and control and manage the purse strings of the NHS!

Once again, the way in which this second sliding door arose–and the innovative multiprofessional and interdisciplinary health care environment that, by stepping through it, we were enabled to create over the coming years–placed my work within a still wider everyday practical context of health care services and their community and industry relationships, which were becoming increasingly central to the evolving field of health informatics.

It was in this new environment that the GEHR project, the antecedent of openEHR, was nurtured into life, as described in Chapter Eight and a Half. Alongside, we made new connections with others in the academic community that Lesley Southgate and her predecessor, Mal Salkind, had drawn together. They included Ann Bowling, a national figure in health services research, and Brian Jolly, engaged in a nationally funded higher education project exploring the teaching of medical ethics, clinical communication skills and health informatics. Another close colleague of subsequent years, Jeannette Murphy, joined us at that time, to spearhead the connecting of health informatics with the medical education curriculum. And it was from there that the third sliding door of those transitional years of my professional life presented itself, three years later.

Door Three

Our Charterhouse Square group's combined profile in health informatics and multiprofessional education, and success in leading the Bart's Skills Centre project and the GEHR project focused on a standardized health record architecture in Europe, was seen by new eyes. These matched us with ideas for new academic developments at the nearby UCL Medical School and its Whittington Hospital campus at Archway, in North London. This complementarity led to the invitation for our combined team to move there to create, and me to lead, a new department, christened CHIME (Centre for Health Informatics and Multiprofessional Education) by its facilitators and founders at UCL and the Whittington, David Patterson, John Pattison, Helene Hayman and Derek Roberts.

The unfolding story of the creation and lifetime of this new academic environment is told in Chapter Nine. The experience of creating and leading CHIME, and of the multiple new local, national and international relationships and roles that I was drawn into, there, became the central context of my evolving sense of the priorities and necessary steps to position health informatics appropriately on the changing landscape of health care, in its transition through the Information Age into the Information Society. This was also closely informed by two of my children's experiences as trainee doctors of those times, and my wife's experience, informed by her time as a doctor in a different country.

The work on the major projects I led, the changes in assessment of clinical skills and performance that Jane and Lesley led, and my switch in those years to leading teams envisaging and creating new foundations for digital care records, internationally, confirmed for me the oncoming inevitable migration of informatics, as a discipline, to the heart of medical science and health care. This migration occurs alongside transformational change in the nature and ways of working of health professions, in their skills and services. I was probably one of only a few people working in academic medicine and health care services of those times who was seeing things from that blue-skies and transitional perspective. But fortunately for me, I was trusted and supported to engage in that spirit, imagining and working to help create new environments supportive of transition towards future Information Society health care.

I had also come to believe that no amount of talking or writing about these still nebulous ideas was likely to enable much of significance to be learned about them, created and sustained–rather the opposite, in fact. A head-down focus on the practicalities of implementation, and thereby learning by doing–as Jo Milan brilliantly exemplified at the Royal Marsden, as described in Chapters Five, Seven, and Eight–was the order of the day! I draw on this experience in Part Three of the book, where I consider the challenges faced in creating and sustaining a future care information utility, designed, operated, led and governed across the disciplines, professions and supporting industries of health care services, in partnership with the citizens and communities they serve.

Reversing back through these three sliding doors, I continue now with the overview of the purposes and methods of modelling and simulation.

As Tools of Design and Engineering

In this section, I move into the world of design and engineering, where models are used to observe, predict, make decisions about and control behaviour of diverse systems, from small-scale devices to industrial plants and national power grids. They may embody algorithms for sampling, filtering and analyzing measurements of the system under consideration, fitting parameters that characterize the model to match as closely as possible to the observed experimental data collected, and estimating how precisely the model predictions can be known and relied upon. The validation and usefulness of the model rests on how well performance aligns with purpose.

As a young boy, I spent many happy hours making a quite large model aeroplane, from balsa wood struts, parchment-based bodywork hardened with cellulose dope, and a miniature diesel engine to drive the propeller. It was a thing of beauty and the maiden flight on a nearby hill a memorable event. I filled the small fuel tank, flicked the propeller to start the motor, and gave it a gentle launch. It took off and climbed with immaculate trim, soared higher, disappeared into cloud–to crash somewhere unseen and be found, broken-winged, with me broken-hearted, an hour or so later! It was a model aeroplane, a real thing but not the real thing. It represented many of the features of the real thing, enough to give me a sense of the real thing. I had fun making it and may have learned a bit about design, construction and flying of aeroplanes, but clearly nothing about controlling them! No harm done!

Real plane crashes cause loss of life, however. The de Havilland Comet passenger jet aircraft crashes of my 1950s childhood, arose for lack of prediction of the impact of metal fatigue in propagating the collapse of its structure under pressure in flight, and failure to design accordingly, to minimize that risk. To reduce fuel consumption in flight, holes were made in struts to reduce their weight. Windows had rectangular shape–creating seeds of dislocation and fracture at the corners of the surrounding metal structure. I have seen them, preserved by aircraft manufacturers and shown to school children attending their aeronautics open days. These early passenger flights were essentially experiments with what proved fatally flawed aircraft designs. They were learned from in those years at the expense of lives. The crashes derailed the nascent jetliner business in the UK–the site of the de Havilland airfield at Hatfield is just a mile from our house and now houses commercial warehouses, elite-car showrooms and open common land for walkers. The old runway can still be traced and a plaque there commemorates the Comet.

In the early 1960s, I saw the prototype engineering systems for the Concorde supersonic plane laid out within a huge hanger at the Filton aerodrome, in Bristol, to test the evolving design concepts in play. A small, odd-looking paper-dart-like plane was built and flown, to simulate the delta wing design. A Vulcan bomber aircraft was fitted, and flight tested, with the prototype Olympus jet engine. The cramped cabin interior was mocked up in wood–I walked inside and wondered how those rich enough to fly in it would fare in such cramped conditions. The prototype flying models were star attractions at the site, for avid visiting school children, me among them, and at the annual Farnborough Air Show, where businesses and spectators merged for this national showcase of aeronautics.

Computer models of aeroplanes and flight simulators are now extraordinarily realistic. Engineers iterate aircraft design concepts using them, and pilots learn to fly using them. Of course, there is always an inaugural first flight, but the Comet-like disasters of former times are now avoidable, albeit that it seems, just recently, that commercially driven short cuts led to unsafe, unstable designs that persisted into large scale production and early flights of the Boeing 737 Max aircraft.

Flight testing of a new aircraft design and construction is now closely linked with tests performed with simulations. The models are used to explore intermediate ranges of behaviour of the modelled system, where there is limited or unduly expensive opportunity to measure and monitor the full range that would be encountered in the real world. Multiple simulated test flights replace real ones in the programme of trials employed. A test that forces the trim upwards until the plane stalls may also be easier to envisage conducting in a simulation, provided, of course, that one already has sufficient confidence in the results obtained, when extending the model set up that far!

Models of buildings are made to show off architectural designs and Lego model villages are built as tourist attractions. The dressmaker's dummy for fashioning and making clothes is a model still widely used. The catwalk human model shows off the finished product to potential retailers and purchasers, promoting a world of glamour and make believe. Today, body profile can be scanned, and used to build and calibrate a three-dimensional computational model, embodying both form and movement, using Computer-Aided Design (CAD) software. The clothes designer has access to database archives of clothing materials and their properties, from which to select when creating a new design. A real prototype can then be constructed, and the modelled design iteratively improved, until the product is approved. The computational model then integrates with cutters and sewers, setting out patterns of materials to be cut out and stitched together in its largescale production. In the clothes shop or online, the model of the tailored garment can be calibrated and displayed, based on the size and preferences of a specific potential purchaser.

A final contemporary example, exhibiting the power of bioinformatics, has been the speed of design of candidate Covid-19 virus vaccines. The development cycle, from the identification of viral genomic sequence, modelling and picturing of the viral surface, and selection of candidate binding targets, through to detailed design and testing of the vaccine, is a process drawing on multiple scientific and computational methods and resources. And the shrinking of the timescale, from conception to approved use in at risk populations, an outstanding achievement.

Within Products and Services

As just illustrated in the case of design and production of clothes, nowadays the design and visualization of manufactured goods, and plans for their production, are often supported by computer models built with CAD software. Prototypes of new products are made and tested at key points in their production cycle; the underlying computer models connect and integrate with design, production and lifetime maintenance and repair, and with quality control and monitoring at all stages of the product life cycle. Costs throughout are estimated, based on historic accountancy data.

The model is thereby integral with related production facility, organization and personnel plans. A similar integrative approach is available for much larger-scale engineering and infrastructure projects. It provides a rigorous and consistent framework of workflow and cost projections required to underpin management and oversight of the process.

In the area of services, models of weather and climate are used to forecast outcomes in detail over coming hours and days and, in broader-brush trends, over coming months. Models of traffic flow simulate how the networks of transportation will be affected in different operating contexts, such as bad weather, scheduled repair and breakdown.

Models created to simulate behaviour of a system may take a quite different form than models used to control that same behaviour. In one case, they are used to predict outcomes of choices under consideration in the design of a new device or system. In the other, the purpose concerns control of its behaviour in practice. In control theory, a class of methods is the model-based control system. In this, a model of the behaviour of the system is built into a system controller integral with the system itself. When the system diverges from the desired operating state, or transition to a new state is required, potential changes to the system's adjustable parameters are tried out first in the onboard model and tuned iteratively to a level that would be expected to achieve the desired change, as predicted by the model, before being applied to the live system.

Models beyond Experimental Validation

In the early 1970s, Jay Forrester (1918–2016) and the Club of Rome, sought to model the global economy. It was a widely ridiculed but nonetheless worthwhile attempt, if perhaps not a realistic expectation. It seemed unimaginable that such a model could achieve more than the broadest of broad-brush approximations to reality or reach more than largely common-sense conclusions. As Walter Sellar and Robert Yeatman might have said, as in their 1930 spoof history of England, *1066 and All That*, 'wrong but wromantic'![10] The quest fizzled out. At this level, only one experiment is conceivable–the uncontrolled experiment of how events play out in real life. In the modelling of complex and interconnected systems, rigorously controlled experiment is a rarity and may be impossible. Clinical practice uses controlled trials in its efforts to tame variability in experimental

---

10   W. C. Sellar and R. J. Yeatman, *1066 and All That. A Memorable History of England Comprising, All the Parts You Can Remember Including One Hundred and One Good Things, Five Bad Kings, and Two Genuine Dates* (London: Methuen, 1930).

observation and measurement of human subjects, to home in on and quantify outcomes reliably ascribable to interventions made.

Models and simulations have found their way into the parlance and practice of economic and social systems–domains where human thought and behaviour are closely embedded, and experimental method not of the essence. My Daniel Kahneman inukbook, *Thinking, Fast and Slow*, describes how patterns of human thought influence economic choices–for example, weighing risk of gain and loss disproportionately.[11] In another quite recent inukbook, *The End of Alchemy*, Mervyn King cautions that mathematical and computational models and simulations addressing such matters, should be supped with a long spoon.[12] He argues that narrative and storytelling should feature more strongly in what he describes as a current crisis of ideas, more than of institutions and methods employed.

Governments have the unenviable task of setting fiscal and monetary policies in the context of economies which are extremely difficult to understand and predict. They review policy options using computer models that describe the underlying principles and behaviours that mathematicians, scientists and economists believe to be in play, and chose policies guided by these model-based predications. And in the world of commerce, computer models of financial markets are used to drive trader advantage–for example, by anticipating market movements and being first to the start gate for buying and selling of shares, thereby achieving first mover advantage, or by gambling to nudge their market value in a preferred direction that would benefit the trader.

Models that Can Lead Astray

Richard Feynman (1918–88) notably once remarked that you can prove anything by analogy. That amounts to the same as saying that you can prove nothing by analogy and mirrors Whitehead's cautionary advice quoted at the head of this chapter. Ability to help clarify and guide understanding are aspects of the usefulness of a model but the quest for a perfect model is an illusory goal.

One can make a simulation fit with experimental data in many ways, providing that one has enough requisite adjustable input parameters of the model at one's disposal, to shape the predictions it makes to achieve that fit. In mathematical language, these might be called degrees of freedom.

---

11   D. Kahneman, *Thinking, Fast and Slow* (New York: Macmillan, 2011).
12   M. King, *The End of Alchemy: Money, Banking and the Future of the Global Economy* (New York: W. W. Norton and Company, 2016).

The process may work for the data at hand, but what about data yet unseen, where a continued good fit may require further embellishment of the model, introducing more degrees of freedom. Where are Occam's Razor and Popper's advantageous simplification, here? This can become disadvantageous complexification. The validation of a model must combine assessment of its purpose, performance and usefulness, and its feasibility depends on ability to test and evaluate these under suitably managed and controlled conditions. The more complex and extensive the system modelled, and the context in which it operates, the harder this is to achieve. An unvalidated model is essentially a loose analogy.

In science, experimental validation is the arbiter of theory, however enthralling the theoretical abstraction. The modelling process is a creative one, and especially so if it stimulates new ideas and leads to tractable new experiment to test and confirm them. Many models will prove unsuccessful or misleading, but failure is there to be learned from. Problems and disputes easily arise where belief rather than experiment becomes the arbiter of the validity of a model.

With the generally more tightly bounded models used for design and engineering purposes, there is less excuse for, or tolerance of, getting the models wrong or misusing them. Unforeseen behaviours–such as the lock-step lateral vibrations that built up in the Millenium Bridge across the Thames, between Tate Modern and St Paul's Cathedral, when first opened for public use–can quickly derail the designs that the modelling had led to, quite apart from tripping up both designers and users in that case! The Tacoma Bridge must presumably have had a test outing *in silico*, too, but rigorous perturbation testing, to simulate the traffic and wind-induced vertical resonance that destroyed it, must have been lacking in the test schedule.

Where human understanding of the modelled domain is complex and uncertain, the model may sometimes be taken as offering beguiling and yet spurious certainty. As Voltaire (1694–1778) wrote, 'doubt is uncomfortable, certainty is absurd'.[13] All models rest on assumptions, simplifications and approximations. As with the wobbly bridge over the Thames, where these are wobbly, the predictions and their consequences may prove wobbly, too! Returning to Whitehead's caution, we must be cautious about tendency to allow the model to supplant the reality in our thinking and reasoning about the domain it represents. We must always keep in mind the purpose that the model is intended to fulfil, and the evidence that it can and does fulfil that purpose for the situation at hand. This can only be achieved if there is

---

13   Letter to Prince Frederick William of Prussia (28 November 1770).

clear and rigorous connection of the concepts, structures and behaviours embodied in the model and the real-world evidence and experience it relates to.

For this reason, we should be cautious of predictions based on opaque models. Models that should best be open to critical review and inspection are sometimes kept under wraps, for a mixture of academic, commercial or political reasons. We should be cautious, too, when modelling seeks to accommodate the uncertainties of human behaviours, however relevant these might be for the purposes the model serves, because they may also, likely, prove very difficult to handle confidently.

Given the intrinsic limitations of their model formulations, modellers often perform a sensitivity analysis to explore how the model predictions change in response to perturbation of the model parameters and initial conditions, and thereby to place confidence limits on predictions made when simulating future events. This has become a talking point in the context of the wide-ranging predictions of different teams simulating the expected impact of different lockdown strategies for limiting the spread of Covid-19 infection. The proof of the pudding is in the eating, but here it must also take account of what was cooked, how and why, and who was eating, when and where! Bland assertion of reliance on science, engenders public scepticism and suspicion that it is the books that are being cooked!

Notwithstanding these caveats, computational models are now central to the study of complex systems and the mathematics and science of complexity has moved forward alongside efforts to build such models. There is now greater understanding of the practical difficulties that modelling, and simulation methods pose, and their intrinsic limitations. Clarity of purpose is essential. Models should correctly utilize the methods and materials they employ but cannot be relied on as correct representations. They can perform well or badly for the purposes they serve, and the struggle to make them better and thereby more useful, is a strong motivation for exploring, using and learning from them. This may necessitate long-term endeavours and require sustained capacity and resource.

The next section visits physics, life science, clinical science, and health care, for examples of models used to explore and represent systems—what they aimed for, how and why they prospered and how and why they failed. These are stories I have personally encountered, firsthand, and some in which I also participated. They illustrate how models have become central to the creation of new knowledge and the taming of its related and exploding data sources, over the timeline of my career.

Pioneers of Computational Modelling

Physics–John Houghton–Modelling Weather and Climate

We share weather and climate. They connect our lives locally and our welfare, globally. This is not to say that the local weather is ever the same at different times and places–it clearly is not, anywhere: minute by minute, a rainstorm moves. This is not to say that the climate of Malaysia, central Europe or sub-Saharan Africa are ever the same–they clearly are not, either. But to model weather and climate in any of these contexts, one must understand and be able to compute with the same science and know how to use that knowledge in the different contexts in which one seeks to understand and make forecasts. One must know how to allow for the differences of local environment that play out in determining the weather there, from locality to locality, and time to time, and how accurately these can be forecast.

Why start with physics and weather? Well, illness is like bad weather and good health is like a sunny climate. Illness and health are local and global. Okay, a bit sophistic, but pandemic and health can learn from weather and climate. Discipline from around the circle of knowledge is now in play in these models, and mathematics and physics is where the weather and climate models started from. Arguably, though, machine intelligence may now sometimes prove a better bet for making accurate short-term forecasts, exploiting the measurements available. Zobaczymy [we will see]![14]

Weather forecasting has a basis in measurement, science and engineering that have all advanced steadily through the Information Age. It is now largely based on mathematical models and simulations, extending over large-scale patterns and local variations of weather. Today's forecasts are based on hundreds of millions of data points, from land, sea and air radiosondes, covering the earth's surface on a one kilometre square grid. Forecasts have improved–in recent decades they have been shown capable of predicting accurately one day further ahead in time, each decade.

In my childhood, the village doctor diagnosing and treating illness in a child and the local weather forecaster predicting weather over the coming period, shared some common traits. There was science and craft in play–skilled observation of what could be seen and felt, combined with limited measurement, put together with a wealth of knowledge and experience. A rough and ready seaside hydrometer was a strand of seaweed hung on an outside door of the house. Its feel reflected moist or dry air, and this in turn reflected and helped in anticipating changes in the weather.

---

14   On this Polish expression, see Preface.

There was good reason to want answers about what was going on and about to happen. Is it going to rain? Is this child's fever a serious concern? Of course, the doctor could, or was expected, to do something about the illness. Weather forecasters were not expected to do anything about the weather, but villagers could put on raincoats and the farmer could act in anticipation of a storm. Similarly, the village general practitioner (GP) might take one look at a sick child and know what was wrong and what to do (or not to do)!

Life has moved beyond invocation and sacrifice to unseen gods, or employment of mystical rainmakers to dance and bring on rain for the crops. But predicting the weather remains a part of culture and folklore. In England, weather arrives mainly from the west and departs mainly to the east. In Poland, the unpleasant damp clouds come from the west and the unpleasant dry and dusty winds come from the East–a metaphor of how Polish people feel, and with good reason, about the currents that have buffeted the history of their lovely country! According to Somerset folklore: 'Lundy high, fine and dry; Lundy low, it's going to snow', reflects how this small island appears on the horizon, from land several miles away. Cynical doubters had a (very English!) variant: 'If you can see Lundy in the morning, it's going to rain; if you can't see it, it's already raining!'

Weather stations at home were quite common in my childhood–anemometer, hydrometer, thermometer and barometer used in creating personalized weather forecasts. Early morning and late-night radio intoned the shipping forecast, based on measurements and observations from a network of lightships and weather stations, at sea and around the coast. These forecasts were published as contour maps of atmospheric pressure and temperature, and patterns of air movement reflecting the rotation of the earth. They were correlated with winds circulating air across warmer and cooler areas of the earth's surface, and seasonal variations according to position of the earth in its orbit, with rotational axis inclined to the ecliptic.

Now, a worldwide network of sensors and satellites collects data for creation of images and calibration of models that span continents. These depend on a functioning global digital network of communications, as do the telescope terrestrial networks and solar system voyagers through which astronomy and astrophysics advance. These networks were being invented and piloted at the time I attended Peter Kirstein's (1933–2020) lectures on telecommunication in the late 1960s, at the London Institute of Computer Science, later incorporated into UCL. He set up the first transatlantic connections with the US Arpanet and is recognized as a founding father of the Internet. This was five years before Conway Berners-Lee (1921–2019) and Ted Coles were selling computers into hospitals, for International Computers and Tabulators (ICT), and Conway's son, Tim Berners-Lee, arrived at Oxford to study physics, before going on to the Conseil Européen pour la Recherche Nucléaire (CERN) in Geneva, where he conceived and implemented the software network protocols which formed the basis of the World Wide Web.

One of my Oxford physics lecturers in the mid-1960s was John Houghton (1931–2020). His course on atmospheric physics was memorable–clear, concise and well presented. Olympian erudition, in welcome contrast to the bafflingly unexplained, but clearly brilliant and enthusiastic, genius of some. I occasionally attend physics alumni events in the department, today, and the standard of presentation all round is now hugely better. Houghton started his course by considering only a small volume of moist air, for which understanding at the level of the gas laws of Robert Boyle (1627–91) combined with the later understanding of the solid, liquid and gas phases of water, enable modelling and prediction of its behaviour in terms of pressures, volumes and temperatures. He was fluent in thinking on his feet, showing how the vector methods and calculus that we were coming to grips with in our first, highly mathematical year of study, could translate into a set of equations that modelled this small volume of air. These, in turn, became the core of generalization to more extensive and complex models of the atmosphere.

Imagine a weather forecast predicting that, on the one hand, the country may be covered in cloud and snow, at -25 degrees Celsius, or, on the other hand, it may enjoy a clear sky and heatwave at +25 degrees Celsius. Those sorts of swings occur naturally over several months from winter into summer–the frozen Niagara Falls giving way to a steam bath, between January and July, as I have seen with colleagues and friends, during visits to the nearby McMaster University. Such swings get wider and more erratic as climate becomes more chaotic. Earthly air temperatures now range over approaching 150 degrees Celsius. Life is tolerant of extreme cold but less so of extreme heat.

And hurricanes do happen in Hampshire, although hardly 'hever', as intoned in George Bernard Shaw's (1856–1950) play, *Pygmalion*.[15] Our children's home summer camp on a farm near Beaulieu in Hampshire, opposite the Isle of Wight, was hit by one in the mid-1950s–trees everywhere were uprooted. My dad's ten carefully erected bell-tents, sheltering twenty-five young campers, withstood the storm. He always brought one-metre wooden tent pegs to the camps and was teased for his caution. He sledge-hammered them into the soft ground at the height of the night-time torrential storm, and ours was the only camp still standing by the next morning, that had not been blown away in the night, like all the others! Drenched scouts and guides had been hurriedly decamped to shelter in the farmer's huge

---

15   G. B. Shaw, *Pygmalion and Major Barbara* (New York: Bantam Classics, 2008).

hay barn, where we saw them as we walked to the milking parlour next morning, to collect our day's supply of delicious fresh, cooled milk!

The physics of the atmosphere from sea level upwards, is extremely complex. It is in a dynamic balance with circulating ocean currents and land masses, small islands and major continents–some moistly forested and some aridly dry regions. Gyroscopic forces from the earth's rotation, solar energy incident, scattered, absorbed, and radiated, from air, cloud, icecap, desert and ocean, all interact. The modelling of ocean depths and flows, such as the El Niño, entraining with atmospheric weather conditions, is still rudimentary. The underwater geography channels a complex system of ocean currents and tides, such as the Gulf Stream, which mixes, ebbs and flows, through tides and seasons.[16] Given these still intractable unknowns, how has weather forecasting bootstrapped from mystical prognosis to everyday utility?

Weather forecasting evolved along complementary axes, of measurement, modelling and simulation. Limited intermediate goals and methods could be framed and explored, with a clear measure of success of the exercise–how well did the forecasts based on these simulations perform in relation to measurement and observation? There was a well-understood and articulated purpose and value in achieving increasingly accurate local forecasts–guiding farmers in planting crops and reaping harvests, and all of us in what to wear.

Chaos theory came into the discussion, through the butterfly wings metaphor describing the widescale magnification and propagation of minute influences. Analysis of the mathematical properties of the underlying equations of the models and their measured parameters enabled probabilities to be attached to forecasts–for example, a model predicts that the probability that it will rain in St Albans between 10am and 11am today, is nine percent.

Paradoxically, places where the weather patterns are predominantly very stable and predictable are difficult places about which to model the disturbances that do arise. Daily alternating patterns of heavy rain and fierce sunshine in Singapore and Malaysia, were highly consistent, but disturbances to this stable pattern cropped up quickly and unpredictably. Snow in desert-encircled Riyadh is not unknown and is a somewhat mystical event. For me, venturing outside from the air-conditioned, refrigerator-like hotel lobby, to travel to the University Hospital to run courses there, was like walking into an oven. Travelling in the desert wadis nearby on a weekend

---

16   The General Bathymetric Chart of the Oceans (GEBCO) is being pieced together from robotic surface vessels, commercial and public data, and crowd sourcing of sonar measurements from large ships and private yachts. Six percent of the area was charted by 2017, twenty percent is expected to be accomplished by the end of 2020, and the survey completed by 2030.

trip, one felt extreme vulnerability when walking even a short distance away from the air-conditioned vehicle and supply of cooled water. It was extraordinary to pick up coral from the sand, showing how much landscape and climate can change. One understood how Saudi colleagues who I once accompanied on a winter visit to cold, windy, rainy and gloomy, Wuthering Heights-like Lancashire and Cumbria (to visit a shipyard there, during my time working in the heavy engineering industry) found it an ecstatic experience of beauty and wonder!

Uncertainty in the prediction that it will rain, reflects both the quality of measurements on which the forecast is based, the appropriateness and reliability of the model itself, and the assumptions it rests on. It may reflect that the system modelled is intrinsically variable, perhaps in some statistically well-characterized or assumed manner. This may favour a stochastic modelling approach rather than a deterministic model of the relationships. It may reflect pragmatic choices made to model the system as an assumed average representation, fitted to averages of measurements made. The uncertainty may relate to the quality and coverage of measurements employed–how many sensors, where situated, how often sampled and how finely calibrated.

As previously discussed, all models are simplifications of the reality they represent. All are created with some purpose in mind, and this focus colours the simplifications made. Statisticians, quite rightly, caution against extrapolating models of data beyond the range of measurements on which they are based. The key test is one of utility and there may be qualitatively different considerations in play. A highly accurate forecast computed slowly may come too late to be useful. If fitting model to measurement requires highly granular measurement, the limited availability or high cost of making those measurements, may render such use infeasible.

In weather forecasting, new challenges have emerged, as capability, need and ambition have grown. This ambition now extends to how well we can model climate, in a way that accommodates both normal patterns and extremes and provides a useful and trusted handle on predictions made. Houghton went on to lead the meteorological service in the UK and to serve as co-chair and chair of the scientific advisory group of the UN Intergovernmental Panel on Climate Change (IPCC), from its inception in 1988 until 2002. He is quoted as having become pessimistic about the capacity of institutions at that level to act cohesively, saying that 'If we want a good environmental policy in the future, we'll have to have a disaster'.[17] He sadly died from complications of Covid-19 infection, in April 2020, as I started to write about him in this book. His commentary, and this coincidence, adds poignancy to the connection of global weather and pandemic.

---

17   Interview of Houghton, 'Me and My God', *Sunday Telegraph* (10 September 1995).

Health care faces arguably even more complex challenges in the modelling and simulation of its personal, local and global contexts. But whereas tackling climate change requires action at a global level, medicine can (the need for global collaboration on pandemic mitigation, notwithstanding) make progress in battling the inequalities of health, through local and regional, private and public, institutions and initiatives. There is a lot to do.

Biology and Medicine–Modelling the Human Body

Having started by opining that illness and weather have much in common, and affect us all, I must now row in another direction. They are also very different. There are marked differences in what is possible: in observation and measurement, experiment and modelling, and connecting these together to deliver useful outcomes.

It would be a daunting challenge, and not very useful, to attempt a full account of the many ways in which the modelling of living systems has evolved and contributed to understanding of human biology, medicine and health care services. Writing and reading about such models can only scratch the surface and provide only partial knowledge of their purpose, what they embody, and how well they contribute. They must be used and understood in context, to be appreciated. Most published models and simulations appear rarely to have been used or further developed beyond their place and time of origin and have thus provided little of sustained value for the domains that they represent. The same ideas and work are often repurposed into new publications, over and again, as I discovered when researching my 1991 Royal Society of Medicine (RSM) talk.

Through these decades of my songline, the evolving story of computational biomedical science was, in significant measure, one of human connections made across disciplines, professions and organizations. I focus here, once more, on examples that I know best, and why and how they stood out. They are of teams and innovations I observed or participated in, as researcher, colleague or reviewer. They differ greatly in their goals and methods. Some illustrate innovation that increased understanding and moved a field forward, while perhaps of little practical application or ambition to extend beyond research into practice. Some have been transformative of ways of thinking and working, more widely. Some have accomplished their immediate goals well, only to be soon rendered obsolete; remembered as historical artefacts of no further consequence.

When considering potential topics for a PhD, in the early 1970s, I explored two broad options. One was to focus on improving medical records, with the example of devices and algorithms for monitoring patients in intensive care. Modular instrumentation systems were becoming widely available and the use of the computer to aggregate, process and summarize the increasing amounts of data, and relate them to clinical decisions, in an accessible manner, was an interesting possibility. Instruments signalling false alarms had become an increasing problem for busy clinical staff.[18] The other option arose by chance when I met John Dickinson, who became my sponsor, head of department and close colleague for twenty-five years. I have my diary of 1970/1971 to refresh my memory of early meetings with him. John introduced me to his interest in clinical physiology and proposed that we work together on modelling the human circulatory system. It is interesting to reflect that having spent twenty years pursuing option two, I switched, when John came towards retirement, to spending the next twenty largely centred on option one!

John, with Moran Campbell (1925–2004) and Jeremy Slater ('Willie', 1928–90) wrote the authoritative textbook of clinical physiology of that era. His career-long interest was in the aetiology of essential hypertension, on which he was a world authority. My parachute into medical informatics was thus an unusual one–from the modelling of physics of the atmosphere into the modelling of human circulation. From an environment of excellence in physics into an environment of world leaders in physiology and medicine. It was a scary jump into a foreign land. It was a road less travelled and, as expressed in Robert Frost's (1874–1963) poem 'The Road Not Taken', it did make all the difference.

In Europe at that time, Jan Beneken (1934–2021) was also modelling the circulatory system, working at the pioneering Netherlands Organization for Applied Scientific Research (TNO) in Utrecht. He worked there, alongside another physicist, Jan van Bemmel, a founding father of medical informatics and its worldwide organization. Van Bemmel originally investigated methods of signal analysis in the electrocardiogram of foetal monitoring. In Scotland at that time, Peter MacFarlane was a notable pioneer of the computerized electrocardiogram, and we touched base many times as I followed his work in analyzing and modelling the electrocardiogram (ECG) signal. Van Bemmel became Professor of Medical Informatics at the Vrije Universiteit Amsterdam in 1973 and then, in 1987, at the Erasmus University Rotterdam, where he became Rector of the University between 2000 and 2003. He led the International Medical Informatics Association (IMIA) in its formative years. I visited TNO, and met the two Jans, when travelling to present a paper at a meeting of the European Society of Clinical Investigation, of which Dickinson was a prominent member.

---

18   This has not changed—the incessant din from unattended multiple alarms in nursing homes was a sad and worrying feature of my parents' care towards the end of their lives.

One of my other early encounters nearby in UCL was in life science. Working in the Biochemistry Department nearby to me in 1971 was Ted Chance, who was interested in mathematical modelling of enzyme kinetics, using newly available timesharing computer services of the early 1970s, to express and solve the equations and create a computer simulation of the reactions. Ted Chance's father was Britton Chance (1913–2010), a luminary biochemist and biophysicist of the era. As so often, the personalities connect. I was introduced to Ted Chance by Peter Sheppard, a junior doctor working with John Dickinson in the UCH Department of Medicine, who subsequently became joint supervisor of my PhD programme, with the bioengineer Stephen Montgomery. Through Ted Chance, I was introduced to the computational problems arising in the solution of non-linear and so-called stiff differential equations, which embodied markedly different rates of change and were costly to integrate, in computer processor time.

This was a problem I encountered later, when studying the behaviour of the Guyton-Coleman model and the Mac Series simulations of circulatory system physiology, which I worked on with John, as discussed in the following examples that interleaved with one another along my songline. The first describes my extended visit to the laboratory of a colossus of modelling of medical physiology of the era, Arthur Guyton (1919–2003), at his home base in Jackson, Mississippi.

Arthur Guyton–Modelling the Human Circulatory System

To consolidate my knowledge of the wider context of my PhD research with him, the run up to which I describe in the next section, John Dickinson wanted me to gain a grounding in the physiology of circulatory system function. He thought the best way to approach this would be to arrange for me to visit the team and study the work of his colleague and friend Arthur Guyton. Arthur had pioneered animal models for studying the circulatory system–it was the then predominant experimental paradigm, pursued also by John in his own research. These labs of yesterday would rightly cause a shudder, today, and be much more tightly constrained and regulated. The experimental findings were used to elucidate the building of computer models of the system.

John and Arthur had become close colleagues because of their shared interest in the aetiology of essential hypertension. In John's case, cerebrovascular hypertension was the focus; in Arthur's, it was his characterization of the 'infinite gain' bestowed on the system by the kidneys that was central. It was interesting to me that two such towering intellects, so pre-eminently aware of the multiple complexities of the control of blood pressure, were, nonetheless, so focused on the idea of one primary mechanism. Would thinking of it as an emergent property, arising in some deeply embedded way from the very complexity of the system, be equally realistic, I wondered? Of course, I had no ideas to offer by way of traditional cause and effect-focused scientific experiment, that might be applicable in that kind of hypothetical arena, and, in any case, the money was directed elsewhere.

Both John and Arthur were clinically trained, but Arthur was no longer active in the profession. They were blessed with similar polymath and practical engineering talents and highly complementary focus and expertise in physiology and clinical medicine. They were also quite different personalities and an example of opposites attracting. Arthur was patriarchal and utterly focused on his work; he told me he had no time for the arts–preferring to relax at home with Disney cartoons. John was libertarian and loved music and opera and the good things of life. He smoked considerable numbers of cigars, sometimes just to annoy what he saw as the unduly censorious attitudes of colleagues, I suspect! It was a long time ago!

Funded and supported by long-term research grants and local patronage, Arthur and his extremely bright and motivated team of colleagues took the physiology of the circulatory system to a new level. An initially threatened and defensive scientific establishment widely disparaged them, and a wiser, unblinkered future world acclaimed them. They studied blood pressure and flow, cardiac output, interaction between vascular, interstitial and cellular body compartments and control mechanisms providing regulation, from the immediate to the long term. Arthur, himself, worked on the interrelationship of resistance and capacitance of blood vessels, blood flow and cardiac pump performance, interstitial fluid and gel dynamics and renal function, with the multifocal eyes of life scientist, clinician and engineer. It was a grand challenge fitting to the grand person.

Arthur was indeed, as I discovered, an amazing person. Initially training to be a surgeon, he contracted polio and became wheelchair-dependent for the rest of his life. He switched to the study of medical physiology and was the last person, John told me, to write a textbook covering this huge domain, single handed. He attained a chair at the University of Mississippi in his twenties–maybe his father, as the Dean of the times, played a part in that early promotion, as some said to me, but it was surely destined to be.

He designed his own crutches, to assist him to get to and fro between car and wheelchair. He adapted the car to enable him to drive. He designed and supervised construction of his family home–he and his wife, Ruth, had a large family and they were harmonious patriarch and matriarch there. Their children, his colleagues told me, were all extremely clever, too. Arthur also designed and supervised the construction of a boat to enjoy sailing on a local lake. He was polymath and poly-competent, as thinker, researcher and engineer, a power in the historic land of Mississippi.

Recognized later in his career, and by dint of his amazing energy and focus, Arthur became President of the American Physiological Society. He was quite conservative in the Mississippi of his times, born into a leading family of the State. But also quite radical, confident and unafraid to be his own person and challenge orthodoxy, as well. Talking about science funding, he argued in one conversation with me, when meeting him and his wife for a meal they invited me to at their home, that overspending on research and focusing too much on large grants, led not just to less research productivity but sometimes to negative outcomes, taking science backwards! He showed me his most recent application for a multi-million-dollar grant to support his laboratory, saying he had already largely accomplished the goals set out there, to be pursued. He said, the grants system coerced researchers to hold back their results and use each grant to publish and promote what was already in the bag and set the scene, experimentally, for success in the next one. He quizzed me about nuclear fusion and the safety of fusion reactors– not something I knew much more about than he did!

I had raised a grant to pay for the air fare to get to Jackson, and John and Arthur paid the living costs. My diary tells me I travelled there on 8 November 1971. I even have the flight numbers, such is the longevity of the paper record! I rather doubt that electronic diaries will persist that long! Arthur put me up in the University Medical Centre Alumni House, an extremely comfortable small hotel on the campus. This was, I discovered, also in use at the time by the Governor of Mississippi, while his official residence was being renovated. There were darkened glass limousines and armed guards in constant attendance. Breakfast in the drug store across the road was eggs sunny side up, grits, orange juice and coffee. It was my introduction to the languid south of the era of Martin Luther King. Over the Thanksgiving holiday later that month, I was invited to stay on a cotton plantation owned by relatives of the family I had stayed with in Kentucky, in school days. They were hunting, shooting and fishing family folk. Half the year was American football and half was dawn to dusk cotton. I made my excuses for not getting up at three in the morning to climb into trees on the plantation, ready to shoot unsuspecting deer, grazing at dawn.

Arthur was the most welcoming and generous of hosts during my month with him. He looked after me very generously, no doubt at John's request as I was a young newcomer and scarcely worthy of so much of his time. He presided over one of the smoothest running and focused teams and departments I have ever experienced. Everyone there (Aubrey Taylor (1933–2015), Thomas Coleman (1941–2021), John Hall, Alan Cowley and Harris Granger (1945–2018)) was either already a tenured professor or destined to become one. Physiologist and biomedical engineering colleagues of theirs of those times, whose work I also followed, were Fred Grodins (1915–89), known for his work on biological control systems, at the University of Columbia; Howard Milhorn, a mathematician and physicist, turned physiologist, doctor and author; and Vincent Rideout (1914–2003), an electrical engineer at the University of Wisconsin.

I was allocated to the different teams in the department for several days each, to see their work and hear their ideas. Arthur himself spent a lot of time with me, describing his work on an integrative model, that he and Tom Coleman collaborated on, and which Tom revised and updated throughout his career, providing it as a resource for teaching, worldwide. The Guyton-Coleman physiological models have proved of widespread educational interest and value and provided important insight guiding world-leading research. They put together all that was known about circulatory system dynamics, to create a model representation. The focus was on synthesis of knowledge about the whole system. On how different mechanisms identified through animal experiment and clinical investigation, came together within the body to regulate blood flow and blood pressure.

Arthur and Ruth Guyton at their home in Jackson Mississippi, where I visited them in 1972

The highly complex 1984 Guyton-Coleman model of circulatory system dynamics, photographed from a print provided to me by the authors

Fig. 4.2 Left: Arthur and Ruth Guyton at their home in Mississippi. Photographer and date unknown. Right: the extraordinarily complex circuit diagram of the Guyton-Coleman model of blood pressure regulation (1974).[19] CC BY-NC.

---

19   YouTube hosts a fulsome tribute to the Guytons (UMMCnews, 'Remembering the Guytons: The Story of Dr. Arthur and Ruth Guyton', online video recording, *YouTube* (3 May 2019), https://www.youtube.com/watch?v=pWKMjYd8748).

Arthur and Tom published these models in successive papers and books. The most notable was that published in the *Annual Review of Physiology*, in 1972.[20] This drew together experimental quantification of functional relationships between different variables throughout the system, operating on different timescales and impacting on blood pressure and body fluid and electrolyte distribution and regulation.

This was John's special area of clinical knowledge, being relevant to measurement and observation in the management of conditions such as essential hypertension, haemorrhage, heart attack, Addison's disease and Conn's syndrome. John's rubric for testing these computer models was his immense knowledge and experience of clinical physiology and practice. He would let the models run freely and observe how changes to different parameters played out–taking blood from the circulation, dropping the pumping power of the left ventricle, disabling hormonal control of aldosterone on sodium metabolism, for example. A bit like iterative modelling of the evolution of the early universe from the Big Bang, conditioned only by current observation and theory of physical law.

Tom and Robert Hester continued the Guyton and Coleman work of the 1960s and 1970s, in the form of the Human and HumMod models. You can see Hester's talk about this venture on TED.[21] Many models now assert their prowess by enumerating how big they are–numbers of variables and their interconnections. Modellers aiming to see what can usefully be omitted sometimes look to have given up in the context of complex biological systems such as this. The goal seems now directed more towards keeping many variables tractably within computational scope!

Over the coming years, I used our Mac Series models (which are described in the next case study, here) to analyze clinical data collected prospectively in clinical care. Could they be used to gain useful insight into the condition of individual patients, and provide useful guidance about whether, and how, to intervene to support and treat them over time? As I demonstrated in my PhD thesis, they were able to represent persuasively the sequence of changes in the circulatory system over time–after a heart attack, for example. But they were much less successful in diagnosing and predicting a pattern of disease within the circulatory system, when matched to clinical measurements made, in the way that a weather forecasting model

---

20 A. C. Guyton, T. G. Coleman and H. J. Granger, 'Circulation: Overall Regulation', *Annual Review of Physiology*, 34.1 (1972), 13–44, https://doi.org/10.1146/annurev. ph.34.030172.000305

21 Hester's TED Talk on this venture is available at TEDx Talks, 'The Most Complete Computer Simulation of Human Physiology | Robert Hester | TEDxJackson', online video recording, *YouTube* (16 July 2019), https://www.youtube.com/ watch?v=HP6wA-H1R7M

can be used to predict the weather, when matched to measurements from weather station sensors.

The reasons for this are illuminating, more generally. The Guyton-Coleman model, though an intellectual *tour de force*, is hugely overdetermined in relation to the measurements that can be made in the real system. Insufficient amount and detail of data is available to be sampled and there are too many adjustable parameters of the model. And thus, as Feynman observed in another context–that of the modelling of elliptical orbits of the planets–the model is not useful as a theory to explain the measurements. Biological variation, subject by subject, is considerable in both healthy and diseased states. There is also considerable overlap and redundancy of feedback mechanisms within physiological systems–as we can see in the Guyton-Coleman model, where there are very many components of the model contributing to its description of blood pressure regulation. This makes the goal of identifying a unique configuration of the model, matched to an observed patient state, impossible to achieve with any confidence or usefulness. To have a chance of success, a much simpler model would be required, and its usefulness assessed in relation to a more closely defined purpose–in terms of scope of model and context in which applied. All this, I learned through trial and error, although many looking back in time, might now suggest it should have been obvious.

I am not knowledgeable about econometric models but imagine that similar parallels must exist there–usefulness in gaining understanding and interpreting 'what if' scenarios, in general terms, but of less value in predicting and deciding on action in response to events unfolding, in highly variable context, day by day. Here, there is also an intrinsically complex and interrelated set of dynamic relationships in play. There is, perhaps, greater ability to measure and observe data collected in the modelled, real-world system, but more limited scope for controlled experiment to inform building or tuning of the model.

Living systems have evolved in a labile manner, accumulating much redundancy of their mechanisms in the interests of maintaining homeostasis and ability to survive in diverse and challenging contexts. For the Guyton-Coleman model, this means that very many parameters of the model can be plausibly adjusted to mirror an observed behaviour of the modelled system. This is because of limitations in the measurements possible, but also a reflection of their intrinsic biological variability. Such intrinsic variability also challenges statistical modelling of data collected, in the ways that statistical methods characterize and model the distributions of interacting variables observed.

As discussed above, one way of ameliorating this problem is by sensitivity analysis of the model, revealing the extent to which its simulated outputs vary with changes made in its defining parameters. Another is to model variables and processes as stochastic phenomena, characterized by defined probability distributions. One way or another, a level of confidence must be stated for the results reported.

I had experience in another area of research, seeking to characterize confidence in correctness of diagnostic decisions. Confidence limits on the probability of a correct diagnosis, based on the measured data and the assumptions and simplifications made in framing the model, yielded a range from zero to one hundred percent. Not a particularly earth-shattering or helpful result! Neither would be the prediction that numbers of deaths in a pandemic will lie somewhere between 5,000 and 5,000,000. Might we better accept, in some such situations, that many estimates about admittedly potentially devastating outcomes are likely to prove very unreliable, signifying that, essentially, we do not know. We should not dwell too long in modelling the unknown but recognize and communicate that we are coping as best we can, and couch our statements and decisions, accordingly.

In contrast to the science of weather forecasting, it is apparent that in modelling human physiology, both purpose and related model must be framed precisely, and tied down experimentally, to a considerable and sometimes still unachievable extent, before the range of predictions of future behaviour of the system modelled can be usefully narrowed. Such models of narrower scope and greater simplicity have proved useful in achieving practical clinical goals. This was the approach adopted by James Kirklin (1917–2004) and Louis Sheppard, whose centre I visited after leaving Jackson, and whose work I describe in another of my examples, in the section on exploratory clinical applications of models, below.

A personal note, here, about the late and great Arthur Guyton. When he came to London, many years later, to deliver the prestigious annual Harveian Lecture at the Royal College of Physicians, in the year of its five hundredth anniversary, no doubt arranged by John Dickinson in his time as a censor of the College, he asked me to sit with him, to help with set up and delivery, when needed. It was a great honour to be beside him, there, and hear his masterly presentation of his life's work. Prince Philip and some of his friends were in attendance, further along the front row. It is hard to know what they might have made of it! I stood aside outside the building, afterwards, while the Royal Party departed. Guyton heaved himself past me on his crutches, pausing to enquire why I chose to wait on royalty! He probably did not think of himself as southern states royalty, but he was!

In his eyes, his work had made understanding of the circulatory system simpler. And yet to more traditional, less practical and differently educated eyes, he made it very much more complex. It is more complex than they saw, and their perspective was not of a kind that could piece together all that was known. Charles Sherrington (1857–1992) wrote a hundred years ago about the integrative role of the human nervous system and its central role in neuroscience. Guyton did the same for the circulatory system in physiological science, seventy years later. His Harveian Lecture was a fitting commemoration of William Harvey (1578–1657), described as the leading medical scientist of the seventeenth century for his discovery of the human circulatory system, as recorded in *de Motu Cordis* (1628), and as the founder of modern physiology. It felt, and still feels, such a privilege, for me, to have been there with him.

John Dickinson–Modelling Clinical Physiology–The Mac Series Models

Fig. 4.3 John Dickinson–one photo chosen by his family; one with Khursheed Ahmed and the author, at McMaster University (1970s); and one with the author in his office at Bart's (*c.* 1985), CC BY-NC.

My story of John Dickinson interleaves at many points along my songline, such was his personal importance to and for me. It has already featured in the previous example in this section, based on his connection with the pioneering work of Guyton. Here, I track back to the beginning, to place my story of him in wider context. There is thus some overlap of the narrative of these two sections. Having described, above, three sliding door moments that marked my career around the time of this picture, my Bart's office sliding door that it shows is symbolic (Figure 4.3). Indeed, my first meeting with John proved a life-changing sliding door moment. The picture hangs on the wall of my office at home, today.

After leaving Oxford, I worked in London for two years in the medical engineering company which had funded my industrial scholarship to study physics at Magdalen. In those years, I saw the early stages of development of a new technology for automated chemical pathology laboratory testing in hospitals and the computer system being developed to control it. I also saw the operation of commercial consortia bidding for hospital development contracts in different countries.

A new beginning was then forced on to me after the company lost its way and I had to leave. A deferred national Science and Industry Scholarship award for postgraduate research, secured as a safety net on leaving Oxford, provided me with a working salary for a three-year PhD programme, which I decided to use to venture into the nascent field of computation in medicine. It was a testing and anxious time in our family life. Such a shift in career direction was full of risk, of a kind that would be hard to contemplate other than through necessity. Things could easily have gone badly wrong. In the times ahead, I stepped, nervously, through many sliding doors.

Stephen Montgomery an engineering faculty academic at UCL, who had a consulting connection with the company, generously sheltered me there while I found my feet, offering to become my academic supervisor. He kindly allowed me to work in his office in the Engineering Building in Malet Place and arranged for me to start by attending courses on the Master of Science (MSc) Computer Science programme at the London Institute of Computer Science, nearby to UCL. Keith Wolfenden (–2003), who taught the database module on the programme, had a growing interest in medical databases. He took me under his wing, there, and we kept in close touch for many years.

I had for some time been looking for a good clinical environment in which to pursue a computational medicine research project. Assisted by Bernard Lucas (a consultant anaesthetist who was also a consultant for the company in which I had worked, advising them on equipment design), I started to meet clinicians in different academic departments and attend ward rounds. For some reason, he decided that I should attend during cardiac bypass surgery in theatre, which was an eye opener to the sophistication of innovative technology deployed, as well as nearly an eye closer emotional shock for me!

Very generously, I was allowed to set up a second base for myself at the University College Hospital (UCH) Medical School Rockefeller Building on Grafton Way, working in the computer room on the fifth floor of the building, adjacent to the surgery and anaesthetics academic unit. I also got to know the hospital physics department led by John Clifton (1930–2023) and formed a close link with him as he, too, had a developing interest in computing in medical physics. Through him, I joined the Hospital Physicists' Association and Institute of Physics, to widen my network. John Clifton became its President a year or two later.[22]

The computer room housed the then very modern Digital Equipment Corporation (DEC) PDP-8 minicomputer. It doubled as the radioisotope lab and was not used and looked after as safely as it should have been, as I soon realized. A situation reminiscent of the old aircraft hangar used for testing linear accelerators, that I described in Chapter Three! Health and Safety procedures are, fortunately, very much more protective of such exposure, today.

At this point, it was by amazing chance and good fortune that I met and got to know John Dickinson, who became my luminary mentor and academic sponsor for the next twenty years. We were introduced by the biochemistry laboratory director in the Metabolic Unit downstairs, David Cusworth, who worked with Charles Dent (1911–76), a world authority on calcium metabolism. Realizing that I was struggling to find my way to a viable PhD topic, David very kindly introduced me to John, one day in December 1970. He had recently returned from an extended sabbatical break at the ground-breaking new Medical School at McMaster University in Canada, as I describe further below. I have a diary record of my early meetings with John, from that time.

It was from this fleeting encounter that our close working relationship and friendship developed in the following years, until his death in 2018– the most important and consequential of my professional life. John was one of a kind–an extraordinary mix of humane clinician and experimental physiologist. He had polymath skills and abilities (doctor, physiologist, organist, squash player, engineer–maintaining his ancient electric typewriter, car and Honda mopeds; designing and installing a central heating system and fairground organ into his family's Hampstead home, and more!). His father had been an engineer at the North London Polytechnic, later City University. Above all, he was a selfless, quite shy, and not personally ambitious person, blessed, though, with a strong drive and sense of self that marked his charisma and personality. He was truthful to a fault and able

---

22   Medical Physics is now an academic department within the UCL Engineering Faculty, and the now very much larger UCL Biomedicine estate extends across the entire previous UCH hospital building: to newly merged and constructed research institutes and teaching hospitals across central London, out to the Royal Free Hospital, in Hampstead, the Whittington Hospital in Archway and the Royal National Orthopaedic Hospital in Stanmore. Biomedicine has thus expanded to comprise some fifty percent of the academic constituency of the University.

to ignore irrelevant nastiness and vanity in life, to focus on what he was interested in and found fun.

At the time we met, John was a clinical senior lecturer in medicine and rising star in the academic medical unit, then led by Max Rosenheim (1908–72). Rosenheim was one of the first professors of medicine in London, subsequently President of the Royal College of Physicians and elevated through multiple civil honours to a baronetcy in 1970. He was originally appointed as a professor in the days when the University was sceptical that medicine deserved such academic status. Somewhat like professors of computer science in the 1960s. How times change!

John and Stephen co-supervised me through my extended PhD years at UCL up until 1975. John, in turn, introduced me to a world where my interest and engagement with the nearby early flowering of computer science at the Institute of Computer Science, and my mathematics and physics background, made me a good fit with his own growing research interest in medical computing, as the field was then called. He had just returned from a sabbatical at McMaster University in Hamilton, Ontario, invited there with his lovely and sparky wife, Elizabeth, by their long-term friend and colleague Moran Campbell, a doyen of respiratory medicine and physiology of the era. Moran had gone there from the academic powerhouse of the Hammersmith Hospital in London, invited by the then Dean of the new McMaster University Medical Centre, John Evans (1929–2015), to become its new Dean and plan an innovative curriculum of medicine for a new, graduate-entry medical school. Evans went on to become the ninth President of the University of Toronto from 1972–78. MUMC, as it was affectionately known, was an inspiring new building and environment, and a humming academic community. John and Moran shared a career-long interest in clinical physiology, having published the first edition of their key book in the field.[23]

John determinedly stuck to his guns with his hypothesis that the primary cause of essential hypertension was resistance to blood flow in the cerebral arteries. The mechanisms regulating blood pressure in the circulatory system were a multifaceted research conundrum, challenging any human brain to fit together the breadth and variety of data from animal and clinical research, into a plausible integrative hypothesis. Over his career, and well into his active retirement years, John charted the hundreds of mechanisms that impacted on and were impacted by blood pressure in the circulatory system. Later in his retirement, he continued to review and summarize the literature, working with Julian Paton, now a Professor in New Zealand

---

23   E. J. M. Campbell, C. J. Dickinson and J. D. H. Slater, ed., *Clinical Physiology* (Oxford: Blackwell Scientific, 1961).

At McMaster, John got to know the other newly appointed faculty members there. He discovered the computer unit and its Hewlett-Packard (HP) computer system, installed there by David Sackett (1934–2015), the Professor of Epidemiology. It was he who nurtured, and was the founding spirit, of evidence-based medicine, a notably important and influential new way of thinking in the context of burgeoning numbers of new methods of clinical intervention and treatment, coming to the fore in the Information Age.

Computer Centres were not common features of any academic environment in those times–least of all in medicine. Sackett's department's primary use of the facility was for the development of the SPSS statistical software. He wrote about how new online resources of medical knowledge and practice could be integrated with ward-based teaching of clinical medicine. In later years, I was the international appointee in a Canadian Government team reviewing his successors' work, for the Canadian Research Council.

John became engrossed in thinking up potential uses he might make of this Hewlett-Packard 3000 computer, then state of the art. It was installed in a carefully protected, air-conditioned computer room. McMaster was intent on breaking the established mould of separate modules of life science and clinical practice in the curriculum, preferring to mix and interrelate the two from the start. It also focused on recruiting students who were already graduates, and some from non-scientific disciplines, who wished to move on into medical studies. It had a magnificent building but no laboratory facilities for students. John became interested in how computer simulation might usefully augment the medical curriculum.

He set to work to write a quite simple computer programme to simulate blood pressure and flow in the human circulatory system, which he christened MacMan. This was the start of the work he and I developed in London and at McMaster, with Khursheed Ahmed, George Sweeney, Ralph Bloch, Moran Campbell, Norman Jones (1931–2021) and others, over the coming fifteen years. It became known as the Mac Series of physiological models and, in addition to MacMan, covered body fluid and electrolyte distribution and renal function, respiration and pharmacokinetics–the latter the brainchild of Ralph Bloch. These were christened MacPee, MacPuf and MacDope and my subsequent graphics-based implementations were published in 1984.[24] These versions were favourably reviewed in detail in

---

24   As mentioned above, over the past year, I have resurrected the last published editions of the Mac Series, in the graphical form that I wrote them in the 1980s, sucking them from still extant three-and-a-half-inch floppy discs and implementing them, with the help of a very obliging hobbyist in the Netherlands

the *Times Higher Education Supplement*. They became of interest to groups eager to explore ways of minimizing animal experimentation and details were published also in this movement's journal, ATLA Abstracts.[25]

I visited McMaster with John several times over those fifteen years, funded in part by money I had raised by packaging up and distributing the Mac Series programs around the world, first on huge magnetic tapes and then on floppy discs and in manuals published by IRL Press. Khursheed and his family became wonderful and very hospitable friends. I used to stay with them, while John and Elizabeth were hosted by the MUMC Dean. Over the final two years of my PhD programme, I had created versions of MacMan for the PDP-8 and on the University mainframe, and devised methods to optimize parameters for this model and its extension to cover body fluid and electrolyte mechanisms and renal function–Guyton's main interest.[26] What John had constructed in his effective (but difficult to disentangle) working code, I distilled into sets of functional relationships with analytical solutions and differential equations amenable to numerical integration methods. This involved substantial rewriting of the code, replacing some of the iterative solutions of short-term adaptations, such as the baroreceptor reflex adjustments in vascular tone, by analytical solutions. It also involved introducing a computational framework for numerical optimization, fitting parameters of the model to clinical measurements in myocardial infarction, both from published papers and a study based on data collected in intensive

---

on the DOSBox platform. This is a cloud-based resource that simulates the Microsoft PC operating system used at that time, MS-DOS. DOSBox is the only surviving platform for many computer games of the era. It is lovingly preserved, open-source, by gaming afficionados, who delight in wielding soldering irons and hoarding electronic components, to keep the hardware and software of their beloved games, alive, as I further describe in Chapter Five. It was a heart-dropping moment for me when, after some struggles with indecipherable error codes, a tiny code patch arrived from the Netherlands and all four programs were reincarnated, in a flash!

25   C. J. Dickinson, D. Ingram and K. Ahmed, 'The Mac Family of Physiological Models', *Alternatives to Laboratory Animals*, 13.2 (1985), 107–16, https://doi.org/10.1177/026119298501300204.

26   I vividly recall the first outing of these early versions of the programs, at a 1971 meeting of the Physiological Society, at UCL. John showed the MacPee programme, connecting with it through a slow, ten characters per second teleprinter, and I used the PDP-8's much more dynamic oscilloscope display, transferred by a novel scan converter device to a television screen in the nearby lecture theatre, to demonstrate MacMan. Its simulations of the haemodynamic consequences of blood loss, cardiac insufficiency or vascular hypertension attracted a large audience. John was discussing much more detailed topics involving renal and interstitial fluid dynamics, on the other side of the room, and came over with Lord Rosenheim, as he then was, to see what the excitement was all about!

care unit (ICU) patients at UCH. Numerical optimization methods of this kind were in an early stage of evolution, and I experimented with the main exploratory approaches. At the time, there was much research into computational solutions for stiff systems of differential equations, and I implemented these methods, too, to replace the quite simple iterative program loops whereby many, including Dickinson and Guyton, were simulating these dynamics.

My changes speeded computation in some parts of the simulation, but the non-linear differential equations were too unwieldy to be integrable with available numerical integration packages of the time. John, unaware of these issues, had ploughed his way through to the endpoint he had sought, which served his purpose well, by using numerical smoothing functions to ease the 'stiffness' of the modelled changes as the simulation evolved forward in time, ensuring the calculations did not become unstable, and the solutions oscillate. Thankfully, the body, as a distributed system, does not normally face unstable oscillations of this kind, although instability in its biological control systems does arise in some contexts–such as in periodic breathing of the immature lungs of premature babies.

I mined the literature to unearth published sources of clinical haemodynamic data for patients treated for myocardial infarction–these were very few and far between–and wrote numerical optimization procedures to match the model to these, adjusting model parameters according to patient height and weight and optimizing the cardiac pump performance parameter to match the published blood pressure, heart rate and cardiac output values. With considerable effort, I collaborated with John's clinical house officer of the time, and ICU nursing staff, to collect data from their patients, recorded over ten days following heart attack. I used further numerical optimizations to match the model to haemodynamic and body fluid and electrolyte measurements, to estimate the cardiac pump performance, day-by-day. As an independent check, I correlated these estimates with enzyme studies, used routinely to assess extent of cardiac tissue damage. In this way, the time course of damage and recovery of heart pump performance was charted, and the results checked against the enzyme picture.

All this was very laborious, a considerable burden on routine clinical care, and very approximate–and completely useless in any practical sense! But I did learn a lot that I drew on in subsequent years, for example as a reviewer of major EU modelling research projects, such as the Oncosimulator developed by Georgios Stamatakos and Norbert Graf, in the EU Advancing Clinico-Genomics Trials on Cancer (ACGT), p-Medicine and Computational Horizons in Cancer (CHIC) projects, as further discussed, below, in the final example of this section.

Denis Noble and Peter Hunter–Virtual Physiological Human and In Silico Medicine

In the early 1970s, physiologists were exploring the mechanical performance of human muscle fibres and the stimulation of their contraction that gives rise to the rhythmic pumping action of the heart ventricles. From the time of Ernest Starling (1866–1927), the heart pump performance had been characterized as a function curve, relating the pressure from venous blood entering through the right atrium to the rate of flow of blood into the systemic circulation via the aorta (cardiac output). One of the first books John Dickinson gave me to read on clinical physiology was Guyton's monograph, *Cardiac Output and Its Regulation*.[27] This was a topic I also encountered at conferences addressed by the UCL and Oxford physiologist, Denis Noble, whose interest was at a more granular level, recording muscle tension and length in laboratory experiments, twitching muscle fibres electrically and observing the effect of perfusion with catecholamine hormones, mirroring the manner in which the body stimulates and regulates cardiac performance. Other researchers that I got to know, such as Derek Gibson (–2021) at the Brompton Hospital in London, a founding father of echocardiography, later extended this knowledge into a three-dimensional model of the left ventricle, integrating individual muscle fibre mechanics into the muscle wall dynamics, shaping the contraction phase that ejected blood from the ventricle and the following relaxation phase that allowed incoming blood flow from the pulmonary circulation to re-expand it.

An increasing number of research teams experimented with physiological models. Noble's work extended into the modelling of cardiac cell metabolism, to study metabolic aspects of cardiac disease. His work was ground-breaking in the methods developed for modelling across domains of physics, chemistry, biology and physiology of the cell and cellular transport. The Guyton-Coleman model was essentially an integrative assembly and simulation based on experimentally derived function curves, from clinical and physiological studies of the circulation. Noble dug deeper into the modelling of function within the cell, developing and generalizing modelling methods to assist integrative understanding of more complex systems of biological and clinical science, bridging from genomics to immunology. In Oxford, he teamed up with Peter Hunter in the Oxford Engineering Department, which had long pioneered bioengineering, from the time of Brian Bellhouse (1936–2017) in the 1960s, developing artificial heart valves. I remember Bellhouse as a fellow of Magdalen College in my

---

27   A. C. Guyton, C. E. Jones and T. G. Coleman, *Circulatory Physiology: Cardiac Output and Its Regulation* (Philadelphia, PA: Saunders, 1973).

time there. Lionel Tarassenko, a subsequent head of the same department, has pioneered signal analysis methods applied to clinical data analysis and decision making.

In the USA, through the 1980s and 1990s, the Visible Human Project was established in support of the study of anatomy. This interdisciplinary field of endeavour extended into bioscience and medical science, more widely, under umbrella terms such as systems biology and systems medicine. Hunting for a unifying initiative, in 1997 the International Union of Physiological Sciences (IUPS) launched plans for its Physiome Project. The scope of this was well exemplified by the Oxford–Auckland Cardiac Physiome Project. In short order, genome led to epigenome, transcriptome, metabolome and biome, propelled by the explosion of bioinformatics data, both experimentally and in clinical contexts. The quest for integration was championed by one of Guyton's key team members that I had spent time with in Jackson, Alan Cowley, who had subsequently moved to a chair at Milwaukee. By then President of the IUPS, he wrote in 2004: 'now is the time to begin building the scientific infrastructures that will enable an integrated understanding of the function of complex organisms and chronic diseases'.[28]

The European Union has championed brave attempts to implement this mission and it is likely on a very long runway; possibly even longer than that of controlled nuclear fusion! Building on ideas developed in the Physiome Project, EU research funding was invested in the Virtual Physiological Human (VPH) Network: 'to enable collaborative investigation of the human body as a single complex system'.[29] This brought together academia, clinical practice and industry, to explore how deeply and widely this synthesis might run. The present day International Virtual Physiological Human Institute was established to take this work forward. Noble's colleague, Hunter, then working in New Zealand, became a leading light.

The term, *in silico* medicine, arrived, championed in the work of another group that I became close to in the early 2000s, the Advancing Clinico-Genomics Trials (ACGT) on Cancer initiative of the European Union. One question has recurred throughout VPH-style research: How well can the advancing science of *in silico* medicine connect with the practicalities of improving clinical care? For example, in confronting the panoply of experimental and clinical data from a patient with nephroblastoma, and using these to match a model of chemotherapy, Graf and Stamatakos and their colleagues and teams tracked the impact of treatment on a

---

28   *IUPS Newsletter*, 7 (September 2004).
29   STEP Consortium, *Seeding the EuroPhysiome: A Roadmap to the Virtual Physiological Human* (n.p.: STEP Consortium, 2007), p. 2, https://www.vph-institute.org/upload/step-vph-roadmap-printed-3_5192459539f3c.pdf

tumour's growth and its sought for reduction and elimination. Their work in the ACGT project and its successors is described in my next and final example of pioneers of innovation in modelling the human. In the choice of treatment regimens and their outcomes, there are harder challenges, where the uncertainties that I had come up against in my comparatively tiny PhD study, now five decades ago, still persist. Intrinsic biological variability, the uniqueness of each clinical problem and of the people and teams facing and addressing it, and the wider context in which the treatment applied plays out all interact and may confound feasibility of transition from the science to its effective and useful application in clinical care.

In silico medicine is a natural science and it is natural to be curious about and study it. In a clinical context, it is another specialism and, as with all such specialization, it has the potential to integrate and inform, and to fragment and confound. As has unfolded since the beginning of my songline–from mathematics and physics into biophysics, physiology, medicine and health care in everyday contexts–even the most sophisticated and well-endowed clinical environments have struggled to keep abreast of all that can now be measured and analyzed. In health care, information technology has enabled the advance of the best of the best. It has not achieved comparable impact at the other end of the spectrum of excellence–the worst of the worst. In some respects, through wasteful expenditure on pursuit of unrealistic goals, and commandeering of resource for elite priorities, it has arguably caused and allowed the gap, relatively, to widen.

Interest in what now comes under the banner of VPH research has persisted through six decades, since the 1960s,[30] seeking to help establish and consolidate progress in what is still a rapidly evolving field. A notable early team, whose work I collected, was that of Ed DeLand. He obtained a mathematics PhD at UCLA, at age thirty-four, and worked in the innovative environment of the RAND Corporation in Santa Monica, from the 1960s. When I came across his work, he was modelling red blood cell membrane transport equilibria, based on computation of the Gibbs function of statistical thermodynamics, with a view to applying the model to the interpretation of clinical laboratory measurements. The model was impressive in its capacity to predict these equilibria very precisely, in changing conditions. DeLand was a colleague of Thomas Lincoln (1929–2016), the clinician I mentioned in the Introduction as someone I met in London in my early PhD days with John Dickinson and Stephen Montgomery.

---

30   W. Ware, *RAND and the Information Evolution: A History in Essays and Vignettes* (Santa Monica, CA: RAND, 2008), https://www.rand.org/content/dam/rand/pubs/corporate_pubs/2008/RAND_CP537.pdf

The breadth of ambition for the Virtual Physiological Human has brought new levels of synthesis and insight into play, just as Sherrington did, in 1906, when he first envisaged the integrative character of the nervous system. When researching this connection, I alighted on Sherrington's reply, when asked about the purpose of his university, which still echoes a hundred years on:

> After some hundreds of years of experience, we think that we have learned [...] how to teach what is known. But now with the undeniable upsurge of scientific research, we cannot continue to rely on the mere fact that we have learned how to teach what is known. We must learn to teach the best attitude to what is not yet known. This also may take centuries to acquire but we cannot escape this new challenge, nor do we want to.[31]

A University discipline teaching about the unknown–Dick Cheney might have been pitching for a faculty position! The Information Age is expanding the domain of what is known and creating new dimensions of unknowing. The physicist, Max Born (1882–1970), once poetically described scientific discovery as a process of opening windows onto the stars, that simultaneously increases our vision of the unknown–that has stuck with me, not having read his works since my college days. Perhaps the common ground being sought for the Information Society is as much about coping with the unknown as it is about sharing of the known. One wonders what Sherrington might have made of a Novacene concept of computers that can know, where humans do not and cannot.

Georgios Stamatakos and Norbert Graf–The Oncology Simulator

In the early 2000s, I was appointed to several UK medical and engineering and physical sciences research council boards, and, as with my work for the NHS and EU, was involved in oversight of 'e-science', as it came to be termed. The EU boards were especially interesting and satisfying because they provided continuity over many years between reviewers and research teams, drawn from across academia, health care and industry. The EU Commission worked us hard and for little financial reward, but the relationships both ways became deep and enduring. One such incredibly hard-working and creative initiative, that I especially enjoyed working with, was the Advancing Clinico-Genomics Trials on Cancer (ACGT) project.

---

31   J. Eccles and W. Gibson, *Sherrington: His Life and Thought* (Berlin: Springer International), p. 24.

This set out to build a master ontology of data used in management of clinical trials, linking with advances in genomics science. The cancers studied were nephroblastoma, breast cancer and leukaemia. In parallel, a computer model and simulation of chemotherapy, christened Oncosimulator, was pioneered and pushed forward with amazing energy and commitment by Georgios Stamatakos and Norbert Graf. Through dedication and hard work over many years, they became much-admired pioneers in the advance of *in silico* medicine.

Norbert was the inspirational and hard-working clinical leader of the ACGT team. Biomedical scientists from leading cancer centres across Europe were also members. Norbert encouraged the initially sceptical clinical academics, himself included, to build a very fruitful and data rich environment for Georgios and his team. Manolis Tsiknakis and Mario Cortelezzi from the Hellenic Mediterranean University, led and held together the technical teams, including researchers from the prestigious Fraunhofer Institute in Germany and strong industry and health care institution partners. These people, and their enthusiastic colleagues of all ages became a memorably motivated community. Olle Björk, an oncologist from the Karolinska Institute in Stockholm and head of the Barncancerfonden [Swedish Childhood Cancer Foundation], and Elena Tsiporkova, an incisive biomedical scientist and mathematician, were colleagues with me in the review and advisory boards appointed for the project and its p-Medicine and CHIC successors, over the following ten years.

The master ontology was an ACGT project workstream pursued by a subgroup linked closely with Barry Smith's international biomedical ontology movement, mentioned in connection with the world of medical knowledge bases, in Chapter Two. The project loyally followed this lead as it was the vision on which the grant had originally been made It nearly became the project's undoing further downstream, as the messiness of clinical reality came up against the philosophical drivers of formal ontology. The focus on the master ontology initially pulled activities together and, as it creaked against the realities of harmonizing real data and real database implementations, nearly pulled them apart. This goal had gradually to be deemed to have failed and was downgraded in priority.

Norbert was the powerhouse for development of a tool to formalize clinical trials design and consistent collection of data across sites. The engineers loyally tackled data aggregation and descriptive metadata, across the different institutions and sites. The ethico-legal framework for the sharing of data was a notable success story–ably and professionally handled by Nikolaus Forgó, a professor of law and subsequently Dean, at the University of Hannover.

ACGT and its successor projects were an outstanding conjunction and collaboration of many teams and aspirations. It received many tens of millions of euros of European Commission investment, over three rounds of five-year funding, to create and sustain its teams and environments. As with all such projects, it produced many volumes of written reports, keeping their reviewers awake to the small hours, preparing for the regular three-day review meetings!

The clinical goals were well-expressed, and the clinicians and life scientists involved were already world authorities, joining research across many centres, in Europe, America and Japan, including my twin alma maters, UCL and the University of Oxford, in the UK. There was great success in pulling together clinical and genomics science data and building informatics infrastructure for research on different cancers. These wider connections allowed the research outputs to find a place in many international conference proceedings and journals. The range of expertise and the age and gender balance and culture of the teams was excellent. It proved the fundamental importance of good environment–not just as something nice to have, but as essential.

Georgios emerged as a world figure in *in silico* multiscale modelling– scaling from modelling chemotherapy at a molecular level, to its impact on tumour angiogenesis and growth, and tumour destruction by chemotherapy. The model utilized finite element methods from engineering science to model at multiple levels and scales of cellular and organ function. The Oncosimulator work brought different groups of modellers into a productive conjunction–mathematicians at Oxford working on analytical models of angiogenesis and the finite element approach of Georgios's team in Athens working on cellular mechanisms. Norbert, already a world figure in paediatric nephroblastoma research, and running a wonderful paediatric cancer service and caring community in Saarland, was the father figure across all domains of the project–an energetic, humane and infectiously enthusiastic clinician who also held together the project's links in Japan and the USA.[32]

---

32 As I write today, the Pfizer/BioNTech Covid-19 vaccine is announced to be approved for use in the UK. The earlier press releases had connected its inventors, two Turkish doctors working in Germany, to the University of Saarland, Norbert Graf's University, where they had met as students. Norbert became a dean of this medical school. He told me in an email last week, that he knew them well from the time they collaborated on research with him. Another inspiring story of international connection between people and teams, and the environments that enable them and their work to prosper.

Exploratory Clinical Applications

The examples now move on further, to models of clinical decision making and intervention in the everyday practice of health care. In the early 1980s, I worked with my Mac Series colleague at McMaster, Ralph Bloch, to draw together and edit a two-volume collection, *Mathematical Methods in Medicine*, to accompany the Wiley six-volume *Handbook of Applicable Mathematics*. The first volume, focused on statistical and analytical techniques, included a chapter on clinical decision analysis.[33] The second volume focused on clinical applications.[34] In this section, the examples are drawn from a range of clinical applications of modelling that I connected with in the first half of my career in medical and health informatics.

Statistical Modelling of Diagnosis–The Royal College of Physicians of London Computer Group

Classification and statistical analysis of clinical observations and measurements has long been used to segment patient populations within diagnostic and therapeutic groupings. These have ranged from simple scoring to intricate mathematical methods. Mathematical methods for analyzing and guiding clinical decision making took root in the 1970s, bringing together academic departments of medicine, statistics, and psychology, in the context of everyday clinical practice. Bayesian statistical methods were championed by Dennis Lindley (1923–2013), head of statistics at UCL, and later by Adrian Smith, whose later career was as Vice-Chancellor of Queen Mary University of London, UK Government Chief Scientist and Director of the Alan Turing Institute, established close to UCL as a national initiative in data science. I first came across Adrian Smith's work in the early 1980s, when he published a novel method for forecasting renal allograft rejection.[35] This was based on mathematical analysis of serial measurements of creatinine clearance in urine, using a Kalman filter technique, and showed that the event could be predicted up to several days before clinically manifested in

---

33 D. Ingram and R. F. Bloch, ed., *Mathematical Methods in Medicine, Part I: Statistical and Analytic Technique* (Chichester, NY: John Wiley and Sons, 1984).

34 D. Ingram and R. F. Bloch, ed., *Mathematical Methods in Medicine, Part II: Applications in Clinical Specialities* (Chichester, NY: John Wiley and Sons, 1986).

35 A. F. M. Smith, 'Change-Point Problems: Approaches and Applications', *Trabajos de Estadistica Y de Investigacion Operativa*, 31.1 (1980), 83, https://doi.org/10.1007/BF02888348; I. M. Trimble, M. West, M. S. Knapp, R. Pownall and A. F. Smith, Detection of Renal Allograft Rejection by Computer', *BMJ*, 286.6379 (1983), 1695–99, https://doi.org/10.1136/bmj.286.6379.1695

patients. This work has an interesting connection with the contemporary unfolding story of artificial intelligence, as discussed in Chapter Two.

Wilfrid Ingram Card (1908–85) was head of gastroenterology in Glasgow and a leading figure in the profession in the 1960s, with a special interest in medical education. I remember him visiting UCL and speaking at the Royal College of Physicians in London in the 1970s. The Glasgow University Record describes his distinctive contribution: '[...] in October 1966 he was appointed to a personal Professorship at the University of Glasgow in the Department of Medicine by Mathematical and Statistical Methods [...] In 1967 he published a classic article entitled "Towards a Calculus of Medicine" (*Medical Annual* 1967, 85, 9-21)'. Henrik Wulff credits him with 'a new paradigm of clinical thinking'.[36]

Card had collaborated with Lindley in further developing his ideas for mathematical modelling of medical decisions. In this they coined the term 'indicant' to cover clinical measurements and observations used to confirm a diagnosis, and linked these indicants with candidate diagnoses, using a Bayesian model of probability. There were several competing, but not necessarily conflicting perspectives on the nature of clinical diagnosis at that time, leading to different approaches to its formal study. Was it based on the weighing of statistical probabilities connecting what was observed and measured with potential underlying causes? Was it a human acquired skill based on recognition of patterns in these indicants? Was it a Popperian hypothetico-deductive method, acquiring evidence and gradually homing in on a conclusion about the causes of a presenting complaint, by ruling out alternative possibilities? What kind, specificity and sensitivity of evidence and model was needed? How did clinicians weigh multiple kinds and amounts of such evidence, in practical context, often when working under extreme pressure in seeking to save lives? Moran Campbell, on a sabbatical break from McMaster, took an interest in the topic, advocating for the framing of diagnosis of disease as a hypothetico-deductive method.[37]

The experiments conducted with these different approaches, exploring their technical and clinical contexts, and the accompanying debates within associated scientific and professional communities were the focus of the Royal College of Physicians of London (RCP) Computer Group. This was established through connections of Card with clinical professional luminaries of the era, including the RCP President from 1977–83, Douglas

---

36   'Measuring Gut Feelings: The Scientific Basis for Clinical Medicine', talk given at a Memorial Festschrift, RCP London, 17 June 1986.

37   E. J. M. Campbell, J. G. Scadding, and R. S. Roberts, 'The Concept of Disease', *BMJ*, 2.6193 (1979), 757–62; E. J. M. Campbell, 'The Diagnosing Mind', *The Lancet*, 329.8537 (1987), 849–51, https://doi.org/10.1016/S0140-6736(87)91620-5

Black (1913–2002). Membership of the group was drawn widely from across UK academic medicine and statistics. David Spiegelhalter, (an alumnus of Oxford and UCL, and student of Adrian Smith, who went on to become President of The Royal Statistical Society and Professor of Public Understanding of Risk at Cambridge, and a nationally prominent advisor and commentator on statistical aspects of public policy) teamed up with Robin Knill-Jones (a Glasgow gastroenterologist working alongside Card) to develop a Bayesian model for differential diagnosis of acute abdominal pain. A system they christened Gladys, standing for Glasgow dyspepsia! Abdominal pain was readily recognized, but what character of pain, how exemplified and with what underlying aetiology? And in context of clinical management, what presenting situations required urgent action and what manifestations were deemed non-specific of underlying disease, and best to be watched over, to see how they evolved.

Another luminary figure of that time, Timothy (Tim) de Dombal (1937–95), also shone there. He was a surgeon at Leeds, who, with a mixture of persuasive charm and iron determination, master-minded large-scale collections of data relating to problems of differential diagnosis in gastroenterology. His field trials were conducted first in the hospitals in which he worked, collecting cohort sets of a standardized group of indicants for the most common diagnoses of acute abdominal pain, and then using these to predict the most likely diagnoses for newly presenting patients. The work extended to many countries under the auspices of the World Gastroenterology Organization and the International Federation for Information Processing, where Tim played leading roles. He was less well supported near to home–seen as neither a proper surgeon nor a proper statistician, perhaps. It seemed that he rather relished that notoriety, and he was better respected and anchored in the wider world community in which he worked. But it cannot have been an easy mix of roles and reputations to sustain.

Tim's method for modelling the diagnosis of acute abdominal pain combined standardized methods of clinical data collection and a simple Bayesian method for estimating the probabilities to be assigned in linking an observed patient profile with the six diagnoses he chose to work with as explanatory of the pain. For each of these six diagnoses, he collected learning sets of a hundred cases–in some rare conditions only fifty–with which to calibrate his method. The approach was based on assumption of conditional independence of these data indicants, when calculating the probabilities assigned. This assumed property of the data was recognized not to hold, but the limitation was glossed over. It functioned more as a scoring system, as the highest estimated probability was chosen as indicative of the correct diagnosis and the actual probabilities assigned were not assessed for their accuracy.

Nonetheless, the method (sometimes referred to as 'Idiot Bayes'!) produced some persuasive evidence that it could assist clinical management, for example in avoidance of negative laparotomy through misdiagnosis of non-specific abdominal pain. The method was straightforward to compute, in comparison with the more complex Bayesian models of these probabilities that were used by others. Implementation of these mathematically more rigorous Bayesian models proved difficult and lacked sufficient range and granularity of available clinical data, on which to calibrate the model and compute its predictions. The computational resource required increased steeply alongside the increasing complexity and variety of clinical measurements arising in the modelled domain.

Tim faced professional opposition from some senior clinical colleagues who disparaged the importance of his work and obstructed its adoption, meaning that his progress had to be very hard-won–a not uncommon scene for such pioneers! The message that a program algorithm might, to some quantifiable degree, parallel human diagnostic skill and performance, was an uncomfortable idea for many, if not most. It challenged the self-belief of practitioners and brought the nature of their roles and contributions under a new spotlight. Tim was feisty, as well as testy, at times, but created a loyal team around himself and battled on, with notable charisma and *sangfroid*. Sadly, he died very young from unsuccessfully managed complications of cardiac surgery.

I got to know Tim and tracked his work for several years. He shared his data with me, as I tried to support a colleague clinical lecturer in the Department of Medicine at Bart's, Huw Llewellyn, with his MD (Doctor of Medicine) research project. Huw had envisaged a novel method of reasoning about diagnosis, based on manipulation of mathematical sets, expressing linkage of indicants with diagnoses. To help him, I wrote software to implement his approach, as a way of testing and presenting his ideas in his MD thesis. His reasoning was not wrong, it seemed to me, but the method did not provide useful clinical results in the work we did together. It estimated a range of probabilities whereby the observed indicants could be linked with candidate diagnoses and suggested a rationale for step-by-step investigation in reaching a diagnostic decision. The confidence limits it could assert were quickly too wide-ranging to have practical significance in guiding decision. Huw faced difficulty in defending the ideas presented in his MD thesis. He battled on and won through to the award of the degree, and still pursues those ideas, today. He was a strong and goodhearted professional doctor, hugely proud and loyal to the Welsh valley origins of his family. I noted, as I made checks in writing this section, that he is now a co-author of the prestigious *Oxford Handbook of Clinical Diagnosis*. Clearly, he was talent, grit and staying power personified! I watched a short video connected with the promotion of his book. He sounded exactly the Huw I knew.

In the discipline of psychology, there was continuing focus on how humans could structure, refine and improve decision making. Was there a structured tree of decision points, traversed systematically according to questions asked and findings reported? Did humans learn their skills through experience whereby a decision could be made in a 'blink', based on a recognized pattern of observation and measurement? How many variables could the brain hold in mind, when interpreting and deciding the diagnostic significance of all this information? Some studies had suggested the magic number of seven variables, after which human capacity, having initially steadily improved, started to decline, and quality of decision making likewise declined. The phenomenon of information overload became of interest in the study of clinical risk, pioneered at UCL by my colleagues, Charles Vincent and Pippa Bark, in the Psychology department. Pippa subsequently joined my department and Charles moved to Imperial College London, working under Ara Darzi, who also pioneered innovations in surgical robotics and clinical informatics.

Many people contributed to the RCP Computer Group throughout its life, with Jeremy Wyatt becoming a notable participant, writer and advocate of the work. The group fulfilled a valuable coordinating focus but its role as a national forum declined as key personalities moved on and momentum was lost. It was replaced by a more generically focused activity, concerned with the impact of information technology on medical records and terminology. This new unit was led by colleagues and friends of those days, Martin Severs, John Williams and Iain Carpenter, who put tremendous energy into seeking national consensus on the structured content of clinical records. They were doughty pioneers at the coalface of informatics in clinical practice, health policy and research, for several decades.

Martin maintained his clinical professional work in care of the elderly, and as Dean of faculty at his local University of Portsmouth. He led the formative years of the International Health Terminology Standards Development Organization (IHTSDO), as described in Chapter Two and went on to become Medical Director of the NHS Health and Care Information Centre, subsequently NHS Digital and NHSX. These organizations metamorphosed and changed their name many times over these years, as described in Chapter Seven. John and his wife, Jane, pioneered a gastroenterology record-keeping system in Swansea, and John went on to lead Research and Development for the NHS in Wales. He created and led the RCP Informatics Unit that grew from the Computer Group. This works collaboratively with the NHS, still, in standardization of the clinical content of care records.

Operational Research–Clinical Trials and Epidemiology

In the mid-1980s, UCL established a Clinical Operational Research Unit (CORU). It was led by Ray Jackson, a mathematician who came to the fore in battling the orthodoxy of clinical trials methodology, proposing that clinical outcomes from treatments could be modelled mathematically, drawing on operational data from care records of populations of patients, thereby lessening the requirement for costly, independently established and extensive randomized trials. This proposition did not persuade minds, but Ray was a wily politician as well as a skilled mathematician, and he succeeded in broadening the academic focus of CORU, extending mathematical methods across health services research and biomedical informatics. Ray's contributions to government operational research are recorded on a civil service website.[38]

It was an era when mathematics and engineering were both pitching for ownership of the fledgling discipline of computer science, not unreasonably given its founding fathers. Alan Turing (1912–54), Alonzo Church (1903–95) and John von Neumann (1903–57) were mathematicians, and the field was lifting off, powered by advances in semiconductor physics and electrical engineering. Operational research had a clear pedigree in mathematics and CORU remains in that UCL faculty to this day. With Steve Gallivan and Mark Leaning, colleagues of mine from those times, Ray initiated a programme of mathematical modelling, widely across biology and medicine. He was a battling individualist, and a very able and successful one.

I first met the world of mathematical models in medicine, in reading work of the mathematician, John Maynard Smith (1920–2004). He became a professor of mathematics, much interested in its applications in evolutionary biology and genetics, having started as an aeronautical engineer. Pure mathematics is a pursuit that treasures its isolation and sometimes almost scorns its wider application, relevance and importance! It does not do 'trade' and exists on a level of abstraction and within community that can defend an ivory tower-like existence and perspective. That aside, where would we all be without it? Maynard Smith brought mathematical insight to the centre of biological and medical discipline, as Ian Stewart has, today.

My closer contact with mathematical epidemiology arose through my work for the Wellcome Foundation in the late 1980s, on computer-assisted learning–my main interest in those years. A project had been established to build an educational resource based on the Henry Wellcome (1853–1936)

---

38   M. Hudson, *A History of the Government Operational Research Service 1968–1980* (n.p.: GORS, 2018), p. 20, http://www.operational-research.gov.uk/public_docs/history-of-gors.pdf

collection of historical items, known as the Wellcome Museum of Tropical Medicine, later incorporated into the Wellcome Collection Museum of Medical Science, and now to be closed. The Wellcome Foundation had traditionally had strong worldwide roots in research in this domain. The Foundation's original major shareholding in the Burroughs-Wellcome drug company was sold, and the proceeds reinvested more widely into the recast Wellcome Trust. The Trust has enjoyed stellar subsequent growth of its investments. This enabled its rapid development as a major international funder of research and public awareness of biomedical science. It was led through this transitional period from 1991–98 by its then Director, the parasitologist Bridget Ogilvie, who I worked with closely at that time.

Among its luminary Trustees of the time was the mathematical biologist Roy Anderson, author, with Robert May (1936–2020), of the highly cited book, *Infectious Diseases of Humans: Dynamics and Control*.[39] May went from mathematical epidemiology to become Government Chief Scientist and President of the Royal Society. Anderson led departments at both Imperial College and Oxford and succeeded the formidable former Chairman of GlaxoSmithKlein, Richard Sykes, when becoming Rector of Imperial College. He reviewed the museum project that Bridget had asked me to look after when it had got into difficulties, after conflict within its senior team.

Anderson was one of an extremely talented grouping of mathematical biologists and tropical disease researchers, working closely with Wellcome. Neil Ferguson, who studied physics at Oxford and migrated into mathematical epidemiology, became a senior member of Anderson's team, at Oxford and Imperial. He was prominent in the modelling and simulation controversies that populated academic and public discussion of policy options for containing the Covid-19 pandemic. My UCL colleague head of academic medicine of earlier years, Patrick Vallance, presided over the furore, as the Government Chief Scientist of the time. Chris Whitty, a University College London Hospitals (UCLH) physician and epidemiologist, acted, also remarkably calmly, as Chief Medical Officer (CMO) alongside him. The preceding Chief Scientist, Mark Walport, also a former chief of the Wellcome Trust, and formerly also a chief of medicine, at Imperial College, acted in support to help carry the public load. The preceding CMO, Sally Davies, was also a physician from Imperial College. They all needed to know and trust one another well, and they gave sterling service.[40]

---

39 R. M. Anderson and R. M. May, *Infectious Diseases of Humans: Dynamics and Control* (Oxford: Oxford University Press, 1992).

40 Sparkling academic and medical careers often lead to high office in universities and leadership of government and international agencies. Some migrate into academic leadership from careers in industry and some in the reverse direction,

In the Covid-19 context, a wide range of assumptions, simplifications and models has been in play among proposing and competing groups of modellers: about susceptibility to and degree of infection, transfer within populations, and the course of illness arising–unnoticed, mild, serious and fatal. Experimental data that would help to pin these down more precisely is only slowly possible, dependent on clinical interventions, reliable testing methods and population level sampling of virus and viral response. Predictions about the degree of infection, interactions with containment measures, vaccination and treatment regimens, and expected clinical outcomes have been wide-ranging. Such predictions must, necessarily, be hedged with caveats that render them difficult to interpret as a basis for what are major policy decisions, balancing the safeguarding of personal safety and livelihood alongside capacity of the caring services.

My Polish nephew, who is working at a high level in investment banking in New York, believes the world has committed catastrophic error of overreaction, in response to what was, he admits, a terrible pandemic. Different assumptions used in designing and calibrating models, and fitting them to contemporary measurement and observation, led to radically different predictions and strategies. Countries that took early and more drastic action on containment seem to have succeeded better at first, than those where policy was gambled and nuanced more in favour of 'play it by ear' and 'wait and see'. Events in such as New Zealand and China, have more recently been reversing this trend. In whatever way a pandemic is modelled, the policy choices made in seeking to contain it involve choices about values. Information has been assembled, communicated and weighed, worldwide and in new ways, in this pandemic. Being the first of the modern scientific era and Information Age, it seems destined to become a set piece of future analysis by epidemiologists and historians.

---

and to and fro, vitalizing connections. Those who are London-based or close to London appear to have a stronger hold on levers of political power and influence in these echoing hallows. I owe it to my NHS-employed family members, further north, to make that observation, which they would, no doubt, have me say, more loudly! Bridget Ogilvie once remarked to me about the three-fold talent of leadership she observed in academia—brain, political nous and human insight, I seem to recall. This categorization reminds me now of the philosopher Immanuel Kant (1724–1804), who wrote about the threefold resources—intelligence, power and money. He also wrote about the three degrees of evil: frailty, impurity and depravity or perversity! Everything in the world maps to three dimensions, it seems, but time always tells—especially so with simulations! Zobaczymy!

Electrophysiology

From the 1970s, electrophysiology was expanding into the computer domain with methods for signal analysis of the electrocardiogram (ECG), accumulation of large data banks, and automatic characterization of disorders of cardiac rhythm. This led to new methods for their detection, mitigation and correction in patients. Jan van Bemmel, in Utrecht, Peter Macfarlane, in Glasgow, and Bruce Sayers (1928–2008) and Richard Kitney at Imperial College, were pioneering colleagues of those times. There was parallel work in other areas of signal analysis, notably study of the electroencephalogram (EEG) and its importance in brain science and clinical neurology.

Physicists and electrophysiologists developed what were termed inverse methods for the modelling of cardiac function. These worked backwards from electrical signals propagated through the chest wall and detected by an array of sensors fixed to the skin around the chest surface. The signals were combined and analyzed with software, to infer the structure of a postulated model of the beating heart as a transmitter of electrical signals. This was akin to the methods of axial tomography image reconstruction, used in imaging devices, such as X-ray, MRI and PET scanners.

Modelling Ventilation Management

Among the Mac Series models, MacPuf achieved the greatest success. It was envisaged by John Dickinson, in close collaboration with Moran Campbell and Norman Jones at McMaster University, both titans in the field of respiratory physiology. Other teams developed simpler programs that modelled limited aspects of lung function and achieved success, for example in matching these to measurements in gaseous anaesthesia and as tools for practical classes exploring lung mechanics and gas exchange. The idea of MacPuf was more ambitious–its goal was to model the cardiorespiratory system of the body, in clinical context.

MacPuf found its way into an unusual book, explaining line by line the clinical and physiological rationale of the program. It was an adventurous idea and won appreciative reviews–a polymath clinician writing about how he wrote a program to simulate what he saw as the essence of the system he was describing. My signed copy from John is one of my most valued books, a superinukbook! The program also found its way into preclinical courses of physiology, notably through the graphics versions that I created for the International Business Machines Corporation (IBM) PC microcomputer, when it made its appearance in the 1980s. I took it into undergraduate and postgraduate clinical teaching of anaesthetics and intensive care medicine, in combination with structured learning materials that I developed with colleagues at Bart's and McMaster.

The question of how the Mac models might assist clinical insight and guide treatment had been the basis of my early 1970s PhD research at UCL. The example developed there had used two of the other models–of circulation and fluid and electrolyte balance–to investigate recovery from acute myocardial infarction. In the following years at Bart's, I worked with an anaesthetics and intensive care doctor, Charles Hinds. Charles went on to become Professor and Head of Department at Bart's, author of a very successful textbook and President of the Intensive Care Society. From the experience of the earlier PhD project, it seemed that a situation where extensive measurement of the body system was required for traditional management, combined with a clinical scenario where there was a small set of possible choices and adjustments of treatment, would be a good candidate area in which to explore the applicability of a model-based approach to patient management.

We set out to investigate how the MacPuf respiratory model might be used to interpret and guide ventilation management of patients in the ICU. This involved extensive collaboration with the anaesthetics research laboratory team at Bart's, in connection with new modalities of measurement and monitoring of patients. Mass spectrometry was being tried as an *in vivo* respiratory measurement device, along with routine measurements of blood gases, gas exchange and body metabolism. This involved a considerable investment of time and effort in liaison with industry partners involved in the project. Little of this came to fruition but it did provide useful context for the modelling work, when considering how improved measurement might enable the model to be matched more accurately with the clinical interventions being simulated. Rather, in the way that the expanded network of atmospheric sensors has underpinned advances in modelling of the weather.

It was a long haul over some five years, to bring these developments into alignment and devise a numerical optimization of just four key model parameters to match them to the measured respiratory variables. The high quality and dependable software productivity tools of today for mathematical analysis and software development–MATLAB, Mathematica, Eclipse and many more–were a distant vision, and those rudimentary ones that were already available, stuttered, changed and most of them quickly became obsolete. These were the temperamental equivalent of early motor cars, in need of constant, competent and time-consuming adjustment and maintenance.

The project succeeded in its primary goals and the model predictions were used in two ways. First, to explore options for managing patients with severe respiratory failure, such as in viral pneumonia, and correlate them with the clinical pathway that unfolded.[41] Second, within interactive computer-assisted learning courses for anaesthetics and ICU trainees, published in collaboration with Charles's opposite number at UCL, Rod Armstrong.[42]

There were several reasons why this line of research came to an end. First, it proved of little interest as a research topic for the research council funding schemes of the times. Second, it would have required a larger team, working across the clinical and technical domains, which was not available to me and beyond my personal capacity to create at the time. And perhaps most significantly, the pilot project was likely to prove difficult, if not impossible, to improve and generalize more widely, beyond our setting at Bart's and the protective sponsorship provided there. I had been fortunate beyond words in the trust John Dickinson had shown in me, but as he approached retirement and I achieved a personal chair, it was important to look for new opportunity to extend the range of my academic activities.

The MacPuf model of human respiration was the most generic and widely used of its kind of its time. John was not a respiratory physician. He was interested in the challenge of representing clinical physiology and its system behaviours with computer models. Principally, he did this to explore their use as educational resources. He was not very interested or engaged in their validation and application in clinical practice, although he encouraged me to pursue that line. He saw his own experience, published research and expert colleague practitioners as providing the best available, realistic and reliable guides to their improvement. That was his nature and reflected the roles he had to balance in his professional work.

---

41   C. J. Hinds, D. Ingram, L. Adams, P. V. Cole, C. J. Dickinson, J. Kay, J. R. Krapez and J. Williams, 'An Evaluation of the Clinical Potential of a Comprehensive Model of Human Respiration in Artificially Ventilated Patients', *Clinical Science*, 58.1 (1980), 83–91, https://doi.org/10.1042/cs0580083; C. J. Hinds and C. J Dickinson, 'The Potential of Computer Modelling Techniques in Intensive Care Medicine', in *Computing in Anesthesia and Intensive Care*, ed. by O. Prakash, Developments in Critical Care Medicine and Anesthesiology (Dordrecht: Springer Netherlands, 1983), pp. 153–69, https://doi.org/10.1007/978-94-009-6747-2_13; C. J. Hinds, M. J. Roberts, D. Ingram and C. J. Dickinson, 'Computer Simulation to Predict Patient Responses to Alterations in the Ventilation Regime', *Intensive Care Medicine*, 10.1 (1984), 13–22, https://doi.org/10.1007/BF00258063

42   C. J. Hinds, D. Ingram and C. J. Dickinson, 'Self-Instruction and Assessment in Techniques of Intensive Care Using a Computer Model of the Respiratory System', *Intensive Care Medicine*, 8.3 (1982), 115–23, https://doi.org/10.1007/BF01693430; J. B. Skinner, G. Knowles, R. F. Armstrong and D. Ingram, 'The Use of Computerized Learning in Intensive Care: An Evaluation of a New Teaching Program', *Medical Education*, 17.1 (1983), 49–53.

My work with Hinds was specific to the topic of respiratory system management in the ICU. It would have been possible to iterate further, in new clinical series of patients and with new kinds of data and optimization methods, but it appeared that the benefits this might bring to the everyday management of patients would prove very limited. Some modelling research groups that combined clinical and technical membership iterated their contributions in this way, within a single narrow domain of application. They succeeded for a while in publishing and republishing their work, maintaining a high profile, thereby. Extremely few of such outputs established and sustained useful clinical application. I would guesstimate that, twenty years on from publication, at least ninety-nine percent of them had already disappeared beyond the event horizon of research endeavour. Such is the anarchy of transition into the Information Age and its information explosion!

Modelling and Controlling Cardiovascular Dynamics

In the early 1970s there was much interest in what were termed model-based control systems. The design of feedback control systems was already a well-established engineering discipline and practice, enabling continuous adjustment of the system's controls to achieve a desired level of its performance. As represented, for example, by the control of the operating pressure of a steam engine by a steam governor, a purely mechanical device, or of the temperature of a water bath by a thermostat, typically in the form of an electromechanical device. How could a computer model of the controlled system be used to achieve this control, by predicting the effect of possible adjustments and using a numerical method to compute an optimum adjustment of the settings?

The PID (Proportional-Integral-Derivative) Controller was the basis of one engineering design that applied a corrective change in system settings, according to the magnitude, integral over time and rate of change, of the difference between actual and desired operating level, or performance, of the system. Another approach experimented with was to model the system to be controlled in purely mathematical terms–as a generically structured black box connecting inputs and outputs, with no attempt made to represent what was known about the actual structure and function of the system concerned. With this method, experimental perturbations of the inputs and measurements of consequent changes in outputs, were used to infer and update detail of the structure of the model. This model was then used to predict and control behaviour of the real system being modelled. It is a method akin to machine learning algorithms of today.

In order to characterize such models, various methods of signal analysis, pioneered in electrical engineering, were employed. These techniques involved decomposing measured signals into a linear combination of different frequency components (Fourier series), and experimental perturbations of the system settings, based on a pseudorandom binary sequence of inputs. This was the approach adopted in a leading clinical cardiology research centre of the 1960s and 1970s in Birmingham, Alabama. I flew there after my visit to Guyton and his team in Mississippi, in November 1971. It was soon after the era of loud gubernatorial politics of George Wallace, and the protests and peace movement of Martin Luther King. It was a place I approached with some trepidation. After the visit, I stood anxiously for an hour, alone outside on a humid, gloomy, stormy evening, waiting for an expected, but late arriving taxi, to take me back to my hotel. I can still see that alarming scene, in my mind, now.

At the hospital, I had arranged to meet a clinical cardiologist whose work I had read about and who was investigating cardiac muscle biomechanics in the context of cardiovascular disease. The more lasting and impactful event, by chance, was a visit he arranged for me, as we spoke, to the hospital's postsurgical intensive care unit, run by an already luminary, but still young, cardiac surgeon and medical computing pioneer of the era, James Kirklin. He had worked earlier at the Mayo Clinic and in collaboration with IBM at its Yorktown Heights research centre.

I was not able to meet Kirklin himself. I gathered that he worked through the day in theatre, came to the academic department in the evenings and worked there through to the small hours, before going home to sleep and arriving back to repeat the cycle, early next day! The informatics focus of his department was on the opportunity provided by real-time sensors to monitor and manage post-operative recovery of patients in the ICU. He had for some time been working to improve clinical outcomes for these patients, by introducing frequent measurement and a related set of 'house rules', as he termed them, for determining clinical management. The unit conducted extensive studies of the outcomes achieved through this close attention to detail of management, based on regular measurement of key variables. The computer system used to capture and process the data was developed and run by an engineer, Louis Sheppard, who welcomed me to the unit. The air-conditioned computer suite, located immediately above the ICU, was almost as large as the ICU itself, I recall.

Lou Sheppard later came on leave from his employment, and then on regular subsequent visits, to Bruce Sayers's (1928–2008) (subsequently Richard Kitney's) electrical engineering department at Imperial College, to complete a PhD there. He developed a model-based approach to patient management, based on data collected in the practical clinical setting in Alabama, with Kirklin. We continued to meet from time to time, over several years. In his PhD project, he developed a linear frequency domain model of the response to infusion of sodium nitroprusside, for control of blood pressure. This used pseudo-random binary pulsed administration of the drug dose prescribed, under Kirklin's clinical supervision, to identify the defining parameters of the model when configured to represent an individual patient, and from this to predict and optimize the time-course of actual administration of the drug, to achieve and maintain stable blood pressure at a desired target level.

Lou's methods showed impressive results in controlling blood pressure and was extraordinarily successful in adjusting continuous infusion to cope with all manner of changes in clinical situations, acutely and over time, smoothly and effectively. A subsequent PhD student at Birmingham, John Slate, built on this to design and commercialize a model-based controller for infusion devices. I have a personal copy of his excellent doctoral thesis. I recall the remark of the then Professor of Medicine at The London Hospital Medical College, Robert Cohen (1933–2014),[43] when I shared these results at a meeting. He said that an interesting question arising was whether these patients would have done okay in their recovery, anyway, cared for with the prevailing human clinical skills of the time, even if perhaps a bit more chaotically.

In other words, another kind of control was required: a controlled clinical trial involving a suitably large number of cases, to demonstrate and convince that the new approach was clinically viable as part of everyday treatment and good practice, beyond the special environment in which it had been developed and brought to fruition. Such investigation and regulatory process is central to the approval of new pharmaceuticals but has proven harder to organize in gaining support for new devices–especially one such as this, which substitutes for human decision and uses a closed loop controller, impacting directly on treatment of the patient. This new possibility was inevitably unnerving for all concerned, including the regulators. Problems that such machines address, and the scope of the methods adopted for solving them, must be closely pinned down, to meet legal requirements for governance and accountability of clinical care.

---

43   Robert (Bob) Cohen was a close colleague of John Dickinson, then his opposite number at Bart's. They transcended politics through the turbulent years of rivalry leading to merger between the two hospitals, and incorporation of their medical schools within Queen Mary College (now QMUL). He was active in a leading initiative at the London Hospital, computerizing its patient administration, as I describe in Chapter Seven.

Where did the legal responsibilities and accountabilities traditionally carried by a clinician lie, when the actions taken were being determined, closed loop, by an algorithm. These questions posed both ethical and philosophical dilemmas, and they have been further highlighted as informatics has moved into the era of artificial intelligence. It is not dissimilar to the ethical issues surfaced in some debates about how model-based reasoning about epidemics has been used to decide policy for managing the Covid-19 epidemic. That said, at least the latter do not embody closed loop control. The decisions are human decisions.

Parenthesis–Purpose

Philosophers have debated noumenon and phenomenon over many centuries, in seeking clarity of reasoning about the world–the reality of the world underpinning what is experienced and observed. The golden rule when embarking on creation of a model of observed appearances, as Whitehead characterized the ways in which we experience the world, is to start with purpose. What are the appearances of the world that we seek to represent in a model, and why are we doing it? Purpose is a human quality; it embraces human values and goals communicated in the language of stories. There are machine goals, but not machine values–at least, not yet!

The 1972 mathematical model of the global economy, *Limits to Growth*, championed by the group called The Club of Rome, led to vocal controversy about assumptions, methods and predictions of models. The model became the focus of attention and argument, incapacitating as much as enabling debate and leadership on the issues. The exercise might perhaps have been better described as dealing with limits to our capacity to think about and act on the limits to growth! In such situations, the tails of special interest wag the dog of common purpose and goal. Conference of the Parties (COP) conferences seeking political traction on climate change have continued to navigate this familiar obstacle course.

Seeking illusory perfection, and losing sight of usefulness, models may become overly elaborate and intractable for the purposes they serve. They may equally be framed too simply, also limiting their usefulness. They may be overly restrictive or permissive of customization within different contexts of use, in both cases making their use more complicated. In *The End of Alchemy*, Mervyn King discussed the past twenty years of crisis in finance and banking and how '[In] the space of little more than a year, what had been seen as the age of wisdom was viewed as the age of foolishness.

Almost overnight, belief turned into incredulity'.[44] He attributed this not to failure of banking or policy but rather to a crisis of failed ideas. He cautioned wariness of over-dependence on rational models of economics–this was the alchemy he dramatized in his title. He emphasized, by contrast, the importance of narrative and storytelling.

When thinking about purpose, and goal of care information utility for the Information Society, we must also confront values. Machines that we create may come to embody and lead us to act according to values we do not hold–unwitting and unrecognized, but implicitly the case. A story illustrates how, unbeknown to us, such a machine may take us somewhere we would not wish to be, open to massive criticism about our values and governance.

Some decades ago, a medical school introduced an algorithm to assist the admissions team in selecting among students applying to study there. Courses in medicine are typically manyfold oversubscribed in relation to the numbers of places available. The algorithm was based on analysis of the school exam grades achieved by previously selected students, prior to entry, and their final exam results on completing the medical course. This was combined with the data provided by prospective students on their application forms. The goal of the algorithm was to predict which applicants were most likely to succeed in the course and guide the admissions team in their selections, accordingly. The discriminant analysis came up with a system to score applicants, based on these data. This was duly put into use, aiming to lighten the workload of admissions tutors, pressed for time in reviewing thousands of applications and deciding which of the applicant to invite for interview. A while later, the school discovered to its horror that it had been assigning points according to ethnicity!

---

44   M. King, *The End of Alchemy: Money, Banking and the Future of the Global Economy* (New York: W. W. Norton and Company, 2016), cover note.

5. Information and Engineering– The Interface of Science and Society

Engineering is positioned at the interface of science and society. In health care, it connects the creators, commissioners and users of information systems, shaping and navigating pathways leading to success or failure in supporting the quality and improvement of services. This chapter celebrates engineers, with stories of their focus, skill and dogged persistence. I draw first on Samuel Smiles (1812–1904) and his 1881 book, *Men of Invention and Industry*, a wonderful account of engineering innovation through the English Industrial Revolution, to draw parallels with innovation in the information revolution of our age.

The chapter associates the kinds and groupings of data that are captured, processed, stored and retrieved with the devices and systems employed to do this. It describes how these have evolved, from the remote village life of my childhood, through school and university days, to my desktop today, in my now global village life, and the Cloud of computational resource that it immediately connects me with. It highlights how characteristics and limitations of devices and evolving computer programming paradigms have channelled both theoretical and practical developments, and determined their usefulness. It connects the discussion of models and simulations in the preceding chapter with data models, information models and knowledge models of today.

The chapter tracks the parallel evolution of software and algorithm, from early empirical methods closely aligned to the underlying machinery of the computer, to programming languages based on theory of data and algorithm, tuned to different domains of application, seeking tractable solutions for the computational challenges they pose. It concludes with a discussion of the standardization of computer systems and methods and the transformational infrastructure of the Internet and World Wide Web. The closing reflection, which concludes Part One of the book and sets the scene for Part Two and Part Three, looks towards a new interface of science and society, as the anarchic transition through the Information Age leads into a reinvention of health care supported by care information systems construed and sustained as a public utility.

    https://doi.org/10.11647/OBP.0335.05

He alone invents to any good purpose who satisfies the world that the means he may have devised had been found competent to the end proposed.

–Doctor Samuel Brown[1]

Too often the real worker and discoverer remains unknown and an invention beautiful but useless in one age or country can be applied only in a remote generation or in a distant land. Mankind hangs together from generation to generation; easy labour is but inherited skill. Great discoveries and inventions are worked up to by the efforts of myriads ere the goal is reached.

–Henry Mayers Hyndman (1842–1921)[2]

The wonder of yesterday becomes the common or unnoticed thing of today.

–Samuel Smiles (1812–1904)[3]

The stories and connections made in the chapters thus far have spanned philosophy, mathematics and science. These might be headlined as about musings, measurements and models! This chapter moves to another emanation–that of machine! The computer is a machine, and it is principally engineers that give it life and connect it with health care and society.

The engineering domain is sometimes described as lying at the interface of science and society–connecting the two. It is where theory and practice meet, pushing forward the boundaries of science and developing and improving technology whereby lives can improve, and society move forward. It is where material, method and construction meet, in making and doing things that serve and protect us–scaling from prototype to everyday device and method, system and infrastructure, and creating and nurturing new communities and environments where these products are used and supported. I started as a mathematician and physicist, immersed myself in connecting the computer with medical science and health care, and ended up as a chartered engineer and honorary physician, so I declare my interest in promoting this cause.

Information is sometimes described as data enhanced with added meaning and context. Some descriptions work backwards from knowledge. As previously mentioned, David Deutsch described knowledge as information with causative power, and Charles West Churchman (1913–2004) and

---

1   Quoted in S. Smiles, *Men of Invention and Industry* (London: Read Books, 2013), p. 50.
2   Quoted in ibid., p. 50.
3   Ibid., p .58.

Richard Ackoff (1919–2009) described information as knowledge for the purpose of taking effective action. These descriptive connections indicate cross-reference. As discussed in Chapter Three, information has come to occupy a middle ground between knowledge and data, distilled and ordered for the purpose of guiding action that determines what is then made and done. Chapter Six explores how the concept of information entered scientific discourse in the context of the search for scientific understanding of the unique nature of living systems. This chapter is about the engineering of information systems for everyday use.

In Praise of Engineers

In my book, and in this book, engineers emerge as heroes, often unsung. Elena Rodriguez-Falcon has proposed calling them 'ingeniators'–a term stressing the role of ingenuity and imagination rather than mere technical proficiency. I like the idea–Spanish, German, French and Norwegian languages follow it, and it would be good for English, too, although the word itself feels a bit cumbersome. Engineering is about making and doing. It is an imaginative approach to life and a state of mind. I have observed and followed people trained in science who have made fundamental advances in their fields. Many such people also possess the heart and skill of engineers. It is a two-way street–many trained in engineering have paved the way for scientific advances.

The father of my career-sponsoring professor of medicine, John Dickinson (1927–2015), was an engineer and John inherited energetic engineering genes. As well as being an internationally renowned doctor and teacher, in his limited spare time he was often busy working with motorbikes, cars, musical organs, central heating systems, electric typewriters and computers! Experimental physiology captivated him early in his career; he wrote his first book about the electronic circuits he had devised, empirically, for capturing physiological signals. Clinical research involving experimental treatments and numbers did not have the same practical resonance for him and he did not engage substantially in that field. His everyday clinical practice was a synthesis of art and science, education and professionalism. In his more reflective time, amidst his six-day working week, he spent much energy in keeping abreast of research on essential hypertension, on which he was a world authority, and, with me alongside, in experimenting with computer simulations of human physiology, to the perplexity of many of his colleagues!

John had prodigious energy–playing squash competitively and organ music assiduously, and attending scientific, professional and musical events voraciously. The ennobled former Regius Professor colleague of his, sitting beside me at his Festschrift memorial meeting, asked if John had ever been put forward for a national honour. I thought likely not–in truth he would have been a worthy candidate but probably never gave such matters a second thought. People captivated by making and doing things seldom think like that.

Thus far in the book, I have shuffled on and off academic hats of mathematics and science and will now put on the hat of engineering, conferred on me, as a Chartered Engineer, by the United Kingdom (UK) Engineering Council. I did my doctoral work in the early 1970s in a mixture of academic departments of engineering, physics, medicine and computer science. My experience of engineering started between school and university, when I spent three months travelling the country as a prospective future management trainee in the heavy engineering industry. For a month, one summer, I worked in the machine-shop of an apprentice training school of a huge factory in the North-East, and out on the factory shopfloor, subject to shopfloor discipline. I learned to operate metal lathes and milling machines. One weekend, some of the many machine workers I got to know there were running a summer fair social event, where whole families turned up and showed off and shared their hobbies. They invited me along. These engineers, almost universally, had model-making hobbies–amazing model steam engines, aeroplanes and the like. A wonderful spectacle of working models and they and their families loved them. Engineering was in their blood.

Academic science envisages and explores the way forward in discipline, on stepping-stones and sometimes in timely or lucky long jumps. It is fuelled and refreshed by joy of discovery and refinement of knowledge. Engineers are artisans–building bridges, experiencing the practical realities of the world where their work is used and appreciated, sustained by joy in making and doing things that work and are useful.

There is sometimes a clash between the kinds of people who are motivated by and wish to learn by making and doing things within societal context, and those who prefer to learn at a safer distance from the societal shopfloor. Such protected places may indeed be ivory towers, but such are not confined to universities. It is good fortune, but perhaps increasingly rare, to have a working environment where the risks and opportunities of learning and practice can coexist and support one another. Engineers gravitate to places where interesting challenges present in working contexts. They tend to be robust and down-to-earth people. Maybe that is why there are few engineering pioneers visible in the higher echelons and corridors of politics and power! Engineering is hard and often unsung and unrewarded work. It exists within wide social contexts, facing multi-faceted challenges.

Engineering in Context

Problems reflecting poor understanding and a lack of practical grip have perennially bedeviled policy, design and implementation of complex engineering projects at a national level. An inherent difficulty faced is the often very wide range of contexts in which engineers must design and make things that work. First, an amusing story, that caricatures the national scene.

Sometime around 2000, I was asked to chair the national launch event for a new policy document on education and training in information technology for National Health Service (NHS) staff. A key theme was to be the joining together of disparate professional groups within a shared common initiative. The meeting was addressed by a health minister and was organized by an NHS manager who was also looking after an initiative to create a national Health Informatics Academic Forum, which I was helping to pull together at that time. A glossy brochure was prepared for the occasion and on its cover was a diagram of three cogwheels, arranged and meshed–a visual metaphor of gearbox and traction. Similar diagrams appear all over the Internet, intended as a metaphor for how different roles and functions integrate with one another in an organization or system. Here is a slide I used to use to illustrate this sort of pitch (see Figure 5.1). Some do not enmesh the cogs, thus unintentionally implying, to an engineering mind, freely spinning wheels connecting nothing with anything!

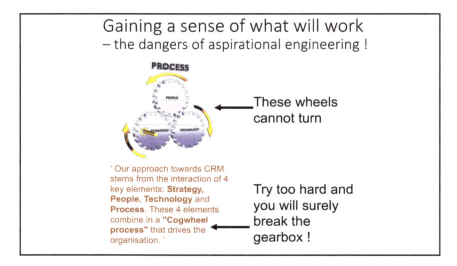

Fig. 5.1 Three gear wheels engaged like this lock together and cannot turn. This image appears frequently as a supposed metaphor of a smoothly functioning organization. It is, rather, an ironic metaphor of the widespread lack of understanding and appreciation of engineering! Image created by David Ingram (c. 2010), CC BY-NC.

At the beginning of the meeting, I glanced at the pile of brochures, one for every attendee at the occasion, and saw a problem–I mentioned it quietly to my colleague, who blanched and swore me to secrecy, which of course I respected. The problem was, as anyone who has played with Meccano, studied mechanics, made, or done anything with, any kind of gearbox would know, this arrangement cannot work. The gears are locked in a deadly embrace and torque applied to any of the cogwheels will be totally resisted by the other two. Increasing the force applied will inevitably break the machine. Rather like an early car, hurtling along (well, thirty miles per hour say, in those days!) and being accidentally thrown into reverse, causing the gearbox to explode!

Deadly embrace is a term describing a fault in program code where several threads of program logic, operating asynchronously, pause in a closed loop of dependencies, one on another. It is a set of mutually self-defeating current states and planned actions–faulty engineering–nothing happens! The metaphor of the three cogs is not the intended one for a smoothly functioning human organization. It is a cautionary metaphor for unsuspected deadly embrace–the danger of unwittingly putting together machines or organizations that cannot, by the nature of their assumptions, specifications and design, be implemented and function as intended. Unwisely forced action in such circumstances, can incapacitate or break technology and burden or break organizations required to use the product. Most do not have eyes to look under the bonnet to observe the workings of computer systems. Many information gearboxes, lashed together and grinding, have populated the Information Age. And many have failed before launch.

Nowhere are costs sunk more deeply than into and around strategic national infrastructure, of which information infrastructure is an increasingly large component. Physical infrastructure is there for all to see while information infrastructure is hidden from view. But the strictures that its malfunction creates and imposes are widely felt and experienced, as much as are the traffic jams queued up on motorways undergoing repair. There is wasted time, cost, frustrated effort and disappointment.

There is also an underlying problem of professional status. Engineering has long been short-changed in national life. The snobberies and vanities of profession and discipline have often labelled it pejoratively as for 'nerds'; I have listened to eminent doctors describe engineers (and implicitly me!) as such. James Watt (1736–1819), who pioneered steam power–an innovation and infrastructure that changed human society for the better and for good– was one such nerd. I will tell his story, and those of similar engineers, below, as they have the power of metaphor to illuminate the story of information engineering of the past seventy-five years. Charles Babbage (1791–1871)– who pioneered the engine of information, the computer–was more erudite, but he, too, was typecast as a nerd. Given what these two faced and what they made and did, perhaps it was something of a compliment! Nerdish, as in 'not easily repressed or daunted'!

Engineering reputation typically rests on a lifetime of sustained practical achievement. Academia bestows and defends status through purity and advance of bounded discipline. Engineering is applied science, obligated to both god of discipline and mammon of practice, and thus not pure enough for the pinnacles of academic honour. The guilds of academia and society perennially debate and adjudicate the relevance and impact of academic work. Professions have feet in both camps, but trades are not considered professions. There is no Nobel prize for engineering; but none for mathematics either, so none the less admirable for that. But the engineering contributions to the scientific advances that have won many Nobel prizes, are noteworthy.

Engineering is about learning by doing. Learning requires memory– personal, occupational and institutional. Information is easily lost and forgotten, especially, now, in its burgeoning, mutually disjoint and contradictory electronic forms. Archaeologists uncover physical evidence that guides current understanding of former times. The wonderfully preserved Roman aqueduct in Segovia is remembered and visited by tourists, like us, of today. The Information Age is not leaving discoverable Egyptian temple or Rosetta stone decorations and traces of culture and language. Failed or outdated software and digital records are easily lost beyond recovery.

My local council transferred its historic records of the city's domestic properties to microfilm. I needed to check ours and had a look–they were already faded, some no longer legible with the reader provided at the office. There is supposedly a national database–it is substantially incomplete. I suggested it might be a good idea to let the local community know about this reality, in case anyone wished to check and secure what they still could of the records of their own properties, for themselves. The council shrugged its shoulders, pleading budget cuts.

What about our medical records? Maybe we should more urgently work to enable personal possession of these, once again, as is still the practice with personal paper and film records, in many countries. As further discussed in Chapter Seven, information infrastructure, like most public utilities, is judged by how successfully it recedes from sight and is only noticed when it goes wrong. In health care, we must take special care to ensure that this does not mean when the cost of remedy is a ransom, or it is simply too late, as already with much of our property's council microfilm record.

Very few early computers and their running software are conserved in science museums. Very many products of human endeavour, building and operating the information infrastructures of today's world, have already disappeared into the mists of time. It is hard to build and sustain for posterity the engineering reputation of a Christopher Wren (1632–1673), Watt, George Stephenson (1781–1848), Isambard Kingdom Brunel (1806–59) or Gustave Eiffel (1832–1923), without leaving behind beautiful churches, steam engines, ships, bridges and towers, for later citizens to see and enjoy. This is not wholly true–Tim Berners-Lee, Larry Ellison, Bill Gates, Steve Jobs, Jeff Bezos, Elon Musk and Mark Zuckerberg will surely be long remembered by historians. There are many others who created the science and engineering underpinning their achievements.

Buried deep in all information infrastructure are many ground-changing intellectual and practical achievements, of stature comparable to those that led into the Cloud and the World Wide Web. The Turing machine and lambda calculus of computation, the interplay of engineering with mathematics and science in the development and manufacture of computer devices, the methods of programming languages and formal logic, the relational calculus of databases, have provided foundations of discipline and infrastructure of immense significance.

Polymaths breach the defended boundaries of discipline and are not always liked for it, on either side of the battle lines. Babbage was variously mathematician, philosopher, inventor and mechanical engineer. In his later career he rose to become Lucasian Professor of Mathematics at the University of Cambridge but was first a lecturer in astronomy at the Royal Institution in London. In those times, laborious use of tables of astronomical data was required for the purposes of navigation. This spurred his inventive mind to devise machines to automate the work of creating them. The Babbage machine was dismissed with disdain by George Airy (1801–81), the Astronomer Royal of the times, in his advice to the government, when it enquired of him about its significance. He was quoted as follows: '[...] I replied, entering fully into the matter, and gave my considered opinion that it was worthless'![4] He was clearly given to airy judgements!

Stepping forward to the twentieth century, when mathematics, after such as Gottlob Frege (1848–1925), Alfred North Whitehead (1861–1947) and Bertrand Russell (1872–1970), was moving into a new era, theory of computation evolved from strong mathematical roots and credentials. And early electronic computers–valves, resistors, inductors, capacitors– arrived from a mixture of government, electrical engineering industry and academic partnerships. A new academic discipline, as computer science then was, tends initially to be classified as a sub-discipline of an existing and accepted one. Some, such as materials science, which draws together physics, chemistry, metallurgy and ceramics, become disciplines and schools of study. Computer science was originally owned by mathematics and then by electrical engineering. With its increasing academic credentials and popularity with students, it now lays claim to its own hybrid sub-disciplines, such as computational physics, computational biology and computational medicine–even bioinformatics in some places! I felt impelled to keep track of them all through the anarchic transitional years of the Information Age. Their significance and academic traction were hard to predict, and different constituencies and interests batted names to and fro. Information and informatics, as disciplines, have ramified ever more widely over all disciplines and thus faced similar challenge of identity. Connecting widely across disciplines, they have a distinctive home with none. 'What is reality', 'What is information?' and 'What is life?' have turned out to be closely connected and deeply enigmatic questions, as Chapter Six explores.

---

4   Quoted in G. B. Airy and W. Airy, ed., *Autobiography of Sir George Biddell Airy* (Cambridge, UK: Cambridge University Press, 1896), p. 152.

There are few if any polymaths, today, who can journey widely across the increasing numbers of connected disciplines of academic discourse, all around the circle of knowledge that has exploded in the Information Age. The lone investigator has been supplanted by the diversely and widely connected team. As now also in health care, where multidisciplinary and multiprofessional teams oversee complex treatments and care pathways. Neil Gershenfeld proposed the regrouping of academic discipline around grand challenges facing society, in which all disciplines had a part to play—ageing society, artificial intelligence, clean energy. Many Universities have tussled with the difficulty of reframing their missions in this way, while, at the same time, remaining focused on narrowly framed research metrics that emphasize identity and profile of individual disciplines. This dual approach was articulated by Derek Roberts (1932–2021), when he was University College London (UCL) Provost, himself coming from a stellar career in the engineering industry. UCL's research mission has been noteworthy in bringing disciplines together in this way. Framing and painting a picture of the grand challenges facing society, requires an institutional framework and a palette of colours drawn from across academia and across society.

The famous Maurits Escher (1898–1972) lithograph entitled *Drawing Hands* (1948) is an optical illusion that illustrates, for me, the paradox arising when depicting a grand challenge from multiple perspectives of discipline and practice—each hand is clasping a pen and drawing the other.[5] The image is a visual metaphor for the writing of individual stories about grand challenges. All disciplines and professions write the story of medicine and health care. This lithograph also emotes complementarity of perspectives in storytelling. From theory comes practice; from practice comes context and test of theory, as well as recognition of the need for and shape of new theory. Theory moves into practice and practice moves into theory. Translational medicine has often been thought of and presented as a one-way street from science into practice. Likewise, development of software has traditionally been thought of in terms of a succession of one-way 'waterfalls' from requirements, downstream to systems analysis, down again to coding, and then to a (guaranteed!) successful implementation. Software engineers learned that this does not work well, and moved to

---

5   M. C. Escher, 'Drawing Hands', *National Gallery of Art*, https://www.nga.gov/collection/art-object-page.54237.html. Escher used visual paradox to illustrate complex ideas. I often used this image when describing how health and care, theory and practice, health care and informatics, are co-evolving through the Information Age. It illustrates the important idea of complementarity that I highlighted in the Introduction, drawing on the immediate post-war Reith Lectures of Robert Oppenheimer. Escher's many woodcuts and lithographs, which I refer to several times in the book, are readily viewed online.

rapid prototyping and agile design, embodying the ebb and flow of design, development and implementation in practice.

If engineering fails and a bridge wobbles, buckles or collapses, the problem can be diagnosed and rectified. Living systems adapt to errors, mistakes and misfortunes–the errors of transcription and mutation of DNA, and other accidents and chance events. In their structure and through their function, they have evolved able to defend themselves. Medicine provides additional armoury, outside as well as inside the body, and care for the individual helps them towards recovery, rehabilitation and renewed self-reliance. Information is subject to malignancy and degeneration, and work is needed to keep it relevant and in good shape. The peer reviewers of science and the editors of Wikipedia perform roles of maintenance and repair. And the engineers of information systems maintain and sustain them, and keep them relevant, sound and safe.

The past fifty years have often exposed lack of capability and capacity to achieve ambitions for innovation in information systems. It has been costly learning within multiple and chaotic contexts of change. Issues of discipline, profession, organization, scale and standard became entangled and muddled. Success and failure are not well summarized and acted on in binary terms: 'distributed practice is dreadful, we will impose central control'; 'central control has not worked, we will leave it to local practice'. A bit like management of the national economy, where, devoid of more sensitive and specific control levers, policy and practice interact and the economy tends to bump along in limit cycles of oscillation.

Many problems at the policy interface of science and society pose intractable challenges; they have been characterized as wicked problems and I discuss these in Chapter Seven. Leadership in coping with and adapting to wicked problems is a uniquely human challenge. As the saying goes, 'leaders go first'. Leaders protect followers and build trust. But pioneers–who sometimes, but by no means always, succeed into positions of wider leadership–can be awkward souls. They are not always good at, or interested in, being judged by or judges of their peers. As one illustrious pioneer, Galileo Galilei (1564–1642), who suffered greatly from peer judgement, remarked: 'I would rather discover a single fact, even a small one, than debate the great issues at length without discovering anything at all'![6]

---

6   Quoted in D. L. Goodstein and J. R. Goodstein, ed., *Feynman's Lost Lecture: The Motion of Planets around the Sun* (New York: W. W. Norton and Company, 1996), p. 17.

Engineers as Innovators—From Steam Engines to Information Engines

I had a close connection with the contemporary worlds of heavy engineering along five years of my songline, when at university and then working in the industry, in the 1960s. Beside me today, as I write, is my grandfather's 1889 school prize; the leather-bound, now somewhat tattered edition of Samuel Smiles's (1812–1904) *Men of Invention and Industry*, cited above. Published in 1884, it is an enthralling account of people, inventions and struggles in the preceding centuries, and the contexts and communities in which their ideas crystallized, and their projects developed. It describes major changes, such as in steam power, railways, shipping, cloth making and printing, that heralded massive change in society.

These events saw determined agonists pitted against equally determined, more powerful, antagonists—defenders of *status quo* and vested interest. Their battles stretched over many decades. The final chapter of the book is a series of accounts of people Smiles had met in his travels around the country, who worked in their own homes and pursued hobbies that had risen to the level of national acclaim, one such the principal engineer of the pioneering era of fabrication of reflector telescopes, which he mastered to pursue his hobby of astronomy. The chapter is entitled 'The Pursuit of Knowledge under Difficulties'. Pioneering invention and innovation are difficult!

I have used Smiles's accounts in tracking back through several hundreds of years, to collect engineering parables: of shipbuilding and its connection with commercial, military and government establishment from the Middle Ages, and of steam power and its connection with unfolding physics, industry and transport, from the eighteenth century. As with the story of library classifications in Chapter Two, used there to give a historical context to contemporary struggles in formalizing computable knowledge, these stories illustrate features in common with contemporary struggles of pioneers of information engineering in medicine and health care.

What we often cannot recognize or discuss well, in the here and now, because too complex, uncertain and contentious, can sometimes be better framed and said more acceptably, but still authentically, in the context of parallels drawn with historical events and different domains, separated at a safe psychological distance. In making these connections, I in no way intend to compare humans with steam engines and ship propellers, although they do, on occasion, share a tendency to get a bit too hot, blow off steam and create a lot of froth! Engineering history is relevant because it is at the engineering interface of information and health, and how this is thought about and managed, that things have often gone wrong in information for health care. There has been a lot of bubbling, hissing and scolding!

Of course, things do now play out quite differently, as well. Lifestyle today has become entrained to rapid pendulum swings of technological change, occurring in Internet time. Human minds and institutions adapt more slowly, entrained to a human dynamic that is more akin to the slowly shifting orbit of the Foucault pendulum of long ago. Today, we know that pendulums constructed with multiple degrees of mechanical freedom can exhibit chaotic patterns of motion. Ideas and their agonists and antagonists, sponsors and detractors are buffeted by events, chance or otherwise. They emerge, progress, survive and die, often chaotically.

Smiles's book features some great quotations as chapter headings. As with all such citations, I have not accepted Microsoft Word's kind offers to correct for grammar or style! Here is a bold claim from Sir Humphry Davy (1778–1829) that sets the scene–a plug for the importance of engineering, I think:

> The beginning of civilization is the discovery of some useful arts by which men acquire property comforts or luxuries. The necessity or desire of preserving them leads to laws and social institutions. In reality, the origin as well as the progress and improvement of civil society is founded on mechanical and chemical inventions.[7]

In one of his autobiographical records, Isaac Newton (1643–1727) wrote: 'It is certainly apparent that the inhabitants of this world are of short date seeing that all arts, as letters, ships, printing, the needle etc, were discovered within the memory of history'.[8] One hundred and fifty years later, Smiles remarked that:

> Most of the inventions which are so greatly influencing, as well as advancing, the civilization of the world at the present time, have been discovered within the last 100 or 150 years. We do not say that man has become so much *wiser* during that period; for, though he has grown in knowledge, the most fruitful of all things were said by 'the heirs of all the ages' thousands of years ago.[9]

Here are reflected the contemporary musings and angst of the Information Age–new inventions are changing the world extremely quickly but what matters to humankind remains as expressed thousands of years ago.

---

7   H. Davy, 'Progress of the Arts and Sciences', *The Saturday Magazine*, 416 (1838), 246–47 (p. 246).

8   Quoted in Smiles, *Men of Invention*, p. 2.

9   Ibid., pp. 1–2.

Smiles notes 'recent triumphs with electric power and electric light', but places James Watt's invention of the condensing steam engine in the front rank:[10] an invention that provided power for pumping water from mines, propelling ships and railway engines, transforming transport and manufacturing, and powering printing presses to communicate the information of William Caxton's (*c.* 1422–91) printed word.

The story of the development of the steam engine is a parable of engineering at its interface with the society of the times. In counterpoint was its interface with physics–the stories of Robert Boyle (1627–91), Nicolas Carnot (1796–1832) and Rudolf Clausius (1822–88), unravelling the gas laws in terms of pressures, temperatures and volumes of gases, and the theory of thermodynamics, linking concepts of heat, work, energy and entropy. In later times, with these properties modelled and quantified in terms of velocity distributions of the atoms and molecules comprising the gases, physics moved on to a statistical theory of thermodynamics, seeding a new concept of information linked with the enumeration of states of order and disorder in physical systems, pioneered by Ludwig Boltzmann (1844–1906). Later, John von Neumann (1903–57) progressed these concepts into the language of quantum theory and Claude Shannon (1916–2001) built on them in his theory of communication of signals, which was termed 'information theory'.

The story of steam power is rich in historical interest and insight, with parallels to the present-day story of information and health care. It was a powerful vector of transforming change of organizations and society at large, challenging entrenched thinking and assertions of status that were not ready to give way. It forced open a way to the Industrial Revolution and powered its plant. It created the railways and challenged the moguls of shipping, and their carefully guarded wealth and influence of the times. The contemporary study of organizational change and its implications for health care policy have been an interesting focus for anthropologists, such as Donald Berwick. Their observations and links with design science have interested and guided policy makers, as they sought to chart their way through the Whitehead anarchy of transition into the Information Society.

Shipbuilding, at the heart of trade and battle over empire, had been in continuous transition over centuries, from wood to iron construction, from oars and sails to steam and paddles and propellers. Opposition to innovation from threatened commercial, political and professional vested interest was a recurring theme of those times. Smiles records that Humphry Davy and Walter Scott (1771–1832), luminary figures of the age, ridiculed

---

10   Ibid., p. 2.

the idea of using gas for lighting, as advocated by Watt's entrepreneurial genius colleague, William Murdock (1754–1839).[11] This seems, he says, to have been the root of the term 'gaslighting', for shaming and ridiculing opponents! Murdock was ultimately awarded a gold medal of the Royal Society in 1808, for his work!

I have selected some other stories from different areas of engineering, to illustrate the feel of the times. Take, for instance, Phineas Pett (1570–1647), who proposed a radically new design of ships for the Navy in the early seventeenth century. This had shipwrights in a flurry. The Venetian galleys they were used to had evolved and were suited to calm Mediterranean seas but ill adapted to stormy seas further north. Judicial review was commissioned by the Royal Court–government and politics were royal matters in those days. Eventually, his new-fangled ship, christened The Princess Royal, triumphed, and reset ship design thereafter, as 'the parent of the class of shipping which continues in practice even to the present moment'.[12]

The first model steamboat was, Smiles suggests, made by Denis Papin (1647–1713), a Huguenot physician and Professor of Mathematics at Marburg. In 1707, he fitted a steam engine to a small boat. A more practical design was patented by Jonathan Hull (1699–1758) of Campden, in Gloucestershire, in 1736. He tested it on the Avon River nearby at Evesham. James Watt's double acting condensing steam engine of 1769 was the first power source capable of 'impelling a vessel'. It was not until 1815 that the first such boat appeared on the Thames.

The story of this condensing steam engine is particularly instructive: with Watt as inventor, Matthew Boulton (1728–1809) as promoter and sponsor (the firm of Boulton and Watt) and Murdock as developer and improver.[13] It rested on the tripod of their cooperating skills and abilities, that allowed it to make progress in design, broaden its scope, create new market, survive adversity and be sustained. Watt's engine arose from him playing with a model built by Thomas Newcomen (1664–1729). Boulton was already a successful businessman. They collaborated in business and their original application for the engine was, as mentioned above, to pump water from coal pits. Uncanny that computers likewise 'pump' data!

Murdock got involved as a young man, in 1779, sorting out practical difficulties with the pumps in use by the Boulton and Watt company in Cornwall. Smiles describes his improvements thus: 'these had William Murdock's genius stamped upon them by reason of their common-sense

---

11   Ibid., p. 141
12   Ibid., p. 38.
13   Ibid., p. 123.

arrangements which showed that he was one of those original thinkers who had the courage to break away from the trammels of traditional methods and take shortcuts to accomplish his objects by direct and simple means'.[14]

Watt was, by all accounts, a determined struggler–something of a tortured genius. As Smiles records:

> Watt lived on until 1819; the last part of his life was the happiest. During the time that he was in the throes of his invention, he was very miserable, weighed down with dyspepsia and sick headaches. But after his patent had expired, he was able to retire with a moderate fortune, and began to enjoy life. Before he had cursed his inventions; now he could bless them. He was able to survey them and find out what was right and what was wrong. He brought his head in his hands to his private workshop and found many means of enjoying both pleasantly.[15]

Smiles prefaces his sixth chapter on the inventor of the steam-printing engine, Frederick Koenig (1774–1833), with a quotation from Daniel Defoe (*c.* 1660–1731): 'The honest projector is he who having by fair and plain principles of sense, honesty and ingenuity, brought any contrivance to a suitable perfection, makes out what he pretends to, picks nobody's pockets, puts his project in execution, and contents himself with the real produce as the profit of his invention'.[16] If perhaps idealistic to today's ear, this captures Smiles's admiration for the character, commitment and staying power of inventors such as Watt and Koenig.

The struggles over steam power continued, on multiple fronts. The story of George Stephenson (1781–1848) and the railways, and the powering of factory machines, is well known. I highlight, here, the contentious battles over sea power and naval conflict on land. An innovation of that era was John Harrison's (1693–1776) chronometer, for use in determining longitude at sea[17] (the story of which I told in Chapter Three, in context of the impact of innovation in measurement). As with Babbage's engine, it was the eminent Astronomer Royal of the time who covertly opposed and obstructed the idea, in this case being interested only in lunar tables. It took forty-five years for the invention to gain parliamentary approval, in 1773.

---

14   Ibid., p. 145.
15   Ibid., p. 146.
16   Ibid., p. 156. I have known someone remarkably like that, who died too young, a couple of years ago. He was my career long colleague and friend, Jo Milan (1942–2018), whose endeavours in creating the information systems at the Royal Marsden Hospital, in England, enabled and accompanied its progress as a centre of excellence in cancer care. I tell his story in Chapter Eight.
17   Ibid., p. 104.

His wooden clocks ended up in the Science Museum in South Kensington and four chronometers are housed at the Royal Observatory in Greenwich.

Other controversies raged over ships. Smiles describes a Dr Lardner (I take this to be Professor Dionysius Lardner (1793–1859)), who had argued in a Royal Institution lecture in 1838 that coal- and steam-powered ships, that were struggling to be accepted, would never cross the Atlantic because they could not carry enough coal to raise the steam required.[18] The feasible marriage of electrically powered vehicles and weighty battery technology power sources are debated in similar terms, today! He also writes that Sir William Symonds (1782–1856), 'the surveyor and principal designer of Her Majesty's ships, was opposed to all new projects. He hated steam power and was utterly opposed to iron ships. He speaks of them in his journal as "monstrous". So long as he remained in office, everything was done in a perfunctory way'.[19]

Steam power triggered similar letting-off of steam in a quite different kind of innovation–the steam printing press. This attracted venomous opposition from printers of the times, as did computer typesetting in our era. Smiles records the secrecy surrounding its initial introduction: 'Great was the secrecy with which the operations were conducted. The pressmen of the *Times* office obtained some inkling of what was going on and they vowed vengeance to the foreign inventor who threatened their craft with destruction'.[20]

The idea of the propeller had first been conceived by Watt around 1770. He described it in a letter to a friend as 'a spiral oar'; it became known, derisively, as the 'screw'. This term had, from the 1600s, been associated with application of pressure or coercion, echoing the rack of torture. Few merchant ships were built and fitted with the screw up until 1840. The Admiralty was strongly opposed and made slow progress in adapting it for the Royal Navy. There was, however a very determined developer of the propeller screw, Francis Pettit Smith (1808–74), who faced down the Admiralty's obstruction antics, albeit at considerable personal cost. He succeeded in the staging of an experiment. Paddle steamers and screw-propelled boats were put into a racing competition and the propeller triumphed. As Smiles writes, 'Francis Pettit Smith, like Gulliver, dragged the whole British fleet after him'.[21] Eventually, the Admiralty had to give in.

Commenting on the struggle, Smiles observes that Smith derived no dividend for his invention: 'Smith spent his money, his labour and

---

18   Ibid., p. 3.
19   Ibid., p. 70.
20   Ibid., p. 169.
21   Ibid., p. 70.

his ingenuity in conferring a great public benefit without receiving any adequate reward and the company, instead of distributing dividends, lost about £50,000 in introducing this great invention, after which, in 1856, the Patent Right expired'. He comments on the determination that had been required, as follows:

> Sir Francis Pettit Smith was not a great inventor. He had, like many others, invented a screw propeller but, while those others had given up the idea of prosecuting it to its completion, Smith stuck to his invention with determined tenacity and never let it go until he had secured for it a complete triumph. As Mr Stephenson observed at the Engineers meeting, Mr Smith had worked from a platform which might have been raised by others, as Watt had done, and as other great men had done; but he had made a stride in advance which was almost tantamount to a new invention. It was impossible to overrate the advantages which this and other countries had derived from his untiring and devoted patience in prosecuting the invention to a successful issue.[22]

The political establishment later caught up. Robert Stephenson (1803–59), a Member of Parliament, convened a meeting in later years to commemorate Smith's achievements. Also illustrating the support that comes only after such contentious and disruptive battles of ideas have been won, Smiles quotes Baron Charles Dupin (1784–1873), who compared the farmer Smith with the barber Richard Arkwright (1732–92), inventor of the spinning frame: '"He had the same perseverance and the same indomitable courage. These two moral qualities enabled him to triumph over every obstacle". This was the merit of Screw Smith–that he was determined to realize what his predecessors had dreamt of achieving; and he eventually accomplished his great purpose'.[23]

These stories have common features. They are parables for our times about the challenge of engineers and engineering and the struggle to innovate. They are stories of invention and traction, talk and distraction; of inventors who innovate and create, and detractors who block and procrastinate; of those who join in and those who observe and judge. If there are three priorities that should be learned from this history, by any who would aspire to create and innovate in health informatics, they are implementation, implementation, implementation–in making and doing things; creating and sustaining necessary new communities and environments; scaling and standardizing methods. And in all this, learning by doing. This was the maxim I adopted for openEHR, which features as an example of a

---

22   Ibid., pp. 71–72.
23   Ibid., p. 72.

mission for clinically grounded, technically rigorous and professionally and organizationally engaged engineering in health informatics–the subject of my parenthetical Chapter Eight and a Half.

The Information Technology Industry

This section is a rapid scan along the timeline of the evolving information technology (IT) industry–snapshots more than full video. It glosses over some technical details that are introduced, more systematically, in later sections. Its aim is to illustrate the depth and scale of evolutionary advance in the nascent IT industry, where many technology teething problems have spilled over into, and interacted with, wider disruption and advance of health care.

Automation of clerical work using mechanical and electronic devices, called Hollerith tabulator machines, was the innovation that gave birth to the first International Business Machines (IBM) Corporation. It was founded by Thomas J. Watson Sr. (1874–1956), one hundred years ago in 1920. Caxton's printing press metamorphosed into an electro-mechanical information automaton. IBM Worldwide Trading Corporation was established in 1949 and taken forward from 1952 to 1971 under the leadership of Watson's son of the same name, Thomas J. Watson Jr. (1914–93). The business based on Hollerith machines, pioneered by the father over the preceding half century, metamorphosed, under the leadership of the son, into mainframe computers and commercial data processing software for automation of clerical work. This strategy, that had been doubted as viable by the autocratic father, triumphed under the diplomatic son!

This was the era of change and transition after the end of the Second World War in 1945, when a new international order emerged under the auspices of the League of Nations. In America, East and West, and in England, two embryonic worlds of computation evolved and enmeshed– those of the hardware and software of computing machines. Two wider worlds also enmeshed and engaged in this endeavour–the commercial world of computers and tabulators and the world of academic science and engineering. In America, this history played out around the evolution of the IBM computer.

The new hardware evolved rapidly over the next decade, starting with thermionic valve-based designs that were the successors of the ENIAC machine of the early 1950s, and moving on to transistor-based machines from the mid-1950s, based on William Shockley (1910–89) and colleagues' Nobel Prize-winning advances in electronic technology. The IBM series of mainframe computers spread into the commercial world and the military, underpinning the space missions of the 1960s. A key design focus of the early machines was in finding the best trade-off between what capabilities should be built into the machine as hardware, with an early focus on hardware to perform floating point arithmetic, and what should be the preserve of stored programs running on the hardware. The design of software to run on these stored program machines played out in the evolution of two pioneering languages, FORTRAN and LISP. The former name arose from FORmula TRANslation and the latter from LISt Processing. FORTRAN led the way in the world of numerical computation and LISP in the world of symbolic reasoning.

IBM created and positioned itself at the epicentre of major technological change. It amassed huge wealth, starting with large mainframe computers and, over many decades, adapted and metamorphosed its product line into aggregations of smaller and smaller, minicomputer and microcomputer machines, and larger and larger software platforms and research and consultancy services. It has been the great survivor. Microsoft, Google, Apple and Amazon have likewise lifted on these currents of transition into the present-day Internet Cloud resources of the Information Age. The race now, in university and industry laboratories, is for quantum computers, where the dream is of tens of quantum qubits, now stuttering into life, emerging on a larger scale, with computing power matching the billions of nanoscale transistor circuits lined up in the largest of today's devices.

I recall being told the story of a customer who purchased an IBM mainframe in the 1960s and later chose to upgrade it to the next machine up in the range, which computed much faster. The new contract was signed and had a suitably hefty price tag, doubling the power of the machine. A support engineer arrived to perform the upgrade. He switched off the power, removed a cover on the side of the sizeable machine, reached inside and, with a pair of pliers, cut a small metal link between two components on one of the circuit boards. He put the cover back on, switched on the power, ran some tests, and departed! It may be completely apocryphal–I have no means of knowing–but it says something with a ring of truth about the disconnect between cost to provide and price to purchase, in the world of IT!

IBM pioneered new technology in many domains, including health, where the Watson software, commemorating IBM's founder, is a machine intelligence guru of medical knowledge today. The Digital Equipment Corporation (DEC) pioneered the smaller scale minicomputers of the 1960s and 1970s. It grew into an international conglomerate and made similar efforts to innovate in health, in niche areas of database (such as the MUMPS language), imaging and laboratory systems, by giving customers the wherewithal to create bespoke systems interfaced with the devices they made and used. Its co-founder, Kenneth Olsen (1926–2011), was another mogul of the times and became wealthy Massachusetts aristocracy.

A story told to me by one of DEC's salesmen of the times, went as follows. One year, Olsen addressed the company's public meeting of shareholders, shortly after a major power failure had occurred, plunging the East coast of the USA, including the DEC home base near Boston, into protracted darkness. This led to a noticeable population boom, nine months later. Taking questions at the end of his talk, a small lady sitting near the front raised her hand and asked: 'Mr Olsen, the electric grid breakdown has been such a disaster, can you reassure me that it wasn't our computers that caused it?' To which, it is said, Olsen replied: 'no mother, it wasn't!'

Many companies–Control Data Corporation, Sperry-UNIVAC and Honeywell in America, ICT in the UK, Bull in France, Siemens Nixdorf in Germany and more–competed with IBM at mainframe level. Control Data put major effort into a large-scale computer-assisted learning system that they christened Plato, with a graphical interface that was both innovative and appealing to users. The venture quickly folded once the company's priming investment had been expended. A mainframe of the scale of the CDC7600, dedicated solely to educational courses, was beyond almost anyone's scope for investment. Just as well, as such courseware was highly experimental, limited to CDC systems, and soon obsolete.

Many more companies–Hewlett-Packard, Data General, Modular One, Norsk Data and more–competed with DEC at minicomputer level. The minicomputer manufacturers were selling into an engineering-literate customer community, and these people wished and needed to know their products inside out. They deployed the increasing power of the minicomputer to provide general purpose multiuser systems for small communities of users, such as the HP 3000 set up introduced at McMaster and the early PDP-11/45 system that I later introduced, configured and operated for a while, at St Bartholomew's Hospital (Bart's).

I was developing software through these early years: largescale simulation programmes and clinical applications in radiotherapy, nuclear medicine, and neonatal intensive care records, starting on the IBM mainframes of UCL in the late 1960s, then on the DEC minicomputers of the University College Hospitals (UCH) in the early 1970s, and at Bart's in the 1980s. The early work in medical physics involved the writing of machine code software and the construction of hardware required to interface hospital physics devices with the minicomputer, as well as the adaptation of the computer operating system software to accommodate the high data transfer rate of some of the imaging systems. Developers needed to know and work on all these components of the computer system. This breadth of knowledge and skill had to be acquired alongside the work of developing and operating the clinical applications the systems were used for.

The wider market developed differently, leaving the DEC approach of offering highly customizable computer systems, focused on technically knowledgeable customers and users, increasingly outmoded. Device manufacturers had gradually caught up and incorporated digital signal processing and data management circuit boards within their own products. The mid-1970s were a key turning point in the market. The industry started to offer machines and software tools and packages that were accessible, not just by specialist programmers but by anyone with the wish and perseverance to build their own applications. These users required no knowledge or insight into how the machine and operating system were designed and functioned–just the ability to follow rules in using them. Like the progression from early cars, where every function and need had to be carefully monitored and catered to, to cars that people just fill up with fuel and oil, inflate tyres, drive, park and occasionally clean!

The pace of advance in computational power and data storage capacity of semiconductor devices was characterized in Moore's Law, reflecting new technology of miniaturization of chip manufacture–from companies such as Intel, Texas Instruments, Zilog, Acorn and AMD.[24] The Unix operating system was born in the early 1970s at the pioneering industrial research Bell Laboratories.[25] Unix became established as an operating system for minicomputers used in science and engineering, implemented across different manufacturers' machines.

Database design evolved more coherently and generically after Edgar Codd (1923–2003) succeeded in formalizing rigorous set-based algebra and practical heuristics for representing and managing complex data relations. Prior to this, it was principally the physical properties and limitations of magnetic tapes and spinning discs that shaped approaches to data storage and retrieval, leaving little scope for optimizing these methods according to the structures of the data themselves, and how they would be used in

---

24 Gordon Moore was a co-founder of the Intel chip manufacturing company. In 1965, he asserted that the number of transistors that could be fabricated onto a silicon chip would double every year over the coming decade, and the cost of computers would fall by a half. In 1975, he revised the estimate to doubling every two years. With some fluctuations, this relationship has held through to 2020. It looks set to continue for some years more, with nanometre scale size of transistor being demonstrated this year.

25 The original Bell Company was named after Alexander Graham Bell (1847–1922), the Scottish founding father of practical telephony. Ownership now rests in the Nokia Group. Bell Labs has been a stellar performer in technological innovation, with nine Nobel Prizes arising from its historic work.

practice. Diverse database management methods came and went. Oracle reigned supreme in this software revolution and business–the wealth of its founder, Larry Ellison, later devoted to his yacht-racing passion. Network technology advanced in parallel over several decades, from Arpanet to Ethernet and Internet, from browser technology to World Wide Web to client-server architecture, from parallel and GRID to Cloud computing. As oncoming waves, these advances created new turning points in the market.

The major computational infrastructures for physics, astronomy and biology advanced, with government investment and drawing on a scientific community culture of cooperation and sharing of key components (although there were, of course, rivalries!). The teams innovated to improve network, processor and database architectures, and software methods, where commercial products of the time fell short of meeting need. Innovation embodied in the robotic arm that is central to operation and maintenance of the Culham prototype fusion reactor, near Oxford, emerged within that kind of science and engineering community. The design of reactor and robotic technology were parallel and interrelated challenges, proceeding together–a shared journey of discovery.

With software, the focus evolved from packages to mega-suite applications, supplied expensively by mega corporations. These became one-stop shops for business applications–Systems Applications and Products in Data Processing (SAP) for the organizational back office. Oracle started to sell mega-suites for managing large institution back-office applications, such as finance systems. The cost of adapting such products to suit the needs of the client institution was typically high. Variations in user needs were ironed out through procurements that included consultancy and training, to persuade and support the purchasing organization in changing its working practices, rather than leave the onus resting on the software supplier to adjust its product to meet those needs–sometimes beneficially and acceptably, but sometimes not. Changes in information systems and related working practices could take months and years to bed in, running alongside existing systems and then supplanting them.

Faults in software are continuously identified and fixed, and new ones created. Continuing support contracts for system hardware and software, to keep them functioning and updated, became a necessity for the user and a reliable source of revenue for the software supplier. The supplier's business model shifted from outright purchase to leasing.

Likewise in device markets, with customers tied into a proprietary brand of product, the cost of operating the device (for example, buying a supply of idiosyncratically designed ink cartridges for a printer) became more expensive over the device lifetime than the original purchase cost of the printer itself. These evolutionary trends were mirrored in the world of health care IT systems, as I explore further in Chapter Seven.

In the hospital, the institution was stirring and responding to the computer suppliers knocking on their doors, with futuristic sales pitches designed to entice and secure orders. The building of local team capacity had started in the physics departments, which were active in supporting clinical services where clear new roles were foreseen for computers–for example, in clinical measurement, radiotherapy, nuclear medicine and clinical laboratory services. Computerized patient administration systems were a major focus of interest of the times. Information technology became a bastion that enhanced and reinforced the power base of management professionals in their perennial battles with clinicians at the coalface, in the running of health services. They had allies in government and the politics of increasingly expensive and unaffordable health care service delivery and IT became ensnared in power struggles over central and local policy and directive, and clinical professional autonomy. This was where the big money for IT innovation in health care came to reside and where mega-projects arose.

Health care, and public sector organizations, more generally, switched their attention towards knowing how best to buy IT from suppliers and manage large contracts with them. This was, itself, a complex and impactful interplay, but it lessened the focus on knowing how to innovate, and catalyze and lead change, in the growing range of IT systems needed for effective and efficient delivery of services. Scientific and technological advance, fragmentation of incompatible IT systems, and fragmentation of health care services went hand in glove through this era. And few focused on where IT fitted in the development, upskilling and support of the evolving and future interdisciplinary and multiprofessional health care workforces, in adjusting their working practices to this new world, thus increasing their already heavy burden. I recently had my Covid booster and seasonal flu vaccinations. The jabs took a couple of minutes at most, including answering a few simple questions about my health, and me adjusting my sleeve. The completion of screens of computer questionnaire, entering information about me, already many times known, to many systems, in disparate health care contexts, by the friendly clinician, took about ten minutes!

The outsourcing of services has provided easy targets for blame when failure looms! But outsourcing can be a very risky strategy when it involves procuring a service that you, the purchaser, do not understand and cannot articulate in a satisfactory way. 'Any colour of car so long as it is black', Henry Ford's supposed motto, indicated power of the producer to dictate; 'no one got sacked for buying IBM' indicated the protective attitude of the wary purchaser of computers. They reflected newly enforced realities and defences of the day. Focus on the wholeness of health and care services suffered as a result.

By the early 1980s, desktop microcomputers with graphical user interface became the norm, taking over from text-based display devices. New competing empires of microcomputer and operating system arose. The machines started as small boxes, with keyboard, cassette or floppy disc drive for program and data storage and attached television screen–such as the Acorn BBC micro, Sinclair Spectrum, Atari and Commodore PET computers. Prices came down to hundreds of pounds. They were both cheap and accessible, stimulating a domestic consumer market for systems running games and simple applications for word-processing, accounting and database management. They also gave opportunity for novice users to experiment with their own simple code–inspirational for school children and hobbyists of the era. Today, the Raspberry Pi has taken the cost of such apparatus down to tens, from hundreds, of pounds.

IBM returned to see off its established minicomputer and fledgeling microcomputer challengers, plunging into the microcomputer era of the 1980s with the IBM PC. DEC tried but could not quite make this transition. I bought one of their early microcomputers, the DEC Professional, for my work on educational software and interactive videodisc systems. I spent many weeks implementing the Mac Series software on top of its cumbersome operating system. I quickly switched to the IBM PC and the MS-DOS operating system. Apple and IBM took their time and learned their way to dominance of the desktop computer market. Dedicated word processors became the 'must have' equipment of every office, disrupting the previous pattern of secretarial services.

Microcomputer operating systems progressed from the simple functionality of CPM and DOS to Microsoft DOS (MS-DOS) which evolved to several stages of Windows, and of Apple iOS, consolidating experience in early minicomputer operating systems. Microsoft operating systems were licensed to many manufacturers and suppliers, to use for running their computer systems, packaged with office software and rudimentary databases. Apple kept hardware and software inhouse within an integrated offering–in time creating a proprietary smartphone technology stage and charging actors for the right to perform on the platform it provided. Linux, an open-source Unix-like operating system and its Ubuntu derivative, colonized desktop, server and autonomous device domains. Android and Ubuntu arose as open-source operating systems–Android to colonize smartphone devices, pitching as rival to Apple's proprietary iOS.

Applications software development became the expensive part of the business and the hardware and its operating software a buried utility. Programming languages and tools migrated across different manufacturers' systems. Intellectual Property Rights in software were difficult to defend, street markets became the office front of software piracy. Eastern Europe, although constrained and held back for decades by limited resources and trade embargo, applied brain power and persistence to the cloning of the computers themselves. There was a weirdly amusing episode that I encountered about one such cloning.

Around 2000, I was invited to Timisoara, in Romania, to give a keynote lecture at a national meeting. On the following evening, I found myself in conversation with the local University's head of computing services. He told me of the pride his team had experienced during the isolation of the country in the Ceausescu era, in succeeding in cloning the DEC PDP-11/34 computer to produce a more powerful home-grown version. He told me an interesting story concerning the uprising, which ultimately displaced President Nicolae Ceausescu, catalyzed by the brave public stand of a Lutheran priest in Timisoara. There had been demonstrations in the streets of Bucharest, close to the central telephone exchange building. The exchange was controlled by the PDP-11/34 surrogate computer, which was the pride and joy of the regime, symbolizing national triumph over its enemies.

Concerned that the crowds would invade and destroy the treasured machine, the regime placed a tank outside the exchange, to defend it. Inside the exchange, the computer was ticking away, acting as a social media telephony hub of the uprising, connecting, and communicating events and coordinating tactics across the country. The regime was oblivious–their actions defeated their own attempts to contain and isolate the protesters! The complex world of IT is fertile domain in which to let loose unintended consequences!

I have had similar experience of the practical engineering skills and persistence of physicists in Poland, in building and operating a radio telescope, during the country's locked down years. It still runs, lovingly maintained by staff who have dedicated their careers to preserving its machinery and maintaining the electronic and machining materials and skills needed in support of their science. It is a treasured artefact of its times, housed, alongside other classic optical telescopes of earlier times, at a hillside observatory near Krakow; our friend, a physicist who runs the radio-telescope, took us to explore it.

Returning to software development, the needs of research, and concern for independence from commercial constraints of software copyright, reinforced cooperation on software for data analysis. Collaborative developments of software packages for statistical analysis of research datasets stemmed from the 1960s–designing algorithms to migrate mathematical methods that were formerly enacted with pen and paper and aided by pocket calculators, into ubiquitous software. Some such endeavours spun into businesses with their products marketed internationally. New statistical methods that required substantial amounts of calculation, which had not previously been feasible to perform, became tractable with the use of software packages. What had previously engaged 'Huxley summers' of devoted wheel turning of hand-operated calculators, to solve their Nobel Prize-winning equations governing the nerve action potential, surrendered to a few milliseconds of computer muscle power.

There was a downside, of course! Any user, not just a trained statistician, could set the machine to churn through huge numbers of calculations, quickly and precisely. 'P fishing', or 'data dredging'–combing datasets to uncover correlations deemed statistically significant–became something of a plague. The boundaries of statistical significance and practical significance became quite blurry in some disciplines. The five-sigma threshold level of significance used in physics in hypothesis testing, to render a result worthy of designation as a discovery of new knowledge, would rule out significance of the results from all experiments in biology and medicine! Such would be completely inappropriate, of course, but much that passes as significant research finding in clinical studies–when reflecting on money spent and benefit realized–seems hardly worth knowing. And as science spreads far beyond laboratory experiment into population studies, the experimental biases implicit in design, conduct, analysis, interpretation and dissemination of the work have rightly come under greater scrutiny–selection bias, detection bias, observer bias, publication bias and more. All these assumed greater importance as the scale and range of data science started to explode.

Many advances in information technology have had their origins in academia and moved swiftly to richer and better funded environments in private industry. Harvard University had brief early connection with the founders of Microsoft (Bill Gates and Paul Allen (1953–2018)) and then Facebook (Mark Zuckerberg); Stanford University was the starting point of Google (Larry Page and Sergey Brin). The UK e-science program was an exciting era of cooperation in which I collaborated and helped to oversee. This and many similar government-funded programmes have shared learning with industry-funded and -led research laboratories, underpinning fundamental technological innovation, and gaining wide commercial traction across the world–the Cloud arose in that way. In recent years, Google has absorbed and hugely progressed ideas of artificial intelligence that were nucleated in academic environments, and developed ground-breaking quantum computing technology. These kinds of synergy have mirrored long-established pioneering establishments in the USA, such as the Bell and IBM labs.

Today the provenance of Cloud-based technology has focused applications development on web technologies. Many overlaying layers of 'technology stack' specialize and standardize subdomains of design, such as the user interface. A new legacy has started to raise its head–that of the diversely evolving patterns of programming languages and their specialization to different kinds of computational task, and the generation, testing and maintenance of code for these. Faults (bugs) that creep from the system and program design stages into operational systems are hard to detect, diagnose, and correct. As they interact with other computational processes, they can accrete incremental noisy complexity and vulnerability.

Good system design and poor program implementation is clearly problematic. Poor design and competent program implementation–in other words, done by the books–can be equally troublesome. I have seen an operationally fault-prone design of a software system for posting patients' laboratory test results to their electronic records, albeit correctly coded, proving vulnerable to an unforeseen contingent 'event' and sending some results to the wrong record. In this case the event was an accumulation of too long a queue of results held up in the system before they could be posted to the associated record. I have not heard that a programming error was the cause of the faulty control of the early Boeing 737 MAX aircraft. It was, one gathers, due to oversight of an unforeseen contingent event, which led to a design vulnerability. The aircraft relied on a single sensor to activate software to correct for incipient instability encountered during flight, to which the plane was more vulnerable because of an implicit design imbalance in its flight trim; that, in turn, arising from technically suboptimal positioning of its engines. These concerns had, apparently, been overridden in its subsequent manufacture, due to commercial pressure to maintain the aircraft's production schedule and contain its costs. From this picture, one might imagine a potential vulnerability in the operation of an autonomous health care software system, in the context of the contingent variability which is so characteristic of individual health care 'events'. How can we be sensitive to, mitigate and guard against such risk? We should remember that that is what human clinicians seek to do every day. That is why they must be interested in the patient's story as well as their data. The record must centre on the individual patient and capture and communicate its clinical meaning.

An urgent problem today is how to cope with the accumulating and costly legacy of obsolete code and methods of coding. The solution must involve writing and communicating better code. Mutual coherence of system design with programming language and method is fundamental. In the world of software technology, this evolving quest has devolved into two competing factions–functional programming and object orientation.

And new buzzwords abound for platforms that themselves write code for applications, with a hundred or more of what are called 'no-code' or 'low-code' environments.

It will not surprise that I am concerned about the entropy of legacy systems code created along this anarchic pathway. We cannot escape the fact that the battling of entropy that naturally accumulates in this way involves continuous work, and sometimes disruptively so! And it will also not surprise that I have found the domain of health care to be almost paradigmatically prone and vulnerable to this entropic disease, and thus a place where we must place special emphasis on the mutual coherence of our efforts to computerize. Not always popular with legacy landlords of decaying properties, but true.

Data Processing

A key message of the Information Age is that quality of health care depends increasingly on how well its information systems connect and deal with both the syntax and semantics of data–how they are structured and what they mean. This resonates with the words of Florence Nightingale (1820–1910) quoted in the Preface, from a hundred and fifty years ago. This may sound superficially obvious, but its underlying practical implications have taken many decades to be understood and sink in. The meandering course of the marriage of health care with information technology over the past five decades has been manifested, expensively and consequentially, in the failure to understand, capture and manage data well–coherently, consistently, conveniently, sustainably and in context. It is not a surprising history–this has been an anarchically changing, complex and contentious period in which to plan, navigate and learn the nature and significance of data, in the context of understanding and promoting health and combating disease, and providing the care services that are needed.

Learning from the experience of those decades is important if information systems are to avoid emulating the crisis of the world's monetary system in 2008. Information pandemic is prospectively overwhelming. Much of what we connect with *in silico*, and depend on to persist, will wither in time. As clay tablets and papyrus weather and wither, so too do digital media. Information technology is no more immortal than life itself. Semiconductor junctions decay, and the silicon crystals used to make them will, no doubt, eventually merge slowly back into the sand they came from. Our virtual worlds are mortal, too!

The next section recalls the history of electronic data storage technologies and introduces data models that link theory and practice in the design and implementation of database systems. Data are often described as a sea. We slip from classical correctness in treating the word as a plural noun (*data* from *datum*) into a modern usage of data instead of datum as a (singular) sea. I will no doubt continue to slip between the two–my meticulously insistent classicist, Latin and Greek scholar school headteacher has long disappeared from my shoulder! The following section adopts a parallel approach to knowledge models and knowledge-based systems. The story then moves to theory and practice of software, as algorithm and programming language.

The engineering challenges encountered in using hardware and software to represent and integrate data, information and knowledge, in systems that embody observation and measurement, database and knowledge base, record keeping, logic and computation, extend beyond these elements into considerations of information models and information architecture. These in turn lead to consideration of software systems and software standardization, within and between different domains of application, with the goal of achieving coherence and meaningful computational interoperability within and between information systems. The final sections address system architecture and the drive for standardization, which have been greatly influenced by the advent of the unifying framework of the Internet and World Wide Web, and the global information infrastructures and user communities these have enabled to gain traction, develop and grow.

Data Storage

Data models and information models feature in the design and formal specification of databases used for storing and accessing data. They operate at different levels of abstraction. The former is focused on the logical arrangement of data, to facilitate its rigorous and secure storage in the machine database. The latter on the characteristics and flow of data, in the context of services and organizations that the database supports. The database system is software that relates logical model to physical layout of data within the storage medium–managing secure and efficient access and maintaining integrity of the data stored.

As discussed in the previous chapter, models serve purposes, and modes and methods of modelling reflect those purposes. There are not intrinsically right or wrong ways to model data. It can be done accurately or inaccurately, reliably or unreliably, well or badly, using different methods that are proposed and find use. Alighting on successful ways to model data requires a combination of insight, experiment, and experience. The past fifty years have been highly experimental.

I do not seek, here, to catalogue the many paradigms and methods of data modelling and storage that have featured along my songline. It would serve no great purpose and the text would quickly disappear into the thicket of anarchy, obsolescence and confusion that has characterized the domain. It would be a headache to write, as much as to read. What seems more relevant is to focus on the story of how the different paradigms and methods arose, the purposes they served, the compromises they represented and the diversity they displayed. I will trace a path through this evolving story.

Information systems are programmed in software and there is therefore an intimate connection between the physical representation of data within systems and the algorithms, computer languages and programming paradigms employed. Information systems also support reasoning about data and knowledge, making inferences and guiding decisions in the context of both data and knowledge. There is thus also intimate interaction between representations of data and representations of knowledge, and the software that programs and enacts the reasoning connections made.

All this is a long story and following and absorbing it requires mental persistence. Information engineering requires another kind of persistence– the term has been appropriated there to mean storage of data on a physical medium. Device technology, data persistence method and database performance–data in and data out–are closely coupled, but deeply below the surface of what a user sees. Unfortunately, but rather inevitably, it is often a matter of 'out of sight, out of mind', and the consequences of that short-sightedness can be profound. The unfolding story starts with the engineering that underpins data storage devices.

I have pondered from time to time over many weeks, now six months into writing this book, over how to tell the evolving story of data storage, data models and databases, along my songline. It has cropped up in many places in the first drafts of the ten chapters and not very satisfyingly. As a fifty-year scan quickly reminds one, the topic has been a muddle; one that students of today, seeking skill in the domain, would be well-advised not to attend to in any detail! The standard approaches to description and organization of data are coursework and textbook stuff for the student of today but they were an anarchy of discovery and change in the making. Technical detail of methods employed has been captured in classic textbooks, such as the well-known one by Christopher J. Date–his 1975 textbook now into its eighth edition–but these quickly date.[26] There are increasingly clear and structured overviews of the field in Wikipedia. The story has continuing impact on and

---

26   C. J. Date, *An Introduction to Database Systems* (Delhi: Pearson Education India, 1975).

interaction with health care information systems, and these are the aspects I focus on here.

I am sitting down to reorganize the material for this section on a Monday morning, and it is the first morning I have overslept beyond an early start. I came to, knowing that the matter had been drifting around in my dreaming consciousness through the night. I awoke, decided upon introducing it as a story of my childhood village community, village data and everyday devices, seventy-five years ago at the beginning of the Information Age. Zobaczymy [we will see]![27] The kinds of data stored today have much in common with those of this childhood, although utterly different in variety, scale, methods employed and purposes served. What has happened to these data in the intervening years? How were they and are they stored and accessed, now, and where are they?

In my childhood in the small village in rural Hampshire, maybe five hundred people lived there. There were similar, even smaller hamlets dotted around in the countryside, with the nearest small town five miles away. There was a village shop, which doubled as the bakery and post office, a primary school for fifty pupils, coming from the surrounding area, a church and church hall, a grocer, doubling as a much-frequented sweetshop, a pub, a farmyard and a woodyard, and the village bobby's (police) house. Stately homes and estates of country squires and landed gentry dotted the surrounding landscape. Prince Philip and pals were sometimes at play with guns and dogs, in the fields surrounding the twenty acres occupied by the children's home run by my parents. A game keeper appeared with a brace of pheasants after each shoot, as a reward for us children not straying to disturb the birds and shooting.

The village data was written down in numerous forms. Simple financial accounts featured in running a household and sat alongside diaries, address books, letters, lists and documents, with notebooks acting as catch-all *aide-memoires*. A small amount may already have been recorded onto early magnetic tapes. At the start of my songline, financial data recording the income and expenditure of a business was recorded in books, often huge ledgers. Data was entered in tabular form, recording details of individual transactions as they arose, and later summarized in sets of accounts, drawn together and presented in a standard manner so they could be viewed and independently verified by auditors, as full and correct representations. The accounts and records covered employment of staff, purchase of material items or services, income from sales of goods or services. From these were derived further tables recording assets held, profit and loss, taxation and

---

27   On this Polish expression, see Preface.

the like. These would be just one part of the documentary record required by law. Documents and correspondence by letter were filed in hefty racks and cabinets.

Imagine me, now, as a social historian, arriving to learn about and document village life, as in Gilbert White's idealized *Natural History of Selborne* (1789).[28] Such a history is often remembered and told through stories. The aim is to collect as much data as possible to complement and support those stories. Who lived there? In what families? When were they born? Where did they live? How did they earn their living and how much did they earn? Why did they choose that way of life? These are: who, what, when, where, how and why questions. They are used in navigating the provenance of lots of different kinds of data and their contexts.

Waves of data flowed, pervading and proliferating in the village. In the school: school classes, teachers, classmates, attendance records, exam results, the annual school play in the village hall. The village shops, pub, bobby, church and church hall, even the farm, and wood yard, all have stories to tell and records to keep, connected one with another through people and contexts of events that they share–the villagers, extreme winter snow or summer drought, harvest festival, outbreaks of contagious disease. They form narrative accounts and each person, and every family, has stories to tell. Over time, these play out further and connect more widely, within and beyond the village.

Much of this history is an oral history, as told, sung and persisted along the Aboriginal songlines. The data persist: as written and printed words, as symbols and numbers, as media, and in association with features of the landscape. They are evidence in court: presented by professionals, told, listened to, read, made sense of and adjudicated, through the eyes, ears, thought and experience of judges and jurors. They are assimilated nearer to home: in family and kinship, culture, practice and life of the village. *Family and Kinship in East London* in the 1950s, was one of my dad's inukbooks, from his difficult and impoverished childhood there.[29] The human authors of the recorded data, and their authenticity and authority, wax and wane and become established and trusted, or forgotten, over time.

Times changed and technologies for recording and communicating data shaped and were shaped by those changes. Data was communicated in greater amounts and more quickly, to and from afar, through broadcasts, letters, newsprint, books and travel. Clerking of entries in ledgers had earlier given way, in larger businesses, to recording on punched cards that could

---

28   G. White, *The Natural History of Selborne* (London: Gibbings, 1890).

29   M. Young and P. Willmott, *Family and Kinship in East London* (London: Routledge, 2013).

be printed from and sorted. Mechanical typewriters arrived in the village in similar very small numbers as did early cars. In my childhood, there were just two or three car owners in the village, many bicycles, quite a few horses and, of course, many Shanks's ponies (of travellers on foot!). Few houses had phones and television was equally slow in arriving. My great aunts living in a tiny Cotswold Hills hamlet, had no electricity and used oil lamps and solid fuel. Some hand-operated calculators assisted the tallying of numbers for financial accounts. Dictaphones accompanied doctors on their rounds, keeping an *aide-memoire* on the move, for later transcription to paper by a secretary. Files of correspondence, reports and accounts proliferated, and administration became data heavy and ever more complicated. Postal services ferried and telegraphed data from person to person, organization to organization, and place to place.

And Pegasus took wing as the name of an early vacuum-tube computer, programmable to process text and calculate with numbers. Computers received program instructions and data, punched onto paper tape and card, and read into the machine by tape and card readers, calculated and printed out in new forms. Program and data were also read and written, using flexowriter, which doubled as typewriter and slow printer, operating noisily to print ten characters per second. Postal telegram gave way to telex. The computer had a small memory store that could be addressed and worked with directly, providing space for both program and data. Outside the machine, the data was stored on card, paper tape and as printout. A laborious workflow was tended to by teams of computer operators, processing the work in discrete batches.

There was another industry evolving rapidly and in parallel—that of radio and television, recording and broadcasting for the entertainment industry, on sound and then video media. Records of music had long been based on mechanical devices—folding paper card for pianola and rotating spiky disc for musical chimes. This merged into the world of electrical transducers of mechanical vibration, vinyl record, stylus, amplifying horn; and then loudspeakers arrived. We had one of the early phonographs at home, beloved by my parents; they had much of Mozart's music on inflexible early records, played at seventy-eight revolutions per minute (rpm), that cracked rather too easily. In my mind's eye, I can still see the horn. And with the advent of electrical recording onto magnetic tape media, tape recorders became a rapidly growing new domestic market.

The recording and editing of such tapes, reel to reel, became a home-based hobby. Dictated oral history and record found its way onto magnetic tape. Editing—adding to and erasing bits of the record—was a time-consuming labour of love! Data was recorded sequentially along the tape, and the tape scanned with playback machines that could skip fast forwards and backwards to locate content. The tape player incorporated a counter that ticked up the number of rotations of the tape cassette as it recorded onto or played from the device. Positions of pieces of music on the tape were written down in a notebook index. Of course, as the long tape wrapped around the spindle, the length of tape signified by each tick upwards on the counter, increased in proportion to the increasing diameter of spooled tape. This index did not signify amount of music, just its start position, and that with decreasing precision.

On vinyl records, the music was recorded and sensed as a time varying mechanical indentation along one long track–helical along the surface of a cylinder or spiral from outer rim towards the centre of a disc. The physical recording of a given loudness, frequency and length of note (p, f; B-flat; crotchet or minim) was associated with different physical magnitude, frequency of indentation, and distance along this track. Along a magnetic tape track, it was recorded and sensed as a change in strength of magnetization of the tape. In contrast to the disc and stylus arrangement, and in like manner to the phonograph cylinder, this was recorded uniformly, always occupying the same length of tape for the note recorded. In all these ways, characteristics of device and recording technology determined quality of performance–in this case the oral quality of the sound. Some still hold vinyl preeminent, although the entertainment industry has long been built on the shoulders of digital devices and systems, and now of Cloud-based streaming services.

Calculation and computation moved from mechanical (Babbage engine and hand-operated calculator) and analogue (Napier's bones, slide rule and analogue computer) devices into the electronic era. Magnetic tapes became the leitmotiv of digital data storage. One track of audio changed to seven and then nine parallel tracks of binary data on reels of magnetic tape, spinning on large tape-drive devices attached to computers. Programs running in the computer controlled this device and transmitted data to and fro between tape and computer memory. The data was organized on the tape in sequential files–one following the other down the tape–and the tape was annotated with electronic markers, indicating the beginning and end of files and first and last positions of the tape where they were recorded. Detection of these markers alerted the device hardware about where files were positioned. Software indexes were used to facilitate jumping forward or backward from one to the other. Indexed sequential files, and fixed and variable length records were introduced as new persistence methods, to adapt to changing needs and speed of access.

Writing and reading data involved spinning the tape to the position required and transferring to and from there, bit by bit, byte by byte and file by file, rotating the tape drive forward a step at a time under program control. The tapes grew to hundreds of feet in length and electronic circuitry was devised that searched for the markers, thereby enabling a program command such as 'skip forward' or 'skip back', to the start or end of the next file or the start or end of recorded information on the tape. In these operations, the tape could be spun past the read/write sensor very much faster than when inching a step at a time, to write and read data.

So far, so good, but as with the manual editing of audio cassette tapes, or the splicing of paper tapes used for the input of computer programs and data, the sorting and editing of material on the tape under program control became a significant block on productivity. Allocation of space on the tape, and recovery of space freed up after data previously stored there had been either erased or edited and repositioned in revised form elsewhere, was time-consuming and laborious. If a file is deleted, is that section of tape still available for reuse? In charming technical language, this discarded data is termed 'garbage', and recovering and recycling the space it occupied, for further use, is termed garbage collection! Garbage became a term of derision in castigating misuse of data–Garbage In, Garbage Out (GIGO) became a catch phrase.

The deletion or repositioning of data and reassignment of the storage space freed up had to be recorded as an update to whatever index the program was using to identify and locate data recorded on the tape. Material that had been placed sequentially, with associated items located near to one another, became fragmented, as files were split into sections and recorded in non-adjacent sections of the tape. Reconnecting the separated pieces of a file required for use in a computation involved waiting for the tape to spin (described as a latency period), and this could slow the writing and retrieval of data considerably. Managing the positions of files on the tape, with multiple edits, deletions and re-recordings, made for laborious program software. Often the simplest approach was reel-to-reel editing, as with audio tapes, copying from one tape to a fresh new one, which could be done at greater speed, leaving out the pieces no longer required and adding new pieces as the tapes spun by.

The programming effort required to accommodate and adjust to the characteristics of the recording device again became a significant matter of tail wagging dog. The purpose of the exercise was not simply to achieve and facilitate accessibility of data and data storage–it was to compute with the data, and this involved searching through, calculating with and reordering the data, such as by time, place or person it described. Optimization of these data-processing tasks involved an interplay between properties of devices and properties of the data themselves. Ingenious mathematicians and engineers devised new algorithms to improve the efficiency of such manipulations of data; the utility of each pitched against characteristics of the device for which it was implemented. Theory of data-processing stretched theory of software and database design.

As far as the data were concerned, magnetic tapes were essentially automated filing cabinets. The digitized files comprised text and numbers, occupying pigeon-holes on the tape, termed fields and grouped in records of fixed, sometimes variable length, and records grouped together in files. The file held groupings of data from lists and tables previously recorded in paper documents. Where the purpose was to keep all the data in the document together, it made sense to design storage and retrieval, document by document, accordingly. Where the purpose was to work with the content of multiple documents–accessing and processing pieces of data and updating other stored documents, accordingly–granularity and flexibility of access within records was a more complex challenge.

At the time of my first practical encounters with mainframes and minicomputers (in 1969, on London's first Master of Science (MSc) course in computer science), tape and disc technologies were equally poised–I worked with and programmed them both.[30] Pictures of spinning magnetic

---

30   Computing was a puzzling newcomer in the academic world and especially so
     in a medical school. To stabilize and find my bearings in my initial foray into
     this new world, I decided to enrol to attend a pioneering Masters course in
     computer science, at the then quite new London Institute of Computer Science
     (ICS) in Gordon Square. This was a London University Institute, not connected
     to any College at the time, directed by Richard Buckingham (1911–94), a particle
     physicist and mathematician, turned computer scientist. The combination of
     lectures and practical work was a congested curriculum. The luminary Peter
     Kirstein (1933–2020), credited as a founder of the Internet for his work in
     creating the ARPANET network link between the USA and the UK and early
     banking networks, was the very bright lecturer in systems programming. He
     owned a DEC PDP-15 in the basement and much coursework for him involved
     machine-code punched with flexowriters onto paper tape, read into the machine
     and used to explore the coding of operating systems and device drivers. With
     London University's decision to disband the ICS, the staff were reemployed to
     establish new departments at the six principal Colleges of London University at
     that time. Peter took a small core group of the staff into nearby UCL, first as part
     of a new joint Department of Statistics and Computer Science, and subsequently
     as the first Head of a newly created Department of Computer Science. In later
     years he collaborated with my Department at UCL, CHIME, in piloting the
     Internet IPv7 protocol in medical applications, as part of a research project in
     the EU Framework Programme. Keith Wolfenden—dry and slightly lugubrious
     in manner, but generously warm-hearted—was the lecturer on data processing.
     He took us through sorting algorithms, such as bubble-sorting, and we wrote
     and tested programs. The vagaries of processing data to and from magnetic tape
     were expounded—very much an example of device technology considerations
     dominating data manipulation in the balance of theory and practice. I learned,
     there, perhaps for the first time, how closely software engineering methods were
     coupled to the practical properties of devices. True of theory and practice of

tapes were iconic images of the times but magnetic tape technology soon ran out of steam in keeping pace with the scope and scale of data-processing requirements. However, they were not rendered obsolete and were still in use in the petabyte data stores established at places like the Central Computer Laboratory of the Research Councils (CCLRC) laboratory at Harwell, which I was shown when attending advisory board meetings there in the early 2000s. The robotically controlled modular array of tape cartridge drives was used to archive the increasingly massive datasets of e-science that were processed by powerful connected grids of computers. The backup would have required many days if carried out across a network connection and was instead achieved by placing tape cartridges in a white van and driving them to a secondary backup centre elsewhere, we gathered!

But just as tapes and tape recorders for analogue audio recordings had given way to more flexible, robust and manageable vinyl records and record players, magnetic drum and disc stores arrived in the computer room, storing megabytes of digital data. Such devices had been experimented with in the world of immediate post-war crystallography laboratories, where the world's first drum store was claimed by an inventor working with John Bernal (1901–71), friend of John von Neumann (1903–57), at Birkbeck College in London, as mentioned in Chapter Three. The storage of digital data, serving the needs of audio and video media and computation, spawned the compact disc, DVD, floppy disc, video disc and dynamic RAM data sticks.

---

measurement, more generally. This was quite tedious stuff, and I was delighted to find a higher-level language, APL, which coped elegantly and satisfyingly with the mathematical aspects of such algorithms. The mainframe of the day was the Ferranti Atlas, which occupied most of the ground floor of the Institute. Its design, which included extraordinary thin metallic strips of firmware code, was lovingly described in lectures on machine and operating system design, by Alan Fairbairn. Eric Nixon introduced us to computer science through the vehicle of a virtual machine he had devised which was programmed and ran on the Atlas. We were introduced to theory of computation by one of the research fellows, in a course encompassing Turing machine and the language of set theory and formal logic. Other lecturers covered circuit design, operating systems, and programming languages. We did coursework that introduced us to languages such as FORTRAN, PL/1, and ALGOL, but much of the time we wrote native machine code. These were early days, with none of the structural and conceptual clarity, expressive power and efficiency of today's programming languages and their platform implementations to support program design and testing. Languages tuned, rather pragmatically, to the needs of different domains of application were, and for coming decades continued to be, an exploratory maze. They sought to balance evolving theory of the design of programming languages with the changing requirements of the domains in which they were applied.

With the new devices arose new ambition to manage increasing scale and complexity of data, as well as a new challenge in developing better means for optimizing them to work well. New data storage and management methods led to stronger bonds between data structures and software. Data modelling became a mainstream preoccupation and concern. As the doyen of software paradigms Niklaus Wirth was to write in 1976: 'Algorithms + Data Structures = Programs'.[31]

Moving on from magnetic tapes, my experience in 1970 progressed to digital data stored, uniformly, in concentric rings, on spinning magnetic discs. As with magnetic tapes, there was access delay (latency) in rotating the disc to the required positions for reading and writing data, although considerably less than for spinning tapes. The discs were in continuous rotation and latency was determined by speed of rotation and time for movement of a sensor arm between the periphery and inner regions of the disc, much as a stylus reads from a vinyl record. Drum-like rotating storage devices had an array of read/write sensors positioned parallel with the axis of rotation, enabling faster access to larger data stores, but at a cost in terms of the extra hardware and control circuitry required.

Allocation of space on these devices, and recovery of space freed up, was a similar optimization challenge, and an index of the space allocation enabled the device control software to move the head directly to access the required data. Initially the discs were fixed in place within the device. Quite swiftly, technology improved to the point where discs could be housed in demountable cassettes, thus achieving an archival function akin to magnetic tapes on racks. In due course, disc technology was miniaturized, and its storage capacity expanded; floppy discs and minidiscs became consumer items at home.

Early disc devices were very temperamental–most prototypes are. Their electrical circuitry and physical components were annoyingly prone to failure and sometimes to spectacular and damaging crashes of the read/ write sensors–destroying sensor, spinning disc and stored data. Risk of corruption of sections of disc and data meant that great care was needed to keep backups and test and compensate for the prevalent presence of blemishes in the magnetic surface. My first disc storage device was of suitcase size, incorporating a thirty centimetre diameter spinning metal disc which stored just thirty-two kilobytes of data–it seemed quite impressive at the time! It was always going wrong, however, and a maintenance engineer took several days to come to sort things out, bringing the bulky oscilloscopes and

---

31   N. Wirth, *Algorithms + Data Structures = Programs* (Englewood Cliffs, NJ: Prentice-Hall, 1976).

signal generators of the maintenance trade of that era. Essential recurrent maintenance contracts became an expensive budget item.

Design and performance limitations restricted most databases to storage of files similar in structure to those stored on magnetic tape. Searching within these files involved software for locating them on disc, reading them into memory, record by record, and analyzing the data, field by field. It was all down to the program one wrote. Products with more elaborate functionality began to emerge as disc technology settled and became more reliable. And early pioneers were already hard at work, exploring new horizons. Constraints of computer memory size forced economy towards concise, albeit not easily humanly readable, program code. Constraints of storage device performance motivated exploration of new methods of data persistence. Requirement to accommodate multiple simultaneous users of a computer, working in different domains of application, led to a need for new optimization among program algorithm, data storage and the operating system software of the computer itself.

Exploratory medical physics applications of the era worked at this interface, linking imaging devices, such as nuclear medicine scanners and cameras, with minicomputers to capture their fast data streams, to process and generate higher quality and dynamic images. And most significantly, the Massachusetts General Hospital Utility Multi-Programming System (MUMPS) was conceived and developed in Boston, in the late 1960s, in the laboratory and team of the doyen of medical informatics, Octo Barnett (1930–2020). It led hospital information systems into the Information Age and has endured, underpinning principal hospital information systems and many other domains of IT systems today.

As the speed and capacity of disc storage increased, and ambition rose, attention switched to characteristic organization of the data themselves, when determining data storage requirements and methods for accessing and processing them–issues of type, interrelationship and scale of data, and of their context and usage. It was an era of experiment and learning–prototyping, refining, discarding and generalizing. From it emerged new theories and models of the logical structure of data, independent of its chosen means of physical storage. Theory of algorithm advanced alongside experiments in programming. Theory of computation paralleled advances in processor and network technology.

Data Model and Database

The term data model came to mean an abstract model that sets out a description and logical organization of data elements, defining their characteristics and how they are related to one another. It is an abstraction in the sense of existing independently of the technology used to store and access the modelled data.

Pursuing the village data analogy, the physical compilation of lists, financial accounts and other records became increasingly burdensome. First hand-written, stored in ledgers and filing cabinets, later dictated to a secretary, or captured on an audio device and typed out, it became an increasingly expensive process. Requirements for sharing, analysis and regulation of data expanded; this led to their being organized and expressed in different ways, and increased the number and size of sets of data required to be kept in the records. Keeping records up to date occupied more time.

The school and church kept written records. These would be descriptive of people living in the neighbourhood and the many kinds of issues and events connecting with their roles and activities. In a general way, providing answers to questions about who did what, when, where, how and why. Much of the content might well be common between these two sets of records, but, being designed and maintained independently, it was likely to be expressed differently and include different levels of detail.

The management of changes in interrelated sets of records brings new complexity. In my secondary school years, I was given the task of organizing and keeping a diary of all the school sports fixtures; setting dates and times; negotiating with all the different schools involved to make their different diaries fit together; organizing transport; and handling problems arising when, for whatever reason, the pattern broke down. We might nowadays call this a workflow–the work was mine and there was good reason to call the sports diary a 'fixture' list. We fought like crazy to keep the pattern fixed from season to season–competing with certain schools in certain weeks of the term, each year! As soon as one fixture broke down and could not be played on the usual date, in the usual location and at the usual time, the knock-on effects ramified through many school fixture lists.

It was hard work to adjust the pattern and make sure it was still consistent with every match required being played by the end of the season, with transport, availability of referees, refreshments and so on, all arranged. As a mathematical and procedural problem this was difficult enough. As a human problem, with the many possible reasons calling for changes–weather, school term dates, special events, illnesses, personal whims of teachers–a good deal of interpersonal brokerage and persuasion was required. It was a highly contingent world–imagine from there to health care service diaries!

Nowadays, we might call this process 'logistics'–in my experience, the process was not formally all that logical! A timetabling automaton would struggle to cut the mustard in resolving such matters, without much human brokerage of the compromises required to reach agreement, each issue being felt differently in different schools. 'The computer says no' would come to rule the roost!

These rather simple examples reveal underlying complexity in the challenge faced in modelling data, especially where purposes served are shared purposes. Translated from paper to the computer domain, such models must be clear, coherent and consistent, both in the definition of the data they embody and in how they are understood, communicated and used. Human language is inexact and brokers differences and uncertainties. The computer domain is unforgiving–such limitations propagate as errors. To compensate, the usage of language on the human side of the communication becomes progressively narrowed and appropriated to more specific computer domain meanings. And concern for precision of communication of the meaning and context ascribed to data leads to ever more detailed recording of data about data–metadata. In his book *Homo Deus*, Yuval Noah Harari describes the debasement of human language and communication to fit the needs of consistently computable data, a data religion or 'dataism'–a term first used by David Brooks in the *New York Times* in 2013.[32]

Continuing with the computerization of village data analogy, data were seen to be of different kinds and groupings–there were numbers and character strings, and villagers, families, school classes, church attenders, shop customers–unbounded and ever-changing groupings. Times are seconds and years, weekdays and anniversaries, before lunch and during sleep. Locations are the home, the school, the shop, the bus stop. The groupings exist in hierarchies: children within family, school class within school. And such hierarchies break down and become blurred in their precision and usefulness.

Here natural language starts to depart company with and give in to computer-speak. In appropriated use of the terms, each 'element of data' within any such 'grouping' is called an 'instance' of that 'grouping' and the 'grouping' is called a 'class'–hence 'school class' as a 'class'! 'Class' and 'instance' became appropriated terms to describe such 'groupings' more generally, as did the word 'classification', to describe how its 'members' were determined. Each 'school class' is an 'instance' of the 'set' of all 'school classes' in the school. Each pupil is an 'instance' in the 'membership' of a 'school class'. My primary school Years 1 and 2 'school class', taught first by Miss Broadhurst and then by Miss Simpson, is where I was first

---

32   Y. N. Harari, *Homo Deus: A Brief History of Tomorrow* (London: Random House, 2016); D. Brooks, 'Opinion | The Philosophy of Data', *New York Times* (4 February 2013), https://www.nytimes.com/2013/02/05/opinion/brooks-the-philosophy-of-data.html

'instantiated' as a pupil of Woolton Hill Church of England Primary School, in the village of Woolton Hill, in Hampshire, in England... the computer is a hard task master in its insistence on normalizing language. I will give in and not attempt too great a precision in my normalization of these terms, not being (or for my purposes here, not needing to be) too pernickety about them.

In this way of structuring and reasoning, one person's set of data can feature in many data instances within the ensemble of groupings (classes) used to model the village data. This hierarchy of data and classes might be modelled as analogous to tree structures of the village data, with successive groupings ramifying (branching) one from another. The village data is represented in this model as leaves on trees. To search for the data we seek, we must climb and navigate the tree, through its hierarchy of branch and twig groupings, to arrive at the leaves of data we seek. But it is not always useful or appropriate to atomize data in fine detail. There are many ways of doing it, serving different purposes, and represented as different tree structures. And some groupings of data are best kept together within a single document and the document stored and retrieved as a whole, prior to any further consideration and computation. There can thus be many trees modelled in this village data wood. One can easily lose sight of the wood, faced with the tangle of trees.

The analogy of modelling data hierarchy as a tree may fail us on other counts as these are often not normal branching trees. Branches can combine as well as diverge, and a network of connections is another way to model and populate the links between the different groupings. The network may be a highly regular structure which we think of as a lattice or a highly variable structure where the more complex mathematics of graph theory may come into play. And the data tree hierarchy can, in the mind, be uprooted and inverted, to be climbed the other way up, starting from some element of data and discovering the groupings and locations where it is instantiated. For 'content addressable' file storage, a new kind of index is needed, like an alphabetical book index that points to pages in the book where the indexed topic or detail is described.

Experiments in data modelling and data storage progressed on multiple axes of information engineering, treating the data as: entity and attribute; document; tree, network, lattice and graph. These brought new richness of linkage and relationship among the data and associated new complexity in methods to keep them rigorous, up-to-date and secure. As new application domains were explored, device features and limitations became less dominant in determining and constraining database design; however, requirements to represent diversity of structure, content, extent and context of the records themselves, that changed over time, became more ambitious and thus more difficult to accommodate and implement.

Any more detailed description of the many different paradigms of data structures that have been explored, and their aetiology, would quickly ramify into a book itself. Some have evolved and endured, and others have disappeared or been superseded. The hierarchical paradigm is still used for the Microsoft Windows Registry. However well they are defined, though, data models cannot hope to accommodate the full semantic richness of the real-world data domains they seek to represent, just as formal logic struggles to accommodate the verbal language nuances of human argument. But data quality matters in everyday life, irrespective of whether computerized or not.

The exploration of different paradigms of data modelling has focused new light on data quality more widely, informing a clearer sense of the balance that must be struck between rigour, expressiveness and ease of use of information systems. The inefficiencies and harm arising from poor or inadequate discipline in the capture and handling of data, and the cost penalties these impose, is today more apparent. What is less appreciated is that this pattern persists also in the domain of algorithms, which come together with data models in the representations implicit in computer programs. There is considerable and costly accumulated legacy of obsolete software. This issue is further addressed in the software section of the chapter, below.

A full, rational and consistent data structure, fit and performant for all potential purposes that the data may serve, is readily understood to be often unachievable, and would, in any case, need to adapt and change over time. In the village, the church decides what it wishes to computerize in its records–about births, marriages and deaths, about families, baptisms, confirmations and tithes–and models its data accordingly. Others, if so minded or required to, also structure and keep their own different records. Some stick with paper records!

However, what happens when a 'Who?' question is asked by the village doctor–such as 'Which of the children are in this Sunday class and that school class?' And why would the doctor need to seek this information? Perhaps to check against their medical records to see who has not had their measles vaccinations, after a child who is a member of both these groupings shows up one morning with early signs. Maybe a bit far-fetched–bush telegraph among parents at the school gate would likely have got there before the doctor. But the general issue here is that data exist within multiple groupings and contexts, any of which may prove relevant to a question that needs a consistent and trusted answer.

Over time, personal data came to be seen as the property of the data subject and an ethical obligation was recognized, which became an increasingly closely defined legal obligation, that they be kept up-to-date, consistent and confidential, used only for purposes for which that person had given informed consent. Thus, the need for rigorous and robust standardization of data became a new kind of both moral and legal imperative. And providing the means to meet these new requirements encountered further complexity when different aspects of a data subject's personal data were being held in multiple disjoint databases, conformant with different data models and handling their access control security differently.

When reflecting on these intrinsic complexities of handling data in computer systems, combined with concern for its confidentiality, it is perhaps not surprising that medical records have persisted so long in paper form, insecure though this may prove to be in reality–at risk of physical theft as much as cybertheft. The combined complexity of these multiple sets of requirements has been nowhere more vividly exemplified than in personal health care records.

And it was through pioneers in medicine of the 1960s and 1970s–people like Barnett, Neil Pappalardo and Howard Bleich (1934-2021), in Boston, at the Massachusetts General Hospital and Beth Israel Hospitals–that ground-breaking innovation occurred. The MUMPS language was conceived of, developed and commercialized, and used to build and operate early clinical department and hospital-wide computer applications and information systems. Jo Milan (1942–2018), my colleague at the Royal Marsden Hospital in the UK, pitched in alongside. The MUMPS-based systems perform extremely flexibly, efficiently and powerfully in clinical context, to this day, and MUMPS spread and persisted in other domains–notably in records of banking transactions.

From its origins, MUMPS had proceeded from a simple and pragmatic set of choices. It treated a persistent data store as a virtual array addressable directly by a MUMPS language program as a global program variable. To the programmer, it was like a coiled snake of extending magnetic tape, directly addressable anywhere along its length. The MUMPS language was implemented as a 'program interpreter', working line by line through the program code, and enabling direct and efficient control of the still very limited power and capacity of the machine environment, for multiple users. It implemented the storage of the snakelike data array on disc (its 'persistence', as the term became appropriated), such that programs could efficiently access and retrieve data from this array, even if data instances along the snake were located few and far between on the disc surface, and only very sparsely populating the virtual storage array structures that the language and program provided for. This was a major advance of the times.

By inspired and original use of indexing keys, it populated these sparsely occupied arrays such that, for example, elements 1, 10 and 1000 in the array only used three storage locations, and array elements could be inserted, edited and removed equally simply, with access to each element achieved via a quick and continuously 'balanced tree' search strategy, called a 'B-Tree', adjusted over time to keep database access operations optimally efficient.

A legacy of the fixed structures of data records implemented in early databases, utilizing indexed magnetic tape and disc files, was program styles and capabilities that were inflexible and inefficient, when the records were highly varied and changeable, in structure and extent. MUMPS gave the programmer direct control of computer, disc-based data and processing algorithm. It fell short, as became clearer in time, in not providing for different data types and data relationships. This was compensated for by merging a fully relational database modelling approach (which I discuss next), on top of a MUMPS-style programming environment and data persistence engine. This was the major achievement of Milan and his team, at the Royal Marsden Hospital, as described in Chapter Eight, when discussing the ETHOS software that they pioneered. Their achievements speak for themselves. As a persistence engine, MUMPS has not been surpassed in the world of leading hospital and financial systems. As an innovation it was a *tour de force* of achievement and impact. It passed the so-called 'ACID test' of database transactions–atomicity, consistency, isolation and durability–guaranteeing integrity of data despite program errors, power failures or other mishaps.

From the late 1950s and in parallel with the, in some ways similar, evolution of MUMPS, the CODASYL consortium (the Conference/Committee on Data Systems Languages) worked on specification and standardization of a network paradigm data model and language for manipulating data in records. This was the era of COBOL (Common Business-Oriented Language) that hit a sweet spot of ease and simplicity for much of the industry that was writing finance applications at the time, and it endures in many applications to this day. The trend though was towards separating the description of data structure from the language used to manipulate data. Edgar Codd's 'relational model' fulfilled this purpose, arriving a decade later and quickly becoming the dominant database paradigm in the industry. The term 'relation' thereby acquired specific new meaning in the language of, and reasoning about, data structures and databases.

The relational model proposed a mathematically rigorous and generic pattern for describing data, anchored in the mathematics of sets and the logic of propositions and predicates. Anyone following the relational paradigm shared this one rigorous theoretical model. To produce a database to meet their individual needs, they organized their data using the same relational database methods. To do this well was an art, much as proving a mathematical theorem is an art, and some are better at it than others.

To return to the village school data computerization analogy, there are data about teachers on the staff, subjects taught and lessons delivered to consider. To organize data descriptive of these lessons, it is necessary to have a means to identify each of them uniquely in the database–this mechanism is called a 'database key'. For example, every lesson might be assigned a number to identify it uniquely. For every lesson, various fields of data–the teacher, subject and other details such as its time and location–are to be stored, referred to individually as 'data attributes', each of a particular 'data type'–number, text string etc.–and together as a grouping called a 'tuple'. A convenient way to think about relations was as a two-dimensional table structure, with attributes as columns and tuples as rows. The set of tuples populating this table formed the body of what was called a 'relation' and within the 'calculus of relations', each relation was a named 'variable'. Mathematically speaking, each row is a 'proposition', and the relation is a 'predicate'. Theorems arising in the mathematical manipulation of these variables are expressed in a 'relational algebra'.

The school needed to record other kinds of data about teachers, pupils, school classes and subjects. To avoid 'redundancy'–for example recording the same details of teachers and pupils in multiple contexts, such as in school, year group and school class membership lists, for example, as well as in the list of lessons delivered–such data was organized once, within separate teacher and pupil relations, again with tuples uniquely identified. Special relations are then created providing means to join and cross-reference between these separate relations, expressed as mathematical manipulations of the sets of data described in the associated table structures.

This was bread and butter mathematics but required careful attention to detail. Incautious design risked inefficiency and error in both the recording and manipulation of the associated data. Associated with Codd's relational model was a set of rules tying down the forms in which tables were to be designed and linked to model the village data, rigorously and safely. These stipulated practices to guarantee integrity of storage, retrieval and maintenance of the data instances that comprised and populated the records held within the physical medium that embodied the database.

Refinement of the relational database domain was further complicated by requirements to compute with the data held in the database. Dates and times might need to be expressed and viewed differently in different contexts. In some cases, it proved simpler and more efficient to store the data in a standardized Julian date format and provide algorithms for its translation to meet the different display formats required. This was more efficient and less prone to error than recording the same time in different ways in different places. Database software started to incorporate stored programs for such data manipulations as this, that were commonly required. It was in keeping with new thinking of data as 'data objects', comprising both content and methods associated with manipulating and sharing that content, within and between objects.

The database software implementing and processing data structures conformant with the relational model, provided the interface between the abstract form of the tables and the physical layout of data thereby stored on and accessed from the storage medium, according to the patterns defined in the data model. This enabled flexible storage and finely detailed and speedy search. Database systems were originally designed for storage on peripheral devices such as rotating discs. In time, the hugely increased size of memory banks available made it feasible to store small databases within the computer processor's directly connected memory store, accessible there by program. Small-scale and mass-produced cassette tapes and floppy discs were introduced to store programs and data for early microcomputers, using simple filing systems. These rotated slowly but were robust and skilfully engineered with smaller disc read/write heads. In time, fast-spinning micro disc drives and solid-state storage devices became available for microcomputers, in parallel and keeping pace with the increasing sophistication of their operating systems. The interplay of program and disc access had by now clearly departed way beyond the long-winded and slowly winding capabilities of early magnetic tape media.

Standardized methods arrived for querying data within relational databases (Structured Query Language, SQL), and this had a profound impact on the industry. The database software market developed rapidly and was a highly competitive one. Keeping pace, as a user, was hard. Products came and went. IBM's database management system (DBMS) blossomed early and died away; Oracle stayed the course and reaped rich rewards. Ingres metamorphosed into the widely used and open-source PostgreSQL database. Document-oriented databases proved widely applicable, still, and MongoDB scaled to huge numbers of downloads. Web applications led to Resource Description Framework (RDF) as a serialization format for data exchange, and SPARQL as a corresponding query language. Extended Markup Language (XML) emerged from Structured Generalized Markup Language (SGML) as a widely used, easily read and machine processable, flexible markup language, to accommodate the transfer of a wide range of structured data in web environments. JavaScript Object Notation (JSON), likewise, and the Representational State Transfer (REST) standard provided Application Programming Interfaces (APIs) to manipulate XML representations of data in web resources. Each packet of data transferred was understood independently of any preceding transfer and state of the system, the process thus described as 'stateless'.

Capacity and performance requirements became more demanding as databases spread more widely into industry and commerce. As complexity and volumes of data expanded, the engineers enhanced the functionality of their products by providing shortcuts in the processing required, within the database, and implementing more efficient storage, retrieval and querying operations. Intractable problems arose in the early era of implementation of these very large databases–what was termed 'Big Data'. These challenged the applicability and scalability of the relational model of data. 'Non-relational data models' re-emerged, to cope with the new requirements for accessing large aggregations of less well-structured data.

The explosion of scientific measurement, described in Chapter Three, and the emergence of Internet and web resources over the passing decades brought new priority to the storage and processing of largely unstructured data, or data too complex, diverse and largescale to be managed efficiently within the relational paradigm. Free text, medical images, geographical maps and observations and measurements from almost every domain were being collected in ever greater amounts, and users needed to search and analyze them in novel ways. This led to experiments with new algorithms and data structures. Networks of processors and data storage devices led to experimentation with new operating system paradigms, dividing up and implementing processing tasks across multiple machines and storage devices, located both close-by and at a distance.

This period led to the rediscovery of earlier pioneering non-relational database paradigms, notably those based on the storage of 'key-value pairs'. This was a push for greater simplicity, resembling that which had motivated the MUMPS community many decades before, in the late 1960s. The territory first explored by MUMPS was revisited. Packages focused on management of 'big data', such as Apache Spark and Apache Cassandra, originated in academic departments in America and were freely licensed, open-source. Apache Hadoop, also made available under open-source license, tackled the combined challenge of scale of data and computational load. These new systems were described as 'no-SQL' databases and, interestingly, computer languages used to program them revisited another software paradigm from the 1960s and 1970s, that of 'functional programming', which I discuss in the section below on software.

The compromises required to be made between ideas and ideals for modelling data structure and storing it physically, to support rapid and efficient data processing, have always been stark and limiting ones, dependent on the properties of the data, device and system concerned, and the purposes served. Experience of experimental methods deployed to organize data and the context of its creation, helped to elucidate theories of data model, that in turn guided and harmonized the underlying data and metadata models used for implementations–a virtuous circle of theory and experiment, but, in practice, a slow, tortuous and costly one. This evolutionary process led to clearer language for description of the types and classifications of data, and their aggregations. The wish to describe and formalize the purposes served by the data, and actions based upon it within its user communities brought new challenges into focus, and another era of experimentation evolved.

Information Model

Thus far in the village data processing analogy, we have moved from village documents and lists to village databases. We now move from the village to the nearby town and its organizations and businesses. Here reside developers of systems, makers and sellers of products and services, and those who manage and regulate them. Connections ramify widely with other people and organizations, as collaborators, suppliers, customers and competitors.

The data arising in these wider contexts, and how they are used, reflect wider purposes that draw on and contribute to the evolving knowledge of the people and organizations involved–describing how, and how well, they function. A full circle of meanings answering to questions that might be asked of the data come into play–the who did what, when, where, how and why questions about what it represents and the context in which it arises. This is the domain of semantics. Put simply, what are the meanings that the data represent? This wider scope extends the design of information systems into new areas of modelling of data, covering the processes involved and the outcomes achieved in its capture and use. It also introduces requirements for describing and linking between different kinds of data and databases, and into the world of knowledge bases.

To begin with, additional semantics were layered into systems by way of programs that interrogated existing databases and organized them to serve the additional purposes that exceeded the functionality provided by those sources alone. The market was looking for ways to generalize the specifications for such systems so that a design might be implemented on more than one database provider's product. Here emerged the next stage of abstraction in the design of systems, setting out in more detail, at a higher level, the definitions, interrelationships and flow of data within a system or organization.

This came to be known as an 'information model'. From the mid-1990s, pioneers of database theory, and the companies in which they worked, collaborated to envisage and design an abstract modelling language to express these new requirements. This built on the 'object-oriented software' paradigm, whereby the classes of relational database theory were represented as objects in information models. These objects described both the data themselves and incorporated program methods to manipulate them, stored within the database.

This idea, and that of 'inheritance' of data attributes between data objects in a hierarchical arrangement–a distinguishing feature of object orientation– stretched modelling beyond the focus and potential of relational database theory. Mapping from one to the other presented computational difficulties and imposed limitations on what could be implemented in practice.

As with models in general, the information model is designed to meet the purposes it serves. Just as the relational database model provided a language and mathematically sound underpinning for the design of compliant systems, the information model required its own language theory. Over the following two decades, through multiple incarnations, Unified Modelling Language (UML) became a dominant formalism for expressing information models. It provided a metamodeling framework for all such models. It is not without its detractors who highlight requirements that it cannot satisfy. As ever, the particular case solution veers towards a bespoke, all or nothing approach, and the general case solution counsels an 80:20 perspective of wider applicability. They are not right or wrong choices–they are empirical judgements, and the proof of the pudding is in the eating.

The information model is a further stepping-stone in the design of a database. The data persisted, conformant with the information model, enables application software to cater more straightforwardly for the needs of all users of the data, in their different user and organizational contexts. This database will still require all the previous data modelling capabilities that underpin the way data are stored, searched and retrieved from physical devices.

Seen within the context of a spectrum that spans from data representation to knowledge representation, an information model lies intermediate between data model and its associated data storage schema, and knowledge model and its associated formal methods of inference. It represents a middle layer of semantically enhanced data and knowledge customized to support action. As rehearsed in Chapter Two, knowledge expressed as information with causative power (Deutsch) and information as knowledge for the purpose of taking effective action (West Churchman and Ackoff), appears to be grasping at much the same philosophical nettle. When building everyday computer systems, we should best avoid descending too far into philosophical rabbit holes!

Information models can in principle be mapped to and persisted within different paradigms of database. In the Internet age, the focus has shifted to less formally structured data, modelled with tools such as the XML markup language. Databases have exhibited a mixture of model paradigms–native XML, key-value stores of the MUMPS kind, as well as relational.

Knowledge Management

Chapter Two drew on histories of philosophy, mathematics and logic in its discussion of knowledge, and reasoning with knowledge. Chapter Three placed knowledge in the context of theory and experiment in the sciences, and the 'omnuscular' world of data that they embody. Chapter Four extended knowledge and data into the world of modelling and simulation using computers. This chapter pursues a further angle on these matters–that of the design of computer systems to represent, communicate and reason with knowledge and data in their practical contexts.[33] In the mid-1950s, the use of computer software to reason in this way became a curiosity and subject of experiment. The exploratory software systems developed came to be called 'expert systems' and a prominent seedbed of this movement of several decades was Stanford University in California. The team and developments there were early forerunners of knowledge-based systems and artificial intelligence, today. The history of these endeavours is interesting, and I latched onto it as I started to read my way into computer science and information engineering in the late 1960s.

I recall fascinating work by the electrical engineer and computer scientist, Ivan Sutherland, that caught my mind at the time. In 1988, Sutherland received the prestigious Alan Turing Award, for his pioneering and visionary contributions to computer graphics. His 1963 Sketchpad software set the scene for human/computer graphical interface. The paper set out two connected problems concerning the readily tangible example of the arrangement of a system comprising three oblong wooden blocks. He showed the complexity of writing a program that would receive as input an arbitrary set of coordinates defining a three-dimensional grouping of these blocks, represent their arrangement as a data structure, and then answer the question: is this an arch? This work addressed a problem of representation

---

33 As mentioned before, there is some overlap and repetition in the text as I connect overlapping endeavours, chapter by chapter. This is to serve the interests of open-access online publication of the book, where individual chapters are framed as separately downloadable components.

and reasoning with knowledge. This sort of mental gymnastics was the stuff of punitive coursework in the London Institute Computer Science MSc course, along with rather duller, but equally bemusing, exercises in writing machine code to perform floating point arithmetic! Sutherland's program, tackling a question that a human eye might decide in a blink, albeit with some edge cases, was bespoke to this one geometrical problem and ran to many pages of printout. A thought-provoking juxtaposition!

On the east coast of America, the story of IBM was starting to unfold, and on the west coast, Stanford University was an academic nexus of experiment with the new machines. IBM established its own research centre in New York State. In 1956, just a few years after Francis Crick (1916–2004) and James Watson experienced their double helix Eureka moment, Arthur Samuel (1901–90)–a latter-day game-playing Demis Hassabis–who coined the term 'machine learning', wrote a program for an early IBM 704 computer, to play the game of checkers (draughts, in England). This played the game and learned from its experience to play it better, just as DeepMind's AlphaGo has learned to be the best at Go and AlphaFold to be capable of folding proteins.

In the 1950s, IBM Checkers was the nucleus of an excited explosion of interest and litany of terms: expert system, knowledge representation, knowledge management, knowledge engineering, machine learning and artificial intelligence took flight. Discipline struggling for identity tends to struggle over its name–my own a foremost culprit! Writing about this confusion takes too much time, has too much imprint and has little meaning, other than as struggle for a yet unreachable clarity. The volume of words is noise more than signal, reflecting that we do not yet, and maybe still cannot, understand. In this buzz, all manner of flowchart, decision tree, statistical transformation and program logic have been claimed to have a place in the oeuvres of the day. The unfolding of the story of the encounter between computer and knowledge is a still-evolving story of insight and understanding, all around the circles of knowledge and of available computational theories and methods.

In this chapter, the focus has been on engineering. The information model lay in the middle, between the quest to model and engineer data and the quest to model and engineer knowledge. Knowledge representation and access to and reasoning with knowledge are in themselves lofty goals. The next step of integrating a knowledge model descriptive of how a system works, with a database of records collected from the working system, is still a highly experimental challenge. In 1950, Escher made a lithograph illustrating the contrast of imagined and perceived order in a messy world, entitled *Contrast (Order and Chaos)*.[34] The lithograph is a telling metaphor for how we speak of computer systems and methods, and what they are often made up of, under the bonnet!

Experiments involve trial and error, and the world-weary aphorism about experiments in computerization has it that 'to err is human, to really mess things up, buy a computer'. The computer is a hard task master in exposing inadequate or inconsistent thinking. Computer programs are unforgiving in their insistence on clarity and consistency in what they are required to enact.

The term model, as used in the data model for representation and manipulation of data collected from a system and stored in databases, assumes new significance when used in the context of representation and reasoning about the structure and function of the system itself. This model is informed by a mixture of current understanding and ideas about the system, and data collected from it, historically and prospectively. Here, concern for integrity of data widens into concern also for correctness of reasoning about the structure and function of the system itself. Representation of knowledge and reasoning draws on theory informed by philosophy, logic, linguistics and mathematics, and computational method rooted in changing science and engineering. Data are not just things we need to acquire and record. They have a wider context, representing our quest for knowledge and classification–exemplifying our understandings and ideas about the nature of things and the organization of our knowledge about them. 'Thing theory' became a thing–occupying abstract and philosophical minds! It is a bit like string theory. I am eagerly awaiting strings of things theory!

There are multiple ways in which knowledge and reasoning draw on data and make logical inferences, far exceeding the making, manipulating and optimizing of lists. Knowledge engineering describes all kinds of description of reasoning about things. Things may be kinds and parts of other things. A Ford car is a kind of car; a Ford car wheel is a kind of wheel and a part of a Ford car. 'Kind of' and 'part of' are relationships. These can be pieced together in trees or networks of relations, in like manner that we saw with groupings of data. Logical propositions drawing on these relations may be true or false, and theorems based on them may be proved logically correct or incorrect.

As with the proliferation of connections made in the early experimental exploration of data models, this field quickly also connected very widely. The language of mathematics and formal logic is the proper and safe place in which to discuss theory underpinning data and knowledge representation.

---

34   M. C. Escher, 'Contrast (Order and Chaos)', *National Gallery of Art*, https://www.nga.gov/collection/art-object-page.63273.html

I have touched the surface of this discourse in a limited and general manner. Further curiosity is best pursued into specialist literature. It is a difficult domain to express, communicate and interpret. It is often expressed confusingly. What can one make of the self-reference in a definition of relation as 'a set of concepts and categories in a subject area or domain that shows their properties and the relations between them'? Having dumbed down on meaning, it is just then a short hop to statements like 'what's new about our ontology is that it is created automatically from large datasets'!

Knowledge bases have a two-fold purpose: capture of the knowledge relevant to a domain of interest, in some computable form, and formal and computable method for reasoning with that knowledge, in the context, also, of new and prospective data collected in the domain. The representation of knowledge in this way is reasonably termed a knowledge model, although all forms of knowledge might also reasonably be said to model reality, in one way or another. As we saw above, the earlier term used to describe systems of this kind was 'expert system', deriving from early attempts from the 1960s, to represent complex human decision making. Some early systems involved simple programs to enact the logic of a decision tree. Others showed ground-breaking potential. I introduced some early examples of knowledge-based systems in Chapter Two, in the discussion of formal logic.

Having tracked the American story, another story connects this new world back to the English genius of Turing and Donald Michie (1923–2007), a luminary founder of artificial intelligence (AI) in the UK. His expertise spanned an Oxford degree in classics, wartime contributions in code breaking at Bletchley Park, alongside Turing, an MA in human anatomy and physiology, and then a DPhil in mammalian genetics. Long classified as secret, Michie's work on using the Colossus computer to help decode messages from a German encryption device, more sophisticated than ENIGMA and nicknamed Tunny (the encrypted messages were called 'fish'!), was fundamental. Michie and Turing shared a hobby in programming computers to play chess and were captivated by the idea of machines that might learn from experience.[35]

In his next appointment within the medical school in Edinburgh, Michie co-wrote an early textbook of molecular biology and then, from 1960, switched his attention back to AI. He created Freddy II, the world's first robot that could work from computer vision to assemble complex objects

---

35   The team at Bletchley Park included the three times British chess champion, Harry Golombek (1911–95), as I discovered at a recent visit there. Members of the team wrote a letter pleading for more funding for the code-breaking effort. Golombek took this to Winston Churchill, who responded within twenty-four hours, issuing instruction for 'action this day' to provide the funding!

from a pile of parts. His wide-ranging and speculative research interests disturbed his academic chiefs and, in 1973, the UK Science Research Council commissioned James Lighthill (1924–98) to report on the prospects for AI. I knew him as the then Provost of UCL, where I was at the time engaged on my PhD. The dismissively critical Lighthill Report derailed robotics research in the UK and wider afield. Another example of 'Airy' dismissal of new ideas that has cropped up several times in these pages–in this case, more aristocratic academic hubris than pretence of knowledge! Not so much losing the plot as just not finding it in the first place![36] Japan did not make this mistake and its industrial developments in robotics of the 1980s helped power a burgeoning economy. The Japanese progress towards '5th Generation Computing' and AI led, fearful of competition, to a revival of interest in robotics in Europe and the USA. In the mid-1980s, Michie headed the Turing Trust in Cambridge and established the Glasgow Turing Institute, where he pursued work on robotics, machine intelligence and computer vision into his retirement in the 1990s. Among his later interests were microcomputer systems dedicated to surgical audit and patient administration, word-processing and spreadsheets.

The previously described Escher lithograph, *Drawing Hands*, might be taken to symbolize information as a self-referencing complementarity of knowledge and data–information as knowledge from data and data from knowledge, perhaps. It might capture the complementarity of an engineer making and doing something and knowing how to make and do it. It might symbolize informatics as a co-evolving science and engineering of information. To continue in this way of looking at information engineering, we must now consider the algorithms and software that specify the instructions that the computer enacts. This then leads on to the design of information systems and efforts to promote their coherence and mutual compatibility through information standards and standardization. The final section considers the profound changes that the Internet and World Wide Web have brought to information engineering.

---

36 It is both interesting and slightly ironic that Demis Hassabis emerged from a PhD combining computer science and neuroscience at UCL, the institution where James Lighthill had been Provost, and took his world-beating skill in the games of chess and Go into computer games and then into DeepMind. Also, that Go, the hardest of board games, should have a name which, in life science, is the acronym for Gene Ontology, and that, in this domain, the DeepMind AlphaFold software looks to be mastering the highly complex three-dimensional combinatorial problem of life science, that of protein folding.

Software–Algorithm, Data Structure and Computer Program

The story and timeline of the evolution of computer software has been convoluted and long, as have been those of data model and database, and knowledge model and knowledge base. Wirth wrote in the mid-1970s, that 'Algorithms + Data Structures = Programs'. Algorithm is an abstract concept used to describe a method for manipulating data in a computation. Programs enact computation. There has been a continuous tug-of-war and coevolution on these three fronts, under countervailing pressures of theory and practice. Let us start with program as language.

Many different programming languages have emerged, traditionally grouped within four principal programming paradigms, although there are admixtures of these. Procedural, object-oriented, functional and logical paradigms constrain the ways in which a program can be expressed, based principally on abstractions of process, data, algorithm and logic. Each programming language provides a distinctive repertoire of methods and styles for the programmer to use in expressing and representing the algorithms and data required to implement their desired computation. Programming languages have evolved to address requirements arising in different application domains, and learning acquired through experience in their use there. It has been a chaotic era–new technologies and capabilities arriving in rapid succession, onto a landscape of then current practice rendered quickly obsolete. The story continues to unfold. Quantum computation is a window opening onto another new world–or multiple worlds!

The combined mathematical and computer science foundations of today's programming languages were set in the first half of the twentieth century, notably in the 1930s by Turing's universal computing machine and Alonzo Church's (1903–95) lambda calculus. These provided a mathematical framework for formalizing the language of computation, rather as Frege's predicate calculus had cast a mathematical net over the language of logic. And, as introduced in earlier sections of the book, the first electronic computers evolved in the early 1950s, from wartime prototypes in the USA and England–the ENIAC with its connection to the mathematician von Neumann and weapons research at Los Alamos, and the Colossus with its connection to code breaking endeavours at Bletchley Park in the UK. Early programmable computers implemented a generic design of a computing machine (central processing unit or CPU), known as the von Neumann architecture. Programmed instructions for each machine were expressed as a numeric machine code and loaded into the computer memory along with data, to instruct the machine to perform the calculations required.

Early programs were expressed directly in these numbers. Programmers became fluent in the language of machine code, often expressed as a sequence of hexadecimal numbers, one hex number for each four bits (binary digits) of machine code. Early symbolic languages arose in the 1950s, in the form of assembly languages (assemblers) that translated from symbols representing instructions for the processor to execute, and locations within the CPU registers or computer memory, where program and data were to be located. Machine and assembly language expression focused on the inner workings of the computer rather than on the structure of the computation that the program was designed to perform.

Programs at this level were able to exert a fine level of control over machine operation and program execution. They could easily contain erroneous code that halted or otherwise crashed the operation of the machine. Such programs were opaque and cumbersome to correct or 'debug'. In early days this often involved the flicking of switches on the computer console, to inch, one step at a time, through the program instructions and observe the binary contents of machine registers and memory displayed on panels of console lights. I've done my share of puzzling over these twelve- and sixteen-bit binary numbers and their hex-codes, including times when the lights were intermittently faulty! You can imagine the emoji-like frustration–but it did teach one about what was happening beneath the bonnet of the machine and help keep one's feet grounded!

High-level programming languages were experimented with to express the steps required in a computation, independently of the features and vagaries of the machine on which it was to be performed. The design of these early languages reflected the kinds of computation their designers had in mind–FORTRAN focused on numerical calculation and LISP on symbolic reasoning tasks, for example. The needs of compact and expressive data structure and algorithm, and efficiently performant programs, might easily have pulled in different directions, albeit that they all, necessarily, interacted in execution of the task at hand.

From these beginnings, numerous clans emerged, championing many threads of imperative programming and declarative programming languages. Imperative programming focuses on describing *how* a program operates. Declarative programming focuses on describing a program's desired results rather than on steps the program is to perform to achieve them. In those embryonic times, FORTRAN was more imperative in style, and LISP more declarative. It was a highly experimental era and theory came later. Over time, two principal paradigms and priesthoods took hold on the landscape of experiment–temples of object-oriented programming, dedicated to gods and genes of data, and functional programming, dedicated to those of algorithm. Genetic recombinants drew pragmatically from both gene pools. Bespoke languages were created to focus on the characteristics and needs of particular subject domains–domain-specific languages.

Having toured and ramified to the horizons of data-oriented and functionally oriented programming styles (implemented for ensembles of mainframes, minicomputers and microcomputers, on the uncharted and shifting sands of new domains of computation), program language and software discipline are now drawing together under the unifying hardware technology umbrella of the Cloud and the software and network technology ecosystem of the World Wide Web. The history of language is that it evolves and ramifies, unifies, breaks and regroups. It is inevitable that we have not seen the end of new paradigms and languages of computation!

Maybe someday there will be a priesthood of all software believers, but one must rather doubt it, as science and technology continue to evolve. Maybe the music of all software will one day be tuned to the key of F-sharp Major (F# is the name of a favoured modern functional programming language!)[37] It could have Mahler's Tenth Symphony as its theme music, but, then again, that was unfinished! The challenges of writing and transcribing music for the different instruments in a full orchestra will forever characterize the quest for a universal language for programming, and indeed for mathematics. All theories, and florid analogies, like this one, break down somewhere! There has been a Mozart Programming system since 1991, though, and the pursuit of harmony is a good goal, countering countervailing pressures that tolerate or actively seek unnecessary and undesirable division![38] But I should not be too sceptical and dismissive–there has been a lot to admire in what this often-chaotic era has achieved, in evolving, clarifying and tidying the world of computer programming, for those who enter seriously and practise it today.

Moving on now to algorithm, the term itself has an ancient pedigree connected with the mathematics of algebra. Algebra dates from the early

---

37   F-sharp major is the key of the minuet in Haydn's 'Farewell' Symphony, of Beethoven's Piano Sonata No. 24, Op. 78, of Chopin's Barcarolle, of Verdi's 'Va, pensiero' from *Nabucco*, of Liszt's Hungarian Rhapsody No. 2, of Mahler's unfinished Tenth Symphony, of Korngold's Symphony Op. 40, of Scriabin's Piano Sonata No. 4. Wikipedia contributors, 'F-sharp Major', *Wikipedia, The Free Encyclopedia* (6 July 2023), https://en.wikipedia.org/wiki/F-sharp_major

38   'The Mozart Programming System combines ongoing research in programming language design and implementation, constraint logic programming, distributed computing, and human-computer interfaces. Mozart implements the Oz language and provides both expressive power and advanced functionality'. *The Mozart Programming System*, http://mozart2.org/

recorded history of the Middle East, in the arithmetic of number and the use of symbols and words to represent and reason with numbers, in reaching solutions of equations. The word is traced to the Arabic title of a treatise of the seventh-century Persian mathematician Muhammad ibn Mūsā al-Khwārizmī (780 CE–850 CE) on the solution of linear and quadratic equations. He is credited as the father of algebra. Later, Latin translations of his work transcribed his name as Algorithm. The meaning and usage of this term has evolved also from Greek αριθμός [*arithmos*] ('number'), Medieval Latin 'algorismus', Middle English 'algorism' to 'algorithm' in seventeenth-century English. It has become specialized within the language of mathematics and computer science. For example: 'In mathematics and computer science, an algorithm is a finite sequence of well-defined, computer-implementable instructions, typically to solve a class of problems or to perform a computation';[39] or, more generally, 'a process or set of rules to be followed in calculations or other problem-solving operations'.[40]

As with the history of mathematics, that of the algorithm is a story of coevolution of theory and practice. What has happened over millennia in mathematics has occurred in a century of coevolution of mathematics and computer science, and more recently in five decades of Internet time. It is a daunting field to seek to summarize here. I take courage from a Faraday Lecture at the Institute of Electrical Engineering in London, some fifteen years ago, on this subject. It was delivered by Donald Knuth, the American computer scientist and mathematician. Hopefully, he will be remembered, millennia from now, as the father of the analysis of algorithms–maybe they will then be called knuthisms! Knuth had drawn from the practice into the theory of algorithm–how programs systematize computation. As I started my journey into computer science in 1969, Knuth was already publishing his seminal encyclopaedic volumes on *The Art of Computer Programming*,

---

39   Wikipedia contributors, 'Algorithm', *Wikipedia, The Free Encyclopedia* (1 July 2023), https://en.wikipedia.org/wiki/Algorithm

40   'algorithm', in *Concise Oxford English Dictionary*, ed. A. Stevenson and M. Waite (Oxford: Oxford University Press, 2011), p. 31. In like manner, mathematics has evolved in the form of number theory, geometry (measuring the earth) and analysis, and in modern times through the study of combinatorics, probability, statistics and numerical methods. The monumental *Wiley Handbook of Applicable Mathematics*, published from 1980–1984, with a supplement in 1990, has volumes on Algebra, Probability, Numerical Methods, Analysis, Combinatorics and Geometry (parts A and B) and Statistics (Parts A and B). With my McMaster colleague Ralph Bloch, and halfway along my songline, still immersed in mathematical modelling of human physiology, I assembled and edited a companion handbook in the series, entitled *Mathematical Methods in Medicine*. This was published in two parts, in 1984 and 1986, covering statistical and analytical techniques and clinical applications, respectively.

which he started in 1962, envisaging a seven-volume series.[41] By 1973, the first three were in print from his handwritten text. Part one of volume four (IVA) took another thirty years and part two of volume four (IVB) was published in 2022. Along the way, the typesetting technology used to set his elaborate notation became obsolete and he spent eight years developing TeX, to enable publication of the fourth volume to progress.

After this build up, you can imagine the keen anticipation of those attending the lecture. Except that a lecture did not take place. The huge auditorium was packed out for this annual event commemorating the scientist who pioneered electromagnetism and electrochemistry, Michael Faraday (1791–1867). The hall hushed and Knuth, by then quite elderly, came slowly to the lectern, said one sentence, and sat down. 'I will take questions', he said! Slightly startled at first, the audience revived to pump him with questions, and he to respond thoughtfully, for the allotted hour. It was a memorable occasion and quite interesting as a reflection on the way one, such as he, oversaw the almost limitless potential scope of their topic.

An algorithm is an abstract representation of steps taken in computing with numbers and symbols, organized into useful and tractable data structures and operated on with useful and powerful functions. It can be expressed and implemented in different ways, employing different kinds of computer language, running on different kinds of computing machinery and serving different kinds of purpose. How programmers choose to pick their way through this combinatorial set of options and opportunities is up to them. Thereby, their program may or may not work, be efficient to code and execute, and reach a correct answer in line with the question asked. As with Knuth's audience of programmers, what did they need and want to know about algorithms, which they could draw on in their programs and deploy.

Algorithms are manifested and used throughout academic and professional discourse. This summer (2020) they have guided, and then been derided, in the context of the grading of student performance, when national school-leaver examinations were cancelled. They are sometimes slow and laborious to articulate and program. An arbitrary list of numbers might contain different types and properties of numbers–for example: integer or real, odd or even. They might contain prime numbers. The

---

41   Completed volumes are as follows: Volume I: Fundamental Algorithms; Volume II: Seminumerical Algorithms; Volume III: Sorting and Searching; Volume IVA: Combinatorial Algorithms, Part 1. Planned volumes are as follows: Volume 4C, 4D: Combinatorial Algorithms, Part 3 and 4; Volume V: Syntactic Algorithms; Volume VI: The Theory of Context-Free Languages; Volume VII: Compiler Techniques.

programmer might wish to sort and order the list in different ways. Given a representation in computer memory, using what methods can the list be sorted, to be presented as a sequence ordered by size of number, further ordered into two groups of integers and reals, or two groups of prime and non-prime numbers?

Algorithms for achieving desired ends, such as these, might, in principle, be enacted in the head, or with pencil and paper, or by implementation through a computer program. There may be a variety of potential methods that come to mind; some easy to envisage and others more brain-aching. Some are easy to enact mentally and some too hard or time and resource consuming, that way. The first two of the above orders are mentally tractable, and practical to achieve, depending on perseverance and length of list. Prime numbers get more complicated to reason with, both mathematically and mentally. New theorems about prime numbers gain Fields Medals in mathematics. Contemporary cryptography depends on the identification of the large prime numbers it is based on, being computationally intractable.

Some algorithms for achieving a desired end may be correctly described in a concise conceptual form, and others equally correctly, but more laboriously. This may reflect the intrinsic nature of the task itself, or the expressiveness of the language used in expressing, reasoning with, and programming it. Equally correct algorithms and programs may vary hugely in their comprehensibility to a human reader trying to understand them, and in the efficiency of their execution by the computer, which likewise may reflect the characteristics of its hardware and operating software. Proof of the correctness of an algorithm is a matter of mathematics and logic. Mathematical and logical proofs are expressed in mathematical and logical languages and notations.

Computer programs enact algorithms. Program is written in programming language and its correctness is partly a matter of the correct use of that language and partly its correct implementation within the computer. As Knuth is quoted as saying, 'Beware of bugs in the above code; I have only proved it correct, not tried it'[42] and 'An algorithm must be seen to be believed'.[43] Good program design reflects a match and balance between the form of a particular algorithm and how it can be expressed in a particular programming language and computing environment. These are attributes of the language, the numbers, texts and symbols of its datatypes, and the methods whereby it accesses, manipulates and stores these in

---

42   From 'Notes on the Van Emde Boas Construction of Priority Deques: An Instructive Use of Recursion' (1977), n.p.
43   D. E. Knuth, *The Art of Computer Programming, Volume 1: Fundamental Algorithms,* 3rd ed. (Reading, MA: Addison-Wesley Professional, 1997), p. 4.

enacting the algorithm. These considerations have reflected in the different programming paradigms that have evolved over time, in turn reflecting the problems or tasks being computerized, the data structures being processed and the computer systems in which programs operate and interoperate with others.

There is a framework and hierarchy of good order in all this–traversing theory and practice of mathematics, logic, algorithm, data, program and machine–on which we depend so that the computation tackled by the program can be relied on to do what the programmer and user want it to do. This framework requires discipline grounded in all these domains, both one at a time, and taken as a whole. Practically, there are differences in assumptions made and approximations implicit in different parts of the system deployed. There are impedances to free flow of information between them–a so called impedance mismatch, drawing on analogy with electrical circuit design. Philosophically, there are differences of belief and perspective about reasoning.

In 1962, Knuth was a graduate student in mathematics at California Institute of Technology (Caltech), close by to Richard Feynman (1918–88). At the time, he conceived of his project as a single book in twelve chapters. The sceptical publisher sought his academic adviser's support in deciding whether to take it on. The project has still only reached halfway in shining light to illuminate an expanding universe of algorithm. The light cannot reach the boundaries. It is the ultimate missed publisher's deadline! James Lovelock wrote *Novacene* at age one hundred, so there is still hope that Knuth's volumes on syntactic algorithms, context-free languages and compiler techniques may yet see light of day!

Software is everywhere; it conditions and reflects everything it touches. It is approach and paradigm, art and creativity, experiment and interface, ecosystem and legacy. Faced with a boundless challenge of encapsulating all this, my approach in this book has been to place the co-evolving computer machines and programming paradigms of each era in the context of my career in health care information systems, and the projects I designed, wrote programs for, led, collaborated with and reviewed, over those years. In this chapter and Chapter Seven, I tell these stories, indexed to both timelines.

Software as Art and Creativity

Painting and drawing, sculpture, music, theatre and dance are creative arts. Reasoning with abstract mathematics is a creative art. The arts fire imagination, stimulating and satisfying feeling and emotion. Those who know and practise the arts bring knowledge, skill and experience to its interpretation and appreciation. They have insight, talent and taste, and they have preference. Writing poetry is an art and so is writing computer programs.

My second cousin and her husband are art gallery junkies, and they take me along to exhibitions and educate me. Jim is a textile designer, who trained in art school alongside David Hockney. His appreciations and preferences in colour, texture and design are a great resource to draw on in interpreting art, such as when we viewed the pre-Raphaelite decorated rooms of the Edward Burne-Jones (1833–98) house on the bank of the river Thames, in London. Skills of artists and designers, and properties of tools and materials, blended and intermingled creatively.

Mathematics, science and engineering are creative, in similar and different ways. My late sister's family are talented mechanical engineers in their work and hobbies, building model engines and restoring and maintaining vintage motor bikes and cars, displaying them at fairs and competing in races. They make and maintain things and derive great pleasure in these skills and pursuits, albeit demanding and sometimes frustrating. In *Zen and the Art of Motorcycle Maintenance*, Richard Pirsig (1928–2013) mused on the engineering of motor bikes and the meaning of quality of machines.[44] Another inuksuk book of mine.

It is not difficult for someone observing from the outside to recognize quality in a practical skill and achievement on view, and the joy it brings to its practitioners. It would be a rare person who visited the experimental nuclear fusion reactor at the Culham Laboratory near Oxford, and heard its story, who did not come away feeling mightily impressed. It speaks for itself, we say. It is more difficult, though, to appreciate abstract worlds of mathematics and computation in the same way. Their qualities and pleasures are experienced within the domain, but not readily beyond it, where they may easily be unappreciated, taken for granted or evoke opposite feelings, especially when they fail, or fail to connect–brain box, nerd etc.!

Although most can rise to playing a hand in cards and board games, excellence in chess or Go verges on an artform. What, then, would Pirsig have made of AlphaGo, I wonder? In *The Creativity Code*, Marcus du Sautoy has written memorably about artificial intelligence and creative art.[45] I have used the 2022 released Stable Diffusion artificial intelligence-based software to create images from text (see Figure 1.1), to illustrate how new artforms are coming into existence in the Information Age.

44   R. M. Pirsig, *Zen and the Art of Motorcycle Maintenance: An Inquiry into Values* (London: Bodley Head, 1974).

45   M. du Sautoy, *The Creativity Code: How AI Is Learning to Write, Paint and Think* (Cambridge, MA: Harvard University Press, 2019).

These parallels of software with art and creativity occurred to me recently, when observing the vivid and detailed communications online, worldwide, minute by minute, among enthusiasts keeping alive the hardware and software of vintage computer games. My younger son, Tom, now a cardiologist, had told me a week before about the open-source software created to emulate the now obsolete MS-DOS microcomputer disk operating system, on which Microsoft was built forty or more years ago. He had used it to show his children the early computer games and exploratory worlds he played with in his teenage years. It occurred to me that my long-forgotten copies of the computer simulation programs, the Mac Series, that I described in Chapter Four, might be coaxed into running again on this open-source DOSBox platform.

I collected the 1987 floppy discs that we published with IRL Press, which are, as far as I know, the sole surviving implementations, and bought a floppy disc drive to try to read them again. This arrived the next day and I succeeded in reading the discs onto my backup Windows-XP laptop, not wanting to take any unforeseen risks in loading them onto my current machines. The appearance of the initial screen of the simplest of the programs made my heart jump, only to be immediately disappointed as the software crashed as soon as the first user input was requested from the keyboard. After digging around in the online manual, I adjusted the configuration of the DOSBox software but achieved only minor correction of the opening program graphics–the keyboard crash persisted. I joined the online community and scanned its extensive lists to try and find reference to the problem I had encountered, but to no avail. Responding to my enquiry to the DOSBox development team, a very helpful person in the Netherlands got in touch immediately. After hearing my description and seeing the details of the crash from the screen dumps that I emailed to him, he came back with a patch that instantly solved my problem. All four programs sprang to life. He told me in subsequent emails about the DOSBox open-source community he worked in, as a hobby, with colleagues around the world.

In this process, I saw a humming beehive of communication among games afficionados, maintaining a honeycomb of long-extinct computer hardware and software for running a huge range of computer games. This was vintage motorbike community writ large in vintage computer games community. Joyful hobbyists, wielding soldering irons, not standing at lathes; tuning software set up, not engine timing. And competing in virtual reality, online, not in driving spluttering vehicles up muddy hillsides!

Computer programming involves theory, skill, practice and creativity. It has evolved from and illuminated theoretical foundations of mathematics and computer science of the past one hundred years and more. The practical capabilities of computers and software have balanced with the elucidation of theory, both for the methods used and applications devised. The field has advanced on an Internet timescale, rendering hard-won skills and achievements quickly obsolete, creating a Whitehead socio-technical anarchy of legacy and confusion. Theory and practice of computation, and its devices, software and systems, continue to co-evolve. The art and creativity of programming is expressed with a continuously evolving palette of algorithm and language on an ever-growing landscape of applications.

Software as Experiment

It is quite rare for non-programmers to write good code, but some do create innovative software for their own domains of specialism, with impact that it is hard for those versed only in programming to improve on. Some of the most original software I have studied was developed by people who had the inspiration to experiment with use of the computer in a creative way, in a new domain. Many have been talented and polymath scientists and clinicians–John Dickinson, Arthur Guyton, Bill Aylward, Sam Heard, Octo Barnett. Some of their code reflected limited finesse in engineering and design, but it had the merit of a clear goal for how the program was intended and needed to fit and work within its planned context of use. They equipped themselves with sufficient skill to bind the computer to their will, working within its features and around its limitations, to achieve the purposes they had in mind. The code they produced was sometimes a tangle of data and algorithm. Their creative triumph was to express their huge knowledge and insight in physiology and medicine in a computable form. Their work broke new ground across both scientific and technological domains. They made connections. In doing so they were, in themselves, inuksuks in the landscape of software advance.

These people were architects more than designers of the programs they produced. Architects must learn and understand, by iterative experiment, how their planned work will fit and function within its intended setting. They must bridge from the user of the system to the science and technology embodied in its software and hardware. Lacking the expertise provided by bridging insight and experience, the construction team building a bridge may fall into the sea below. Of course, pioneers sometimes fall from their novel bridges into the same sea. But they tend to be strong, and know how to swim there, then get out of the water and go back doggedly to build a better bridge; or know when to abandon the effort!

This analogy with bridge-building came to mind when recalling the Eiffel bridges that I was once told about, in Porto in Portugal, during a European Union (EU) project team meeting there. Eiffel designed novel and beautiful bridges as well as the iconic Eiffel tower in Paris and the American Statue of Liberty. His creative vision led him to take risks in experimenting with new construction methods and materials. There was sometimes doubt that they were sound, and the first unshuttering of the new structure was a public spectacle, with the audience assembled wondering whether the new design would collapse! Even fully accredited engineers make mistakes in the design and oversight of their constructions, as the wobbling and buckling London Thames and Tacoma bridges have attested.

Software as Struggle with Imperfection

In 1977, I listened to a memorably entertaining keynote lecture delivered at the closing conference of the UK's National Development Programme for Computer-Assisted Learning, at the University of Surrey. The speaker was Judah Schwartz[46] and his title was something like 'How to do maths with a broken calculator'. The talk was about his experiments in teaching maths by challenging his students to calculate using a limited subset of the calculator's keys–the others being effectively 'broken', hence the title. The message was about the nature of fluency in mathematics and how it is taught, and the implications for the teaching profession and education technology. Schwartz showed that much can be taught and learned about the nature of calculation by seeing how one can get along when our methods of calculation are broken, or not available in some way.

There is something of this challenge in the writing of software with 'broken' programming languages–akin to 'broken' formal logic limiting our ability to express nuance of logical argument. All use of language involves struggle to express what the originator wishes to say, and to be heard and understood. All computer systems represent a struggle between the imperfections of what they can and cannot do, and the requirements of the domains in which they are employed. Quite human, really! I wonder how Schwartz might have turned this struggle with imperfection into useful learning about those domains. There's a lot to learn, here, about future health care.

Software development selects and draws on available methods and resources and invents new ones. It homes in on goals–what is to be achieved, where it is to be enacted and how it will be tackled. There is an ever-expanding and evolving variety of programming tools and resources to choose from in

---

46   Schwartz was a luminary figure in educational technology whose career spanned physics at Tufts University, engineering at Massachusetts Institute of Technology (MIT), and education at Harvard University. He published his 'broken calculator' software for the Apple Mac computer. He died in May 2020, from Covid-19.

tackling these tasks more effectively and efficiently. As creative art, these are akin to knives, brushes and pencils; to canvases, chapel ceilings and street side walls; to oils, charcoal and ceramics. The result may be a Leonardo, a Michaelangelo, a Banksy, a graffiti or a first attempt. They are frequently experimental, with preferences and choices highly contextualized.

In the early days, the available methods for writing and testing software were very limited and rather onerous and unreliable. Akin to vintage cars needing to be coaxed to perform, hands on, with crank handles and fine adjustment of timing of ignition and carburation of fuel-air mix. It was said to me by one prominent early supplier, that most of the code written for a large-scale system, like a hospital information system, was taken up with handling situations arising when the desired program operation went wrong in some way. Computer systems are still far from smooth functioning utilities, that merge unseen and unremarked into the background of life.

One learns language as a child by struggling to express one's growing self with a limited vocabulary of words, and sometimes a florid vocabulary of frustration. Natural language takes a long time to learn well and there are natural linguists and struggling linguists. And older minds struggle more than younger ones. Coders like me learned to write programs in similar manner, with the vocabulary of machine code, assembler language, and a limited choice among higher level program languages. Some of these were implemented as line-by-line language interpretation of the program code and some through a preliminary step of language compilation, to translate the code into a block of essentially machine code that could be fed to and digested by the machine.

Programming languages embrace data representation and algorithm. In their varieties, they evolve and enable fluency tuned to different domains of discourse. They can bring rigour and efficiency to the writing of software, and they can tie the process in Gordian knots of unfathomable complexity, when too elaborate and beyond the feasible skills, available time, or interests of their supposed users. Until you have experimented with framing a problem and solving it with the tools available to you, you cannot learn how to do it well. Doing it well, or better, may involve, using the tool better or using a different tool, or combination of tools. This is how crafts and disciplines interact. And all this struggle for learning costs time and creative effort.

The manipulation of bits and bytes, such as is needed in controlling devices, has remained in the world of machine code, assembler and low-level language, notably C and its descendants–not all judged as improvements! Scientific computation was programmed early on, and still exists, in FORTRAN–labelled as an imperative language, describing a process that does what it says it does, step by step. Focus on improvements in structure and flow of these programs led Wirth to develop Pascal. There was a long-running struggle to balance imperative and declarative elements in the style of program language. Theory and technology of computation and program language, interacting with formal linguistics and grammar, have co-evolved beyond measure along my songline. There was a pattern of continuous experiment and improvement, characterizing and exploring the principal program paradigms.

These were all struggles to find good and feasible ways to express and communicate about fuzzy and grey areas of development and application of program languages. Early programming languages were invented *de novo* and became the shaky foundations of software because there were no others. Inflexible and massive foundations, and the methods, materials and structures of buildings constructed on them, do not easily survive subsidence or shifting sands. Early programs, too, were rather fragile edifices. Keeping such edifices intact and functional is costly and exhausting work!

In the continuing efforts to tame such challenge of imperfection, the languages and skills of programming have become progressively more specialized and commoditized, within software and computing platforms. This has greatly improved the construction and maintenance of new systems but also accelerated obsolescence of the old. Valuable resources that embody useful learning and capability are no longer supported or supportable by these new paradigms, skills and infrastructures. The languages in which they were framed and communicated are no longer spoken. It is a cruelly wasteful process but very natural from an evolutionary perspective. The alarming feature is that the disruption it entrains is in significant part a global phenomenon. It is a largely unseen, underground threat, with overground consequences. It is not a meteorite leading to global winter or viral pandemic. It is, in this sort of lurid analogy, like a continuing liquefaction and reconsolidation of the foundations underpinning every building.

The world of software platforms has created much new and valuable common ground, but also unleashed unproductive competition between factions competing to enclose parts of this new territory for themselves. Markets and market forces are important but they, too, are always a struggle with imperfection. We are coming to see that new mechanisms of collaboration and regulation are needed, as these markets assume global dimensions, such as those created by software systems operating in the earthly Web and computational Cloud of the Information Age.

Software as Ecosystem and Legacy

Software development has become a massive industry, in which platforms and tools have evolved to keep pace, to make programming more efficient, reliable and automated. Generic and standardized approaches have evolved, honed within changing theoretical, practical and commercial contexts. The common framework of the World Wide Web, disseminating information and linking applications, has been an immense driver of this process in recent decades. Multiple new opportunities and risks have arisen. The competing platforms of IBM, Microsoft, Apple, Google, Amazon and Facebook have acquired immense power. When their products are commoditized as services, through Cloud-based networks, they can lead to monopoly that defies displacement by the innovations of newcomers and imposes unavoidable cost on users who are bereft of viable alternatives. This has brought new commercial and governance pressures that are now operating and impacting on a global scale.

The rapidly changing scope and context of users' requirements brings continuing need for investment in the new applications required to support them. This investment focuses on programming methods to integrate with an existing or new, usually proprietary, implementation platform, to maintain an interoperating ecosystem of applications. Choices are limited and based, in large part, on rules imposed for achieving compatibility with the platform. Very sizeable investments are then vulnerable to industry developments and behaviours that may quickly render the chosen platform no longer cost-effective or efficient.

Within a chosen shared software platform ecosystem, different parts of the user organization, and their different supporting specialist suppliers of software, have different needs, rules and priorities for managing change. They may need to move faster than the supplier of the proprietary platform can adapt and change the product to accommodate their special needs. If they act independently, they may choose and implement software that fragments the coherence and integrity of the local software ecosystem, fall behind and harm themselves. If they do not act, they also fall behind. It is a catch-22. And in such contexts, the implementation, testing and maintenance of needed changes can take much time and prove very costly, or indeed unachievable. They wait for something to break and then pick up the pieces.

The evolving combination of inflexible and dysfunctional software brings dissatisfaction and inertia for users, software providers and markets. Powerful software monopolies–powerful because customers become locked to them–acquire a rigidity and inflexibility that makes customization to local need ever more difficult. The user must bend to the system rather than the other way around. This is not the stuff of innovation. But it is the stuff of accumulating information entropy and disorder.

It is a natural feature of evolution that the underpinning framework and integrity of the software languages and paradigms are challenged by evolving requirements and experience of them in use. Each generation or paradigm is in a sense broken by purposes for which it is found to be suboptimal, outmoded or otherwise unfit. Oftentimes, opaque and intractable code is kept alive by highly intelligent and capable coders who have struggled to keep it operational, leading to more complex and severe code disasters, when the inevitable collapse happens. Cyber-attacks reveal these vulnerabilities, rather as a viral epidemic reveals vulnerability of health care.

Continual bending of software to overcome problems all too easily results in entropic disorder–spaghetti piles of code threads. Arguably, this is a good time to think afresh and, where possible, to start again, having learned important lessons about purposes, methods and tools of software development. Sometimes this will not be possible, for any number of good and bad reasons. In real life, a patch and move on approach often prevails, or proceeds by default. Failed or faulty code is patched; the unsafe bridge is reinforced, and this increasingly unsound legacy builds further towards future collapse.

This is a gloomy scenario of cost and waste. The hidden danger in public information infrastructure was the subject of an article just two weeks before, as I wrote this, in the *New Scientist* magazine. This is true to life and no one's 'fault' but does need to be recognized for what it is. Unfortunately, too many high-level minds set off to build cardboard bridges across turbulent rivers, employing a workforce of skilled but non-swimming stone masons. They throw their hands up when all seems lost, just a few metres from the bank, and proceed to plan a tunnel, which turns out to be through granite and bankrupts the Treasury with the cost of diamond rock cutters!

In case you doubt this graphically polemic language, investigate the story of the planned replacement, twenty-five years ago, of the UK west coast railway line, described as a '£10 billion rail crash'! Googling 'signalling west coast main line 10 billion disaster' should do the trick. In this plan, a budget escalation, a massive amount of which was hypothecated to expensive wired signaling systems, was 'solved' by a decision to do away with these systems. The project was given the go-ahead by the government, with the condition that it would implement a computerized wireless signaling system (connecting between trains and a central control room), which at that time were non-existent and thus operationally unproven. The project collapsed at that time, the congestion of traffic remained unsolved, and is now the target of the one hundred-billion-pound HS2 high-speed rail link from London to the North of England.

You might also come across another project, nearer to home, characterized as a '£10 billion NHS IT project disaster'. More on that in Chapters Seven and Eight. Software ecosystems are complex socio-technical edifices; an interface of user requirements, organizations and ways of working, with engineering methods, skills and tools, employing development and maintenance teams, management and money. Planning for their design and implementation shares the features of the wicked problem of social policy that features in my critique of the architecture of health care information systems, in Chapter Eight. This chapter's engineering focus now moves from software methods to systems architecture.

System and Architecture

One can make a car from scratch by breaking the task down into multiple component actions of design and production and setting up multiple departments to enact them: for wheels, engines and parts of engines, chassis, bodywork and internal fittings. One can repeat this for successive car models, each designed to catch the buyers' eyes and entice them with new features.

Someone is needed who has learned and knows about users of cars and the needs and preferences that influence their purchases, and about the car as a whole–how it is built and performs, where and when it will be driven, how safely and how it feels to its occupants. Just as buildings need architects and designers, so, too, do information systems. They bring a higher-level perspective of the human needs they serve. Such architecture is hard enough when making a product like a car or a submarine, but tractable with experience, authority, money and time. For the enterprises of health care–evolving rapidly, alongside human lives being turned upside down, for patients and carers, for their professionals and for the funders, suppliers and regulators involved–the complexity in the making is of a different order.

Architects are chiefs among creators of systems, as archbishops are chiefs among bishops. Architecture is associated with the names of its architects, and architects create and belong to schools and fashions of their times. There are professional architects of buildings and ships. Information architecture is the bridge between the requirements and design of information systems, and the glue bonding together their implementation and operation.

Architects of buildings work from a brief that sets out a vision of the requirements to be met by a new building. They envisage and formulate plans for how that vision might be achieved, within specified constraints of applicable regulations and available money, materials and workmanship. They talk the languages of users and commissioners of buildings, and of designers and constructers of buildings. They draw on a pedigree of expertise, experience and reputation. There are guidelines that inform their proposals for access, space allocation, insulation, heating and lighting and so on, to support the intended uses. They combine materials and structures to create an aesthetically pleasing functioning environment. At the heart of each work of art there is an artist.

Painters start from a blank canvas and architects of buildings may often be asked to do so, as well. 'What might a family home look like at this clifftop seaside location we have just purchased?', a wealthy family who have just won the national lottery, might ask. Information architecture in support of health care has also developed from blank canvases along my songline. 'Make a computer do this' is a blank canvas to work on, where what 'this' is, and its operational context lack clarity and consistency. How best to represent requirements, plans and designs, such that they can be safely realized by system developers, in the anarchic context of the information revolution and its mushrooming and chaotic technologies, has often been anyone's guess.

It is a situation akin to that described in the age-old tale of the car traveller—that I have already invoked, in the Introduction—who was lost when trying to reach Dublin. They stopped to ask directions from someone standing at the roadside, who thought for a moment and then replied, 'If I were you, I wouldn't start from here!' This story is somewhat near the knuckle, as a metaphor for information architecture in our era. It is the situation facing many an information system architect, asked to show how the goals that have been set, and how they can and will be achieved. The destination, as defined, lies somewhere at the end of a rainbow; the car in which the traveller expects to reach the destination is destined to break down irreparably within five miles, and is, in any case, almost out of fuel; the road ahead is beset by floods and landslides, and some has not yet been built! Information architects are often troubled by not knowing where to start. In my lectures of those times, I used statistics quoted in the December 1996 *Software Magazine* about failed IT projects. It reported that, in 1995, more than one hundred and forty billion US dollars was spent on IT projects in the USA that were either cancelled or 'redefined'. And eighty four percent of projects failed to deliver what the stakeholders needed and wanted. Judging by recent reports, as discussed in the Introduction, this reality has not improved.

My first encounter with information systems was in the heavy engineering industry of the mid-1960s, when systems analysis was the focus and paradigm for representing work and data flow within organizations, with a view to improving or streamlining them more cost-effectively. Formal project management and control methods split component sub-tasks within integrated production processes, along time critical pathways. In later years, I learned, in similar manner, how the modelling of bodily functions differentiated and atomized them into respiratory, cardiovascular and endocrine subsystems, and many more. In the body, no such differentiation pertains–the system works as one entity, a whole. High positive airway pressure applied in the intensive care unit to promote respiratory gas exchange, may also apply a reverse hydrostatic pressure inhibiting the circulation of venous blood back into the heart and lungs, thus countering delivery of oxygen and removal of carbon dioxide throughout the body. Managing the complexity and interconnection of biological systems led in time to the integrative study of systems biology and systems medicine. Although integrative in intent, these new entities led to new boundaries and contexts of discipline that were rather arbitrarily defined and defended.

In the world of engineering, information systems became systems of systems. Everything was broken down into components and connections, rather like complex electrical circuits. Within organizations, patterns of working practice, mixing actors, actions, products and services, were laid out on extensive flow charts and maps. The goal was towards reorganization and automation of working practices, enabled by computer systems that would carry out what might at one time have involved pen, paper and filing cabinets, with communication via postal and telephone service. Just as data could, and needed to, be modelled in various ways to reflect different purposes and perspectives, the same applies to the related information systems when specifying how the data were to be collected, analyzed and used. Having atomized the tasks to be performed into discrete components and connections, developers proceeded to automate them by writing software that represented and enacted this design. There was no way of knowing how the combined new system of people and computers would work in practice, whether the computational part was reliable and efficient, and the human part comprised satisfactory and sustainable work.

This era exposed limitations arising from the continuous and chaotic evolution of methods for representing and programming computations and information flows. The continuous evolution also extended to computational, data storage and communication technologies. There was frequent frustration with failures to understand the requirements for a system that could and would do the job it was envisaged it would do, at the time it was expected to do it, at a cost that had been budgeted for, staffed and operated by people available and trained to use it. Mismatch with the users' needs, capabilities and expectations led to a culture of default. Expression of user resignation defaulted to the *Little Britain* TV show actor

David Walliams and 'computer says no'! Failures identified in the workings of organizations and society, more generally, were ascribed to problems of 'the system', deeply entrenched and termed 'systemic'.

In the hospital context, one must only suffer the misfortune of lying for an extended period in a hospital ward–or sit, anxiously, with a very sick relative, over long periods of months, as I have done, or attend clinics where little is known that connects with why one is there and what is or should already be known about a patient's presenting condition–to understand that fragmentation of computer systems is mirrored in atomization of services. A close colleague wrote to me, recently, after his own similar experience as a hospital inpatient. Tails of poorly conceived and executed computerization have wagged dogs of attentive clinical care. Extremely hard-pressed professional and clerical staff pore over badly designed screens, battling demands for entry of data that disappears, to appear later in spreadsheets or orders for actions to be taken.

This burdensome practice cannot coexist at all well with an orderly and reassuring environment and atmosphere, at the point of care, in the clinic or on the phone, answering to the anxiety of patients and their relatives, distinguishing between the real urgency of pressed alarm bells and the false alarms from bedside monitors. These are systems of poor utility.

The father of utilitarian philosophy was Jeremy Bentham (1748–1832)– utility as an end guided by and pursued for the good it confers. Common services, such as for energy, water and communications, are utilities; as Joel Birnbaum said, they function best when least noticed. His worldview of information as a utility is discussed in Chapter Seven. Statistics quantifies utility of an action, such as a clinical intervention, in terms of probabilities and values ascribed to its various potential outcomes. We often seem caught, confusingly, between high probabilities of low-value outcomes and low probabilities of high-value outcomes. Confusion and disconnection of ends (what is aimed for) and means (how it is approached) can readily lead to the creation of costly information systems that prove of low utility. How much money was spent on track and trace systems during the Covid pandemic, I wonder? This chaotic and wasteful panorama is long-standing– what are its mitigations and remedies?

Fred Brooks was Professor of Computer Science at the University of North Carolina (UNC) and worked in the mainframe computer era at IBM as architect of the famous IBM/360 series computers. He was a colleague of Edward Feigenbaum's collaborating team at Stanford and is widely known for his book, *The Mythical Man-Month*.[47] In this he distilled his professional

---

47   F. P. Brooks Jr., *The Mythical Man-Month: Essays on Software Engineering* (New Delhi: Pearson Education, 1995).

experience of an era where engineering of systems became rather lost in the woods. He pinpointed the consequences of poor architecture and implications for design leadership of software systems.

'Systems need architects' was one of his memorable aphorisms. Another was: if you are falling behind in making a new system work, adding numbers to the team can easily make matters worse. In coining the term, 'mythical man-month', he was highlighting that innovation does not come in quanta of months of effort. As experienced with the RSX operating system toothing troubles in DEC, which I lived and worked though, a small team can move faster and crack open and solve problems that have defeated much larger teams, even ten times the size. The large team becomes so consumed in internal communication about the problems and failures, as to be unable to solve them. The stripped-down team, liberated from an incumbency that has grown to tackle and cover for confusion, works together more easily, and works things out.

Man-months do pay salaries, however, and there is perverse incentive in play. New hype and mantra expressed in the pursuit for new resource wins often befuddled political support. Politics commands public purse strings and seeks to show how modern and imaginative it is. Innovative and disruptive thinking does not often win in this arena and is seen as an opponent to be suppressed.

Failed engineering projects often also result from a combination of invalid assumptions and undue expectations. These lead to poor decisions about method to be employed, capability and planning. And the diagnosis and blame for failure is often attributed to somewhere within the technical domain, where indeed the symptoms often do arise, with cost and time overruns, key expectations not met and systems performing poorly. In large-scale information systems, failure is evidenced in wide-ranging breakdown and malfunction, akin to sepsis or proliferating bodily cancer. Its causes may rather reside not in a localized defect but in the architecture of the whole system: of knowledge, actions, roles and responsibilities. From ambulance to recovery ward, data on a single arriving patient may pass through tens of separate computer systems. It does little to improve continuity and coherence of care, and services of care. An atomized set of systems adds administrative cost and workload along the line.

Uncovering the detail of historic software systems is like visiting an archaic domain–akin to the library in Umberto Eco's novel, *The Name of the Rose*, with disconnected custodians preserving its hidden away and guarded secrets.[48] This is software entropy. Antiquated software often reveals itself

---

48   U. Eco, *The Name of the Rose* (London: Pan Books, 1984).

like a rusty old car tottering along the road and coming to a teetering halt. Along the road are many abandoned burnt out wrecks, blocking the way ahead for newcomers.

Delving beneath the bonnet of an archaic information systems, one may find a morass of rusty databases and smoking information circuitry. It may not catch on fire, but it has grown old and dysfunctional through accumulation of entropy. The code is populated with string and sealing wax software patches that have been hurriedly added, to meet new needs and cover previous defects, and then forgotten about. It creaks and judders, having grown old and out of tune with changing methods in the vanguard of the industry. Whole industries have existed to keep such legacy on life support. The original coder may have long since departed, leaving little if any documentary record of their programs–not just what it is but why it is as it is and the compromises and limitations it embodies. Sometimes, the code can no longer be compiled from source to machine-code form, and exists only as an impregnable binary object, and encryption which may defy even costly reverse engineering.

Many of us have experienced such information system jalopies and car crashes. I have been thanked for writing this, here, as it was. It is not something to be conveniently forgotten! Fifteen years ago, I was asked to chair an NHS group set up to monitor implementation of a plan for common prescribing practice across all general practice (GP) and pharmacy IT systems. It proceeded at a snail's pace as each supplier struggled to adapt their code and databases in line with the new common requirements that had been nationally mandated. It was an archaic and painful process, far removed from the promise of agile development that was the mantra of the age.

Another illuminating example of the general weakness of system architecture came with the looming arrival of the year 2000. This had engendered a peak of concern about the robustness of software and demand for perusal of code, to search for and iron out weaknesses arising due to the way all dates were being recorded and processed in programs and databases. A common programming heuristic of those times had been to represent and store the year as two digits, implying a date relative to 1 January 1900–or 1901 if 00 was reserved for 'date not known'! In this model, as the clock struck midnight on 31 December 1999, time would come to an end and the recorded date of a new entry would be reset to 'unknown' or 0. This threat was perceived as a pending national emergency and a huge amount of time and resources was spent scanning through virtual acres of program listings, throughout the economy, to find and fix date representation problems that might be revealed there. There was bated breath in high places as the striking Big Ben clock–which the dangerously crushed crowds on the Thames riverbank were waiting for, expectantly and drunkenly–hailed a new century. The wave of fireworks propagating along the river, that had been promised to celebrate that same moment, proved a damp squib, and the feared systemic breakdown of software throughout the economy did not happen either. This confirmed the prediction of my colleague, then UCL Professor of Computer Science, Anthony Finkelstein, who had risked reputation and demonstrated his clear head and safe pair of hands, in sagely opining that it would be that way. He went on to become a government scientific advisor and then University Vice-Chancellor at the alma mater of his formidably learned and accomplished father, Ludwig Finkelstein (1929–2011), a doyen of the field of measurement and control engineering who, with his protégé, Ewart Carson, had a special interest in medicine.

The key learning from this story is not that the feared Year 2000 disaster did not happen, but rather that there had been so little confidence in the industry and user domains, that information systems would prove robust to this obvious challenge. And yet, some good engineers and leaders of engineering were certain, without investigation, that their own systems would not prove vulnerable. One such was my colleague, Jo Milan, architect and designer of the nationally preeminent cancer information systems he and his team built and sustained throughout most of my songline, at the Royal Marsden Hospital, in London and Sutton. Why and how could he be so sure? Because, as Jo explained to me, the coherent, concise and superbly functional data models that underpinned the whole of the information systems of the Marsden (my words, not his, he was a very modest man; I tell his story in Chapter Eight), invoked just one very small date function. He had written it and knew it was robust. To satisfy his untrusting hospital managers, who failed to recognise the jewel in their crown that Jo and his team and their systems represented, Jo did pull it briefly to his office screen and took a few moments to scan and verify its correctness, before confirming in an email that this had been done–keeping his managers in the clear, upwards in their hierarchy of NHS managers.

Teams responsible for supporting systems with much less complex requirements, but exemplifying code threads more akin to a pile of spaghetti, dedicated many months to this task, diverting their attention from other important work. There are immense burdens of cost and opportunity imposed everywhere by poor information engineering. Many projects never make the transition into everyday practice–the first Covid-19 App of NHSX is one from today. National bank software systems have crashed and malfunctioned several times over recent years, their maintenance and update procedures unsound, bedevilling both businesses and public services.

And information system security flaws expose their user organizations to unavoidable ransom demands. Knowledge of flaws in software and databases does bring opportunity for the virtuous, as well as for the less virtuous, on occasion. I remember giving a talk at a Research Council strategy board meeting, and listening to another speaker there, from an eminent bioinformatics research group. The discussion was about errors in genome sequence databases. In a seemingly not entirely tongue-in-cheek manner, they remarked that teams sometimes did not quickly report errors they discovered in shared databases. They could adjust for these for themselves, but competing scientists might not be aware and would be left to independently discover them, at a cost to the accuracy of their own analyses and the productivity of their work!

Science is well equipped with intelligent minds, well able to look after themselves and the impact of such error and imperfection within science is unlikely to cause a Challenger Space Shuttle scale of disaster. But health care services are more vulnerable. They exist to provide a human service, keeping on top of scientific advance and increasing and changing demand, and must contend with incoherence and complexity of information. Overloaded senior managers easily lose sight of systemic problems and of the human efforts and values that hold everyone's efforts together within the service. As pressures escalate, it is understandable that highly motivated people lose heart.

Health care policy makers have sought to protect the service risks they are accountable for, by substantially outsourcing problems and their solutions to others. It is a bit like outsourcing any service central to the running of a business. Common good advice is only to outsource things you understand and that are not core to what makes you special. If you do, you are admitting to a weakness and setting yourself and your business up for mistakes and exploitation. And no amount of court cases and governance checks can put right the damage that may ensue. This adds further cost and intractable complexity. Health care services have endured and accumulated both.

Solutions to wicked problems can only be found in cooperation and collaboration–from the centre and from the ground–in the clinical and caring professions and with the patient communities they serve. This will be a trajectory of David Goodhart's head, hand and heart, to generate new roles and capabilities that will be needed on the other side of the Whitehead–and in the UK context, Whitehall–information systems anarchy of the past fifty years.[49] That is the trajectory that I trace and anticipate in Parts Two and Three of this book.

---

49   D. Goodhart, *Head Hand Heart: The Struggle for Dignity and Status in the 21st Century* (London: Penguin Books, 2020).

Norms, Standards and Standardization

The essential thing in form is to be free in whatever form is used.[50]

On holiday in the small seaside town of Port Bou, in Northern Spain, the flat where our family was staying in the 1980s overlooked the beautiful beach and sea, on one side, and the railway line emerging from a tunnel from Perpignan in France into Spain, on the other. The intercity express trains crept very slowly into a long shed covering the tracks. Emerging at the far end, they accelerated away. On the inside of the shed, the wheels and axles of the bogies suspending the train carriages underwent a conversion between two national standards. To the north, the gauge of the railway track was that of France and to the south that of Spain. The diverging/converging rail tracks going each way through the shed, combining with the bogies, performed a standards conversion and the wheels emerged with new separation along the axles to conform with the new standard required. A bit complicated and time consuming, and maybe frustrating for passengers eager to get to Barcelona, but better than a train wreck, coming off the rails at the border between countries! A quick check on Wikipedia indicates this divergence of standards still pertains, forty years on. It shows how difficult it is to shift and modernize infrastructure. Information infrastructure is no different.[51]

I read an equally illuminating story, recounted by the historian, Norman Davies, about Russian history, and the merger of armies after a war. Weapons and ammunition from the opposing armies were collected and pooled in preparation for new campaigns, only to discover that rifles and bullets did not align; the precision necessary in this case is likely much greater than that for train wheels. This was one of many complicating logistical and organizational problems arising from the conquest and the merger of armies. Another case of standards not aligning, with potentially explosive consequences.

---

50   Wallace Stevens (1937), quoted in C. J. Date, *An Introduction to Database Systems* (Delhi: Pearson Education India, 1975), p. 263.

51   I came across another connection with Port Bou when listening to a recent podcast about Walter Benjamin (1892–1940), a highly influential German-Jewish literary critic and sociologist of culture of the past century. His philosophy was a practical one, seeking to connect his thinking with everyday life and experience. He was not a fan of wordy and generalized abstract thinking, saying that 'I have nothing to say, only things to show'. Clearly an engineering minded philosopher, and a committed networker. In 1940, he was escaping from Paris and the German army's advance and proceeded to the Spanish border at Port Bou. He was refused entry, and committed suicide there.

The terms 'norm' and 'standard' are loaded with meaning. *Norma* in Latin meant square, and we still talk of square meals and square deals, implying something appropriate, balanced and fair. As discussed in relation to the theme of measurement in Chapter Three, according to Ivan Illich (1926–2002), nineteenth-century English geometry took over the term and normal came to mean to be at right angles. A connotation of principal axes spread into normalization and normal forms and by the late nineteenth century had come to symbolize conformity to a common type. These terms have acquired specific meanings and appropriations within the language of computer science and database design. In France, the École normale supérieure was established to train teachers in correct usage of the French language in French-speaking countries. Likewise in France, Auguste Comte (1798–1857) introduced a new medical connotation to the term, and, by the end of the nineteenth century, these norms became bound up with criteria for diagnosis and treatment of disease.

The term 'standard' also had a more proprietorial tone. Something to be expected in polite society and in the husbandry of animals and crops, and of resources, more widely. They became components of more formal governance; rules that should be adhered to in pursuit of social and material goals, allowing life to function harmoniously, and things to fit and work together well. With a motor-driven electric power generator situated in the garden, supplying the house, it did not much matter what exact voltage it supplied to power domestic appliances, provided one had a kettle or lights that were compatible. Providing electrical power as a utility for the whole village and nationally, it again did not matter a lot; there were pros and cons of different transmission line technologies, but what did matter was that there should be one standard that providers and consumers adopted and adapted to.

Technical standards like this serve many purposes in design, development, manufacture and supply of goods and services, and in simplifying their efficient updating and maintenance; this contributes to the creation of a coherent workforce of support engineers, trained and up-to-date with the technology. Such standards can simplify work, enabling the realization of economies of scale and providing a seamless service, where disharmony of incompatible products and services imposes unnecessary costs and increased overhead.

Standards for information systems enter wider realms of complexity and contention, reflecting their wide and pervasive contexts and the methods adopted for creating, making, using, maintaining and regulating them. There are good and almost unanswerable points in favour of standardization of some areas of endeavour. It is difficult to see why any developer writing software for an information system embodying representation of time would think it a good idea to reinvent ISO 8601, the international standard covering the exchange of date- and time-related data first published in 1988. Perhaps physicists probing towards Planck limits of time might think it largely irrelevant to their needs! However, the choice and adoption of information standards, more generally, has proved a costly, time-consuming and difficult area, exposing and brokering among many differences of perspective and conflicts of interest. I have seen it first-hand, as a wicked problem of health care IT, and will return to this topic in Chapter Seven.

Often in the domain of standards-making, the process adopted to arrive at a consensus about the standard reveals more about the purposes it will serve and ways of brokering conflict of interest about these, than it does about performance of the standard when implemented. Standards have spread from properties of devices–where the scope of a proposed standard is more easily defined and policed within a predominantly scientific or technological domain–to properties of systems and services–where scope and purpose are more widely open to debate and disagreement, on other levels of commerce, policy and law.

Before embarking on the challenge of defining a standard, it is well to establish a basis for discussion about what is to be standardized, why and how. It is not a good idea to start a process towards standardization from a blank canvas of the field to be standardized. In discussions of information systems, there is a need to focus on what is often called a reference model. According to the Organization for the Advancement of Structured Information Standards (OASIS):

> [a reference model is] an abstract framework for understanding significant relationships among the entities of some environment, and for the development of consistent standards or specifications supporting that environment. A reference model is based on a small number of unifying concepts and may be used as a basis for education and explaining standards to a non-specialist. A reference model is not directly tied to any standards, technologies, or other concrete implementation details, but it does seek to provide a common semantics that can be used unambiguously across and between different implementations.[52]

A reference model provides information about a particular kind of environment and the types of things that exist there, how they mutually connect and interact with one another. It is an abstract model and does not talk in terms of specific methods of implementing them. It is not in itself a standard but can provide a framework for standardization, creating

---

52 'OASIS SOA Reference Model (SOA-RM) TC', *OASIS Open*, https://www.oasis-open.org/committees/soa-rm/faq.php

standards that ease the work of developers and making them more useful and applicable in wider contexts. In that a standard provides a basis for discussion, good standards can play useful roles in education, communication and organization. When different approaches to standardization are under review, it is good to have concrete and implemented proposals at the centre of debate, where they can be compared, when reaching decisions.

Standards-making processes can all too easily become contentious and bogged down, papering over differences and forcing resolution based on votes cast by representatives of different interest groups rather than on a basis of both theory and implementation practicality. In the political domain, they can be used as instruments of control and manipulation, promoting interests of proposers of a standard, and blocking those of their competitors. They may appeal as convenient garments to clothe emperors, who use them in name only, as cover for their lack of knowledge and experience about the basis or impact of the standard in practice.

Viewed top-down, there is a strong temptation to tackle lack of practical understanding of a domain by prior assertion of an answer about how it should be standardized. Better by far to pursue standardization through incremental and experimental method, leading to the definition and adoption of specific standards, based on both evidence and declared intent. That is the basis whereby science can persuasively align its theories and engineering usefully its designs. No process of standardization can disguise or compensate for lack of understanding of a domain, but confession of that reality is not always seen as an option. The pretence of knowledge is maintained through a combination of abstract confabulation and wishful thinking. Benjamin Disraeli (1804-81) once described a windbag colleague politician as being 'intoxicated with the exuberance of his own verbosity'.[53] In the Information Age, echoing Mervyn King's remarks about damaging hubris and pretence of knowledge in the world of high finance, practitioners of the Information Age are too often overloaded with the burden of inconsequential detail.

We rely on a supply of electricity, gas and water, to flow in networks and arrive at a standardized interface with house and home. We need information that flows, just as water flows to create and support life. The electrical engineering of information flow is now a well-designed, polished and maintained infrastructure, although with continuing scope for improvement. The flow of information, with its causative power, can be a turbulent flow of rivers, bursting banks and flooding across landscapes. This can be a destructive power, different in kind and feel from that

---

53   Quoted in *The Times* (29 July 1878).

appealing to the optimism of David Deutsch, about the power of knowledge (as information with causative power) to resolve the ills of the world. In calmer water analogy, the experience of the Alhambra Palace in Granada, on a hot, sunny summer day, is overwhelming. Here is beautiful architecture and design, here is free flowing and calming water. Here is a simple and functional engineering system, delivering water from the mountains behind to the fountains, in the sunlight and shade.

Information flow is not sweetness and light; it will always exhibit bias and inaccuracy, and harbour destructive and criminal potential. It will be contentious and there will be competition. But it can be a lot better than at present. It has become increasingly corralled, entrained and attacked within and between adventitious global monopolies that then seek, first and foremost, to protect and preserve their own expanding ambitions and interests. Standardization of information for health care needs to grow and embody a better balance of global and local perspectives; the local anchored foursquare within local community and democratic politics. That square should be the new norm. There is much work to be done. It is to that square that the book heads in Part Three.

Information systems nowadays are procured and bolted together from products of industries that address international markets. The purchasers' choices are binary: between a contract to do it all and a suite of contracts to piece it together. These require different skills sets, resources and appetites of those making decisions on purchases. The former requires very deep pockets and willingness to tolerate the supplier's system largely as is. There exists only limited, and expensively disincentivized capacity to adapt locally. The latter approach requires methods and local capability and capacity to support local standardization, at a level that is not yet easily achieved.

When researching the purchase of a new car recently, I read that the full range of Volkswagen cars now rests on a production platform of modular components that fit together in their product range of cars. The benefits extend throughout the business: in design, production and maintenance, and in the back-office as well. In developing the theme of this book, I am seeking to show how we can reach this win-win in health care IT. In this, we need to marry the benefits and imperatives of global coherence, with the needs and interests of the local, marrying together both the local and global villages of health care we now populate. For this, we need good standards that promote what has been described as 'co-opetition'–the combination of cooperation and competition.

These two villages form the starting point for my discussion of the evolution of health care in the Information Age, in Chapters Six and Seven. I will describe examples of coherent information architecture, pulled together across major hospital systems and the benefits and user satisfaction that these have created. In Chapter Eight, I devote a half chapter to two open initiatives I have nurtured and supported from their beginnings, a prelude to discussion of Open Data and other 'open' movements in Chapter Nine. The first is the story of the openEHR mission to provide open specifications for a generic platform architecture for health care records, now lifting off in implementations around the world. The second, which I introduce more briefly, is the OpenEyes open-source software application. Adoption of the current release is accelerating and already providing records for approaching fifty percent of eye consultations in the UK, including in national programmes for the whole of Scotland and Wales.

In Chapter Nine, I come to how we can frame and lead the combined pursuit of continuity and change in the Information Age, from Whitehead transitional anarchy through to a new local- and global-village order of care information utility, in a manner that promotes what Robert Axelrod described in his book, *The Evolution of Cooperation*.[54] This may be destined to come about chaotically and destructively, driven from science or from society. It can, though, come in more stable and just ways, at their interface, supported through the rigorous, engaged, and trusted efforts of engineers and engineering. Which path plays out will depend on how the challenge is approached–whether inclusive or exclusive. My anthropologist colleague at UCL, Paul Bate, surveyed implementation of health care innovations. He described what he saw as an 'implementation gap' in health care innovations and quoted Donald Hambrick and Albert Cannella,[55] who observed 'outcomes and levels of success that are less–sometimes considerably less– than originally planned or predicted'. He concluded that 'it is not so much the improvement method itself, or even the strategy, but how it is done (and in the case of imports, how it is customized) that determines ultimate success'. The music hall song line 'It ain't what you do, it's the way that you do it' comes to mind! Especially so, in the context of wicked problems!

The Internet and World Wide Web

The arrival of the Internet and World Wide Web have had a powerfully formative influence on almost all areas of information engineering and standards impacting on information systems. Volumes of data stored in Cloud data stores and accessible throughout the world have multiplied from petabytes to many multiples of exabytes. Iceland became an early home

---

54   R. M. Axelrod, *The Evolution of Cooperation* (London: Penguin Books, 1990).

55   D. C. Hambrick and A. A. Cannella Jr., 'Strategy Implementation as Substance and Selling', *Academy of Management Perspectives*, 3.4 (1989), 278–85.

for ice-cooled data stores, and the Microsoft Azure cloud is implementing new datastores, cooled deep undersea. Data storage with Azure is held in triplicate and the network of linked processors offers computational resource on virtual machines, worldwide. Google Docs, Amazon Web Services and Apple iCloud have similar Cloud infrastructures.

The explosion in number and scale of data sources and the standardization of browser technology interfacing with users of systems, has brought new paradigms of data management, programming language and client-server architecture of applications. The scale and diversity of large datasets captured in scientific research, has tested data management paradigms to the limit. The scale and complexity of processing required in analyzing data has forged new priorities for networks of computers and programming methods that allow computational tasks to be shared among them. There is a growing preponderance and focus on large datasets, hosting what is termed unstructured data, annotated using standardized markup languages, but non-relational in form.

This revolution has placed pressure on the working practices of standards organizations. Internet timescales could not survive the five or more years in which an International Standards Organization (ISO) standard typically took to mature and reach publication. The demand for immediate results, in the context of both software and standard, became both imperative and declarative: 'I don't want anything in particular, but I want it now'!

ISO has deprecated detail derived from specific implementation, wishing to remain vendor- and product-neutral in its standards. Its constituency has been based on 'one country, one vote', and is thus, inevitably, a political mix. The Object Management Group (OMG) was born out of industry frustration with the ISO process, as an industry collaboration to meet industry needs, and voted on by its member companies. OMG happily takes on board methods of standardization where there is an existing implementation, if these can be freely published and accessed by all its members, who pay a fee for their membership to cover the costs of the organization. To cover its costs, ISO makes a charge for downloading of its standards documents. In many cases, OMG standards have progressed, verbatim, as fast-tracked ISO standards, but some years later.

The missions and goals of OMG and ISO are quite similar in their wish to facilitate standardization to the benefit of all sectors of the economy. But their methods, constituencies and loyalties differ considerably. In the realm of politics, determining international standards from on high, the ISO method lines up with national preoccupations and concerns. In the realm of industry, the pursuit of business opportunity favours the OMG approach. OMG is investing in the concept of architecture driven modernization of systems and services, providing tools based on a Business Architecture

Core Metamodel (BACM), to align and support suppliers in modernizing their products within the changing information landscape.

The address hierarchy of Internet-connected devices and services has been under the management of the Internet Corporation for Assigned Names and Numbers (ICANN), a not-for-profit organization responsible for Internet Protocol (IP) and Domain Name Services (DNS) that transport and navigate data throughout the Internet. Originally established in different form under US Government contract, the organization works collaboratively across all countries and sectors, to maintain the global Internet.

An IP (Internet protocol) address is a numerical code divided into sections, which enables electronic connection to the domain of a specific device and location. To avoid or minimize unnecessary use of complicated numbers, this allocation is managed by the DNS as a symbolic domain name, mapping between symbolic names of domains and their IP numerical sequences. If I am a domain, my house number, road, city and country might constitute my IP address. If I move to a new house, I can take me with me, but my current IP address stays where it is. I can reroute my postal mail by notifying the postal service of a new location. My Internet communications are routed to the IP address of any location where I log on.

Skipping back to information systems, resources hosted within devices and domains need unique identifiers, called Uniform Resource Identifiers (URIs). They are strings of characters that unambiguously identify a particular resource. They follow defined syntax and are extensible to unique identification of separate resources within subdivided domains. A Uniform Resource Locator (URL), or web address, references a resource by specifying its location on a computer network and a mechanism for accessing it. URLs are used most commonly to reference web pages (http: and https:), but also for file transfer (ftp), email (mailto), database access (JDBC) and many other applications.

The Status Quo

In the 1960s, pioneering NHS colleagues that I first encountered–like John Anderson (1921–2002), a professor of medicine; Frederick Flynn (1924–2011), a head of chemical pathology laboratory services; and John Clifton (1930–2023), my chief of medical physics at UCH–needed all their skills of management and persuasion to deal with a health service that was then placing all things computer in its central Supplies Division, with staff overseeing purchase of chairs one week and computers the next. How health care has navigated through now seven decades of scientific and technological advance, in and through the Information Age and its associated reorganizations of services and strategies, is an extraordinary story. The convergence of politics, commercial interest, hubris and pretence of knowledge, ambition, immature new technologies and practical realities of health care can create chaotic situations akin to Macbethian cauldrons of 'double, double toil and trouble'! Burn, bubble, boil and bake sounds about right, not to mention sting and charm! Where connection and influence are global, what might once have been contained and localized, becomes of global impact. A detailed account of the coevolution of health care and information technology is rehearsed in Chapter Seven.

This final section of the chapter takes a brief look at how evolution in information engineering has impacted the governance of public services, with a story of a seemingly common misadventure uncovered in one government ministry. In company with many large organizations, governments have come to realize that they have not been good at designing and implementing information systems. Of course, such difficulties are not unique to health care.

In the late 1990s and early 2000s, I worked closely with Al Aynsley-Green when he was director of clinical research at the Great Ormond Street Hospital for Children and UCL Medical School. He led the creation of a database of all the research teams there, and their projects, to assist in the development of the research plans at the Institute of Child Health.[56]

Al became a supportive colleague in this project. He was subsequently appointed as the first Children's Commissioner for England, in which role he took an interest in information systems at the government Department for Education (DfE). One initiative at the time had seen external consultants brought in to analyze and propose improvements in its information management. Inevitably, this extended into schools and universities, courts and hospitals, and interfaced throughout government departments. Uncovering rock by rock, as on a seashore, to see what lay beneath, the

---

56   The then chief of medicine of the UCL Medical School, Leon Fine, asked me to help in creating something similar for all of the UCL Biomedicine Division (which was, by then, accounting for about a half of the one billion pounds annual financial turnover of UCL), and its linked NHS Hospital Trusts (which multiplied this one billion several times over). I could not say no, of course! It was a tough ask, but a good way to get to know the wider institution and community. I was looked to, to take on several such aspirational tasks and integrative roles in those years. Though distracting from a more focused academic mission, these roles were implicit in my appointment and the expectation of those appointing me regarding my broader contributions to the University and local health services. Striking a delicate balance, we were able to create and sustain a rich interdisciplinary and multiprofessional environment for the CHIME department. Its challenges and achievements are reflected on in Chapter Nine, in the context of our experience in creating a new working environment for the Information Age.

consultants discovered an extraordinary complex of databases. Not dissimilar to what, I later understood, was embodied in the large collection of databases maintained under the aegis of the NHS Information Centre.

Al asked me to come to a meeting at the DfE, where the consultants' report was to be discussed. There were serious mandarins in attendance, baffled and bemused by the spider's web of data relationships that had been identified and charted in the consultants' systems analysis. A heap of spaghetti would have writhed in embarrassment! I had come across many such intractable data networks over the course of my career and was sympathetic, asking, simply and innocuously, what they felt they had discovered in the project. The enigmatic response from the department's commissioner of the report was that they now had a 'clearer view' of the chaos! Were this a discovery about plans for an aeroplane that would likely not fly, or a submarine that would likely sink, there would be the option, and perhaps imperative, to start afresh. But no one there felt responsible for the situation in question. All present experienced the reality but did not, or could not, diagnose and connect the problems revealed with how to set about solving them. I imagine they could have done no more than put the report aside and move on to other pressing concerns.

The consultant's very detailed systems analysis had revealed a lack of architecture and design in the many preceding systems analyses that had led to this set of atomized and uncommunicating databases. The use of a consultant to conduct what looked to have been a rather fruitless exercise was a classic example of what Mariana Mazzucato and Rosie Collington have described in their recent book–the final inukbook that I have drawn on in writing this one.[57] It describes the present-day double bind that pushes organizations to commission external consultants to study and diagnose their problems and propose solutions, which end up costing a lot and adding little to the inhouse capability that would be implicit in the capacity to enact necessary remedial action and change.

Such anarchic assembly of databases is widespread. Some organizations have sufficient resources, opportunities and capabilities to wipe the slate clean and start afresh, but most in the public sector do not. In health care, this situation is also demonstrated in the several hundreds of non-communicating, small-scale and isolated systems in use in major university

---

57   M. Mazzucato and R. Collington, *The Big Con: How the Consulting Industry Weakens Our Businesses, Infantilizes Our Governments and Warps Our Economies* (London: Allen Lane, 2023). The 'Con' in their cross wires is Consultancy, playing with the implication that it can be akin to a confidence trick. Being a bit provocative, myself—to match the outspokenness of these authors in addressing their theme— is there sometimes another kind of contemporary 'Con' in play, captured in their 'Big Con' title—namely, the 'Con' of the 'Big'!?

hospital Trusts. These may, indeed, each be performing essential everyday work. But few have specifications extant, showing how they were designed and implemented. And the software tools used and the computers and peripheral devices, themselves, may mostly now be obsolete. The situation was also revealed in project dissertations of students I supervised, who enrolled on postgraduate courses in health informatics with us at UCL, from their day jobs in hospital Trusts. Projects all over the world have battled with, and sought to integrate, non-coherent software systems. Such an endeavour costs a lot of money and often fails. And even a successful short-term outcome may quickly be rendered technologically or functionally obsolete.

As in these sorts of example, many IT projects, large and small, have defied the wisdom of Fred Brooks and paid too little attention to integrative, health-economy-wide architecture and design of information systems. This has occasioned a very great loss of money, impairing and destroying existing in-house capabilities, while distracting from other health care priorities. Each new such venture can impose an additional burden at the coalface of care and constitute a further burden for its central management, in coping with and unravelling the further complexities and inconsistencies that lack of coherent data generates.

Knowledge and experience that bring the capability and capacity to make and do things in-house, has too often been lacking. Battle-hardened folk, like Mervyn King, author books which are more open about the limitations and failures they have observed and worked through. They provide and encourage a culture of honesty and humility, which is essential in learning to make and do better. This is not about prescience; it is about coping better and adopting more realistic ways of working. Policy for health care practices and services cannot be wholly evidence-based. Its implementation is not a controlled or controllable experiment. It is the navigation of an unfolding future of problems that must be coped with and resolved. In this we need traction, balance, purpose and capability to make and do–the parenthetical topics I have highlighted in my chapter-by-chapter reflections, to this point in the book.

One response to these difficulties, seeking to tame proliferation of new and speculative initiatives, is to require prior evidence of effectiveness. This has the sound motivation to achieve safety and cost effectiveness of health care services, as well as absolve from blame when things go wrong. It has created some important and influential new voices–the National Institute for Health and Care Excellence (NICE) in the UK, concerned with cost-benefit evaluation of new treatments, has been a notable success story.

But undue focus on evidence in a domain that can and must be navigated, while still substantially unexplored, is a bit hard on brave explorers. David Sackett (1934–2015), the father of evidence-based medicine (EBM), who

I first encountered at McMaster University before his invention of the field had crystallized, was clinically and epidemiologically grounded and exploratory in his approach. In the heat of the Covid debate, the evidence adduced, and the predictions made in advising on policy, brought many voices and their conflicting views into play. In reality, no one could have known how potentially black swan events–such as harmful viral mutation, ineffective vaccine development and poor behavioural compliance of the public with quarantine and distancing injunctions–would land. Evidence must be weighed, and nowadays, so must evidence about evidence!

The interaction of information engineering with health care has sometimes felt akin to a goldrush in a warzone. We need to become better grounded in the context of health care services as experienced, and not just as described and predicted to be, by people far from the biting of bullets at the coalface of care–patients, relatives and their supporting professionals. We need to find common ground and stand up for what matters to them, and why. We need to co-create new environments in which information can evolve and be sustained as a utility and not as a technology. We need local people, teams and alliances to carry a global flag. If I know my nine grandchildren well, I trust that their generation will prove to be one that can and will make and do this. They look to be up to, and up for, the challenge of finding the common ground required, and helping to create the future there.

Parenthesis–Making and Doing Things Differently

This chapter parenthesis completes Part One of the book. It is a reflective handover into Part Two–perhaps a Mervyn King-style, audaciously pessimistic perspective, but not without some Barack Obama-style, audacious hope, I hope! Erwin Schrödinger (1887–1961) cautioned that what he wrote risked foolishness, when prefacing his attempt to answer the question 'What is life?', as I recalled in the Preface. 'What is health care?' is equally puzzling and one inevitably risks foolishness when seeking to respond adventurously to that important question, as well. Part Two of the book places these two questions side by side, in context of the anarchy of transition of life science and health care services through the past seventy-five years of the Information Age. Where we have got to with these questions and concerns is central to how we can and must now set about reimagining, inventing and creating health care for the Information Society of the future. There is a lot to reflect on!

Information engineering has become integral to the delivery of health care services and will remain hugely consequential for its future reinvention and reform. It has involved massive investments and implementation endeavours, in multiple dimensions and directions, globally, played out along an evolving timeline over seven decades. It has been at the heart of advances in health care services and instrumental in bringing them to their knees. I reflect, here, on key issues necessitating the reinvention of services, their interrelationship with new requirements for information systems, and challenges in the implementation of such systems. It is safe to say that success in the reinvention of affordable, safe, effective and sustainable health care services (and their associated disciplines, professions and governance) will depend on success in the implementation of a wholly new concept of care information ecosystem. Implementing and sustaining this, incrementally and iteratively, will be how we learn how to do it. It will not be easy and will take a long time, but it is an essential goal.

It is in the engineering domain, where implementation realities are faced and pushes come to shoves, that things oftentimes go badly and expensively wrong, as we develop and deploy new technology and implement it on new terrain. In evidence of this today, we can follow the many years of delay and budget overruns in the construction of the Crossrail line in London. Or the design failures and subsequent crashes of the Boeing 737 MAX aircraft in the 2010s, mirroring those of the de Havilland Comet in the 1950s, which exposed vulnerability to unstable aerodynamic balance and control, and metal fatigue in flight.

Great expectations are vested in new technologies. They were so in the Comet, as expressed by a government minister at the time:

> During the next few years, the UK has an opportunity, which may not recur, of developing aircraft manufacture as one of our main export industries. On whether we grasp this opportunity and so establish firmly an industry of the utmost strategic and economic importance, our future as a great nation may depend.[58]

In retrospection of what happened with the UK avionics industry, there was more rhetorical clutching at straws than grasping of opportunities in this encomium. People talk today about grasping opportunity in health care in a somewhat like manner. Health care information policy has clutched at straws. We may not always need the engineering that makes modern aircraft, but we will always need that which supports and sustains our

---

58   Duncan Sandys (1908–87), Minister of Supply, 1952, quoted in P. J. Lyth, 'American Aerospace Dominance and the British Challenge in Jet Engines', in *Tackling Transport*: Volume 3, ed. by H. Trischler and S. Zeilinger (London: NMSI), pp. 81–98 (p. 90).

health care services and their information ecosystem. Safety of health care traverses many more dimensions of complexity than does safety of aircraft.

New engineering methods are intrinsically experimental and developmental, and thus prone to mistakes and reappraisal, as they evolve. Where policy and governance are tuned to, and retransmit, signals from a disappearing era of technology, services and society, they can prove vulnerable and maladroit when responding to, seeking to cope with and adapting to radical change, as several of the examples in this chapter have illustrated. Better framing and implementation of plans is about a culture of realism, agility, learning by doing and ability to learn from mistakes. Significant and costly failures can arise when these qualities are lacking or experiment happens at an inappropriate scale—running before walking, as it were. Of course, some experiments can only be conducted at scale, but they remain experiments, nonetheless. And some problems only reveal themselves when explored for real, at scale, or when they emerge from left field. As the French physician and anthropologist Paul Broca (1824–80) reputedly said, 'The least questioned assumptions are often the most questionable'.

There are major and interlinked challenges beckoning as we progress towards the reinvention and reform of the NHS and health care in the UK, today. In a nutshell, these encompass:

- Demographics—an ageing population and associated preponderance of support and cost in providing care for those with chronic conditions, for which there is no cure;

- Social inequalities—with multifactorial causes and impacts on health;

- Separation of health and social care services—despite sharing in common many citizens that they both care for;

- Ineffectiveness of interventions and services—much that is done is deemed to achieve poor cost-benefits;

- Discontinuity—fragmentation of specialisms and professions, leading to disconnected and redundantly repetitive processes;

- Overburdening of workforce—a crisis of ends and means and expectations at all levels—with much human need ending up inappropriately positioned as health care service workload;

- Affordability—an ever-increasing range of improved but costly therapeutic options;

- Rapid and far-reaching changes in life and medical science and device technology–these create difficulties in keeping abreast and up-to-date;

- Burdensome, mutually non-coherent and inflexible information systems;

- Physical estate–much is decrepit and not fit for purpose.

Looking forward, policy is increasingly focussing on:

- Awareness of experience of care and what matters to citizens, in context of quality of life as well as cure of disease;

- Prevention, early intervention and self-care;

- Integration of services at a local level;

- Delegation of authority within health care teams and professions, to prescribe and enact interventions.

These policy perspectives reflect core information engineering challenges:

- Care information systems must be reinvented to be centred on the citizen at home, in the context of care services that connect with them there and within their local community, enabling and eliciting their participation and feedback;

- Data sources are currently highly fragmented and noncoherent, discontinuous, serially redundant and centred on services not citizens. This issue must be addressed head on, as a public domain concern and with suitable new governance;

- A new concept of citizen-centred data repository and related computable knowledge resources must be developed from the ground, gradually supplanting the current legacy with, wherever possible, globally shared and governed public domain specified methodology. This endeavour will target improvement in the cost-effectiveness of information services that directly support health care. It will enable an iteratively and incrementally evolving and improving, and sustainable, marketplace for products and services. It will provide coherent context of data supporting health care governance, management, professional education and research;

- Data volumes have exploded in size and databases have grown serendipitously. The workload of capturing data in the context of everyday health care delivery must be massively streamlined, to enable more time for engaging with the need for more personal empathy and care.

There are several principal and related challenges embodied in all this.

First, the current mismatch of need and capacity is not sustainable with current concepts and models of health care services. Social care cannot continue to be envisioned and enacted independently of the health service. There must be a better way and creating it must be a central goal that focuses efforts on the support and enablement of citizens and carers, to participate in and manage the meeting of their needs, at or as near as possible to where they live. Closer bonding of health and social care services requires new professionalism, environment, teamwork and community, and new information systems that mirror these needs. Health care services are basic to society and must have their foundations in teamwork that is anchored and supported more strongly at local level.

Second, the principal information engineering challenge–which will be a long-term, iterative and incremental one, implemented in a spirit of learning by doing–is to create and sustain a locally customized and globally standardized care information utility. This must be based on a shared vision of the balance, continuity and governance of the care services supported and meet the needs of those working at all levels of health care in providing them. It must, as well, enable and support citizens acting in support of their own health care needs, and of those carrying caring burdens within families and local communities, focused on what matters to them. The citizen-facing information architecture of this new utility and the engineering methods employed in implementing and sustaining it will be fundamental to the successful reinvention and reform of health care. As I seek to demonstrate in Chapters Eight and Eight and a Half, there is already implemented and provenly applicable technology and method on which to base such a plan and platform, moving forward. It is growing widely across the world. Plans for technology promoting new scientific advance and related change and reorganization of services, must be aligned and adjusted around this core mission, with much greater attention to the radical change in services and society that may flow from them, and to proceed cautiously to secure benefits and avoid disbenefits.

In thinking about what can and should now be done along these lines, to help make the current situation better, we need first to understand why past failure to make progress, set against a backdrop of huge investments, has persisted for so long, and at such cost and expense. In a nutshell, it is because government and professional policy has championed an increasingly fragmented concept of health care, and information technology has accelerated this fragmentation. That is the nut of it, and the shell is the championing of proprietary and fragmenting industrial models of information and information technology over the cultivation of a coherent common ground of requirement for information systems. This fragmentation persists across all the personal, professional, public and proprietary domains that must work together, coherently, in support of the balance, continuity and governance of cost-effective health care.

A patient may ask or expect their doctor to 'make me better'–in reality, it is a team effort, with the patient and their carers central to the team. A vituperative professor of surgery that I once trailed on his ward-rounds angrily rasped at his senior registrar, and delegated to him the task to 'get that patient well'! No amount of such rant helps anything get better but is the way of frustrated authority in difficult or chaotic times. Policy makers and other leaders have sometimes acted like that, implicitly, even if unknowingly so, delegating to engineers–way down stream, out of sight and mind–the task of realizing their dreams of future information for health. They have been frustrated that the levers they pulled, seeking to achieve their aspirations, proved unconnected with the outcomes they wished for and expected. Lacking provenly implementable ideas for how to proceed, the pattern of recurrent illustrious reviews and policy resets, the papering over of past failure with promise (and re-promise) of new and better futures, dressed in new clothes that have seldom arrived on time, and when they did, often failed to fit–all this has led to repeated failure.

This deliberate caricature is all a bit polemical. But given the continuing and escalating, costly and burdensome implications of its underlying truths, it needs to be considered, reflected on and learned from–because it has not needed and does not need to be this way. In Chapter Seven, I track, in detail, fifty years of reports, policies, strategies, reorganizations and initiatives in health care IT. This reveals the accumulated depth of problems that have become entrenched in a hard to improve and hard to dislodge, legacy of rapidly obsolete information systems, inflexible to meet the evolving needs of medical science and health care. I have had my account of the scene reviewed by central actors of those times, who have not demurred. It is by no means only a problem of the health care sector. A forward-facing and evolutionary approach to creating a sustainable care information utility, to support the changing needs of health care, is put forward and further elaborated from Chapter Eight onwards in the book. To some eyes, it will, no doubt, appear a naively optimistic and inappropriate Dreaming.[59] But it is now a demonstrably tractable proposition, since it is already happening

---

59   On the Aboriginal concept of the Dreaming, see Preface.

and halfway there. I will now zoom out and cool down somewhat, to reflect on the wider societal context of all this.

The Information Age and the UK NHS arrived in tandem–the seventy-five-year evolution of information technology being mirrored in that of the NHS. They arrived in an era of upswing in society, reflected in a concern to address the causes of social deprivation and create a universal health care service. Robert Putnam characterized the sixty years of American society that followed from around the 1890s, as an upswing from 'I to we'. The subsequent sixty years, from around the 1950s, as a downswing from 'we to I'.[60] He charted these two eras using a wide range of timeseries population datasets, each exhibiting an upswing and following downswing, in the form of an inverted letter U (∩).

As the NHS arrived, UK society entered a similar transition from upswing to downswing. The parallel upswing of information technology has aligned with, and perhaps accentuated and powered, the fragmentation of the 'we' of community and the assertion of the 'I' of individualism that Putnam describes. Health care services swung to an industrial and corporate managerial model of delivery, channeling new methods enabled by technology and new patterns of health care organizations and specialized professional services. From the mid-1960s, information technology sputtered into life, portended as a potent elixir–a solution to problems of supply and demand for boundless health care services. An echo of what the *Scientific American* journal said about the arrival of the motorcar, at the turn of the twentieth century, as I recalled in this book's Preface! The 2020s are poised at the limit of the Putnam downswing cycle, at an uncertain saddle point that can break, both up and down. Putnam is reassuringly positive that a new generation will bring energy and commitment to regeneration of upswing. There is much uncertainty, and much to make and do if this is to become a reality, just as in former and similarly uncertain times, as he recounts.

Befuddled by thwarted attempts to cope with the anarchic transition, government policies have been slow in recognizing the many and related integrative challenges of the fragmenting Information Age, and slow in adapting and evolving accordingly, to cope. Some of the disruption of health care services by information technology has been reminiscent of the battles over steam engines and steam power in the eighteenth and nineteenth centuries, as my examples in the chapter illustrated! It has been a costly anarchy of transition, tending to block the softer, more humble voices of experiment and learning which some that I have introduced in this book,

---

60   R. D. Putnam, *The Upswing: How America Came Together a Century Ago and How We Can Do It Again* (London: Simon and Schuster, 2020).

have represented, and argued for. The latest scientific or technological advances and buzzwords of organization have tended to be bandied with abandon, and successive reviews of past policies and future projections have mainly served to kick the can down the road. Genomics science, artificial intelligence and robotics have heralded an immense new adventure of ideas. They must be channelled in support of principled reinvention and reform of health care. This will open society to a new world, where a new Pandora's box of problems and concerns will, as ever, be poised to emerge. How we cope with and adapt to them, and what we make and do about them, is what will count.

It is as well to remember what David Graeber (1961–2020) wrote about the creation of the future, as quoted at the head of my Prologue. We all make the future and have choices in what we make, and how we make it, including about matters affecting our own health care. In these contexts, services are personal, and much information is personal. The quality of future health care services will reflect their enablement of all of us, as citizens, to become more instrumental, wherever possible, in making and doing much more of what we need and wish for, for ourselves and for one another, supported by related communities, professions, and institutions. The *how* of this will be common ground for all health care services, and a coherent and citizen-centred care information utility will be needed to support its emergent reality over the coming decades. This utility will need to look quite different from that created by the enclosure and commercialization of knowledge and personal data in the downswing era, if it is to help turn the inverted U (∩) world right-side up to U again, enabling and powering upswing in a new cycle of Putnam's 'I to we'.

The primary enabler of a successful care information utility will be trust on all sides, and trust is not something that can be hand-on-heart created; it is earned slowly and quickly lost. Like reputation, it arrives on foot and departs on a fast horse! The evolution towards a shared, sustained and trusted care information utility will be a slow one, but one that can start to be articulated, and gain traction, now. I have made a first, Aunt Sally-like, attempt in Part Three of this book. It will have multiple faces and must function securely and efficiently. It must span diverse locations and contexts, globally, while supporting balance, continuity and governance of services, locally. It must embody personal and professional co-ownership, social inclusion and community governance, tuned to the needs and expectations of all citizens of the Information Society. Who will make this happen, what will they do, where and how? There is a considerable legacy of existing stuff that will not do for this endeavour, and much new stuff taking shape to help us make and do things better, now. Progress in this direction is emerging in many countries–in Europe, for example, in Sweden, Norway, Spain,

Slovenia and Finland, including in whole health economy programmes of reform that I have been observing and engaging with.

An architectural blueprint is needed, covering all bases of the who, what, when, where, how and why of principled mission, goal and plan for the utility. Such a mission has proved beyond the individual scope and capacity of governments, professions, services, and industries, especially in large health economies. It is a community interest and will need to embody all of these participants, but also to be created afresh on new common ground, with citizen focus and ownership, and that not just in name. I have characterized this community interest and mission as 'care information utility with you in charge'–palindromic CIU with uic! ! More catchily, perhaps, as openCare! The primary users will be individual citizens in partnership with the professionals who serve and support them. Its scope will embrace both health and social care, signifying their joint identity and chemistry, held together in a rewarding exchange between the two domains. This characterization suggested itself to me when reading descriptions, today, of the covalent organic frameworks of chemistry.

Part Three of the book starts to articulate a Dreamtime-like vision of the creation of the future openCare utility. Before addressing the challenge of the future, it is necessary to describe and seek understanding of the past and present reality. In that regard, Chapter Seven in Part Two includes a good deal of critical commentary, but I hope it is fair. Part Three is an optimistic perspective which I likewise hope is not too starry-eyed. I have listened to and been guided by my colleagues closest to the health care service realities of recent decades, who have mentored me in both aspects.

One final personal reflection at this point, from one now long retired from the everyday fray of working life. There is a clearly identified group in society who will always have a special interest in the coherence and continuity of the services that the care information utility will support, being typically more aware of and engaged in their own side of the bargain in keeping well. This is the community of lucky and able, young-at-heart, retired citizens, who often seek and need new human connections through which they can feel needed and valued, for a hoped-for ten to twenty years of not-so-busy but still healthy and active retirement. There could be an appealing and win-win opportunity to articulate and support recognized roles for this group. They are present in families and communities everywhere, and are well-placed to help create, populate and operate a coherent common ground of care information utility. They have much to offer in this way for the reinvention of health care, by sharing their varieties of experience and skill, and, as importantly, their time and concern. I like the idea that care of the elderly might in this way have a reflection in the elderly of care!

Of course, very many citizens, and certainly not just the retired, have always contributed to care, in their everyday personal lives and the voluntary sector, as well as in professional careers and roles. The re-invention of health care for the Information Society must seek to better recognize and draw together all who provide care. Roll on openCare!

Acknowledgements

This book draws together many and diverse stories about people, organizations and events, and the ideas, endeavours and experiences that have connected them with me, along my songline. There are very many people acknowledged in this way, throughout the chapters. Writing about them is itself an acknowledgement of my good fortune in the insights, opportunities and enjoyment they have brought me. Rather as with authors of papers in science who have sometimes listed very many co-authors, only few of them having put pen to paper or tapped keys in preparing the manuscripts, I feel concerned not to be selective in their acknowledgement here.

Acknowledgement is also about recognizing the inspiration, enjoyment and support we have received in other ways. Words cannot adequately acknowledge and convey my gratitude and indebtedness to my family and friends, past and present. They have been my rocks. I hope I have done okay in showing them that.

There have been some friends and colleagues who were especially close by, and without whom the songline of the book might easily have played out very differently. Chris Mullard, my early childhood friend, is family with us, still. John and Diane Bailey have been the most inspiring, stalwart and sustaining of friends here in St Albans over half a century.

I have had some great teachers; we owe our teachers so much. My primary school head teacher, Mildred Maggs, in the tiny village of Woolton Hill in Hampshire, is still occasionally an actor in my dreams: chalking up weekly arithmetic test exercises on the blackboard and warming herself near to the coke burner in the classroom, as she read from books to the assembled pupils at the end of the school day! My maths teacher at the Cathedral School in Bristol, Dai Davies, showed me the difference between getting to a problem solution and getting to it clearly, concisely and elegantly, using the best available methods for the task. My lovably eccentric head teacher, Cecil Rich, kept me tuned to classical education while my eyes turned to maths and science. At Magdalen College, University of Oxford, where I then alighted, James Griffiths gently cajoled and pointed the way through physics tutorials, and the altogether complementary Dirk ter Haar, entrained us to keep going in solving the taxing problems of theoretical physics that he threw our way, flamboyantly scribbling down his own solutions, chalk on blackboard or pencil on paper as he spoke, before his students' goggling eyes. Geoff Redman, Robin Muers, Ian Phillips and Duncan Gallie were neighbours and good friends at Magdalen, who have stayed in touch to this day.

In later years, Stephen Montgomery took care of me as I transferred chaotically from my early career in the medical engineering industry to doctoral research in medical computing at University College London. John Clifton then introduced me into the world of medical physics, where Andrew Todd-Pokropek and David Delpy were colleagues who remained nearby over many of the following years, as their academic careers in medical imaging and clinical measurement methods prospered. John Dickinson and Jo Milan, who are remembered in the book's dedication and who feature in several of its chapters, entered my songline at that time, in the early 1970s, as did Christopher Taylor who was embarking on his stellar work in medical imaging, at Manchester.

I worked at two great institutions in my subsequent academic career. The Medical College of St Bartholomew's Hospital (Bart's) in London and the Medical School of University College London (UCL). I owe special acknowledgement to these iconic communities and to the Deans and Provosts who had me under their wings there. The many acknowledgements due in relation to the second half of my academic career, at UCL, are covered very widely in the text and further drawn together in the additional resources archive.[1] Reggie Shooter was my first Dean at Bart's. He used to tease me as to what on earth I was doing there, and secretly shepherded me along the way! Lesley Rees (1942–2022), my last Dean there, was hugely supportive and facilitating of my career. She was the first woman Dean of Bart's, and conferred on me, as her first professorial appointment, the first chair in Medical Informatics in the UK, that linked information technology and health care. It was notable that even though information technology (IT) was predominantly a male professional domain, it was often women colleagues, perhaps sensitive about the struggles they themselves faced in gaining senior academic position, who best understood the struggles involved in simultaneously carving out a career and creating a new field. With John Dickinson, Lesley backed me to take on important new leadership roles for the Medical College, which helped lift my career to a different plane. Jim Malpas, Mal Salkind, Gerry Slavin, Paul Turner and Donald

---

1   Available at https://www.openbookpublishers.com/books/10.11647/
     obp.0335#resources

Jeffries, as professorial seniors, Celia Burrage, David Perret, Huw Llewelyn and Andrew Gorsuch, as Medical Unit colleagues, and Sam Heard, Lesley Southgate, Jane Dacre and Peter Cull, the famous medical artist, also in charge of educational support services, were great colleagues through those career-forming years.

Two other very significant acknowledgements are due here, which I express simply. They are of my indebtedness to the hugely consequential and inspirational, now evolving worldwide communities of openEHR and OpenEyes. These started in the Dreamings of ones and twos, grew to tens of key creators and anchors, then to hundreds of engaged implementers and adopters, and are now climbing to many thousands. They are the ones showing how such movements can catch a moment, internationally, and contribute widely to the reinvention of health care in society, which the advent of the computer has both enabled and necessitated. All these wonderful people have inspired me with their staying power and vitality and are one of the principal reasons why I have felt determined and energized to write this book.

The book has been taxing to envisage, scope and write. Indeed, writing it has played a large part in discovering how to write it, and hence its three substantive drafts over three years of solid efforts—more learning by doing! It was a tiring and revealing process but, at the same time, one that had to be attempted or forgotten. If forgotten, it would have quickly disappeared over the horizon and beneath the waves. As a unique eyewitness history, that would have been a pity. I have had the support of nine professional colleagues who have read and advised on different drafts of the manuscript. Unsurprisingly they have not always concurred—with one another or with me! The many appreciative and supportive comments they provided have encouraged and spurred me on to complete the book.

My longstanding nearby St Albans friends, John and Diane Bailey—well-read English language and literature teachers and leaders in school, college and adult learning education—read sections of my early attempts to pitch the language and tone of the book, discussing and advising about its interest, relevance and accessibility to wider audiences. My former doctoral student and now good friend, Seref Arikan, did me the huge service of reading for style, content and accessibility, from the earliest drafts, chapter by chapter. He brought the capable knowledge of a developer of health computing systems over thirty years, and experience from his insightful, much downloaded UCL PhD with me, in the field. Jeannette Murphy and Evelyn Hovenga have read from educational perspectives; Martin Severs, Bill Aylward and Norbert Graf from international organization and governance, medical science, clinical practice and management perspectives; Georgios Stamatakos and Alan Rector from computer science, mathematical modelling and formal logic perspectives. All these reviewers have variously approved, put me right, reassured and criticised me for the content they reviewed–in its correctness, balance of personal and professional perspective, length and accessibility. I am indebted to them all for their advice and guidance.

The final form has been adjusted with guidance from Open Book Publishers (OBP), as to what is in the printed book and e-books, and downloadable online, and the connectivity with the book's archive of additional resources kept online. I am indebted to the OBP founders and directors, Alessandra Tosi and Rupert Gatti, their independent peer reviewers of the manuscript, and the OBP team–Jeevan Nagpal, Laura Rodriguez Pupo, Cameron Craig and Adèle Kreager. They have been patient, cheerful, clear, prompt, helpful and supportive. No author could ask for more. It has been a huge benefit to have the final manuscript copy-edited by a publisher traditionally centred in the humanities. Adèle has caught many mistakes in my manuscript, tidied awkward phrasing to achieve greater clarity, and chased down, corrected and completed incomplete citations. I applaud their mission and hope that the book does well for them. It was a tricky challenge to prepare the diagrams and photos to a quality suitable for printing. Tony Briscoe, a professional photographer and local friend in St Albans, very generously took my source materials to his studio and computers and transformed them into book and archive material that solved the problems as best possible. Recognizing that the book was being written and published open access, Tony waived his fees. The costs incurred for book production and making it available open-access, have been generously supported by a crowd-funding appeal. All contributors, at the time of publication and later, are and will be acknowledged, in the book itself and its updating archive of additional resources.

Regarding what the book now contains, of course the buck stops with me. I hope it is interesting and useful, as well as thought-provoking and controversial. As I wrote at the end of the Preface, nothing useful could be written about this very complex, wide-ranging, and rapidly evolving field, that was not!

I have given it my best, but, as with dancing, there is always much room for reinterpretation and improvement! The principal reason it now exists at all has been Bożena's love and support–wanting me to write it and ensuring in a million everyday ways that I could and did. She keeps us dancing.

Donors

We thank the following donors who have generously contributed to the publication of this book, and to our initiative:

openEHR International

The Apperta Foundation CIC

Better Ltd

Sebastian Iancu

Jordi Piera-Jiménez

Kanthan Theivendran

Vanessa Pereira

Rachel Dunscombe

Tony Shannon

Ian McNicoll

Seung-Jong Yu

Sam Heard

We also thank the sixteen anonymous donors who have kindly supported this publication.

Contents in Detail

VOLUME 1

VOLUME 2

Page numbers may be found in the Table of Contents of Vol. 2

PART TWO – ANARCHY OF TRANSITION

6. Life and Information – Co-evolving Sciences

    Life in Evolutionary Context

    Life in Historical and Scientific Context

    Information in Context of Physical, Engineering and Life Sciences

        New Frontiers of Information

    From Life and Information to Mind and Intelligence

        Artificial Intelligence

    Landmark Contributions

        1944 – Erwin Schrödinger: *What Is Life?*

        1956 – John von Neumann: *The Computer and the Brain*

        1978 – John Zachary Young: *Programs of the Brain*

        1996 – Richard Feynman: *Feynman Lectures on Computation*

        1998 – Ian Stewart: *Life's Other Secret*

        2007 – Douglas Hofstadter: *I Am a Strange Loop*

        2012 – John Scales Avery: *Information Theory and Evolution*

        2015 – Nick Lane: *The Vital Question*

        2019 – Marcus du Sautoy: *The Creativity Code*

        A Pause for Reflection

        2020 – Paul Davies: *The Demon in the Machine*

List of the Inukbooks

Avery, J. S., *Information Theory and Evolution*, 2nd ed. (Singapore: World Scientific Publishing, 2012)

Axelrod, R. M, *The Evolution of Cooperation* (London: Penguin Books, 1990)

Barnes, J., *A History of the World in 10½ Chapters* (New York: Knopf, 1989)

Becker, A., *What Is Real?: The Unfinished Quest for the Meaning of Quantum Physics* (London: John Murray, 2018)

Chatwin, B., *The Songlines* (New York: Random House, 2012)

Date, C. J., *Database Design and Relational Theory: Normal Forms and All That Jazz*, 2nd ed. (n.p.: Apress, 2019)

Davies, N., *Europe: A History* (Oxford: Oxford University Press, 1996)

Davies, P., *The Demon in the Machine: How Hidden Webs of Information Are Solving the Mystery of Life* (Chicago, IL: University of Chicago Press, 2021)

Dickinson, C. J., *A Computer Model of Human Respiration: Ventilation, Blood Gas Transport and Exchange, Hydrogen Ion Regulation* (Baltimore, MD: University Park Press, 1977)

Ernst, B., *The Magic Mirror of M. C. Escher*, trans. J. E. Brigham (New York: Barnes and Noble, 1994)

Fermi, L., *Atoms in the Family: My Life with Enrico Fermi* (Chicago, IL: University of Chicago Press, 2014)

Gawande, A., *Better: A Surgeon's Notes on Performance* (New York: Metropolitan Books, 2007)

—, *Complications: Notes from the Life of a Young Surgeon* (London: Penguin Books)

Gibbon, E., *The History of the Decline and Fall of the Roman Empire* (London: Strahan and Cadell, 1788)

Goodhart, D., *Head Hand Heart: The Struggle for Dignity and Status in the 21st Century* (London: Penguin Books, 2020)

Guyton, Arthur C., 'Cardiac Output and Its Regulation', *Circulatory Physiology*, 1973, 353–71

Feynman, R. P., *Feynman Lectures on Computation*, ed. A. Hey (New York: CRC Press, 2018)

Fisher, R., and W. Ury, *Getting to Yes: Negotiating Agreement without Giving In*, 2nd ed. (New York: Penguin Books, 1991)

Harari, Y. N., *Homo Deus: A Brief History of Tomorrow* (London: Random House, 2016)

Hellerman, H., *Digital Computer System Principles* (New York: McGraw-Hill, 1967)

Hodges, A., *Alan Turing: The Enigma* (New York: Simon and Schuster, 1983)

Hofstadter, D. R., *I Am a Strange Loop* (New York: Basic Books, 2007)

Hogben, L. T., *Man Must Measure: The Wonderful World of Mathematics* (London: Rathbone Books, 1955)

Illich, I., *Deschooling Society* (London: Calder and Boyars, 1971)

—, *Limits to Medicine: Medical Nemesis: The Expropriation of Health* (London: Boyars, 1995)

Institute of Medicine, *Computer-Based Patient Record: An Essential Technology for Health Care* (Washington, DC: The National Academies Press, 1991)

—, *Crossing the Quality Chasm: A New Health System for the 21st Century* (Washington, DC: The National Academies Press, 2001)

Ishiguro, I., *Klara and the Sun* (New York: Knopf, 2021)

Kahneman, D., O. Sibony and C. R. Sunstein, *Noise: A Flaw in Human Judgment* (New York: Little, Brown Spark, 2021)

Khayyam, O., *The Rubaiyat of Omar Khayyam*, trans. E. Fitzgerald (London: George G. Harrap & Co. Ltd., 1928)

King, M., *The End of Alchemy: Money, Banking and the Future of the Global Economy* (New York: W. W. Norton and Company, 2016)

Kuhn, T. S., *The Structure of Scientific Revolutions: 50th Anniversary Edition* (Chicago, IL: University of Chicago Press, 2012)

Kurzweil, R., *How to Create a Mind: The Secret of Human Thought Revealed* (New York: Viking Books, 2012)

Land, F., *The Language of Mathematics* (London: Murray, 1960)

Lane, N., *The Vital Question: Energy, Evolution, and the Origins of Complex Life* (New York: W. W. Norton and Company, 2015)

Lane Fox, R., *The Invention of Medicine: From Homer to Hippocrates* (London: Penguin Books, 2020)

Levi, P., *Other People's Trades* (London: Sphere Books, 1990)

Lovelock, J., *Novacene: The Coming Age of Hyperintelligence* (Cambridge, MA: MIT Press, 2019)

Maddox, J., *What Remains to Be Discovered: Mapping the Secrets of the Universe, the Origins of Life, and the Future of the Human Race* (New York: Macmillan, 1998)

Mazzucato, M., and R. Collington, *The Big Con: How the Consulting Industry Weakens Our Businesses, Infantilizes Our Governments and Warps Our Economies* (London: Allen Lane, 2023)

McEwan, I., *Machines like Me* (Toronto: Knopf Canada, 2019)

Meyer, B., and J.-M. Nerson, *Object-Oriented Applications* (Englewood Cliffs, NJ: Prentice Hall, 1993)

Minford, J. trans., *Sun Tzu: The Art of War* (London: Penguin Books, 2002)

Oppenheimer, J. R., *Science and the Common Understanding* (Oxford: Oxford University Press, 1954)

Perutz, M. F., *I Wish I'd Made You Angry Earlier: Essays on Science, Scientists, and Humanity* (Oxford: Oxford University Press, 2002)

Piketty, T., *A Brief History of Equality* (Cambridge, MA: Harvard University Press, 2022)

Pinker, S., *The Better Angels of Our Nature: The Decline of Violence in History and Its Causes* (London: Penguin Books, 2011)

Popper, K., *The Open Society and Its Enemies* (Abingdon: Routledge, 2012)

Putnam, R. D., *The Upswing: How America Came Together a Century Ago and How We Can Do It Again* (New York: Simon and Schuster, 2020)

Rees, M., *On the Future: Prospects for Humanity* (Princeton, NJ: Princeton University Press, 2018)

Russell, B., *Authority and the Individual: The Reith Lectures for 1948–49* (London: Allen and Unwin, 1949)

—, *History of Western Philosophy: Collectors Edition* (New York: Routledge, 2013)

Sandel, M. J., *The Tyranny of Merit: What's Become of the Common Good?* (London: Penguin Books, 2020)

Sautoy, M. du, *The Creativity Code: How AI Is Learning to Write, Paint and Think* (Cambridge, MA: Harvard University Press, 2019)

—, *What We Cannot Know: Explorations at the Edge of Knowledge* (London: Fourth Estate, 2016)

Schrödinger, E., *What Is Life?* (Cambridge, UK: Cambridge University Press, 1948)

Schumacher, E. F., *Small Is Beautiful: A Study of Economics as if People Mattered* (London: Abacus, 1973)

Simard, S., *Finding the Mother Tree: Uncovering the Wisdom and Intelligence of the Forest* (London: Penguin Books, 2021)

Sinclair, D. A., *Lifespan: Why We Age–and Why We Don't Have To* (London: Harper Collins, 2019)

Smiles, S., *Men of Invention and Industry* (London: Read Books, 2013)

Stewart, I., *Life's Other Secret: The New Mathematics of the Living World* (New York: John Wiley and Sons, 1998)

Sunstein, C. R., *Infotopia: How Many Minds Produce Knowledge* (Oxford: Oxford University Press, 2006)

Susskind, R. E., and D. Susskind, *The Future of the Professions: How Technology Will Transform the Work of Human Experts* (Oxford: Oxford University Press, 2015)

Taleb, N. N., *Antifragile: How to Live in a World We Don't Understand* (London: Allen Lane, 2012)

Tett, G., *Anthro-Vision: A New Way to See in Business and Life* (New York: Simon and Schuster, 2021)

Thaler, R., and C. Sunstein, *Nudge: Improving Decisions about Health, Wealth and Happiness* (New Haven, CT: Yale University Press, 2008)

Topol, E., *Deep Medicine: How Artificial Intelligence Can Make Healthcare Human Again* (London: Hachette, 2019)

Universität Bern. Akademische Kommission, and Law Symposium on Human Genetic Information Science, *Human Genetic Information Science, Law and Ethics*, Ciba Foundation Symposium 149 (Chichester, NY: John Wiley and Sons, 1990)

Vincent, B., *Haydn's Dictionary of Dates* (Frankfurt: Salzwasser-Verlag, 2020)

Von Neumann, J., *The Computer and the Brain*, Mrs. Hepsa Ely Silliman Memorial Lectures (London: Yale University Press, 1958)

Weizenbaum, J., *Computer Power and Human Reason: From Judgment to Calculation* (Harmondsworth: Penguin Books, 1993)

Whitehead, A. N., *Adventures of Ideas* (New York: Macmillan, 1933)

Wilson, F. M., *In the Margins of Chaos: Recollections of Relief Work in and Between Three Wars* (New York: Macmillan, 1945)

Young, J. Z., *Programs of the Brain: Based on the Gifford Lectures, 1975–7* (Oxford: Oxford University Press, 1978)

List of Figures

Many of the figures in the book have been made accessible via a QR code. This originally served the dual purposes of magnifying figures containing smaller text and providing access to figures that were originally omitted from the printed publication, to reduce the page count. With the book now cast as a two-volume work, the latter was no longer necessary and thus these images are now included in the printed version as well.

Fig. 4.2 Left: Arthur and Ruth Guyton at their home in Mississippi. Photographer and date unknown. Right: the extraordinarily complex circuit diagram of the Guyton-Coleman model of blood pressure regulation (1974). CC BY-NC.

Fig. 4.3 John Dickinson—one photo chosen by his family; one with Khursheed Ahmed and the author, at McMaster University (1970s); and one with the author in his office at Bart's (*c.* 1985), CC BY-NC.

Fig. 5.1 Three gear wheels engaged like this lock together and cannot turn. This image appears frequently as a supposed metaphor of a smoothly functioning organization. It is, rather, an ironic metaphor of the widespread lack of understanding and appreciation of engineering! Image created by David Ingram (c. 2010), CC BY-NC.

List of Additional Resources

All additional resources are available at
https://www.openbookpublishers.com/books/10.11647/obp.0335#resources

Appendix I: Royal Society of Medicine Talk Notes, 1991

Appendix II: NHS Acts of Parliament, Policies and Organizations Relating to Information and Information Technology since 1946

Appendix III: Forty Years of Policy and Implementation in the UK NHS

Appendix IV: A Reflection on Health Informatics

Appendix V: A Wider Acknowledgement of Contributions

Appendix VI: Annexes to Chapter Eight and a Half–openEHR Documents of Record:

    Annex I: The Original openEHR Manifesto, 1999

    Annex II: Origins of openEHR

    Annex III: Transcript of Lecture about openEHR for Medinfo 2007, Brisbane

    Annex IV: openEHR History from 2002–18

    Annex V: openEHR Vision and Mission–Co-written with Thomas Beale, 2018

    Annex VI: openEHR Today

Appendix VII: Digital Preservation of the Mac Series of Physiological Models

References

Aaronovitch, D., 'DeepMind, Artificial Intelligence and the Future of the NHS', *The Times* (14 September 2019), https://www.thetimes.co.uk/article/deepmind-artificial-intelligence-and-the-future-of-the-nhs-r8c28v3j6

Adams, D., *The Hitch Hiker's Guide to the Galaxy: A Trilogy in Five Parts* (London: Random House, 1995)

Ahmed, K., D. Ingram and C. J. Dickinson, *Software for Educational Computing: A General-Purpose Driver for Computer-Assisted Instruction, Interrogation and System Simulation ('MACAID')* (Lancaster: MTP, 1980)

Airy, G. B., and W. Airy, ed., *Autobiography of Sir George Biddell Airy* (Cambridge, UK: Cambridge University Press, 1896)

Allardice, L., 'Kazuo Ishiguro: AI, Gene-editing, Big Data... I Worry We Are Not in Control of These Things Anymore', *The Guardian* (20 February 2021) https://www.theguardian.com/books/2021/feb/20/kazuo-ishiguro-klara-and-the-sun-interview?CMP=Share_iOSApp_Other

Amiri, I. S., S. R. B. Azzuhri, M. A. Jalil, H. M. Hairi, J. Ali, M. Bunruangses and P. Yupapin, 'Introduction to Photonics: Principles and the Most Recent Applications of Microstructures', *Micromachines*, 9.9 (2018), 452, https://doi.org/10.3390/mi9090452

Anderson, J., and A. Graham, 'A Problem in Medical Education: Is There an Information Overload?', *Medical Education*, 14.1 (1980), 4–7, https://doi.org/10.1111/j.1365-2923.1980.tb02604.x

Anderson, R. M., and R. M. May, *Infectious Diseases of Humans: Dynamics and Control* (Oxford: Oxford University Press, 1992)

Aristotle, *Prior Analytics*, ed. and trans. by R. Smith (Indianapolis, IN: Hackett Publishing Co., 1989)

Arnold, M., *Culture and Anarchy: An Essay in Political and Social Criticism* (Cambridge, UK: Cambridge University Press, 1869)

Astbury, W., 'Molecular Biology or Ultrastructural Biology?', *Nature*, 190 (1960), 1124, https://doi.org/10.1038/1901124a0

Audit Commission, *Setting the Records Straight: A Study of Hospital Medical Records* (London: HMSO, 1995)

Avery, J. S., *Information Theory and Evolution*, 2nd ed. (Singapore: World Scientific Publishing, 2012)

Axelrod, R. M, *The Evolution of Cooperation* (London: Penguin Books, 1990)

Bacon, F., *Advancement of Learning*, ed. J. Devey (New York: P. F. Collier, 1901)

Bailey, N., *Dictionarium Britannicum* (London: T. Cox, 1730)

Barber, B., R. D. Cohen and M. Scholes, 'A Review of the London Hospital Computer Project', *Medical Informatics*, 1.1 (1976), 61–72

Barnes, J., *A History of the World in 10½ Chapters* (New York: Knopf, 1989)

Batley, S., *Classification in Theory and Practice* (Oxford: Chandos Publishing, 2014)

Becker, A., *What Is Real?: The Unfinished Quest for the Meaning of Quantum Physics* (London: John Murray, 2018)

Beckman, M., *Math Without Numbers* (New York: Penguin Books, 2022)

Benenson, P., 'The Forgotten Prisoners', *Observer* (28 May 1961)

Berlin, I., *The Hedgehog and the Fox* (London: Weidenfeld and Nicolson, 1953)

Bertalanffy, L. von, *General System Theory: Foundations, Development* (New York: George Braziller, 1968)

Black, D., 'The Aims of a Health Service', *The Lancet*, 319.8278 (1982), 952–54, https://doi.org/10.1016/S0140-6736(82)91945-6

— 'Data for Management: The Körner Report', *BMJ* (*Clin Res Ed*), 285 (1982), 1227–28, https://doi.org/10.1136/bmj.285.6350.1227

Blackburn, S., *The Oxford Dictionary of Philosophy*, 2nd ed. (Oxford: Oxford University Press)

Bochaberi, S., V. Rathod and C. Fourie, 'Digital Square Announces New Software Global Goods Approved through Notice G', *Digital Square* (16 February 2023), https://digitalsquare.org/blog/2023/2/16/digital-square-announces-new-software-global-goods-approved-through-notice-g

Brooks, D., 'Opinion | The Philosophy of Data', *New York Times* (4 February 2013), https://www.nytimes.com/2013/02/05/opinion/brooks-the-philosophy-of-data.html

Brooks Jr., F. P., *The Mythical Man-Month: Essays on Software Engineering* (New Delhi: Pearson Education, 1995)

Buchanan, B. G., and E. A. Feigenbaum, 'DENDRAL and Meta-DENDRAL: Their Applications Dimension', *Artificial Intelligence*, 11.1–2 (1978), 5–24

Buchanan, B. G., G. Sutherland and E. A. Feigenbaum, *Heuristic DENDRAL: A Program for Generating Explanatory Hypotheses in Organic Chemistry* (Stanford, CA: Stanford University Department of Computer Science, 1968)

Burke, E., *The Works of the Right Honorable Edmund Burke*, vol. I (New York: Little, Brown, 1877)

Burns, F., *Information for Health: An Information Strategy for the Modern NHS 1998–2005* (London: NHS Executive, 1998)

Campbell, E. J. M., 'The Diagnosing Mind', *The Lancet*, 329.8537 (1987), 849–51, https://doi.org/10.1016/S0140-6736(87)91620-5

Campbell, E. J. M., C. J. Dickinson and J. D. H. Slater, ed., *Clinical Physiology* (Oxford: Blackwell Scientific, 1961)

Campbell, E. J. M., J. G. Scadding and R. S. Roberts, 'The Concept of Disease', *BMJ*, 2.6193 (1979), 757–62

'Celebrating G. Octo Barnett, MD', *Journal of the American Medical Informatics Association*, 27.8 (2020), 1187–89, https://doi.org/10.1093/jamia/ocaa170

Chatwin, B., *The Songlines* (New York: Random House, 2012)

Chown, M., *Infinity in the Palm of Your Hand: Fifty Wonders That Reveal an Extraordinary Universe* (London: Michael O'Mara Books, 2018)

Christensen, C., M. E. Raynor and R. McDonald, *Disruptive Innovation* (Boston, MA: Harvard Business Review, 2013)

Cimino, J. J., 'Desiderata for Controlled Medical Vocabularies in the Twenty-First Century', *Methods of Information in Medicine*, 37.4–5 (1998), 394–403, https://doi.org/10.1055/s-0038-1634558

Cimino, J. J., and X. Zhu, 'The Practical Impact of Ontologies on Biomedical Informatics', *Yearbook of Medical Informatics*, 15.01 (2006), 124–35, https://doi.org/10.1055/s-0038-1638470

Cobb, M., *The Idea of the Brain: The Past and Future of Neuroscience* (New York: Basic Books, 2020)

Coleridge, S. T., *Lay Sermons* (London: Edward Moxon, 1852)

Congress of the United States Office of Technology Assessment, *Coastal Effects of Offshore Energy Systems* (Washington, DC: Congress of the United States Office of Technology Assessment, 1976)

—, *Computer Technology in Medical Education and Assessment* (Washington, DC: Congress of the United States Office of Technology Assessment, 1979), https://www.princeton.edu/~ota/disk3/1979/7903/7903.PDF

—, *Policy Implications of Medical Information Systems* (Washington, DC: Congress of the United States Office of Technology Assessment, 1977), https://www.princeton.edu/~ota/disk3/1977/7708/7708.PDF

Conyngton, T., 'Motor Carriages and Street Paving', *Scientific American Supplement*, 48 (1899), 196660

Cooper, J., 'Healthcare Expenditure, UK Health Accounts Provisional Estimates: 2020', *ONS* (1 June 2021), https://www.ons.gov.uk/

peoplepopulationandcommunity/healthandsocialcare/healthcaresystem/
bulletins/healthcareexpenditureukhealthaccountsprovisionalestimates/2020

Côté, R. A., and S. Robboy, 'Progress in Medical Information Management. Systematized Nomenclature of Medicine (SNOMED)', *JAMA: The Journal of the American Medical Association*, 243.8 (1980), 756–62, https://doi.org/10.1001/jama.243.8.756

Dacre, J., M. Nicol, D. Holroyd and D. Ingram, 'The Development of a Clinical Skills Centre', *Journal of the Royal College of Physicians of London*, 30.4 (1996), 318

Darwin, C., *On the Origin of Species by Means of Natural Selection, or, The Preservation of Favoured Races in the Struggle for Life* (London: John Murray, 1860)

Date, C. J., *An Introduction to Database Systems* (Delhi: Pearson Education India, 1975)

David, R., 'New Vaccine Promise', *Nature Reviews Microbiology*, 11.5 (2013), 298, https://doi.org/10.1038/nrmicro3019

Davies, P., *The Demon in the Machine: How Hidden Webs of Information Are Solving the Mystery of Life* (Chicago, IL: University of Chicago Press, 2021)

Davies, N., *Europe: A History* (Oxford: Oxford University Press, 1996)

—, *Heart of Europe: A Short History of Poland* (Oxford: Oxford University Press, 1984)

Davy, H., 'Progress of the Arts and Sciences', *The Saturday Magazine*, 416 (1838), 246–47

Dawkins, R., *The God Delusion* (Boston, MA: Houghton Mifflin Company, 2006)

—, *The Selfish Gene* (Oxford: Oxford University Press, 1976)

De Rougemont, D., *Penser avec les Mains* (Paris: A. Michel, 1936)

Department of Health, *A First Class Service: Quality in the New NHS* (London: The Stationery Office, 1998)

—, *Delivering 21st Century IT Support for the NHS: National Specification for Integrated Care Records Service* (London: Department of Health, 2002)

—, *New NHS: Modern, Dependable* (London: The Stationery Office, 1997)

—, *Our Healthier Nation: A Contract for Health* (London: The Stationery Office, 1998)

Dewey, J., *The School and Society and the Child and the Curriculum* (Chicago, IL: University of Chicago Press, 2013)

Dickens, C., *A Tale of Two Cities* (London: Chapman and Hall, 1868)

Dickinson, C. J., D. Ingram and K. Ahmed, 'The Mac Family of Physiological Models', *Alternatives to Laboratory Animals*, 13.2 (1985), 107–16, https://doi.org/10.1177/026119298501300204

Dobbs, M., *House of Cards* (London: Harper Collins, 1990)

Drake, N., 'Alien Hunters Detect Mysterious Radio Signal from Nearby Star', *National Geographic* (18 December 2020), https://www.nationalgeographic.com/science/article/alien-hunters-detect-mysterious-radio-signal-from-nearby-star

Du Sautoy, M., *The Creativity Code: How AI Is Learning to Write, Paint and Think* (Cambridge, MA: Harvard University Press, 2019)

—, *What We Cannot Know: Explorations at the Edge of Knowledge* (London: Fourth Estate, 2016)

Duignan, B., 'Willard Van Orman Quine', *Encyclopedia Britannia* (21 June 2023), https://www.britannica.com/biography/Willard-Van-Orman-Quine

Eccles, J., and W. Gibson, *Sherrington: His Life and Thought* (Berlin: Springer International)

Eco, U., *The Name of the Rose* (London: Pan Books, 1984)

Einstein, A., *The Einstein Reader* (New York: Citadel, 2006)

—, *Ideas and Opinions* (New York: Crown Publishers, 1954)

Eliot, T. S., *Little Gidding* (London: Faber and Faber, 1943)

Ernst, B., *The Magic Mirror of M. C. Escher*, trans. J. E. Brigham (New York: Barnes and Noble, 1994)

Errington, T. M., A. Denis, N. Perfito, E. Iorns and B. A. Nosek, 'Reproducibility in Cancer Biology: Challenges for Assessing Replicability in Preclinical Cancer Biology', *Elife*, 10 (2021), e67995, https://doi.org/10.7554/elife.67995

Eve, A. S., *Rutherford–Being the Life and Letters of the Rt. Hon. Lord Rutherford* (Cambridge, UK: Macmillan, 1939)

Fairey, M., *A National Strategic Framework for Information Management in Hospital and Community Health Services* (London: DHSS, 1986)

Fennell, L. A., 'Ostrom's Law: Property Rights in the Commons' (John M. Olin Program in Law and Economics Working Paper No. 584, 2011), https://chicagounbound.uchicago.edu/cgi/viewcontent.cgi?article=1356&context=law_and_economics

Fermi, L., *Atoms in the Family: My Life with Enrico Fermi* (Chicago, IL: University of Chicago Press, 2014)

Feynman, R. P., *Feynman Lectures on Computation* (New York: CRC Press, 2018)

—, *What Do You Care What Other People Think?* (New York: Bantam, 1989)

Feynman, R. P., R. B. Leighton and M. Sands, *The Feynman Lectures on Physics* (Beijing: Beijing World Publishing Corporation, 2004)

Fisher, R., and W. Ury, *Getting to Yes: Negotiating Agreement without Giving In*, 2nd ed. (New York: Penguin Books, 1991)

Forster, E. M., *Howards End* (London: Edward Arnold, 1910)

Fortescue, M., 'The Colours of the Arctic', *AMERINDIA*, 38 (2016), 25–46

Foskett, D. J., 'The Dewey Decimal System', *Britannica*, https://www.britannica.com/topic/library/The-Dewey-Decimal-system

Friedman, T. L., *The World Is Flat: A Brief History of the Twenty-First Century* (New York: Picador/Farrar, Straus and Giroux, 2007)

Fukuyama, F., *The End of History and the Last Man* (London: H. Hamilton, 1992)

Gawande, A., *Better: A Surgeon's Notes on Performance* (New York: Metropolitan Books, 2007)

Gebreyes, K., A. Davis, S. Davis and M. Shukla, 'Breaking the Cost Curve', *Deloitte Insights* (9 February 2021), https://www2.deloitte.com/xe/en/insights/industry/health-care/future-health-care-spending.html

Gershenfeld, N., 'Bits and Chips', *New Scientist*, 169 (2001), 55

General Medical Council, *Tomorrow's Doctors: Recommendations on Undergraduate Medical Education* (London: GMC, 1993)

Gibbon, E., *The History of the Decline and Fall of the Roman Empire* (London: Strahan and Cadell, 1788)

Goodhart, D., *Head Hand Heart: The Struggle for Dignity and Status in the 21st Century* (London: Penguin Books, 2020)

Goodstein, D. L., and J. R. Goodstein, ed., *Feynman's Lost Lecture: The Motion of Planets around the Sun* (New York: W. W. Norton and Company, 1996)

Gould, S. J., and N. Eldredge, 'Punctuated Equilibrium Comes of Age', *Nature*, 366.6452 (1993), 223–27, https://doi.org/10.1038/366223a0

Graeber, D., *The Utopia of Rules: On Technology, Stupidity, and the Secret Joys of Bureaucracy* (New York: Melville House, 2015)

Guyton, A. C., T. G. Coleman and H. J. Granger, 'Circulation: Overall Regulation', *Annual Review of Physiology*, 34.1 (1972), 13–44, https://doi.org/10.1146/annurev.ph.34.030172.000305

Guyton, A. C., C. E. Jones and T. G. Coleman, *Circulatory Physiology: Cardiac Output and Its Regulation* (Philadelphia, PA: Saunders, 1973)

Hambrick, D. C., and A. A. Cannella Jr., 'Strategy Implementation as Substance and Selling', *Academy of Management Perspectives*, 3.4 (1989), 278–85

Harari, Y. N., *Homo Deus: A Brief History of Tomorrow* (London: Random House, 2016)

Haskell, D. G., *The Songs of Trees: Stories from Nature's Great Connectors* (London: Penguin Books, 2018)

Hawking, S., *A Brief History of Time: From Big Bang to Black Holes* (London: Random House, 2009)

Healthcare Facilities Today, 'Healthcare Information Technology Market to Reach $441 Billion by 2025', *Healthcare Facilities Today* (26 April 2019), https://www.healthcarefacilitiestoday.com/posts/Healthcare-information-technology-market-to-reach-441-billion-by-2025--21259

Helman, C., *Culture, Health and Illness*, 4th ed. (Oxford: Butterworth/Heinemann, 2000)

HIMSS, '2022: Future of Healthcare Report' (2022), https://pages.himss.org/rs/420-YNA-292/images/PDF-FOH%20Report-2022-08.pdf

Hinds, C. J., and C. J. Dickinson, 'The Potential of Computer Modelling Techniques in Intensive Care Medicine', in *Computing in Anesthesia and Intensive Care*, ed. by O. Prakash, Developments in Critical Care Medicine and Anesthesiology (Dordrecht: Springer Netherlands, 1983), pp. 153–69, https://doi.org/10.1007/978-94-009-6747-2_13

Hinds, C. J., D. Ingram, L. Adams, P. V. Cole, C. J. Dickinson, J. Kay, J. R. Krapez and J. Williams, 'An Evaluation of the Clinical Potential of a Comprehensive Model of Human Respiration in Artificially Ventilated Patients', *Clinical Science*, 58.1 (1980), 83–91, https://doi.org/10.1042/cs0580083

Hinds, C. J., D. Ingram and C. J. Dickinson, 'Self-Instruction and Assessment in Techniques of Intensive Care Using a Computer Model of the Respiratory System', *Intensive Care Medicine*, 8.3 (1982), 115–23, https://doi.org/10.1007/BF01693430

Hinds, C. J., M. J. Roberts, D. Ingram and C. J. Dickinson, 'Computer Simulation to Predict Patient Responses to Alterations in the Ventilation Regime', *Intensive Care Medicine*, 10.1 (1984), 13–22, https://doi.org/10.1007/BF00258063

Hill, C., *The World Turned Upside Down: Radical Ideas During the English Revolution* (New York: Viking Press, 1972)

Hoffer, E. P., G. O. Barnett, B. B. Farquhar and P. A. Prather, 'Computer-Aided Instruction in Medicine', *Annual Review of Biophysics and Bioengineering*, 4.1 (1975), 103–18

Hoffer, E. P., M. J. Feldman, R. J. Kim, K. T. Famiglietti and G. O. Barnett, 'DXplain: Patterns of Use of a Mature Expert System', *AMIA Annual Symposium Proceedings* (2005), 321–24

Hofstadter, D. R., *Gödel, Escher, Bach: An Eternal Golden Braid* (New York: Basic Books 1979)

—, *I Am a Strange Loop* (New York: Basic Books, 2007)

Hogben, L. T., *The Loom of Language* (New York: W. W. Norton and Company, 1944)

—, *Man Must Measure: The Wonderful World of Mathematics* (London: Rathbone Books, 1955)

—, *Mathematics for the Million: A Popular Self Educator*, 2nd ed. (London: Allen and Unwin, 1937)

—, *Science for the Citizen* (London: George Allen and Unwin, 1938)

Hudson, M., *A History of the Government Operational Research Service 1968–1980* (n.p.: GORS, 2018), http://www.operational-research.gov.uk/public_docs/history-of-gors.pdf

Hutchins, W. J., ed., *Early Years in Machine Translation: Memoirs and Biographies of Pioneers* (Amsterdam: John Benjamins Publishing, 2000)

Huxley, A., *Brave New World* (n.p.: DigiCat, 2022)

Illich, I., *Deschooling Society* (London: Calder and Boyars, 1971)

—, *Limits to Medicine: Medical Nemesis: The Expropriation of Health* (London: Boyars, 1995)

Ingram, D., and S. S. Arikan, 'The Evolving Role of Open Source Software in Medicine and Health Services', *Technology Innovation Management Review*, 3.1 (2013), 32–39, https://timreview.ca/sites/default/files/article_PDF/IngramArikan_TIMReview_January2013.pdf

Ingram, D., and R. F. Bloch, ed., *Mathematical Methods in Medicine, Part I: Statistical and Analytic Technique* (Chichester, NY: John Wiley and Sons, 1984)

—, *Mathematical Methods in Medicine, Part II: Applications in Clinical Specialities* (Chichester, NY: John Wiley and Sons, 1986)

Ingram, D., R. V. H. Jones, I. Finlay and A. Lant, 'An Interactive Videodisc "Cancer Patients and Their Families at Home", Designed for Education in Primary Health Care', *Journal of Audiovisual Media in Medicine*, 15.2 (1992), 73–76

Institute of Medicine, *Computer-Based Patient Record: An Essential Technology for Health Care* (Washington, DC: The National Academies Press, 1991)

Institute of Medicine, *Crossing the Quality Chasm: A New Health System for the 21st Century* (Washington, DC: The National Academies Press, 2001)

'International Classification of Diseases (ICD)', *World Health Organization*, https://www.who.int/classifications/icd/en/

'International Classification of Primary Care, 2nd edition (ICPC-2)', *World Health Organization*, https://www.who.int/standards/classifications/other-classifications/international-classification-of-primary-care

Ireland, B., 'Millions of Hours of Doctors' Time Lost Each Year to "Inadequate" IT Systems', *BMA* (5 December 2022), https://www.bma.org.uk/news-and-opinion/millions-of-hours-of-doctors-time-lost-each-year-to-inadequate-it-systems

Ishiguro, K., *Klara and the Sun* (New York: Knopf, 2021)

Jahanbegloo, R., *Conversations with Isaiah Berlin* (London: Peter Halban, 1992)

Johnson, R., *School of Computer Science and Information Systems: A Short History* (London: Birkbeck, University of London, 2008), https://www.dcs.bbk.ac.uk/site/assets/files/1029/50yearsofcomputing.pdf

Justinia, T., 'The UK's National Programme for IT: Why Was It Dismantled?', *Health Services Management Research*, 30.1 (2017), 2–9

Kahneman, D., *Thinking, Fast and Slow* (New York: Macmillan, 2011)

Kahneman, D., O. Sibony and C. R. Sunstein, *Noise: A Flaw in Human Judgment* (New York: Little, Brown Spark, 2021)

Kawamura, K., *BSO–Broad System of Ordering: An International Bibliography* (Koshigaya: K. Kawamura, 2011), https://repository.arizona.edu/handle/10150/129413

—, 'In Memoriam: Eric Coates, 1916–2017', *Knowledge Organization*, 45.2 (2018), 97–102, https://doi.org/10.5771/0943-7444-2018-2-97

Khayyam, O., *The Rubaiyat of Omar Khayyam*, trans. E. Fitzgerald (London: George G. Harrap & Co. Ltd, 1928)

King, M., *The End of Alchemy: Money, Banking and the Future of the Global Economy* (New York: W. W. Norton and Company, 2016)

King's Fund, The, 'Time to Think Differently' (2012–13), https://www.kingsfund.org.uk/projects/time-think-differently

Knuth, D. E., *The Art of Computer Programming, Volume 1: Fundamental Algorithms*, 3rd ed. (Reading, MA: Addison-Wesley Professional, 1997)

Kuhn, T. S., *The Structure of Scientific Revolutions: 50th Anniversary Edition* (Chicago, IL: University of Chicago Press, 2012)

Kurzweil, R., *How to Create a Mind: The Secret of Human Thought Revealed* (New York: Viking Books, 2012)

—, *The Singularity Is Near: When Humans Transcend Biology* (New York: Viking Books, 2005)

Lane, N., *The Vital Question: Energy, Evolution, and the Origins of Complex Life* (New York: W. W. Norton and Company, 2015)

Lane Fox, R., *The Invention of Medicine: From Homer to Hippocrates* (London: Penguin Books, 2020)

Lawrence, T. E., *Seven Pillars of Wisdom* (Chatham: Wordsworth Editions Limited, 1997)

Leatherman, S., and K. Sutherland, *The Quest for Quality in the NHS: A Mid-term Evaluation of the Ten-year Quality Agenda* (London: The Stationery Office, 2003)

Lee, L., *Cider with Rosie* (London: Penguin Books, 1959)

—, *Down in the Valley: A Writer's Landscape* (London: Penguin Books, 2019)

Leibig, C., M. Brehmer, S. Bunk, D. Byng, K. Pinker and L. Umutlu, 'Combining the Strengths of Radiologists and AI for Breast Cancer Screening: A Retrospective Analysis', *The Lancet Digital Health*, 4.7 (2022), e507–19

Leonardo da Vinci, *Notebooks*, comp. I. Richter (Oxford: Oxford University Press, 2008)

Levi, P., *Other People's Trades* (London: Sphere Books, 1990)

Lindsay, R. K., B. G. Buchanan, E. A. Feigenbaum and J. Lederberg, 'DENDRAL: A Case Study of the First Expert System for Scientific Hypothesis Formation', *Artificial Intelligence*, 61.2 (1993), 209–61

Lovelock, J., *The Ages of Gaia: A Biography of Our Living Earth* (Oxford: Oxford University Press, 2000)

—, *Novacene: The Coming Age of Hyperintelligence* (Cambridge, MA: MIT Press, 2019)

Lu, Z., D. Mandal and C. Jarzynski, 'Engineering Maxwell's Demon', *Physics Today*, 67.8 (2014), 60–61

Lyth, P. J., 'American Aerospace Dominance and the British Challenge in Jet Engines', in *Tackling Transport: Volume 3*, ed. by H. Trischler and S. Zeilinger (London: NMSI), pp. 81–98

MacAskill, W., *What We Owe the Future* (New York: Basic Books, 2022)

Maddox, J., *What Remains to Be Discovered: Mapping the Secrets of the Universe, the Origins of Life, and the Future of the Human Race* (New York: Macmillan, 1998)

Marmot, M., *Fair Society, Healthy Lives: The Marmot Review: Strategic Review of Health Inequalities in England Post-2010* (London: Marmot Review, 2010)

—, 'Health Equity in England: The Marmot Review 10 Years On', *BMJ*, 368 (2020), m693, https://doi.org/10.1136/bmj.m693

Mazzucato, M., *The Entrepreneurial State: Debunking Public vs. Private Myths in Innovation*, rev. ed. (London: Anthem Press, 2014)

Mazzucato, M., and R. Collington, *The Big Con: How the Consulting Industry Weakens Our Businesses, Infantilizes Our Governments and Warps Our Economies* (London: Allen Lane, 2023)

Mazzucato, M., and R. Collington, 'Trillion-dollar Con Trick: Advice that Makes Things Worse', *The Times* (10 February 2023), https://www.thetimes.co.uk/article/ trillion-dollar-con-trick-advice-that-makes-things-worse-pgrs5jc5j

McEwan, I., *Machines like Me* (Toronto: Knopf Canada, 2019)

McGuinness, T. D., and H. Schank, *Power to the Public: The Promise of Public Interest Technology* (Princeton, NJ: Princeton University Press, 2021)

McIntyre, N., *How British Women Became Doctors: The Story of the Royal Free Hospital and Its Medical School* (London: Wenrowave Press, 2014)

Mearian, L., 'Study: Digital Universe and Its Impact Bigger than We Thought', *Computerworld* (11 March 2008), https://www.computerworld.com/ article/2537648/study--digital-universe-and-its-impact-bigger-than-we-thought.html

'Medical Subject Headings', *National Library of Medicine*, https://www.nlm.nih.gov/mesh

Middleton, B., D. F. Sittig and A. Wright, 'Clinical Decision Support: A 25 Year Retrospective and a 25 Year Vision', *Yearbook of Medical Informatics*, 25.S 01 (2016), S103–16

Milan, J., C. E. Munt and M. W. Dawson, 'A Model Based Approach to the Evolutionary Development of a High Performance Hospital Information System', in *Medical Informatics Europe '90*, ed. by R. O'Moore, S. Bengtsson, J. R. Bryant and J. S. Bryden, Lecture Notes in Medical Informatics (Berlin: Springer-Verlag, 1990), pp. 457–61

Miller, R. A., 'INTERNIST-1/CADUCEUS: Problems Facing Expert Consultant Programs', *Methods of Information in Medicine*, 23.01 (1984), 9–14

Minford, J. trans., *Sun Tzu: The Art of War* (London: Penguin Books, 2002)

Monod, J., *Chance and Necessity: An Essay on the Natural Philosophy of Modern Biology* (New York: Knopf, 1971)

Muggleton, S., 'Obituary: Donald Michie', *The Guardian* (10 July 2007), http://www.theguardian.com/science/2007/jul/10/uk.obituaries1

Musen, M. A., B. Middleton and R. A. Greenes, 'Clinical Decision-Support Systems', in *Biomedical Informatics*, ed. by E. H. Shortliffe and J. J. Cimino (Cham: Springer Nature, 2021), pp. 795–840

Nayler, R., 'Parliaments of the Future', *New Scientist*, 257.3427 (2023), 27

Naylor, C., 'The Case for Public Service Reform', *BBC Radio 4* (6 March 2022), https://www.bbc.co.uk/programmes/m0014x7v

NHS Executive, *Priorities and Planning: Guidance for the NHS 1996/97* (Leeds: HMSO, 1996)

NHS Executive, *Seeing the Wood, Sparing the Trees. Efficiency Scrutiny into the Burdens of Paperwork in NHS Trusts and Health Authorities* (London: HMSO, 1996)

Nicholson, L., 'Setting the Records Straight: A Study of Hospital Medical Records Undertaken by the Audit Commission', *Records Management Journal*, 6.1 (1996), 13–32 https://doi.org/10.1108/eb027083

Nightingale, F., *Notes on Hospitals*, 3rd ed. (London: Longman, Roberts and Green, 1963)

Nuffield Provincial Hospitals Trust, *The Flow of Medical Information in Hospitals* (London: Oxford University Press, 1967)

Obama, B., *The Audacity of Hope: Thoughts on Reclaiming the American Dream* (New York: Crown Publishers, 2006)

Obama, M., *The Light We Carry: Overcoming in Uncertain Times* (London: Penguin Books, 2022)

Oppenheimer, J. R., *Science and the Common Understanding* (Oxford: Oxford University Press, 1954)

Orwell, G., *Nineteen Eighty-Four* (London: Hachette, 2021)

Oxford English Dictionary, The Compact Edition (London: Book Club Associates by Arrangement with Oxford University Press, 1979)

Penrose, L. S., 'The Elementary Statistics of Majority Voting', *Journal of the Royal Statistical Society*, 109.1 (1946), 53–57

Perutz, M. F., *I Wish I'd Made You Angry Earlier: Essays on Science, Scientists, and Humanity* (Oxford: Oxford University Press, 2002)

Piketty, T., *A Brief History of Equality* (Cambridge, MA: Harvard University Press, 2022)

Pinker, S., *The Better Angels of Our Nature: The Decline of Violence in History and Its Causes* (London: Penguin Books, 2011)

Pirsig, R. M., *Zen and the Art of Motorcycle Maintenance: An Inquiry into Values* (London: Bodley Head, 1974)

Popper, K., *The Open Society and Its Enemies* (Abingdon: Routledge, 2012)

—, *The Open Society and Its Enemies: The Spell of Plato* (London: Routledge and Kegan Paul, 1957)

—, *The Open Universe: An Argument for Indeterminism from the Postscript to the Logic of Scientific Discovery*, ed. by W. W. Bartley III (Abingdon: Routledge, 2012)

Poskett, J., *Horizons: A Global History of Science* (London: Penguin Books, 2022)

Pray, L. A., 'Discovery of DNA Structure and Function: Watson and Crick', *Nature Education*, 1.1 (2008), 100, https://www.nature.com/scitable/topicpage/discovery-of-dna-structure-and-function-watson-397/

Protti, D., *World View Reports* (London: NHS CFH Press, 2005)

Pullman, P., *His Dark Materials Trilogy* (London: Scholastic, 1997)

Putnam, R. D., *The Upswing: How America Came Together a Century Ago and How We Can Do It Again* (New York: Simon and Schuster, 2020)

Raleigh, W., *The Works of Sir Walter Raleigh* (New York: Burt Franklin, 1966)

Ranganathan, S. R., *Colon Classification*, 6th ed. (Bangalore: Sarada Ranganathan Endowment, 1989)

—, 'Colon Classification Edition 7 (1971): A Preview', *Library Science with a Slant to Documentation*, 6 (1969), 204–05

—, *The Five Laws of Library Science* (Bangalore: Sarada Ranganathan Endowment, 1989) https://repository.arizona.edu/handle/10150/105454

—, *Philosophy of Library Classification* (Bangalore: Sarada Ranganathan Endowment, 1989), https://repository.arizona.edu/handle/10150/105278

Rector, A., S. Schulz, J. M. Rodrigues, C. G. Chute and H. Solbrig, 'On Beyond Gruber: "Ontologies" in Today's Biomedical Information Systems and the Limits of OWL', *Journal of Biomedical Informatics*: X, 2 (2019), 100002, https://doi.org/10.1016/j.yjbinx.2019.100002

Rees, M., *On the Future: Prospects for Humanity* (Princeton, NJ: Princeton University Press, 2018)

Riedel, S., 'Edward Jenner and the History of Smallpox and Vaccination', *Proc (Bayl Univ Med Cent)*, 18.2 (2005), 21–25, https://www.ncbi.nlm.nih.gov/pmc/articles/PMC1200696/

Rittel, H. W. J., and M. M. Webber, 'Dilemmas in a General Theory of Planning', *Policy Sciences*, 4.2 (1973), 155–69, https://www.jstor.org/stable/4531523

Roberts, M., 'Machine Churning', *New Scientist*, 250.3335 (2021), 23, https://doi.org/10.1016/S0262-4079(21)00873-3

Roberts, M., et al., 'Common Pitfalls and Recommendations for Using Machine Learning to Detect and Prognosticate for COVID-19 Using Chest Radiographs and CT Scans', *Nature Machine Intelligence*, 3.3 (2021), 199–217

Rosleff, F., *European Healthcare Trends: Towards Managed Care in Europe* (London: Coopers and Lybrand, 1995)

Rosse, C., and J. L. V. Mejino Jr., 'A Reference Ontology for Biomedical Informatics: The Foundational Model of Anatomy', *Journal of Biomedical Informatics*, 36.6 (2003), 478–500, https://doi.org/10.1016/j.jbi.2003.11.007

Russell, B., *Authority and the Individual: The Reith Lectures for 1948–9* (London: Allen and Unwin, 1949)

—, *An Inquiry into Meaning and Truth* (New York: Routledge, 2013)

—, *History of Western Philosophy: Collectors Edition* (New York: Routledge, 2013)

—, *My Philosophical Development* (London: George Allen and Unwin, 1959)

—, *The Problems of Philosophy* (Oxford: Oxford University Press, 1912)

Sandel, M. J., *The Tyranny of Merit: What's Become of the Common Good?* (London: Penguin Books, 2020)

—, *What Money Can't Buy: The Moral Limits of Markets* (New York: Farrar, Straus and Giroux)

Saunders, L., D. Ingram and S. H. D. Jackson, *Human Drug Kinetics: A Course of Simulated Experiments* (Oxford: Oxford University Press, 1989)

Saunders, L., D. Ingram and S. J. Warrington, 'The Pharmacokinetics and Dynamics of Oxprenolol: A Simulation Study with Six Subjects', *Journal of Pharmacy and Pharmacology*, 37.11 (1985), 802–06

Saunders, L., D. Ingram, C. J. Dickinson and M. Sherriff, 'A Comprehensive Computer Simulation of Drug Metabolism and Pharmacokinetics', *Computers & Education*, 6.2 (1982), 243–52

Schopenhauer, A., *Parerga and Paralipomena: A Collection of Philosophical Essays* (New York: Cosimo, 2007)

Schrödinger, E., *What Is Life?* (Cambridge, UK: Cambridge University Press, 1948)

Schumacher, E. F., *Small Is Beautiful: A Study of Economics as if People Mattered* (London: Abacus, 1973)

Secretary of State for Health, *The Health of the Nation: A Consultative Document for Health in England* (London: HMSO, 1991)

Sellar, W. C., and R. J. Yeatman, *1066 and All That. A Memorable History of England Comprising, All the Parts You Can Remember Including One Hundred and One Good Things, Five Bad Kings, and Two Genuine Dates* (London: Methuen, 1930)

Shannon, C. E., 'A Mathematical Theory of Communication', *The Bell System Technical Journal*, 27.3 (1948), 379–423

Shannon, C. E., and W. Weaver, *The Mathematical Theory of Communication* (Urbana, IL: University of Illinois Press, 1949)

Shaw, G. B., *Pygmalion and Major Barbara* (New York: Bantam Classics, 2008)

Shirres, D., 'Digital Delusion: A Lesson from Not-so-long Ago', *Rail Engineer* (3 September 2018), https://www.railengineer.co.uk/digital-delusion-a-lesson-from-not-so-long-ago

Shortliffe, E., *Computer-Based Medical Consultations: MYCIN* (New York: Elsevier, 2012)

Simard, S., *Finding the Mother Tree: Uncovering the Wisdom and Intelligence of the Forest* (London: Penguin Books, 2021)

Simard, S., D. Perry, M. Jones, D. Myrold, D. Durall and R. Molina, 'Net Transfer of Carbon between Ectomycorrhizal Tree Species in the Field', *Nature*, 388 (1997), 579–82, https://doi.org/10.1038/41557

Sinclair, D. A., *Lifespan: Why We Age–and Why We Don't Have To* (London: Harper Collins, 2019)

Skinner, J. B., G. Knowles, R. F. Armstrong and D. Ingram, 'The Use of Computerized Learning in Intensive Care: An Evaluation of a New Teaching Program', *Medical Education*, 17.1 (1983), 49–53

Smiles, S., *Men of Invention and Industry* (London: Read Books, 2013)

Smith, A. F. M., 'Change-Point Problems: Approaches and Applications', *Trabajos de Estadistica Y de Investigacion Operativa*, 31.1 (1980), 83, https://doi.org/10.1007/BF02888348

Smith, R., 'The Future of Healthcare Systems', *BMJ*, 24.314 (1997), 1495–96, https://doi.org/10.1136/bmj.314.7093

Smith, S., *Spiceland Quaker Training Centre, 1940–46: Cups without Saucers* (York: W. Sessions, 1990)

Snow, C. P., *The Two Cultures and the Scientific Revolution* (Cambridge, UK: Cambridge University Press, 1959)

STEP Consortium, *Seeding the EuroPhysiome: A Roadmap to the Virtual Physiological Human* (n.p.: STEP Consortium, 2007), https://www.vph-institute.org/upload/step-vph-roadmap-printed-3_5192459539f3c.pdf

Stevenson, A., and M. Waite, ed., *Concise Oxford English Dictionary* (Oxford: Oxford University Press, 2011)

Stewart, I., *Life's Other Secret: The New Mathematics of the Living World* (New York: John Wiley and Sons, 1998)

Stroetmann, V., J.-P. Thierry, K. Stroetmann and A. Dobrev, *eHealth for Safety: Impact of ICT on Patient Safety and Risk Management* (Luxembourg: Office for Official Publications of the European Communications, 2007)

Sullivan, T., 'Why EHR Data Interoperability Is Such a Mess in 3 Charts', *Healthcare IT News* (16 May 2018), https://www.healthcareitnews.com/news/why-ehr-data-interoperability-such-mess-3-charts

Sunstein, C. R., *Infotopia: How Many Minds Produce Knowledge* (Oxford Oxford University Press, 2006)

Susskind, R. E., and D. Susskind, *The Future of the Professions: How Technology Will Transform the Work of Human Experts* (Oxford: Oxford University Press, 2015)

Sutherland, G., *Heuristic DENDRAL: A Family of LISP Programs* (Stanford, CA: Stanford University Department of Computer Science, 1969)

Sutton, D. R., and J. Fox, 'The Syntax and Semantics of the PRO Forma Guideline Modeling Language', *Journal of the American Medical Informatics Association*, 10.5 (2003), 433–43

Syed, M., 'Piers Morgan's Idiotic rants Reduce Subtle Arguments to Soundbites', *The Times* (24 January 2021), https://www.thetimes.co.uk/article/piers-morgans-idiotic-rants-reduce-subtle-arguments-to-soundbites-d2zpchbjv

Taleb, N. N., *Antifragile: How to Live in a World We Don't Understand* (London: Allen Lane, 2012)

—, *The Black Swan: The Impact of the Highly Improbable* (New York: Random House, 2007)

Tett, G., *Anthro-Vision: A New Way to See in Business and Life* (New York: Simon and Schuster, 2021)

Times Health Commission, 'Rising Levels of Ill Health Costing Economy £150bn a Year', *The Times* (16 January 2023), https://www.thetimes.co.uk/article/rising-levels-of-ill-health-costing-economy-150bn-a-year-x5dkcn5jg

Topol, E., *Deep Medicine: How Artificial Intelligence Can Make Healthcare Human Again* (London: Hachette, 2019)

—, *The Topol Review: Preparing the Healthcare Workforce to Deliver the Digital Future* (London: National Health Service, 2019), https://topol.hee.nhs.uk/wp-content/uploads/HEE-Topol-Review-2019.pdf

Tribus, M., and E. C. McIrvine, 'Energy and Information', *Scientific American*, 225.3 (1971), 179–88

Trimble, I. M., M. West, M. S. Knapp, R. Pownall and A. F. Smith, 'Detection of Renal Allograft Rejection by Computer', *BMJ*, 286.6379 (1983), 1695–99 https://doi.org/10.1136/bmj.286.6379.1695

Ulam, S., 'John von Neumann 1903–1957', *Bull. Math. Soc.*, 64.3 (1958), 1–49, https://www.ams.org/journals/bull/1958-64-03/S0002-9904-1958-10189-5/S0002-9904-1958-10189-5.pdf

'Unified Medical Language System', *National Library of Medicine*, https://www.nlm.nih.gov/research/umls/index.html

Universität Bern. Akademische Kommission, and Law Symposium on Human Genetic Information Science, *Human Genetic Information Science, Law and Ethics*, Ciba Foundation Symposium 149 (Chichester, NY: John Wiley and Sons, 1990)

Vincent, B., *Haydn's Dictionary of Dates* (Frankfurt: Salzwasser-Verlag, 2020)

Vincent, C., ed., *Clinical Risk Management: Enhancing Patient Safety*, 2nd ed. (London: BMJ, 2001)

Von Neumann, J., *The Computer and the Brain*, Mrs. Hepsa Ely Silliman Memorial Lectures (London: Yale University Press, 1958)

Wachter, R., *Making IT Work: Harnessing the Power of Health Information Technology to Improve Care in England* (London: Department of Health, 2016)

Walker, J., E. Pan, D. Johnston, J. Adler-Milstein, S. W. Bates and B. Middleton, 'The Value of Health Care Information Exchange and Interoperability: There Is a Business Case to Be Made for Spending Money on a Fully Standardized Nationwide System', *Health Affairs*, 24.Suppl1 (2005), W5-10-W5-18, https://doi.org/10.1377/hlthaff.W5.10

Wanless, D., *Securing Our Future Health: Taking a Long-term View* (London: HM Treasury, 2002)

Ware, W., *RAND and the Information Evolution: A History in Essays and Vignettes* (Santa Monica, CA: RAND, 2008), https://www.rand.org/content/dam/rand/pubs/corporate_pubs/2008/RAND_CP537.pdf

Warner Jr., H. R., 'Iliad: Moving Medical Decision-Making into New Frontiers', *Methods of Information in Medicine*, 28.04 (1989), 370–72

Wedgeworth, R., ed., *World Encyclopedia of Library and Information Services* (Chicago, IL: American Library Association, 1993)

Weinberg, S., *The First Three Minutes* (New York: Bantam Books, 1979)

Weizenbaum, J., *Computer Power and Human Reason: From Judgment to Calculation* (Harmondsworth: Penguin Books, 1993)

Wheeler, J. A., 'Information, Physics, Quantum: The Search for Links', in *Feynman and Computation*, ed. by A. Hey (Boca Raton, FL: CRC Press, 2018), pp. 309–36, https://doi.org/10.1201/9780429500459-19

White, G., *The Natural History of Selborne* (London: Gibbings, 1890)

Whitehead, A. N., *Adventures of Ideas* (New York: Macmillan, 1933)

—, *The Aims of Education and Other Essays* (New York: Macmillan, 1929)

—, *Symbolism, its Meaning and Effect* (New York: Macmillan, 1927)

—, 'Universities and their Function', *Bulletin of the American Association of University Professors (1915–1955)*, 14.6 (1928), 448–50

Whitehead, A, N., and B. Russell, *Principia Mathematica* (Cambridge. UK: Cambridge University Press, 1925–27)

Willis, K., 'Russell and His Obituaries', *Russell: The Journal of Bertrand Russell Studies*, 26 (2006), 5–54, https://doi.org/10.15173/russell.v26i1.2091

Wiltshaw, E., *A History of the Royal Marsden Hospital* (Middlesex: Altman, 1998)

Wilson, F. M., *In the Margins of Chaos: Recollections of Relief Work in and Between Three Wars* (New York: Macmillan, 1945)

Wirth, N., *Algorithms + Data Structures = Programs* (Englewood Cliffs, NJ: Prentice-Hall, 1976)

Wu, C. Q., transl., *Thus Spoke Laozi: A New Translation with Commentaries of Daodejing* (Honolulu: University of Hawaii Press, 2016)

Wyke, A., 'Peering into 2010: A Survey of the Future of Medicine', *The Economist* (19 March 1994), 1–20

Young, J. Z., *Programs of the Brain: Based on the Gifford Lectures, 1975–7* (Oxford: Oxford University Press, 1978)

Young, M., and P. Willmott, *Family and Kinship in East London* (London: Routledge, 2013)

Yust, W., ed., *Encyclopaedia Britannica: A New Survey of Universal Knowledge* (Chicago, IL: University of Chicago Press, 1945)

Zimmerli, W. C., 'Who Has the Right to Know the Genetic Constitution of a Particular Person?', *Ciba Foundation Symposium*, 149.93 (1990), 93–110, https://doi.org/10.1002/9780470513903.ch8

Index of Names

More recent participants along the author's songline are included in the extended acknowledgements of Appendix V and documented on the openEHR website.

About the Team

Alessandra Tosi was the managing editor for this book.

Adèle Kreager copy-edited, proof read and indexed this book.

The Alt-text was created by Anja Pritchard.

Jeevanjot Kaur Nagpal designed the cover. The cover was produced in InDesign using the Fontin font.

Tony Briscoe provided his services as a professional photographer, to optimize the print quality of many of the images and slides.

Cameron Craig typeset the book in InDesign and produced the paperback and hardback editions. The text font is Tex Gyre Pagella; the heading font is Californian FB.

Cameron also produced the PDF, EPUB, HTML, and XML editions. The conversion was performed with open-source software such as pandoc (https://pandoc.org/), created by John MacFarlane, and other tools freely available on our GitHub page (https://github.com/OpenBookPublishers).

This book has been anonymously peer-reviewed by experts in their field. We thank them for their invaluable help.

This book need not end here...

Share

All our books — including the one you have just read — are free to access online so that students, researchers and members of the public who can't afford a printed edition will have access to the same ideas. This title will be accessed online by hundreds of readers each month across the globe: why not share the link so that someone you know is one of them?

This book and additional content is available at:
https://doi.org/10.11647/OBP.0335

Donate

Open Book Publishers is an award-winning, scholar-led, not-for-profit press making knowledge freely available one book at a time. We don't charge authors to publish with us: instead, our work is supported by our library members and by donations from people who believe that research shouldn't be locked behind paywalls.

Why not join them in freeing knowledge by supporting us:
https://www.openbookpublishers.com/support-us

Follow @OpenBookPublish

Read more at the Open Book Publishers **BLOG**

You may also be interested in:

Non-communicable Disease Prevention
Best Buys, Wasted Buys and Contestable Buys
Wanrudee Isaranuwatchai, Rachel A. Archer,
Yot Teerawattananon and Anthony J. Culyer

https://doi.org/10.11647/obp.0195

Undocumented Migrants and Healthcare
Eight Stories from Switzerland
Marianne Jossen

https://doi.org/10.11647/obp.0139

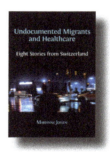

Intellectual Property and Public Health in the Developing World
Monirul Azam

https://doi.org/10.11647/obp.0093

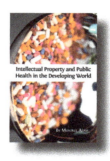

www.ingramcontent.com/pod-product-compliance
Lightning Source LLC
LaVergne TN
LVHW061954050326
832903LV00036B/4826